SOUTHWEST CAMPING DESTINATIONS

RV And Car Camping Destinations In
Arizona, New Mexico, and Utah

MIKE *and* TERRI CHURCH

D1605628

ROLLING HOMES PRESS

Published by
Rolling Homes Press
161 Rainbow Dr., #6157
Livingston, TX 77399-1061

www.rollinghomes.com

Printed in the United States of America
First Printing 2008

Publisher's Cataloging in Publication

Church, Mike, 1951-
Southwest Camping Destinations : RV and car camping destinations in Arizona,
   New Mexico, and Utah / Mike and Terri Church-Second Edition
   p.cm.
   Includes index.
   Library of Congress Control Number: 2008937907
   ISBN 978-0-9749471-9-8

1. Camping–Southwest–Guidebooks. 2. Recreational vehicle living–Southwest–
Guidebooks. 3. Camp sites, facilities, etc–Southwest–Guidebooks. 4. Southwest–
Guidebooks. I. Church, Terri. II. Title.

Warning, Disclosure, and Communication With The Authors and Publishers

Half the fun of travel is the unexpected, and self-guided camping travel can produce much in the way of unexpected pleasures, and also complications and problems. This book is designed to increase the pleasures of Southwest camping and reduce the number of unexpected problems you may encounter. You can help ensure a smooth trip by doing additional advance research, planning ahead, and exercising caution when appropriate. There can be no guarantee that your trip will be trouble free.

Although the authors and publisher have done their best to ensure that the information presented in this book was correct at the time of publication they do not assume and hereby disclaim any liability to any party for any loss or damage caused by errors, omissions, or any other cause.

In a book like this it is inevitable that there will be omissions or mistakes, especially as things do change over time. If you find inaccuracies we would like to hear about them so that they can be corrected in future editions. We would also like to hear about your enjoyable experiences. If you come upon an outstanding campground or destination please let us know, those kinds of things may also find their way to future versions of the guide or to our internet site. You can reach us by mail at:

Rolling Homes Press
161 Rainbow Dr., #6157
Livingston, TX 77399-1061

You can also communicate with us by sending an email through our web site at:

www.rollinghomes.com

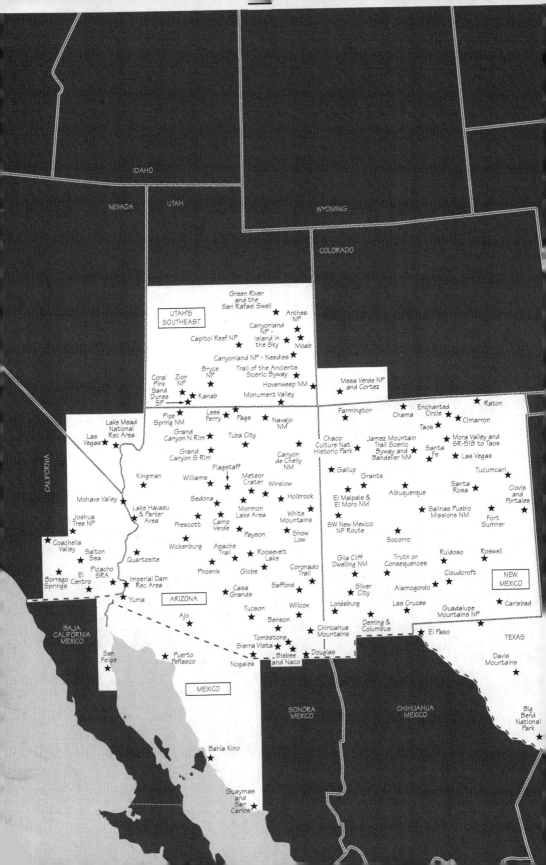

TABLE OF CONTENTS

Destinations and Their Campgrounds

CHAPTER 5

CHAPTER 6

10

Preface

Southwest Camping Destinations is one of two books in our Camping Destinations Series. The other is *Pacific Northwest Camping Destinations.* We plan to write more of these guides in the years ahead. We also write and publish the Traveler's Guide Series including the books *Traveler's Guide to Alaskan Camping, Traveler's Guide to Mexican Camping, Traveler's Guide to Camping Mexico's Baja,* and *RV and Car Camping Vacations in Europe.*

Both series are designed for both RV and car camping travelers in the continental U.S. and adjoining Canada and Mexico. These books are travel guides aimed at a large part of the traveling public that has been virtually ignored by traditional travel book publishers – camping travelers. There are lots of travel guides available, but very few include the details that the camping traveler needs for a fun-filled and comfortable trip.

We have not attempted to include all of the campgrounds in the Southwest in this book, the large catalog-style guides take care of that. Instead, we've selected destinations then picked out campgrounds that stand out as good places to stay while visiting those destinations. You'll find a brief description of what each area has to offer in the way of attractions, then a listing of some of the better campgrounds in the area.

Our campground entries deserve a little explanation. You'll note that we've made heavy use of icons or pictograms to convey information in a compact format. We think you'll find them very useful. By using the pictograms we've allowed ourselves room to use text to try to give you a better feel for what the campground offers and to give useful driving instructions for finding it. You'll also find latitude and longitude so that you can easily use a GPS-based mapping program for navigation and we've included maps showing approximate locations for each campground.

There's another great feature in this book. Many of the RVers visiting the Southwest come as Snowbirds. They stay in large RV parks that just aren't quite like the ones designed for traveling RVers. We developed a new format to cover those parks and it makes up Chapter 8 of this book.

The Southwest is a wonderful car camping and RVing destination all year long. We hope you'll enjoy it as much as we do.

SOUTHWEST

VALLEY OF THE GODS

Chapter 1

Introduction

The Southwest is one of the most popular camping and RV destinations in North America. It's a unique destination too, because it attracts visitors all year long.

In the summer there are vacation and outdoor-oriented travelers and week-end campers from around the state. They generally head for the high Southwest, the area that has comfortable temperatures because, generally, the higher you are the cooler it is. That's important in the Southwest. Chapters 4, 5, 6, and 7 of this book are dedicated to these camping travelers. These chapters describe the various destinations and the campgrounds that are available. We've also included coverage for the lower altitude destinations in these chapters, because they become viable destinations in Spring, Fall, and Winter as the temperatures there become very nice.

We've provided only limited coverage in these chapters for the Snowbird towns where most RV parks are really optimized for Snowbird travelers. Our coverage of those towns list camping areas and RV parks that are the most suitable ones available for vacationing and traveling campers and RVers.

Of course the Snowbirds are the other Southwest campers. Several hundred thousand Snowbird campers visit the Southwest every winter. Chapter 8 is dedicated to those Snowbird travelers. It has a huge amount of information about the parks in the main Snowbird "roosts". These are Casa Grande, the Coachella Valley (Palm Springs), Lake Havasu and the Parker Strip, Las Vegas, the Mohave Valley, Phoenix (including Mesa, Tempe, Apache Junction, and the remainder of the Phoenix area), Quartzsite, Tucson, and Yuma.

If you are a Snowbird, however, and want to stay in a town not covered in Chapter 8, we have information for you too. You'll find that the campground descriptions in Chapters 4, 5, 6, and 7 contain more than enough information to allow you to decide which campgrounds you need to call to get the information that will allow you to make your final choice.

You may be wondering which areas are considered High Southwest destinations and which are in the Low Southwest. The fact is that the dividing line changes depending upon the time of year.

For Snowbirds, who visit the Southwest in the dead of winter, the dividing line appears to be at about 3,000 feet. Every one of the most popular Snowbird destinations is below that altitude. A "second tier" of Snowbird destinations is above this altitude and up to about 4,500 feet. Included in this group are towns like Benson, Willcox, Deming, Las Cruces, Truth or Consequences and Alamogordo. There is a map showing these altitudes and the areas they cover in Chapter 8 on page 435.

In summer another dividing line is handy. This is the Mogollon Rim, the edge of the Colorado Plateau, which runs across Arizona and New Mexico. In general the rim altitude is from 6,000 to 8,000 feet. Many winter Snowbirds move above the rim for the great summer weather up there, and most of the vacation travelers and weekend campers from the big cities in the Southwest are up there too. Of course people do camp at lower altitudes in the spring, summer and fall; but it's important to be prepared for the sun and heat when you do.

Camping Travel

Not everyone who uses this book will be an experienced camper and certainly not everyone will have an RV – or even would want one. Camping travel has always been popular in the US and now it's more comfortable and easy than ever. Traveling in your own car or RV, sleeping in your own mobile bed, visiting the great outdoors but having the comforts of home, and saving lots of money doing it – that's camping travel.

You don't need an RV to travel this way. During the summer months you can comfortably camp out of the back of your car. For just a small investment you can equip yourself with everything you need to stay in a campground. Today's camping equipment is inexpensive and usually pretty well designed. You don't need expedition quality gear for car camping, and there is no reason to spend extra money to get equipment that is ultra-light weight. You're not going to be carrying this equipment on your back. It is much more important to get equipment that will be comfortable. Get a big tent, they're not really expensive. You don't have to sleep on the ground, there are foam and air mattresses, not to mention cots, that are almost as comfortable as your bed at home.

If sleeping in a tent seems a little more like roughing it than you are willing to accept you still can camp. Rental RVs are readily available. Later in this chapter you'll find information about renting RVs in Los Angeles, Las Vegas, Phoenix, and Albuquerque. When you check prices remember that the RV provides both transportation and lodging, you'll also spend less on food because you can easily cook in an RV and won't have to eat every meal in a restaurant. It won't take long to feel at home at the wheel of your rental RV, most roads aren't crowded, and you'll be surprised at the views that you'll have from that high RV seat. When renting we recommend that you don't get a RV that is larger than you need. Big is not necessarily better with RVs, especially when you are traveling most of the time. If you have kids along consider having them sleep in a tent, they'll probably like it better anyway.

This is a good place to mention RV maneuverability. When you are parked comfortably in a campsite you want the biggest RV possible, but when you are on the road you want the smallest one possible. We've all seen the huge RVs traveling the interstate, usually pulling a tow car. Those RVs are fine when you are in an RV park but they're not really very convenient when on the road, particularly when you leave the interstate. For the type of traveled outlined in this book you'll be much happier in a smaller RV. It will be easier to park when shopping, easier to fill with fuel at a station, and be more economical to operate. Most importantly, a smaller RV gives you many more choices when it comes to picking a campsite.

Once you reach the destinations you're going to want to be able to drive around to see the sights, go shopping, and conveniently get around. Fortunately, many of the destinations in this book aren't crowded urban areas so you can use an RV for local access. Those with really big RVs will want to have a tow car or (in the case of those pulling trailers) use their towing vehicle. Rental motorhomes in the 18 to 22 foot range are not too difficult to maneuver and park so you won't need a tow car if you have one of those.

Tour Routes

In Chapter 2 of this book we outline three tours that you can follow to enjoy much of what the Southwest has to offer. Two of these tours start in Flagstaff, a city convenient for touring northern Arizona and southern Utah. The other starts in New Mexico's largest city, Albuquerque. Each includes six or seven destinations that offer good RV facilities and things to see and do. The idea is that you can spend a week traveling and know that you will enjoy each of the stops you make. Actually, it would be easy to spend two or three weeks on each route, but that is up to you. These routes are just ideas. You can take it from there.

Travel Campgrounds

Travel campgrounds in the Southwest can be classified in many ways, but we think of them as described below. When they are available we've tried to provide a range of campground types to choose from at each destination. The type you like will depend upon how much you value hookups, amenities, natural settings, convenience and cost.

Commercial campgrounds provide the widest range of amenities. They are owned by companies or individuals and must make at least a small profit to stay open. This does not necessarily mean that they are always the most expensive campground choice since the government-owned campgrounds have been raising their rates in recent years. Commercial campgrounds almost always offer hookups, dump stations, and hot showers, they also often have swimming pools and other amenities. They seldom limit the time of your stay. A big advantage of commercial campgrounds is that they usually will accept reservations over the phone with no additional charge. They are almost always the only type of campground that is located near or inside a town. Parking sites in commercial campgrounds are usually closer to each other than those in government campgrounds, land is a big cost to a commercial campground but is pretty much free to the government. Commercial campgrounds have been forced to enlarge sites to remain viable so most can deal fairly well with large RVs.

Arizona, New Mexico, Utah, and California state campgrounds are similar to each other. Most are located in scenic or historical locations, or on a reservoir offering fishing and boating opportunities. Government campgrounds tend to have lots of land so parking sites are spread farther apart than in a commercial campground. Sites themselves can be large enough for the largest RVs although this varies, older campgrounds were built when RVs were smaller and many have not been updated. State campgrounds in all of these states often have hookups, but not always. They also often provide showers, although there is sometimes a small charge in the form of a coin-operated timer. State campgrounds are much more likely to allow campfires than commercial campgrounds, usually wood can be purchased at the campground. During the busy season most state campgrounds now have an on-site "host". Usually the host is an RVer who parks in one of the sites and helps run the campground by collecting fees, marking reserved sites, providing information, and helping state employees keep the facility clean, safe, and organized. There is often a 14 or 21-day stay limit in state campgrounds.

Federal campgrounds in the area covered by this book are either National Park Service (in National Parks and National Monuments), Forest Service (in National Forests), or BLM (on BLM lands). These campgrounds vary a great deal and it's hard to generalize. Big efforts are being made to increase site size to deal with modern big RVs, and to provide wheelchair accessible facilities. Since these facilities vary so much you will find the individual listing in Chapters 4, 5, and 6 to be invaluable since they tell you what size RV will fit, whether hookups are available, and whether reservations can be made. Federal campgrounds often have a 7 or 14-day stay limit.

For many RVers camping is just not camping without a campfire. European visitors seem to particularly enjoy them, maybe because they don't find campfires in European campgrounds. Many commercial campgrounds do not allow campfires, probably due to burning restrictions in urban areas and the supervision and clean-up that fires require. Most state, provincial, and federal campgrounds do allow campfires although burning restrictions are often in effect in dryer areas.

DESERT CAMPING NEAR QUARTZSITE

You will not be able to find sufficient firewood on the ground in any of the campgrounds listed in this book. That means that you must either bring your own or purchase it at the campgrounds. Most campgrounds that allow fires do sell firewood.

Boondocking Areas

The Southwest offers a kind of camping experience not found in other parts of the country. Large areas of desert have been set aside for boondocking – parking RVs in the desert with no hookups. Some Southwest RVers spend months and months each year doing this. Many others do it for at least a short period of the winter. It's great to be out in the desert away from civilization, and it's free or almost free. We've described a great many of these campgrounds in the Arizona chapter, and there's a section giving you the rules titled *BLM Land Camping* at the beginning of that chapter.

Snowbird Campgrounds

Snowbird campgrounds are the ones that are designed to be used by Snowbird visitors from the north. There are hundreds of these in the Southwest. While Snowbird campgrounds do also accept traveling campers that's not their primary purpose. Often Snowbird campgrounds do not accept children, many have a fifty-five and older rule. Many do not accept smaller RVs or tents and many require RVs to be self contained. Amenities are aimed at the Snowbird and long-term stays rather than children and travelers. You'll seldom find a playground at a Snowbird campground.

Chapter 8 in this book is about Snowbird campgrounds in the most popular Snowbird destinations. Snowbirds also spend the winter in a few other towns in the Low Southwest and you'll find many of the campgrounds they use described in other chapters in the book.

Campground Reservations

The destinations in this book are popular. If you are traveling during the period from Memorial Day (end of May) to Labor Day (beginning of September), as most RV travelers do (see below for Snowbirds), you will find that campgrounds are sometimes full when you arrive. To avoid a late-in-the-day search for a place to stay all you have to do is take the time to reserve a space. We have indicated whether campgrounds accept reservations in the individual campground listings in this book.

It is easy to make a reservation at virtually all commercial campgrounds. Almost all accept MasterCard or Visa charges and some even have toll-free numbers. Best of all, there is almost always no additional charge for making a reservation.

State and federal campgrounds are another story. The good news is that many now accept reservations. The bad news is that most charge a substantial fee to make the reservation and most use a sub-contractor for the reservation-taking process. It is usually necessary to make the reservation several days in advance. One bright spot, more and more the government reservation contractors have information about site sizes so you will actually know which site you will be parking in and how big it is. Information about how to make state and federal reservations is listed at the beginning of Chapters 4, 5, and 6.

Snowbird reservations are another ballgame. For a stay at any Snowbird park in December, January, February or March you should have reservations. Take the time to carefully read Chapter 8 in this book and then call the parks that seem interesting and ask lots of questions. Know as much about the park and the location you will occupy as possible, after all, you will be committing to stay there for quite a while. You will find that most RV parks are anxious to have you make a three month reservations. Some will hesitate to make a reservation for a shorter period until they know how many three month reservations they will have for that year. They don't really know this until December so you may have to call then if you want to stay for a shorter period.

Renting An RV

It is not necessary to own your own RV to enjoy the destinations and campgrounds described in this book. You can easily rent an RV in Los Angeles, Las Vegas, Phoenix or Albuquerque. Here are a few of the firms in that business. Give them a call or drop them a line for information about RVs and rates. Don't forget to ask if they will pick you up at the airport if that is important to you.

Los Angeles Area

Adventure Touring, Los Angeles Depot, 400 West Compton Blvd, Gardena, CA 90248; (866) 672-3572, (250) 837-4555

Cruise America – Los Angeles, 2233 E 223rd St, Carson, CA 90810; (310) 522-3870

El Monte – Santa Fe Springs LAX Location, 12818 Firestone Blvd, Santa Fe Springs, CA 90670; (888) 337-2214, (562) 404-9300

Happy Travel Campers, 14318 Lemoli Ave, Hawthorne, CA 90250; (310) 675-1335, (800) 370-1262

Moturis Los Angeles, 400 West Compton Blvd, Gardena, CA 90248; (877) 668-8747, (310) 767-5988

Road Bear RV, 28404 Roadside Dr, Agoura Hills, CA 91301; (818) 865-2925, (866) 491-9853

Las Vegas

Adventure Touring, Los Vegas Depot, 6590 Boulder Hwy, Las Vegas, NV 89122; (866) 672-3572, (250) 837-4555

Cruise America – Las Vegas, 6070 Boulder Hwy, Las Vegas, NV 89122; (702) 456-6666

El Monte RV – Las Vegas, 13001 Las Vegas Blvd South, Las Vegas, NV 89044; (702) 269-8000, (888) 337-2214

Moturis Las Vegas, LTD, 6590 Boulder Hwy, Las Vegas, NV 89122; (800) 559-8228, (702) 597-5978

Road Bear RV, 4730 Boulder Hwy, Las Vegas, NV 89121; (818) 865-2925, (866) 491-9853

Phoenix Area

A Car and Truck Rental of Surprise (Cruise America), 17150 N 134th Dr, Surprise, AZ 85374; (623) 584-6708

Cruise America – Phoenix, 11 West Hampton Ave, Mesa, AZ 85210; (480) 464-7300

Sun Rentals (Cruise America), 3535 West Indian School Rd, Phoenix, AZ 85019; (602) 242-0181

Albuquerque Area

KOA Kampgrounds (Cruise America), 12400 Skyline Rd, Albuquerque, NM 87123; (505) 275-3550

El Monte - Albuquerque, 118100 Central Ave SE, Albuquerque, NM 87123; (888) 337-2214

Visitor Information

We're strong believers in the usefulness of local traveler's information offices. Arizona, New Mexico, Utah, and California all have fine offices in virtually every town covered in this guide. We've given their addresses at the end of each chapter so that you can send for information before you leave home. If no address is available we give telephone numbers so that you can contact them that way. When you are on the road you will find that the offices are well signed from most town approaches, just follow the signs to the office. They can provide you with maps, a listing of sights to see, opening times, and locations for any service you may require. Most towns also maintain a website with useful information, you can find links to them on our website, www.rollinghomes.com.

Internet Resources

Every day there are more and more websites devoted to information about destinations, campgrounds, interesting sites, parks, and transportation. New websites appear and old ones disappear or change addresses. We've found that the only way to maintain a current listing is to set up our own Internet site. The address is www.rollinghomes.com and it has current links to a large variety of sites that will be of interest to readers of this guide. Don't ignore this resource, it can make your trip much more rewarding.

When To Go

There are two Southwests, the High Southwest and the Low Southwest. The best time for visiting one isn't necessarily the best time for visiting the other. See the introduction to this chapter to determine whether the destinations you are most interested in are high or low.

The high country is best from Spring to Fall. Higher destinations have shorter seasons so if you're planning, for instance, to visit the Enchanted Circle in New Mexico, you'd want to start your travels a little later in the spring than if you were headed to Santa Fe with no plans to go up into the mountains. Another good example is Zion National Park versus Bryce National Park. Although they're just 60 driving miles from each other the altitude of Bryce is twice that of Zion, Bryce has a much shorter season. A good way to determine the camping season for a particular destination is to look at the open and close dates for government campgrounds in that area. These campgrounds are used by tenters and many do not have hookups so their users are temperature-sensitive. Many are closed outside the best season for visiting an area.

The low country is winter country, winter weather is ideal with highs in the high 60s or low 70s and nights in the upper 30s and 40s. It's pretty comfortable in the fall and spring too and many travelers choose that period to explore the Southwest because they can also see the Low and High Southwest during the same trip. Mexico is a special case. Because the ocean is popular year-round you will find that the ocean-side campgrounds there are used throughout the year. The reservoir campgrounds in the Southwest are similar with state reservoir campgrounds in Arizona, New Mexico, and Utah as well as Colorado River campgrounds being used throughout the year. Snowbirds are thickest from the first of January until the middle of April, but they come late because they want to spend Christmas at home, not because they fear the winter in the fall. There is a lot of information in this book about temperatures in the Low Southwest, just look at the average temperature tables in the Snowbird chapter.

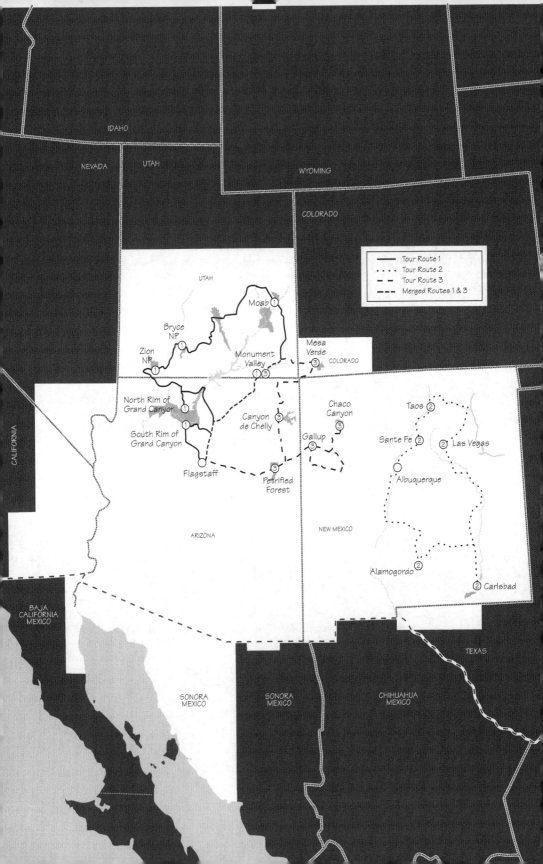

Chapter 2

Suggested Touring Routes

This chapter contains 3 tours of the Southwest. We've included these tours because the Southwest has so much to see and do that it can be difficult to narrow things down. There is no reason to regard the tours as set in stone, you can expand them or leave destinations out, you can spend a week or a month.

Each suggested tour has six or seven driving days. To complete one in a week you have to drive and then see the sights on the same day. Better would be to spend two weeks so that you can drive, see the sights the next day, and then drive on the following day. If you have only one week you could cut out one or two destinations to give yourself more time at one of the places that seems most interesting to you.

TOUR 1 – CANYON COUNTRY

Summary: This tour visits the majority of the national parks that pack Northern Arizona and Southern Utah: Grand Canyon National Park, Zion National Park, Bryce National Park, Capitol Reef National Park, Arches National Park, and Canyonlands National Park. It also visits the Navajo Nation's Monument Valley.

High Points

- » South Rim of the Grand Canyon
- » Marble Canyon and Navajo Bridge
- » North Rim of the Grand Canyon
- » Pipe Springs National Monument
- » Zion National Park

- » Bryce National Park
- » Capitol Reef National Park
- » Arches National Park
- » Canyonlands National Park – Island In the Sky District
- » Canyonlands National Park – Needles District
- » Newspaper Rock
- » Natural Bridges National Monument
- » Moki Dugway
- » Goosenecks State Park
- » Monument Valley
- » Flagstaff

General Description

The tour begins and ends in Flagstaff. Driving northwest you spend the first evening in Grand Canyon National Park at the south rim. The next day you move on to the north rim, which requires a long but interesting drive far to the east. Zion National Park is day three, then Bryce on day four. The fifth day is the long driving day, a total of 235 miles through extremely scenic country including the Journey Through Time Scenic Byway and Capitol Reef National Park. The destination is Moab, your base for exploring both Arches National Park and Canyonlands National Park. If you have an extra day, spend it in Moab. Then it's south to Monument Valley with the possibility of either the Needles District of Canyonlands National Park or Natural Bridges National Monument thrown in.

The total distance of this tour is 1,067 miles, driving time about 27 hours over 7 days.

The Roads

Roads on this tour are, for the most part, paved two-lane highways suitable for any vehicle. There are two sections you may want to bypass if you have a large RV although many people travel them with no problems. The first is the section of SR-12 between Bryce National Park and Torrey known as the Hogback. You'll be going up it, which is the least challenging direction, see the section titled *Journey Through Time Scenic Byway* (page 378) for a discussion of driving the Hogback.

The second section that some people don't like, although many travel it, is called the Moki Dugway. It's actually on a side trip that you don't have to take if you don't want to. See the *Trail of the Ancients Scenic Byway* section (page 393) for a discussion of the Moki Dugway.

Practical Tips

This tour visits many national parks. It is worth your while to buy a National Parks Pass at the first national park entrance you reach. The $50 pass entitles you to visit as many national parks as you wish for an entire year for no additional fee. It also covers anyone traveling in your vehicle with you.

This trip is best taken in the spring or early fall to avoid the crowds. The rocks are just as beautiful during those times of the year and the parks are more enjoyable with fewer people. Tent campers need to be aware, however, that evenings during the shoulder season can be cool at higher altitudes. The best months are May and September. Snow is possible in some places from October to April.

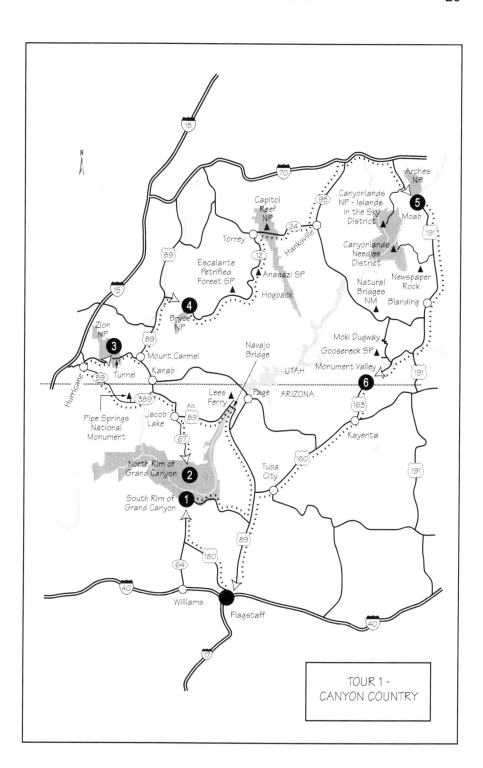

TOUR 1 -
CANYON COUNTRY

▄ DAY 1 – FLAGSTAFF TO SOUTH RIM OF THE GRAND CANYON – 74 MILES, 2 HOURS

From Flagstaff the most scenic route to the South Rim is US-180. It leads northwest from Flagstaff for a distance of 50 miles to connect with SR-64. It's another 24 miles up to the canyon.

The **South Rim of the Grand Canyon** is one of the busiest of the national parks, but also one of the most impressive to visit. Review the *South Rim of the Grand Canyon* section (page 99) for information about things to do and campgrounds choices.

▄ DAY 2 – NORTH RIM OF THE GRAND CANYON – 211 MILES, 5 HOURS

Today's fairly long drive will take you about eight miles. You can almost see your destination from your starting point. The problem is, there are few places to cross the Colorado River so you're going to have to drive quite a distance to reach the closest crossing.

From the South Rim head eastward on SR-64. The highway will lead you out the east entrance of the park and, after 55 miles, connects with US-89 near Cameron. Turn north on US-89 and after 59 miles take the left to Navajo Bridge and Kanab.

You'll descend toward the river and in 14 miles spot the **Navajo Bridge** ahead. You should stop at the parking area and get out to take a look. One span here is just for pedestrians so you can walk out and look down into **Marble Canyon**, the river is almost 500 feet below. It is sometimes possible to spot California condors from here, or perhaps a raft passing on the river below.

This is a good place for a short side trip. Just north of the bridge a road goes right to **Lee's Ferry**. It's a nice paved road and will lead you about 5 miles down into the canyon to the river level. For many years there was a ferry across the river here. It's the place where most Colorado rafting trips start out, maybe you'll be lucky enough to see a group getting ready. For more about this area see the *Lees Ferry* section (page 125).

Back on the highway it's another 41 miles west to Jacob Lake where you'll turn south to drive the 42 miles south to the **North Rim**. Stop at the ranger station in Jacob Lake and check the availability of campgrounds in the area if you don't have reservations. You might want to stake out a spot in one of the nearby campgrounds before heading south.

See the *Grand Canyon North Rim* section (page 97) for information about what to do and where to stay in the area.

▄ DAY 3 – ZION NATIONAL PARK – 150 MILES, 3.5 HOURS

Heading north from the North Rim, take a left on US-89 Alt at Jacob Lake and follow it across the Kaibab Plateau toward Kanab. Rather than going all the way to Kanab, take a left on SR-389 after traveling about 30 miles from Jacob Lake.

This route will take you around the south end of Zion National Park so that you can enter from the west. After 13 miles on SR-389, it's convenient to stop at **Pipe Springs National Monument**. There is a visitor center and a pleasant area to take a stroll. More information is in the *Pipe Spring National Monument* section (page 153).

Back on the road you'll reach the town of Hurricane, Utah in 41 miles. This is a good place to stop if you need supplies. Then drive west on SR-9 to **Zion National Park**, you'll reach it in 23 miles. See the *Zion National Park* section (page 398) for information about the park.

⬛ Day 4 – Bryce National Park – 85 miles, 2 hours

Today's drive is a short one. You might want to do a little more exploring in Zion before leaving or you should have no problem using the time when you arrive in Bryce.

The route leaves Zion by the east entrance which means that you have to negotiate the tunnel. It's not much of a problem, but take a quick look at the required procedure in the *Zion National Park* section of the book (page 398). Heading east you'll reach an intersection with US-89 near Mt Carmel and turn north. Drive north for 43 miles and turn east on SR-12. It's only another 17 miles to **Bryce National Park**. See the *Bryce National Park* section (page 367) for more about the area.

⬛ Day 5 – Moab – 235 miles, 7 hours

Today's drive is a long one and requires an early start. If you have any extra time you might consider breaking the drive at Capital Reef National Park to spend an extra day there or perhaps plan to stay in Moab for an entire day tomorrow.

From Bryce we'll head northeast on SR-12 to Torrey near Capital Reef National Park. SR-12 is extremely scenic, it is designated as a scenic byway. See our section titled *Capital Reef National Park and the Journey Through Time Scenic Byway* (page 378) for more about this route. That section is written as if you were traveling the opposite direction so here are some important sights and their distance from the Bryce junction: **Escalante Petrified Forest State Park** – 44 miles; **Hogback** – 62 miles, **Anasazi State Park Museum** – 73 miles, Torrey – 110 miles.

From Torry head eastward through **Capital Reef National Park** to the intersection with SR-95 in Hanksville, a distance of 47 miles. Then drive north on SR-24 for 44 miles to I-70. Thirty-three miles east on I-70 near Crescent Junction turn south on US-191 and in another 30 miles you'll reach Moab.

Moab is a good base for many activities. See the *Arches National Park* section (page 365), the *Canyonlands National Park – Island in the Sky* section (page 372), and the *Moab* section (page 389) for more about the area and what it has to offer. Once you've done that you may decide that Moab is worth at least two days.

⬛ Day 6 – Monument Valley – 146 miles, 3.5 hours

If you drive directly south from Moab to Monument Valley this is a pretty easy driving day. You should arrive in plenty of time to get some great photos of the sandstone plateaus in the "magic" evening light. You just travel straight down US-191 for 105 miles and then take a right onto US-163. In another 41 miles you're approaching **Monument Valley**. See the *Monument Valley* section (page 392) for more about this area.

However, there are plenty of ways to spend more time. Fifty miles south of Moab you might consider a side trip out to **Newspaper Rock** and the **Needles District of Canyonlands**. See the *Canyonlands National Park – Needles District* section (page 375) for more about that trip.

Or, you might want to detour west from just south of Blanding to visit **Natural Bridges National Monument**, the **Moki Dugway**, and **Goosenecks State** Park. See our *Trail of the Ancients Scenic Byway* section (page 393) for more about that region.

⬛ Day 7 – Return to Flagstaff – 166 miles, 4 hours

The return to Flagstaff is straightforward. Just drive south on US-163 for 24 miles to the intersection with US-160 near Kayentna. US-160 will take you 82 miles southwest to intersect with US-89, then follow US-89 some 60 miles south to Flagstaff.

TOUR 2 – NEW MEXICO

Summary: The tour starts in Albuquerque. It travels up the Rio Grande Valley to Santa Fe and Taos, then crosses the Sangre de Cristo Mountains eastward to the plains. Traveling south it visits Las Vegas, Fort Sumner, Roswell and Carlsbad. Then it swings northwest to Alamogordo and the return to Albuquerque.

High Points

> » Turquoise Trail
> » Santa Fe
> » Taos
> » Enchanted Circle
> » Cimarron
> » Fort Sumner
> » Roswell
> » Carlsbad Caverns National Park
> » Guadalupe Mountains National Park
> » Alamogordo and the Tularosa Basin
> » White Sands National Monument
> » Valley of Fires
> » Albuquerque

General Description

This tour doesn't include all of New Mexico, but it sure includes a great deal of it. You'll get to see the big tourist towns of Santa Fe and Taos. Then you'll drive a good portion of what must be the most heavily promoted driving route in the state, the Enchanted Circle. On the eastern side of the mountains you'll visit many of the most interesting of the small towns scattered about the plains. Once you've traveled south there's the Carlsbad Caverns and Guadalupe Mountains. Even the route back is great with a visit to the very interesting Tularosa Basin.

The tour states in Albuquerque and on the first day travels only as far as Santa Fe. There's so much to do there that it's a great place to spend two or three days if you have the time.

On the second day it's on to Taos, but if you have a smaller vehicle it's fun to drive the High Road and see some of the small Hispanic towns in the foothills overlooking the Rio Grande Valley. If you have a large RV with a tow car consider driving this route in the smaller vehicle from either Santa Fe or Taos. That, of course would require another day.

From Taos the route crosses the Rockies and reaches the Great Plains. The Santa Fe Trail and the great cattle drive trails are the story here and you can visit Cimarron, Las Vegas, and Fort Sumner. Also worth a stop is Roswell for a chance to make up your own mind on the alien question.

Carlsbad is a destination where an extra day or two would be handy too. The caverns

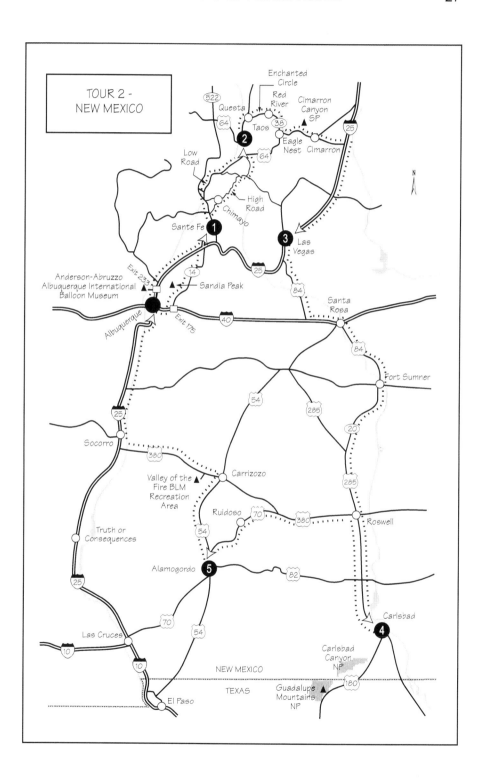

are worth several hours, and so is a hike in McKittrick Canyon in the Guadalupe Mountains.

Heading north and west you end up in the Tularosa Basin which has a wealth of things to see and do. Among them are White Sands National Monument, the White Sands Missile Range, Three Rivers Petroglyph Site, and the Valley of Fires.

Back in Albuquerque after you finish the tour there are still more possibilities with a great Old Town and many museums, not to mention the nearby pueblos.

The total distance of this tour is 990 miles, driving time about 23.5 hours over 6 days.

The Roads

The tour travels a variety of roads. Some time is spent on the interstates but a lot more on major secondary roads. The Rockies are crossed twice, once eastward north of Taos (highest altitude is 9,820 feet) and once westward through Ruidoso. The Ruidoso crossing (maximum altitude about 7,600 feet) was chosen over the Cloudcroft crossing just to the south because the highway is considerably less steep. Neither of the crossings in the tour should present much of a challenge to a well-driven RV of any size except in the winter, see *Practical Tips* below.

Practical Tips

This is a spring, summer, fall tour. In winter the mountain crossings are very likely to have snow and many campgrounds in the mountains are closed. Outer limits for a comfortable trip would be May 1 to October 15, and there is the possibility of a little snow even then. If, on the other hand, you love snow, then this trip can be done all year long. Some campgrounds will be open in all of the destination areas and roads are usually open, you could even get in a little skiing at Santa Fe, Taos, Red River, Ruidoso, or even Albuquerque.

🚐 DAY 1 – SANTA FE – 75 MILES, 2.5 HOURS

One way to get from Albuquerque to Santa Fe is to drive directly up I-25, a distance of about 60 miles. With no stops the trip should take a little over an hour. If you do feel like a stop you might consider the **Anderson-Abruzzo Albuquerque International Balloon Museum** (Exit 233) in Northern Albuquerque, or **Coronado State Monument** (Exit 242). See *Albuquerque* (page 231) for details.

The other route you might take is called the **Turquoise Trail**. It's a little longer but more scenic. Drive east on I-40 as it climbs into the mountains. In a short time take Exit 175, the Tijeras Exit, and head north on SR-14. If you have a smaller vehicle you may want to take the side trip up to Sandia Peak on the **Sandia Crest Byway**. The Turquoise Trial and Sandia Crest Byway are briefly described in the *Albuquerque* section (page 231).

Santa Fe is full of things to see and do. See the *Santa Fe* section (page 326) for information about the city and its campgrounds.

🚐 DAY 2 – TAOS – 68 MILES ON LOW ROAD, 1.5 HOURS; 74 MILES ON HIGH ROAD, 2.5 HOURS

There are two routes between Santa Fe and Taos. For large or wide-body RVs the low road is best. For smaller vehicles the high road is more scenic and interesting. Both are described in the *Santa Fe* section (page 326).

▇ DAY 3 – LAS VEGAS – 169 MILES, 4.5 HOURS

Rather than taking the direct route to Las Vegas we'll drive a longer and more interesting route. You'll drive the more scenic part of the **Enchanted Circle** traveling clockwise. Then descend through the Cimarron Canyon to Cimarron and the Great Plains to over- night in Las Vegas.

From Taos head north on US-64. This is the beginning of the *Enchanted Circle* so take a look at that section (page 272). Continue straight at the intersection in 4 miles and follow SR-522 another 20 miles north to Questa. Turn right onto SR-38 and climb up the valley through Red River to cross the Bobcat Pass. When you reach Eagle Nest, 29 miles from Questa, turn east and descend through **Cimarron Canyon State Park** to the wild west town of Cimarron, a distance of 24 miles.

By the time you reach **Cimarron** you're probably ready for a break so take a look around. See the *Cimarron* section (page 253) for information about Cimarron.

Back on the road, travel 19 miles east on SR-58 to intersect I-25 and follow it 73 miles south to **Las Vegas**. The *Las Vegas* section (page 303) has information about Las Vegas and its campgrounds. If you arrive early in the day you may want to continue south an- other 66 miles to *Santa Rosa* (page 334) or perhaps an additional 44 miles to *Fort Sumner* (page 284) so that you'll have more time in Carlsbad tomorrow.

▇ DAY 4 – CARLSBAD – 275 MILES, 6 HOURS

Today, from Las Vegas follow I-40 just 6 miles south and leave the freeway to travel southeast on US-84 to intersect I-40 in another 41 miles. Head east on I-40 for 19 miles to *Santa Rosa* (page 334) and leave the freeway to again travel southwest on US-84. In 44 miles you'll reach **Ft Sumner**, you can stop and take a look at the visitor center at the State Monument or perhaps visit **Billy the Kid's grave** or his museum in town. Informa- tion is in the *Fort Sumner* section (page 284)

Back on the road the next stop is **Roswell**, 84 miles to the south. Follow SR-20 south out of Fort Sumner until it meets US-285 and then continue south to Roswell. You'll want to park and take a look at the UFO Museum, see the *Roswell* section (page 316).

Back on the road again the next stop is **Carlsbad**, 81 miles south. Information about the town, **Carlsbad Caverns National Park**, and **Guadalupe Mountains National Park** to the south, are in the *Carlsbad* section (page 245) and the *Guadalupe Mountains National Park* section (page 295).

▇ DAY 5 – ALAMOGORDO – 195 MILES, 5 HOURS

From Carlsbad we'll retrace our steps northward 78 miles to Roswell and then turn east to cross the Sacramento Mountains on US-380 and US-70. Some 71 miles from Roswell you'll reach **Ruidoso**. The town has a number of campgrounds and RV parks and if it's the middle of the summer you may want to stop here to spend the night because it will be cooler than in Alamogordo. See the *Ruidoso* section (page 319) for information. Oth- erwise continue on down the west slope of the mountains for 34 miles to intersect with US-54. **Alamogordo** is just to the south. See the *Alamogordo* section (page 227) for information about things to do and campgrounds in this area.

▇ DAY 6 – ALBUQUERQUE – 208 MILES, 4 HOURS

From Alamogordo drive north on US-54 for 56 miles and take a left on US-380. Just 4 miles farther on you might want to stop and take a look at the **Valley of Fires BLM**

Recreation Area where you can stretch your legs by taking a walk through the lava. Back on the road it's 61 miles until you intersect I-25. The freeway will carry you the 87 miles north to **Albuquerque**. See the *Albuquerque* section (page 231) for information about the town.

Tour 3 – Four Corners and Indian Country

Summary: This is a tour of the sights of the Four Corners area including quite a bit of the Navajo Nation. There's also a visit to the Zuni Pueblo as well as Petrified Forest National Park.

High Points

- » Navajo National Monument
- » Monument Valley
- » Valley of the Gods
- » Sand Island Campground and Petroglyph Sites
- » Hovenweep National Monument
- » Mesa Verde National Park
- » Four Corners
- » Canyon de Chelly
- » Hubble Trading Post National Monument
- » Zuni Pueblo
- » El Moro National Monument
- » El Malpais National Monument
- » Chaco Canyon
- » Petrified Forest National Park
- » Meteor Crater

General Description

The tour begins and ends in Flagstaff. It quickly takes you northwest to Monument Valley. Then, the next day circles northward and then east to Mesa Verde National Park. From there you'll drive south through the Navajo Nation to Canyon de Chelly and then Gallup. There's a back-roads trip out to Chaco Canyon and then a return to Flagstaff through Petrified Forest National Park.

The total distance of this tour is 1,154 miles, driving time about 29 hours over 7 days.

The Roads

The roads traveled on this tour includes two and four lane highways and also some back roads. The paved two lane roads leading to Hovenweep National Monument are no problem for any RV, just hold down your speed. The roads out to Chaco Canyon, as we say in that section, could be hard on larger RVs, so the tour is set up to allow you to travel there as a day trip in a tow car if you desire.

Practical Tips

This trip can actually be done any time of year. In summer temperatures can be very high and in winter it would be uncomfortable to be in a tent. The best seasons for travel, as in much of the Southwest, are late spring and early fall.

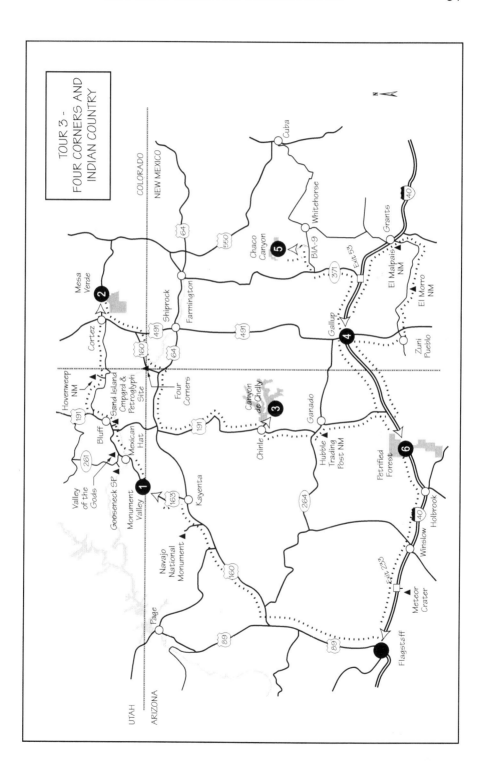

TOUR 3 -
FOUR CORNERS AND
INDIAN COUNTRY

▄ DAY 1 – FLAGSTAFF TO MONUMENT VALLEY – 166 MILES, 4 HOURS

From Flagstaff drive north on US-89. Sixty-two miles north of town turn northeast on US-160. Some 63 miles from this turn it makes an interesting side trip to drive out to **Navajo National Monument**. There's a visitor center and views of a cliff-side pueblo, you'll see lots more up at Mesa Verde. The attraction here is that this is a fairly isolated spot, often pretty quiet. If you have a smaller RV or car and tent you might consider overnighting at one of the two campgrounds here. For more information about the place see *Navajo National Monument* (page 134). Note that the monument is about 9 miles off the main highway so a stop takes a while.

Continuing north, at Kayentna turn north on US-163. This is 83 miles north of where you turned onto US-160 and 22 miles north of the turn-off for Navajo National Monument. After your turn north it's 23 miles to **Monument Valley**, see *Monument Valley* (page 392) for campgrounds and information.

▄ DAY 2 – MESA VERDE – 130 MILES, 4 HOURS

From Monument Valley drive north on US-163 for 56 miles to a point about ten miles north of the town of Bluff, Utah where we will turn east toward Hovenweep National Monument. On the way north there are several items of interest. These places are further described in the *Trail of the Ancients Scenic Byway* section (page 393). Twenty-one miles north of Monument Valley the highway crosses the San Juan River and climbs up to pass through the little town of **Mexican Hat**. Just beyond watch to your right for the namesake rock, you'll have no trouble recognizing it.

In 4 more miles you'll reach the intersection with SR-261. If you turn left here and drive .8 mile, you can turn left at the entrance road to **Goosenecks State Park**. A paved 3.5-mile access road leads you to an overlook of sharp bends in the San Juan River. The water is about 1,000 feet below and has cut its way down through the rock to that point, it's very impressive.

Return to the main road and then turn right to return to SR-163. Turn north and in another 4 miles you'll see a dirt road going off to the left. This is the entrance to **Valley Of The Gods**. It's a BLM administered area with rock formations much like those at Monument Valley to the south. This one's free however, but the road is not suitable for RVs over about 25 feet. It's a 17-mile road that connects with SR-261 a few miles north of Goosenecks State Park.

Continuing north watch for the intersection with US-191. It is about 12 miles north of the Valley of the Gods entrance. Don't turn at the junction, but just to the north turn into the entrance to **Sand Island Campground and Petroglyph Site**. Here you'll find a cliff covered with Indian petroglyphs next to the camping area.

Heading north once again on what is now called US-191 you'll pass through Bluff and then about ten miles north of the town find a sign pointing east to Hovenweep National Monument. This is the first of a series of signs that will lead you Hovenweep. Roads are not for high speed driving but they're paved and fine for any RV. **Hovenweep** is a small archeological site but again, the magic here is the isolated location and, usually, few visitors. Actually, it's a very attractive site with a number of small ruins, some with towers, in a small canyon. A trail runs around the rim of the canyon, it's all on a small scale. There's a campground too, and if you're in a smaller RV or tent you might consider spending the night. For more information see the *Hovenweep* section (page 386).

Heading eastward follow the signs for Cortez. They'll lead you to an intersection with

US-160 just south of Cortez. Turn north and you'll soon be in Cortez, **Mesa Verde** is a few miles to the east. See the *Mesa Verde National Park and Cortez* area (page 307) for information.

🚐 DAY 3 – CANYON DE CHELLY – 140 MILES, 3 HOURS

From Cortez follow US-160 south to **four corners**, a distance of 40 miles. This is, of course, the place where four states come together in one place. Drive on over and take a look, you'll usually find a number of Indian vendors selling crafts.

In another 6 miles the highway will intersect US-64. Take a right and drive west 31 miles to the intersection where US-191 goes south. Head south yourself and drive across the Navajo reservation. In 63 miles you'll reach the town of Chinle. Turn left at the sign for **Canyon de Chelly** and in 2.6 miles you'll see the visitor center with the campground behind it. The *Canyon de Chelly* section (page 76) describes the attractions and campgrounds in the area.

🚐 DAY 4 – GALLUP – 275 MILES, 7 HOURS

The tour route today actually passes through Gallup once before returning quite some time later. There are opportunities for a number of stops along the way in fascinating places.

From Chinle drive south on US-191 to Ganado, a distance of 38 miles. There's an interesting stop in Ganado, the **Hubble Trading Post National Monument**. Here you can sort through a stack of $4,000 Navajo rugs in the corner of what seems to be a forgotten back room.

NAVAJO RUGS FOR SALE AT THE HUBBLE TRADING POST

Traveling on south you'll reach I-40 in about 37 miles. On I-40 drive eastward for 47 miles to Gallup. The plan is to come back here in the evening but for now take Exit 20, marked NM-602, and head south on US-191. In 31 miles you'll reach the **Zuni Pueblo**, you may wish to stop at the visitor center here and do some shopping. See the *Gallup* section (page 286) for more about this.

Now drive eastward on SR-53. Twenty-four miles from the turn you'll see the entrance to **El Morro National Monument** and in another 18 miles the entrance to **El Malpais National Monument**. Both are worth a stop to look around. See the *El Malpais and El Moro* section (page 268).

From El Malpais continue north until you meet I-40 and turn west. Gallup is a good place to spend the night, see the *Gallup* section (page 286) for information about things to see and places to stay in town.

⛺ DAY 5 – CHACO CULTURE NATIONAL HISTORIC PARK – 95 MILES, 3 HOURS

Chaco Canyon is pretty remote and you have to drive a few miles of terrible roads to reach the place, but it's worth it. If you have a small vehicle the drive isn't really that bad. You could conceivably take any vehicle in here, the roads are passable when dry, but big RVs are fragile and just not built for really rough roads. We'd be afraid that a few things might shake loose or break. If you have a tow car leave the big rig in Gallup and make a day trip out of this day's drive.

From Gallup drive east to Exit 53, about 30 miles, and turn north on SR-371. In 28 miles turn right on BIA-9 and drive 13 miles. Now turn left on SR-57, which is gravel, and drive north, slowly, the 20 miles to the park. When you reach it the roads are paved and the visitor center not far ahead. See the *Chaco Culture National Historic Park* section (page 249) for more about the area.

There is a campground at Chaco, suitable for tent campers and no-hookup RV camping for RVs to about 30 feet. It's fun to spend the night in such a remote location.

⛺ DAY 6 – PETRIFIED FOREST – 233 MILES, 5.5 HOURS

If you spent the night at Chaco you can begin the day's tour by driving back out to Gallup. Then enter I-40 and head west to the entrance to **Petrified Forest National Park**. It's at Exit 311, about 70 miles from Gallup.

This is a drive-through park. If you have a large RV and tow car you'll find that it can be hard to find a place to park during the busy summer season. You might want to drive on to Holbrook to leave the RV in a campground and use the tow car to drive through the park. See the *Holbrook and Petrified Forest National Park* section (page 103) for more about this park.

⛺ DAY 7 – FLAGSTAFF – 115 MILES, 2.5 HOURS

Westbound it's only 115 miles to Flagstaff. There are some places to stop, take a look around, and stretch your legs along the way.

The town of **Winslow**, which you can easily drive through on the business loop by taking Exit 257, is known for its "Standing on the Corner" statue and the La Posada hotel. See the *Winslow and the Hopi Mesas* section (page 204) for more information.

It's easy to stop and take a look at **Meteor Crater** at Exit 233. See *Meteor Crater* (page 127) for information.

Chapter 3

How to use the Destination Chapters

The chapters titled Arizona, New Mexico, and Utah are laid out in a similar manner. Each starts with an index map, it's the easiest way to find the information you need. The chapters begin with general descriptions of the landforms and regions of each state. Then there's information about the government campgrounds and their reservations systems (if any).

Chapter 7, the Mexico Destinations chapter, is slightly different. The first part of that chapter has a lot of information about traveling to and camping in the country.

Next; in Chapters 4, 5, 6, and 7; you'll come to the *Destinations and Their Campgrounds* section. Each destination section includes a map to give you the lay of the land and to pinpoint campground locations. The maps are for the most part pretty easy to interpret. We've included a key to the symbols on the following page.

We have selected destinations that are great places to visit as a camping traveler. These are places with convenient campgrounds as well as lots to see and do. Some of these are cities and towns, others are general recreational areas that may cover quite a bit of territory. We give you some background information about the place and also describe some of the attractions that you might want to visit.

Chapter 8, the Snowbirds Destinations chapter, is so different from the other destination chapters that it includes special How to Use instructions at the beginning of the chapter and none of the following applies to it.

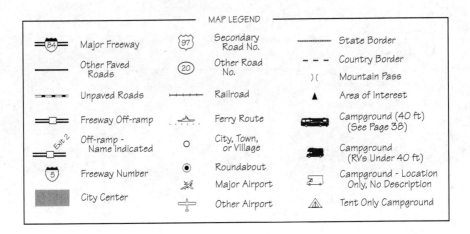

MAP LEGEND

Major Freeway	97 Secondary Road No.	State Border
Other Paved Roads	20 Other Road No.	Country Border
Unpaved Roads	Railroad	) (Mountain Pass
Freeway Off-ramp	Ferry Route	▲ Area of Interest
Off-ramp - Name Indicated	○ City, Town, or Village	Campground (40 ft) (See Page 38)
5 Freeway Number	◉ Roundabout	Campground (RVs Under 40 ft)
City Center	✈ Major Airport	Campground - Location Only, No Description
	✈ Other Airport	⚠ Tent Only Campground

Campground Information

Immediately after the name of the campground we give the opening and closing dates. Then there is contact information for making reservations or making inquiries by phone or email.

A location line gives the campground location with respect to some nearby landmark. The latitude and longitude data can be used if you have an electronic mapping program, a dashboard navigation system, or handheld GPS. At the end of the line is the approximate elevation of the campground.

Next is a line of pictograms or symbols. These are designed to convey important information about the campground at a glance. For your convenience abbreviated keys to these symbols are located on the back inside cover to this book.

FREE	Free	$ $$$	Over $15 and up to $20
$	Up To $5	$$ $$$	Over $20 and up to $25
$$	Over $5 and up to $10	$$$ $$$	Over $25 and up to $30
$$$	Over $10 and up to $15	Over $$$ $$$	Over $30

The first symbols are for price. Since campground prices do change frequently this is really an approximation, but it is the price that was in effect when the book was issued. It is the price for a standard full-hookup site with 30-amp power (if available) for a 30-foot RV. If you are tent camping you may find that no-hookup tent sites are often available for considerably less. If you are in a larger RV requiring a pull-thru site, 50-amp power, or yours is a premium or view site, you will probably find that the price is higher.

The remaining symbols are as follows:

 Tents – The campground does allow tent campers.

Rentals – The campground has rental cottages of some kind for those who do not want to sleep in a tent or RV. They may be yurts, motel rooms, cabins, or even te-pees.

 20 Amp Electric – Low amp electrical hookups are available. Air conditioning use not possible. Most low amp electrical hookups have 20 amp breakers but occasion-ally you'll find a 15 or even 10 amp circuit.

 30 Amp Electric – 30 amp electrical outlets are available.

 50 Amp Electric – 50 amp electrical outlets are available.

 Water – There is water at some or all of the sites. If there is no symbol then water is at faucets or a pump not at the sites. If there is no water we indicate so in the text section.

 Sewer – The sewer symbol means that there are sewer drains available at some or all sites.

 Dump – Indicates that there is a dump station (sani-station) available.

 Flush Toilets – Almost all of the campgrounds listed in this book have toilets, the toilet symbol in our descriptions shows which ones are flush toilets. You may also run into pit or vault (outhouse-style) toilets, particularly in federal campgrounds.

 Showers – Hot showers are available. There may be an additional fee for showers, usually in the form of a coin box that takes quarters.

 Fires – Campfires are allowed, usually at individual sites but sometimes at a central fire pit. Plan on either bringing firewood along with you or buying it at the camp-ground, you won't be able to pick wood off the forest floor either because it is prohib-ited or because there have been too many folks there ahead of you. Cutting standing trees is never permitted. Temporary fire bans are sometimes in effect.

 Swimming – Swimming is available either on-site or very nearby. It may be a swim-ming pool, lake, river, or even the ocean if folks customarily swim there. There are almost never lifeguards, you swim at your own risk. If the swimming is outdoors (not an inside pool) it may be seasonal.

 Playground – There is a playground for children with swings, slides and the equiva-lent or there are horseshoes, a play field, or provisions for some other type of sports.

 Telephone – There is a pay phone or courtesy phone available.

 TV – TV hookups are available at some or all sites.

 Internet – Internet access of some kind is available. It may be an outlet (data port) for you to plug in your computer modem cable or it may be a computer with internet access that you will be allowed to use.

 WI-Fi – Indicates that Wi-Fi (wireless internet) is available in the campground. Wi-Fi access is the fastest changing amenity offered by campgrounds today. Campgrounds are adding Wi-Fi access at a pretty good clip. If this is important to you don't hesitate to ask before making a reservation or perhaps call ahead as you approach your desti-nation to determine the current offerings of the campgrounds you are considering.

Free Wi-Fi – Wi-Fi is not only available – it's free. Since Wi-Fi is such a new thing many campground owners are feeling their way on this. We're finding that many that charged at first are now offering it for free, but also that some that originally didn't charge now are. If you like free Wi-Fi you should let campgrounds owners know it.

 Groceries – Many campgrounds have small stores. We've included this symbol if the store appears to have enough stock to be useful, or if there is an off-site store within easy walking distance.

 Restaurants – Few campgrounds in the U.S. or Mexico have restaurants, but if they do, or if there is one within easy walking distance, we include the restaurant symbol.

 Laundry – The campground has self-operated washers.

 Propane – The campground offers either bottled propane or a propane fill station.

 Ice – Either block or cubed ice is available for ice chests or drinks.

 Wheelchair – The wheelchair symbol indicates that some provision has been made for wheelchair toilet access. These provisions vary considerably, you should call the information number listed for the campground to get more details if this is a consideration for you.

 No Pets – No dogs or cats are allowed. Virtually all campgrounds require leashes and the majority restrict number, size, and breed. Call the information number to inquire if this might apply to you.

 Reservations – Reservations are taken. Please refer to the *Campground Reservations* sections at the beginning of the Destinations chapters for information about making reservations at government campgrounds. Commercial campgrounds are easier, just call the listed telephone number.

 Credit Cards – Either Master Card or Visa is accepted.

 Good Sam – Many campgrounds give a discount to members of the Good Sam Club. We include the symbol if they are official Good Sam campgrounds. We find that the standards required for listing by Good Sam mean that in general these campgrounds stand out as having decent facilities, good management, and relatively fair prices. For club information call (800) 234-3450 or see their website at www.goodsamclub.com.

 Escapees – The Escapee symbol means that discounts are offered to members of the Escapees RV Club. Call (888) 757-2582 or (936) 327-8873 for more information or see their website – www.escapees.com.

 FMCA – Discounts are available to FMCA members. Call (800) 543-3622 or (513) 474-3622 for more information if you own a qualifying motorhome, or check the website at www.fmca.com.

 Passport America – Passport America discount cards are accepted. Most campgrounds offering this discount also will sell you the card.

 40 Foot RVs – Coaches to 40 feet will fit in the park. See *RV Size* below for more about this.

In the text portion of the campground listing we try to give you some feeling for the campground as well as detailed instructions for how to find it. We've included a count of the number of available sites in the campground, sites occupied by permanently situated mobile homes, park units, or RVs are not counted. These are our count and may vary from the owner's count, particularly if there are tent sites at the campground since it is sometimes difficult to count these.

RV Size

Our Big Rig symbol means that there is room for coaches to 40 feet to enter the campground, maneuver, and park. Usually this means we've seen them do it. The driver we saw may have been a better driver than most so exercise caution. If you pull a fifth-wheel you'll have to use your own judgment of how your RV handles compared with a coach. If you drive an even larger 45-foot coach you can at least use our symbol as a starting point in making your campground decisions. There's often more in the write-up itself about this, and we also usually mention pull-thrus if available. Always evaluate the campground and assigned space yourself before attempting to maneuver and park, the final decision is yours. A properly trained outside spotter is essential, most RV accidents occur during the parking phase.

Units of Measurement

The region covered by this guide uses two different sets of measurements. Mexico is on the metric system while the U.S. uses miles and gallons.

Here are some handy conversion factors:

1 km = .62 mile	1 liter = .26 U.S. gallon
1 mile = 1.61 km	1 U.S. gallon = 3.79 liters
1 meter = 3.28 feet	1 kilogram = 2.21 pounds
1 foot = .3 meters	1 pound = .45 kilogram

Convert from °F to °C by subtracting 32 and multiplying by 5/9
Convert from °C to °F by multiplying by 1.8 and adding 32

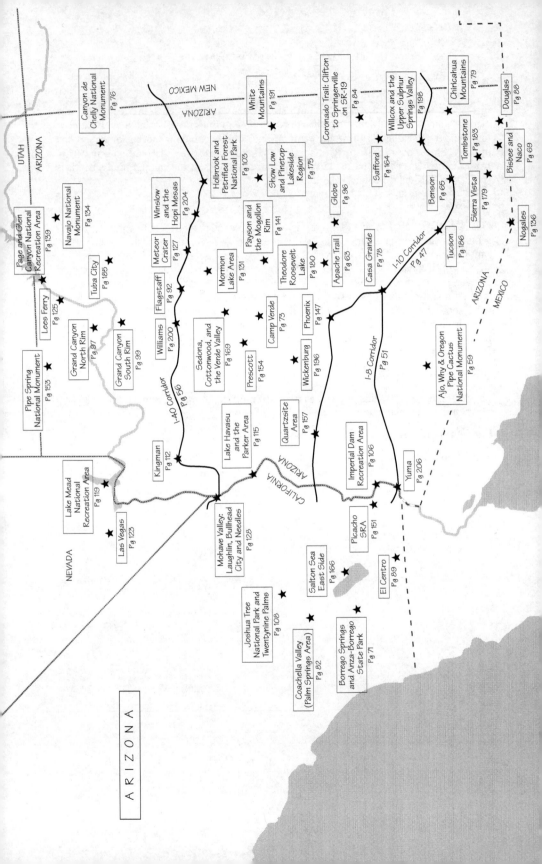

ARIZONA

NEVADA

UTAH

ARIZONA

NEW MEXICO
ARIZONA

CALIFORNIA
ARIZONA

ARIZONA
MEXICO

Page and Glen Canyon National Recreation Area Pg 139

Canyon de Chelly National Monument Pg 76

White Mountains Pg 191

Chiricahua Mountains Pg 79

Willcox and the Upper Sulphur Springs Valley Pg 198

Douglas Pg 88

Navajo National Monument Pg 134

Holbrook and Petrified Forest National Park Pg 103

Show Low and Pinetop-Lakeside Region Pg 175

Coronado Trail: Clifton to Springerville on SR-19 Pg 84

Tombstone Pg 183

Lees Ferry Pg 125

Tuba City Pg 185

Winslow and the Hopi Mesas Pg 204

Safford Pg 164

Bisbee and Naco Pg 69

Grand Canyon North Rim Pg 97

Meteor Crater Pg 127

Payson and the Mogollon Rim Pg 141

Globe Pg 96

Benson Pg 65

Sierra Vista Pg 179

Nogales Pg 136

Pipe Spring National Monument Pg 153

Grand Canyon South Rim Pg 99

Flagstaff Pg 92

Mormon Lake Area Pg 131

Theodore Roosevelt Lake Pg 180

Apache Trail Pg 63

Tucson Pg 186

Williams Pg 200

Camp Verde Pg 73

Phoenix Pg 147

Casa Grande Pg 78

I-10 Corridor Pg 47

Lake Mead National Recreation Area Pg 119

Sedona, Cottonwood, and the Verde Valley Pg 169

Prescott Pg 154

Wickenburg Pg 196

Las Vegas Pg 123

I-40 Corridor Pg 56

Lake Havasu and the Parker Area Pg 115

Quartzsite Area Pg 157

I-8 Corridor Pg 51

Ajo, Why & Oregon Pipe Cactus National Monument Pg 59

Kingman Pg 112

Imperial Dam Recreation Area Pg 106

Yuma Pg 206

Mohave Valley: Laughlin, Bullhead City and Needles Pg 128

Picacho SRA Pg 151

El Centro Pg 89

Joshua Tree National Park and Twentynine Palms Pg 108

Salton Sea East Side Pg 166

Coachella Valley (Palm Springs Area) Pg 82

Borrego Springs and Anza-Borrego State Park Pg 71

Chapter 4

Arizona

When you look at our Arizona map you'll see that we've also included a bit of both California and Nevada in this chapter. These areas of other states fit well with the Arizona camping and RVing scene and it just didn't make sense to add separate California and Nevada chapters.

The population of Arizona is about 5.2 million people, that's almost 3 times that of New Mexico next door. The land area is 114,006 square miles. That's less than New Mexico but not by much, the state is 6th in size in the US.

About half of the people in Arizona live in the Phoenix metropolitan area. That means that Arizona has a relatively small population in the rest of the state. A big reason for this is the lack of water. There are only a few agricultural areas in the state and those that are there are require intensive irrigation.

Altitude means a lot when you are traveling or camped in Arizona. North of Mogollon Rim on the Colorado Plateau the state has cold winters and comfortable summers. South of the rim there are very comfortable winters and extremely hot summers. As you travel in Arizona you will be very aware of this, and you must take it into account when planning your trips.

Arizona's low country experiences a remarkable migration. Each winter the Snowbirds arrive. These are people, a great many of them in RVs, who come here to enjoy the wonderful winter weather.

In this book we have a special chapter just for Snowbird RVers. The huge Snowbird RV parks are designed for this type of living, not really for traveling car campers and RVers. For that reason we have treated them separately. You'll find that the big Snowbird destinations are presented twice, once in this chapter from the perspective of camping travelers, and a second time in the Snowbird chapter from that of the Snowbird resident.

REGIONS AND THEIR CAMPGROUND RESOURCES

The destinations in this book are listed alphabetically. To help you place them in a useful mental framework it might help you to think of them as falling into the following regions.

Northwest Arizona

The northern half of Arizona is almost all part of the Colorado Plateau. That means it's high, usually over 6,000 feet. If you are a traveler you'll want to visit his area in the summer. To the west the plateau subsides and becomes the wide Mohave Valley, actually part of the Colorado River Valley.

Flagstaff is the largest city in northwest Arizona but the biggest attraction for visitors has to be the Grand Canyon. Before going you might take a look at the *Williams* section too, it makes a great base for such a visit.

In this book you'll find the following sections covering this northwest area: ● *Flagstaff*, ● *Grand Canyon North Rim*, ● *Grand Canyon South Rim*, ● *Kingman*, ● *Lees Ferry*, ● *Mormon Lake Area*, ● *Pipe Spring National Monument*, and ● *Williams*.

Northeast Arizona

Northeast Arizona is, above all, Indian country. The huge Navajo reservation occupies much of the northeastern corner of the state. The Hopi Reservation is there too, totally surrounded by the Navajo reservation. This area too is high and primarily a summer destination:

Destinations in this book in northeast Arizona are: ● *Canyon de Chelly National Monument*, ● *Holbrook and the Petrified Forest National Park*, ● *Meteor Crater*, ● *Navajo National Monument*, ● *Page and Glen Canyon National Recreation Area*, ● *Tuba City*, and ● *Winslow and the Hopi Mesas*.

The Rim Country

The Mogollon Rim is the edge of the Colorado Plateau. It runs right through the middle of Arizona with a northwest – southeast slant. The rim country is a region of pines and junipers. Much of it is in National Forests. In some places the rim is clearly defined with a drop 2,000 feet or more. In others it is more gradual. For the most part the rim country is a summer destination.

Rim destinations in this book include: ● *Coronado Trail*, ● *Payson and the Mogollon Rim*, ● *Prescott*, ● *Show Low and the Pinetop Region*, ● *Sedona, Cottonwood and the Verde Valley*, and the ● *White Mountains*.

Southwest Arizona

Southwest Arizona is where most of the people in the state live. It's also where most of the snowbird destinations are located. The altitude is low, mostly below 2,000 feet, so it's definitely a winter destination.

Southwest Arizona destinations described in this book include: ● *Ajo, Why, and Organ*

Pipe Cactus National Monument, ● *Casa Grande,* ● *Phoenix,* ● *Quartzsite Area,* ● *Sierra Vista,* ● *Theodore Roosevelt Lake,* and ● *Wickenburg.*

Southeast Arizona

In southern Arizona, as you travel east, the land gradually rises until at the Arizona – New Mexico border it's at about 4,000 feet. Although the basins are fairly flat there are a number of small north-south trending mountain ranges. These are known as "Sky Island", mountain ranges because their flora and fauna is so different from the deserts that surround them. Most are part of a national forest.

Destinations in this area include: ● *Apache Trail,* ● *Benson,* ● *Bisbee and Naco,* ● *Chiricahua Mountains,* ● *Douglas,* ● *Globe,* ● *Nogales,* ● *Safford,* ● *Sierra Vista,* ● *Tombstone,* ● *Tucson,* and ● *Willcox and the Upper Sulphur Springs Valley.*

Colorado River Valley

The Colorado River Valley forms the border between Arizona and California. There are a number of dams and reservoirs here and water-related activities like boating and fishing are popular in the summer. As this is also a low-altitude area it's a popular winter destination. In fact, it's one of the few places in Arizona that gets lots of both summer and winter visitors.

Colorado River Valley destinations described in this book include: ● *Imperial Dam Recreation Area,* ● *Lake Havasu and the Parker Area,* ● *Mohave Valley: Laughlin, Bullhead City, and Needles,* ● *Picacho State Recreation Area,* and ● *Yuma.*

Southern California Desert and Las Vegas

The southern California desert and the southern tip of Nevada are very much like the desert country to the east in Arizona. They're also very easy to access from Arizona. It doesn't seem like there should be a state border here at all, so we've ignored it and included the area in the Arizona chapter.

Destinations in California and Nevada included in this book are: ● *Borrego Springs,* ● *Coachella Valley,* ● *East of the Salton Sea,* ● *El Centro,* ● *Picacho State Recreation Area,* ● *Lake Mead National Recreation Area,* ● *Joshua Tree National Park and Twentynine Palms,* and ● *Las Vegas.*

I-40 Corridor

I-40 crosses the state of Arizona, a distance of 359 miles from the California border to New Mexico. You'll find the following destinations listed in this chapter along the route. The numbers are the distance from the California border. From west to east: ● *Needles* (actually 13 miles west of the border in California), ● *Kingman* (48 miles), ● *Williams* (161 miles), ● *Flagstaff* (195 miles), ● *Meteor Crater* (233 miles), ● *Winslow* (252 miles), and ● *Holbrook* (285 miles). For an overview see *Interstate 40 Corridor – Arizona* on page 56.

I-10 Corridor

I-10 also crosses the state, it takes 390 miles to do it. The destinations in this chapter along the corridor (and their miles from the California border) are as follows: ● *Palm Springs* (118 miles west of the border in California), ● *Quartzsite* (17 miles), ● *Phoenix* (124 miles), ● *Casa Grande* (194 miles), ● *Tucson* (255 miles), ● *Benson* (303 miles), and ● *Willcox* (340 miles). For an overview see *Interstate 10 Corridor – Arizona* on page 47.

I-8 Corridor

I-8 only makes it half way across the state, then connects with I-10 after 179 miles. The destinations in this chapter along the corridor (and their miles from the California border) are as follows: • *El Centro* (56 miles west of the border in California), • *Yuma* (1 mile), and • *Casa Grande* (172 miles). For an overview see *Interstate 8 Corridor – Arizona* on page 51.

GOVERNMENT LANDS AND THEIR CAMPGROUND

Arizona State Campgrounds

The state of Arizona doesn't have nearly as many campgrounds as you might expect. There are only 14 of them, all are included in this book.

You'll find that most state campgrounds have electricity and water hookups available. In fact, only Lost Dutchman and Lake Havasu State Park do not have electric hookups. Some even have sewer hookups. All have dump stations as well as restrooms with showers. Generally there are big sites in these campgrounds with at least some able to accept the largest RVs, see the individual entries in this book about this. All Arizona State Park campgrounds are open all year long.

Most Arizona state campgrounds do not accept reservations for individual sites although they generally do for group sites. Only Roper Lake and Buckskin Mountain accept reservations, you make them directly with the park.

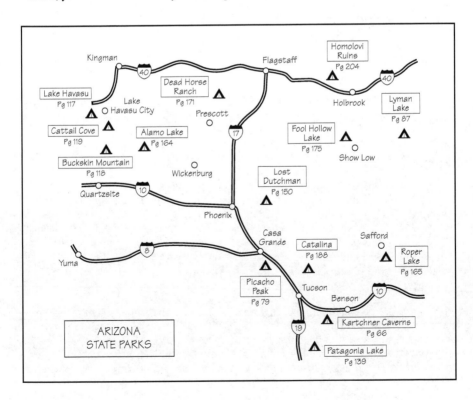

Federal Campgrounds

The Arizona (and California) chapter includes federal campgrounds in seven national forests: Apache, Coconino, Coronado, Kaibab, Prescott, Sitgreaves and Tonto. There are also National Park campgrounds at Canyon de Chelly National Monument, Glen Canyon National Recreation Area, Grand Canyon National Park, Joshua Tree National Park, Lake Mead National Recreation Area, Navajo National Monument, and Organ Pipe National Monument.

Trying to camp in federal campgrounds in a large RV can be a frustrating experience. Many of them just don't have adequately sized sites for modern RVs. Some do, however, and we've tried to give you the information you need in the individual campground write-ups to help you decide which ones will work for you. Some federal campgrounds now offer hookups. You'll find a few in our *Glen Canyon National Recreation Area*; *Grand Canyon North Rim*; and *Sedona, Cottonwood and the Verde Valley* chapters.

Seniors can get a discount on fees for most federal government campgrounds. If you're a US citizen or permanent resident and 62 years old you can buy a Senior Pass. The cost is $10 for life, it gets you half off on most federal campground fees as well as free access to National Parks and other federal lands.

Federal and state campgrounds often have a time limit of 14 days. This is to keep campers from setting up a long term residence in a federal or state campground with low fees and a wonderful location. However, there are federal lands where you can stay longer, see below.

BLM Land Camping

Arizona and southern California have a great deal of Bureau of Land Management federal desert lands. They also get a large number of long-term RV visitors. This combination has created a unique type of camping in the region.

Southwest Arizona and southeast California have campgrounds designated as LTVAs or Long Term Visitor Areas. These are large areas with few facilities. Usually there is a camp host, vault toilets, and sometimes a nearby dump station. Here are the LTVAs and the sections where you'll find a full description of each of them in this book:

Hot Springs LTVA – See *El Centro* section
Imperial Dam LTVA – See *Imperial Dam Recreation Area* section
La Posa LTVA (4 areas) – See *Quartzsite Area* section
Midland LTVA – See *Quartzsite Area* section
Mule Mountain LTVA – See *Quartzsite Area* section
Pilot Knob LTVA – See *Yuma* section
Tamarisk LTVA – See *El Centro* section

Camping vehicles must have at least a 10 gallon waste tank onboard. Port-a-potties are not allowed. An exception is made in the La Posa, Imperial Dam, and Mule Mountain LTVAs for vehicles within 500 feet of one of the toilets. Tents can be used in these same locations but not farther than 500 feet from the toilets and not in the other LTVAs.

LTVAs operate from September 15 to April 15 each year. During that time you can stay in one location without moving or you can move to another LTVA. Or, of course, you can go off and do something else. The fee is either $40 for 14 consecutive days or $180 for the full September 15 to April 15 period.

LTVA permits can be purchased at the La Posa LTVA during busy periods or at the following offices:

BLM Yuma, 2555 E Gila Ridge Road, Yuma, AZ 85365; (928) 317-3200
BLM El Centro, 1661 S 4th St, El Centro, CA 92243; (760) 337-4400
BLM Palm Springs, 690 W Garnet Ave, N Palm Springs, CA 92258;
   (760) 251-4800

In the off season the LTVAs normally become free dispersed camping areas like those described below. However, Imperial Dam and La Posa have a special fee of $15 per overnight stay or $75 per year. Self-pay stations have been set up at the LTVAs.

Camping on other BLM lands is known as dispersed camping. In general, the BLM lets you camp on any BLM land as long as it isn't posted against camping and as long as you're not interfering with some other use, or in some way adversely affecting wildlife species or natural resources. There are absolutely no facilities, you must pack in and pack out everything. This type of camping is usually free, but there is one major condition. You can only camp in one area for 14 days out of any 28 day period. Once your 14 days are up you must move to another site that is at least 25 miles distant – as the crow flies.

Although the BLM says you can camp on much of their land it is often hard to tell what's theirs and what is not. For that reason dispersed camping RVers tend to camp in areas where they see other RVers already parked. You'll find that a few even have a host. There are many very popular areas, we have listed a number of them in the book. Additionally, there is a short term dispersed camping area associated with almost every LTVA,

CAMPING AT THE DARBY WELLS ROAD BLM DISPERSED CAMPING AREA

ARIZONA

although they are often less conveniently located and always a mile or two away. Ask the host at any LTVA about this.

Here are some of the BLM short term dispersed camping areas described in this book:

Chiriaco Summit – See *Joshua Tree National Park and Twentynine Palms Area* section

Craggy Wash – See *Lake Havasu and Parker* Area section

Darby Wells Road – See *Ajo, Why, and Organ Pipe Cactus National Monument* section

Dome Rock Mountain – See *Quartzsite Area* section

Gunsite Wash – See *Ajo, Why, and Organ Pipe Cactus National Monument* section

Hi Jolly/MM 112 – See *Quartzsite Area* section

Plomosa Road – See *Quartzsite* section

Road Runner/MM 99 – See *Quartzsite Area* section

San Joaquin Rd – See *Tucson* section

Scaddan Wash – See *Quartzsite Area* section

Standard Wash – See *Lake Havasu and Parker Area* section

Yuma VFW – See *Yuma* section

DESTINATIONS AND THEIR CAMPGROUNDS

INTERSTATE 10 CORRIDOR – ARIZONA

Interstate 10 (I-10) is one of two main corridors running across Arizona and New Mexico. I-10 is the preferred winter route since it travels across much lower country than I-40 to the north and therefore has much better driving conditions. In summer you might prefer I-40, it's more scenic and a little cooler.

In Arizona I-10 is 390 miles long. Mileage markers (and therefore highway exit numbers) start on the western border. The campgrounds listed below are all in Arizona. See the *Interstate 10 Corridor* section in the New Mexico chapter for campgrounds in that state.

You will note that many of the campgrounds along the highway are described in other places in this book. Rather than including them twice we've given the page number where you can find the detailed descriptions. Some are listed in our Snowbird Chapter. From December until April these Snowbird campgrounds are very busy but often do have a few spaces available for travelers. The rest of the year they're often pretty empty, but still a possible option for travelers.

I-10 runs through the Phoenix metro area. You might think this area would be full of campgrounds, and it is. However, few are conveniently located for an overnight stop when you're traveling I-10. You'll see there is a big gap in the list below between Exit 124 to the west of Phoenix and Exit 185 in Casa Grande, that's Phoenix. Keep that in mind if you're traveling so that you don't get caught in Phoenix traffic trying to find a campground.

Interstate Corridor 10 Campgrounds

➲ *Exit 11*

▦ **DOME ROCK MOUNTAIN BLM DISPERSED CAMPING AREA** *(Listed under Quartzsite on page 161)*

ARIZONA

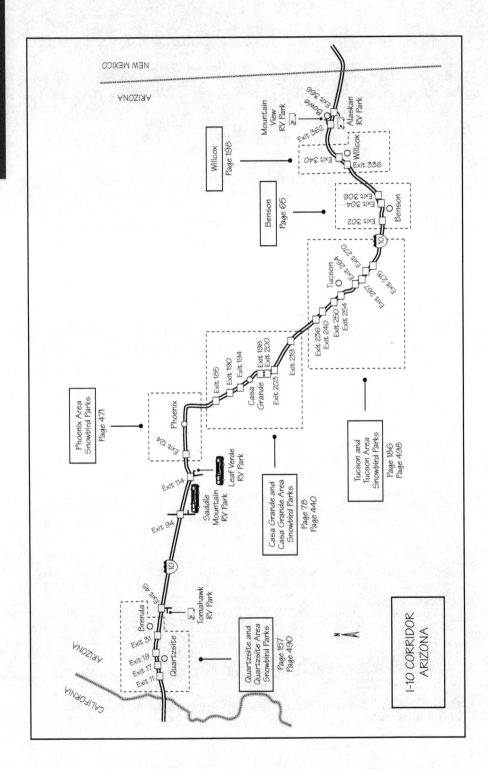

➲ *Exit 17 and Exit 19*

QUARTZITE WITH MANY COMMERCIAL RV PARKS AND BLM DESERT CAMPING
LOCATIONS *(See Quartzsite Area on page 157 and also the description of Quartzsite in Chapter 8 – Snowbird Destinations on page 490)*

➲ *Exit 31*

BRENDA RV RESORT *(Listed as a snowbird park under Quartzsite Area in Chapter 8 – Snowbird Destinations on page 494)*

BLACK ROCK RV VILLAGE *(Listed as a snowbird park under Quartzsite Area in Chapter 8 – Snowbird Destinations on page 494)*

DESERT GOLD RV RESORT *(Listed as a snowbird park under Quartzsite Area in Chapter 8 – Snowbird Destinations on page 495)*

GATEWAY RANCH RV RETREAT *(Listed as a snowbird park under Quartzsite Area in Chapter 8 – Snowbird Destinations on page 496)*

WAGON WEST RV PARK *(Listed as a snowbird park under Quartzsite Area in Chapter 8 – Snowbird Destinations on page 497)*

➲ *Exit 94*

SADDLE MOUNTAIN RV PARK *(Open All Year)*
Res and Info: (623) 386-3892, smrvpark@aol.com
Location: Tonopah, *N 33° 29' 19", W 112° 56' 12", 1,008 Ft*

340 Sites – This is a big modern RV park designed for snowbirds but also a good option for traveling RVs. Amenities here include a swimming pool. Sites are paved or gravel off wide paved access roads. They are back-ins and pull-thrus to 60 feet. Take Exit 94 from I-10 and drive south for .5 mile, the park is on the left.

➲ *Exit 114*

LEAF VERDE RV RESORT *(Open All Year)*
Res and Info: (623) 386-3132, leafrv@aol.com
Location: Buckeye, *N 33° 25' 54", W 112° 34' 26", 1,000 Ft*

400 Sites – This is a large RV park located close enough to Phoenix for a driving visit but far enough out to avoid the urban traffic when accessing the campground. It's also very close to the freeway. Sites here are back-ins and pull-thrus to 65 feet. All are full-hookup sites. Take Exit 114 and then follow the access road on the south side of the freeway toward the east. After 1 mile turn right into South Apache Road, the campground entrance will be on the left in a short distance.

➲ *Exit 124*

DESTINY RV RESORTS PHOENIX WEST *(Listed as a snowbird park under Phoenix in Chapter 8 – Snowbird Destinations on page 487)*

COTTON LANE RV AND MOBILE HOME RESORT *(Listed as a snowbird park under Phoenix in Chapter 8 – Snowbird Destinations on page 487)*

ARIZONA

➲ **Exit 185**

🚐 **FOOTHILLS WEST RV RESORT** *(Listed as a snowbird park under Casa Grande in Chapter 8 – Snowbird Destinations on page 443)*

🚐 **LEISURE VALLEY RV PARK** *(Listed as a snowbird park under Casa Grande in Chapter 8 – Snowbird Destinations on page 444)*

🚐 **VAL VISTA WINTER VILLAGE RV RESORT** *(Listed as a snowbird park under Casa Grande in Chapter 8 – Snowbird Destinations on page 445)*

➲ **Exit 190**

🚐 **CASITA VERDE RV PARK** *(Listed as a snowbird park under Casa Grande in Chapter 8 – Snowbird Destinations on page 443)*

🚐 **SUNDANCE 1 RV PARK** *(Listed as a snowbird park under Casa Grande in Chapter 8 – Snowbird Destinations on page 444)*

🚐 **PALM CREEK GOLF AND RV RESORT** *(Listed as a snowbird park under Casa Grande in Chapter 8 – Snowbird Destinations on page 444)*

➲ **Exit 194**

🚐 **FIESTA GRANDE AN RV RESORT** *(Listed as a snowbird park under Casa Grande in Chapter 8 – Snowbird Destinations on page 443)*

➲ **Exit 198**

🚐 **CAMPGROUND BUENA TIERRA** *(Listed under Casa Grande on page 79)*

➲ **Exit 200**

🚐 **LAS COLINAS RV PARK** *(Listed as a snowbird park under Casa Grande in Chapter 8 – Snowbird Destinations on page 444)*

🚐 **QUAIL RUN RV PARK** *(Listed as a snowbird park under Casa Grande in Chapter 8 – Snowbird Destinations on page 444)*

➲ **Exit 203**

🚐 **DESERT VALLEY RV PARK** *(Listed as a snowbird park under Casa Grande in Chapter 8 – Snowbird Destinations on page 443)*

🚐 **HIGH CHAPARRAL MOTORHOME AND RV PARK** *(Listed as a snowbird park under Casa Grande in Chapter 8 – Snowbird Destinations on page 443)*

➲ **Exit 219**

🚐 **PICACHO PEAK STATE PARK** *(Listed under Casa Grande on page 79)*

🚐 **PICACHO PEAK RV RESORT** *(Listed under Casa Grande on page 79)*

➲ **Exit 236**

🚐 **VALLEY OF THE SUN RV RESORT** *(Listed as a snowbird park under Tucson in Chapter 8 – Snowbird Destinations on page 503)*

➲ **Exit 240**

🚐 **A BAR A RV PARK** *(Listed as a snowbird park under Tucson in Chapter 8 – Snowbird Destinations on page 501)*

➲ **Exit 250**

🚐 **SOUTH FORTY RV RANCH** *(Listed as a snowbird park under Tucson in Chapter 8 – Snowbird Destinations on page 502)*

➲ *Exit 254*

▣ **PRINCE OF TUCSON RV PARK** *(Listed as a snowbird park under Tucson in Chapter 8 – Snowbird Destinations on page 502)*

▣ **TRA-TEL TUCSON RV PARK** *(Listed as a snowbird park under Tucson in Chapter 8 – Snowbird Destinations on page 502)*

➲ *Exit 264*

▣ **BEAUDRY RV RESORT AND RALLY PARK** *(Listed under Tucson on page 501)*

➲ *Exit 267*

▣ **CRAZY HORSE RV PARK** *(Listed as a snowbird park under Tucson in Chapter 8 – Snowbird Destinations on page 501)*

➲ *Exit 270*

▣ **VOYAGER RESORT** *(Listed as a snowbird park under Tucson in Chapter 8 – Snowbird Destinations on page 503)*

➲ *Exit 275*

▣ **PIMA COUNTY FAIRGROUNDS** *(Listed under Tucson on page 189)*

▣ **ADVENTURE BOUND CAMPING RESORTS** *(Listed as a snowbird park under Tucson in Chapter 8 – Snowbird Destinations on page 501)*

➲ *Exit 302*

▣ **COCHISE TERRACE RV RESORT** *(Listed under Benson on page 67)*

▣ **KARTCHNER CAVERNS STATE PARK** *(Listed under Benson on page 66)*

➲ *Exit 304*

▣ **BENSON KOA** *(Listed under Benson on page 68)*

▣ **QUARTER HORSE MOTEL AND RV PARK** *(Listed under Benson on page 67)*

▣ **BENSON I-10 RV PARK** *(Listed under Benson on page 67)*

▣ **RED BARN RV PARK** *(Listed under Benson on page 68)*

▣ **BUTTERFIELD RV RESORT** *(Listed under Benson on page 67)*

➲ *Exit 306*

▣ **PATO BLANCO LAKES RV PARK** *(Listed under Benson on page 68)*

➲ *Exit 336*

▣ **FORT WILCOX RV PARK** *(Listed under Wilcox on page 199)*

➲ *Exit 340*

▣ **MAGIC CIRCLE RV PARK** *(Listed under Wilcox on page 199)*

▣ **GRANDE VISTA RV PARK** *(Listed under Wilcox on page 199)*

▣ **LIFESTYLE RV RESORT** *(Listed under Wilcox on page 199)*

INTERSTATE 8 CORRIDOR – ARIZONA

Interstate 8 (I-8) runs 178 miles from Yuma on the California border to intersect with I-10 near Casa Grande. Mileage markers (and therefore highway exit numbers) start at 0 near Yuma and increase as you travel east.

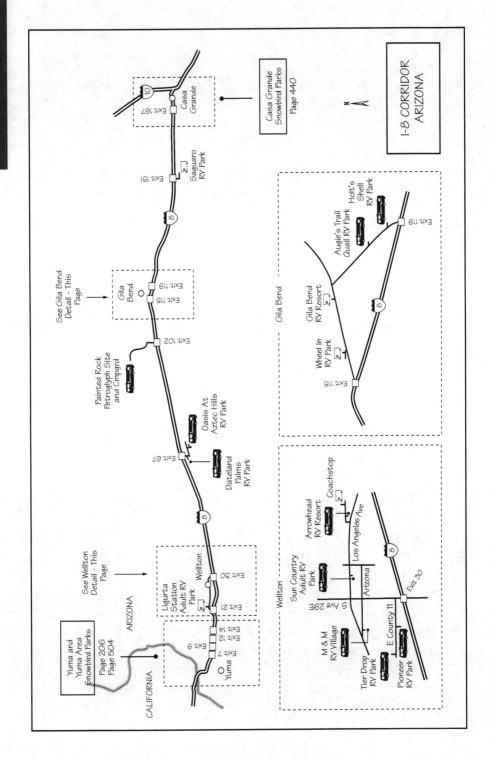

You will note that many of the campgrounds along the highway are described in other places in this book. Rather than including them twice we've given the page number where you can find the detailed descriptions. Some are listed in our Snowbird Chapter. From December until April these Snowbird campgrounds are very busy but often do have a few spaces available for travelers. The rest of the year they're often pretty empty, but still a possible option for travelers.

Interstate 8 Corridor Campgrounds

➲ **Exit 7**

🚐 EL PRADO ESTATES RV PARK *(Listed as a snowbird park under Yuma in Chapter 8 – Snowbird Destinations on page 509)*

🚐 WINDHAVEN RV PARK *(Listed as a snowbird park under Yuma in Chapter 8 – Snowbird Destinations on page 513)*

🚐 ARABY ACRES RESORT *(Listed as a snowbird park under Yuma in Chapter 8 – Snowbird Destinations on page 508)*

🚐 ARIZONA WEST RV PARK *(Listed as a snowbird park under Yuma in Chapter 8 – Snowbird Destinations on page 508)*

🚐 SUN VISTA RV RESORT *(Listed as a snowbird park under Yuma in Chapter 8 – Snowbird Destinations on page 512)*

➲ **Exit 9**

🚐 DESERT PARADISE RV RESORT *(Listed as a snowbird park under Yuma in Chapter 8 – Snowbird Destinations on page 509)*

🚐 CACTUS GARDENS RV PARK *(Listed as a snowbird park under Yuma in Chapter 8 – Snowbird Destinations on page 508)*

🚐 WESTWIND RV AND GOLF RESORT *(Listed as a snowbird park under Yuma in Chapter 8 – Snowbird Destinations on page 513)*

🚐 BONITA MESA RV RESORT *(Listed as a snowbird park under Yuma in Chapter 8 – Snowbird Destinations on page 508)*

➲ **Exit 12**

🚐 BLUE SKY RV PARK *(Listed under Yuma on page 207)*

🚐 WESTERN SANDS RV PARK *(Listed as a snowbird park under Yuma in the Chapter 8 – Snowbird Destinations on page 512)*

🚐 ADOBE VILLAGE RV PARK *(Listed as a snowbird park under Yuma in Chapter 8 – Snowbird Destinations chapter on page 508)*

🚐 SUNRIDGE RV PARK *(Listed as a snowbird park under Yuma in Chapter 8 – Snowbird Destinations on page 511)*

🚐 SUNSET PALMS RV PARK *(Listed as a snowbird park under Yuma in Chapter 8 – Snowbird Destinations on page 512)*

🚐 LAS QUINTAS OASIS RV RESORT *(Listed as a snowbird park under Yuma in Chapter 8 – Snowbird Destinations on page 510)*

🚐 SHANGRI-LA RV RESORT *(Listed as a snowbird park under Yuma in Chapter 8 – Snowbird Destinations on page 511)*

🚐 CARAVAN OASIS RV PARK *(Listed as a snowbird park under Yuma in Chapter 8 – Snowbird Destinations on page 509)*

➲ **Exit 14**

📷 **FORTUNA DE ORO RV RESORTS** *(Listed under Yuma on page 207)*

📷 **SUNDANCE RV PARK** *(Listed as a snowbird park under Yuma in Chapter 8 – Snowbird Destinations on page 512)*

📷 **GILA MOUNTAIN RV PARK** *(Listed as a snowbird park under Yuma in Chapter 8 – Snowbird Destinations on page 510)*

📷 **FOOTHILL VILLAGE RV RESORT** *(Listed as a snowbird park under Yuma in Chapter 8 – Snowbird Destinations on page 509)*

➲ **Exit 30**

📷 **TIER DROP RV PARK** *(Open All Year)*
Res and Info: (928) 785-9295
Location: Wellton, *N 32° 39' 49", W 114° 09' 17", 200 Ft*

200 Sites – The Tier Drop has a swimming pool. Sites are back-ins and pull-thrus to 50 feet. From I-8 take Exit 30 and head north. Take the first left onto E County 11th Street. The campground entrance is on the right in .7 mile.

📷 **PIONEER RV PARK** *(Open All Year)*
Res and Info: (928) 785-3579, www.yumarvparks.com
Location: Wellton, *N 32° 39' 48", W 114° 08' 59", 200 Ft*

336 Spaces – The Pioneer is a popular 55+ snowbird-type park. Like the other campgrounds in Wellton it's very full in winter and empty in the summer. Sites are back-ins to 55 feet with full hookups. Amenities include a pool and spa. From I-8 take Exit 30 and head north. Take the first left onto E County 11th Street. The campground entrance is on the left in .4 mile.

📷 **ARROWHEAD RV RESORT** *(Open All Year)*
Res and Info: (928) 785-3648
Location: Wellton, *N 32° 40' 28", W 114° 07' 15", 200 Ft*

160 Sites – The Arrowhead has full-hookup back-ins and pull-thrus to 60 feet. Amenities include a swimming pool and spa. From Exit 30 of I-8 drive north on Ave 29 E for .7 mile. Turn right on Los Angeles Avenue (Old Hwy 80) and drive .8 mile. Turn left into Mohawk Blvd. After one block turn right and you'll soon see the entrance.

📷 **SUN COUNTRY ADULT RV PARK** *(Open All Year)*
Res and Info: (928) 785-4072
Location: Wellton, *N 32° 40' 25", W 114° 08' 17", 200 Ft*

180 Sites – The Sun Country is one of Wellton's snowbird parks, it's a 55+ adult park. Sites are full-hookup back-ins and pull-thrus to 40 feet. Take Exit 30 from I-8 and drive

north on Ave 29 E for .7 mile. Turn right on Los Angeles Avenue (Old Hwy 80) and you'll see the park on the right in one block.

M & M RV VILLAGE *(Open All Year)*

Res and Info: (928) 785-4273, (800) 365 6966, tsmangine2@aol.com
Location: Wellton, *N 32° 40' 14", W 114° 09' 00", 200 Ft*

90 Sites – The M&M is one of the older parks in Wellton but does sometimes accept tents. Railroad noise is a big problem here with tracks right next to the park. Sites are full-hookup back-ins and pull-thrus to 40 feet. From Exit 30 of I-8 drive north on Ave 29 E for .6 mile. Turn left on Los Angeles Avenue (Old Hwy 80) and drive .6 mile. Turn left into Arizona Ave. After one block you'll reach the entrance on your right.

➲ **Exit 67**

DATELAND PALMS RV PARK *(Open All Year)*

Res and Info: (928) 454-2772
Location: Dateland, *N 32° 47' 57", W 113° 32' 28", 400 Ft*

50 Sites – Dateland is a popular stop for gas and a quick date shake while traveling across the desert. The RV park is some distance behind the gas station and restaurant so it's pretty quiet. Sites are back-ins and pull-thrus to 50 feet. The facility is on the south side of I-8 at Exit 67.

OASIS AT AZTEC HILLS RV PARK *(Open All Year)*

Res and Info: (928) 454-2229, oasisrvpark@hughes.net
Location: Dateland, *N 32° 48' 17", W 113° 30' 08", 500 Ft*

40 Sites – Sites here are mostly full-hookup although a few have water and electric service only. There are back-in and pull-thru sites to 50 feet. From I-8 at Exit 67 drive south for .3 miles. Turn left and drive east for 2.1 miles to Ave 66E. Turn right and in .2 miles you'll see the entrance to the park on the left.

➲ **Exit 102**

PAINTED ROCK PETROGLYPH SITE AND CAMPGROUND *(BLM) (Open All Year)*

Information: (623) 580-5500
Location: 11.5 Miles N of I-8 Exit 102, *N 33° 01' 18", W 113° 02' 47", 600 Ft*

60 Sites – This is an interesting place to spend the night, the petroglyphs here are chipped into the rocks of a large boulder pile just a short stroll from the campground. There are no hookups and water is not available. Sites have picnic tables and firepits and are scattered over a fairly large area with lots of room to park any size RV and good maneuvering room. Toilets are vault style. During the winter this is a popular campground, but in the heat of the summer there are few visitors. Take Exit 102 from I-8, turn north, and follow Painted Rock Road for 11.5 miles to the campground.

ARIZONA

➲ **Exit 119**

▣ HOLT'S SHELL **RV PARK** *(Open All Year)*
Information: (928) 683-2449
Location: Gila Bend, *N 32° 55' 50", W 112° 40' 21", 800 Ft*

24 Sites – This is a modern but basic campground located behind the Shell station that is just north of the exit. It has back-in and pull-thru sites to 60 feet with full hookups. There are showers and a laundry in the dedicated restroom building. The Shell station out front is a big one with lots of truck parking, you'll often see RVs overnighting with the trucks or across the road in a large lot.

▣ AUGIE'S QUAIL TRAIL **RV PARK** *(Open All Year)*
Res and Info: (928) 683-2850, augieqtrv@earthlink.net
Location: Gila Bend, *N 32° 56' 14", W 112° 40' 52", 800 Ft*

115 Sites – This campground has back-in and pull-thru sites to 80 feet. Parking is on gravel. To reach the park take Exit 112 from I-8. Drive north for 1 mile, the campground is on the right.

➲ **Exit 167**

▣ CASA GRANDE GOLF AND **RV RESORT** *(Listed as a snowbird park under Casa Grande in Chapter 8 – Snowbird Destinations on page 443)*

INTERSTATE 40 CORRIDOR – ARIZONA

Interstate 40 (I-40) is one of two main corridors running across Arizona and New Mexico. I-10 is the preferred winter route since it travels across much lower country than I-40 to the north and therefore has much better driving conditions. In summer you might prefer I-40, it's more scenic and a little cooler.

In Arizona I-40 is 360 miles long. Mileage markers (and therefore highway exit numbers) start on the western border. The campgrounds listed below are all in Arizona. See the *Interstate 10 Corridor* section in the New Mexico chapter for campgrounds in that state.

You will note that many of the campgrounds along the highway are described in other places in this book. Rather than including them twice we've given the page number where you can find the detailed descriptions.

Interstate 40 Corridor Campgrounds

➲ **Exit 48**

▣ FORT BEALE **RV PARK** *(Listed under Kingman on page 113)*

▣ ADOBE **RV PARK** *(Listed under Kingman on page 113)*

➲ **Exit 53**

▣ KINGMAN **KOA** *(Listed under Kingman on page 114)*

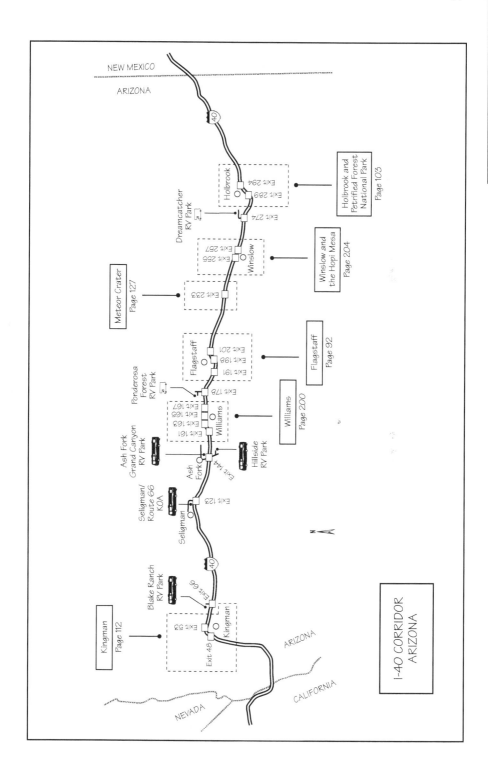

ARIZONA

NEW MEXICO
ARIZONA

Holbrook and Petrified Forest National Park
Page 103

Holbrook
Exit 289
Exit 294

Dreamcatcher RV Park
Exit 274

Winslow and the Hopi Mesa
Page 204

Winslow
Exit 255
Exit 257

Meteor Crater
Page 127

Exit 233

Flagstaff
Page 92

Flagstaff
Exit 191
Exit 198
Exit 201

Ponderosa Forest RV Park
Exit 178

Williams
Page 200

Williams
Exit 161
Exit 163
Exit 165
Exit 167

Ash Fork Grand Canyon RV Park

Hillside RV Park

Ash Fork
Exit 144

Seligman/Route 66 KOA

Seligman
Exit 123

N

Blake Ranch RV Park

Exit 66

Kingman
Page 112

Kingman
Exit 53

Exit 48

ARIZONA
CALIFORNIA
NEVADA

I-40 CORRIDOR ARIZONA

ARIZONA

➲ **Exit 66**

🚐 **BLAKE RANCH RV PARK** *(Open All Year)*

Reservations: (800) 270-1332
Information: (928) 757-3336, www.blakeranchrv.com
Location: 15 Miles E of Kingman, *N 35° 10' 52", W 113° 47' 20", 4,200 Ft*

60 Sites – This is a good campground with a very convenient location right off I-40. There are full-hookup pull-thrus and back-ins to 65 feet. Take Exit 66 from I-40, the campground is about .2 mile to the north.

➲ **Exit 123**

🚐 **SELIGMAN/ROUTE 66 KOA**

Reservations: (800) 562-4017, www.koa.com
Information: (928) 422-3358, www.seligmankoa.com
Location: Seligman, *N 35° 19' 25", W 112° 51' 22", 5,300 Ft*

80 Sites – A KOA with the normal KOA amenities, a good stop if you have kids along. Amenities include a pool, a playground, and Wi-Fi. There are tent sites as well as pull-thru RV sites to 55 feet. Some are water and electric sites, others are full-hookup. Take Exit 123 from I-40 and drive north. You'll see the campground on the left in 1.3 miles.

➲ **Exit 144**

🚐 **ASH FORK GRAND CANYON RV PARK** *(Open All Year)*

Res and Info: (928) 637-2521
Location: Ash Fork, *N 35° 13' 20", W 112° 29' 31", 5,100 Ft*

50 Sites – This is an older campground located in a small town along the freeway. The main business here seems to be production of sandstone building blocks. The town is on the old Route 66 and was once the site of the Escalante Harvey House. The campground has back-in and pull-thru sites to 50 feet. Most have water and electric hookups but a few are full-hookup sites. There are some shade trees in this campground, also a swimming pool. Take Exit 144 and follow the road north and then east for .5 mile. Turn right on 8th Ave, then right on Pine, you'll see the campground ahead.

🚐 **HILLSIDE RV PARK** *(Open All Year)*

Location: Ash Fork, *N 35° 13' 08", W 112° 29' 42", 5,100 Ft*

When we last visited this campground was temporarily closed but a new operator was expected to take it over soon. It's located next to a Texaco station on the hillside south of the freeway. Given the great visibility of the location from the highway one must assume that it will be open in the future. We have not included prices or a contact number because these are not known at this time. Sites here are back-ins and pull-thrus to about 40 feet. Restrooms are in the gas station. Take Exit 144 and then follow the access road east on the south side of the freeway for just a short distance to the campground.

⊃   *Exit 161*

🚐 CATARACT PARK *(Listed under Williams on page 204)*

🚐 CATARACT LAKE CAMPGROUND *(Listed under Williams on page 203)*

⊃   *Exit 163*

🚐 CANYON GATEWAY RV PARK *(Listed under Williams on page 201)*

🚐 GRAND CANYON RAILWAY RV PARK *(Listed under Williams on page 202)*

⊃   *Exit 165*

🚐 CANYON MOTEL AND RAILROAD RV PARK *(Listed under Williams on page 202)*

🚐 RAILSIDE RV RANCH *(Listed under Williams on page 202)*

⊃   *Exit 167*

🚐 WILLIAMS/CIRCLE PINES KOA *(Listed under Williams on page 203)*

⊃   *Exit 191*

🚐 WOODY MOUNTAIN CAMPGROUND *(Listed under Flagstaff on page 94)*

⊃   *Exit 198*

🚐 BLACK BART'S RV PARK *(Listed under Flagstaff on page 93)*

⊃   *Exit 201*

🚐 FLAGSTAFF KOA *(Listed under Flagstaff on page 93)*

🚐 J & H RV PARK *(Listed under Flagstaff on page 94)*

⊃   *Exit 233*

🚐 METEOR CRATER RV PARK *(Listed Under Meteor Crater on page 127)*

⊃   *Exit 255*

🚐 WINSLOW PRIDE RV PARK *(Listed Under Winslow and the Hopi Mesas on page 205)*

⊃   *Exit -257*

🚐 HOMOLOVI RUINS STATE PARK *(Listed Under Winslow and the Hopi Mesas on page 204)*

⊃   *Exit 289*

🚐 OK RV PARK *(Listed Under Holbrook and Petrified Forest National Park on page 104)*

🚐 HOLBROOK/PETRIFIED FOREST KOA *(Listed Under Holbrook and Petrified Forest National Park on page 104)*

⊃   *Exit 294*

🚐 ROOT 66 RV PARK *(Listed Under Holbrook and Petrified Forest National Park on page 105)*

AJO, WHY, AND ORGAN PIPE CACTUS NATIONAL MONUMENT

The strip from Ajo south to Organ Pipe National Monument is a popular destination during the winter. Temperatures are mild and there are lots of places to camp, many free or almost free.

Ajo (population about 3,000) is the large town in the area. This was a former copper mining town with a big open pit mine to the south of town which is now closed. Probably the most attractive feature of the town is its **Hispanic-style square** bordered by a few res-

ARIZONA

taurants, the post office, and a grocery store. There's a larger supermarket north of town, the only one in the area. Sights include the **New Cornelia Open Pit Mine** which can be viewed from an overlook south of town where there is also a small visitor center which is only open in the winter, and not always then. Nearby is the **Ajo Historical Museum**. Ajo has a nine-hole golf course north of town.

Next stop to the south is **Why**. Really little more than an junction, RV parks, service stations, and a restaurant, the town is a winter home to hundreds of snowbird RVers. From Why a two-lane paved road runs east to Tucson through the Tohono O'Odham reservation, a distance of about 120 miles. The tribe operates the tiny slot-machine Golden Hasan Casino and gas station just east of Why.

The **Organ Pipe Cactus National Monument** is 33 miles south of Ajo and 22 miles south of Why. The visitor center is 6 miles north of the Mexico border crossing at Sonoyta. It's a 331,000 acre area filled with the unusual organ pipe cactus, not to mention lots of other types of Sonoran Desert vegetation. Actually, the organ pipe cactus is common in Mexico but almost all examples of the species in the US is within the boundaries of the monument. This is beautiful desert county, some of the most attractive anywhere. There is a visitor center, a campground (see below), hiking trails, and two long dirt driving routes through the outback.

Ajo, Why, and Organ Pipe Cactus National Monument Campgrounds

AJO HEIGHTS RV PARK *(Open Oct 1 to May 1)*
   Res and Info: (520) 387-6796, www.ajorvparks.com, rose@ajorvparks.com
   Location: Ajo, *N 32° 23' 36", W 112° 52' 17", 1,600 Ft*

40 Sites – Ajo Heights is a newer park, it's neat and well kept with nice desert landscaping. Sites are back-ins and pull-thrus to 45 feet with paved drives and parking on gravel. Sites have paved patios. The campground is well-signed on the east side of SR-85 some 1.2 miles north of the 90° bend at the entrance to central Ajo.

BELLY ACRES RV PARK *(Open Oct 1 - April 15)*
   Res and Info: (520) 387-6907, (520) 387-5767
   Location: Ajo, *N 32° 23' 38", W 112° 52' 18, 1,600 Ft*

49 Sites – The Belly Acres is one of the older parks in town. Sites are back-ins and pull-thrus to 45 feet. Parking is on paved strips with brick patios. This campground has a dump station and boondockers can pull in and dump for a fee. The campground is well-signed on the east side of SR-85 some 1.2 miles north of the 90° bend at the entrance to central Ajo. It's next to the Ajo Heights RV Park.

SHADOW RIDGE RV RESORT *(Open All Year)*
   Res and Info: (520) 387-5055, www.shadowridgervresort.com
   Location: Ajo, *N 32° 22' 30", W 112° 52' 26", 1,700 Ft*

125 Sites – The Shadow Ridge is the largest of Ajo's campgrounds and has the nicest facilities. Sites are back-ins and pull-thrus to 55 feet. Each site has a paved patio and picnic table. Amenities include Wi-Fi, lounge, fitness room, game room, craft and workshop,

and some planned activities in the winter. The park is located at 90° bend as you enter Ajo from the north on SR-85.

⊒ Lᴀ Sɪᴇsᴛᴀ Mᴏᴛᴇʟ ᴀɴᴅ RV Rᴇsᴏʀᴛ *(Open All Year)*

Res and Info: (520) 387-6569, www.ajolasiesta.com, reservations@ajolasiesta.com
Location: *Ajo, N 32° 24' 10", W 112° 52' 20", 1,600 Ft*

22 Sites – In winter this little RV park behind a motel is popular with snowbirds, probably because of the good facilities for such a small park. It's also one of the few places in town that will accept tent campers. Sites are back-ins with patios to about 45 feet. There's a nice swimming pool as well as a tennis court and recreation room. The campground is on the west side of SR-85 about 1.4 miles north of the 90° bend at the entrance to central Ajo.

⊒ Dᴀʀʙʏ Wᴇʟʟs Rᴏᴀᴅ BLM Dɪsᴘᴇʀsᴇᴅ Cᴀᴍᴘɪɴɢ Aʀᴇᴀ *(Open All Year)*

Information: (623) 580-5500, www.az.blm.gov
Location: *Ajo, N 32° 20' 25", W 112° 51' 56", 1,800 Ft*

Scattered Boondocking – Camping is on small roads branching off Darby Wells Road south of Ajo. It's a BLM short term dispersed camping area so camping is free but limited to 14 days out of every 28. It's one of the more scenic dispersed areas in Arizona with

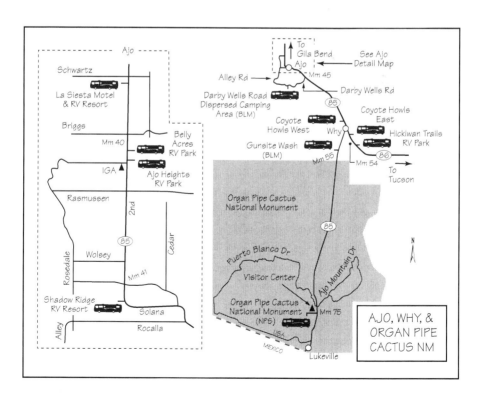

ARIZONA

lots of saguaros and a hilly terrain. There is generally no host in this area. To reach the camping area drive south on SR-85 from Ajo for about two miles from the southern edge of town. Darby Wells Road goes right and loops around to enter Ajo from the west.

COYOTE HOWLS EAST *(Open All Year)*

Information: (520) 387-5209, coyotehowls.com, coyotehowls@coyotehowls.com
Location: Why, *N 32° 15' 49", W 112° 44' 07", 1,700 Ft*

500 Sites – This huge campground offers very low monthly rates ($120) for what is essentially desert boondocking with some amenities and social activities. Sites are widely scattered in desert vegetation. There are restroom buildings with flush toilets and hot showers and several dump stations. Water is available at faucets throughout the park. Generators are allowed during certain daytime and evening hours. The campground is .3 mile east of the intersection of SR-85 and SR-86 in Why, it's on the north side of SR-86.

COYOTE HOWLS WEST *(Open All Year)*

Res and Info: (520) 387-5933, coyotehowls.com, coyotehowls@coyotehowls.com
Location: Why, *N 32° 16' 11", W 112° 44' 29", 1,700 Ft*

37 Sites – This is a small beautifully landscaped RV park which is affiliated with the Coyote Howls Primitive Campground. Sites have full hookups, some are pull-thrus to 45 feet. There are no bathrooms at this park so only self-contained units are allowed. Guests here participate in the planned activities at the larger Coyote Howls Primitive Campground. There is no laundry at the park but a laundromat is located nearby. The campground is located about .3 miles north of the intersection of SR-85 and SR-86 in Why, it's on the west side of SR-85.

HICKIWAN TRAILS RV PARK *(Open All Year)*

Information: (520) 362-3267, http://hickiwantrailsrvpark.com
Location: 2 Miles SE of Why, *N 32° 14' 37", W 112° 43' 27", 1,700 Ft*

190 Sites – This large campground is owned by the local Tohono O'Odham Nation. It is located behind the small Golden Hasan Casino, gas station and convenience store. The facilities were pretty good when constructed but have suffered since, probably because the place is pretty much abandoned in summer. Sites have full hookups. They're back-in sites but many are aligned in a way that allows their use as pull-thrus when the campground isn't full, which it usually is not. The amenity building has flush toilets and hot showers as well as a laundry but needs some maintenance. The campground is located on the north side of SR-86 about 1.9 miles east of the intersection in Why and is behind the casino.

GUNSITE WASH BLM DISPERSED CAMPING AREA *(Open All Year)*

Information: (623) 580-5500, www.az.blm.gov
Location: 2 Miles S of Why, *N 32° 14' 22", W 112° 45' 04", 1,700 Ft*

Scattered Boondocking – Campers in this BLM area are scattered across a large area of scenic desert with many cactus of various sorts. In winter there is a host here and campers should register with him so that their location is known. It's a BLM dispersed camping area so stays are free but limited to 14 days out of every 28. The campground is on both sides of SR-85 about 2 miles south of the Why intersection.

ORGAN PIPE CACTUS NATIONAL MONUMENT *(Open All Year)*
  Information: (520) 387-6849, www.nps.gov/orpi
  Location: 21 Miles S of Why, *N 31° 56' 34", W 112° 48' 40", 1,600 Ft*

208 Sites – This is a huge campground set in a very scenic desert environment. The campground is a huge fan-shaped area with paved access roads and cement parking pads. Sites are as long as 70 feet but the access roads are narrow and entering the sites requires a 90 degree turn so RVs over 40 feet will have some maneuvering problems. Two rows of sites are limited to RVs under 25 feet and tenters with no generator use, generator use in the rest of the campground is limited to 12 noon to 4 pm. Sites have picnic tables and raised barbecue grills. Restrooms have flush toilets and no showers and there is a dump station. The park and campground entrance road go west from SR-85 some 21.2 miles south of Why and 6.3 miles north of the US-Mexico border. It's 1.5 miles to the campground from the highway.

APACHE TRAIL

The well-publicized Apache Trail leads eastward from Apache Junction (just east of Phoenix) for 44 miles to Theodore Roosevelt Lake. The road follows the Salt River Canyon, to the south is the Superstition Wilderness. Many trailheads are along the trail or on short roads off it and hiking trails lead back into the wilderness. Actually, most people think of this as a loop drive with the return on good paved highways through Globe and Superior, a total distance for the loop of 129 miles. The road from Apache Junction to Theodore Roosevelt Lake is designated as SR-88. Portions of it are narrow two-lane (sometimes 1.5-lane) dirt road with precipitous drop-offs and steep grades. These sections are not appropriate for folks who hate heights or for vehicles over about 25 feet long. In fact, it's better not to travel them in any kind of wide-body RV or with a trailer.

Heading east from Apache Junction, after 3.8 miles you may want to stop at the **Goldfield Ghost Town**, a privately-run reconstructed mining town with lots of attractions including an **underground mine**, the narrow-gauge **Superstition Scenic Railroad**, **Goldfield Superstition Museum**, the **Bordello Museum**, and the **Mammoth Steakhouse and Saloon**.

About 12 miles east of Apache Junction you'll reach **Canyon Lake**, a reservoir behind Mormon Flat Dam. You can take a boat tour of the lake on the Dolly Steamboat, there is also a commercial campground, see below.

Tortilla Flat is 16 miles east of Apache Junction. There's a café here as well as a post office and small store. Across the road is a forest service campground, see below.

The pavement ends 23 miles east of Apache Junction, from there to the intersection with SR-188 at Theodore Roosevelt Dam the road is dirt and gravel. Signs warn that vehicles over 40 feet are not allowed. The hairiest section of road is **Fish Creek Hill**, 25 miles east of Apache Junction. Here the road descends 1,500 feet in three miles along a cliff face.

ARIZONA

Some 31 miles east of Apache Junction you'll reach **Apache Lake**. This lake is a reservoir behind Horse Mesa Dam. It's a long lake, about 15 miles, and has a commercial campground and a forest service campground along its shore.

The trail ends by climbing past **Theodore Roosevelt Dam**, an impressive sight as it fills the gorge next to the highway. This was originally the largest masonry dam in the world and was built during the Theodore Roosevelt administration, not later during Franklin Roosevelt's term as were many of the huge dams in the west. Later there were concerns about the dam's safety, and it was encased in concrete and enlarged with the project finished in 1996. The lake behind this dam is an important recreation area, see the *Theodore Roosevelt Lake* destination section below where many campgrounds are described.

Apache Trail Campgrounds

CANYON LAKE MARINA *(Open All Year)*

Information: (480) 288-9233, www.CanyonLakeMarina.com
Location: 15 Miles NE of Apache Junction, *N 33° 32' 07", W 111° 25' 19", 1,600 Ft*

29 Sites – Canyon Lake Marina is probably best known for the Dolly Steamboat, a boat that tours Canyon Lake. The marina also has camping in a large paved lot near the lake. Only no-hookup or electricity and water sites are available, there is a dump station. The campground is located along SR-88 about 14.9 miles northeast of the intersection of US-60 and SR-88 in Apache Junction.

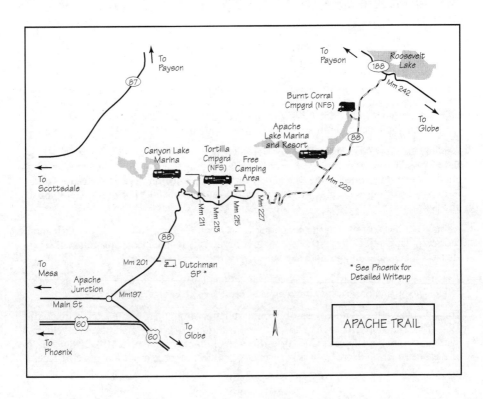

TORTILLA CAMPGROUND *(Open Oct 1 to April 30)*
  Reservations: (877) 444-6777, www.recreation.gov
  Information: (480) 610-3300
  Location: 17 Miles NE of Apache Junction, *N 33° 31' 37", W 111° 23' 42", 1,700 Ft*

77 Sites – Tortilla is a Tonto National Forest campground just across the road from Tortilla Flats, a popular tourist stop. There are tent and back-in RV sites to 45 feet. The restrooms have flush toilets and there is a dump station. The campground is located along SR-88 about 17 miles northeast of the intersection of US-60 and SR-88 in Apache Junction.

APACHE LAKE MARINA AND RESORT *(Open All Year)*
  Res and Info: (928) 467-2511, www.apachelake.com
  Location: 32 Miles NE of Apache Junction, *N 33° 34' 32", W 111° 15' 11", 1,900 Ft*

12 Sites – This lodge along the shore of Apache Lake offers tent camping along the shoreline as well as 12 RV sites along the water. A long, steep entrance road would make getting in and out difficult for larger RVs. We recommend that anyone with reservations about their RVs capacity to handle either up or down grades avoid this campground. Management says the largest they've seen here is 34 feet. In addition to the camping you'll find a restaurant, a small store, and launch facilities for boats. The campground is located along SR-88 about 32 miles northeast of the intersection of US-60 and SR-88 in Apache Junction.

BURNT CORRAL CAMPGROUND *(Open All Year)*
  Information: (928) 467-3200
  Location: 39 Miles NE of Apache Junction, *N 33° 37' 29", W 111° 12' 04", 1,900 Ft*

79 Sites – This is a Tonto National Forest campground on the shore of Apache Lake. In addition to 79 developed sites this campground has a dispersed camping area. The developed sites are mostly back-ins, some to 40 feet. The Forest Service recommends a maximum trailer size of 22 feet. Sites have picnic tables, fire pits, and raised barbecues. There is a swimming beach in addition to a boat ramp. The campground is located along SR-88 about 39 miles northeast of the intersection of US-60 and SR-88 in Apache Junction.

BENSON

Benson (population about 4,000) is located just south of US-10 about 40 miles east of Tucson.

Kartchner Caverns is the biggest tourist attraction in the area. It's on SR-90 just west of town. The caverns were discovered in 1974 and opened as a state park in 1999. This is a living limestone cave and it has been protected since it was discovered so there has been very little damage to the delicate formations inside. You must visit as part of a ranger-led tour and it can be hard to get a slot in one unless you reserve ahead.

Even though Benson, at 3,600 feet, is above the altitude normally considered optimum by snowbirds it is a popular snowbird RV town. Fall and spring weather is ideal and

ARIZONA

winter weather, while cool, features many sunny days. The town has Safeway and Super Walmart stores and two eighteen-hole golf courses. The local museum is the **San Pedro Valley Arts and Historical Museum**.

Benson celebrates **Territorial Days** on the second weekend of February each year and the **Butterfield Overland Stage Day** on the second Saturday of October.

Benson Campgrounds

KARTCHNER CAVERNS STATE PARK *(Open All Year)*

Information: (520) 586-4100, www.azstateparks.com
Location: 12 Miles SW of Benson, *N 31° 50' 11", W 110° 20' 44", 4,500 Ft*

60 Sites – Kartchner is the newest of the Arizona state parks. The reason for the park is the nearby Kartchner Caves. The campground has nice back-in and pull-thru sites to 75 feet, some with electric and water hookups. They have paved access roads, paved parking, and metal picnic tables. Restrooms have flush toilets and showers. There are good hiking trails from the park as well as tours of the caves. Reservations are required for cave tours, call (520) 586-CAVE well in advance of your planned visit. To visit the park leave I-10 at Exit 302, just west of Benson. Drive south on SR-90 for 9 miles, the entrance is on your right.

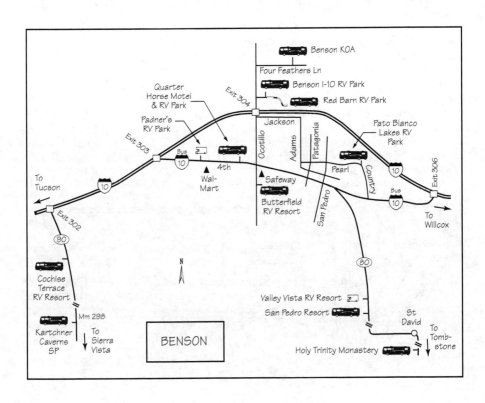

COCHISE TERRACE RV RESORT *(Open All Year)*

Res and Info: (520) 586-0600, (800) 495-9005, www.cochiseterrace.com
Location: 3 Miles W of Benson, *N 31° 57' 08", W 110° 20' 43", 4,100 Ft*

308 Sites – Cochise is the largest and newest RV park in the Benson area. It's nearer Kartchner Caverns than the rest but is situated on an exposed hilltop rather than down in the San Pedro Valley like the other Benson parks. The campground is a luxury big-rig campground with modern facilities and nice wide paved access roads. Sites are mostly back-ins to 50 feet and there are a few longer pull-thrus. Most sites have gravel parking surfaces and no patios. Amenities include a pool and a spa as well as a recreation hall and game room. Take Exit 302 off I-10 just west of Benson. Drive south for .9 mile, the RV park is on the right.

QUARTER HORSE MOTEL AND RV PARK *(Open All Year)*

Res and Info: (800) 527-5025
Location: Benson, *N 31° 58' 15", W 110° 18' 43", 3,600 Ft*

46 Sites – This older motel and RV park has pull-thru sites to 55 feet, all with full hook-ups. It's located near central Benson, in fact it is very near the new Walmart. From I-10 take Exit 304. Drive south for .5 mile to the I-10 business loop, there's a Safeway on the corner. Turn right and you'll see the campground on the right in .2 mile.

BUTTERFIELD RV RESORT *(Open All Year)*

Res and Info: (800) 863-8160, (520) 586-4400, www.rv-resort.com
Location: Benson, *N 31° 58' 01", W 110° 18' 23", 3,600 Ft*

The Butterfield is one of Benson's nicer resorts. It's right beyond the Safeway and across from the post office, very convenient. Also, the Butterfield has an astronomical observatory, the only one we've ever seen in a campground. This is the place to come if you've ever wanted to learn about stargazing. There are 175 back-in and pull-thru sites to 60 feet. All are full hookups. There's a pool and spa as well as a wood and hobby shop and an exercise room. From I-10 take Exit 304. Drive south about .6 miles passing the Safeway and you'll see the RV park on your left.

BENSON I-10 RV PARK *(Open All Year)*

Res and Info: (800) 599-0081
Location: Benson, *N 31° 58' 51", W 110° 18' 20", 3,500 Ft*

88 Sites – Sites here are big, both back-ins and pull-thrus to 80 feet. From I-10 take Exit 304. Drive north just a hundred yards or so and turn right. The park will be on your left almost immediately, just before the road turns to gravel.

RED BARN RV PARK *(Open All Year)*

Information: (575) 586-2035
Location: Benson, *N 31° 58' 44", W 110° 18' 02", 3,500 Ft*

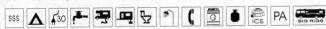

50 Sites – The campground has pull-thru sites to 50 feet. There are also dedicated tenting sites near the entrance with small shared shelters. From I-40 take Exit-304. Drive north about a hundred yards and turn right. You'll pass the I-10 RV Park, the road will turn to gravel, and after an s-turn to the right you'll reach the Red Barn.

BENSON KOA *(Open All Year)*

Reservations: (800) 562-6823, www.koa.com
Information: (520) 586-3977
Location: 1 Mile N of Benson, *N 31° 59' 18", W 110° 18' 07", 3,500 Ft*

105 Sites – This KOA has partial and full hookups sites. They are back-ins and pull-thrus to 50 feet. There's a pool and a spa. The campground is north of the freeway, about a mile from the business district. From Exit 304 of I-10 drive north. In .6 miles turn right on Four Feathers Lane, you'll see the entrance on the left.

PATO BLANCO LAKES RV PARK *(Open All Year)*

Res and Info: (520) 586-8966
Location: Benson, *N 31° 58' 17", W 110° 17' 18", 3,500 Ft*

105 Sites – The Pato Blanco Lakes is one of the newer parks in town. It is a 55+ park. The location is separate from any of the other parks in town and there is nice landscaping and a pond at one side of the park. The 105 sites are both mostly back-ins to 55 feet although there are a few longer pull-thrus. Amenities include a pool and spa, freshwater fishing in the pond, and a recreation hall. For easiest access take Exit 306 from I-10 just east of Benson. On the south side of the highway drive west on business I-10 for .7 mile. Turn right on Country Road and drive north for .4 mile. It bends to the left and you'll see the campground entrance on the right.

SAN PEDRO RESORT *(Open All Year)*

Res and Info: (520) 586-9546
Location: Benson, *N 31° 56' 54", W 110° 17' 14", 3,600 Ft*

160 Sites – This is a combination mobile home and RV park. It's also an age 55+ park. RV sites are pull-thrus and back-ins to 55 feet, all full hookups. There's a pool, a spa, and a recreation room. The campground is south of Benson on SR-80 toward St David. Take Exit 304 from I-10. Drive south .5 mile to the stoplight and turn left. This puts you on SR-80. After driving east for 1 mile the road curves right toward Tombstone and St David, you'll see the campground on the right 2.3 miles from where you turned onto SR-80.

HOLY TRINITY MONASTERY *(Open All Year)*
Information: (520) 720-4016
Location: St David, *N 31° 52' 35", W 110° 12' 44", 3,600 Ft*

20 Sites – The Holy Trinity Monastery in St David has a small RV park in the rear. As you enter the grounds from the highway the road curves left and then right. At this second turn there is a bookstore, that's where you check in if it's open. If not just continue to the back of the property. There are back-in and pull-thru sites, a few will take a 45 footer although most are smaller. Restrooms are nearby. From Benson drive south on SR-80 about 9 miles, the entrance is on the right.

BISBEE AND NACO

Like Ajo to the west Bisbee (population about 6,000) is an old copper mining town with mines that have been closed for years. Miners have been replaced by folks who just like living in this somewhat offbeat town. Unlike Ajo however, Bisbee is far from flat.

Bisbee's center, including **Brewery Gulch**, contains many historical buildings, it's a unique place. Many streets are nothing more than staircases. The Chamber of Commerce has walking tour maps. Be careful which tour you choose, one has over 1,000 stairs.

Since mining is Bisbee's history you shouldn't be surprised that mining is the central

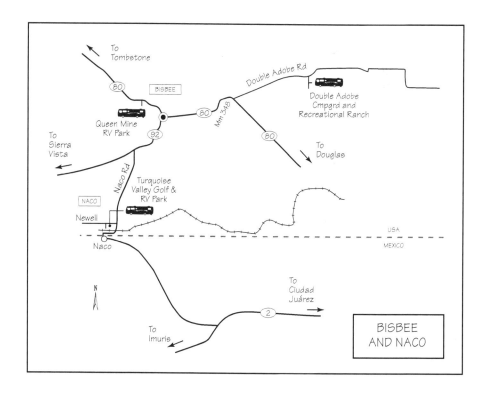

focus of the tourist attractions here. The **Bisbee Mining and Historical Museum** depicts the town's history. Tours of the **Queen Mine**, an underground mine, are possible. The **Lavender Open Pit** is located just southwest of the central area of town, there's an overlook off US-80 a mile or so south. The Queen Mine RV Park as a great view of the pit too.

Naco, 10 miles south of Bisbee, is a quiet little border town. Neither the US nor the Mexico side are tourist towns but if you do walk across there are a few restaurants and shops. On the US side there is an RV park (see below) and a golf course.

Bisbee and Naco Campgrounds

QUEEN MINE RV PARK *(Open All Year)*

Res and Info: (520) 432-5006
Location: Bisbee, *N 31° 26' 21", W109° 54' 42", 5,300 Ft*

25 Sites – This campground has an interesting setting perched above a huge open pit mine with views of the mine and historic Bisbee. Sites are all back-ins around the circumference of the park. An office and restroom building provides flush toilets, showers, and laundry. The campground is located right across SR-80 from old central Bisbee, watch for the sign.

DOUBLE ADOBE CAMPGROUND AND RECREATIONAL RANCH *(Open All Year)*

Reservations: (800) 694-4242, doubleadobe@theriver.com
Information: (520) 364-4000, www.doubleadobe.com
Location: 11 Miles E of Bisbee, *N 31° 27' 34", W 109° 45' 16", 4,100 Ft*

103 Sites – The Double Adobe is popular with snowbirds and travelers. It's a full-service park that is a little out of the way. Sites here are back-ins and pull-thrus with some sites large enough for 45-footers. There is also a tent camping area. The central building houses a kitchen, laundry, restrooms, telephone, crafts room, meeting room and library. This campground also has a trap and sporting clays shooting range, it's open to expert and novice alike. There's also a horse hotel for those traveling with horses or stables for those wanting to keep horses for the season. To reach the campground travel east from central Bisbee on US-80 for 6 miles. Turn left on W Double Adobe Road and drive another 5 miles to the campground.

TURQUOISE VALLEY GOLF AND RV PARK *(Open All Year)*

Res and Info: (520) 432-3091, www.turquoisevalley.com, golfer@turquoisevalley.com
Location: Naco, 9 Miles S of Bisbee, *N 31° 20' 23", W 109° 56' 36", 4,500 Ft*

100 Sites – This campground is part of a facility including an 18 hole golf course. The clubhouse is located right across the road from the campground. Sites are back-ins and pull-thrus to 50 feet. Restroom, a laundry, and a meeting room are located in the campground. There's a restaurant at the golf course across the road. Winter activities, in addition to golf, include dinner dances and art and music instruction. From central Bisbee travel south for 1.5 miles and at the roundabout take US-92 southwest. In 2.7 miles turn

left on Naco Road and drive 4.5 miles to Naco. You'll see signs for the campground pointing right just as you enter the little border town.

BORREGO SPRINGS AND ANZA-BORREGO STATE PARK (CALIFORNIA)

Borrego Springs (population about 3,000) is completely surrounded by the Anza-Borrego State Park. The little town is very scenic with mountains in three directions. Golf is popular here, there are three 18-hole championship golf courses. It's a great base for exploring the state park.

Anza-Borrego State Park is California's largest state park. In fact, this is the continental U.S.'s largest state park. It covers an area of 600,000 acres. Anza-Borrego is particularly well known for its spring bloom of desert wildflowers. Timing for this varies from year-to-year depending upon rainfall and other factors but generally happens late March and early April. You can even arrange to have the park send you a postcard warning you that the time is getting close.

Ocotillo Wells State Vehicular Recreation Area is an 80,000 acre area set aside for off-road vehicles of all types. It adjoins the eastern side of Anza-Borrego state park and is accessible off SR-78. It has free camping and facilities including a dump station and shelter ramadas. Additional off road areas adjoin it including large BLM tracts to the south and east and Anza-Borrego state park to the west, however, that park allows vehicle travel only on established vehicle trails.

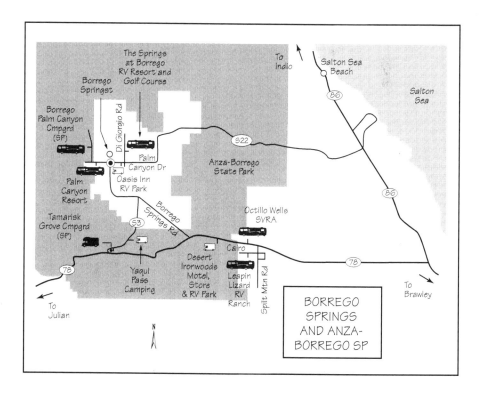

ARIZONA

Borrego Springs and Anza-Borrego State Park Campgrounds

PALM CANYON RESORT *(Open All Year)*

Res and Info: (760) 676-5341, (800) 242-0044, www.palmcanyonresort.com
Location: Borrego Springs, *N 33° 15' 19", W 116° 23' 55", 700 Ft*

140 Sites – The campground here is a large one behind a hotel. Sites are all back-ins, some to 40 feet. Tents are allowed, but not tent pegs, so your tent must be free-standing. There is a swimming pool with a spa and a restaurant in the hotel. The resort is located at the west end of the town's main drag, Palm Canyon Drive. It's 1.3 miles west of the traffic circle that marks the center of town.

THE SPRINGS AT BORREGO RV RESORT AND GOLF COURSE *(Open All Year)*

Res and Info: (760) 767-0004, (866) 330-0003, www.springsatborrego.com
Location: Borrego Springs, *N 33° 15' 57", W 116° 21' 55", 500 Ft*

90 Sites – The Springs is a new, very upscale RV resort build overlooking a 9-hole golf course. Sites are pull-thrus to 90 feet. Prices range from $35 to $60. Facilities, in addition to the golf course, include a clubhouse with a full kitchen, a weight room, individual bathroom/shower rooms, a pool, 4 spas, and 2 tennis courts. RV guests are given discounts on playing the championship 9 hole course which was designed by David Pfaff of Carmel. From the traffic circle which marks the center of town drive east on Palm Canyon Drive for .5 mile. Turn north on Di Giorgio Rd, you'll see the entrance on the right in .6 mile.

ANZA-BORREGO STATE PARK – BORREGO PALM CANYON CAMPGROUND
   (Open All Year)

Reservations: (800) 444-7275, www.parks.ca.gov
Information: (760) 767-5311, www.parks.ca.gov
Location: 1 Mile W of Borrego Springs, *N 33° 16' 07", W 116° 24' 18", 700 Ft*

120 Sites – This is the main campground for the park, located about a mile from the visitor center. Sites vary from paved pull-thrus to 45 feet to short no-hookup sites for small vehicles. Restrooms have flush toilets and showers and Wi-Fi can be picked up in some sites. The park entrance is at the west end of Palm Canyon Drive, 1.4 mile from the traffic circle that marks the center of Borrego Springs. Some .2 mile from the entrance turn right onto the campground access road, you'll reach the campground in .9 mile.

ANZA-BORREGO STATE PARK – TAMARISK GROVE CAMPGROUND *(Open All Year)*

Reservations: (800) 444-7275, www.parks.ca.gov
Information: (760) 767-5311, www.parks.ca.gov
Location: 5 Miles SW of Borrego Springs, *N 33° 08' 18", W 116° 22' 29", 1,300 Ft*

27 Sites – Sites in this campground are short. Trailers are limited to 21 feet, it's hard to see how an RV of any kind over 25 feet could use the campsites. There are not hookups but a new building with flush toilets and showers has just been added. There are faucets only for non-potable water, some drinking water is available however. A number of hik-

ing trails leave from the park. It's located near the intersection of SR-78 and the Yaqui Pass Road about 5 miles southwest of Borrego Springs.

OCOTILLO WELLS SVRA *(Open All Year)*
  Information: (760) 767-5391, www.ohv.parks.ca.gov
  Location: 10 Miles SE of Borrego Springs, *N 33° 09' 01", W 116° 09' 00", 200 Ft*

Scattered Boondocking – The State of California's 80,000-acre Ocotillo Wells State Vehicular Recreation Area allows boondocking off any of the roads through the area. Some areas off SR-78 are accessible to any size RV. This main camping area has about 30 sites with sheltered tables, fire pits, and raised grills with vault toilets nearby. Just to the west is the headquarters area where you'll find a dump station ($10 to use) as well as showers and a pay phone. No one comes here in the summer, it's too hot. In fall, winter, and spring it's pretty quiet during the week and very busy on weekends. Campers are limited to 30 days per year. The area is off SR-78 near Ocotillo Wells about 10 miles southeast of Borrego Springs.

LEAPIN LIZARD RV RANCH *(Open Oct 1 to May 31)*
  Res and Info: (760) 767-4526, www.leapinlizardrvranch.com
  Location: 11 Miles SE of Borrego Springs, *N 33° 08' 23", W 116° 08' 08", 100 Ft*

60 Sites – If you love the Ocotillo Wells OHV area but want hookups this is the place. There are 60 back-in sites to 60 feet with full hookups. Parking is available for OHVs and a trail lets non-street-legal vehicles get to the OHV area just to the north. The campground is in Ocotillo Wells about a mile east of the OHV area headquarters. Follow the signs a block off the road to the south and then turn right for the campground.

CAMP VERDE

The Verde River drains a valley between Flagstaff and Phoenix that is a popular tourist and summer RV playground. One of the attractions is the altitude. At between three and four thousand feet the weather is cooler than Phoenix but not as cool, particularly in winter, as Flagstaff which is at least 3,000 feet higher. We've broken the valley into two parts, that around Camp Verde, this section, and the area upstream where Cottonwood and Sedona are located. See *Sedona, Cottonwood, and the Verde Valley* for information about that section.

Camp Verde (population about 10,000) is the oldest town in the Verde Valley. Due to its location on the southeast side of I-15 it is not really on the tourist routes to the attractions near Sedona and Cottonwood. It's primarily a ranching and farming town but does have some interesting sights nearby. It also tends to be a little more economical than the better known destinations in the valley to the north.

Right in town is the **Fort Verde State Historic Park**. The fort here was built in the 1870s and is along the General Crook Trail between Prescott and Fort Apache (see *Show Low and Pinetop-Lakeside* Region).

Montezuma Castle National Monument is a Sinagua cliff dwelling. It is easy to visit with just a short walking trail to a point where you can get a good look. Other Sinagua dwellings are located at Tonto National Monument which is described in the *Theodore*

ARIZONA

Roosevelt Lake section. Montezuma Castle is a few miles north of Camp Verde and can be easily reached by following signs from Exit 289 of I-17.

Montezuma Well is nearby. This is a small lake used by the Sinagua for irrigation. There are some small ruins nearby. The well is part of Montezuma Castle National Monument and can be reached by taking Exit 293 from I-17 and following signs for about five miles.

Camp Verde Campgrounds

🚐 **DISTANT DRUMS RV RESORT** *(Open All Year)*
Reservations: (877) 577-5507, info@distantdrumsrvresort.com
Information: (928) 554-8000, www.distantdrumsrvresort.com
Location: 5 Miles N of Camp Verde, *N 34° 36' 46", W 111° 51' 51", 3,200 Ft*

156 Sites – The Distant Drums RV Resort is a new big-rig campground associated with the Cliff Castle Casino across the highway. Sites here are back-in and pull-thrus to 45 feet. In addition to full hookups the sites have instant-on telephones which are included in the price, that's about $35. There's a pool and spa, an exercise room, a community room, and a shuttle to the casino. For a fee the dump station is available to those not staying in the park. Take Exit 289 from I-17, the campground is just north of the freeway.

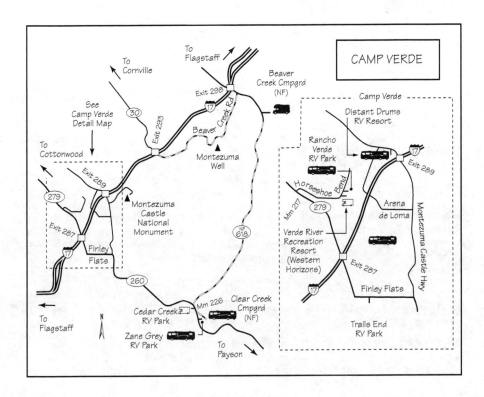

⬛ TRAILS END RV PARK *(Open All Year)*

Reservations: (888) 706-0555, TrailsEndRV@aol.com
Information: (928) 567-0100, www.trailsend-rvpark.com
Location: Camp Verde, *N 34° 33' 55", W 111° 52' 13", 3,100 Ft*

39 Sites – Trails End is located just to the west of central Camp Verde. The sites are unadorned back-ins and pull-thrus to 70 feet. This is a 55 and over park. From Exit 287 of I-17 follow SR-260 southeast toward Camp Verde. The campground will be on the right in 1.2 mile.

⬛ BEAVER CREEK CAMPGROUND *(Open All Year)*

Information: (928) 282-4119
Location: 15 Miles NE of Camp Verde, *N 34° 40' 14", W 111° 42' 46, 3,800 Ft*

13 Sites – This is a Coconino National Forest campground. Most sites here are small, good for tent campers and RVs to 25 feet. Two more are large, about 45 feet long, but this is a small campground and maneuvering room is limited. Both fishing and swimming are possible in Beaver Creek, it's also a convenient place to stay if you are going to tour nearby Montezuma Castle National Monument and Montezuma Well. Easiest access is from I-17 at Exit 298. Travel east for 2.6 miles to the campground.

⬛ RANCHO VERDE RV PARK *(Open All Year)*

Information: (928) 567-7037
Location: 4 Miles N of Camp Verde, *N 34° 36' 03", W 111° 53' 01", 3,000 Ft*

41 Sites – This is a well-kept popular snowbird park. Sites are back-ins and pull-thrus to 50 feet. To reach the park exit I-17 at Exit 287. Drive north for 3.3 miles and turn right on W Horseshoe Bend Road. Follow it for 1.2 miles as it curves around to the left, the campground entrance is on the right.

⬛ CLEAR CREEK CAMPGROUND *(Open All Year)*

Information: (928) 282-4119
Location: 7 Miles SE of Camp Verde , *N 34° 30' 58", W 111° 46' 03", 3,100 Ft*

17 Sites – Clear Creek is another Coconino National Forest campground. Sites here are off a gravel loop with large sycamore trees and junipers. The sites are all back-ins as long as 45 feet, with careful maneuvering the campground can take larger RVs. Each site has a picnic table and fire pit. There's a covered picnic pavilion, fishing and swimming are possible in Clear Creek. To reach the campground travel southeast from Camp Verde on SR-260, the General George Crook Trail, for 6 miles. Turn left on Yulee Road and follow it .7 miles to the campground.

⬛ ZANE GREY RV PARK *(Open All Year)*

Reservations: (800) 235-0608, info@zanegreyrvpark.com
Information: (928) 567-4320, www.zanegreyrvpark.com
Location: 6 Miles Southeast of Camp Verde, *N 34° 31' 00", W 111° 46' 28", 3,100 Ft*

ARIZONA

43 Sites – This is a park located along Clear Creek southeast of Camp Verde. Sites are back-ins and pull-thrus to 60 feet. Amenities include a spa. To reach the campground travel southeast from Camp Verde on SR-260, the General George Crook Trail, for 6 miles. The campground is on the left.

CANYON DE CHELLY NATIONAL MONUMENT

The Canyon de Chelly is jointly managed by the National Park Service and the Navajo nation. There are actually two canyons here: Canyon de Chelly and Canyon del Muerto. These are spectacular places with narrow flat valley floors and sheer sandstone walls rising a thousand feet to the rims. A few Navajo families live and farm down in the valleys.

The visitor center is located outside the canyon near the foot. Access to the canyon, except on one trail, must be with a guide. There are commercial truck and jeep tours and also hiking tours. The one trail that you can hike by yourself is the White House Ruin trail which is actually a great hike. It descends from the south rim of the canyon from Mile 5.9 of the south rim road and crosses the valley floor to a small ruin, it's 2.5 miles round trip.

There are two rim drives. The South Rim Drive follows the south rim of Canyon de Chelly for 21 miles, there are 8 different overlooks to visit. The North Rim Drive follows the north rim of Canyon del Muerto. It's also a 21-mile road and has 5 overlooks.

The monument is located just east of the Navajo town of Chinle which has shops, restaurants, gas, and supermarkets.

WHITE HOUSE RUIN AT CANYON DE CHELLY

Canyon de Chelly National Monument Campgrounds

COTTONWOOD CAMPGROUND *(Open All Year)*
Information: (928) 674-5500
Location: Chinle, *N 36° 08' 55", W 109° 32' 21", 5,500 Ft*

93 Sites – Cottonwood is a pleasant campground adjacent to the visitor center at Canyon de Chelly National Monument. It's a great base for exploring the canyon. Sites are almost all back-ins suitable for tent campers and RVs to about 30 feet but there are a few pull-thrus including one or two that we've seen 40-footers squeeze into. The cottonwoods provide shade and there are water faucets (no water in winter) but no individual hookups. Restrooms have flush toilets but no showers. There is a dump station with a water fill hose. From US-191 in Chinle turn east on BIA-7 following signs for Canyon de Chelly. In 2.6 miles you'll see the visitor center on your right, turn right just past the visitor center and then right again at the next Y to enter the campground.

SPIDER ROCK RV PARK AND CAMPING TOO *(Open All Year)*
Reservations: (877) 910-CAMP, spiderrock@earthlink.net
Information: (928) 674-8961, www.home.earthlink.net/-spiderrock
Location: 10 Miles E of Chinle, *N 36° 04' 36", W 109° 24' 48", 6,700 Ft*

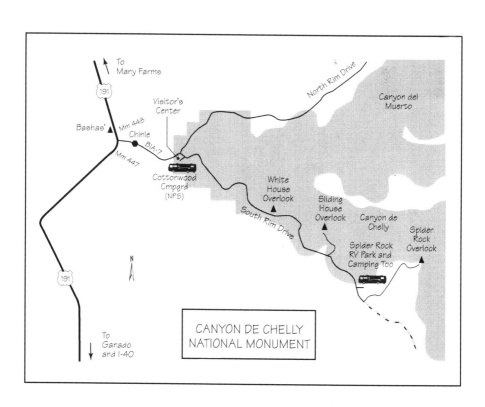

ARIZONA

45 Sites – This is a Navajo-owned campground near the canyon rim. The owner also offers guided tours including overnight camping stays down in the canyon. The canyon rim campground will accommodate tent campers or RVs. A few sites near the front will take RVs to 40 feet although most sites are much smaller. There are solar-heated showers and a dump station. Limited potable water is available. From Chinle drive past the visitor center and then on along the south rim of Canyon de Chelly. The campground is 9.8 miles beyond the visitor center.

CASA GRANDE

Casa Grande (population 30,000) was originally a farming town. With its convenient location midway between Tucson and Phoenix and relatively low land prices it has become an RVing destination for Snowbirds.

The town has a museum, the **Casa Grande Valley Historical Society Museum**. There's also an outlet mall, Outlets at Casa Grande off I-10 at Exit 198.

Casa Grande Ruins National Monument is the main tourist attraction in the area. The ruins here are primarily one large building, four stores high but with only 11 rooms. It's made of Adobe, of course, so a roof has been constructed over the building to protect it from rainfall. Other much smaller ruins are in the same area and there's a visitor center which has exhibits about the Hohokam people who built Casa Grande. The monument is located about 20 miles northeast of Casa Grande, take Exit 185 from I-17 and follow the signs.

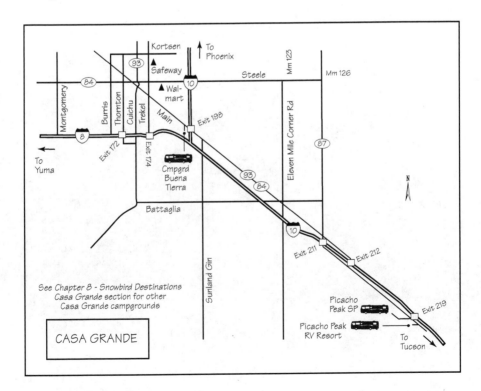

ARIZONA

Nearby **Picacho Peak State Park** offers hiking trails and a campground. It also has a popular annual celebration. Civil War in the Southwest, on the second weekend in March, is a Civil War battle re-enactment with Union and Confederate soldiers conducting battles and showing off their camps.

On the President's Day weekend in February the **O'Odham Tash Indian Days Celebration**, a Native American heritage get-together, offers crafts, a rodeo, and dances.

For more about Casa Grande, and particularly snowbird winter RV parks, see the *Snowbird Destinations* chapter of this book. Many of the campgrounds listed in that chapter also have spaces for travelers, our charts in that chapter give overnight rates for the ones that do.

Casa Grande Campgrounds

CAMPGROUND BUENA TIERRA *(Open All Year)*

    Res and Info: (520) 836-3500, www.campgroundbuenatierrra.com
    Location: Casa Grande, *N 32° 49' 53", W 111° 41' 18", 1,400 Ft*

145 Sites – This handy campground has back-in and pull-thru parking on gravel to about 75 feet. It's located just west of I-10 and just north of the intersection of I-10 and I-8. Take Exit 198 from I-10, the entrance road is just west of the overpass.

PICACHO PEAK STATE PARK *(Open All Year)*

    Information: (520) 466-3183, www.azstateparks.com
    Location: 28 Miles SE of Casa Grande, *N 32° 38' 46", W 111° 24' 06", 1,800 Ft*

85 Sites – The campground in this state park occupies the north-facing slope of Picacho Peak. There are lots of hiking trails in this park. Sites in the campground are off 3 paved loops, sites themselves are paved and have a picnic table and fire pit. Some of the picnic tables have roofs for shade. Loops B and C have electric hookups, there are back-ins and pull-thrus to 45 feet. Winter is the busy season here, there is a very popular Civil War battle reenactment in March. From I-10 some 21 miles east of its intersection with I-8 take Exit 219. Follow the road up the hill to the park.

PICACHO PEAK RV RESORT *(Open All Year)*

    Res and Info: (520) 466-7841, www.picachopeakrv.com
    Location: 28 Miles SE of Casa Grande, *N 32° 38' 36", W 111° 23' 17", 1,700 Ft*

300 Sites – All sites here are full hookup with back-ins and pull-thrus to 50 feet and parking on gravel. There is a pool and a spa as well as a recreation room. Take Exit 219 from I-10 some 21 miles east of its intersection with I-8. Follow the access road on the south side of the highway eastward to the campground entrance.

CHIRICAHUA MOUNTAINS

The Chiricahua Mountains rise to the southeast of Willcox and northeast of Douglas near the New Mexico border. Most of the range is part of the Coronado National Forest, the southern portion is the Chiricahua Wilderness. The range has a number of forest service campgrounds and it is possible for cars and smaller RVs to cross the range through Onion Saddle on Forest Road 42 (it's dirt and rough, but usually passable) from the Chiricahua National Monument to Paradise on the east side. The pines and cooler weather at higher altitudes make this a popular summer destination for folks in southeastern Arizona.

At the northern end of the range, the most scenic part, is the **Chiricahua National Monument**. Here you can drive for six miles on a paved road through Bonita Canyon and up to Massai Overlook at 6,900 ft. There are great views from Massai of impressive rock formations. The monument has some great hiking trails and also a campground, see below. RVs over 29 feet are not allowed to go past a parking area near the entrance where you can leave your RV if you want to use a tow car to drive to Massai Overlook. The monument is located about 55 miles southeast of Willcox, see the campground write-up for driving directions.

North of Chiricahua National Monument, on an extension known as the Dos Cabezas Mountains, is **Fort Bowie National Historic Site**. Fort Bowie was built in Apache Pass, an important route for east/west travel in the 1800s, the Butterfield Stage ran through the pass. Apaches under Cochise and Geronimo frequented the area and at times there were conflicts. Ruins of the fort remain, you must walk in approximately 3 miles on good trails to reach them. Access to the site is from Exit 362 off I-10 about 22 miles east of Willcox. Drive south some 12 miles on Apache Pass Road to the fort. The last mile is gravel. You can drive another 8 miles of gravel across the pass to meet SR-186 south of Willcox.

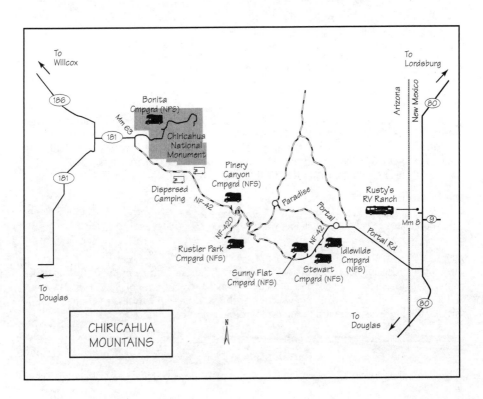

Chiricahua Mountains Campgrounds

RUSTY'S RV RANCH *(Open All Year)*
Res and Info: (575) 557-2526
Location: 10 Miles E of Portal, *N 31° 55' 40", W 109° 02' 09", 4,100 Ft*

40 Sites – This hookup campground sits by itself in the flats east of the Chiricahua Mountains. It's actually in New Mexico but fits best in this section of our book. The sites here are very long pull-thrus. RVs must be self contained. From I-10 at Exit 5 in New Mexico drive south on SR-80 for 28 miles, the campground is on the right.

IDLEWILD CAMPGROUND *(Open May 1 to Oct 31 - Varies)*
Information: (520) 364-3468
Location: 2 Miles SW of Portal, *N 31° 53' 39", W 109° 09' 57", 5,000 Ft*

10 Sites – Idlewild is a small Coronado National Forest campground. Sites are very small, the campground is only suitable for tent campers and small vans and pickup campers. Most sites have picnic tables and fire rings. From Portal on the east side of the Chiricahua Mountains follow paved NF-42 for 1.8 mile to the campground, it's on the left.

STEWART CAMPGROUND *(Open May 1 to Oct 31 - Varies)*
Information: (520) 364-3468
Location: 2 Miles SW of Portal, *N 31° 53' 24", W 109° 10' 06", 5,000 Ft*

6 Sites – Another Coronado National Forest campground with very small sites suitable only for tent campers and small RVs like vans or pickup campers. Most sites have picnic tables and fire rings. From Portal on the east side of the Chiricahua Mountains follow paved NF-42 for 2.1 miles to the campground, it's on the left.

SUNNY FLAT CAMPGROUND *(Open All Year)*
Information: (520) 364-3468
Location: 3 Miles SW of Portal, *N 31° 53' 04", W 109° 10' 35", 5,200 Ft*

14 Sites – Sunny Flat is a modernized Coronado National Forest campground. The access ring road is paved as are the sites. They have picnic tables and fire rings, those not naturally shaded are provided with shade roofs for the picnic tables. Sites are all back-ins, they'll take RVs to about 28 feet. From Portal on the east side of the Chiricahua Mountains follow paved NF-42 for 2.9 miles to the campground, it's on the right.

RUSTLER PARK CAMPGROUND *(Open April 15 to Oct 15 - Varies)*
Information: (520) 364-3468
Location: 16 Miles SE of Chiricahua National Monument,
N 31° 54' 22", W 109° 16' 40", 8,500 Ft

25 Sites – Rustler Park is a fairly remote Coronado National Forest Campground. Reaching the campground requires driving quite a few miles on rough and narrow dirt roads

ARIZONA

so most folks probably wouldn't want to come here in an RV over about 25 feet. Sites are large, many are parallel parking types that will take any size RV. They have picnic tables and fire rings. From Portal it's 14 miles to the campground, about 10 miles of that is rough gravel. Easier access is from the west side of the Chiricahuas near the entrance to Chiricahua National Monument. From the intersection about .1 mile west of the monument entrance follow NF-42 for 12 miles, then take the right and follow NF-42D another 2.8 miles to the campground. Although all of this route is gravel, it's generally in better condition that the road from Portal.

PINERY CANYON CAMPGROUND *(Open All Year)*

Information: (520) 364-3468
Location: 10 Miles SE of Chiricahua National Monument,
N 31° 56' 02", W 109° 16' 18", 7,700 Ft

4 Sites – This Coronado National Forest campground is on the west side of the range. It's suitable for tent campers and small RVs like vans and pickup campers. From the intersection about .1 mile west of the monument entrance follow NF-42 for 10 miles to the campground.

CHIRICAHUA NATIONAL MONUMENT – BONITA CAMPGROUND *(Open All Year)*

Information: (520) 824-3560
Location: Chiricahua National Monument, *N 32° 00' 44", W 109° 21' 16", 5,300 Ft*

22 Sites – This is a nice park service campground in a beautiful setting, overlooked by the red rocks of Bonita Canyon. Sites in this campground are all back-ins, and although some stretch to 40 feet access is limited to 29 feet. This makes sense in view of the lack of maneuvering room. Roads in the campground are paved, sites are gravel, and they have picnic tables and raised barbecues. Restrooms have flush toilets but no showers. The campground is near the entrance to the monument, just past the visitor center. To reach the monument leave I-10 at Exit 331 and follow US-101 southeast for 29 miles. Turn left onto SR-181 and follow it 2.9 miles until reaching a 90 degree right turn where the monument road exits and heads east another 4 miles to the monument.

COACHELLA VALLEY (PALM SPRINGS AREA)

The Coachella Valley's (valley population about 375,000) best known town is probably Palm Springs, but really there are a string of cities here. As you arrive from the Los Angeles in the west Palm Springs is first. To the north on the far side of I-10 is Desert Hot Springs. Then there are a string of towns toward the southeast. Hwy 111 was the original highway here and most of the towns are along it. Traveling south there are Cathedral City, Rancho Mirage, Palm Desert, Indian Wells, La Quinta, and Indio.

Palm Springs was the first destination town here and continues to have most of the visitor attractions. These include the **Palm Springs Aerial Tramway**, the **Palm Springs Desert Museum**, the **Palm Springs Air Museum**, and the **Indian Canyons**. Not to be missed if you're in town at the right time (November through May) is the **Fabulous Palm Springs Follies,** certainly the best "over 55", vaudeville show on the planet.

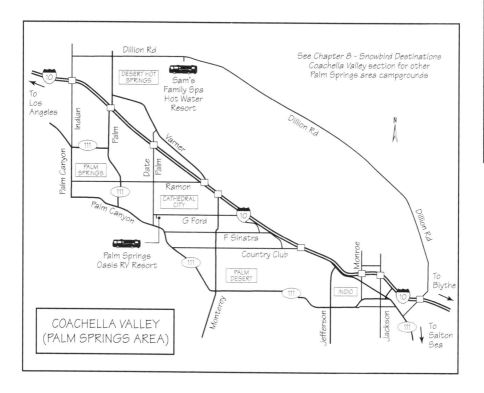

To the north, squarely on the San Andreas Fault, is **Desert Hot Springs**. Because of the fault-top location Desert Hot Springs has a number of hot water springs. It's also the location of some of the more affordable snowbird RV resorts in the area.

Moving south, **Cathedral City** seems to have a bit of a strip-mall feel to it with lots of small stores and auto dealerships. To the east, though are some nice residential areas and country clubs.

Farther south, **Rancho Mirage**, **Palm Desert**, **Indian Wells**, and **La Quinta** are more upscale and very golf-oriented. There are large shopping malls and country clubs. In Palm Desert you'll find the **Living Desert Wildlife and Botanical Park**, in case you couldn't tell – it's a zoo.

Indio, at the south end of the valley, is really the oldest town along here. It has agricultural roots. It's also the home of two big casinos: **Fantasy Springs Casino**, and **Spotlight 29 Casino**.

For more about the Coachella Valley, and particularly snowbird winter RV parks, see the *Snowbird Destinations* chapter of this book. Many of the campgrounds listed in that chapter also have spaces for travelers, our charts in that chapter give overnight rates for the ones that do.

ARIZONA

Coachella Valley (Palm Springs Area) Campgrounds

PALM SPRINGS OASIS RV RESORT *(Open All Year)*

Res and Info: (800) 680-0144
Location: Cathedral City, *N 33° 47' 11", W 116° 27' 26", 1,200 Ft*

140 Sites – This is a age 55+ campground near CA-111 in Cathedral City, a nice central location. The price is in the neighborhood of $40 per night. Sites are all full-hookup back-ins to 40 feet. Parking is on cement pads with gravel surrounding the sites The park has two swimming pools and a spa. In winter you'll want to call ahead for a reservation. The park is located at the corner of Date Palm Drive and Gerald Ford Drive. From I-10 take the Date Palm Drive Exit and drive south on Date Palm Drive for 4.3 miles. Turn left on Gerald Ford Drive and then immediately right into the entrance of the RV park.

SAM'S FAMILY SPA HOT WATER RESORT *(Open All Year)*

Res and Info: (760) 329-6457, www.samsfamilyspa.com
Location: Desert Hot Springs, *N 33° 55' 23", W 116° 25' 31", 1,000 Ft*

175 Sites – Sam's is an older spa, mobile home park, and RV park. The price for RV parking is a little under $40 per night. These are full-hookup back-in sites to 45 feet with parking on gravel and a cement patio. There is a big outdoor pool, a wading pool, and outdoor therapeutic pools which are drained and refilled each day. Other amenities include a 36 washer laundry, RV supplies and groceries sold in the office building, horseshoes, a grassy picnic area with barbecue grills (near the pools), volleyball and basketball courts, exercise room, sauna, a recreation hall, pool & ping pong, and planned activities during the winter. From I-10 as it passes north of Palm Springs take the Palm Drive/Desert Hot Springs exit and head north on Palm Drive. In 3 miles turn right on Dillon Road. You'll see the entrance on the right in 4.3 miles.

CORONADO TRAIL: CLIFTON TO SPRINGERVILLE ON SR-191

The route from Clifton to Springerville is known as the **Coronado Trail**. There are two sections. From Clifton to Alpine on US-191 is a distance of 94 miles. Signs near Clifton warn that vehicles over 40 feet long are not allowed on the road. It's a reasonable request since the road is steep with lots of sharp hairpin curves. From Alpine to Springerville you're on US-180. It's a distance of 27 miles and the road is fine for larger RVs. A word of warning. In winter US-191 is usually closed due to snow although US-180 gets cleared and remains open.

This route is almost entirely within the Apache Sitgreaves National Forest. The first few miles climb through Morenci past the huge (and active) Phelps Dodge Morenci Mine open-pit copper mine. Then you're in the evergreens for the rest of the journey. The road climbs from 3,400 feet in Clifton to 8,000 feet in Alpine, right up and over the Mogollon Rim where it actually reaches 9,300 feet.

The town of **Clifton** (population approximately 2,000) dates from 1872, it has been a copper mining town since that time. Morenci, next door, is a Phelps Dodge company town for the copper mine up the hill. This is its second location, the first town had to be moved when the mine expanded.

ARIZONA

The **Phelps Dodge Morenci Copper Mine** produces more copper than any other in North America. It's a huge operation and tours are available. Contact information is at the end of this chapter. Even if you don't take the tour be sure to stop at the overlook about 10 miles north of Clifton as you're climbing the hill, the view is amazing.

As you continue on up the hill you'll be treated to view after view. Don't expect to make very good time, this is not a high speed road. The Apache National Forest in this area offers a number of hikes and campgrounds, several are listed below.

Alpine (population about 600) is a popular summer destination, many folks have summer homes in the town. **Luna Lake**, east of town, is a wildlife refuge and known for the occasional bald or golden eagle seen there. There's also a state park and campground, see below.

Eager and Springerville (combined population about 6,000) are sister cites located at the north end of the Coronado Trail. It's hard to tell where one ends and the other starts. Together they are an eastern gateway to the White Mountains which are just to the southwest.

Just north of town are the **Casa Malpais ruins**. These are thought to be ruins of a Mogollon ceremonial city and have several unusual features. These include a great kiva and underground ceremonial or burial chambers. Tours to the site meet at a museum in downtown Springerville.

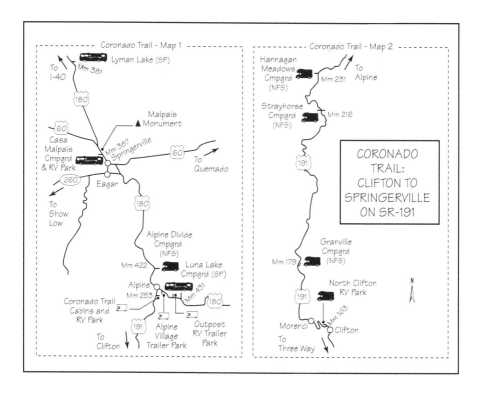

ARIZONA

NORTH CLIFTON RV PARK *(Open All Year)*

Res and Info: (928) 865-9064, (866) 996-2787, www.townofclifton.com,
jvarming@townofclifton.com
Location: Clifton, *N 33° 03' 43", W 109° 18' 06", 3,400 Ft*

55 Sites – This is a really nice little municipal RV park with back-in sites which can accommodate RVs to about 35 feet in length. The interior roads are paved as are the parking spaces. Each site has a gravel patio which has a picnic table and a fire pit. Thirteen of the spaces are full hookups and the remaining 42 are electric and water only. There is a dump station near the entrance to the campground. The campground is on the San Francisco River and river fishing is possible. Other amenities include a recreation hall, playground, and horseshoes. There is a 10 ton limit on a bridge on the entry road.

GRANVILLE CAMPGROUND *(Open April 1 to Nov 30 - Varies)*

Information: (928) 687-1301
Location: 20 Miles N of Clifton, *N 33° 11' 05", W 109° 22' 54", 6,500 Ft*

11 Sites – Granville is an Apache National Forest campground occupying a small oak-filled valley just off US-191. The short entrance road is narrow and rough and closely bordered by trees and vegetation. Sites are small and uneven so the area is only appropriate for tent campers, vans and pickup campers. There are vault toilets and seasonal water. You'll also find a few small cabins farther along the road. Watch for the entrance road and sign on the east side of the highway about 20 miles north of Clifton.

STRAYHORSE CAMPGROUND *(Open All Year)*

Information: (928) 339-4384
Location: 60 Miles N of Clifton, *N 33° 33' 00", W 109° 19' 03", 7,800 Ft*

7 Sites – Strayhorse is a small Apache National Forest campground located just 6 miles below the Mogollon Rim. The spaces here are on both sides of US-191 and have picnic tables and fire rings. Some will take RVs to about 25 feet and are also excellent for tent campers. The campground has two modern vault toilets and also water faucets (no water in winter). There is usually so little traffic at night that the roadside location has never been much of a problem for us. Two trails lead from the campground: Highline Trail goes west to follow the bottom of the Mogollon Rim and Raspberry Trail goes east into the Blue Range Primitive Area.

HANNAGAN MEADOWS CAMPGROUND *(Open May 15 to Sept 15 - Varies)*

Information: (928) 339-4384
Location: 71 Miles N of Clifton, *N 33° 38' 09", W 109° 19' 43", 9,100 Ft*

8 Sites – This is a really beautiful Apache National Forest campground set under a forest of pines, spruce and aspen. There are 8 sites which are very long but the interior roads are narrow and closely bordered by trees so the campground is best for RVs no longer than 30 feet and even with one of those you must be careful. The sites are mostly back-in

(1 pull-thru) and each has a picnic table and fire pit with a grill. The bathrooms are vault style. There are water faucets in the campground but no water in the winter. There is a lodge and restaurant nearby at Hannagan Meadow. The campground is on the west side of SR-191 some 23 miles south of Alpine and 71 miles north of Clifton.

ALPINE DIVIDE CAMPGROUND *(Open May 15 to Sept 15 - Varies)*
Information: (928) 339-4384
Location: 4 Miles N of Alpine, *N 33° 53' 39", W 109° 09' 12", 8,500 Ft*

12 Sites – Some of the sites in this Apache National Forest campground are as long as 40 feet but because of limited maneuvering room it is best for RVs no longer than 30 feet. If you're towing you may need to unhook to turn around at the back of the campground, it's not a circle. The sites are all gravel back-ins off a gravel road. Each site has a picnic table and fire pit with a grill. The bathrooms are vault style. There is a water faucet. The sites are set under lots of shade in a mixed forest of evergreens and cottonwood. This campground has no services in winter but remains open when snow allows. It is located on the east side of US-180 about 4 miles north of Alpine

LUNA LAKE CAMPGROUND *(Open May 15 to Sept 15 - Varies)*
Reservations: (877) 444-6777, www.recreation.gov
Information: (928) 339-4384
Location: 3 Miles E of Alpine, *N 33° 50' 13", W 109° 04' 47", 8,000 Ft*

50 Sites – Luna Lake is the largest Apache National Forest Campgrounds in the area. Family sites are off two loops. Roads and sites are gravel and some will accommodate RVs to 45 feet with careful maneuvering. The campground is set in widely spaced Ponderosa pines and is open and pleasant although it is quite a distance from the lake. To reach the campground drive east on US-180 from Alpine for 3 miles. The entrance is on the left, after turning in you'll pass the day-use area and then drive on around the lake to the campground on the far side.

CASA MALPAIS CAMPGROUND AND RV PARK *(Open All Year)*
Res and Info: (928) 333-4632
Location: 1 Mile N of Springerville, *N 34° 08' 59", W 109° 17' 50", 6,900 Ft*

60 Sites – Sites here are all back-ins to about 50 feet. The campground is located on US-180 about a mile north of Springerville.

LYMAN LAKE STATE PARK *(Open All Year)*
Information: (928) 337-4441, www.azstateparks.com
Location: 18 Miles N of Springerville, *N 34° 21' 39", W 109° 22' 35", 5,900 Ft*

61 Sites – The developed campground here is in two sections, there is also an overflow/ dispersed camping area suitable for large RVs with lakeside camping. The developed sites have paved access road and parking. There are both back-ins and pull-thrus to 50 feet. Each site has a shelter with picnic table and a raised barbecue grill. Hookup sites

ARIZONA

have electricity and water. Some have a sewer connection and there is a dump station. A nice hiking trail lead onto a nearby rock, almost an island, which has a number of pictographs. The campground is on the east side of the US-180 about 18 miles north of Springerville.

DOUGLAS

Douglas (population about 16,000) was founded by the Phelps Dodge Company in 1900 when they built a copper smelter here. Phelps Dodge had mines just to the west in Bisbee, and to the south in Mexico.

Today the mines are closed and so is the smelter. **Agua Prieta** on the Mexican side of the border has become a booming border town with a population exceeding 150,000. Douglas is now little more than a US suburb for the Mexican industrial town to the south.

For folks wanting to walk across to Mexico there's a convenient parking lot. The streets immediately across the border have restaurants and shops, not to mention pharmacies, dentists, and doctors.

Douglas holds the **Cochise Country Fair** on the third week of September with an intercollegiate rodeo. At other times of the year it is possible to camp at the fairgrounds, see below.

Douglas Campgrounds

DOUGLAS GOLF AND RV RESORT *(Open All Year)*
   Res and Info: (520) 364-1588
   Location: Douglas, *N 31° 22' 30", W 109° 32' 27", 4,000 Ft*

28 Sites – These are side by side sites in a large gravel lot, both back-ins and pull-thrus to 55 feet. This is a city-owned golf course and campground and isn't luxurious at all, but it's priced right. From central Douglas drive north on SR-80 and then N Leslie Canyon Road about a mile. The golf course is signed to the right, the campground is in the parking lot.

COCHISE COUNTY FAIRGROUNDS *(Open All Year)*
   Res and Info: (520) 364-3819, cocisefair@theriver.com
   Location: Douglas, *N 31° 22' 31", W 109° 32' 41", 4,000 Ft*

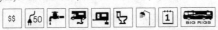

34 Sites – The fairground offers a simple inexpensive place for RV parking. The 34 sites are all back-in sites located along the rock wall to the west of the grounds and the fence to the north between gates 5 and 6. The sites are in a lot with no separation with parking on dirt. Each site has electric and water. There is a dump station. The bathroom building are located near the office at gate 5. They have flush toilets and the women's restroom also has a shower. Reservations are accepted and are a good idea for travelers planning to arrive after 5:00 pm when the office will be closed. From central Douglas drive north on SR-80 and then N Leslie Canyon Road about a mile. The fairgrounds are on the right.

ARIZONA

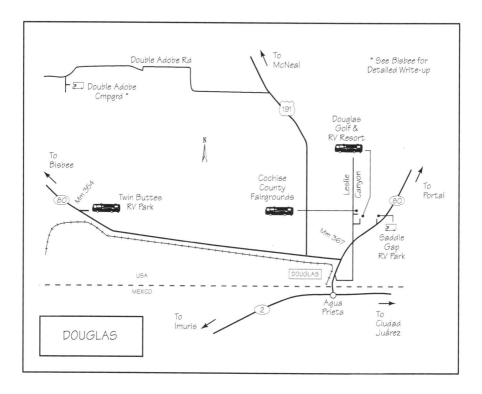

🚐 **TWIN BUTTES RV PARK** *(Open All Year)*
Reservations: (877) 364-7075
Information: (520) 364-7075, www.twinbuttesrvpark.com
Location: 11 Miles W of Douglas, *N 31° 22' 47", W 109° 44' 36", 4,100 Ft*

28 Sites – This is a simple campground in a quiet country setting. The park has 28 RV sites, all are pull-thrus, some to 70 feet. Grass separates the sites, parking is on gravel. An old mobile home unit is used for a clubhouse, restroom building and laundry. A data port is provided in the clubhouse for internet access. From Douglas drive 11 miles west on SR-80, the campground entrance road is on the right.

EL CENTRO (CALIFORNIA)

El Centro (population about 40,000) is a farming community in the middle of the Imperial Valley. A string of towns; Brawley, Imperial, El Centro, Calexico, and Mexicali; are strung from north to south down the valley.

There are a number of snowbird parks here, most are listed below. The area has a pleasant winter climate and Mexicali is close by.

ARIZONA

THE HOT SPRINGS AT THE BLM LTVA NEAR EL CENTRO

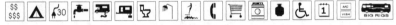

El Centro Campgrounds

🚐 **COUNTRY LIFE RV PARK** *(Open All Year)*

Res and Info: (760) 353-1040
Location: 4 Miles E of El Centro, *N 32° 46' 52", W 115° 30' 12", -200 Ft*

150 Sites – The Country Life is an older mobile home and RV park to the east of El Centro. The park has about 300 sites, half have permanently-located RVs on them. The sites are a little short, about 35 feet, but 40 footers seem to squeeze in. From I-8 east of El Centro take the exit for SR-111. Drive north .5 mile to E Ross Road, turn left, and the campground will be on your left.

🚐 **DESERT TRAILS RV PARK AND GOLF** *(Open All Year)*

Res and Info: (760) 352-7275, www.deserttrailsrv.com
Location: El Centro, *N 32° 46' 13", W 115° 32' 50", -100 Ft*

350 Sites – The Desert Trail is primarily a snowbird residential park with a 9-hole golf course. There are nice pull-thru and golf course sites for large RVs. There is also a gravel overflow area for travelers with electric and water hookups. In addition to the golf course there's a nice pool and spa area and a good clubhouse with restaurant. From I-8 in El Centro take Exit 115 and head south on SR-86. Take the first left, on W Wake Ave and drive .2 mile, the entrance is on your right.

■ **VACATION INN AND SUITES** *(Open All Year)*
Reservations: (800) 328-6289
Information: (760) 352-9700
Location: El Centro, *N 32° 46' 31", W 115° 34' 15", -100 Ft*

31 Sites – This small hotel has a nice little RV park behind it. The sites are small, a couple will take 40-footers, a few more will take 35-footers, the rest are for RVs shorter than 30 feet. These are back-in sites. There's a swimming pool and restaurant that are shared with the hotel and a laundry and restrooms with showers dedicated to the RV park. A call to check if there's a space for you would definitely be a good idea at this campground. From I-8 in El Centro take S Imperial Avenue Exit and drive north. Take the first left, on Ocotillo, and drive around the block to the left to reach the campground entrance behind the hotel.

■ **RIO BEND RV AND GOLF RESORT** *(Open All Year)*
Reservations: (800) 545-6481
Information: (760) 352-7061
Location: 6 Miles W of El Centro, *N 32° 46' 00", W 115° 41' 35", -100 Ft*

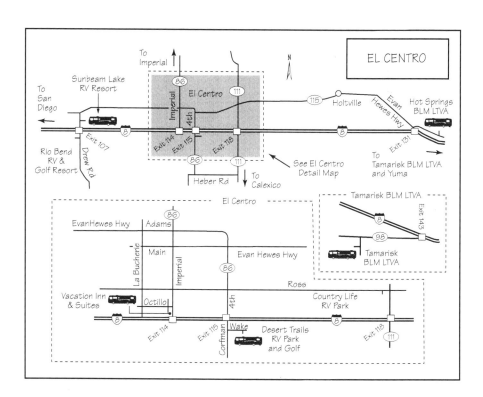

450 Sites – This is a snowbird park with a small executive golf course. About 20 pull-thru sites to 40 feet are available for travelers. The park has a small store and café, a pond for fishing, a pool and spa, and a driving range. From I-8 west of El Centro take Exit 107 and drive south on Drew Road. The campground entrance is on the right in .4 mile.

SUNBEAM LAKE RV RESORT *(Open All Year)*
Reservations: (800) 900-7154
Information: (760) 352-7154, www.sunbeamlake.com
Location: 6 Miles W of El Centro, *N 32° 46' 54", W 115° 41' 05", -100 Ft*

300 Sites – Sunbeam Lake is a spiffy new snowbird park for big RVs. Some sites are alongside little Sunbeam Lake. There are back-in and pull-thru sites to 50 feet. All RVs must be self contained since restroom are locked at night. Amenities include a gym, a clubhouse, library, craft and card room, pool, spa, boat ramp, horseshoes, shuffleboard, laundry, and planned activities. From I-8 west of El Centro take Exit 107 and drive north on Drew Road. The entrance is on the right in .6 mile.

HOT SPRING BLM LTVA *(Open All Year)*
Information: 760-337-4400
Location: 17 Miles E of El Centro, *N 32° 45' 57", W 115° 16' 10", Near Sea Level*

Scattered Boondocking – This BLM LTVA is very convenient. It's known for the hot springs and tub that you can spot if you're traveling eastbound on I-8. There is no dump station at this LTVA, just a vault toilet across the road at the hot springs. See the introductory material in this chapter for the BLM LTVA costs and rules. Take Exit 131 (the CA-115 Holtville Exit) from I-8. Then follow the road on the north side of the highway east 1.1 mile to the LTVA.

TAMARISK BLM LTVA *(Open All Year)*
Information: 760-337-4400
Location: 31 Miles E of El Centro, *N 32° 42' 29", W 115° 07' 41", 100 Ft*

Scattered Boondocking – Tamarisk is the smallest of the LTVAs. There are no facilities, just a large flat area surrounded by a square border of tamarisk trees. See the introductory material in this chapter for the BLM LTVA costs and rules. From Exit 143 of I-10 drive west 2.1 miles on US-98. Turn left and head south, the LTVA is on the right in .1 mile.

FLAGSTAFF

Flagstaff (population about 58,000) is by far the largest town in northern Arizona. It's at an altitude of about 7,000 feet so winters are cool but summers just about ideal. Flagstaff campgrounds are very popular in summer when folks from the low country come up to enjoy the cooler air.

As the largest city in the region Flagstaff has a number of interesting destinations within or near the city. The outstanding museum is the **Museum of Northern Arizona** which lies off US-180 about three miles northwest of town. Sections of the museum include

ARIZONA

archeology, geology, the cultures, and the art of northern Arizona. It's a great place to begin a tour of the north part of the state.

Another favorite is the **Lowell Observatory** on Mars Hill just a mile west of downtown. This observatory has an interesting history. The non-existent "canals", of Mars were discovered here. Still, if you have any interest in astronomy at all you should visit. At night there are sky viewing opportunities for visitors though the historic Clark telescope, the one used to find those canals.

The area surrounding Flagstaff is full of things to visit. East of town along US-40 is **Walnut Canyon National Monument**. Walnut Canyon an extremely scenic little place and there's a nice trail that descends to visit a few simple ruins in the canyon. Take Exit 204 from I-40 about 5 miles east of Flagstaff.

The San Francisco Volcano Field stretches all the way from near Williams to the east of Flagstaff, through the San Francisco Peaks (they're volcanic) and on to the east as far as the Little Colorado River. A great introduction to the area is the Loop Road. It starts 9 miles north of Flagstaff off US-89 and make a 35 mile loop to rejoin US-89 some 14 miles to the north. Along the way you pass the Bonito Campground (see below), **Sunset Crater**, and **Wupatki National Monument**. Wupatki has seven Sinagua and Ancestral Puebloan ruins with either road or trail access.

Flagstaff Campgrounds

BLACK BARTS RV PARK *(Open All Year)*
Reservations: (877) 364-7075, (520) 364-7075
Location: Flagstaff, *N 35° 11' 38", W 111° 37' 01", 6,800 Ft*

175 Sites – For travelers this is undoubtedly the most popular RV park in Flagstaff. It's an older park but big and reasonably priced, also very conveniently located near the freeway. The camp sites are set around the exterior of a large lot and along 4 interior rows. The 4 interior rows are sites 1-134. These can be either used as 134 back-in sites (8 rows) or 67 pull-thru sites (4 rows). As pull-thrus the sites are about 80 feet in length. The sites are mostly full hookup but there are a few which have no hookups for tent campers. There are quite a few pine trees for shade but the park is still light. All the sites have picnic tables and paved patios. There is a data port in the office which can be used for internet access. The park is the home of Black Barts Steak House, Saloon and Musical Revue with nightly performances 7 days a week. The office building also houses an antique store and a few snack items are offered for sale. From I-40 take Exit 198 which is east of the intersection with I-17 and US-180. Head east for just .2 mile to the entrance which is on the left.

FLAGSTAFF KOA *(Open All Year)*
Reservations: (800) 562-3524, www.koa.com
Information: (928) 526-9926, www.flagstaffkoa.com, jsatkoaflag@aol.com
Location: Flagstaff, *N 35° 14' 02", W 111° 34' 35", 6,900 Ft*

200 Sites – The KOA in Flagstaff is a large one with sites set among pines. Due to the trees sites vary considerable in size and layout but they include back-ins and pull-thrus

ARIZONA

to 70 feet in addition to tent sites. Internet access is possible using either data ports or Wi-Fi and there's a small café for a few hours in the evening. Other amenities include basketball, volleyball, a recreation room, and horseshoes. Excellent hiking trails start at the back of the park. The campground is located on the west side of US-89 just 1.2 mile north of its exit from I-40 at Exit 201.

J AND H RV PARK *(Open April 15 to Oct 31)*

Reservations: (800) 243-5264, JHrvpark@aol.com
Information: Summer (928) 526-1829, Winter (623) 551-1577, www.flagstaffrvparks.com
Location: Flagstaff, *N 35° 15' 12", W 111° 33' 23", 6,800 Ft*

65 Sites – The J and H is an RV-only park with back-in and pull-thru sites to 55 feet. There is a mini mart on site which sells gifts, RV supplies, and grocery items. Wi-Fi is available at the sites and a central data port is provided for other internet access. Other amenities at the park include a spa, horseshoes, a recreation hall, a game room, a recreation field, van tours, pet sitting, and a pet run. The campground is located on the east side of US-89 just 2.8 miles north of its exit from I-40 at Exit 201.

BONITA CAMPGROUND *(Open May 1 to Oct 15 - Varies)*

Information: (928) 526-0866
Location: 12 Miles N of Flagstaff, *N 35° 22' 13", W 111° 32' 41", 6,900 Ft*

43 Sites – Bonita is a modern Coconino National Forest campground. It has paved access roads and sites with picnic tables, fire pits, and raised barbecue grills. Sites are back-ins and pull-thrus to 45 feet set among pines. Arrive early as reservations are not accepted, this is a popular campground. From Flagstaff drive north for 10 miles on I-89. Turn right toward Sunset Crater Volcano National Monument and drive 1.8 miles to the campground entrance.

TUTHILL COUNTY PARK *(Open May 1 to Sept 30)*

Information: (928) 774-3464 or (928) 679-8000
Location: 3 Miles S of Flagstaff, *N 35° 08' 35", W 111° 41' 37", 6,900 Ft*

65 Sites – This campground is in the back of the Coconino County fairgrounds. There are 113 no hookup sites under a fairly dense forest of pines. There are back-ins and pull-thrus to about 30 feet. The road through the fairgrounds is paved and becomes dirt once you reach the camping area. Other amenities at the fairgrounds are a picnic shelter, tennis courts, a sports field, volley-ball, and a country store. The fairgrounds are located south of Flagstaff. They're just west of I-17 at Exit 337.

WOODY MOUNTAIN CAMPGROUND *(Open March 15 to Oct 1)*

Reservations: (800) 732-7986
Information: (928) 774-7727, www.woodymountaincampground.com
Location: 2 Miles W of Flagstaff, *N 35° 11' 19", W 111° 41' 24", 7,000 Ft*

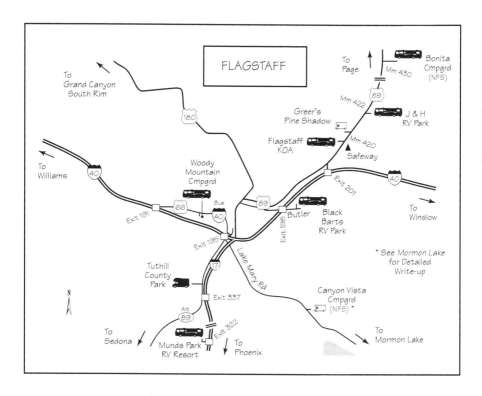

143 Sites – This campground is set in a grove of pines behind the Woody Mountain Store. Parking is on dirt and lots of pine needles. The sites vary from tent sites through full-hookups and are back-ins and pull-thrus to 45 feet. This isn't a fancy campground but it is popular, plan on making reservations for hookup sites all summer long. The swimming pool is outdoor and is heated in the summer. Other amenities include a lounge, arcade games, and horseshoes. The campground is located about 2 miles west of Flagstaff on Business I-40 which is also US-66. One way to get there is to take Exit 191 from I-40 and then drive east on US-66 for 2 miles, the campground is on the right.

MUNDS PARK RV RESORT *(Open April 1 to Nov 1)*

Reservations: (800) 243-1309, mundsparkrv@msn.com
Information: (928) 286-1309, www.mundsparkrv.com
Location: 17 Miles S of Flagstaff, *N 34° 56' 36", W 111° 39' 23", 6,400 Ft*

274 Sites – This large campground along I-17 has a few tent sites, lots of back-ins to about 40 feet, and also some pull-thrus to 65 feet. Sites are separated and shaded by pines. There is a 6,500 square foot clubhouse with planned activities, exercise room, game room, 2 laundromats, nice heated pool, and spa. A central modem is provided for internet access and Wi-Fi is free to the park. Some sites have instant-on telephone. Groceries, RV supplies, propane, ice, gifts & souvenirs are sold. Other amenities include horseshoes,

volleyball, and local tours. The campground is just west of I-17 at Exit 322, about 17 miles south of Flagstaff.

GLOBE

Globe (population about 7,000), along with Miami next door, is another of Arizona's old copper mining towns. The mining boom in the area actually started with the discovery in 1875 of a globe-shaped silver nugget, reportedly complete with the continents visible on its surface. After a few years silver mining gave way to copper mining. During the depression the Globe copper mines were shut down and since that time things have been pretty quiet.

The **Gila County Historical Museum** has exhibits covering the Indian, mining, and ranching history of the area. Just a mile south of central Globe near the Chamber of Commerce is **Besh Ba Gowah**, the ruins of a Salado Indian village. There is a museum with a scale model of the village as it was in 1325 and trails through the ruins.

East of Globe, on the San Carlos Apache Reservation, is the Apache Gold Casino. They have an RV park, the best in the area. It is described below.

Globe Campgrounds

APACHE GOLD RV PARK *(Open All Year)*
Information: (800) 272-2438
Location: 6 Miles E of Globe, *N 33° 21' 23", W 110° 40' 01", 3,100 Ft*

60 Sites – This campground is on the grounds of the Apache Gold Casino. Although it is possible to park for free in the casino parking lot it's not worth the bother, this campground is a real deal. All sixty sites are pull-thrus to 60 feet. They have full hookups including cable TV and the park offers free Wi-Fi service. There is a gas station and convenience store out front and the campground has a swimming pool. It's only a short walk across the lot to the casino which has a restaurant. To reach the Apache Gold drive east from Globe on US-70, it's on the left 6 miles from town.

GILA COUNTY RV PARK *(Open All Year)*
Reservations: (800) 436-5083
Information: (928) 425-4653
Location: Globe, *N 33° 23' 39", W 110° 47' 16", 3,400 Ft*

15 Sites – This is a small county campground within easy walking distance of downtown Globe. There are only 15 back-in sites around the edge of a dirt lot. Most sites have full hookups and a picnic table, any size RV is OK. The only restroom is a portable toilet and there are no showers. Tents are allowed. The campground is at the west end of Cottonwood Street in downtown Globe.

OAK FLAT CAMPGROUND *(Open All Year)*
Information: 928-402-6200
Location: 16 Miles W of Globe, *N 33° 18' 30", W 111° 03' 08", 3,800 Ft*

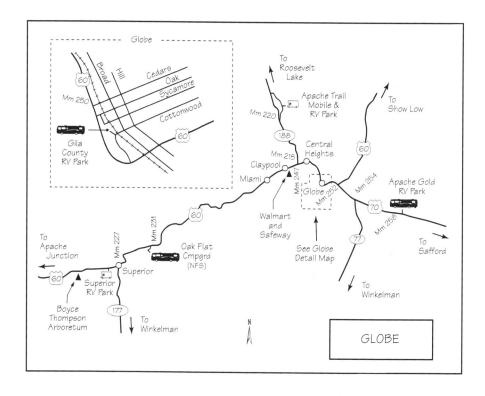

14 Sites – Sites in this Tonto National Forest campground are irregular and of various sizes, some will take large RVs. Parking is on dirt, some sites have shade from pine trees. Each has a picnic table and fire grill. There is no water. There is sometimes a host at this campground. It is located on the south side of US-60 about 16 miles west of Globe.

GRAND CANYON NORTH RIM

The north rim of the Grand Canyon is much quieter than the south rim. It's also about 1,300 feet higher so it's more comfortable in summer and not accessible in winter because the access roads are not kept clear of snow. The season tends to be May through November but varies depending upon snow conditions. Signs at Jacob Lake tell what is open in the off season. The Kaibab Plateau, which is the north rim, is almost all either park, Kaibab National Forest, or BLM land.

The park facility on the north rim is **Bright Angel Point**. There's a lodge and a campground there. Views are spectacular and there are trails into the canyon. Bright Angel, however, takes some driving to reach. The trip from the south rim to the north rim requires driving all the way east to Navajo Bridge and then back to Jacob Lake and then down to the point, a total distance of 190 miles. If you were able to fly directly across it would only be 8 miles.

The **Cape Royal Scenic Drive** lets you travel east from Bright Angel along the rim. The drive heads east from three miles north of the Grand Canyon Lodge and leads 20 miles to

Cape Royal. There are many places to park and view the canyon along the way.

Grand Canyon North Rim Campgrounds

🚐 **NORTH RIM CAMPGROUND** *(Open May 15 to Oct 15 - Varies)*
Reservations: (877) 444-6777, www.recreation.gov
Information: (928) 638-7888, www.nps.gov/grca
Location: North Rim Grand Canyon, *N 36° 12' 37", W 112° 03' 37", 8,300 Ft*

83 Sites – The North Rim Campground is a park service campground located near the lodge and visitor center on the north rim. Sites here are in a forest of pines off a big paved loop. There are tent sites as well as back-in and pull-thru sites as long as 60 feet so even large RVs may find a site. There is a dump station as well as a nearby gas station and a nearby laundry and shower building. Reservations are essential except very early spring or in the fall.

🚐 **DEMOTTE CAMPGROUND** *(Open June 1 to Oct 15 - Varies)*
Information: (928) 643-7395
Location: 17 Miles N of North Rim of the Grand Canyon,
                N 36° 24' 38", W 112° 07' 55", 8,800 Ft

38 Sites – This Kaibab National Forest campground serves as a sort of overflow area

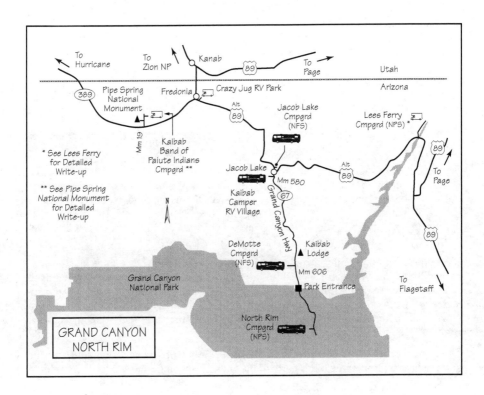

for the north rim. It fills by noon during the summer months. The entrance road crosses DeMotte Park, an open field where you'll often see deer in the evening. The campground is set in pines and firs. The park has recently been rebuilt and now has back-in and pull-thru sites that will take RVs to 45 feet and even larger. There's a gas station and lodge near the campground with a telephone and restaurant. Note the very high altitude of this campground, come prepared for cool nights. Drinking water is available but limited. The campground is located 26 miles south of the Jacob Lake junction and 17 miles north of the North Rim of the Grand Canyon.

JACOB LAKE CAMPGROUND *(Open May 15 to Nov 15 - Varies)*
Information: (928) 643-7395
Location: 43 Miles N of the N Rim of the Grand Canyon,
                  N 36° 42' 57", W 112° 12' 54", 7,900 Ft

54 Sites – Jacob Lake is another Kaibab National Forest campground that serves as an overflow for the North Rim. Get here early in the day or it will be full during the summer months. There's really no lake at the campground, little Jacob Lake is some distance away and is really just the namesake for the junction near the campground. Sites here are back-ins and pull-thrus to about 45 feet. Across the street is the Jacob Lake Inn which has a restaurant, gas station, pay phone, and limited supplies. Jacob Lake is 43 miles north of the north rim at the junction of US-89 and SR-67.

KAIBAB CAMPER RV VILLAGE *(Open May 15 to Oct 15 - Varies)*
Res and Info: (928) 643-7804, www.kaibabcampervillage.com, answers@canyoneers.com
Location: 43 Miles N of the N Rim of the Grand Canyon,
                  N 36° 42' 36", W 112° 13' 48", 7,800 Ft

110 Sites – Kaibab Camper Village is a rustic private campground with hookups. The campground is set in pines and interior roads and sites are gravel and dirt. Sites include back-ins and pull-thrus to 60 feet. It's a busy place in summer as are all of the campgrounds in this area. The campground is located near Jacob Lake. From the intersection head south on SR-67 for just .4 mile. Turn west on the forest service road there (the campground is signed) and drive another .7 mile to the campground. This is 43 miles north of the north rim.

GRAND CANYON SOUTH RIM

The Grand Canyon is justifiably the most popular destination in Arizona. That's why campgrounds as far as a hundred miles away advertise that they're just the place to base yourself while visiting the canyon. You'll probably want to stay a little closer.

The South Rim has a lot to offer. It has hotels, restaurants, information booths, and stores as well as viewpoints that offer the best views in the world and trails both along the canyon and into it. But a word of warning. As a sign warns at the check-in office at Trailer Village, don't buy a ticket for the elevator to the bottom of the canyon from a stranger – there is no elevator.

Most visitor services are in a fairly large area known as the Grand Canyon Village. Both of the main campgrounds are there, also a store, post office, information center, and other

A VIEW OF THE GRAND CANYON FROM THE SOUTH RIM

essentials. See the *Mather Campground* and *Trailer Village* descriptions for more about the campgrounds here.

The first order of business once you have your campsite is probably to see the canyon. If you have a tow car or small vehicle along you can use that, but parking spots can be hard to come by at the overlooks. Instead consider using the free shuttle busses. They hold down traffic and make getting around pretty easy.

If you like to walk the perfect way to see the canyon is the Rim Trail. It extends a total of twelve miles along the south rim, both east and west of the Grand Canyon Village. The main portion is paved and flat, toward the farther ends the trail is narrower and at the west end unpaved.

There are two roads along the South Rim. Hermit Road goes eight miles west from Grand Canyon Village. It is closed to private automobiles, you must travel it in a shuttle. The Desert View Drive goes east for 25 miles along the canyon rim to the east entrance and Desert View Campground. The shuttles only goes east a short distance, as far as Yaki Point. You'll have to use your own vehicle for the rest.

Camping in the canyon can be fun but advance reservations are almost essential. Check the Grand Canyon Website for information.

The Grand Canyon gets more visitors than any other national park in the system except the Great Smokey Mountains National Park. That means that you need to plan ahead if you are going to visit in an RV. With reservations you should be able to get a campsite in the park. Other options are the large campground in Tusayan (called Grand Canyon

Camper Village) or one of the other campgrounds listed below south of the park. You might also consider staying in Williams and visiting the canyon by train.

Grand Canyon South Rim Campgrounds

🚐 **MATHER CAMPGROUND** *(Open All Year)*
 Reservations: (877) 444-6777, www.recreation.gov
 Information: (928) 638-7888, www.nps.gov/grca
 Location: Grand Canyon Village, *N 36° 03' 02", W 112° 07' 16", 6,900 Ft*

323 Sites – Mather is one of two campgrounds at the Grand Canyon Village. There are 323 sites with no hookups, it's excellent for tenters and RVers willing to camp without utility connections. The sites are set on 7 loops named after trees. About half are pull-thrus, some to 60 feet in length. The remaining sites are all back-ins to just 30 feet in length. Although some of the sites are long, the park limits RVs in this campground to 30 feet. The roads are narrow and maneuvering would be tight for larger RVs. The sites are in a forest of juniper and pines and every site has a fire ring and picnic table. Near the manned entrance booth are telephones. Also at the campground entrance is a building which houses showers ($1.50) and a laundry. There is also a dump station. The Market Village, within easy walking distance, has a general store, restaurant, bank, post office, and shuttle bus station. The campground is most easily found by following signs in the Grand Canyon Village area.

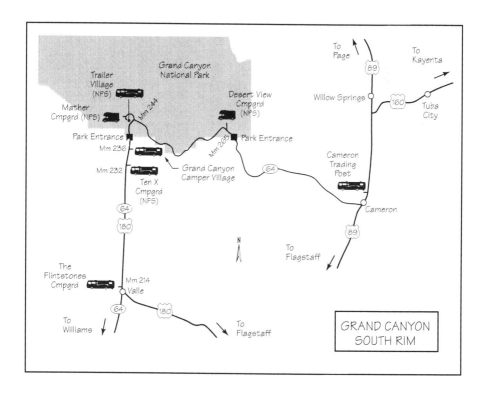

TRAILER VILLAGE *(Open All Year)*
Reservations: (888) 297-2757
Information: (928) 638-2631, www.nps.gov/grca
Location: Grand Canyon Village, *N 36° 03' 09", W 112° 06' 53", 7,000 Ft*

80 Sites – This campground near the Grand Canyon Village in the park has paved sites off of 12 rows (A-L). All of the sites are pull-thrus with full hookups to 50 feet in length. Each has a picnic table and raised barbecue grill. Restrooms have flush toilets and a building at the entrance to nearby Mather Campground has showers and a laundry. Also nearby is the Market Village with general store, restaurant, bank, post office, and shuttle bus station. The campground is most easily found by following signs in the Grand Canyon Village area.

DESERT VIEW CAMPGROUND *(Open May 1 to Oct 15 - Varies)*
Information: (928) 638-7888, www.nps.gov/grca
Location: Grand Canyon South Rim, *N 36° 02' 25", W 111° 49' 32", 7,400 Ft*

50 Sites – Desert View is located near the eastern entrance to the South Rim section of the park. It's convenient to the rim which overlooks a very wide section of the Grand Canyon. Sites will take RVs to 30 feet. From the Grand Canyon Village travel eastward on SR-64 (East Rim Drive) for 22 miles to the campground.

GRAND CANYON CAMPER VILLAGE *(Open March 1 to Nov 30)*
Res and Info: (928) 638-2887
Location: 5 Miles S of Grand Canyon Village, *N 35° 58' 30", W 112° 07' 27", 6,500 Ft*

300 Sites – The Grand Canyon Camper Village is a commercial campground located in Tusayan which is a conglomeration of tourist facilities about two miles south of the south entrance to the park. A variety of site types, including back-ins and pull-thrus to 50 feet, are available. Parking is on gravel in a big open field. It's a pricey place due to the location but facilities are not upscale. Full hookups sites were going for about $50 when we visited. From the Grand Canyon Village on the South Rim drive 5 miles south on US-180, the campground is behind a row of restaurants and other tourist-oriented businesses on the east side of the highway.

TEN X CAMPGROUND *(Open May 1 to Sept 30 - Varies)*
Information: 928-635-5600
Location: 8 Miles S of Grand Canyon Village, *N 35° 56' 14", W 112° 07' 50", 6,600 Ft*

70 Sites – Ten X is a big Kaibab National Forest campground that is convenient to the south rim area so it serves as an overflow campground for the park. It's a real deal compared to other campgrounds in the area and can take big RVs. You can't make reservations so get there before noon if you're traveling during the busy summer season. It has paved back-in and pull-thru sites to 45 feet and longer. From the Grand Canyon Village

on the South Rim drive 8 miles south on US-180, the campground is on the east side of the road.

THE FLINTSTONES CAMPGROUND *(Open All Year)*
Res and Info: (928) 635-2600
Location: 28 Miles S of Grand Canyon Village, *N 35° 39' 16", W 112° 08' 25", 5,900 Ft*

27 Sites – Everything here looks like it's direct from Bedrock City. That includes Fred's Diner as well as the office/store/laundry building known as the Buffalo Lodge. Behind a wall is a theme park called Bedrock City Prehistoric Park. The campground is small and simple with back-in and pull-thru sites to at least 50 feet in a gravel lot with a little dry grass and scattered small trees. There's also a tent area with water and barbecue grills. From the Grand Canyon Village on the South Rim drive 28 miles south on US-180, the campground is on the west side of the road in the little town of Valle.

CAMERON TRADING POST *(Open All Year)*
Res and Info: (800) 338-7385, www.camerontradingpost.com
Location: 29 Miles E of Grand Canyon South Rim,
N 35° 52' 30", W 111° 24' 46", 4,200 Ft

10 Sites – The famous Cameron Trading Post is known for it's southwest Indian artwork. It's also a restaurant, a motel, and even an RV park. RV sites here are very basic, poorly maintained, full-hookup sites that can take 40 foot RVs. All except one are back-ins. There are no restrooms so only self-contained RVs are allowed. The traveler park serves as access for some permanent rigs to the east and has quite a bit of through traffic. Cameron Trading Post is located 1.5 miles north of the intersection of US-89 and SR-64. This puts it 29 miles east of the park.

HOLBROOK AND PETRIFIED FOREST NATIONAL PARK

The **Petrified Forest National Park** and adjoining **Painted Desert** straddle Interstate 40 about 110 miles east of Flagstaff. There are no campgrounds in this national park but the town of Holbrook, 24 miles to the east, has several and serves as a good base for exploring the park.

The park north entrance is at Exit 311 of I-40. This is the Painted Desert section of the park. The road runs for 26 miles, first going north and then looping south to cross I-40 and continue south into the Petrified Forest section and finally to the south entrance. Along the way there are several side roads and pull-offs to stop, look around, and take some pictures. Many people drive this in their RVs which works fine if you don't plan to stop. Parking is limited so if you want to get out and do some walking you'd be better off finding a place to park and driving the park road in a tow car. Consider the two places at the south end of the park mentioned in the *Other Possibilities* section below.

PETRIFIED LOGS AT PETRIFIED FOREST NATIONAL PARK

Holbrook and Petrified Forest National Park Campgrounds

🚐 HOLBROOK/PETRIFIED FOREST **KOA** *(Open All Year)*

Reservations: (800) 562-3389, www.koa.com
Information: (928) 524-6689
Location: Holbrook, *N 34° 55' 25", W 110° 08' 38", 5,200 Ft*

132 sites – This pleasant KOA chain campground is the preferred choice in Holbrook for tent campers and also people traveling with children. There are tents sites, back-ins, and pull-thrus to 60 feet. Facilities include a seasonal swimming pool, dump station, and laundry. To reach the campground take Exit 286 from I-40 and turn north. In .9 mile turn right on Hermosa Dr, the campground is on the right in another .1 mile.

🚐 **OK RV P**ARK *(Open All Year)*

Res and Info: (928) 524-3226
Location: Holbrook, *N 34° 55' 08", W 110° 09' 17", 5,100 Ft*

89 Sites – This is a large RV park with some very long pull-thru sites. These are actually double sites designed for two rigs to about 50 feet, one behind the other, but it seems like we always get one by ourselves so we have 100 feet. These are gravel sites in a large gravel field with some small trees. The sites have concrete patios. The campground is

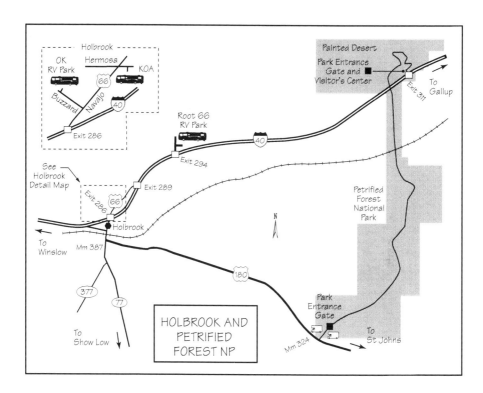

HOLBROOK AND PETRIFIED FOREST NP

located on the north side of I-40. Take Exit 286 and drive north on Navajo, turn left on Buzzard Road after .3 miles, the campground is on the right in another .1 mile.

ROOT 66 RV PARK *(Open All Year)*
Res and Info: (928) 524-2972
Location: 8 Miles E of Holbrook, *N 34° 58' 54", W 110° 03' 22", 5,300 Ft*

22 Sites – This is the smallest of the campgrounds in the area, and the least polished. That said, it's also closer to the highway and to the national park than the ones that are actually in Holbrook. This campground is actually about 8 miles to the east, 17 miles from the north entrance to Petrified Forest National Park. Sites here are on gravel, there are back-ins and pull-thrus and they can accommodate RVs to 45 feet. Tent campers are welcome. There's also a gift shop. Take Exit 294 from I-40. Turn north and then take the first right, the campground entrance is on the right.

Other Camping Possibilities in the Holbrook and Petrified Forest Area

At the south end of the road through the Petrified Forest National Park are two rock shops that offer camping. Boondocking and tent camping is free if you make a minimum purchase ($20 when we visited). Electricity is available at both places with larger purchases or payment of $10. These are actually pretty nice camping areas suitable for big RVs and tents but the only restrooms are those in the shops, there are no showers. These places are at the junction of the park access road and Hwy 180, about 17 miles east of Holbrook.

ARIZONA

IMPERIAL DAM RECREATION AREA

The Imperial Dam Recreation Area on the Colorado River, about 12 miles north of Yuma, is a very popular LTVA and also dispersed camping recreation area. There are also commercial camping facilities and a formal BLM campground. Most of these facilities are in California.

The area around Senator Wash becomes a very active community during the winter and also on summer weekends and holidays. There are lots of opportunities for boating, fishing, and off road vehicle riding.

There are two ways to reach the area. From the east off US-95 follow E Laguna Dam Rd through the Yuma Proving Grounds for about six miles to enter the area.

From the south you can take Exit 172 from I-8 just west of Yuma. Follow S-24 north for 16 miles to Senator Wash.

See the individual entries below for more complete information.

Imperial Dam Recreation Area Campgrounds

HIDDEN SHORES VILLAGE *(Open All Year)*
Res and Info: (928) 539-6700, www.hiddenshores.com, fun@hiddenshores.com
Location: Imperial Dam, *N 32° 52' 58", W 114° 27' 29", 100 Ft*

LAKEFRONT CAMPING AT THE SENATOR WASH RESERVOIR

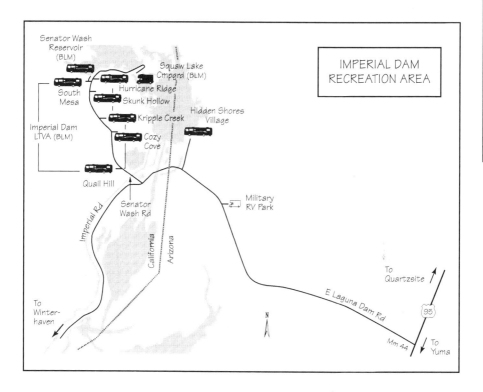

186 Sites – Hidden Shores Village is a large development on the shore of Imperial Reservoir. One section is an RV park. Sites here are back-ins to about 55 feet with paved access roads but parking on gravel. Only RVs less than 10 years old are allowed. Some sites are waterfront. Basic sites are about $55 per day. There is swimming in the reservoir and also a pool. A boat ramp is available and there is a 9-hole executive golf course, golf is free for registered guests. From Yuma drive north on US-95 about 12 miles to E Laguna Dam Rd. Turn left and drive through the Yuma Proving Grounds until a sign at 6.3 miles indicates the entrance to Hidden Shores. Turn right here and drive .5 miles to the manned entrance gate.

🚐 IMPERIAL DAM LTVA *(Open All Year)*

Information: (928) 317-3200, www.az.blm.gov
Location: Imperial Dam, *N 32° 54' 03", W 114° 29' 39", 200 Ft*

Scattered Boondocking – The Imperial Dam LTVA (also sometimes called Senator Wash) encompasses a number of parking areas near the Imperial Dam and Reservoir on the Colorado River north of Tucson. There is a dump station at one of them, the South Mesa camping area, where there is also a host. This is also called the administration area. In summer, outside the LTVA dates, this is a 14-day dispersed camping area with a special $5 per night or $50 per season fee. Overnight costs $10 because that's two days. Starting in Yuma drive north on US-95 about 12 miles to E Laguna Dam Road. Turn left and drive through the Yuma Proving Grounds. At 7.2 miles turn right on Senator Wash

Road and you'll begin seeing signs for the LTVA parking areas. You'll pass Quail Hill, Cozy Cove, Kripple Kreek, Skunk Hollow, South Mesa, and Hurricane Ridge. See the LTVA information at the beginning of this chapter for an explanation of LTVAs and prices.

SENATOR WASH RESERVOIR BLM DISPERSED CAMPING AREA *(Open All Year)*

Information: (928) 317-3200, www.az.blm.gov
Location: Imperial Dam, *N 32° 54' 09", W 114° 29' 50", 200 Ft*

Scattered Boondocking – Just north of the South Mesa LTVA parking area is Senator Wash Reservoir, a lake. Some of the prime sites in the Senator Wash area are along this lake in two areas, North Shore and South Shore. In the past this has been a free 14-day dispersed camping area. It has recently been changed to a $5 per day, $10 per night, or $50 per season area but still with a 14-day limit. Access is signed from the South Mesa administration area.

SQUAW LAKE CAMPGROUND *(Open All Year)*

Information: (928) 317-3200, www.az.blm.gov
Location: Imperial Dam, *N 32° 54' 12", W 114° 28' 39", 100 Ft*

125 Sites – Squaw Lake is a formal BLM campground at the end of the Senator Wash Road. It sits east of a dam with Senator Wash Reservoir on the west side. There are back-in sites that will take RVs to 30 feet with parking on asphalt. There is also an area for tent camping with picnic tables and fire pits near the lake shore. Amenities include a restroom with flush toilets and hot showers as well as a boat ramp. Starting in Yuma drive north on US-95 about 12 miles to E Laguna Dam Road. Turn left and drive through the Yuma Proving Grounds. At 7.2 miles turn right on Senator Wash Road and drive 2.8 miles to a dam. Drive across the top of the dam and then turn right to descend to the campground.

JOSHUA TREE NATIONAL PARK AND TWENTYNINE PALMS

Twentynine Palms (population about 23,000) is a desert town located at the northern border of Joshua Tree. It serves as the main source of supplies for visitors to the national park as well as a place to visit a restaurant if campfire cooking just doesn't appeal.

The 800,00 acre Joshua Tree National Park occupies the high desert to the south of Twentynine Palms, east of the Coachella Valley, and north of I-40. This park is extremely popular for rock climbing, desert hiking, birding (especially in winter) and observing desert bighorn sheep. There are actually two ecosystems in the park. Below 3,000 feet you're in the Colorado Desert with ocotillos and creosote bushes. Above that altitude is the Mojave Desert with the park's namesake, the Joshua Tree.

There are two main roads in the park. In the northern section a loop road called Park Boulevard enters near Twentynine Palms at the Oasis Visitor Center. Nearby is the North Entrance Station. It runs south and then west before looping north to exit at the West Entrance Station, a total distance of 26 miles. The second major road connects the loop with the South Entrance near I-40. This road has several names, we'll call it the South Entrance Road. It's 36 miles from the south entrance up to the intersection with the loop road.

ARIZONA

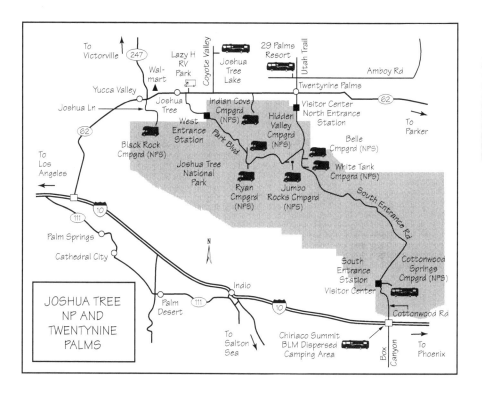

The park has a number of campgrounds. None have hookups and only a few can handle larger RVs. The campgrounds in the interior of the park are very basic but extremely scenic. There is a 30 day per year camping limit in the park, and only 14 of those days can be in the high season, October through May.

Joshua Tree National Park and Twentynine Palms Campgrounds

TWENTYNINE PALMS RESORT *(Open All Year)*

Res and Info: (800) 874-4548, (760) 367-3320, www.29palmsgolf.com
Location: Twentynine Palms, *N 34° 09' 56", W 116° 02' 40", 1,700 Ft*

100 Sites – This resort has many permanently-located units in addition to the RV spaces available for daily, monthly, or seasonal rental. Sites are back-ins and pull-thrus to about 50 feet. The park is adjacent to a golf course and has a pool, spa, clubhouse, game room, exercise room, a putting green, basketball, 2 shuffleboard courts, tennis, horseshoes, and planned activities. In Twentynine Palms from the intersection of SR-62 and the Utah Trail (which is the road that enters Joshua Tree NP at the North Entrance) drive north for 2 miles to Amboy Road and turn left. The campground is on the right in .4 mile.

ARIZONA

JOSHUA TREE LAKE *(Open All Year)*

Res and Info: (760) 366-1213, www.jtlake.com
Location: 5 Miles N of Joshua Tree, *N 34° 12' 21", W 116° 14' 39", 2,400 Ft*

50 Sites – Joshua Tree Lake is on a hillside about five miles north of the town of Joshua Tree. The campground has a small lake where you can fish for catfish, bluegill and bass. The campground has large pull-thru sites with water and electricity hookups. Other amenities include restrooms with showers, bait and tackle, firewood, fishing pole rentals, horseshoes, and off road access. From SR-62 between Twentynine Palms and Joshua Tree turn north on Coyote Valley Road. Drive north for 5 miles and you'll see the RV park on the right.

JOSHUA TREE NATIONAL PARK – BLACK ROCK CAMPGROUND *(Open All Year)*

Reservations: (877) 444-6777, www.recreation.gov
Information: (760) 367-5500, www.nps.gov/jotr
Location: 5 Miles S of Yucca Valley, *N 34° 04' 27", W 116° 23' 23", 4,000 Ft*

100 Sites – Unlike most of the Joshua Tree campgrounds this one is on the edge of the park and access is not from the park roads. That means you don't have to pay an entry fee to get here. It's also unusual because you can make reservations. There are back-ins and pull-thrus to 35 feet. Water is available and there is a dump station. In the town of Yucca Valley, at the intersection where SR-247 intersects SR-62, drive south on Joshua Lane. You'll reach the campground in 5 miles.

JOSHUA TREE NATIONAL PARK – INDIAN COVE CAMPGROUND *(Open All Year)*

Reservations: (877) 444-6777, www.recreation.gov
Information: (760) 367-5500, www.nps.gov/jotr
Location: 3 Miles SW of Twentynine Palms, *N 34° 05' 37", W 116° 09' 24", 3,200 Ft*

101 Sites – Indian Cove is one of the prettiest of the Joshua Tree Campgrounds. It is situated in a rocky canyon overlooking Twentynine Palms. It, like Black Rock, is situated away from the interior roads so access is from its own entrance with its own entrance station. You do not have to pay the park entrance fee to use this campground. The sites here are small but a few will take a 35-foot RV. The campground has only picnic tables, grills, and vault toilets. There is no water in the campground but it is available at the entrance station. The road to the campground goes south from SR-62 between the north entrance station and the west entrance station, just west of Twentynine Palms. From SR-62 it's 2.5 miles into the park on Indian Cove Road.

JOSHUA TREE NATIONAL PARK – JUMBO ROCKS CAMPGROUND *(Open All Year)*

Information: (760) 367-5500, www.nps.gov/jotr
Location: 11 Miles S of Twentynine Palms, *N 33° 59' 30", W 116° 04' 03", 4,400 Ft*

125 Sites – Jumbo Rocks is a pretty campground with scattered granite boulders and outcrops. It's one of the largest campgrounds in the park. The interior roads are paved, there are six loops. Narrow roads and difficult site access mean that 30-foot RVs are the

largest that should use this campground. Amenities are limited to vault toilets, tables, and grills – and, of course, the rocks. There is no drinking water. The campground is located off Park Boulevard, 8 miles from the North Entrance Station and 18 miles from the West Entrance Station.

JOSHUA TREE NATIONAL PARK – RYAN CAMPGROUND *(Open All Year)*
Information: (760) 367-5500, www.nps.gov/jotr
Location: 18 Miles SW of Twentynine Palms, *N 33° 59' 02", W 116° 09' 17", 4,300 Ft*

31 Sites – Ryan is popular with rock climbers. It's a tent and small RV campground with few sites as long as 25 feet. There are picnic tables, grills, and vault toilets. The campground has no water. Ryan is located off Park Boulevard, 14 miles from the North Entrance Station and 12 miles from the West Entrance Station.

JOSHUA TREE NATIONAL PARK – HIDDEN VALLEY CAMPGROUND *(Open All Year)*
Information: (760) 367-5500, www.nps.gov/jotr
Location: 19 Miles SW of Twentynine Palms, *N 34° 00' 56", W 116° 09' 40", 4,200 Ft*

39 Sites – This campground is set in boulders and Joshua trees. Sites are short, park rules limit camping vehicle length to 25 feet. Like most of the campgrounds in the park this one has picnic tables, grills, vault toilets and no water. The campground is located off Park Boulevard, 17 miles from the North Entrance Station and 9 miles from the West Entrance Station.

JOSHUA TREE NATIONAL PARK – BELLE CAMPGROUND *(Open All Year)*
Information: (760) 367-5500, www.nps.gov/jotr
Location: 8 Miles S of Twentynine Palms, *N 34° 00' 08", W 116° 01' 20", 3,800 Ft*

18 Sites – Belle Campground is set in a jumble of granite boulders. The sites here are slightly larger than those at White Tank, the next campground. Narrow roads and difficult access limit RVs to about 30 feet here. This campground is located on the South Entrance Road 6 miles south of the North Entrance and 34 miles north of the South Entrance.

JOSHUA TREE NATIONAL PARK – WHITE TANK CAMPGROUND *(Open All Year)*
Information: (760) 367-5500, www.nps.gov/jotr
Location: 10 Miles S of Twentynine Palms, *N 33° 59' 04", W 116° 01' 07", 3,800 Ft*

15 Sites – This is a tent and small vehicle campground set in a jumble of big rocks. The largest sites are 25 feet long, most are shorter. Park rules limit vehicle length, including the towing vehicle, to 25 feet. There are picnic tables, grills, and a vault toilet, but no water. This campground is located on the South Entrance Road 7 miles south of the North Entrance and 33 miles north of the South Entrance.

🚐 JOSHUA TREE NATIONAL PARK – COTTONWOOD SPRINGS CAMPGROUND
(Open All Year)

Information: (760) 367-5500, www.nps.gov/jotr
Location: 39 Miles S of Twentynine Palms, *N 33° 44' 34", W 115° 48' 52", 3,000 Ft*

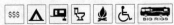

62 Sites – This is probably Joshua Tree's best campground for RVs, particularly big ones. There are two loops. Each has back-in sites in the center and parallel-parking type pull-offs on the outside. Rangers recommend the even number sites for RVs with slide-outs. Some of the pull-offs are as long as 58 feet. There are no hookups here but restrooms have flush toilets (no showers) and there is a dump station just outside the campground entrance. Water is available in the campground. This campground is located on the South Entrance Road 36 miles south of the North Entrance and 5 miles north of the South Entrance.

🚐 CHIRIACO SUMMIT **BLM** DISPERSED CAMPING AREA *(Open All Year)*

Information: (760) 251-4800
Location: I-10 Exit 168, *N 33° 39' 37", W 115° 48' 08", 1,600 Ft*

Scattered Boondocking – See the introductory material in this chapter about the BLM 14-Day dispersed camping areas. This area serves as overflow parking at the south entrance to Joshua Tree National Park. It's also handy because it's a good place to overnight before descending into the Palms Springs area, the first Indio exits are about 20 miles to the west. At the exit the Cottonwood Road extends 1 mile north to the entrance to Joshua Tree National Park and Box Canyon Road runs south and then west. Parking is allowed in three areas. The first is north of the freeway, south of the water district road, and both east and west of Cottonwood Road. The others are both east and west of Box Canyon Road on the south side of the freeway. No facilities are provided, fires are allowed in fire rings.

KINGMAN

Kingman (population about 26,000) is on US-40 about 50 miles east of the California Border and 148 miles west of Flagstaff. Like many other US-40 towns Kingman is a Route 66 town and you'll find authentic Route 66 restaurants and motels in the central area as well as a **Route 66 Museum**. Kingman's main museum the **Mojave Museum of History and Arts**, is excellent.

A good side trip would be a drive to the former gold-mining town of **Oatman**. This tiny place has become a popular destination for everyone from snowbirds in the Colorado River basin to bus tourists from Las Vegas. There are shops and restaurants as well as wandering burros, but it's more fun just to watch the visitors. In a smaller RV it can be fun to drive old Route 66 westward the 28 miles between Kingman and Oatman, but you have to cross 3,550 foot high Sitgreaves pass on narrow roads. You can also approach from the west on a better road, but parking can be tough in a larger RV and maneuvering room is scarce, so come in your tow car if you have one.

STREET ACTION IN OATMAN

Kingman Campgrounds

ADOBE RV PARK *(Open All Year)*
Res and Info: (928) 565-3010
Location: 8 Miles NE of Kingman, *N 35° 13' 20", W 114° 11' 58", 2,800 Ft*

75 Sites – This age 55+ RV park is really in the flat country to the west of Kingman. It's a large lot surrounded by trees. Sites are back-ins and pull-thrus to about 55 feet. The bathrooms are individual tiled rooms. There is a small store selling basic grocery items and RV supplies as well as a recreation room with a kitchen. Planned activities are scheduled in the winter. From I-40 take Exit 48 and drive northwest on US-93. After 3.6 miles take the exit for SR-68 and drive west. In another 4 miles turn right onto Adobe Road and right into the park.

FORT BEALE RV PARK *(Open All Year)*
Reservations: (888) 519-7273, ftbeale@ctaz.com
Information: (928) 753-3355
Location: Kingman, *N 35° 11' 32", W 114° 03' 57", 3,300 Ft*

42 Sites – This is a nice clean simple park in a fenced lot near I-40. A paved road leads through the park with parking on gravel sites. There are a few trees for shade. The interior 12 sites are pull-thrus and the exterior sites are back-ins. Both back-in and pull-thru sites are as long as 65 feet. All sites have full hookups including cable TV. All sites have a

ARIZONA

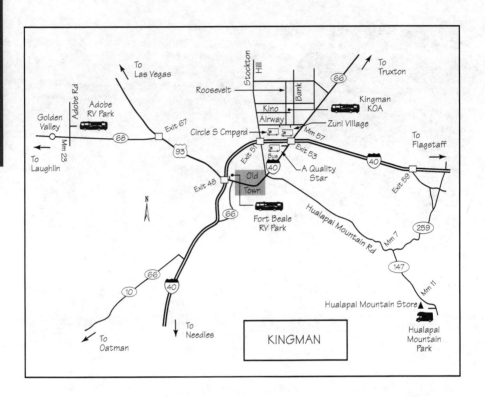

KINGMAN

picnic table. The office building houses a small recreation room. Behind the office is a seasonal outdoor swimming pool. From I-40 take Exit 48. Drive west and immediately turn left onto Metcalfe between the Carl's Jr. and a Chevron gas station. Head north a block to the campground.

🚐 KINGMAN KOA *(Open All Year)*

Reservations: (800) 562-3991, www.koa.com
Information: (928) 757-4397
Location: Kingman, *N 35° 14' 02", W 114° 01' 04", 3,400 Ft*

84 Sites – This KOA is a good one because the RV sites are all pull-thrus to about 50 feet. There are also tent sites, of course, and rental cabins. Amenities include a heated swimming pool and mini golf as well as grocery items in the office. From I-40 take Exit 51 and head north on Stockton Hill Road. In one mile turn right on Kino Avenue and you'll see the campground on the left in 1 mile.

🚐 HUALAPAI MOUNTAIN PARK *(Open All Year)*

Information: (928) 757-0915, (928) 681-5700, www.mcparks.com
Location: 12 Miles SE of Kingman, *N 35° 05' 56", W 113° 53' 04", 6,500 Ft*

ARIZONA

84 Sites – This park sits high on the slope of Hualapai Mountain, the climb from about 3,500 feet at Kingman is a killer and probably should be avoided by most RVs. In summer, though, it's a great place to enjoy some cooler temperatures. This park has a 74 site "campground", a mini RV park with 10 full hookup sites, and 14 rental cabins. All are set in a pine forest. The campground is suitable only for smaller vehicles like vans, pickup campers, and automobile tent campers. Access to the RV park is difficult so that while spaces will take RVs to 32 feet it looks like anything over about 25 feet would have problems getting into them. Eleven pull-thru sites are under construction to the east of the main park. This will be an ATV area but the sites can be used by any RV. These sites will take larger RVs. The new sites have no hookups in the beginning, but plans are for hookups for them eventually. Reservations are accepted only for the cabins but if you call ahead from the foot of the mountain they'll probably tell you what's available and hold a site for you. Nearby is a grocery store and a pay telephone. From SR-66 just east of central Kingman head southeast on Hualapai Mountain Rd. Follow it for 12 miles up the mountain, the park is on the right.

LAKE HAVASU AND THE PARKER STRIP

The lower Colorado River is sometimes called Arizona's West Coast. A popular area of this coast is the 40-mile section from Lake Havasu south to Parker.

There are two reservoirs on this section of the Colorado. To the north is Lake Havasu, the reservoir behind Parker Dam. Below Parker Dam there is a narrow 16-mile-long lake known as Moovalya Lake or more popularly, the Parker Strip. It's wide open to boating and water sports, with few restrictions. From April to October the water is warm and the area full of water-oriented visitors. In winter it's popular with snowbirds, but much quieter. The lower limit of this strip is Headgate Rock Dam, just above the town of Parker.

The town of Parker (population about 3,000) is the main supply town in the southern part of this region. It is on the Colorado River Indian Reservation which stretches south along the Colorado River from Parker almost to Blythe. Parker has stores, restaurants and gas stations.

From Parker roads go north on both sides of the river. On the California side the Parker Dam Road follows the river very closely and there is a long strip of RV parks and other resorts right on the river. Note that RVs, even pickup campers or vans, for security reasons are not allowed to cross the river on the dam at the north end of the Parker Strip. That means that the west side is in effect a kind of cul-de-sac for RVs.

On the east side SR-95, the main north – south highway through the region, is farther from the river but local roads run along giving access to some RV facilities. North of Parker Dam the highway rounds the lower end of Lake Havasu, passes through the Bill Williams River National Wildlife Refuge, and then stays inland for 14 miles until it reaches Lake Havasu City.

Lake Havasu, the reservoir behind Parker Dam, is 45 miles long and up to 3 miles wide. It's a very popular water sports lake.

Lake Havasu City (population about 55,000) is by far the largest city in this region. The town is well known for its **London Bridge**, relocated block by block from London. If you're wondering why the island at the west end of the bride is called Pittsburg Point, not Pittsburg Island, there's a reason. London bridge first spanned a dry gully, only later was it deepened to allow water to flow under the bridge.

ARIZONA

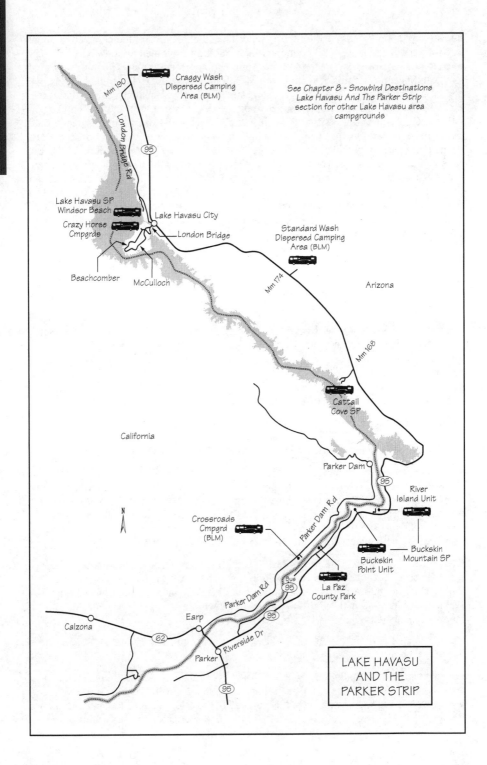

Craggy Wash
Dispersed Camping
Area (BLM)

Mm 190

London Bridge Rd

95

See Chapter 8 - Snowbird Destinations
Lake Havasu And The Parker Strip
section for other Lake Havasu area
campgrounds

Lake Havasu SP
Windsor Beach

Crazy Horse
Cmpgrds

Lake Havasu City

London Bridge

Standard Wash
Dispersed Camping
Area (BLM)

Beachcomber

McCulloch

Mm 174

Arizona

Mm 168

Cattail
Cove SP

California

Parker Dam

95

River
Island Unit

N

Crossroads
Cmpgrd
(BLM)

Parker Dam Rd

Buckskin
Mountain SP

Buckskin
Point Unit

Parker Dam Rd

Bus
95

La Paz
County Park

Calzona

62

Earp

Riverside Dr

95

Parker

95

LAKE HAVASU
AND THE
PARKER STRIP

For more about RV camping in the Lake Havasu and Parker area, and particularly snow-bird winter RV parks, see the *Snowbird Destinations* chapter of this book.

Lake Havasu and the Parker Strip Campgrounds

🚐 **CRAZY HORSE CAMPGROUNDS** *(Open All Year)*

Res and Info: (928) 855-4033
Location: Lake Havasu City, *N 34° 28' 08", W 114° 21' 25", 400 Ft*

600 Sites – This very large RV park is the closest to London Bridge. It's popular with both travelers and Snowbirds. There are back-in and pull-thru sites to 60 feet, some along the waterfront. Amenities include a clubhouse and grocery store and there is a paved bike trail to the bridge. In Lake Havasu City follow signs for London Bridge. After crossing the bridge continue for .4 miles and then turn right on Beachcomber Blvd. The campground entrance will be on your right in just a few hundred yards.

🚐 **LAKE HAVASU STATE PARK – WINDSOR BEACH** *(Open All Year)*

Information: (928) 855-2784, www.azstateparks.com
Location: Lake Havasu City, *N 34° 29' 31", W 114° 21' 28", 400 Ft*

47 Sites – This is a nice park with many of the sites on the lake, it's close enough to use a bicycle to travel into Lake Havasu City. Sites are irregular, mostly back-in or pull-in, some to 55 feet. Restrooms have flush toilets and showers. Swimming is possible in the lake and there are also boat ramp facilities. The park is on the lake shore north of London Bridge. Follow London Bridge Road north along the shoreline from its southern end a block north of the access road to London Bridge. In 1.6 miles you'll see the park entrance on your left.

🚐 **CRAGGY WASH BLM DISPERSED CAMPING AREA** *(Open All Year)*

Information: (928) 505-1200
Location: 6 Miles N of Lake Havasu City, *N 34° 35' 22", W 114° 21' 55", 1,100 Ft*

Scattered Boondocking – Craggy Wash is a BLM camping area. Like other dispersed camping areas there is no charge, there are no facilities, and your stay is limited to 14 days out of a 28 day period. The area is on the east side of SR-95 north of Lake Havasu City near Mile 190.

🚐 **STANDARD WASH BLM DISPERSED CAMPING AREA** *(Open All Year)*

Information: (928) 505-1200
Location: 3 Miles S of Lake Havasu City, *N 34° 26' 06", W 114° 12' 58", 1,100 Ft*

Scattered Boondocking – Standard Wash is a BLM free-camping area. Like other dispersed camping areas there is no charge, there are no facilities, and your stay is limited to 14 days out of a 28 day period. This one is south of Lake Havasu City on the east side of SR-95 near Mile 174.

ARIZONA

ARIZONA

CROSSROADS CAMPGROUND *(Open All Year)*

Information: (928) 505-1200
Location: Parker Strip, *N 34° 12' 40", W 114° 12' 56", 300 Ft*

12 Sites – This small BLM campground is located in the Parker Strip. It's on the shore of the Colorado River and the sites will take larger RVs. The campground has no potable water but does have vault toilets. From Parker cross the river and head north on the Parker Dam Road on the west side of the river. The entrance road is on the right in 5.5 miles.

LA PAZ COUNTY PARK *(Open All Year)*

Information: (928) 667-2069, www.co.la-paz.az.us/LazPazCountyParks/
Location: 8 Miles N of Parker, *N 34° 13' 34", W 114° 11' 24", 300 Ft*

Approx 500 Sites – This big county park is good for both summer use and snowbird stays, it's located on the east side of the river. The hookup-area sites are both back-ins and pull-thrus to 50 feet. They have electric and water hookups and there is a dump station. There are also waterfront no-hookup sites and a huge grass-covered field that can by used for overflow dry tent and RV camping. In winter it's possible to stay here for six months and there's a golf course next door. The campground is located along SR-95 some 9 Miles north of the intersection of SR-62 and SR-95 in Parker.

BUCKSKIN MOUNTAIN STATE PARK – BUCKSKIN POINT UNIT *(Open All Year)*

Reservations: (928) 667-3231
Information: (928) 667-3231, www.azstateparks.com
Location: 10 Miles N of Parker, *N 34° 15' 19", W 114° 09' 43", 300 Ft*

89 Sites – Buckskin Mountain has two units. River Island is described below. The Buckskin Point unit is larger, it has 89 sites including cabana units for tenters and smaller RVs along the river, back-ins, and pull-thrus to 65 feet. Most sites have electricity and water hookups, a few also have sewer. There are picnic tables and raised barbecues at the sites. Amenities include a boat launch, interpretive center, cactus garden, boutique, and even a basketball court. Swimming is in the Colorado River. The dump station here can be used by non-guests for a fee. The campground is located along SR-95 some 11 Miles north of the intersection of SR-62 and SR-95 in Parker.

BUCKSKIN MOUNTAIN STATE PARK – RIVER ISLAND UNIT *(Open All Year)*

Information: (928) 667-3386, www.azstateparks.com
Location: 11 Miles N of Parker, *N 34° 15' 25", W 114° 08' 43", 300 Ft*

37 Sites – The River Island unit of Buckskin Mountain State Park now offers electrical sites that are excellent for large RVs. It's a beautiful campground along the river with tent sites as well as big back-in and pull-thru sites. There are electrical and water hookups and a dump station. Restrooms have flush toilets and showers. The campground is located along SR-95 some 12 Miles north of the intersection of SR-62 and SR-95 in Parker.

CATTAIL COVE STATE PARK *(Open All Year)*
Information: (928) 855-1223, (520) 628-5798, www.azstateparks.com
Location: 23 Miles N of Parker, *N 34° 21' 14", W 114° 10' 00", 400 Ft*

88 Sites – Cattail Cove is a beautiful state park on the shore of Lake Havasu. It's popular in summer, of course, but snowbirds like it in winter too. This park offers discounts for long term stays and sets aside many sites for 6 month tenants. Sites here are both back-ins and pull-thrus to 50 feet. There are restrooms with flush toilets and hot showers, a swimming beach, and a boat ramp. Within walking distance is Sandpoint Marina and RV Park which offers a restaurant, store, and laundry. The campground is located along SR-95 some 24 Miles north of the intersection of SR-62 and SR-95 in Parker.

LAKE MEAD NATIONAL RECREATION AREA (ARIZONA, NEVADA)

The 2,337 square mile Lake Mead Recreation Area centers around two reservoirs. In the north, behind Hoover Dam, is the huge Lake Mead. It's a popular recreational resource, with fishing, water sports, and houseboating the top attractions. At almost every road access point to the lake you'll find a National Park Service campground with no hookups and also a privately run full-hookup RV park. Usually there's also a marina with other attractions including a boat ramp and perhaps docks, houseboat rentals, restaurant, motel and store.

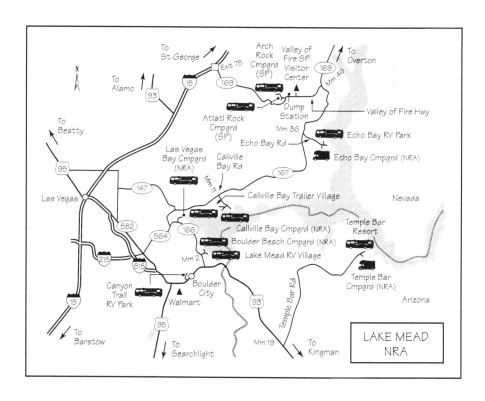

ARIZONA

The **Alan Bible Visitor Center** for the recreation area is located just east of Boulder, right along the road out to Hoover Dam. Just a little farther east you can take a tour of **Hoover Dam**. Traffic currently passes over the dam and there are security checkpoints (RVs are thoroughly inspected) at each end so traffic can get backed up. A bridge is under construction to bypass the dam, completion is expected during 2008.

North of Las Vegas but just west of the Lake Mead Recreation Area is **Valley of Fire State Park**. Two campgrounds in the state park are described below in addition to those in the Lake Mead Recreation Area. Valley of Fire State Park was Nevada's first state park and is a beautiful area of brilliantly colored cliffs and boulders.

To the south is smaller Lake Mohave behind Davis Dam. See the *Mohave Valley* section below for information about Katherine Landing and the campgrounds there.

Lake Mead National Recreation Area Campgrounds

VALLEY OF FIRE STATE PARK – ATLATL ROCK CAMPGROUND *(Open All Year)*

Information: (702) 397-2088, www.parks.nv.gov
Location: 44 Miles NE of Las Vegas, *N 36° 25' 04", W 114° 33' 08", 2,200 Ft*

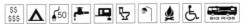

50 Sites – This campground is named after the nearby Atlatl Rock, an important petroglyph site. Some of the pictures here are thought to be over 1,500 years old. Campground sites are off a circular loop with some back-ins as long as 45 feet. Recently 25 sites with electrical and water hookups have been added and restrooms have flush toilets and showers. Nearby is a dump station and the visitor center, also nearby, has a telephone. From the intersection of SR-147 (East Lake Mead Dr) and SR-167 (Northshore Road) east of Las Vegas drive northeast on SR-167 for 43 miles. Turn left on Valley of Fire Highway toward Valley of Fire State Park and drive 7 miles. Turn right and after passing the dump station on your right. Atlatl Campground is on your left. It's shorter but not as scenic to drive north from Las Vegas on I-25 to Exit 75 and then drive 17 miles east to the park on SR-169.

VALLEY OF FIRE STATE PARK – ARCH ROCK CAMPGROUND *(Open All Year)*

Information: (702) 397-2088, www.parks.nv.gov
Location: 44 Miles NE of Las Vegas, *N 36° 25' 10", W 114° 33' 24", 2,300 Ft*

29 Sites – Arch Rock is the secondary campground in Valley of Fire State Park, the nearby Atlatl Campground has nicer facilities. However, Arch Rock is tucked into a red rock canyon and is a beautiful campground. The sites are back-ins and some are as long as 45 feet, a carefully drive 45 foot coach or big fifth wheel should fit just fine. The campground has vault toilets but campers could use the showers at Atlatl Campground and there is a dump station near Atlatl too. To find the campground follow the instructions give above for Atlatl Campground and after passing Atlatl on your left you will arrive at Arch Rock Campground in a half mile or so. Another shorter route is to drive north from Las Vegas on I-25 to Exit 75 and then drive 17 miles east to the park on SR-169.

LAKE MEAD NRA – ECHO BAY CAMPGROUND *(Open All Year)*

Information: (702) 293-8907, www.nps.gov/lame
Location: 48 Miles NE of Las Vegas, *N 36° 18' 30", W 114° 26' 07", 1,200 Ft*

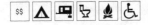

154 Sites – There are campsites at two different locations in this National Park Service (NPS) campground. The upper campground has 115 sites. They're all back-ins to about 30 feet. There is a dump station at this location and restrooms with flush toilets. About .6 miles beyond is the second campground. It is much smaller with most sites being back-ins to about 25 feet. This campground too has flush toilets. Groceries and a boat ramp are available at the nearby marina. From the intersection of SR-147 (East Lake Mead Dr) and SR-167 (Northshore Road) east of Las Vegas drive northeast on SR-167 for 32 miles. Turn right onto Echo Bay Road and in 3.9 miles you'll reach the campgrounds.

ECHO BAY RV PARK *(Open All Year)*
Information: (702) 394-4000, (702) 394-4066, (800) 752-9669
Location: 58 Miles NE of Las Vegas, *N 36° 18' 37", W 114° 25' 55", 1,200 Ft*

58 Sites – Sites here are back-ins to 60 feet. The campground has trees for shade and a restroom building with both showers and laundry. The associated hotel has a restaurant and groceries as well as Wi-Fi in the lobby. To drive to the campground follow the directions given for the Echo Bay Campground above.

LAKE MEAD NRA – CALLVILLE BAY CAMPGROUND *(Open All Year)*
Information: (702) 293-8907, www.nps.gov/lame
Location: 25 Miles NE of Las Vegas, *N 36° 08' 26", W 114° 43' 34", 1,200 Ft*

107 Sites – This NPS campground is away from the water but the sites are very nice. All sites are back-ins, some as long as 40 feet. Parking pads are all paved and restrooms have flush toilets. There is a dump station and showers, a snack bar, groceries, and a telephone are available at the nearby marina. Callville Bay Trailer Park, a short walk away, has a laundry. From the intersection of SR-147 (East Lake Mead Dr) and SR-167 (Northshore Road) east of Las Vegas drive northeast on SR-167 for 8 miles. Turn right onto Callville Bay Road and in 3.6 miles turn right into the campground.

CALLVILLE BAY TRAILER VILLAGE *(Open All Year)*
Res and Info: (702) 565-8958, (800) 255-5561
Location: 25 Miles NE of Las Vegas, *N 36° 08' 39", W 114° 43' 30", 1,300 Ft*

5 Sites – This is a trailer park with five sites available for RVs. It's older but if you need hookups and want to be in this area it's a possibility. Sites are back-ins and are about 45 feet long. They have full hookups. A restroom building nearby has showers and a laundry. Follow the driving instructions given above for Callville Bay Campground and when you turn into the campground take the immediate right for the trailer park and drive to the back for the RV sites.

LAKE MEAD NRA – LAS VEGAS BAY CAMPGROUND *(Open All Year)*
Information: (702) 293-8907, www.nps.gov/lame
Location: 19 Miles E of Las Vegas, *N 36° 07' 41", W 114° 52' 28", 1,200 Ft*

86 Sites – This is one of the nicest of the Lake Mead NPS camping areas although it is nowhere near the water. Sites in this campground are all back-ins, some to about 30 feet

ARIZONA

but a few that are as long as 45 feet. They have picnic tables and fire pits and there are quite a few trees. From the intersection east of Las Vegas of US-93 and SR-166 near Alan Bible Visitor Center drive north on SR-166 for 10 miles. Turn right into Las Vegas Bay and in .1 mile turn left and drive .8 miles to the campground.

LAKE MEAD NRA – BOULDER BEACH CAMPGROUND *(Open All Year)*

Information: (702) 293-8907, www.nps.gov/lame
Location: 13 Miles NE of Las Vegas, *N 36° 02' 09", W 114° 48' 08", 1,200 Ft*

146 Sites – This is the closest of the Lake Mead NRA campgrounds to Las Vegas, and the busiest. The campground has back in sites to about 35 feet and a few pull-thrus to 70 feet. Some sites have a view of the lake. Restrooms have flush toilets but no showers. There is a dump station at the campground and Lake Mead RV Village next door has showers that are available for a fee. From the intersection east of Las Vegas of US-93 and SR-166 near Alan Bible Visitor Center drive north on SR-93 for 2 miles. The campground is on the right.

LAKE MEAD RV VILLAGE *(Open All Year)*

Res and Info: (702) 293-2540, www.LakeMeadRvVillage.com
Location: 13 Miles E of Las Vegas, *N 36° 02' 05", W 114° 48' 01", 1,200 Ft*

115 Sites – The campground terraces up from the lakeshore with back-in and pull-thru sites to about 60 feet. Most sites have paved patios and picnic tables. The office houses a small store and gift shop. From the intersection east of Las Vegas of US-93 and SR-166 near Alan Bible Visitor Center drive north on SR-93 for 2 miles. The campground is on the right.

CANYON TRAIL RV PARK *(Open All Year)*

Res and Info: (702) 293-1200, www.canyontrailrvparknv.com
Location: Boulder, *N 35° 58' 38", W 114° 51' 01", 2,500 Ft*

156 Sites – This campground is a large square gravel lot. There are back-in sites around the edge and pull-thrus in the center. At the west end of Boulder turn north from US-93 on Veteran's Memorial Drive and follow it as it curves around to the right. The campground is on the left 1.4 mile after you turn off US-93.

LAKE MEAD NRA – TEMPLE BAR CAMPGROUND *(Open All Year)*

Information: (702) 293-8907, www.nps.gov/lame
Location: 59 Miles E of Las Vegas, *N 36° 01' 52", W 114° 19' 31", 1,200 Ft*

153 Sites – This is a large NPS campground with back-in and pull-thru sites to about 30 feet. It's a nice campground with trees for shade and site separation. Restrooms have flush toilets. Showers are available at the Temple Bar Resort. The resort also has a restaurant, bar, grocery store, pay telephones, and ice is sold. There are also a few RV sites with hookups, see below. The marina has a boat ramp, a swimming beach, and a fish cleaning station. The campground is somewhat remote. From Hoover Dam drive south on US-93 for 18 miles. Turn east on Temple Bar Road, it's 26 miles to the campground.

TEMPLE BAR RESORT *(Open All Year)*
Res and Info: (928) 767-3211, www.templebarlakemead.com
Location: 59 Miles E of Las Vegas, *N 36° 02' 03", W 114° 19' 21", 1,200 Ft*

30 Sites – The Temple Bar Resort has a motel, cabins, and a trailer park. Most sites in the trailer park are filled by long-term residents but there are sometimes one or two open for travelers. These are back-ins and have full hookups. The resort has a bar, restaurant, and store and is at the marina where a boat launch is available. There is a swimming beach. The RV park has a restroom with shower. Rates are cheaper here in the winter season (Nov 1 - March 31) than what is indicated on the icon line. To reach the resort follow the instructions for the campground above, it's right next door.

LAS VEGAS

Las Vegas (population about 575,000) is a top Southwest attraction. Millions of people visit each year, quite a few of them in RVs. A lot of RVers feel that Laughlin and other outlying gambling towns are easier to visit, and they are, but they're just not Las Vegas.

The main attraction is the **Strip**. This is Las Vegas Boulevard, the most interesting part of which runs for 4 miles from the intersection with Main Street to the Mandalay Bay Casino. Must-see casinos on or near the strip with lots to offer in addition to gambling are, from north to south: Stratosphere; Las Vegas Hilton; Circus Circus; Wynn Las Vegas; Treasure Island; Mirage; Venetian; Caesar's Palace; Bellagio; Paris Las Vegas; Hard Rock Hotel and Casino, MGM Grand; New York, New York; Excalibur; Luxor; and

NEW YORK-NEW YORK ON THE LAS VEGAS STRIP

ARIZONA

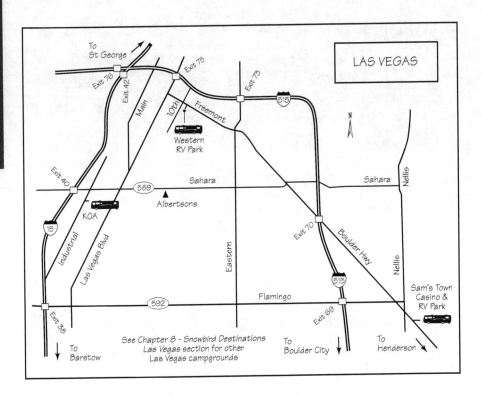

Mandalay. It's fun to walk the strip at night just to see the shows and lights, there's a monorail to the east if your legs get tired.

In addition to the Strip you'll want to see the covered pedestrian mall on **Fremont Street** in the downtown area. It's a quarter-mile stretch with an overhead light show and offers up the older downtown casinos.

For more about Las Vegas, and particularly snowbird winter RV parks, see the *Snowbird Destinations* chapter of this book. Many campgrounds listed in that chapter also have spaces for travelers, our charts in that chapter give overnight rates for the ones that do.

Las Vegas Campgrounds

LAS VEGAS KOA AT CIRCUS CIRCUS *(Open All Year)*

Reservations: (800) 562-7270, www.koa.com
Information: (702) 733-9707, www.lasvegaskoa.com
Location: Las Vegas, *N 36° 08' 24", W 115° 09' 51", 2,000 Ft*

385 Sites – The Las Vegas KOA at Circus Circus is no doubt the best place to stay if you are planning to visit the Strip. It is conveniently located behind Circus Circus casino. Unfortunately, it can be expensive. Prices are "managed". In other words, they vary

dramatically depending upon forecast demand. It pays to call ahead and check prices, then plan your trip for a time when prices are lowest. Parking here is on asphalt, sites are closely packed, some are pull-thrus as long as 60 feet. Tent camping is on grass. This is a well run park, the facilities are in excellent condition. Amenities include an office building with an excellent store and gift shop, an ATM, free Wi-Fi in the park, swimming pool, spa, and playground. Restaurants are in the casino next door. The gate to the campground is a block west of the Strip off Industrial Road. From I-15 take Exit 40 and head west on E Sahara Ave. You'll cross over Industrial and .5 mile west of the freeway take the right exit which will bring you back to Industrial. Then drive south for .3 mile to the well-marked entrance.

SAM'S TOWN CASINO AND RV PARK *(Open All Year)*

Res and Info: (800) 634-6371, (702) 456-7777, www.samstownlv.com
Location: Las Vegas, *N 36° 06' 38", W 115° 03' 35", 2,000 Ft*

287 Sites – Sam's Town is a casino on the Boulder Highway away from the strip. The name may remind you of the RV Club but so far as we know they're not related. There are actually two RV parks related to the casino, this one and the one nearby on Nellis, see *Chapter 8*. Stays in this park are limited to 14 days. Sites are all full-hookup back-ins or pull-thrus to about 50 feet. There is a nice pool area, in addition to the pool there is a spa. The casino is right next door and has restaurants and entertainment. From I-515 on the east side of Las Vegas take Exit 70 and head south on the Boulder Highway. In 2.5 miles you'll see the casino on the left, the entrance road for this RV park is just past the casino, also on the left.

WESTERN RV PARK *(Open All Year)*

Res and Info: (702) 384-1033, (702) 384-4620
Location: Las Vegas, *N 36° 09' 58", W 115° 08' 04", 2,000 Ft*

69 Sites – This is a very utilitarian campground located about a half mile from the covered pedestrian casino mall downtown. It is located in two paved lots near the corner of Fremont and 10th. Sites range from 30 to 50 feet, they all have full-hookups. The office is next to the 10th and Fremont lot, it houses the restrooms and laundry.

LEES FERRY

Historically Lees Ferry was one of the few places where travelers could cross the Colorado River in the Grand Canyon area. It's 14.5 river miles south downstream from the Glen Canyon Dam near Page and is a put-in point for folks floating the Colorado River through the Grand Canyon. It's administered as part of the Glen Canyon Recreation Area by the National Parks Service.

At Lees Ferry you are down at river level. Sandstone cliffs rise on all sides although they're not quite as steep as in other spots in the canyon. For this reason a road could be built down to water level and this was for many years a ferry crossing. There are two boat launching areas, one for power boats headed upstream and the other for rafts headed downstream. The Paria River enters the Colorado here. The Pariah River and its canyon

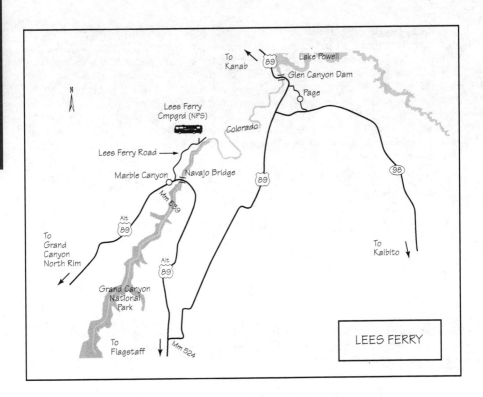

are a popular hiking route, but dangerous due to flash floods, particularly for the unprepared hiker. Ruins of some structures built by Mormon settlers remain in the area.

Upstream to the Glen Canyon Dam the Colorado River is relatively peaceful and can be traveled in a normal boat. This section is a popular trout fishing area because water released from the dam is cold, good for trout.

Below Lees Ferry is Marble Canyon. Although the Grand Canyon proper doesn't start until the Little Colorado enters the river some 61 miles downstream of Lees Ferry, the launching area here is the last place with road access to the river so float expeditions start here.

Marble Canyon itself is impressive. Navajo Bridge, which is located near the beginning of the entrance road down to the river, is 470 feet above the water and the canyon sides are vertical. California Condors are sometimes seen near the bridge.

Lees Ferry is part of the Glen Canyon Recreation Area and there is a visitor center near Navajo Bridge as well as a pay station on the entrance road. See the campground description below for driving instructions.

Lees Ferry Campground

LEES FERRY CAMPGROUND *(Open All Year)*

Information: (928) 608-6404, www.nps.gov/glca
Location: Lees Ferry, *N 36° 51' 34", W 111° 36' 22", 3,200 Ft*

54 Sites – This National Park Service campground (it's in the Glen Canyon Recreation Area) occupies a hillside overlooking the Colorado River. Sites are back-ins and pull-thrus to 75 feet. Each one has a sheltered picnic table and raised barbecue grill. The loop road is gravel and parking at the sites is gravel too. There's a dump site nearby. From the Navajo Bridge drive .3 mile west and turn right on the Lees Ferry Road. Follow the road for 4.3 miles to the campground entrance.

METEOR CRATER

Meteor Crater is an impact crater, not a volcano. It was formed when a 150 foot wide meteor, traveling at 40,000 miles per hour, hit the Earth. Pieces penetrated the surface to a distance of 3,000 feet. The resulting crater is over 500 feet deep and 4,000 feet in diameter.

The tourist facilities here are privately owned. There is a well-run campground near the entrance and a road climbing the outside of the crater to an observation area and museum. Take Exit 233 about 35 miles east of Flagstaff, the paved entrance road is about 5 miles long.

Meteor Crater Campground

METEOR CRATER RV PARK *(Open All Year)*

Reservations: (800) 478-4002
Information: (928) 289-4002
Location: Meteor Crater, *N 35° 06' 20", W 111° 01' 56", 5,300 Ft*

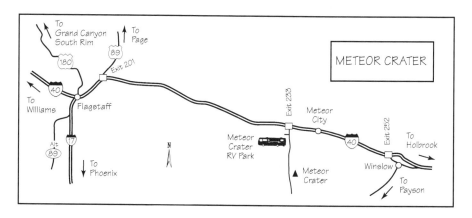

ARIZONA

71 Sites – This is a private campground, a good place to stay while visiting the crater but also a good place to overnight if you're traveling I-40. The sites here are all pull-thrus to about 65 feet. There's also a grass tent camping area. Out front there's a gas station, a Subway sandwich shop, and a store with groceries and souvenirs. The campground is just south of I-40 at Exit 233. That's 35 miles east of Flagstaff.

MOHAVE VALLEY: LAUGHLIN, BULLHEAD CITY, AND NEEDLES

This area covers the very southern point of the state of Nevada and the bordering areas of California and Arizona. Laughlin is in Nevada, Bullhead City in Arizona, and Needles in California. The area is relatively compact, about 25 miles from north to south.

This area is part of the Colorado River Valley. It's flat, and much of this area south of Laughlin and Bullhead City is part of the Fort Mohave Indian Reservation.

Laughlin (population about 8,000) became a gambling destination when Don Laughlin built the Riverside Resort Hotel and Casino in 1966. Today there are 9 large casinos in Laughlin. They occupy a strip along the river.

Across from Laughlin is **Bullhead City** (population about 35,000). Bullhead City started out in the 1940s as a place to house the workers building Davis Dam, just to the north. The town has grown continuously since that time as people settled here, attracted by the climate and recreational attractions.

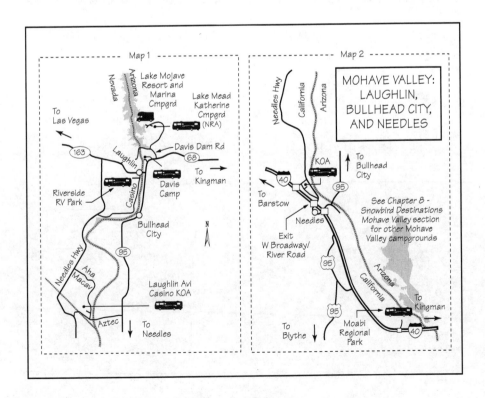

ARIZONA

Just north of the pair of cities is the southern border of **Lake Mead National Recreation Area**. This area encompasses two lakes, in the south is Lake Mohave and in the north Lake Mead. Katherine Landing, on Lake Mohave, offers the most southern access to the recreation area, it's just a few miles north of Bullhead City and has two camping areas, see below.

South of the pair of cities, but close enough so that it is part of the neighborhood, is **Needles, California** (population about 5,000). The town is near the point where I-40 crosses the Colorado River into California. It's a Route 66 town, of course, so the central district has Mother Road-era motels and restaurants. There are a number of campgrounds near Needles.

To the west of this area is the Mojave National Preserve. One of the more interesting sights there are the **Mitchell Caves**. These are limestone caves, the only ones in the California State Park system. You should get a reservation before going since the area is remote and the tours often fill, contact information is at the end of this chapter. You have to call to get a written form mailed to you, then you have to submit it. To get there you drive west from Needles for 41 miles. Take the exit marked Essex Road and proceed north for 15 miles to the cave area which is known as Providence Mountains State Recreation Area.

For more about the Mohave Valley, and particularly snowbird winter RV parks, see the *Snowbird Destinations* chapter of this book. Many campgrounds listed in that chapter also have spaces for travelers, our charts in that chapter give overnight rates for the ones that do.

Mohave Valley: Laughlin, Bullhead City, and Needles Campgrounds

RIVERSIDE RV PARK *(Open All Year)*
Res and Info: (800) 227-3849, (702) 298-3535, www.riversideresort.com
Location: Laughlin, *N 35° 09' 54", W 114° 34' 30", 500 Ft*

740 Sites – Laughlin's downtown RV park is going strong. It's so busy that reservations are always recommended. The campground is right on Casino Drive, which is Laughlin's "Strip", so it's easy to get to the casinos from the campground. All sites are for RVs and have full hookups. Most are back-ins but there are a few pull-thrus as long as 75 feet. The campground entrance is off S Casino Drive about a half mile south of SR-163, which is the road that crosses the river to Bullhead City. One reason this campground is so busy is that RVers are now banned from overnighting in casino parking lots by the county health department.

DAVIS CAMP *(Open All Year)*
Reservations: (877) 757-0915
Information: (928) 754-7250, www.mcparks.com
Location: 1 Mile N of Bullhead City, *N 35° 11' 06", W 114° 33' 57", 500 Ft*

171 Sites – Davis Camp is a Mohave County park with a fantastic location. It's on the Colorado River less than a mile south of Davis Dam which creates Lake Mojave Reservoir. Laughlin's casinos are less than two miles distant across the bridge in Nevada and

ARIZONA

Bullhead City is about 2 miles south. It's a huge park with camping in several locations. There are ramadas with tent/dry camping sites along the river and also full hookup pull-thrus to 50 feet. The park has 2 dump stations, a laundry, RV storage, museum, boat ramp, swimming beach, and wading area. The park occupies the east shoreline of the Colorado upstream from the bridge that joins Laughlin, Nevada and Bullhead City, Arizona. It's hard to miss.

LAKE MEAD – KATHERINE CAMPGROUND *(Open All Year)*

Information: (702) 293-8907, www.nps.gov/lame
Location: 7 Miles N of Bullhead City, *N 35° 13' 20", W 114° 33' 28", 700 Ft*

173 Sites – This is a Lake Mead National Recreation Area campground which means that it is run by the National Park Service. It's a large campground in a pretty setting occupying a slope above the marina at Katherine Landing on Lake Mohave. The sites are all paved back-ins to about 40 feet. They have picnic tables and fire pits. There's a restroom building with flush toilets and showers as well as a dump station. Below, at the marina and within walking distance, there's a general store, motel, swimming beach, and restaurant. From Bullhead City drive north on SR-68 for 3 miles. Turn left on the Davis Dam road and drive 1.1 mile to the sign for the turn to Lake Mead National Recreation Area. Turn right and drive another 2.5 miles to the Katherine Landing area. The campground is ahead and to the left after passing through the entrance kiosk.

LAKE MOHAVE RESORT AND MARINA CAMPGROUND *(Open All Year)*

Res and Info: (800) 752-9669, www.sevencrown.com
Location: 7 Miles N of Bullhead City, *N 35° 13' 27", W 114° 33' 42", 600 Ft*

28 Sites – In addition to the park service campground there's a small commercial RV park at Katherine Landing. Sites in this park have full hookups, they're all back-ins to about 35 feet, most sites are smaller. In fact, they won't accept reservations for RVs over 30 feet. There is a restroom building with flush toilets and showers as well as a laundry. From Bullhead City drive north on SR-68 for 3 miles. Turn left on the Davis Dam road and drive 1.1 mile to the sign for the turn to Lake Mead National Recreation Area. Turn right and drive another 2.5 miles to the Katherine Landing area. Check-in is at the motel, they'll tell you how to reach the well-hidden RV park.

LAUGHLIN/ AVI CASINO KOA *(Open All Year)*

Reservations: (800) 562-4142, www.koa.com
Information: (702) 535-5450, www.avicasino.com
Location: 7 Miles S of Bullhead City, *N 35° 01' 01", W 114° 38' 39", 400 Ft*

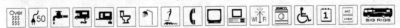

260 Sites – This campground has just become a KOA. Sites here are all full-hookup sites, both back-ins and pull-thrus to at least 45 feet. Parking is on gravel. The campground does not offer monthly rates in the winter. Guests at the RV park can use all of the facilities of the resort including the pools, beach, spas, and boat ramp on the river. In addition to this campground the casino has two large gravel lots for boondocking. This is allowed here since it is on Indian land. The casino is on the Colorado River about 15 miles south of Laughlin. From Bullhead City drive south on SR-95 for about 5 miles. Turn west on

Aztec Road and drive 2.7 miles to cross the river and reach the casino and campground.

MOABI REGIONAL PARK *(Open All Year)*
   Res and Info: (760) 326-3831, www.county-parks.com, moabi@ctaz.com
   Location: 10 Miles SE of Needles, *N 34° 43' 38", W 114° 30' 45", 400 Ft*

140 Sites – Many of the sites here are riverfront sites with water and electric hookups. The sites are in small groups. To reach these sites you drive through the park from the entrance gate about a mile to the riverfront. These river sites are priced at $36 with hookups and $22 without. They are popular in the summer and reservations are necessary then. The remaining sites are individual ones near the entrance of the park. They are back-ins and pull-thrus suitable for RVs to 45 feet, some are partial and some full hookup. There is also a large lot for dry camping in this area. The sites near the entrance have picnic tables and raised barbecue grills. Campfires are not allowed in summer. The park has a dump station which visitors may use for $10, also a swimming beach and a boat ramp. Access is from I-40. Take the first ramp west of the California/Arizona line, marked Park Moabi Road, and enter the campground to the north.

NEEDLES KOA *(Open All Year)*
   Reservations: (800) 562-3407, www.koa.com
   Information: (760) 326-4207
   Location: 2 Miles W of Needles, *N 34° 52' 07", W 114° 38' 35", 500 Ft*

98 Sites – Located just west of Needles this campground has the normal KOA amenities including a pool, a small store, tent sites, and cabins. RV sites will accept 45 footers. To easily reach the campground from I-40 take the W Broadway/River Road exit just west of Needles. Drive north for .7 miles and take the left on National Old Trails Road. The campground is on the right in another .8 mile.

MORMON LAKE AREA

Just southeast of Flagstaff is a plateau area in the Coconino National Forest with many lakes and campgrounds. It's a convenient destination for those ready for some wilderness relaxation near the city. The high season here is summer and since it's so close to Flagstaff the campgrounds fill fast on summer weekends. Spring and fall are a great time to visit if you are in the area.

Mormon Lake, the lake that the area is named for, is the largest natural lake in Arizona. However, it's extremely shallow, no more than 10 feet deep and at times it even dries up. Several campgrounds are off the Mormon Lake Loop Road that circles it at a distance, but they're not waterfront campgrounds. If you want to boat on this lake you'll have to carry your boat to the water.

For boating the only lake that allows engines over 8 hp is **Upper Mary Lake**. This 5 mile-long lake also has a nearby campground but it's across the highway, see Lakeview Campground below.

ARIZONA

Mormon Lake Area Campgrounds

CANYON VISTA CAMPGROUND *(Open May 1 to Oct 15 - Varies)*

Information: (928) 526-0866
Location: 6 Miles SE of Flagstaff, *N 35° 07' 21", W 111° 35' 57", 6,900 Ft*

11 Sites – This Coconino National Forest campground is set up for larger RVs. The access roads are wide and there are long back-in sites to 45 feet. Potable water is available in limited quantities. Trails from the campground access Walnut Canyon and the Arizona Trail. From the intersection of Lake Mary Road and Alternate SR-89 south of Flagstaff drive 5.5 miles southeast on Lake Mary Road. The campground is on the left.

ASHURST LAKE CAMPGROUND *(Open May 1 to Oct 15 - Varies)*

Information: (928) 526-0866
Location: 21 Miles SE of Flagstaff, *N 35° 01' 12", W 111° 24' 29", 7,100 Ft*

25 Sites – Ashurst is a Coconino National Forest campground, one of two on the shore of little Ashurst Lake. This campground is set off gravel loops in mostly junipers and a few pines. There are 25 sites, 6 of which are pull-thrus. Both the pull-thrus and back-ins are fairly short although a few reach 35 feet. The sites all have picnic tables and rock fire

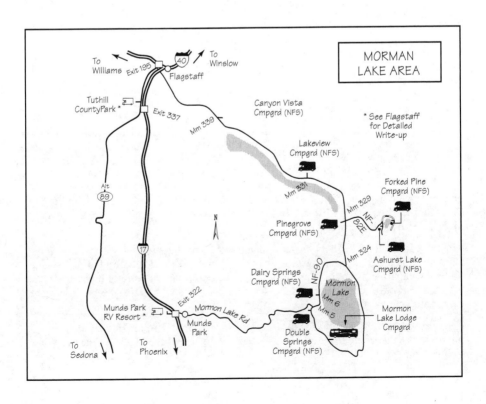

ARIZONA

rings, a few are along the water. Limited potable water is available. The bathrooms are not available from October through May but there is one that is kept open near the boat launch so although the campground is closed people use it anyway. The campground is popular for fishing, it is stocked with trout, bass, and channel cats. Because it can be windy here, it is also popular with wind surfers. Bird-watching can be good here for waterfowl, hawks, and song birds. From the intersection of Lake Mary Road and Alternate SR-89 south of Flagstaff drive 17 miles southeast on Lake Mary Road. Turn left on NF-82E, the Ashurst Lake access road, and drive 4 miles to the lake. The campground is to the right.

FORKED PINE CAMPGROUND *(Open May 1 to Oct 15 - Varies)*
Information: (928) 526-0866
Location: 22 Miles SE of Flagstaff, *N 35° 01' 20", W 111° 23' 52", 7,100 Ft*

25 Sites – Forked Pine is on the opposite side of Ashurst Lake from Ashurst Lake Campground. It's very similar but you need to drive a 1-mile gravel road to reach it. It too gets used all winter long with no restrooms, if you need them you must use the ones near the boat launch on the far side of the lake. Limited potable water is available. Sites are shorter than those at Ashurst and are good for RVs to about 25 feet. To reach the campground follow the instructions above for reaching Ashurst Lake. When you reach the lake turn left and follow the gravel road for 1 mile around the lake to the campground. Note that camping is only allowed in the two established campgrounds at Ashurst Lake.

LAKEVIEW CAMPGROUND *(Open May 1 to Oct 15 - Varies)*
Information: (928) 526-0866
Location: 13 Miles SE of Flagstaff, *N 35° 03' 58", W 111° 29' 42", 6,800 Ft*

30 Sites – This is a recently renovated Coconino National Forest campground located across the highway from Upper Mary Lake. Sites are very good for tent campers and smaller RVs to about 28 feet. They have picnic tables, fire rings and raised barbecues. Both campground access roads and sites are gravel. Limited potable water is available. There's a trail from the campground to the Lake Mary Narrows Picnic Area on the lakeshore. From the intersection of Lake Mary Road and Alternate SR-89 south of Flagstaff drive 13 miles southeast on Lake Mary Road.

PINEGROVE CAMPGROUND *(Open April 21 to Oct 15 - Varies)*
Reservations: (877) 444-6777, www.recreation.gov
Information: (928) 526-0866
Location: 17 Miles SE of Flagstaff, *N 35° 01' 38", W 111° 27' 17", 6,800 Ft*

46 Sites – Pinegrove Campground is a newly constructed Coconino National Forest campground. It occupies a pine grove away from any of the lakes. The Forest Service advises that sites are good for RVs to 33 feet. They have picnic tables, fire pits, and raised barbecue grills. The campground has flush toilets, showers, and a dump station. From the intersection of Lake Mary Road and Alternate SR-89 south of Flagstaff drive 17 miles southeast on Lake Mary Road.

ARIZONA

DAIRY SPRINGS CAMPGROUND *(Open May 1 to Oct 15 - Varies)*
Reservations: (877) 444-6777, www.recreation.gov
Information: (928) 526-0866
Location: 24 Miles SE of Flagstaff, *N 34° 57' 21", W 111° 29' 03", 7,100 Ft*

30 Sites – Sites in this Coconino National Forest campground are set in a forest of pines and firs. It's an older campground and the sites aren't well defined. Although some sites are quite large access can be difficult and the Forest Service recommends that only RVs to 35 feet use the campground. Sites have picnic tables and fire pits, there are water faucets scattered throughout. From the intersection of Lake Mary Road and Alternate SR-89 south of Flagstaff drive 20 miles southeast on Lake Mary Road. Turn right onto NF-90 (Mormon Lake Road) and drive 3.7 miles to the campground.

DOUBLE SPRINGS CAMPGROUND *(Open May 1 to Oct 15 - Varies)*
Information: (928) 526-0866
Location: 25 Miles SE of Flagstaff, *N 34° 56' 33", W 111° 29' 28", 7,100 Ft*

13 Sites – Double Springs is much like its sister campground, Dairy Springs, which is just down the road. Some sites here are large but access is difficult for large RVs, the Forest Service recommends a 35 foot limit. From the intersection of Lake Mary Road and Alternate SR-89 south of Flagstaff drive 20 miles southeast on Lake Mary Road. Turn right onto NF-90 (Mormon Lake Road) and drive 5 miles to the campground.

MORMON LAKE LODGE CAMPGROUND *(Open All Year)*
Res and Info: (928) 354-2227, www.MormonLakeLodge.com
Location: 28 Miles SE of Flagstaff, *N 34° 54' 44", W 111° 28' 04", 6,900 Ft*

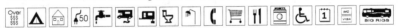

74 Sites – This resort has 74 full-hookup pull-thrus to 60 feet in length with lots of maneuvering room. It also has a grassy tent-camping area. The lodge has rooms, cabins, a restaurant (steakhouse), a general store, gas station, museum, and a post office. Other amenities include basketball, volleyball, horseshoes, a trout fishing pond for kids, a petting zoo, a dinner theatre, a western theme town, a buffalo habitat, horse rides, and a meeting room. The dump station is open to the public for a fee. From the intersection of Lake Mary Road and Alternate SR-89 south of Flagstaff drive 20 miles southeast on Lake Mary Road. Turn right onto NF-90 (Mormon Lake Road) and drive 8 miles to the campground.

NAVAJO NATIONAL MONUMENT

Navajo National Monument is run jointly by the National Park Service and the Navajo nation. The attraction here is three Ancestral Puebloan ruins: Betatakin, Keet Seel and Inscription House. These are canyon ruins protected by overhanging cliffs.

None of the ruins is easily accessible. There are easy 1 mile round trip hiking trails from the visitor center to overlooks where you can view the Betatakin ruins. For a closer look you take a ranger-led hike of five miles round trip. The trail starts at 7,300 feet, it is rough and drops 700 feet, then you must return. Four hours are scheduled for the hike so you

ARIZONA

RANGER LED HIKE TO THE BETATAKIN RUINS IN NAVAJO MONUMENT

can see that it is important to be in pretty decent shape if you want to get a close look at the ruins.

Keet Seel, best of the ruins at the monument and considered one of the most impressive ruins in the southwest is even tougher to visit. It's a 16 mile round trip hike so you must camp overnight. Only 20 permits are issued for visits each day so if you want to make this tour you must plan ahead and make a reservation months in advance. Once you reach the ruins an on-site ranger leads tours.

The final ruin, Inscription House, is closed to the public and cannot be visited.

Access to the monument is by good paved road from US-160 52 miles northeast of Tuba City and 22 miles southwest of Kayenta. Then there's a nine-mile paved road in to the monument. The monument is not particularly big rig friendly. At the visitor center drive around the circle and turn back toward the entrance, you'll see the parallel parking area for big RVs. So far so good, but the campgrounds will not accommodate big RVs, see the campground descriptions below. Alternate places to stay if you can't fit in the campground are Tuba City and Monument Valley.

Navajo National Monument Campgrounds

SUNSET VIEW CAMPGROUND *(Open All Year)*
Information: (928) 672-2700, www.nps.gov/nava
Location: Navajo National Monument, *N 36° 40' 33", W 110° 32' 33", 7,200 Ft*

ARIZONA

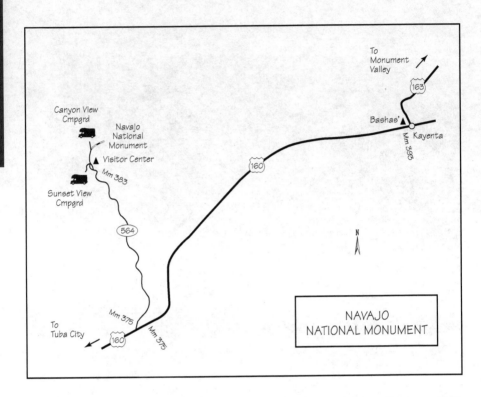

NAVAJO
NATIONAL MONUMENT

31 Sites – This is a beautiful little campground with paved drives and sites. All sites are back-ins, some will take RVs to 28 feet. Restrooms have flush toilets, water is available at outdoor sinks, and there is an indoor grey water disposal unit. Dogs are allowed in the campground but not outside it, a telephone is at the visitor center. The campground entrance is just past the visitor center parking to the left, it's just a short walk between the campground and the visitor center.

CANYON VIEW CAMPGROUND *(Open April 15 to Sept 30)*
   Information: (928) 672-2700, www.nps.gov/nava
   Location: Navaho National Monument, *N 36° 41' 03", W 110° 32' 28", 7300 Ft*

14 Sites – The second park campground is slightly more rustic than Sunset View Campground, it's also a little farther from the visitor center. The location is very nice but roads and sites are gravel and portable toilets are the only restroom facilities. For this reason the campground is only open during non-freezing weather. Again, the telephone is at the visitor center. RV size is limited to 28 feet. The campground entrance is to the right just past the visitor center parking lot.

NOGALES

Nogales (population about 21,000) is the border town south of Tucson. The crossing west of town is the best on the border for RVers heading onto Mexico's mainland. From

Nogales a four lane highway leads south to Mazatlán, three days away. See the *Mexico* chapter in this book for some great destinations in Mexico: Kino Bay and Guaymas/San Carlos.

On the Mexico side of the border is the Mexican town, also called Nogales. It's bigger than the US town with an approximate population of 200,000. Walking across the border downtown is easy here and there are lots of restaurants, shops, pharmacies, dentists and doctors offices.

The artist colony town of **Tubac** is located 20 miles north of Nogales along I-19, accessible from Exit 34. There are shops, galleries, and restaurants. The **Tubac Presidio State Historic Park** is on the south side of town. It protects the site of the Spanish fort that protected this area and has a museum. The **Juan Batista de Anza National Historic Trail** leads 4.5 miles south to **Tumacacori National Historic Park** which has a museum and the ruins of an early mission church. It is also accessible from Exit 29 of I-40.

Nogales Campgrounds

MI CASA RV PARK *(Open All Year)*
Information: (520) 281-1150
Location: Nogales, *N 31° 23' 07", W 110° 57' 05", 3,700 Ft*

60 Sites – The Mi Casa is an older campground with many permanent mobile homes

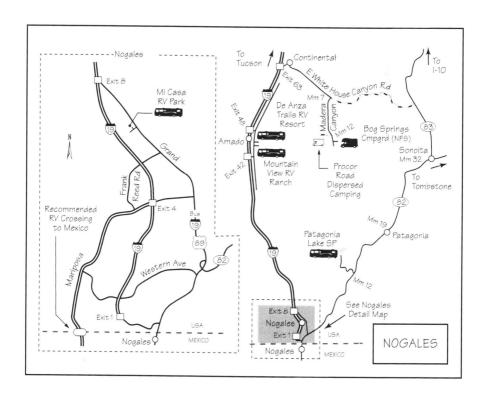

and RVs. It is, however, the only RV park actually in Nogales and does have a row of pull-thru sites to about 50 feet. It can be a good place to stay while preparing to cross the border. Restrooms are old but useable. The campground is located behind a Circle K some .5 miles south of the northern exit for Nogales, Exit 8 off I-19. This exit can only be accessed southbound, northbound follow US-89 from central Nogales to reach the campground.

🚐 DE ANZA TRAILS RV RESORT *(Open All Year)*

Reservations: (866) 332-6022, deanzarv@earthlink.net
Information: (520) 398-8628
Location: 25 Miles N of Nogales, *N 31° 42' 18", W 111° 03' 46", 3,200 Ft*

82 Sites – De Anza is a large modern campground near the freeway. The sites are all back-ins to 45 feet. There is a huge clubhouse which houses a lounge, exercise room, meeting room, ballroom, dining room, game tables, and laundry. Wi-Fi is available in the park for a fee and a modem connection is available for internet. The swimming pool is a covered chlorine-free salt water pool and there is a spa. From I-19 take Exit 48 and travel south on the east side of the freeway for 1.5 miles to the campground.

🚐 MOUNTAIN VIEW RV RANCH *(Open All Year)*

Res and Info: (520) 398-9401
Location: 25 Miles N of Nogales, *N 31° 42' 12", W 111° 03' 50", 3,100 Ft*

72 Sites – This is an older campground but has decent rates. It appears to have been a KOA at one time. RV sites are back-ins and pull-thrus to 45 feet and tents are OK. There's a seasonal swimming pool. It's located very near the De Anza, described above. From I-19 take Exit 48 and travel south on the east side of the freeway for 1.6 miles to the campground.

🚐 BOG SPRINGS CAMPGROUND *(Open All Year)*

Information: (520) 281-2296
Location: 49 Miles NE of Nogales, *N 31° 43' 37", W 110° 52' 33", 5,200 Ft*

13 Sites – Bog Springs Campground is in Madera Canyon, a popular bird-watching venue on the north side of the Santa Rita Mountains. It's a Coronado National Forest Campground and is fairly remote but really still pretty easy to get to. The campground is situated in a forest of juniper and sycamores. A few sites would take carefully driven 35 foot RVs, most are much smaller. To reach the campground start on I-19 between Tucson and Nogales. Take Exit 63 and drive east on E Continental Road for 1.3 mile. Turn right on E White House Canyon Road and follow it for 7.1 miles. Here the main road will turn right and become Madera Canyon Road. Follow it up into the mountains for 5.3 miles, passing an entrance station, and you'll see the campground entrance on the left. The rough entrance road will lead you .5 miles back to the campground.

PATAGONIA LAKE STATE PARK *(Open All Year)*
Information: (520) 287-6965, www.azstateparks.com
Location: 11 Miles NE of Nogales, *N 31° 29' 35", W 100° 51' 16", 3,800 Ft*

106 Sites – Camping sites are located in 2 areas. To the right as you enter the park are 34 sites with electric and water hookups. To the left are 72 developed sites with no hookups. There are also 12 boat-accessible sites. The sites all have picnic tables and fire pits, they are either shaded by trees or have ramadas over the picnic tables. Sites are separated by trees and vegetation although they're near each other. The longest sites are about 45 feet, most are shorter, only a few are pull-thrus. There is a dump station and water fill station. The lake has a swimming beach and fishing is possible for crappie, bass, bluegill and catfish. The bathrooms have flush toilets and showers. A marina store sells fishing license and tackle, bait, ice, supplies and rents boats. Two boat ramps are available. There are 740 acres with hiking trails and 300 species of birds. From Nogales drive 11 miles northeast on SR-82, The campground entrance is on the left.

PAGE AND GLEN CANYON NATIONAL RECREATION AREA

Lake Powell, behind Glen Canyon Dam, has the second largest volume of water in any reservoir in the US. It has a shoreline of almost 2,000 miles and extends well into the valleys of the Colorado and San Juan Rivers. This is an extremely popular lake for water sports and houseboat travel.

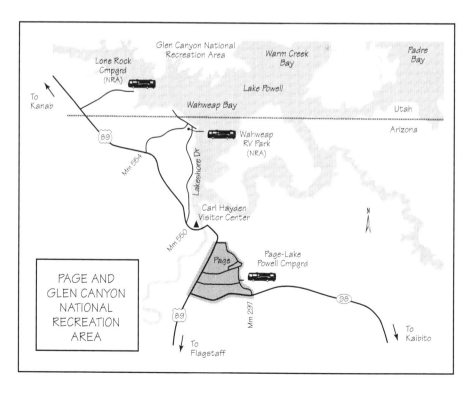

ARIZONA

Page (population about 10,000) only dates from 1957. It was the town constructed to house the workers who built Glen Canyon Dam. Nonetheless, it's the largest town in this part of the state and the place to get supplies. Page is just a mile or so southeast of the Glen Canyon Dam. At the **Powell Museum** you'll find information about the lake's namesake, John Wesley Powell, and the area. You can also book tours of Rainbow Bridge National Monument and Antelope Canyon.

The **Carl Hayden Visitor Center** is right at the dam. It has information about the Recreation Area and the dam. Tours of the dam are also offered.

The boat tour to **Rainbow Bridge National Monument** is extremely popular. The bridge is 290 feet high and 275 feet wide. It's near the lake's south shore. Tours leave from Wahweap Marina, there is a short hike to reach the bridge. This is the largest natural bridge in the world but only the third largest natural arch. Water only penetrates to the arch when the Lake Powell is near full pool.

Photographers love **Antelope Canyon**. It's a deep sandstone slot canyon with wonderful lighting and patterns. The best time to visit is the middle of the day since otherwise sunlight does not penetrate to the canyon floor. There are actually two Antelope Canyon areas, upper and lower. There is also another canyon called Rattlesnake that is reserved for photographers. Fees for taking a tour from Page aren't a lot higher than visiting with your own vehicle.

Off US-89 just south of Page there's a spectacular overlook of the **Horseshoe Bend** of the Colorado River below the dam.

Note that the Lees Ferry area, described in a separate entry in this chapter, is also inside Glen Canyon National Recreation Area.

Page and Glen Canyon National Recreation Area Campgrounds

🚐 **PAGE-LAKE POWELL CAMPGROUND** *(Open All Year)*

Res and Info: (928) 645-3374, www.pagecampground.com
Location: Page, *N 36° 54' 04", W 111° 27' 11", 4,200 Ft*

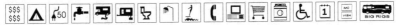

98 Sites – This campground is located on the outskirts of Page. It has tent, partial, and full-hookup sites. Some are pull-thrus to 55 feet. There's also an indoor swimming pool and spa. One way to reach the campground would be to follow SR-98 around the south side of town from US-89. Two and six-tenths mile from where you left US-89 turn left and the campground will be on your right in .6 mile.

🚐 **WAHWEAP RV PARK** *(Open All Year)*

Reservations: (800) 528-6154, (602) 278-8888
Information: (928) 645-1059, visitlakepowell.com
Location: 7 Miles N of Page, *N 36° 59' 54", W 111° 29' 51", 3,900 Ft*

202 Sites – Wahweap is a newer campground in the Lake Powell Recreation Area with excellent facilities. There are both large sites without hookups and large sites with them, some to 60 feet. An office, store, showers, and laundry are located near the entrance and office. RV park guests can also use other nearby facilities including a pool, spa, and

restaurant. Boat tours are available. The access road, Lakeshore Drive, to the Wahweap area leaves US-89 about .7 mile northwest of the west end of the dam crossing. Follow Lakeshore Drive about 4.7 miles to the campground entrance.

LONE ROCK CAMPGROUND *(Open All Year)*
    Information: (928) 608-6404, www.nps.gov/glca
    Location: 9 Miles NW of Page, *N 37° 00' 59", W 111° 32' 43", 3,600 Ft*

Scattered Boondocking – This is an area of dispersed camping along the lakeshore and in the sand behind. The road to the lake is paved to a parking lot which has a restroom with flush toilets. This is about a half mile above the lake shore, but this varies with the level of the lake of course. The surface in many places here is solid and OK for heavy RVs but exercise caution. There are about 10 portable toilets situated near the lake and in the sandy area behind the lake. This is a popular destination for off-road vehicle fans. There is a dump station with water on the main road to the beach. Park hosts sites are located near the dump station. The access road to the camping area leaves US-89 some 7.7 miles northwest the west end of the dam crossing.

PAYSON AND THE MOGOLLON RIM

Payson (population about 15,000) is considered to be the gateway to the Mogollon Rim Country. About 20 miles east of town SR-260 climbs up onto the Mogollon Rim. The whole area, both below and above the rim, is national forest land. Small back roads and campgrounds are everywhere.

Payson itself has a good museum, the **Rim Country Museum**. It's an introduction to the area and has a lot of information about Zane Grey, the prolific western author. He had a cabin here. The museum is located in Green Valley Park which is west on Main St from SR-87.

North of Payson about 11 miles on SR-87 is **Tonto Natural Bridge State Park**. The bridge is a travertine formation and it's huge, 180 feet high. The entrance road is steep and large vehicles are not recommended.

The **Mogollon Rim** forms the edge of the Colorado Plateau. It runs for 400 miles through Arizona and New Mexico with one of the most impressive sections northeast of Payson. Here the difference between the bottom and top of the rim is about 2,000 feet. Some of the campgrounds listed below are quite near the edge of the rim.

Payson and the Mogollon Rim Campgrounds

HOUSTON MESA CAMPGROUND *(Open Feb 1 to Nov 30)*
    Reservations: (877) 444-6777, www.recreation.gov
    Information: (928) 474-7900 or (928) 468-7135
    Location: Payson, *N 34° 16' 16", W 111° 19' 12", 5,200 Ft*

105 Sites – Houston Mesa is a convenient and modern Tonto National Forest campground just outside Payson. There are two campgrounds here, a horse camp section has 24 sites and can only be used by campers with horses. The remainder of the campground has 81 sites off three loops. There are separate loops for tent campers and RVers, some

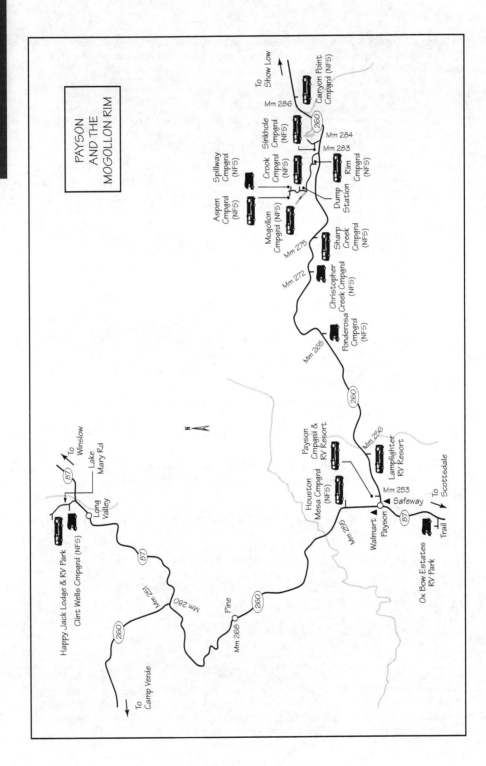

PAYSON AND THE MOGOLLON RIM

sites will take RVs to 45 feet. The campground has paved roads and parking, flush toilets, showers, and a dump station. The campground is on the east side of SR-260 at the northern entrance to Payson.

PAYSON CAMPGROUND AND RV RESORT *(Open All Year)*
   Res and Info: (928) 472-2267, paysoncamp@aol.com
   Location: Payson, *N 34° 14' 33", W 111° 18' 35", 5,000 Ft*

95 Sites – The Payson is an older park which is well maintained. It appears to be a former KOA and has a variety of sites including tents, partial hookup, and a number of full hookups sites, both back-in and pull-thru, to 40 feet. The campground has a seasonal swimming pool and Wi-Fi is available near the office. The Payson is on the north side of SR-260 some .8 miles east of the intersection of US-87 and SR-260 in Payson.

LAMPLIGHTER RV RESORT *(Open All Year)*
   Res and Info: (928) 474-5048, www.lamplighterrvresort.com
   Location: Payson, *N 34° 15' 14", W 111° 15' 39", 4,600 Ft*

265 Sites – Although the Lamplighter is large it really has just a few sites for travelers. Almost all the sites are filled with permanently-located mobile homes and RVs. The available sites are back-ins and are 55 feet long. Reservations are a good idea. The resort is located at the eastern edge of Payson on the south side of SR-260.

OX BOW ESTATES RV PARK *(Open All Year)*
   Reservations: (800) 520-5239
   Information: (928) 474-2042
   Location: 3 Miles S of Payson, *N 34° 11' 00", W 111° 20' 51", 4,700 Ft*

51 Sites – Ox Bow Estates is located near the south side of Payson. The sites are almost filled with long-term campers but there are a few that will take RVs to 38 feet or so. There are also a few tent sites. The dump station can be used by folks from outside the park for a fee. A small store has a few grocery items and bottled propane. From the intersection of US-87 and SR-260 in Payson drive south for 4.2 miles. Turn west on E Trail and follow it for .8 mile to the campground.

PONDEROSA CAMPGROUND *(Open April 1 to Oct 31 - Varies)*
   Reservations: (877) 444-6777, www.recreation.gov
   Information: (928) 474-7900
   Location: 10 Miles NE of Payson, *N 34° 17' 58", W 111° 06' 55", 4,600 Ft*

60 Sites – This Tonto National Forest campground has both short and long sites, back-ins and pull-thrus, to 45 feet. However, maneuvering room is limited and the campground is best for RVs to about 35 feet. Roads and sites are paved. There is a dump station with water. From Payson drive northeast on SR-260 for 10 miles, the campground is on the right.

ARIZONA

CHRISTOPHER CREEK CAMPGROUND *(Open April 1 to Oct 30 - Varies)*
Information: (928) 474-7900
Location: 17 Miles NE of Payson, *N 34° 18' 46", W 111° 02' 20", 5,600 Ft*

42 Sites – This Tonto National Forest campground occupies the valley of Christopher Creek, a cold water trout stream that issues from the Mogollon Rim. There's a grade down to the campground which occupies both sides of the creek, the crossing sometimes has water flowing across it. In addition to tent sites there are smaller RV sites and a few parallel-parking style sites that would accept RVs to about 30 feet, the largest we would want to see try to negotiate the access roads here. Restrooms are vault toilets. From Payson drive northeast on SR-260 for 17 miles to the campground entrance.

SHARP CREEK CAMPGROUND *(Open April 15 to Oct 31 - Varies)*
Reservations: (877) 444-6777, www.recreation.gov
Information: (928) 474-7900
Location: 20 Miles NE of Payson, *N 34° 18' 22", W 110° 59' 44", 6,000 Ft*

28 Sites – Sharp Creek is a Tonto National Forest campground. Sites here are off a long access road and two loops. Some sites can take RVs to 45 feet. From Payson drive northeast on SR-260 for 20 miles, the campground is on the right.

SINK HOLE CAMPGROUND *(Open May 15 to Oct 31 - Varies)*
Information: (928) 535-4481
Location: 27 Miles NE of Payson, *N 34° 18' 17", W 110° 53' 06", 7,500 Ft*

24 Sites – Sink Hole is a newly renovated Sitgreaves National Forest campground in great condition. Sites are off two loops, they extend to 55 feet. There is a designated wheelchair site too. Each site has a table and fire pit and there are vault toilets. Willow Springs trailhead is nearby and Willow Springs Lake is another 1.2 miles down the same entrance road, there is a boat ramp at the lake. To reach the campground from Payson drive northeast on SR-260 for 27 miles and turn left on the road for Willow Springs. The campground is on the left some .3 miles down the road.

RIM CAMPGROUND *(Open May 15 to Sept 15 - Varies)*
Information: (928) 535-4481
Location: 28 Miles NE of Payson, *N 34° 18' 22", W 110° 54' 25", 7,600 Ft*

33 Sites – Rim is a Sitgreaves National Forest campground in the Rim Lakes Recreation Area. Sites are parallel-parking type off two circular roads, each has a picnic table and fire pit off to the side. The unique configuration of the campground means that any size RV can use it. To reach the campground drive northeast from Payson on SR-260 for 26 miles. Turn left onto NF-300, signed for Woods Canyon Lake and Rim Lakes Recreation Area, and follow it for .8 miles. The entrance road is on the left.

MOGOLLON CAMPGROUND *(Open May 15 to Sept 15 - Varies)*
Information: (928) 535-4481
Location: 30 Miles NE of Payson, *N 34° 19' 19", W 110° 57' 19", 7,600 Ft*

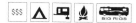

32 Sites – Mogollon is a Sitgreaves National Forest campground in the Rim Lakes Recreation Area. It's configured like the Rim campground, described above. To reach the campground drive northeast from Payson on SR-260 for 26 miles. Turn left onto NF-300, signed for Woods Canyon Lake and Rim Lakes Recreation Area, and follow it for 3.2 miles. Here the road becomes gravel. Continue for another .7 miles to the campground, it's on the left.

CANYON POINT CAMPGROUND *(Open May 15 to Oct 15 - Varies)*
Reservations: (877) 444-6777, www.recreation.gov
Information: (928) 535-4481
Location: 31 Miles NE of Payson, *N 34° 19' 33", W 110° 49' 42", 7,700 Ft*

109 Sites – Canyon Point is a modern Sitgreaves National Forest campground. Interior roads are paved and so are the parking pads. There are back-in and pull-thru sites to 70 feet and even 35 sites with electrical hookups. Restrooms have flush toilets and hot showers and there is a dump station with water. From Payson drive northeast on SR-260 for 31 miles to the campground entrance.

CROOK CAMPGROUND *(Open May 15 to Oct 30 - Varies)*
Information: (928) 535-4481
Location: 30 Miles NE of Payson, *N 34° 19' 04", W 110° 56' 33", 7,500 Ft*

26 Sites – Crook Campground is a Sitgreaves National Forest campground. It's modern, a beautifully laid out campground. Sites are off two circles. In the center of each is a large ramada providing shelter for various activities. Sites radiate outward. They are paved back-ins, some extend to 55 feet. They have picnic tables and fire pits. Some are specially designed wheelchair accessible spaces with raised grills. To reach the campground drive northeast from Payson on SR-260 for 26 miles. Turn left onto NF-300, signed for Woods Canyon Lake and Rim Lakes Recreation Area, and follow it for 3.2 miles. Turn right, straight would be a gravel road, you'll pass a dump station in .5 mile and reach the campground entrance road on the right at .2 miles after the turn.

ASPEN CAMPGROUND *(Open May 1 to Oct 31 - Varies)*
Reservations: (877) 444-6777, www.recreation.gov
Information: (928) 535-4481
Location: 31 Miles NE of Payson, *N 34° 19' 51", W 110° 56' 34", 7,600 Ft*

130 Sites – Aspen is the largest of the Sitgreaves National Forest campgrounds grouped near Woods Canyon Lake, the area is called the Rim Lakes Area. The sites here are off four paved loops, there is a manned entrance booth in the summer. The campground has not been upgraded like some in the area. Paving on the roads and on parking pads has deteriorated and in general the sites are narrow and difficult to access for larger RVs

although some reach 40 feet in length. Many sites would not allow the use of slide-outs. On the access road there is a dump and water station which serves the campgrounds in the area. There are three nearby lakes. To reach the campground drive northeast from Payson on SR-260 for 26 miles. Turn left onto NF-300, signed for Woods Canyon Lake and Rim Lakes Recreation Area, and follow it for 3.2 miles. Turn right, straight would be a gravel road, you'll pass a dump station in .5 mile and reach the campground entrance road on the left at 1.1 miles after the turn.

SPILLWAY CAMPGROUND *(Open May 15 to Sept 15 - Varies)*
  Reservations: (877) 444-6777, www.recreation.gov
  Information: (928) 535-4481
  Location: 31 Miles NE of Payson, *N 34° 19' 51", W 110° 56' 32", 7,500 Ft*

26 Sites – Spillway is another Sitgreaves National Forest campground in the Rim Lakes Recreation Area. It sits next to the outlet spillway for Woods Canyon Lake, hence the name. This is an older campground and has not been upgraded like some in the area. It's great for tent campers and adequate for RVs only to about 35 feet. There's a small store nearby. To reach the campground drive northeast from Payson on SR-260 for 26 miles. Turn left onto NF-300, signed for Woods Canyon Lake and Rim Lakes Recreation Area, and follow it for 3.2 miles. Turn right, straight would be a gravel road, you'll pass a dump station in .5 mile and reach the campground entrance road on the right at 1.1 miles after the turn.

CLINTS WELL CAMPGROUND *(Open All Year)*
  Information: (928) 477-2255
  Location: 36 Miles N of Payson, *N 34° 33' 18", W 111° 18' 56", 6,800 Ft*

7 Sites – This little Coconino National Forest campground is suitable for tent campers and those in vans and pickup campers. Set in pines it's pretty basic with picnic tables, fire rings, and vault toilets. No water is available. From Payson follow SR-260 north for 24 miles through Pine and Strawberry to its intersection with SR-87. Then follow SR-87 north another 12 miles to Lake Mary Road. Turn left and you'll see the campground on the left in another .4 mile.

HAPPY JACK LODGE AND RV PARK *(Open All Year)*
  Reservations: (800) 430-0385, HpyJack@The River.com
  Information: (928) 477-2805, www.happyjacklodge.com
  Location: 37 Miles N of Payson, *N 34° 34' 24", W 111° 19' 45", 6,900 Ft*

75 Sites – The Happy Jack Lodge has tent and RV sites, some are pull-thrus to 75 feet. A huge main building houses a good size grocery store, and a restaurant which is only open during the busy season, summer. There is a dump station which can be used by those camping elsewhere for a fee and water is also sold. From Payson follow SR-260 north for 24 miles through Pine and Strawberry to its intersection with SR-87. Then follow SR-87 north another 12 miles to Lake Mary Road. Turn left and you'll see the campground on the left in another 2 miles.

PHOENIX

Phoenix (metro area population about 3,900,000) covers a huge area. From the foot of the White Tank Mountains in the west to the far east end of Apache Junction is over 50 miles. It can take hours to traverse the city, despite the fact that roads have been built in recent years at a pretty good clip. You'll find that in addition to the freeways there is a grid of boulevards a mile apart, going both east/west and north/south.

Another name for the Phoenix area is "Valley of the Sun", and that describes the area pretty well. It's very hot in the summer and extremely comfortable in the winters. The sun shines almost every day. There are few clouds and little rain except during the "monsoon season", in late July, August, and early September.

Phoenix has lots of museums and attractions, so many that we'll just list a few here. The top museum is the **Heard Museum**. The museum celebrates the Native American culture of the Southwest and is not to be missed. The Heard is located in Phoenix's central area, and once you're there you'll find that many other attractions are pretty close by. These include the old **Arizona State Capitol**, now a museum, the **Phoenix Art Museum**, and a host of smaller museums.

One great feature of the Phoenix area is the system of **Maricopa Country regional parks**. They now pretty much surround the city and many of them have beautiful campgrounds. All of the ones with campgrounds are described below.

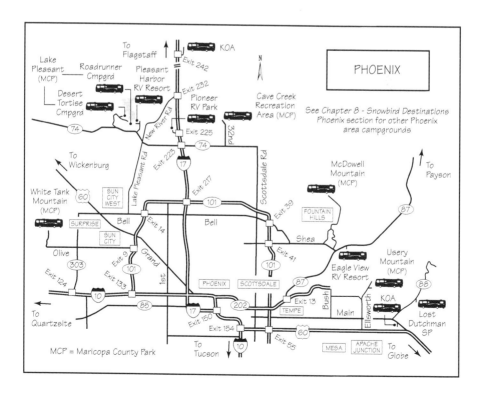

For more about Phoenix, and particularly Snowbird winter RV parks, see the *Snowbird Destinations* chapter of this book. Many of the campgrounds listed in that chapter also have spaces for travelers, our charts in that chapter give overnight rates for the ones that do.

Phoenix Campgrounds

KOA BLACK CANYON CITY *(Open All Year)*

Reservations: (800) 562-5314, www.koa.com
Information: (623) 374-5318
Location: 27 Miles N of Phoenix, *N 34° 03' 38", W 112° 08' 31", 2,100 Feet*

52 Sites – This KOA has tent sites as well as back-in and pull-thru sites as long as 40 feet. There's a pool and a spa. The KOA is off I-17 at Exit 242 on the east side of the highway.

PIONEER RV PARK *(Open All Year)*

Information: (623) 465-7465, 8006585895, www.arizonaresorts.com
Location: 10 Miles N of Phoenix, *N 33° 49' 21", W 112° 08' 53", 1,700 Ft*

285 Sites – This age 55+ park north of Phoenix is handy if you're visiting the city in an RV, the small open-air historical park next door has a number of interesting buildings that have been moved from other places and reconstructed here. RV sites are back-ins and pull-thrus to 50 feet. Roads are paved and sites are gravel. There's a pool, a spa, and a laundry. From I-17 north of Phoenix take Exit 225, the park is on the west side of the highway.

LAKE PLEASANT REGIONAL PARK *(Open All Year)*

Information: (928) 501-1710, www.maricopa.gov/parks
Location: 24 Miles NW of Phoenix, *N 33° 51' 51", W 112° 19' 03", 1,800 Ft*

150 Sites – There are 2 areas in this Maricopa Country regional park campground. The Desert Tortoise area has sites 101-176. The sites are back-in sites as long as 45 feet in length. There are 3 loops. The middle loop has electric and water hookups and the other 2 loops are dry camping. There are showers in the 2nd and 3rd loops. The roads are paved and parking is on gravel. The Roadrunner area has sites 1-75. The sites are located on 4 loops and all have electric and water hookups. In this area parking is paved. There are showers in 3 of the 4 loops. All of the sites in both campgrounds have covered picnic tables and fire pits. The bathrooms are wheelchair accessible and there are specific sites in both campgrounds which are designated wheelchair accessible sites. Many sites in both campgrounds overlook the lake. Primitive camping is allowed for $5, it is possible to do this with an RV along the lakeshore in several spots. Like all Maricopa County regional parks the sites in this campground can not be reserved and there is a 14 consecutive day limit. From Phoenix drive north on I-17 to Exit 223. Turn left on SR-74 and drive 11.5 miles. Turn north on Castle Hot Springs Road and you'll reach the entrance at 2.2 miles.

ARIZONA

PLEASANT HARBOR RV RESORT *(Open All Year)*
   Reservations: (800) 475-3272, mwd@pleasantharbor.com
   Information: (928) 501-5253, www.pleasantharbor.com
   Location: 18 Miles N of Phoenix, *N 33° 50' 58", W 112° 15' 04", 1,800 Ft*

254 Sites – Pleasant Harbor RV Resort is just one section of this large facility. There is also a marina here, some electric-only sites outside the RV park ($23), and dry camping ($6). The RV park does not allow tents but they are allowed in the dispersed camping area. Sites are for long back-ins to about 45 feet and there is a beautiful central area with swimming pool, spa, and small grocery. From Phoenix drive north on I-17 to Exit 223. Turn left on SR-74 and drive 8.2 miles. Turn north on N 87th Ave and you'll reach the entrance at 2.1 miles. There's a gate for the entire facility, they'll direct you to the RV park. The office there also handles the dispersed camping, or you can pay at the gate.

CAVE CREEK RECREATION AREA *(Open all Year)*
   Information: (623) 465-0431
   Location: 18 Miles NE of Phoenix, *N 33° 49' 27", W 112° 01' 04", 1,800 Ft*

38 Sites – Cave Creek is one of the great Maricopa County campgrounds which surround Phoenix. It has a cactus garden setting and well-spaced sites, both back-in and pull-thrus, to 45 feet. The sites have electric and water hookups and there is a dump station. Each site has picnic table and fire pit, restrooms have flush toilets and showers. Like all Maricopa County regional parks the sites in this campground can not be reserved and there is a 14 consecutive day limit. Cave Creek is farther out than most of these county campgrounds. Head north on I-17 until you reach Exit 223. From the exit drive east on SR-74 for seven miles, turn left on N 32nd Street. Drive north for 1.7 miles to the campground entrance.

EAGLE VIEW RV RESORT *(Open All Year)*
   Res and Info: (480) 836-5310, www.eagleviewrvresort.com, jpenberthy@fmcasino.com
   Location: 15 Miles NE of Mesa, *N 33° 34' 27", W 111° 40' 27", 1,300 Ft*

150 Sites – Eagle View RV Resort is affiliated with the nearby Fort McDowell Casino. The sites in the RV park are all back-ins, some are as long as 69 feet in length, it's a big-rig park. Instant-on telephone connections are included in the price of your site, there's also free Wi-Fi. The large clubhouse has a plasma TV, library, billards/game room, and banquet facilities. The swimming pool is heated and there is a spa. A free shuttle is provided to the casino where there are 5 restaurants and to the We-Ko-Pa Golf Club. The Out of Africa Wildlife Park is nearby. Also nearby is a gas station with a convenience store. From Exit 13 of SR-202, the Red Mountain Freeway, drive north on SR-87 for 13.7 miles. Turn south on N Ft. McDowell Road, the campground is .4 miles from the turn.

ARIZONA

McDOWELL MOUNTAIN REGIONAL PARK *(Open All Year)*

Information: (480) 471-0173, www.maricopa.gov/parks
Location: 20 Miles N of Mesa, *N 33° 39' 59", W 111° 41' 46", 1,600 Ft*

80 Sites – This Maricopa Country park is located just north of Fountain Hills. Camping is off of two loops, the north loop (older loop) with sites 1-40 and the south loop (newer loop) with sites 41-80. All sites have electricity and water hookups, a picnic table, fire ring and a raised barbecue grill. There is a dump station. Both loops have restrooms with flush toilets and showers. The park is known for its more than 40 miles of hiking and mountain bike trails (13 miles of competitive trails). It was recently rated one of the top 10 spots in the country for mountain biking. Like all Maricopa County regional parks the sites in this campground can not be reserved and there is a 14 consecutive day limit. From Exit 13 of SR-202, the Red Mountain Freeway, drive north on SR-87 for 11.7 miles. Turn left on E Shea Blvd and drive 3.3 miles. Turn right on N Fountain Hills Blvd and follow it for 7.4 miles to the campground.

USERY MOUNTAIN REGIONAL PARK *(Open All Year)*

Information: (480) 984-0032, www.maricopa.gov/parks/usery
Location: 5 Miles N of Apache Junction, *N 33° 28' 50", W 111° 37' 07", 2,000 Ft*

73 Sites – The sites in this Maricopa Country park campground are off 1 large loop road with a another road and sites running through the interior of the loop. Of the 75 sites 15 are parallel-parking style and the remainder are back-in. Many of both styles will accommodate a 45 foot RV. An overflow lot is available for campers waiting to get a space in the park. All sites have electricity and water hookups, a picnic table, fire pit, and a raised barbecue grill. A dump station is located near the entrance to the park. Fees are collected at a manned entrance booth and credit cards are accepted. The bathroom building has flush toilets. There are about 30 miles of hiking trails as well as ranger-guided hikes. The park also has Arizona's premier outdoor archery range, the only 5 star range in the western US. Like all Maricopa County regional parks the sites in this campground can not be reserved and there is a 14 consecutive day limit. From E Apache Trail in Apache Junction drive north on N Ellsworth Rd. for 4.8 miles to the park entrance.

LOST DUTCHMAN STATE PARK *(Open All Year)*

Information: (480) 982-4485, (602) 542-4174, (800) 285-3703, www.azstateparks.com
Location: 5 Miles NE of Apache Junction, *N 33° 27' 45", W 111° 28' 52", 2,100 Ft*

69 Sites – There are 69 sites in this campground and a hiker/biker campsite. Forty of the sites are extremely long pull-thrus. The sites are widely spaced and are separated by trees, shrubs, and cactus. There are no hookups. All of the sites have picnic tables and raised barbecue grills. A dump station and water fill is available to the right just after entering the park. A number of excellent hiking trails lead from this park. The campground is located along SR-88 about 5 miles northeast of the intersection of the E Apache Trail and SR-88 in Apache Junction.

MESA/APACHE JUNCTION KOA *(Open All Year)*

Reservations: (800) 562-3404, www.koa.com
Information: (480) 982-4015
Location: Apache Junction, *N 33° 24' 05", W 111° 31' 44", 1,700 Ft*

150 Sites – This KOA had a flat gravel site. There are tent sites and both back-in and pull-thru RV sites as long as 60 feet. The campground has a pool and a spa. The campground is off the E Old West Hwy some 1.6 miles southeast of intersection of the E Apache Trail and SR-88 in Apache Junction.

WHITE TANK MOUNTAIN REGIONAL PARK *(Open All Year)*

Information: (623) 935-2505, www.maricopa.gov/parks
Location: 10 Miles West of Phoenix, *N 33° 36' 05", W 112° 30' 04", 1,400 Ft*

40 Sites – This Maricopa County park campground is the only one in the far west of Phoenix. It's also the only one of the big county park campgrounds surrounding Phoenix that has no hookups. It has mostly back-in sites to 60 feet but a few even longer parallel-parking type pull-off sites. Each site has a picnic table, a fire pit, and a raised barbecue grill, a few of the sites have a paved patio. They're widely spaced and separated by trees and desert vegetation. Restrooms have flush toilets and hot showers, there is no dump station. Like all Maricopa County regional parks the sites in this campground can not be reserved and there is a 14 consecutive day limit. In northwest Phoenix (actually Peoria) follow W Olive Ave west until it ends at the park. From SR-101 that's a distance of 14 miles.

PICACHO STATE RECREATION AREA (CALIFORNIA)

This California state recreation area is a remote desert park next to the lower Colorado River. There is access to the river including two paved boat ramps so this is a popular destination for boaters and fishermen. They're after black bass, channel and flathead catfish, striped bass and bluegill.

In addition to the boat ramp there are quite a few miles of jeep roads, only suitable for four-wheel-drive vehicles. In addition to the two campgrounds listed below there are four more primitive campsites upstream that are accessible from the river or by 4-wheel-drive track.

Access to this recreation area is via an 18-mile dirt road. The road can be rough but is usually OK for even large RVs. It would be a good idea to call the park office in Winterhaven (760-996-2963 or 760-393-3059) for more information about road conditions before setting out for the park. This is a desert road and you should have plenty of fuel, water, a spare tire, and tools. To get to the park take Exit 172 off I-8, that is just west of the California/Arizona border. Drive north on Winterhaven Drive for .3 mile and turn right onto Picacho Road. The road is paved for the first 4.5 miles, then turns to dirt for the final 18 miles to the park entrance gate.

ARIZONA

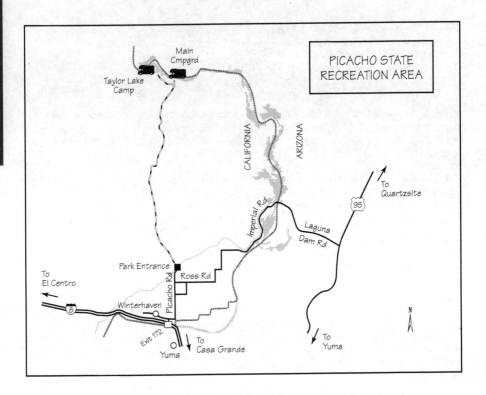

Picacho State Recreation Area Campgrounds

MAIN CAMPGROUND *(Open All Year)*
Information: (760) 996-2963
Location: Picacho SRA, *N 33° 01' 22", W 114° 36' 57", 100 Ft*

54 Sites – Sites here are nicely spaced and have a pretty desert setting but the campground is not on the river. They have picnic tables and fire rings and some even have shelters over the tables for shade. Some will take RVs to 45 feet. Restrooms are chemical toilets and there are solar-heated showers. Water is available and there is a dump station. A host camps at this campground. The campground is easily accessible from the recreation area entrance, just continue straight once you enter to the T, take a left and watch for the entrance on your left.

TAYLOR LAKE CAMP *(Open All Year)*
Information: (760) 996-2963
Location: Picacho SRA, *N 33° 01' 45", W 114° 38' 15", 100 Ft*

4 Sites – This is a tent-only camping area overlooking one of the side channels of the river. Picnic tables and firepits are provided, there are shade shelters over the picnic tables and a chemical toilet. Access is via a dirt road suitable for small vehicles only, RVs

are not recommended but four-wheel-drive is usually not necessary. The road to Taylor Lake Camp goes left just beyond the entrance gate to the recreation area, it's 2.1 miles to the camping area.

PIPE SPRING NATIONAL MONUMENT

The small Pipe Spring National Monument features a Mormon cattle outpost dating from the 1870s. It is located on the Kaibab Paiute Tribe reservation. The park is run as a memorial of both Paiute and pioneer life in the region.

The monument is relatively remote but it is not unusual for travelers to visit since SR-59/389 is the best way to bypass Zion and its restrictive tunnel when traveling from St George toward the east.

Pipe Spring National Monument Campgrounds

🚐 **KAIBAB BAND OF PAIUTE INDIANS CAMPGROUND** *(Open All Year)*
Information: (928) 643-7215, kptwfp@hotmail.com
Location: Pipe Spring National Monument, *N 36° 52' 01", W 112° 44' 12", 5,000 Ft*

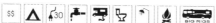

60 Sites – This is a campground set in a gravel lot near the Visitors Center for Pipe Spring National Monument. It's operated by the local Indians. There are 60 sites, some have full

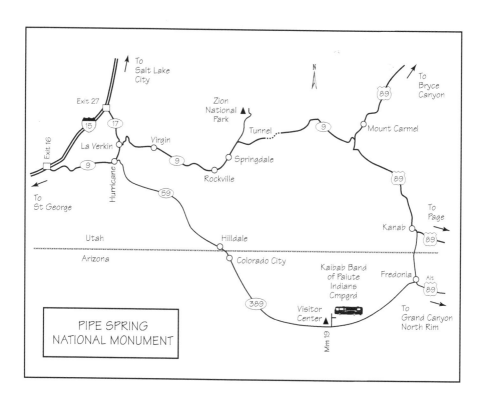

hookups and others have none. Many are pull-thrus to a length of 65 feet. Restrooms are in an older portable building and have flush toilets and hot showers. On the road where you turn off Hwy 389 to go to the campground there is a Mobil gas station which has grocery items for sale. The entrance road to Pipe Spring National Monument goes north from SR-389 about 20 miles southwest of Kanab, Utah. This is pretty empty country, you won't have any problem finding the monument headquarters or the campground.

PRESCOTT

Prescott (population about 35,000) has a scenic valley location in the Bradshaw Mountains. Prescott National Forest extends to the south, east and west so there are national forest campgrounds right on the outskirts of town.

Prescott has a number of museums. These include the **Sharlot Hall Museum**, a collection of historical buildings near the center of town, and the **Smoki Museum** which contains a large collection of Indian artifacts, both historical and current. The **Phippen Museum** north of town is a western fine art museum.

Prescott's big summer celebration is **Frontier Days** which features the "World's Oldest Rodeo". It's a ten day event which includes the Fourth of July weekend.

Prescott Campgrounds

◼ **POINT OF ROCKS CAMPGROUND** *(Open All Year)*
    Res and Info: (928) 445-9018
    Location: 4 Miles N of Prescott, *N 34° 35' 43", W 112° 25' 31", 5,100 Ft*

96 Sites – This is a very popular commercial campground in a scenic area of boulders just north of Prescott. It's so popular that you should always make reservations if you plan to visit, a long time in advance for a summer visit. The sites here are almost all back-ins off gravel access roads. They're full-hookup sites. There are good hiking trails accessible from the campground. From the junction of SR-89 and SR-69 just north of Prescott drive north on SR-89 for 3.7 miles, the campground entrance is on the right.

◼ **WATSON LAKE PARK** *(Open June 1 to Aug 31 - Varies)*
    Information: (928) 777-1100
    Location: 4 Miles N of Prescott, *N 34° 35' 32", W 112° 25' 26", 5,100 Ft*

22 Sites – The camping is in two different areas. One through 15 are on the left as you enter the park. These are back-in spaces in an open lot with trees for shade, they'll take any RV. Sites 16 to 22 are to the right at the first road past the entry gate. These are back in spaces separated by vegetation. Some of the sites are long enough to take RVs to 45 feet. There is a water fill station in the first camping area. There are wheelchair accessible flush toilets and showers between the two camping sites. During the summer there is a manned entrance gate. During the winter the entire park is used only as a day use area. None of the sites are actually on the lake, but it is a short walk away. Swimming and fishing are possible in the lake. Other amenities at the park include horseshoes and a recreation field. From the junction of SR-89 and SR-69 just north of Prescott drive north on SR-89 for 3.6 miles, the campground entrance is on the right.

◪ WILLOW LAKE RV & CAMPING PARK *(Open All Year)*

Reservations: (800) 940-2845
Information: (928) 445-6311
Location: 8 Miles N of Prescott, *N 34° 36' 43", W 112° 26' 15", 5,100 Ft*

198 Sites – The largest part of the sites in this commercial campground are used by monthly tenants. There are about 30 tent sites and 30 RV sites available for overnighters. Some sites are back-in, some pull-thru, a few will accommodate 40-footers. Easiest access from Prescott is by driving north from the intersection of SR-89 and SR-69 north of town for 4.4 miles. Turn left on Willow Lake Road and drive for 2.1 miles. Turn right and after another 1.3 miles turn right on Heritage Park Road, the campground entrance is about a half-mile down this road.

◪ YAVAPAI CAMPGROUND *(Open All Year)*

Information: (928) 443-8000
Location: 5 Miles N of Prescott, *N 34° 36' 07", W 112° 32' 21", 5,600 Ft*

25 Sites – This is a really pretty Prescott National Forest campground set among large boulders, pine trees, and junipers. The sites are located off 1 loop road with lots of separation between them. All sites are back ins and the park limits the size of vehicle here to 50 feet. There are water faucets in two locations in the park. There are 2 sets of wheelchair

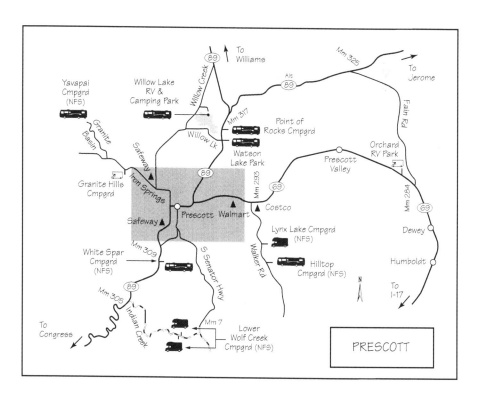

accessible composting toilets. The roads and the camping sites are nicely paved. Each site has a metal picnic table and a fire pit. Some of the sites have sand pads for tenting. Sites 8 and 21 are designated as wheelchair accessible sites. Hiking trails leave from near the campground. Access is slightly convoluted. From central Prescott drive west on W Gurly St. for a few blocks and then head north on Grove Avenue which becomes Miller Valley Road. In 1.1 mile take the left fork onto Iron Springs Rd. Follow it for 3 miles and turn right on Granite Basin Road. You'll reach the campground in 2.1 miles.

LYNX LAKE CAMPGROUND *(Open April 1 to Oct 31 - Varies)*
Information: (928) 443-8000
Location: 5 Miles E of Prescott, *N 34° 31' 02", W 112° 23' 28", 5,500 Ft*

36 Sites – This is a beautiful refurbished Prescott National Forest campground located very near Prescott. It's best for tent campers and smaller RVs, only a few sites will take RVs up to 35 feet, most are better for 25-foot RVs or smaller. The sites are off about 7 small loops, access roads are paved. The parking pads are also paved and the sites have picnic tables and fire pits. Hiking trails leave from near the campground and it is not far from the campground to Lynx Lake. From the intersection of US-89 and US-69 northeast of town drive east on US-69 for 2.8 miles. Turn right on Walker Road, which is paved, and drive 2.3 miles to the campground.

HILLTOP CAMPGROUND *(Open April 1 to Oct 31 - Varies)*
Information: (928) 443-8000
Location: 6 Miles E of Prescott, *N 34° 30' 28", W 112° 23' 03", 5,500 Ft*

38 Sites – Hilltop is a very accessible Prescott National Forest campground. Sites are widely spaced off three loops. It's a modern campground with paved access roads and sites. Most sites are smaller back-ins but there are a few parallel-parking style pull-offs that will take 45-footers. Sites have picnic tables and fire pits, there are vault toilets. The campground is very near Prescott. From the intersection of US-89 and US-69 northeast of town drive east on US-69 for 2.8 miles. Turn right on Walker Road, which is paved, and drive 3.2 miles to the campground.

WHITE SPAR CAMPGROUND *(Open All Year)*
Information: (928) 443-8000
Location: 1 Mile S of Prescott, *N 34° 30' 21", W 112° 28' 39", 5,600 Ft*

60 Sites – White Spar is a large Prescott National Forest campground just outside Prescott, and it's open all year. This campground has 63 very large sites, many over 40 feet in length. About 12 of the sites are pull-thrus. The sites are located in two area, the White Spar Camping Area (sites 1-32) and the North Campground (sites 33-63). The interior roads are paved and the parking spaces are paved with a picnic table and a fire pit. There are wheelchair accessible vault toilets throughout the park. During the winter there is a host but only about 10 of the sites are open. From Prescott drive south on SR-89, the campground is about two miles south of the central business district.

🚐 **LOWER WOLF CREEK CAMPGROUND** *(Open May 1 to Oct 31 - Varies)*
Information: (928) 443-8000
Location: 9 Miles S of Prescott, *N 34° 27' 18", W 112° 27' 37", 6,000 Ft*

19 Sites – This small Prescott National Forest campground is located on both sides of the road. There are 20 small sites, they are best for tent campers and small RVs to about 30 feet. Many sites are not level and maneuvering room is limited. No water is available. Easiest access is by driving south from central Prescott on S Vernon Ave which soon comes to a Y. Take the left fork, this is S Senator Hwy. In 6 miles turn right on Wolf Creek road, the campground is 3 miles down this gravel road.

QUARTZSITE AREA

The small town of Quartzsite is the ultimate RVing spectacle. Even non-RVers know that in January the town becomes a magnet for the southwest RVing community with thousands of RVs parked in the desert for miles around the town.

Quartzsite is located on I-40 just 19 miles east of the California – Arizona border. In the summer very few people live here. Two off-ramps lead to a few gas stations, a restaurant or two, and acres of empty, often rather ratty-looking, RV parks. It's an RV ghost town. Summer temperatures sometimes exceed 110 degrees here, most people have other places to spend the summer.

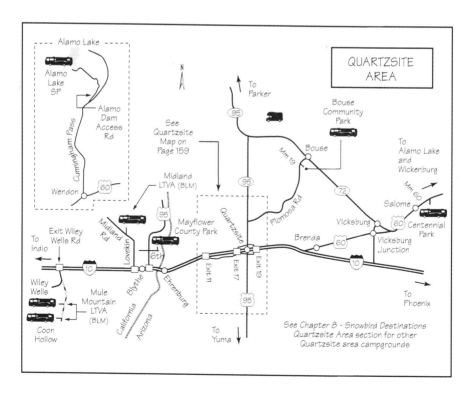

In the fall the town starts to come alive. RV parks start to fill with Snowbird RVers. Then, in early January, RVers from all over the southwest head for Quartzite. They fill the sixty-odd RV parks in the town and in surrounding towns for many miles around. They also fill the desert around the town, boondocking on BLM land that has been set aside for just that purpose.

A number of events are scheduled for January and early February. Most are rock shows or RV events. After so many years of this it has become hard to tell if the RVers are attracted by the shows or the shows by the RVers. Regardless, it's a chance to rally in the desert, a chance to get together with old friends.

Here's a listing of the events and their locations in town (keyed to the map) from November 2008 to February 2009. Dates will change in upcoming years and perhaps the locations and events will too, but you can be sure there will be a lot going on.

General Events
- 6th Annual Christmas Lights Parade (December 7)
- Hi Jolly Daze Parade (January 3)
- 4th Annual Willpower/Pawpower ATV Parade (February 7)

Pow Wow Grounds – Map Key A
- 43rd Annual Pow Wow (January 21 – January 25)
- 6th Annual "It's Chili in Quartzsite", Chile Cook-off & State Salsa Championship – February 28

Big Tent – Map Key B
- 25th Quartzsite Sports, Vacation, & RV Show (January 17 – 25)
- 10th Annual Quartzsite Hobby, Craft & Gem Show (January 28 – February 1)
- 10th Annual Quartzsite Rock & Roll Classic Car Show (January 28 – February 1)

Tyson Wells Grounds – Map Key C
- Tyson Wells Rock/Gem/Mineral Show (January 2 – January 11)
- Tyson Wells Sell-A-Rama (January 16 – January 25)
- Tyson Wells Art and Crafts Fair (January 30 – February 8)
- Blue Grass Festival at Tyson Wells (February 27 – March 1)
- The La-Z-Daze Quartzsite Classic Horseshoe Tournament (Date TBA)

Rice Ranch Grounds – Map Key D
- Rice Ranch "Yawl Come", Show (November 1 – February 28)

Prospector's Panorama Grounds – Map Key E
4 Shows from November 1 – February 15
- Christmas Gold Rush Days
- Gold Show
- Gem and Mineral Show
- Peddler's Fair

The Main Event Grounds – Map Key F
- The Main Event (January 10 – January 25)
- Steam Engine Show (January 23 – January 25)

Desert Gardens Map – Key G
- Desert Gardens Gem and Mineral Show (January 1 – February 28)

ARIZONA

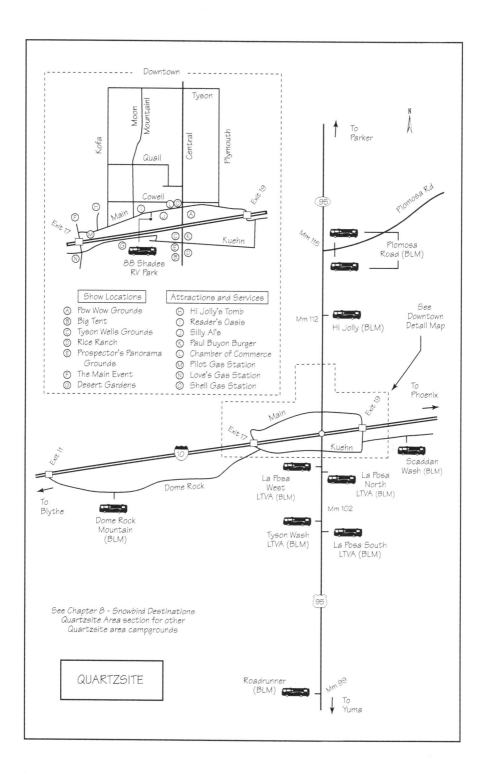

Downtown

Tyson

Moon Mountainl

Kofa

Central

Plymouth

Quail

Cowell

Main

Exit 17

Exit 19

Kuehn

88 Shades
RV Park

To
Parker

N

95

Plomosa Rd

Mm 115

Plomosa
Road (BLM)

Mm 112

Hi Jolly (BLM)

See
Downtown
Detail Map

To
Phoenix

Show Locations	Attractions and Services
Ⓐ Pow Wow Grounds	Ⓗ Hi Jolly's Tomb
Ⓑ Big Tent	Ⓘ Reader's Oasis
Ⓒ Tyson Wells Grounds	Ⓙ Silly Al's
Ⓓ Rice Ranch	Ⓚ Paul Buyon Burger
Ⓔ Prospector's Panorama	Ⓛ Chamber of Commerce
Grounds	Ⓜ Pilot Gas Station
Ⓕ The Main Event	Ⓝ Love's Gas Station
Ⓖ Desert Gardens	Ⓞ Shell Gas Station

Main

Exit 17   Exit 19

10

Kuehn

Exit 11

Dome Rock

Scaddan
Wash (BLM)

To
Blythe

Dome Rock
Mountain
(BLM)

La Posa
West
LTVA (BLM)

La Posa
North
LTVA (BLM)

Mm 102

Tyson Wash
LTVA (BLM)

La Posa South
LTVA (BLM)

95

See Chapter 8 - Snowbird Destinations
Quartzsite Area section for other
Quartzsite area campgrounds

QUARTZSITE

Roadrunner
(BLM)

Mm 99

To
Yuma

ARIZONA

In addition to these shows there are a number of less formal swap meets around town throughout the November – February season.

You'll see that we've included campgrounds for some distance to the west and east in this chapter. For more about Quartzsite, and particularly Snowbird winter RV parks, see the *Snowbird Destinations* chapter of this book. Many of the campgrounds listed in that chapter also have spaces for travelers, our charts in that chapter give overnight rates for the ones that do.

Quartzsite Area Campgrounds

EIGHTY EIGHT SHADES RV PARK *(Open All Year)*
Res and Info: (928) 927-6336, (800) 457-4392 www.grapevine7.com
Location: Quartzsite, *N 33° 39' 54", W 114° 13' 32", 900 Ft*

104 Sites – This is one of a row of parks along the south side of the I-10 business loop through town. It's right in the middle of things. Sites are back-ins and pull-thrus to 50 feet. Take Exit 17 from I-10 and drive north a short distance and follow the road as it makes a 90-degree right. From there go .9 mile, the campground is on the right.

LA POSA WEST BLM LTVA *(Open All Year)*
Information: (928) 317-3200, www.az.blm.gov
Location: 1 Mile S of Quartzsite, *N 33° 39' 07", W 114° 13' 07", 900 Ft*

Scattered Boondocking – This is one of four different camping areas in the La Posa LTVA. See the introductory material in this chapter for the BLM LTVA costs and rules. This LTVA is the very close to the big tent during the shows there. There is a manned entrance house during the busy season which sells permits. A pay telephone is at the entrance house. From Business I-10 in Quartzsite drive south on S Central Blvd.(US-95). You'll pass over the freeway and in 1 mile see the entrance on your right.

LA POSA NORTH BLM LTVA *(Open All Year)*
Information: (928) 317-3200, www.az.blm.gov
Location: 1 Mile S of Quartzsite, *N 33° 39' 07", W 114° 12' 56", 900 Ft*

Scattered Boondocking – This is one of four different camping areas in the La Posa LTVA. See the introductory material in this chapter for the BLM LTVA costs and rules. This LTVA is just across the street from La Posa West and is still close to the action of Quartzsite. There is a manned entrance house during the busy season. During the RV show we've seen private operators bring big portable shower trucks to this location. From Business I-10 in Quartzsite drive south on S Central Blvd (US-95). You'll pass over the freeway and in 1 mile see the entrance on your left.

LA POSA TYSON WASH BLM LTVA *(Open All Year)*
Information: (928) 317-3200, www.az.blm.gov
Location: 3 Miles S of Quartzsite, *N 33° 37' 36", W 114° 13' 08", 1,000 Ft*

Scattered Boondocking – This is one of four different camping areas in the La Posa LTVA. See the introductory material in this chapter for the BLM LTVA costs and rules. Tyson Wash is just south of La Posa West. It has a manned entrance gate during the busy season. It also has vault toilet allowing tenters and RVs without sanitary facilities to camp. From Business I-10 in Quartzsite drive south on S Central Blvd (US-95). You'll pass over the freeway and in 2.8 miles see the entrance on your right.

LA POSA SOUTH BLM LTVA *(Open All Year)*
Information: (928) 317-3200, www.az.blm.gov
Location: 3 Miles S of Quartzsite, *N 33° 37' 36", W 114° 13' 00", 1,000 Ft*

Scattered Boondocking – This is one of four different camping areas in the La Posa LTVA. See the introductory material in this chapter for the BLM LTVA costs and rules. La Posa South is just south of La Posa North. It has a manned entrance gate during the busy season and also dump stations and vault toilets which allow tenters and RVs without sanitary facilities to camp here. You must have a LTVA permit to use the dump station. From Business I-10 in Quartzsite drive south on S Central Blvd (US-95). You'll pass over the freeway and in 2.8 miles see the entrance on your left.

ROAD RUNNER/MM 99 BLM DISPERSED CAMPING AREA *(Open All Year)*
Information: (928) 317-3200, www.az.blm.gov
Location: 6 Miles S of Quartzsite, *N 33° 35' 07", W 114° 13' 02", 1,100 Ft*

Scattered Boondocking – See the introductory material in this chapter about the BLM 14-Day dispersed camping areas. The entrance to this one is near Mile 99 south of Quartzsite. The camping area is west of US-95 between the gas line road and La Paz Valley Road. From Business I-10 in Quartzsite drive south on S Central Blvd (US-95). You'll pass over the freeway and in 5.6 miles see the access on your right.

SCADDAN WASH BLM DISPERSED CAMPING AREA *(Open All Year)*
Information: (928) 317-3200, www.az.blm.gov
Location: 3.5 Mile E of Quartzsite, *N 33° 39' 57", W 114° 11' 15", 900 Ft*

Scattered Boondocking – This 14-Day area is east of Quartzsite on the south side of I-10. See the introductory material in this chapter about the BLM 14-Day dispersed camping areas. To reach the area take Exit 19 from I-10 and travel east just a short distance on the south side of the highway. The parking area is south of the frontage road.

DOME ROCK MOUNTAIN BLM DISPERSED CAMPING AREA *(Open All Year)*
Information: (928) 317-3200, www.az.blm.gov
Location: 6 Miles W of Quartzsite, *N 33° 38' 41", W 114° 20' 02", 1,100 Ft*

Scattered Boondocking – This 14-Day dispersed camping area is west of Quartzsite on the south side of I-10. See the introductory material in this chapter about the BLM 14-Day camping areas. To reach the area take I-10 west from Quartzsite to Exit 11. The parking area is south of the frontage road.

ARIZONA

⊟ HI JOLLY/MM 112 BLM DISPERSED CAMPING AREA *(Open All Year)*

Information: (928) 317-3200, www.az.blm.gov
Location: 5 Miles N of Quartzsite, *N 33° 42' 31", W 114° 12' 58", 800 Ft*

Scattered Boondocking – Hi Jolly is the smallest of the 14-day areas around Quartzsite, still, it's pretty large. See the introductory material in this chapter about the BLM 14-Day dispersed camping areas. From Quartzsite at the intersection of SR-95 and Business I-10 drive north 3 miles to Mile 112. The camping area is on the right.

⊟ PLOMOSA ROAD BLM DISPERSED CAMPING AREA *(Open All Year)*

Information: (928) 317-3200, www.az.blm.gov
Location: 5 Miles N of Quartzsite, *N 33° 44' 51", W 114° 12' 58", 800 Ft*

Scattered Boondocking – This is a 14-day area north of Quartzsite. See the introductory material in this chapter about the BLM 14-Day dispersed camping areas. From Quartzsite at the intersection of SR-95 and I-10 Business drive north 5.8 miles to Plomosa Road (also called the Bouse-Quartzsite Rd.) Turn right, the camping area is on both sides of Plomosa.

⊟ MIDLAND BLM LTVA *(Open All Year)*

Information: (760) 251-4800, www.ca.blm.gov/caso
Location: 16 Miles NW of Blythe, *N 33° 43' 38", W 114° 39' 32", 500 Ft*

Scattered Boondocking – The Midland LTVA occupies land atop a low plateau to the northeast of Blythe, California. See the introductory material in this chapter for the BLM LTVA costs and rules. Midland LTVA has a dump station and a telephone, as well as a host. To reach this LTVA leave I-10 at the second exit west of the California/Arizona border, the exit is marked Lovekin Blvd. Drive north on Lovekin for 5.4 miles and then bear left onto Midland Rd. Follow Midland for another 12 miles to the LTVA entrance, it's on the right.

⊟ MULE MOUNTAIN BLM LTVA – WILEY WELLS *(Open All Year)*

Information: (760) 251-4800, www.ca.blm.gov/caso
Location: 25 Miles SW of Blythe, *N 33° 29' 37", W 114° 53' 16", 600 Ft*

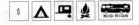

15 Sites and Scattered Boondocking – The Mule Mountain LTVA is unlike the other LTVAs because it actually has two campgrounds, Wiley Wells and Coon Hollow (see below). The sites here at Wiley Wells are in 2 loops. The south loop has sites 1-9 and the north loop has sites 10-15. Some of the sites are longer than 80 feet. All have picnic tables and either raised barbecue grills or fire pits. Some of the tables are sheltered. There are 2 vault toilet buildings, one in each loop. This is a popular place in the winter, most sites fill pretty quickly. Between the Wiley Wells and Coon Hollow campgrounds there is a dump station. In addition to the formal camping areas scattered LTVA camping is possible anywhere between the 2 campgrounds. There's also an associated 14-Day area south of Coon Hollow, ask the hosts at the campgrounds about this. To reach the Wiley Wells campground leave I-10 some 21 miles west of the California/Arizona border at the

exit labeled Wiley Wells. Travel south on Wiley Wells Road for 2.8 miles. The road to Wiley Wells then turns to sand and gravel (and dust) while the paved road curves off to the right to a prison. Continue south another 5.5 miles to the Wiley Wells campground.

☰ MULE MOUNTAIN BLM LTVA – COON HOLLOW *(Open All Year)*
Information: (760) 251-4800, www.ca.blm.gov/caso
Location: 28 Miles SW of Blythe, N 33° 26' 51", W 114° 54' 01", 600 Ft

29 Sites and Scattered Boondocking – The campground here is just like the other one in the Mule Mtn LTVA, but bigger. The sites are in 2 loops. The south loop has sites 1-12 and the north loop has sites 13-29. There are long sites, rock-lined drives, non-potable water, and vault toilets. All the sites have picnic tables and either raised barbecue grills or fire pits. To reach the Coon Hollow campground leave I-10 some 21 miles west of the California/Arizona border at the exit labeled Wiley Wells. Travel south on Wiley Wells Road for 2.8 miles. The road to Wiley Wells then turns to sand and gravel (and dust) while the paved road curves off to the right to a prison. Continue south another 5.5 miles, you'll see the Wiley Wells campground on the right. In another 1.5 miles you'll pass the dump station and 1.8 mile south of that come to the entrance to Coon Hollow campground.

☰ BOUSE COMMUNITY PARK *(Open All Year)*
Information: (928) 667-2069
Location: 24 Miles NE of Quartzsite, *N 33° 55' 41", W 114° 01' 13", 900 Ft*

20 Sites – This community park has limited sites with electricity and water hookups, both pull-thru and back-in sites to 45 feet. There is room in several areas for other dry camping. The park has a gravel drive and parking is on gravel. There is a putting green, a playground, a large ramada, and 4 horse stables. There is also a dump station which non guests can use for a fee and water is sold. Overnight campers pay $5 to dump (slide-in campers $3), if you stay a week you get 1 free dump, and monthly get 1 free dump per week. The campground is on the south side of the Bouse-Quartzsite road, 1 mile west of the Bouse intersection (and 24 miles from Quartzsite).

☰ CENTENNIAL PARK *(Open All Year)*
Information: (928) 667-2069
Location: 5 Miles E of Salome, *N 33° 47' 22", W 113° 33' 30", 1,800 Ft*

24 Sites – The 24 sites in this campground are very widely spaced off a big gravel loop road. Some of the sites are pull-thrus, all of the sites are very long and wide. They sometimes put as many as 3 RVs traveling together in one site. There are no hookups, but there is a dump station with a water fill station. There is a fee of $5 for overnighters to dump. Weekly guests get 1 free dump and monthly guests get one free dump per week. Non guest are allowed to dump for $7. Water for guests is free and for non guests a donation is requested. The park has wheelchair accessible bathrooms with showers. There is a baseball field, basketball court, and a playground. The campground sits next to an 18 hole golf course. The front 9 holes are grass and cost $8, the back 9 are desert and cost $2. There is also a driving range. Golf carts, clubs, and pull carts can be rented. From Salome

drive 3.5 miles north on US-60. Turn right on Centennial Park Road and you'll reach the campground in 1.6 mile. It's 46 miles northwest of Quartzsite.

MAYFLOWER COUNTY PARK *(Open All Year)*

Information: (760) 922-4665, www.riversidecountyparks.org
Location: 5 Miles NE of Blythe, *N 33° 40' 12", W 114° 32' 02", 300 Ft*

182 Sites – This county park has 19 dry sites and 152 sites with water and electric. The sites are all back-in to a length of 40 feet although 45-footers squeeze in since there aren't a lot of obstacles. The main interior road through the park is paved and the roads between the rows of sites are a combination grass/sand. Most of the sites are shaded. Restrooms have flush toilets and showers. The campground sits right on the banks of the Colorado River. The dry sites have the location closest to the river. These sites have raised barbecue grills. Fishing is possible in the river and there is a swimming lagoon and a boat ramp. There is a 14 day stay limit in the summer. Monthly rates are offered from Oct 1 - March 31. Other amenities include a dump station, air for tires, horseshoes, shuffleboard, and lawn bowling. It's a first-come, first-served campground – no reservations. From I-10 in Blythe take Exit 95 marked US-95, Intake Blvd, Needles; and drive north on US-95. In 3.7 miles turn right onto 6th Ave and follow it for 2.7 miles to the river, the campground is to the left.

ALAMO LAKE STATE PARK *(Open All Year)*

Information: (928) 669-2088, www.azstateparks.com
Location: 77 Miles NE of Quartzsite, *N 34° 13' 43", W 113° 34' 40", 1,300 Ft*

202 Sites – Alamo Lake is very isolated, we've listed it under Quartzsite because the route from the south is the closest. This Bill Williams River reservoir has good fishing. There are 19 full hookup sites, 80 water and electric sites and both developed and undeveloped sites with no hookups. The campground has a dump station as well as restrooms with flush toilets and hot showers. There are two boat ramps. From SR-60 about 5 miles northeast of Salome in tiny Wendon turn north and follow the paved Cunningham Pass Rd and then the Alamo Dam Access Road 35 miles to the park. This is 77 miles from Quartzsite.

SAFFORD

The town of **Safford**, population about 9,000, is in the Gila River Valley, one of Arizona's top agricultural areas. It serves as the supply center for quite a large region.

The main attraction here, in addition to **Roper Lake State Park** just south of town, is the **Pinaleno Mountain Range** to the southwest of town. It's one of southeast Arizona's "sky island" mountain ranges and includes Mt. Graham which rises to 10,720 feet. The range is in the Coronado National Forest and has six forest service campgrounds, some suitable for RVs to about 23 feet. The Swift Trail climbs high into the mountains giving excellent access to high country at 9,000 feet with trails leading to the peaks. There are 23 paved miles and then another 13 miles of gravel road. It's a narrow winding road and not recommended for vehicles over 23 feet long. The gravel portion is closed from November 15 to April 15. Swift Trail goes west from US-191 about 6 miles south of Safford.

Safford Campgrounds

ROPER LAKE STATE PARK *(Open All Year)*

Reservations: (928) 428-6760
Information: (928) 428-6760, www.azstateparks.com
Location: 4 Miles S of Safford, *N 32° 45' 25", W 109° 42' 29", 6,300 Ft*

45 Sites – Individual sites in this park are off two loops. They are widely spaced, mostly back-ins but a few pull-thrus. Electricity and water hookups are available, there's 30 amps on the Hacienda Loop and 50 on the Cottonwood Loop. Restrooms have showers and the lake has a swimming beach. An unusual feature here is the hot-spring fed spa. From US-191 some 4 miles south of Safford turn east on Roper Lake Road. It's .5 mile to the entrance road on your right.

LEXINGTON PINES MOTORHOME AND RV PARK *(Open All Year)*

Res and Info: (800) 232-7570
Location: Safford, *N 32° 50' 02", W 109° 43' 35", 6,200 Ft*

54 Sites – The Lexington Pines is a large 55+ mobile home and RV park with about 200 spaces on the western side of Safford near the big box stores. There are a lot of permanently located mobile homes in the park but the northwest corner is use for snowbirds and

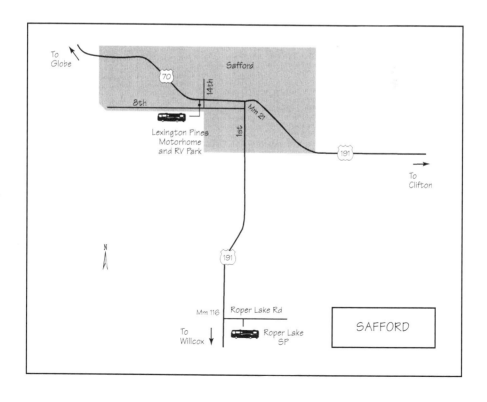

travelers. Sites are all back-ins to about 50 feet with full hookups. Internal access roads are paved and sites are gravel. There is a spa and recreation room. This is a 55 and older park. From the intersection of South 1st Ave (US-191) from the south and east/west US-70 in central Safford drive west on US-70 for 1.1 miles, turn left at the sign, the park is directly ahead with the office in the building to the left just before the entrance.

SALTON SEA EAST SIDE (CALIFORNIA)

California's Salton Sea is the largest lake in the state. It was originally formed when the Colorado River was accidentally allowed to flow into the basin in 1901. This isn't the first time that a lake has been here. The Colorado has formed the lake many times, then it would change course and the lake would dry up. The sea today is about 200 feet below sea level. It is known for water sports, excellent fishing, and birding opportunities.

The sea has its problems. Evaporation and water replacement by drainage from agricultural areas means that the salt content is increasing. It also means that excessive nutrients in the water sometimes cause algae blooms which in turn cause fish and bird die-offs. Scientists are trying to figure out how to save the lake, so far with little luck. You'll find that sometimes this is a nice place to spend time and at others there has been a die-off making the area fairly unpleasant.

The best time to visit is the fall, spring and winter from October to June when temperatures can be very comfortable. In summer it's very hot.

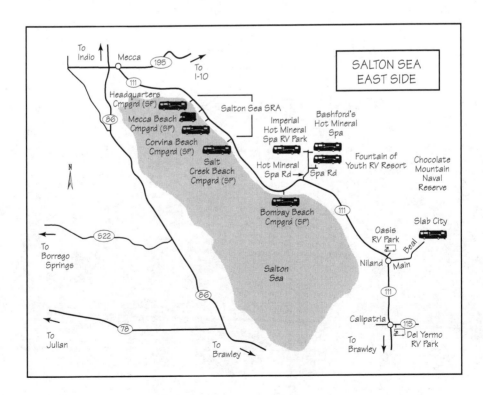

East of the lake there are a number of hot spring resorts with campgrounds. Several are listed below. This is also the location of the famous (or infamous) boondocking area known as Slab City.

Salton Sea East Side Campgrounds

🚐 SALTON SEA SRA – HEADQUARTERS CAMPGROUND *(Open All Year)*
   Reservations: (800) 444-7275, www.parks.ca.gov
   Information: (760) 393-3059, (760) 393-3052, www.parks.ca.gov
   Location: 25 Miles SE of Indio, *N 33° 30' 31", W 115° 55' 05", -200 Ft*

50 Sites – Near the visitor center for the state park is the largest of the park's camping areas. Others are to the south along the lake with separated entrance roads. Here there is a line of 15 long pull-thru full-hookup sites at the back of the large parking area for the visitor center. There are also dry-camping sites nearby. A loop road farther back has parallel-parking type sites with electricity and water hookups. There's also a boat ramp, dump station, and playground. Reservations are accepted from October 1 to May 31. For a hookup site they're a good idea, particularly on weekends. The campground is off SR-111 some 25 miles southeast of Indio.

🚐 SALTON SEA SRA – MECCA BEACH CAMPGROUND *(Open All Year)*
   Reservations: (800) 444-7275, www.parks.ca.gov
   Information: (760) 393-3059, (760) 393-3052, www.parks.ca.gov
   Location: 26 Miles SE of Indio, *N 33° 29' 31", W 115° 54' 04", -200 Ft*

105 Sites – Mecca Beach is 1.5 miles south of the Headquarters Campground. Sites here are fairly short, about 30 feet. Only ten sites have hookups and many of them are taken by park employees or hosts. Only four of the hookup sites can be reserved. The sites are parking spots in two long blacktopped lots with picnic tables and fire pits or raised grills behind. Restrooms have flush toilets and solar-heated showers. Campers use the boat launch and dump station at the Headquarters Campground. The campground is off SR-111 some 26 miles southeast of Indio.

🚐 SALTON SEA SRA – CORVINA BEACH CAMPGROUND *(Open All Year)*
   Information: (760) 393-3059, (760) 393-3052, www.parks.ca.gov
   Location: 28 Miles SE of Indio, *N 33° 28' 34", W 115° 53' 20", -200 Ft*

Scattered Boondocking – This is a dispersed camping area with no formal sites. Parking is along a road running next to the beach. You can park right on the water's edge. The only amenities are portable toilets and a water faucet. This campground is three miles south of the Headquarters Campground, 28 miles south of Indio.

🚐 SALTON SEA SRA – SALT CREEK BEACH CAMPGROUND *(Open All Year)*
   Information: (760) 393-3059, (760) 393-3052, www.parks.ca.gov
   Location: 31 Miles SE of Indio, *N 33° 26' 41", W 115° 50' 40", -200 Ft*

Scattered Boondocking – Salt Creek is another dispersed camping area next to the beach.

ARIZONA

There are portable toilets and a water faucet. The campground is 6 miles south of the Headquarters Campground, 31 miles south of Indio.

SALTON SEA SRA – BOMBAY BEACH CAMPGROUND *(Open All Year)*

Information: (760) 393-3059, (760) 393-3052, www.parks.ca.gov
Location: 40 Miles SE of Indio, *N 33° 21' 03", W 115° 44' 02", -200 Ft*

Scattered Boondocking – Bombay Beach is another dispersed camping area next to the beach, it's just west of the community of Bombay Beach. There are portable toilets and a water faucet. The campground is 15 miles south of the Headquarters Campground, 40 miles south of Indio.

BASHFORD'S HOT MINERAL SPA *(Open Oct 15 to May 31)*

Information: (760) 354-1315, www.bashfords.com
Location: 18 Miles N of Niland, *N 33° 25' 23", W 115° 40' 54", -100 Ft*

70 Sites – This is a friendly age 55+ family-run campground and hot-springs resort. Sites are back-ins and pull-thrus to 50 feet. The water comes out of the ground here at 160 degrees Fahrenheit. Cooled down it is used for six individual mineral pools, fresh water is used for a swimming pool. From a point on SR-111 some 43 miles south of Indio and 14 miles north of Niland, turn east on Hot Mineral Spa Road. The campground is on your right in 3.4 miles.

FOUNTAIN OF YOUTH RV RESORT *(Open All Year)*

Information: (760) 354-1340, (888) 800- 8772, www.foyspa.com
Location: 17 Miles N of Niland, *N 33° 23' 57", W 115° 39' 45", -100 Ft*

500 Sites – The Fountain of Youth is a giant compared to the other two hot spring campgrounds nearby. It's also the nicest of the three. Of the 850 sites here about 300 serviced sits are available for daily, monthly or seasonal rental, plus there are another 200 or so dry sites. This is a gated park with 2 large swimming pools, 3 therapeutic jet pools, and a hot mineral water spa. There are also two artesian mineral water steam rooms. Other park amenities include tennis courts, a beauty salon, a grocery store, cafe, a massage therapist, a scenic 9 hole desert golf course, a fitness room, a card room, pool tables, shuffleboard, a crafts/sewing room and a crafts coordinator, and bocce courts. From a point on SR-111 some 43 miles south of Indio and 14 miles north of Niland, turn east on Hot Mineral Spa Road. In 1.6 miles turn right and the campground will be on your left in another 1.2 miles.

IMPERIAL HOT MINERAL SPA RV PARK *(Open All Year)*

Information: (760) 354-4100
Location: 18 Miles N of Niland, *N 33° 25' 33", W 115° 41' 08", -100 Ft*

100 Sites – This is a mobile home and RV park. They have about 100 back-in sites for traveling RVs or for seasonal rentals. There is also a dry camping overflow area. This

SALVATION MOUNTAIN AT THE EDGE OF SLAB CITY

park has 11 small mineral pools and a larger fresh water pool. There's also a desert golf course. From a point on SR-111 some 43 miles south of Indio and 14 miles north of Niland, turn east on Hot Mineral Spa Road. The campground is on your left in 3.7 miles.

SLAB CITY *(Open All Year)*
   Location: 4 Miles East of Niland, *N 33° 25' 33", W 115° 41' 08", -100 Ft*

Scattered Boondocking – Slab City is the former Camp Dunlap naval base. When it was abandoned the slabs that formed the floors of many of the buildings were left, hence the name. It's a large desert area which is not actively administered by anyone. Some people have been here boondocking for years, others visit for a day or two or for the season. It's really a community occupied, as you might imagine, by all kinds of people. Services including garbage disposal and newspaper and water delivery can be contracted with various individuals. Niland has a dump station at the fairgrounds near the south side of town, a grocery store, and restaurants. In Niland drive east on Main Street. Some 3 miles from the turn you'll pass a giant painted hillside on your right (Salvation Mountain) and enter the camping area just beyond.

SEDONA, COTTONWOOD, AND THE VERDE VALLEY

The Verde Valley to the west of I-17 is an attractive area with much to see and do. People here say the altitude is ideal, above the desert heat and below the cool of the high country. We'll start in the west and move to the east in this description.

Jerome (population about 500) is an old gold and copper mining town with an unusual setting, it precariously clings to the side of Cleopatra Hill overlooking the Verde Valley. The mines closed down in the 30s and today Jerome is a tourist and art town. In addition to art galleries and restaurants there are three interesting museums in town: **Jerome State Historic Park, Jerome Historical Society Mine Museum**, and **Gold King Mine and Ghost Town**. If you have a big RV the best place to camp would be Cottonwood on the flats below. Smaller vehicles can negotiate Jerome's streets and steep grades and use the campgrounds above, including Potato Patch and Mingus Mountain national forest campgrounds.

Cottonwood (population about 11,000) serves as the supply center for the western part of the valley. It has a pleasant downtown and also a strip of businesses on the SR-89 bypass route to the south and west of town. Just two miles northwest is Clarkdale.

Dead Horse Ranch State Park, just north of town, is one of the best places in the region to camp. The park is on the Verde River and has good fishing and birding.

Tuzigoot National Monument is a hilltop Sinagua pueblo that has been partially restored. The visitor center and ruins are just northeast of Cottonwood and accessible from the road leading up to Clarkdale.

The **Verde Canyon Railroad** makes a 25-mile run up through the scenic Verde River Canyon from Clarkdale to Perkinsville. The engines are vintage diesels.

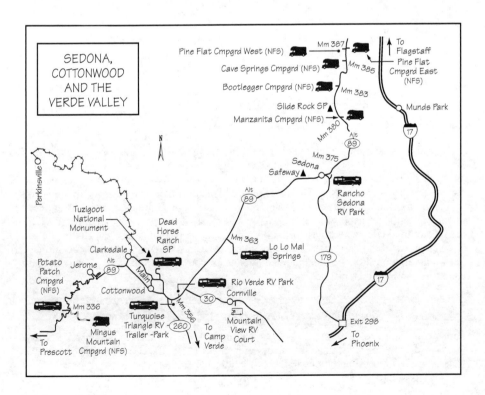

Sedona (population about 11,000) is an upscale artist, retirement and spiritual center sur-rounded by red cliffs at the lower end of Oak Creek Canyon. It's enough of a tourist town that you'll actually find timeshare touts. Sedona is full of galleries, restaurants and shops. Jeep tours and hikes in the surrounding red rock country are very popular. The town is also considered by many to be surrounded by spiritual energy vortices, tour operators know where they are.

Oak Creek Canyon to the north of Sedona is a very popular playground for campers and people who want to enjoy the river. There are several swimming holes and campgrounds. SR-89A runs through the canyon to Flagstaff, only 25 miles away. Campgrounds tend to be small and impossible to get into on weekends during the summer, see the descriptions below.

Sedona, Cottonwood, and the Verde Valley Campgrounds

DEAD HORSE RANCH STATE PARK *(Open All Year)*
Information: (928) 634-5283, www.azstateparks.com
Location: Cottonwood, *N 34° 45' 13", W 112° 01' 18", 3,300 Ft*

127 Sites – This is a large state campground with 127 sites. Camping is off 4 loops. The lower loop is Quail Loop (1-45). The North Campground has Red-Tail Hawk Loop (46-82), Cooper's Hawk Loop (83-110), and Blackhawk Loop (111-127) (tents only). One hundred and ten sites have electricity and water hookups, 23 are dry sites, and 17 are tent sites. Thirty-eight sites (in the Quail and Cooper's Hawk Loops) are pull-thrus to 60 feet. Some sites have fire pits, others have raised barbecue grills, and some have both. There is a bathroom building in the Quail loop with flush toilets and showers. A bathroom build-ing is under construction in the North Campground. Freshwater fishing and a boat ramp are available in 3 lagoons and the Verde River. Trails leave near the Blackhawk Loop. The park is located just east of Cottonwood. From SR-60 just east of town turn north on N 10th St. to enter the campground.

POTATO PATCH CAMPGROUND *(Open May 1 to Oct 31 - Varies)*
Information: (928) 567-4121
Location: 14 Miles W of Cottonwood, *N 34° 42' 35", W 112° 09' 15", 7,000 Ft*

40 Sites – This Prescott National Forest campground is located in the mountains above Jerome and has good big-rig features. There are back-in and pull-thru sites to 45 feet. Twelve have electricity. Interior roads and parking pads are paved, each site has a fire pit and picnic table. There are vault toilets and potable water is available. From a point on US-89A which is 14 miles west of Cottonwood and 24 miles NE of Prescott turn north into the campground entrance. Access through Jerome from the Cottonwood area on SR-89 Alt is not suitable for large RVs due to steep grades, switchbacks, and congestion.

MINGUS MOUNTAIN CAMPGROUND *(Open May 1 to Oct 31 - Varies)*
Information: (928) 443-8000
Location: 18 Miles W of Cottonwood, *N 34° 41' 11", W 112° 07' 07", 7,500 Ft*

25 Sites – Mingus Mountain is a Prescott National Forest campground. It has 6 tent-

ing sites and 19 RV sites to 40 feet with electrical outlets. No water is available at this campground. Access is via a 4 mile dirt road suitable for RVs to about 35 feet in dry weather. From a point on US-89A which is 14 miles west of Cottonwood and 24 miles NE of Prescott turn south and follow NF-104 about 4 miles to the campground. Access through Jerome from the Cottonwood area on SR-89 Alt is not suitable for large RVs due to steep grades, switchbacks, and congestion. It's best to approach from the direction of Prescott.

⌘ TURQUOISE TRIANGLE RV – TRAILER PARK *(Open All Year)*

Reservations: (888) 994-7275
Information: (928) 634-5294
Location: 1.5 Mile SE of Cottonwood, *N 34° 43' 15", W 111° 59' 56", 3,300 Ft*

65 Sites – The sites in this RV park are in 2 large gravel lots behind the office and a tire shop. The drives and parking are all gravel. There are 65 sites, a few of them are pull-thrus. Some of the back-ins and pull-thrus are large enough for 45-foot RVs. The sites all have full hookups including cable TV. There are some trees for shade but no landscaping. A few sites but not all have picnic tables. The office has a modem for internet connection and Wi-Fi is scheduled to be installed. There is a laundry room and a lounge room with a TV. The Reese's Tire Shop has the same ownership and park residents are given a discount on tire purchases. The park is located on the south side of Alt SR-89 about 1.5 miles southeast of Cottonwood.

⌘ RIO VERDE RV PARK *(Open All Year)*

Res and Info: (928) 634-5990, www.rioverdervpark.com
Location: 2 Miles SE of Cottonwood, *N 34° 43' 18", W 111° 59' 22", 3,200 Ft*

76 Sites – This campground is located along the Verde River. The sites here are in 3 locations: the lower campground, the hillside, and the riverfront. All sites except one are back-ins. The one pull-thru would accept a 45 foot RV and there are a few other sites which could take 40 feet RVs, but for most sites the maximum RV size is 35 feet. You should definitely call ahead to check for a suitable site if you're over 35 feet. All are full hookup including cable TV. A computer is provided in the office for internet access and Wi-Fi is provided to the park for no additional charge. The interior roads are gravel and some parking is on gravel and some is on grass. There is a tent camping area on grass near the river at the front of the park. The office sells propane and there's a restaurant next door. The campground is located on the north side of Alt SR-89 about 2 miles southeast of Cottonwood.

⌘ LO LO MAI SPRINGS *(Open All Year)*

Information: (928) 634-4700, www.lolomai.com, lolomaisprings@sedona.net
Location: 10 Miles SW of Sedona, *N 34° 46' 29", W 111° 54' 02", 3,500 Ft*

112 Sites – This is a beautiful park along Oak Creek in a wooded setting. It is a membership park and non-members are allowed to stay here if there is room, but they can not make reservations. The park is usually easy to get into in the winter but from March 1

- Oct 30 it is often full of members. About 52 of the sites are full hookup and the remainder have only water and electricity. The sites have large paved patios, picnic tables, and some have rock fire rings. The sites are almost all back-in and quite a few will take RVs to 40 feet and some will take 45. Tent camping is allowed on the grass near the river. The swimming pool is only open during the summer season. Other amenities at the park include basketball, a dish washing sink, volleyball court, clubhouse, and a store. Wi-Fi is available at some sites in the park. Propane is sold. The price structure here is unusual, it's $30 for a 30-foot RV, then an additional dollar for each additional foot. To reach the campground drive southwest on Alt. SR-89 for some 8 miles. Turn left on Page Springs Road and drive 1.6 miles to the entrance on your left.

🚐 **RANCHO SEDONA RV PARK** *(Open All Year)*
    Reservations: (888) 641-4261
    Information: (928) 282-7255
    Location: Sedona, *N 34° 51' 59", W 111° 45' 35", 4,200 Ft*

84 Sites – Rancho Sedona is the most popular campground for visitors to Sedona. The sites in this park are set under many large sycamore and cottonwood trees along Oak Creek. There are a total of 84 sites, 2 of which are pull-thrus. Quite a few take a 40 foot RV and several will take a 45 footer. The pull-thru sites are 36 feet . All sites except 2 are full hookup. The 2 water and electric sites are for RVs 25 ft and under. The office has a DSL connection for internet and Wi-Fi is provided to the park for free. Reservations are needed, especially for large RVs because all sites will not accommodate 40 footers. Some sites have instant-on telephone. Rates depend on location and run from $29 to $55 per night. A free shuttle to town is provided, but it's only a half-mile or so. Swimming is in the creek. To reach the campground drive south on SR-179 from its intersection with Alternate SR-89 in town. After .3 miles at the 90-degree right turn you want to turn left instead. Drive .25 mile on Schnebly Hill Road and turn left into the entrance of the park.

🚐 **MANZANITA CAMPGROUND** *(Open All Year)*
    Reservations: (877) 444-6777, www.recreation.gov
    Information: (928) 282-4119, www.fs.fed.us/r3/Coconino
    Location: 6 Miles N of Sedona, *N 34° 56' 09", W 111° 44' 41", 4,800 Ft*

18 Sites – The sites in this Coconino National Forest campground sit next to Oak Creek in Oak Creek Canyon. Four of the sites are parallel parking style on pavement and the rest are parking on gravel. These sites are only large enough for tent camping with a small car. Each one has a picnic table and fire pit. The bathrooms are vault toilets. The campground is located about 6 miles north of Sedona on the east side of the highway. It is difficult to see the entrance coming up so take it easy as you approach the turn.

🚐 **BOOTLEGGER CAMPGROUND** *(Open April 1 to Oct 31 - Varies)*
    Information: (928) 282-4119, www.fs.fed.us/r3/Coconino
    Location: 8 Miles N of Sedona, *N 34° 58' 13", W 111° 45' 01", 5,300 Ft*

10 Sites – This Coconino National Forest campground is located in popular Oak Creek

Canyon. The 10 sites in this campground sit above the river. They're very small, only suitable for small cars with tents. There are vault toilets. Swimming in the creek is popular in the summer. Oak Creek is stocked with trout during the summer months so fishing is possible. The campground is located about 8 miles north of Sedona in Oak Creek Canyon.

CAVE SPRINGS CAMPGROUND *(Open April 15 to Oct 15 - Varies)*

Reservations: (877) 444-6777, www.recreation.gov
Information: (928) 282-4119, www.fs.fed.us/r3/Coconino
Location: 11 Miles N of Sedona, *N 35° 00' 02", W 111° 44' 28", 5,300 Ft*

82 Sites – Cave Creek is a Coconino National Forest campground in the Oak Creek Canyon. To reach this campground you must cross the river on a low bridge. It's a large campground with back-in sites long enough for RVs to 35 feet. Space is at a premium here, finding a place to park a tow car would be difficult. The interior roads of the park are paved and most of the parking is on gravel. A few sites have paved parking pads. The sites have picnic tables and fire pits. This campground has hot showers, the bathrooms are vault toilets. Water is available in the park. Swimming is possible in Oak Creek as is fishing. The campground is located about 11 miles north of Sedona, the entrance is on the west side of the highway.

PINE FLAT EAST CAMPGROUND *(Open April 1 to Nov 15 - Varies)*

Information: (928) 282-4119, www.fs.fed.us/r3/Coconino
Location: 12 Miles N of Sedona, *N 35° 00' 43", W 111° 44' 16", 5,500 Ft*

21 Sites – This Coconino National Forest campground is just across Highway 89A from Pine Flat West Campground and Oak Creek. Lack of maneuvering room and uneven terrain (the campground is on a hillside) limits the size of RVs here to about 25 feet, even though some of the sites are longer. The interior roads of this park are paved. Parking is sometimes on gravel and sometimes paved. Every site has a picnic table and either a fire pit or a raised barbecue grill. The bathrooms are vault style. There are no showers. Water is available in the park. The campground is located about 12 miles north of Sedona on the right.

PINE FLAT WEST CAMPGROUND *(March 1 to Nov 15 - Varies)*

Reservations: (877) 444-6777, www.recreation.gov
Information: (928) 282-4119, www.fs.fed.us/r3/Coconino
Location: 12 Miles N of Sedona, *N 35° 00' 43", W 111° 44' 19", 5,500 Ft*

37 Sites – This Coconino National Forest campground is right off Hwy 89A on the west side next to Oak Creek. There are 37 sites. Some of the sites are as long as 35 feet but because of narrow interior roads and trees the campground is appropriate for RVs to only about 30 feet. The interior roads of this park are paved, some but not all parking pads are paved too. Every site has a picnic table and either a fire pit or a raised barbecue grill. The bathrooms are vault style and there are no showers. Water is available and there is a pay telephone at this park. The campground is above the river, swimming and fishing is possible in the river. The campground is located about 12 miles north of Sedona on the left.

SHOW LOW AND PINETOP-LAKESIDE REGION

A string of three towns form the focus of this region: Show Low (population about 8,500), Pinetop and Lakeside (combined population about 4,000). Highway 260 running through these towns is roughly following the **Mogollon Rim** just to the south. This area is surrounded by the **Sitgreaves National Forest**. It's a region of pines and lakes at a altitude of between 6,000 and 7,000 feet. For that reason it's much cooler than the low country to the south and a very comfortable place during the summer.

Because it's cooler and so different than the desert country this is a popular recreation area for Phoenix residents. It's also popular with retirees who spend the winter in snowbird areas at low altitudes and then travel up here for the summer. Access from Phoenix is either via US-60 through Globe, a distance of 169 miles; or via SR-87 and SR-260 through Payson, a distance of 180 miles. Highway 60 is very scenic since it traverses the 1,000 foot deep Salt River Canyon. It's a questionable route for large RVs because it's mostly a two-lane road with quite a few steep ascents and descents. From Pinetop SR-260 continues eastward across the White Mountains to the eastern White Mountain gateways of Springerville and Eager. SR-73 heads south into the White Mountain Apache Reservation.

Supplies are readily available in the area with large grocery stores in both Show Low and Pinetop-Lakeside and a large Walmart in Lakeside.

For outdoors enthusiasts the National Forest and the White Mountains Apache Reservation offer plenty of hiking, fishing, and four-wheeling options. Information is available at the Lakeside Ranger Station and at the Apache Reservation's Hon-Dah Ski and Outdoor Sport next to the Hon-Dah Casino south of Lakeside. See the *Information Resources* listing at the end of this chapter.

The Hon-Dah Casino is located just south of town across the border of the White Mountain Apache Reservation. The campground there is one of three described below.

If you continue south on SR-73 for 23 miles from the casino you'll pass through Whiteriver, administrative center of the White Mountain Apache Reservation, and reach Fort Apache and the **Fort Apache Historical Park**. This fort, established in 1870, later became a boarding school. Next to the fort buildings you'll find the pointed-roofed **Apache Cultural Center and Museum** with exhibits and a shop. It also serves as a visitor center for the historical park. Exhibits about the fort are in a separate building known as General Crook's Cabin. The cultural center staff will sell you an entry pass to tour the historical park and also issue a pass if you would like to tour the nearby **Kinishba Ruins**.

The White mountains to the east of this region are covered in a separate section titled *White Mountains*.

Show Low and Pinetop-Lakeside Region Campgrounds

FOOL HOLLOW LAKE STATE RECREATION AREA *(Open All Year)*
  Information: (928) 537-3680, www.azstateparks.com
  Location: Show Low, *N 34° 15' 48", W 110° 04' 36", 6,300 Ft*

123 sites – This is a beautiful campground with paved back-in sites arranged off paved loops in groves of pines and juniper. Some sites will take RVs to 45 feet. The lake is good

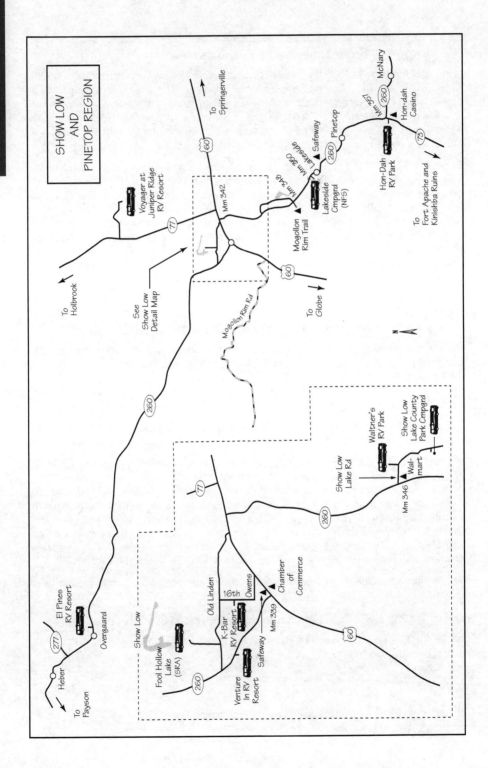

SHOW LOW
AND
PINETOP REGION

for fishing since it's stocked and has a boat ramp, docks, and fish cleaning stations. From the intersection of US-60 and SR-260 just southwest of central Show Low drive 1.9 miles west on SR-260, turn right on Old Linden Road and drive .6 miles, the recreation area entrance is to the left.

VENTURE IN RV RESORT *(Open All Year)*

Res and Info: (928) 537-4443, www.RVontheGo.com
Location: Show Low, *N 34° 15' 05", W 110° 04' 48", 6,400 Ft*

100 Sites – The Venture In is a summer residential park. It's a beautiful modern park with many park models and permanent or semi-permanent residents but there are also many traveler RV sites. It's a 55+ park and has many amenities including a spa, computer room, game room, craft room, and work-out room. The park has about 400 sites with about 100 available for RVs. These are back-ins to 50 feet with big patios. The campground is on the west side of SR-260 about 1.4 mile northwest of its intersection with US-60 in Show Low.

K-BAR RV RESORT *(Open All Year)*

Res and Info: (928) 537-2886
Location: Show Low, *N 34° 15' 07", W 110° 03' 36", 6,400 Ft*

90 Sites – The K-Bar is an older resort but is well maintained. Sites are somewhat irregular and set among pine trees. This is a popular summer park and fills with summer semi-permanent residents with just a few sites set aside for travelers. Sites are full-hookup pull-thrus and back-ins to 60 feet, parking is on gravel and dirt. To reach the park start at the intersection of SR-260 and US-60 in Show Low. Drive northeast on US-60 for .5 mile and turn left onto West Owens Street. Follow Owens west for 7 blocks, a distance of .4 mile and them follow it around a 90 degree right turn to head north on South 16th Street. The park is on the left in another .4 mile.

WALTNER'S RV PARK *(Open May 1 to Oct 15)*

Res and Info: (928) 537-4611
Location: Show Low, *N 34° 12' 20", W 110° 00' 41", 6,600 Ft*

145 Sites – Waltner's is an older campground with nice separated sites in a grove of evergreens. The campground is a popular residential park in the summer and sometimes has sites for travelers. It is a 55+ park. Sites are full-hookup back-ins and pull-thrus to about 40 feet. From the intersection of US-60 and SR-260 in Show Low drive southeast on SR-260 toward Lakeside/Pinetop for 3.9 miles. Turn left on Show Low Lake Road and follow it east for .4 miles. Turn left on S 28th Street and continue for .2 mile, the campground entrance is on the left.

SHOW LOW LAKE COUNTY PARK CAMPGROUND *(Open All Year)*

Reservations: (888) 537-7762
Information: (928) 537-4126
Location: Show Low, *N 34° 11' 35", W 110° 00' 23", 6,600 Ft*

70 Sites – Sites in this county park are in two locations near little Show Low Reservoir. There are a variety of site sizes and shapes but almost all are back-in sites. Sizes vary too, a few sites are as long as 50 feet but most are smaller. Most sites are no hookup sites, just a few have electricity and water. There is a dump station, a visitor center building with the office, restrooms and showers, and a small store. Rental boats are available and there is a boat ramp. From the intersection of US-60 and SR-260 in Show Low drive southeast on SR-260 toward Lakeside/Pinetop for 3.9 miles. Turn left on Show Low Lake Road and follow it east and south for 1.2 miles to the campground.

LAKESIDE CAMPGROUND *(Open May 1 to Sept 31 - Varies)*
Reservations: (877) 444-6777, www.recreation.gov
Information: (928) 333-4301
Location: Lakeside, *N 34° 09' 26", W 109° 58' 36", 6,900 Ft*

82 sites – Unlike most US Forest Service campgrounds this older Sitgreaves NF campground is in an urban location and can handle bigger RVs. There are no hookups but there is a dump station. You'll find it right along SR-260 in the town of Lakeside some 8.1 miles southeast of the intersection of SR-260 with Hwy 77 in Show Low.

HON-DAH RV PARK *(Open All Year)*
Res and Info: (928) 369-7400, www.hon-dah.com
Location: 3 Miles S of Pinetop, *N 34° 04' 47", W 109° 54' 20", 7,000 Ft*

258 sites – This large campground is associated with the Apache casino across the street. Interior streets are gravel and so are parking pads. Pines dot the property. Sites vary in length but many exceed 45 feet so any RV should fit. This is a popular summer campground with many long-term residents. The Hon-Dah Casino does not allow RV camping in the casino parking lot but there is a gravel lot in front of the RV park where casino guests are allowed to park for a fee if the campground has no room. The casino and RV park are located at the junction of SR-260 and SR-73 about three miles south of Pinetop.

VOYAGER AT JUNIPER RIDGE RV RESORT *(Open All Year)*
Location: 10 Miles N of Show Low, *N 34° 21' 33", W 110° 00' 25", 6,000 Ft*

100 Sites – Juniper Ridge is a large development with lots for sale. The RV park is just a small part of the picture. Amenities include a 9 hole golf course, heated pool and spa, and tennis courts. There are about 100 sites set aside for RVs, expect these to be pretty much full during the summer months. It's also a 55+ park. Sites are full hookup and are back-ins and pull-thrus to about 80 feet. Amenities are some distance from the RV parking area, a tow vehicle is very useful here. Juniper Ridge is located 10 miles north of Show Low off SR-77 toward Holbrook. From the intersection of SR-77 and US-60 in Show Low drive north on SR-77 for 7.4 miles. Turn right on White Mountain Lake Road and follow it for 3 miles to the park.

ELK PINES RV RESORT *(Open April 1 to Oct 31)*
Res and Info: (928) 535-3833, www.elkpinesrvresort.com
Location: Overgaard, *N 34° 23' 28", W 110° 32' 17", Alt 6,600 Ft*

68 Sites – This campground sits in tall pines in the town of Overgaard, about 30 miles northwest of Show Low. Sites here are all full-hookup back-ins to about 50 feet. This is a popular summer residential campground but sometimes has space for travelers in the spring and fall and sometimes in the summer. From the intersection of US-60 and SR-260 head northwest toward Payson. The campground is in Overgaard, a distance of 31.2 miles.

SIERRA VISTA

Sierra Vista (population about 41,000) is the largest population center in Arizona southeast of Tucson. The army's **Fort Huachuca**, with a population of about 10,000, is a big part of the town. Fort Huachuca dates from the Apache Indian wars in 1877 and the very good **Fort Huachuca Museum** documents its long and interesting history. Also on the fort grounds is the Army Intelligence Museum which shows off the fort's current activities as an intelligence school and testing center for electronics.

Just east of town is the San Pedro River Valley. Forty miles of the upper river valley are included in the **San Pedro Riparian National Conservation Area**. This is a rare desert

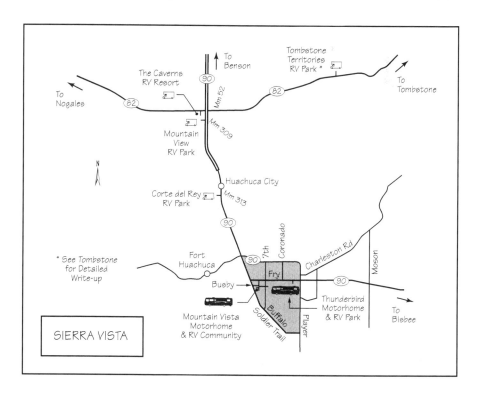

riverside ecosystem and is reported to be home to over 350 bird species, it is called by some the world's best birding area. Primary access is at San Pedro House on SR-90 between Sierra Vista and Bisbee.

The **Huachuca Mountains**, southwest of town are partly on the fort and partly the Coronado National Forest. The high peaks are in the **Miller Peak Wilderness** and the **Coronado National Memorial** is at the southern end of the range near the Mexico border.

In small vehicles you can access several canyons on the north and east faces of the mountains either from the fort or from SR-92 on the east side of the range south of Sierra Vista. One interesting destination is the **Ramsey Canyon Preserve**, run by the Nature Conservancy. It's a sanctuary for hummingbirds with a visitor center, trail, and bird observation area in Ramsey Canyon. The best time to visit to see hummingbirds is summer, turn off SR-92 and head west about six miles south of Sierra Vista.

The **Coronado National Memorial** honors the Spanish explorer Francisco Vásquez de Coronado who came through this area in 1540 searching for the Seven Cities of Gold. There is a visitor center and hiking trails. There is also a gravel road that crosses Montezuma Pass and connects with more gravel routes to Sonoita, Patagonia and Nogales. To reach the memorial drive south from Sierra Vista on SR-92 for 10 miles. Turn right at the signed entrance road and drive another 5 miles on paved roads to the visitor center.

Sierra Vista Campgrounds

🚐 **THUNDERBIRD MOTORHOME AND RV PARK** *(Open All Year)*
   Res and Info: (520) 458-2794
   Location: Sierra Vista, *N 31° 33' 14", W 110° 15' 51", 4,600 Ft*

113 Sites – This is an urban park near the center of Sierra Vista. Sites are both back-in and pull-thrus to 60 feet with parking on gravel. It's in central Sierra Vista on E Fry Blvd between S Calle Portal and Avenida Escuela. This is 2.5 miles east of the intersection of Buffalo Soldier Trail and Fry Blvd at the Fort Huachuca gate.

🚐 **MOUNTAIN VISTA MOTORHOME AND RV COMMUNITY** *(Open All Year)*
   Res and Info: (877) 452-0500
   Location: Sierra Vista, *N 31° 32' 49", W 110° 18' 00", 4,600 Ft*

85 Sites – Sites here are full-hookup back-ins to 80 feet. From the intersection of Buffalo Soldier Trail and Fry Blvd drive east .3 mile. Turn right on Carmichael Ave and drive south .6 mile. The entrance is on the right.

THEODORE ROOSEVELT LAKE

Theodore Roosevelt Lake, usually just called Roosevelt Lake, is a 23 mile long reservoir behind Theodore Roosevelt Dam on the Salt River. The lake is located about 75 miles east of the Apache Junction suburb of Phoenix (via Globe) and is a popular fishing and water sports destination. The lake is entirely within the Tonto National Forest, there are many campgrounds located around it. Downstream the Salt River flows through several more reservoirs and is paralleled by the *Apache Trail*, see that section for more information. Water levels fluctuate dramatically in the lake, you may wish to check with the

FISHING AT THEODORE ROOSEVELT LAKE

Forest Service visitor center in Roosevelt to see which campgrounds and boat ramps have water access before choosing your final destination campground. To stay at the campgrounds you must have a Tonto Pass. It costs $6 per motorized vehicle (plus $4 for boats) and is the only fee collected for staying at the campgrounds. You must buy it at the ranger station or from various commercial vendors in the area.

Tonto National Monument overlooks the south side of the lake. It was created to encompass two Salado Indian ruins. There is a visitor center and trails to the two ruins. Easiest to visit is the Lower Cliff Dwelling although the trail does have 350 steps. The Upper Cliff Dwelling is a three mile round trip hike with a ranger, tours are only conducted from November through April.

Theodore Roosevelt Lake Campgrounds

🚐 **BACHELOR'S COVE DISPERSED CAMPING** *(Open All Year)*
    Information: (928) 467-3200, www.fs.fed.us/r3/tonto
    Location: Theodore Roosevelt Lake, *N 33° 42' 48", W 111° 12' 20", 2,100 Ft*

Scattered Boondocking – Bachelor's Cove is a Tonto National Forest dispersed camping area on the shore of the lake. Staying here requires the Tonto Pass, see the introduction to this section. It's a small area next to a cove that actually penetrates under the highway so that parking is on the west side of the road. The parking area size depends upon the water level. The only amenities are portable toilets. There is no potable water. The camping area is 4.3 miles north of the intersection of the Apache Trail (SR-88) and SR-188 on the west shore of the lake.

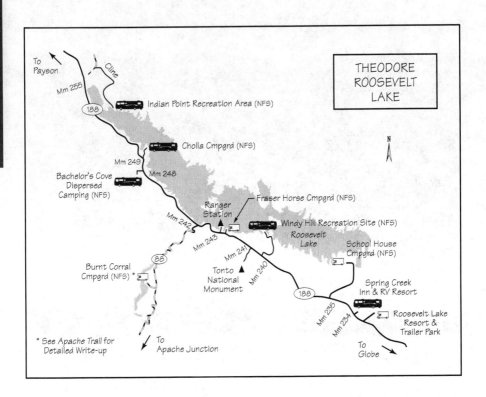

CHOLLA CAMPGROUND *(Open All Year)*

Information: (928) 467-3200, www.fs.fed.us/r3/tonto
Location: Theodore Roosevelt Lake, *N 33° 43' 29", W 111° 12' 17", 2,200 Ft*

206 Sites – This Tonto National Forest campground has 188 RV sites and 18 tent sites on 6 loops. Staying here requires the Tonto Pass, see the introduction to this section. Wheelchair accessible flush toilets are located in every loop and 3 bathroom/shower buildings are centrally located. Most sites are back-ins some to as long as 60 feet, and a few are pull-off style parking. The pull-off sites are not good for RVs with slides. All sites have a blue metal-roofed picnic table and a fire pit. The sites are widely spaced and separated by small trees, cactus, and other desert vegetation. A boat ramp is to the right as you enter the park and there is a fish cleaning station. From Oct 1 - March 31 visitors can stay 6 months - other times only 14 days. The dump station is across Hwy 188. This is the largest solar-powered campground in the US. The camping area is 5.1 miles north of the intersection of the Apache Trail (SR-88) and SR-188 on the west shore of the lake.

INDIAN POINT RECREATION AREA *(Open All Year)*

Information: (928) 467-3200, www.fs.fed.us/r3/tonto
Location: Theodore Roosevelt Lake, *N 33° 46' 10", W 111° 14' 33", 2,100 Ft*

50 Sites and Scattered Boondocking – Indian Point is a large campground away from the

main highway on the northeast shore of the lake. Staying here requires the Tonto Pass, see the introduction to this section. As you enter this recreation site to the right is a camping area which has formal RV sites. The sites are both back-in and pull- thrus. Some have parking on gravel and others have paved parking, they have fire pits. Further in to the recreation area there are several big gravel lots with room for many RVs for dispersed camping. The roads between these lots is gravel. There are no tables, but there are rock fire rings. Both camping areas have vault toilets. There's also boat ramp here, RVs are not allowed to camp in the paved ramp lot. From the intersection of the Apache Trail (SR-88) and SR-188 on the west shore of the lake drive north for 9.8 miles and turn right on Cline Blvd. Follow it southeast for some 6 miles to the campground entrance.

SPRING CREEK INN AND RV RESORT *(Open All Year)*

Res and Info: (928) 467-2888, www.rooseveltlake.com, fish@rooseveltlake.com
Location: Theodore Roosevelt Lake, *N 33° 36' 10", W 111° 00' 22", 2,300 Ft*

81 Sites – Even though this park is mostly occupied by monthly tenants, it is very nice and clean and obviously well run. There are a combination of sites, back-in and pull-thrus to 70 feet. All sites have full hookups and have a paved patio. The park has a nice clubhouse with a big rock fireplace. The RV park is part of a resort which also includes a motel. Out front is a gas station which also has a store and a restaurant. This park is full both winter and summer and reservations are necessary. Rates are higher in summer. One reason for the popularity of this campground is that the other campgrounds in the area, forest service campgrounds, limit generator use in the evening. That means no air conditioning at night, almost essential in summer. From the intersection of the Apache Trail (SR-88) and SR-188 on the west shore of the lake drive south for 14.8 miles to the campground.

WINDY HILL RECREATION SITE *(Open All Year)*

Information: (928) 467-3200, www.fs.fed.us/r3/tonto
Location: Theodore Roosevelt Lake, *N 33° 39' 00", W 111° 05' 09", 2,300 Ft*

347 Sites – The 347 sites in this Tonto National Forest campground are located off 9 loops. Interior roads are paved and parking is on gravel. The sites are a combination of back-ins and many pull-thrus to 70 feet. The sites are mostly side-by-side parking without a lot of separation between sites, just a small tree. Each site has a blue metal-roofed picnic table and a fire pit. Wheelchair accessible toilets are located in all the loops and there are 4 centrally located shower/bathroom buildings. There is an amphitheater and a boat ramp. Several miles of hiking trails leave from the park. Staying here requires the Tonto Pass, see the introduction to this section. This campground allows long term stays of up to 6 months for the period October 1 - March 31. Outside that period the stay is limited to 14 days.

TOMBSTONE

Tombstone (population about 2,000) and its Boot Hill have a prominent place in the history of the west. Who hasn't heard of the gunfight at the OK Corral where Wyatt Earp, Doc Holliday, and Virgil and Morgan Earp shot it out with the Clantons and McLauries?

ARIZONA

The historical Tombstone was a mining town, the ground under the town is honeycombed with mineshafts. In the early 1880's the population was as high as 10,000 – until the mines flooded in 1886.

Today Tombstone is a tourist town. The 1881 gunfight and others are recreated in various locations, sometimes several times a day. **Tombstone Courthouse State Historic Park** in the center of town documents the history. The **Bird Cage Theater** is an old dance hall and brothel that you can tour. You can also visit the **OK Corral and Boot Hill**. The **Crystal Palace Saloon** and **Big Nose Kate's** are still open for business.

With such a tourist orientation it won't surprise you to hear that the town hosts many events during the year. Among them are **Territorial Days** in March, **Wyatt Earp Days** on the Memorial Day Weekend, **Fourth of July in Tombstone**, **Vigilante Days** on the second full weekend in August, **Rendezvous of Gunfighters** on Labor Day, **Helldorado Days** on the third weekend of October, **Tombstone Western Music Festival** on Veteran's Day weekend, and the **Clanton Gang Reunion** sometime in November.

Tombstone Campgrounds

WELLS FARGO RV PARK *(Open All Year)*
Reservations: (800) 269-8266, www.wellsfargorv.com
Information: (520) 457-3966, camp@wellsfargorv.com
Location: Tombstone, *N 31° 42' 50", W 110° 04' 06", 4,500 Ft*

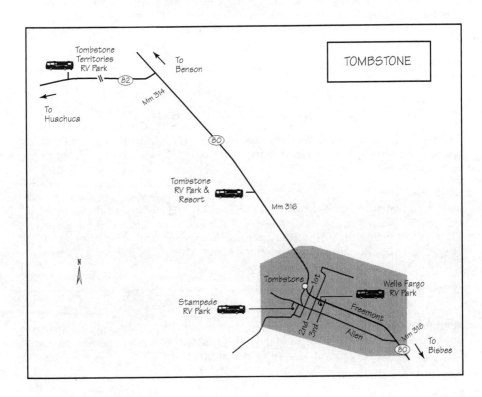

52 Sites – This park is so convenient you may get caught in the gunfire. It sits on the corner of Fremont Street, Tombstone's main street, and N 2ⁿᵈ St. There are back-in and pull-thru sites to 75 feet and tent campers are welcomed. The office has a small store which sells RV parts. A data port is available in the office for internet access. There is also a laundry and a pay telephone.

STAMPEDE RV PARK *(Open All Year)*
Res and Info: (520) 457-3738
Location: Tombstone, *N 31° 42' 50", W 110° 04' 19", 4,500 Ft*

51 Sites – The sites in this campground are in 2 gravel lots separated by a city street. There are pull-thrus and back-ins as long as 60 feet. The sites all have full hookups including cable TV. Parking is on gravel but the sites have green paved patios. One building houses the bathrooms and laundry and has a pay telephone in the front. The park is within easy walking distance of downtown. Approaching Tombstone from the north continue straight where SR-80 makes the 90-degree left onto Freemont St. Go one block, turn right and you'll see the campground a half block ahead on the left.

TOMBSTONE RV PARK AND RESORT *(Open All Year)*
Res and Info: (800) 348-3829, www.tombstone-rv.com, russjenn@msn.com
Location: 1 Mile NE of Tombstone, *N 31° 43' 49", W 110° 04' 48", 4,300 Ft*

86 Sites – The Tombstone has back-in and pull-thru sites to 45 feet. There are also tent sites as well as a few cabins and some motel rooms. The sites are separated by trees and have picnic tables. Almost all RV sites are full hookup with cable TV. A modem is provided for internet access and Wi-Fi is provided to parts of the park for free. There is a swimming pool which is open and heated May - October. The office has a good size store and ice and propane are sold. A pay telephone and laundry are available, campfire rings are available upon request. Reservations and credit cards are accepted. The campground is located one mile north of Tombstone on the west side of SR-80.

TOMBSTONE TERRITORIES RV PARK *(Open All Year)*
Res and Info: (877) 316-6714, (520) 457-2584, ttrvpark@earthlink.net
Location: 11 Miles NW of Tombstone, *N 31° 43' 20", W 110° 13' 25", 4,000 Ft*

102 Sites – This campground is some distance from town but is a nice park. It's a big rig park with all pull-thru sites to 80 feet. There's a pool and a spa. From Tombstone drive north on SR-80 for three miles. Turn left on SR-82 and drive 8 miles to the park, it's on the right.

TUBA CITY

Tuba City (population about 8,000) is located on the Navajo Reservation and serves as the supply and administrative center for the western section of the reservation. It's also a

ARIZONA

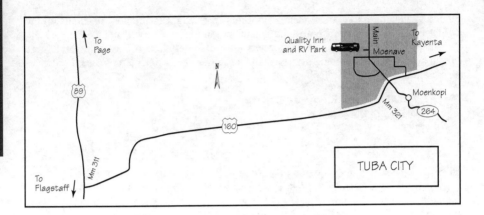

supply center for the Hopi Reservation, 45 miles to the southeast. In fact, the town was named for a Hopi chief by the Mormon settlers who founded it in 1877.

In Tuba city you might visit the **Trading Post** to shop for Navajo crafts. Another nearby attraction is the dinosaur tracks just off US-160 about five miles west of town near Mile 316. Guides are available at the tracks but not necessary, kiosks sell crafts and jewelry.

Tuba City and its RV park make a good place to stay while visiting Navajo National Monument if you have a large RV since the campground at the monument can't take big RVs. It's 62 miles from Tuba City to the monument.

Tuba City Campground

QUALITY INN AND RV PARK *(Open All Year)*
Res and Info: (928) 283-4545, (800) 644-8383
Location: Tuba City, *N 36° 07' 52", W 111° 14' 26", 4,900 Ft*

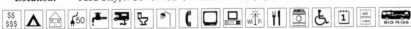

30 Sites – This campground behind a Quality Inn has 24 full hookup RV sites and 6 tent sites. RV sites are back-ins and pull-thrus to 60 feet. Large cottonwood trees separate the sites and provide good shade. The tent sites are nice and have a brown wooden fence separating them. All sites (including the tents) have a paved patio and picnic table. A central area near the restroom/laundry building has raised barbecue grills. The motel out front has Wi-Fi in the lobby, (Wi-Fi not available at the sites). A computer is also provided in the lobby for other internet access. The Hogan Restaurant is associated with the RV Park and Quality Inn and RV guests get a 10% discount. Reservations are only taken the day of your stay and in the summer may be necessary, so call early. In Tuba City from the intersection of US-160 and SR-264 drive north on BIA-101 (Main St.) for 1 mile, the motel is on the left with the campground behind it.

TUCSON

Tucson (population 900,000 for the metro area) is Arizona's second most populous city. It has an interesting Hispanic history, and has lots to see and do, both in the city and in the surrounding area.

ARIZONA

Central Tucson has a lot of historical buildings and two excellent museums: the **Tucson Museum of Art and Historical Block** and the **Arizona Historical Society Museum**. Take the time to go downtown and look around, it's not all museums and history. There are also parks, restaurants, and shops.

Tucson has the largest private collection of historical aircraft in the country, second only to the Smithsonian. The **Pima Air and Space Museum** has over 250 aircraft on display. It's about 12 miles south of downtown. Also extremely interesting are bus tours of **AMARC** where over 5,000 surplus aircraft are stored on 2,600 acres. Tours leave from the Pima Air and Space Museum. And finally, there's the **Titan Missile Museum** where an actual Titan II ICBM, still in its silo, can be visited.

In the high desert **Saguaro National Park West** to the west of Tucson there are a couple of attractions that make a good day trip. The **Arizona-Sonora Desert Museum** is one of the best living natural history museums around, and the **Old Tucson Studios** are a western movie set with lots of activities set up for visitors.

For more outdoor activities consider a trip northeast of Tucson. **Sabino Canyon** has a visitor center at the mouth of the canyon and then shuttle busses that travel a 4-mile road up into the canyon. You can picnic, hike, or swim. The birding is considered excellent. In nearby **Bear Canyon** you can hike to the Seven Falls. After that, if you're ready for a drive, how about the 25-mile **Catalina Highway/Sky Island Scenic Byway** up Mt Lemon to Summerhaven. Several campgrounds are located along this highway, some are described below.

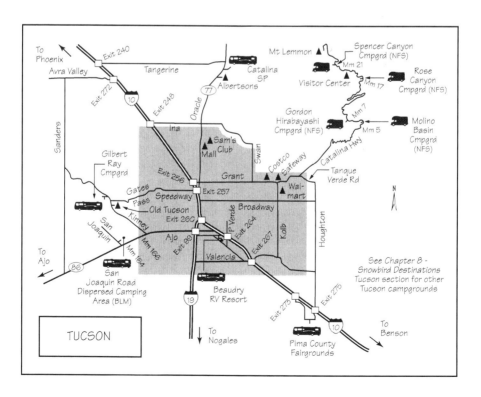

South of town there are good day-trip destinations too. First stop might be **Mission San Xavier del Bac** about ten miles south of Tucson. This colonial-era Spanish mission church, also known as the White Dove of the Desert, dates from 1700.

Kitt Peak Observatory, 6,875 feet high, has many telescopes of various kinds. There's a visitor center and self-guided tour. It's about 55 miles down here from Tucson, but it's paved all the way. Don't bring your RV though, use a smaller vehicle.

For some RVers one of the big events of the year is Tucson's Gem, Mineral, and Fossil Showcase which last two weeks in late January and early February and ends with the three day **Tucson Gem and Mineral Show**.

For more about Tucson, and particularly snowbird winter RV parks, see the *Snowbird Destinations* chapter of this book. Many of the campgrounds listed in that chapter also have spaces for travelers, our charts in that chapter give overnight rates for the ones that do.

Tucson Campgrounds

BEAUDRY RV RESORT AND RALLY PARK *(Open All Year)*
    Res and Info: (888) 500-0789, www.beaudryrvresort.com
    Location: Tucson, *N 32° 09' 33", W 110° 55' 34", 2,600 Ft*

400 Sites – Beaudry, one of the largest RV dealers in Arizona, has built a nice big-rig RV park right next to their sales and RV servicing facilities in Tucson. There's also a Camping World, pretty handy. Sites here are back-ins and pull-thrus to 65 feet. Amenities include a pool and spa, restaurant, instant-on phone connections, and free Wi-Fi in a central location. A few luxury sites even have their own spas. From I-10 take Exit 264 B. Go north just .1 mile on N Palo Verde Rd, turn left on Irving Rd and drive .5 mile. Turn left on Country Club and drive south for .3 miles, the entrance is on the left.

CATALINA STATE PARK *(Open All Year)*
    Information: (520) 628-5798, www.azstateparks.com
    Location: 10 Miles NE of Tucson, *N 32° 25' 02", W 110° 55' 50", 2,600 Ft*

120 Sites – Catalina is well-known as a great desert campground with lots of hiking possibilities. It's popular and, unfortunately, you can't make reservations so getting in can be problematic on weekends or even during the week during the winter season. There are actually 2 side by side loops. Campground A, the older loop, has 48 sites. Half of these sites have electric and water hookups and the other half are dry. These sites are mostly back-ins but a few are pull-thru and many will take 45 foot RVs. Campground B is the newer section and was just opened in October of 2005. It has 72 sites which all have electric and water hookups and are a combination of back-in and pull-thru sites large enough for any size RV. All sites have picnic tables and raised barbecue grills. Ground fires are not allowed. Both campgrounds have flush toilets and showers. The dump station and a pay telephone are near the entrance. Camping fees are paid at a manned ranger station and credit cards are accepted. Easiest access is probably from I-10 northwest of town. Take Exit 240, signed as Tangerine Rd, and head east. After 12 miles the road T's at SR-77. Turn south and the park entrance is on the left in .8 mile.

ARIZONA

TENT CAMPING AT THE GILBERT RAY CAMPGROUND

GILBERT RAY CAMPGROUND *(Open All Year)*
Information: (520) 883-4200 or (520) 877-6000
Location: 10 Miles W of Tucson, *N 32° 13' 12", W 111° 08' 42", 2,600 Ft*

140 Sites – Gilbert Ray is a county campground in a spectacular desert setting. Sites are back-ins, some to about 45 feet. Access roads are paved but sites are gravel. Restrooms have flush toilets but no showers, there is a dump station. A trail leads from the campground to the Old Tucson theme park. Easiest access, particularly for large RVs, is to leave I-19 south of Tucson at Exit 99 (marked Ajo Way) and drive west on SR-86 (W Ajo Way). After 5 miles turn right on S Kinney Road. This paved but narrow road leads you 5.9 miles to an intersection, turn left here and in just .5 mile you'll see the campground entrance on the left.

PIMA COUNTY FAIRGROUND *(Open All Year)*
Information: (520) 762-9100, www.swfair.com, office@Swfair.com
Location: 8 Miles E of Tucson, *N 32° 02' 45", W 110° 46' 57", 3,000 Ft*

400 Sites – There is RV camping in several areas in this large fairgrounds. As you enter there are 5 rows with 28 back-in sites on each row off to the right. These sites have water and 15-amp electric hookups with parking on dirt. To the left in this lot are 22 back-in sites with 20/30/50 amp electric and water with parking on grass or dirt. There are several additional areas with RV hookups on the grounds and two dump stations. Restroom in two locations have showers. The office is in the middle of the fairgrounds, you'll have to

wander a bit to find it. Using the dump station costs $5 and there are daily, weekly, and monthly rates. Campsites are not available during the fair which is held the last ten days or so of April.

🚐 SAN JOAQUIN RD BLM DISPERSED CAMPING AREA *(Open All Year)*

Information: (520) 258-7200
Location: 9 Miles SW of Tucson, *N 32° 09' 21", W 111° 06' 57", 2,400 Ft*

Scattered Boondocking – See the introductory material in this chapter about the BLM 14-Day camping areas. This one isn't very large but there is still room for dozens of RVs. It's particularly handy for two reasons. First, it's near Tucson. Second, it's over 25 miles from the 14-Day areas near Ajo and Why so it's easy to ping-pong between them if you're fond of this area in the winter. Easiest access, particularly for large RVs, is to leave I-19 south of Tucson at Exit 99 (marked Ajo Way) and drive west on SR-86 (W Ajo Way). The area is on the right in 8 miles, in the northeast quadrant formed by SR-86 and S San Joaquin Road.

🚐 MOLINO BASIN CAMPGROUND *(Open Nov 1 to April 25 - Varies)*

Information: (520) 749-8700
Location: 11 Miles NE of Tucson, *N 32° 20' 14", W 110° 41' 28", 4,500 Ft*

37 Sites – Molino Basin Campground is a small Coronado National Forest campground. Most sites here are for tent campers, many are walk-in sites. Just three sites are designated RV sites, a sign at the entrance to the campground limits trailers to 22 feet. Some sites will take much larger RVs but maneuvering room is limited. Each sites has a picnic table, fire pit, a raised barbecue grill, and a metal storage box. Picnic tables are either ramada or tree shaded and the interior roads are newly paved. There is no water. Note that this campground has a reverse season, it's open in the winter and not the summer because it's located low on the mountain where summer temperatures are high. To reach the campground follow the Tanque Verde Road east to the E Catalina Highway. Heading northeast, this highway becomes the Mt Lemon Highway. Some 10.3 miles from the turn onto the E Catalina Highway the campground is on the left.

🚐 GORDON HIRABAYASHI CAMPGROUND *(Open All Year)*

Information: (520) 749-8700
Location: 13 Miles NE of Tucson, *N 32° 20' 21", W 110° 43' 03", 5,000 Ft*

11 Sites – This is a small Coronado Forest National campground. Sites are off one road with a turnaround at the end, it's good for RVs to 30 feet. There is no water. To reach the campground follow the Tanque Verde Road east to the E. Catalina Highway. Heading northeast, this highway becomes the Mt Lemon Highway. Some 12.5 miles from the turn onto the E Catalina Highway the campground is on the left.

ROSE CANYON CAMPGROUND *(Open April 15 to Oct 15 - Varies)*
Reservations: (877) 444-6777, www.recreation.gov
Information: (520) 749-8700
Location: 22 Miles NE of Tucson, *N 32° 23' 42", W 110° 41' 30", 7,100 Ft*

74 Sites – Rose Canyon is a larger Coronado National Forest campground with sites set in pines. Interior roads are dirt and access is via a steep grade. The Forest Service recommends a maximum RV size of 22 feet. Potable water is available. Trout fishing and hiking is possible at Rose Lake, but not swimming or boating. To reach the campground follow the Tanque Verde Road east to the E Catalina Highway. Heading northeast, this highway becomes the Mt Lemon Highway. Some 21.5 miles from the turn onto the E Catalina Highway the campground is on the left.

SPENCER CANYON CAMPGROUND *(Open April 15 to Oct 15 - Varies)*
Information: (520) 749-8700
Location: 26 Miles NE of Tucson, *N 32° 25' 06", W 110° 44' 17", 8,000 Ft*

60 Sites – Spencer Canyon is a Coronado National Forest campground set high on the mountain in the pines. Great for a summer camping trip! Sites are small and only suitable for RVs to 22 feet or so. There's good hiking in the area. To reach the campground follow the Tanque Verde Road east to the E Catalina Highway. Heading northeast, this highway becomes the Mt Lemon Highway. Some 26 miles from the turn onto the E Catalina Highway the campground is on the left.

WHITE MOUNTAINS

Arizona's White Mountains rise above the Mogollon Rim near the eastern edge of the state. They're bordered on the west by the White Mountain Apache Indian Reservation and on the east by the Coronado Trail. Most access to campgrounds in the White Mountains is from SR-260 to the north as the highway crosses between the two gateways: Pinetop-Lakeside and Springerville/Eagar. For information about the Pinetop-Lakeside gateway see our *Show Low and Pinetop-Lakeside Region* section. For information about the Springerville/Eager gateway see our *Coronado Trail* section.

The White Mountains destination campgrounds listed below are all in either the Apache National Forest or the White Mountain Apache Indian Reservation. Few of these campgrounds have hookups or great amenities but this is a very popular destination area because it has very pleasant summer weather and lots of unspoiled country.

The **White Mountain Apache Indian Reservation** has done a great deal to develop the portion of the White Mountains inside the reservation for recreational uses. You'll find that reservoirs have been created for fishing; also roads, campgrounds, and even a ski area. You do not need state licenses for fishing, hunting, or boating on the reservations. You do, however, need permits from the reservation. These are generally sold at stores on the reservation or from stores in the surrounding area.

The **Sunrise Ski Area** is the state's largest. There's also a cross-country ski center nearby called the **Sunrise Sports Center** as well as two nearby campgrounds. It's located

ARIZONA

off SR-260 about 25 miles east of Pinetop. Campgrounds in the area are Sunrise Campground and Sunrise RV Park, see below.

The little town of **Greer** (population 150) is a popular mountain get-a-way. It's just outside the eastern border of the reservation along the headwaters of the Little Colorado River and has three campgrounds either in town or nearby. See the write-up for the Mountain Aire RV Park below for instructions about driving to Greer.

Big Lake, one of the largest lakes in the area, is a popular fishing lake. There are four different Apache National Forest campgrounds, they're listed separately below.

White Mountains Campgrounds

BIG BEAR LAKE CAMPGROUND *(Open May 15 to Sept 15)*

Information: (928) 338-4385
Location: White Mountain Apache Indian Reservation,
N 34° 03' 22", W 109° 43' 35", 7,900 Ft

40 Sites – Big Bear Lake is stocked twice a month in spring and summer with rainbow and Apache trout. It's an 18 acre lake. The campground here is off a large loop in pines next to the lake. Sites are very large, most are back-ins. Some sites have picnic tables and rock fire rings. The campground sometimes has potable water and there is a nice boat ramp. To reach the campground follow SR-260 to Mile 369.3 which is 8 miles east of McNary and 26 miles west of Eagar. Drive north on the gravel access road for .2 mile.

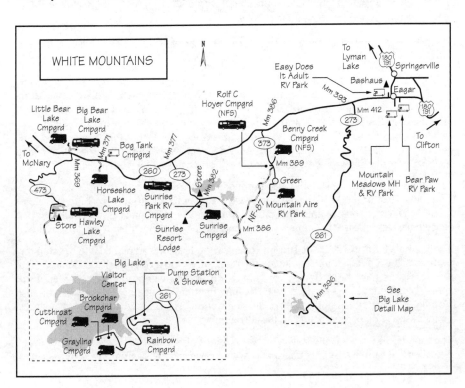

Take the right fork at the Y and you'll be at the campground in another .3 mile. Camping permits are not available on-site and must be purchased before you arrive. They are available at McNary, Honda, and Sunrise store.

LITTLE BEAR LAKE CAMPGROUND *(Open May 15 to Sept 15)*
Information: (928) 338-4385
Location: White Mountain Apache Indian Reservation,
                 N 34° 03' 40", W 109° 44' 00", 7,800 Ft

20 Sites – Little Bear, like Big Bear, is a popular fishing lake. It too is stocked twice a month and produces rainbows, Apache trout, brown trout and sunfish. At 15 acres the lake is a little smaller than Big Bear, and so is the campground. There are about 20 sites and due to narrow roads, a tough turnaround, and small sites the practical RV size limit here is about 30 feet. To reach the campground follow SR-260 to Mile 369.3 which is 8 miles east of McNary and 26 miles west of Eagar. Drive north on the gravel access road for .2 mile. Take the left fork at the Y and you'll be at the campground in another .4 mile. Camping permits are not available on-site and must be purchased before you arrive. They are available at McNary, Honda, and Sunrise store.

HAWLEY LAKE CAMPGROUND *(Open All Year Weather Permitting)*
Information: (928) 338-4385
Location: White Mountain Apache Indian Reservation,
                 N 33° 59' 28", W 109° 45' 32", 8,100 Ft

100 Sites – Hawley Lake is a 260-acre lake that was formed by damming Trout Creek. This was done to create a fishing lake, the first of several of these lakes created on the reservation to attract campers and fishermen to the area. Fishing is considered good, mostly rainbow trout are caught. Hawley Lake Campground is on a rise to the south of the lake with the sites in evergreens. Sites are not well defined, some have picnic tables and metal fire grates but others do not. People park pretty much where they want. You'll see really big rigs in here but drivers have to be very careful when parking. Water is available but not at individual sites. Restrooms are portable toilets. A small store is located about a half-mile beyond the campground. That's where you pay for your camping permit, they also have limited groceries, a restaurant, gas, and a dump station. To reach the campground follow SR-260 to Mile 369.5 which is 8 miles east of McNary and 26 miles west of Eagar. Drive south on Road 473 for 10 paved miles to the campground.

HORSESHOE LAKE CAMPGROUND *(Open May 15 to Sept 15)*
Information: (928) 338-4385
Location: White Mountain Apache Indian Reservation,
                 N 34° 02' 16", W 109° 41' 21", 8,100 Ft

100 Sites – Horseshoe is another reservoir lake created for the fishing. It's within a mile of SR-260 so even in winter people come out here to fish – through the ice. It's a 120-acre lake and is known for its trout fishing. There is a store here with a ramp, dock, and dump station but recently it has been closed and the dump station locked. Sites here are mostly back-ins in trees with some tables and fire pits of various kinds. Large RVs camp here but maneuvering room is limited. There are water faucets and vault toilets. The access road

to the lake is near Mile 370.9 of SR-260. This is 9 miles east of McNary and 25 miles west of Eagar. The gravel access road goes south past the store to the campground. If the store is closed you'll have to have a camping permit when you arrive, they are available at McNary, Honda, and Sunrise store.

SUNRISE CAMPGROUND *(Open May 15 to Sept 15)*
Information: (928) 338-4385
Location: White Mountain Apache Indian Reservation,
N 33° 59' 51", W 109° 33' 07", 9,300 Ft

150 Sites – Sunrise Lake is another popular trout lake on the reservation. It's a big one, about 890 acres. Nearby is the Sunrise Ski Area and two campgrounds. See below for information about the small Sunrise Park RV Campground. Sunrise Campground is a typical reservation no-hookup campground. It is not located at the lake, it's to the south. Site size and narrow roads make 35 feet the practical RV size limit here, and even then caution is essential. Picnic tables and fire rings are provided. Restrooms are outhouses and portable toilets. Water faucets are scattered around the campground. The Sunrise Resort Lodge is about 1.4 miles from the campground, the Sunrise store a half-mile closer. It has basic grocery items, gas, a phone, and sells reservation camping and fishing permits. There's a restaurant at the lodge. The access road to the campground is near Mile 377.5 of SR-260. That is 16 miles east of McNary and 18 miles west of Eagar. Drive south for 4.1 miles and take the first right past the store. The campground entrance road is on the left in another 100 yards.

SUNRISE PARK RV CAMPGROUND *(Open All Year)*
Information: (928) 735-7669
Location: White Mountain Apache Indian Reservation,
N 33° 59' 54", W 109° 33' 12", 9,200 Ft

20 Sites – This campground is nothing more than back-in sites in a lot next to the road near the entrance to the Sunrise Lake Campground. Any size RV will fit but they must be self-contained since there are no restrooms except the portable toilets up in the campground, and they're beyond useful walking range. There are no water hookups either. The Sunrise Store is close by, that's where you check in. The access road to the campground is near Mile 377.5 of SR-260. That is 16 miles east of McNary and 18 miles west of Eagar. Drive south for 4.1 miles and take the first right past the store. The campground entrance road is on the left in another 100 yards.

MOUNTAIN AIRE RV PARK *(Open May 15 to Oct 15)*
Res and Info: (928) 735-7524, (928) 425-3608, www.mountainairerv.com
Location: Greer, *N 34° 00' 16", W 109° 27' 34", 8,300 Ft*

32 Sites – The Mountain Aire is located at the southern end of Greer. It's suitable only for RVs to 34 feet. There are restrooms and a recreation hall. Quite a few spaces are rented seasonally and reservations are a very good idea since RV parks with hookups in this area are scarce. From SR-260 near Mile 385.7 drive south on SR-373. This is 24 miles east of McNary and 10 miles west of Eagar. You'll enter Greer at about 4 miles, the campground is on the left at 4.5 miles.

ROLFE C HOYER CAMPGROUND *(Open May 15 to Sept 30 - Varies)*

Reservations: (877) 444-6777, www.recreation.gov
Information: (928) 333-4301
Location: 1 Mile N of Greer, *N 34° 02' 03", W 109° 27' 13", 8,300 Ft*

100 Sites – This large Apache National Forest Campground is modern and popular. It's set in pines and off six loops. Interior roads are paved and so are the sites. They're all back-ins, some as long as 60 feet. Showers are at a building near the entrance, there is an entrance station. The campground is located about 1 mile north of Greer. From SR-260 near Mile 385.7 drive south on SR-373. This is 24 miles east of McNary and 10 miles west of Eagar. The campground is on the right at 3.1 miles.

BENNY CREEK CAMPGROUND *(Open May 15 to Sept 30 - Varies)*

Reservations: (877) 444-6777, www.recreation.gov
Information: (928) 333-4301
Location: 1 Mile N of Greer, *N 34° 02' 19", W 109° 27' 16", 8,300 Ft*

26 Sites – Benny Creek Campground is another Apache National Forest campground just down the road from the big Rolfe C Hoyer Campground. It's older and not quite so fancy. It's a more open campground (fewer trees) and sits at the side of a meadow. Sites here are smaller, some OK for RVs to about 35 feet. Most are back-ins although there are a few that are pull-offs along side of the access road. The campground is located about 1 mile north of Greer. From SR-260 near Mile 385.7 drive south on SR-373. This is 24 miles east of McNary and 10 miles west of Eagar. The campground is on the left at 2.9 miles.

BIG LAKE – RAINBOW CAMPGROUND *(Open May 15 to Sept 30 - Varies)*

Reservations: (877) 444-6777, www.recreation.gov
Information: (928) 333-4301
Location: 22 Miles SW of Eagar, *N 33° 52' 41", W 109° 24' 18", 9,100 Ft*

153 Sites – This is the largest of the campgrounds in the Apache National Forest's Big Lake Recreation Area. It is also the one suitable for large RVs. The sites here are both back-ins and pull-thrus. Some sites are in the 50-foot range but many are narrow so slide-outs can be a problem. Restrooms have flush toilets. There is a shower building within walking distance of this campground that is also used by people staying at the other campgrounds, but this is the only campground close enough for convenient use without a vehicle. This campground has a manned entry booth, it's a busy place. From SR-260 near Mile 393 just a mile or so west of Eagar head south on SR-273. You'll reach the recreation area entrance road in 21 miles. After turning in you'll see the dump station and showers on the left at .4 miles, a visitor center on the left at .7 mile, and the Rainbow Campground entrance on the left at .8 mile.

BIG LAKE – GRAYLING CAMPGROUND *(Open May 15 to Sept 30 - Varies)*

Reservations: (877) 444-6777, www.recreation.gov
Information: (928) 333-4301
Location: 22 Miles SW of Eagar, *N 33° 52' 19", W 109° 24' 42", 9,000 Ft*

23 Sites – Grayling Campground is the second of the Big Lake Recreation Area campgrounds suitable for RVs. This campground has a narrow gravel road and smaller sites, it's OK for RVs to about 30 feet, many sites are smaller than that. Restrooms here have flush toilets but no showers. The campground is across the road from the lake and a dock/ramp area. Showers and phones are near Rainbow Campground. To reach the campground follow the instructions above given in the Rainbow Campground write-up. The Grayling Campground entrance is 1.5 mile from the recreation area entrance.

BIG LAKE – BROOKCHAR CAMPGROUND *(Open May 15 to Sept 30 - Varies)*
  Reservations: (877) 444-6777, www.recreation.gov
  Information: (928) 333-4301
  Location: 22 Miles SW of Eagar, *N 33° 52' 30", W 109° 24' 52", 9,000 Ft*

13 Sites – Brookchar is a tent-only campground with tent sites away from a paved parking lot. Sites have tables and fire pits. Restrooms have flush toilets but no showers. Showers and phones are near Rainbow Campground. To reach the camping area follow the instructions above given for Rainbow Campground. The Brookchar Campground is 1.8 mile from the recreation area entrance.

BIG LAKE – CUTTHROAT *(Open May 15 to Sept 30 - Varies)*
  Reservations: (877) 444-6777, www.recreation.gov
  Information: (928) 333-4301
  Location: 22 Miles SW of Eagar, *N 33° 52' 30", W 109° 24' 59", 9,000*

18 Sites – The final Big Lake Recreation Area campground is Cutthroat. This is a tent campground with tent sites next to individual parking pads. You'll find a few vans and pickup campers back here too but the sites are small. Each has a picnic table and a fire pit. There are vault toilets. Flush toilets, showers, and phones are near Rainbow Campground. To reach the campground follow the instructions above given for Rainbow Campground. The Cutthroat Campground is 1.9 miles from the recreation area entrance.

WICKENBURG

Wickenburg (population about 6,000) is only 30 miles northwest of Surprise, Phoenix's northwest suburb. It's outside the urban sprawl but close enough to take advantage of the shopping and other amenities of the big city. Surprisingly, there are few RV parks in the town.

The town has a western motif of sorts, many of the downtown buildings reflect the theme and there are western shops and guest ranches as well as a western museum, the **Desert Caballeros Western Museum**. The low elevation here means winter is very pleasant but summer is hot.

Wickenburg was originally a gold town. Mines were located outside town but ore was brought into Wickenburg for processing since that's where the water was. The original **Vulture Mine** can be toured, it's about 15 miles southwest of town. You can also tour the reconstructed town and Nella-Meda Mine at **Robson's Arizona Mining World**. It's 25 miles west of town on US-60 then 4 miles north on US-71.

Three miles south of town is the **Hassayampa River Preserve**. It's managed by the Nature Conservancy and is a great place for birding. While the river is above ground here, it's below the surface upstream toward Wickenburg.

Wickenburg Campgrounds

HORSPITALITY RV RESORT *(Open All Year)*

Res and Info: (928) 684-2519, horspitality@hotmail.com
Location: Wickenburg, *N 33° 57' 08", W 112° 42' 35", 1,900 Ft*

105 Sites – This is by far the largest campground in town. It has tent, partial, and full hookup sites. There's also a dump station. Most RV sites are back-ins to 40 feet although there are a very few longer pull-thrus. Parking is on gravel and there are paved patios There is an internet room with dial-up internet access and Wi-Fi is planned. Amenities include 72 horse pens, a round pen, an arena, and behind the park are 110 miles of riding trails for horses or ATVs. The campground is located just south of Wickenburg. From the intersection of US-89 and US-60 in Wickenburg (corner of Wickenburg Way and Tegner St) drive 2.1 miles toward Phoenix on US-60. The campground entrance is on the right.

DESERT CYPRESS RV AND MOTORHOME PARK *(Open All Year)*

Res and Info: (928) 684-2153, (866) 765-8650, desertcypress @msn.com
Location: Wickenburg, *N 33° 58' 22", W 112° 43' 30", 2,000 Ft*

35 Sites – This is a combination mobile home park and RV park and is a 55 and older park. There are about 35 sites which are available to travelers. The park is very clean and tidy and has nice landscaping including beautiful tamarisk trees (also called Desert Cypress). The sites are mostly back-ins to about 35 feet in length but there are 2 or 3 which will take RVs 40-42 feet in length. The sites are all full hookup including cable TV. Dial up internet access is available in the clubhouse. Pop-up tent trailers are welcome but not tents. The swimming pool is not heated so really is just for summer use. There is a laundry room, bathrooms, and showers, and a recreation room. From the intersection of US-89 and US-60 in Wickenburg (corner of Wickenburg Way and Tegner St.) drive .4 mile toward Phoenix on US-60. Turn left on Jack Burden Rd. and follow it about 100 yards to the park entrance.

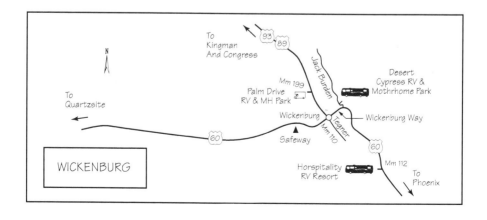

ARIZONA

WILLCOX AND THE UPPER SULPHUR SPRINGS VALLEY

Willcox (population 4,000) occupies a relatively well-watered area along I-10 to the east of Tucson and Benson, about 50 miles from the New Mexico border. Ranching and agriculture form the economic base of the town.

The most famous person from Willcox appears to have been Rex Allen, the Arizona Cowboy. He starred in singing cowboy movies beginning in 1950. Willcox has a **Rex Allen Arizona Cowboy Museum**, a statue of him with his horse Koko, a Willcox Rex Allen Theater (which today shows movies), and Rex Allen Drive is a major street through town. Then there's **Rex Allen Days** the first Friday to Sunday of October each year.

The **Chiricahua National Monument** and the **Fort Bowie National Historic Site**, described in the *Chiricahua Mountains* section above, are easily reached from Willcox so the town makes a good base for visiting them. Just south of town is a large shallow lake called **Willcox Playa** which is home to about 10,000 sandhill cranes each winter. It can be hard to get close enough to see them but the Chamber of Commerce in town can give you directions to two sites where you can watch the birds in the distance. Very popular in the birding world is Wings over Willcox on the third weekend in January, which celebrates the birds in the area.

Cochise Stronghold is associated with the Apache leader Cochise and is fun to visit, it is located about 32 miles south of Willcox and has a campground, see the description below.

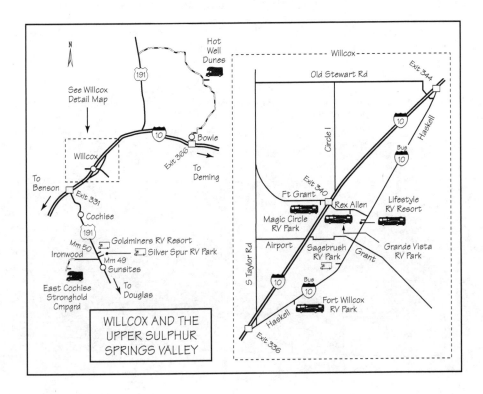

WILLCOX AND THE UPPER SULPHUR SPRINGS VALLEY

The **Amerind Foundation Museum and Fulton-Hayden Art Gallery** are located between Willcox and Benson. The foundation has a large collection of Indian artifacts. Take Exit 318 from I-10 and drive south a mile, then turn left.

Willcox and the Upper Sulphur Springs Valley

◼ LIFESTYLE RV RESORT *(Open All Year)*
Res and Info: (520) 384-3303
Location: Willcox, *N 32° 15' 37", W 109° 49' 38", 4,100 Ft*

60 Sites – Lifestyle has back-in and pull-thru sites to 65 feet. Amenities include a pool and a spa as well as a restaurant and gift shop. Some sites have instant-on telephone. The campground is located on the I-10 business loop which parallels I-10 through town. The easiest route is to take Exit 340 and turn southeast. Drive 1.1 miles to N Haskell (I-10 Bus), turn right, and you'll see the campground entrance almost immediately on the right.

◼ GRANDE VISTA RV PARK *(Open All Year)*
Res and Info: (520) 384-4002
Location: Willcox, *N 32° 15' 46", W 109° 50' 02", 4,100 Ft*

33 Sites – The Grand Vista has pull-thru sites to 55 feet. Amenities include a swimming pool and recreation hall. The campground is located northeast of the center of town. From I-40 take Exit 340 and drive east .6 miles. Turn south on N Prescott Ave, the RV park is at the end of the street.

◼ MAGIC CIRCLE RV PARK *(Open All Year)*
Res and Info: (520) 384-3212
Location: Willcox, *N 32° 15' 54", W 109° 50' 46", 4,100 Ft*

63 Sites – The campground has 63 sites with parking on gravel. They are both back-ins and pull-thrus to 60 feet, all with full hookups. There is a swimming pool and a recreation room. The park is on the northwest side of the freeway. Take I-40 Exit 340 and go northwest. Turn left on Virginia, you'll reach the campground in .1 mile.

◼ FORT WILLCOX RV PARK *(Open All Year)*
Information: (520) 384-4986
Location: Willcox, *N 32° 13' 48", W 109° 51' 33", 4,100 Ft*

26 Sites – The RV park has back-in and pull-thru sites to 50 feet. It's located south of town off I-40 Business. Take Exit 336 from I-40 and drive north toward town on Haskell on the east side of the freeway. The campground will be on your right in 1.1 mile.

EAST COCHISE STRONGHOLD CAMPGROUND *(Open All Year)*
   Information: (520) 364-3468
   Location: 32 Miles S of Willcox, *N 31° 55' 32", W 109° 58' 01", 5,000 Ft*

19 Sites – This Coronado National Forest campground occupies a canyon on the eastern edge of the Dragoon Mountains. Sites are set under granite boulders and are shaded by oaks. It has paved interior roads and paved sites, although you have to drive a dusty dirt road to get here. There are tent sites as well as back-in RV sites long enough for 35 foot RVs although most are smaller. Sites have picnic tables, raised barbecue grills, and fire pits. No drinking water is available. A short nature trail leads from the campground as well as a trail across the Dragoons to West Cochise Stronghold. From I-10 take Exit 331 which is 9 miles southwest of Willcox. Drive south on US-191 for 18.5 miles. Turn right on Euclid St. which becomes Ironwood Road. After 4.9 miles the road turns to dirt. The campground is 3.7 miles from where the pavement ended.

HOT WELL DUNES BLM CAMPGROUND *(Open All Year)*
   Information: (928) 348-4400
   Location: 19 Miles N of Bowie, *N 32° 31' 24", W 109° 25' 35", 3,400 Ft*

10 Sites – Hot Well Dunes is a popular off-road driving area with a campground and two hot tubs. The camping area poorly defined spaces, some with picnic tables and firepits. The hot springs is piped into two nice concrete tubs that are sunk into the ground. The tubs adjoin the camping area and the vault toilets there also serve the camping area. Access requires driving on dirt roads but in dry weather and if you take the route below the road is generally fine for RVs to about 30 feet. Take Exit 362 from I-10 for Bowie, that's about 22 miles east of Wilcox. From the center of town drive 2 miles north on Central Avenue. Turn right on Fan road and drive 1 mile. Turn north on Donahue and drive another mile. Turn right on Rosewood and follow Rosewood east and then north for 6 miles to Haekel Road. Now follow Haekel north for 9 miles to the campground entrance road on the right.

WILLIAMS

Williams (population about 3,000) is 53 miles south of the Grand Canyon south entrance. It's a very good alternative to staying in the park for campers. You can either drive up to the park or ride the popular Grand Canyon Railway. A word of caution, during the very busy middle of the summer there can be lines of one or even two hours to get into the south entrance of the park.

Williams is a **Route 66** town. The freeway bypassed Williams only in 1984, the town was on the last section of Route 66 to remain open. Downtown Williams is well-preserved, a lot like it was during the days when Route 66 was most popular.

The **Grand Canyon Railway** runs daily trains from Williams to the Grand Canyon station near the rim every day. It leaves at 8 am, arrives about 12:15 and returns at 3:15, arriving in Williams at 5:45. In summer a steam locomotive is used, in winter a diesel. There's a small museum, the Grand Canyon Railway Museum, at the depot. The campgrounds in town will be happy to arrange your tickets.

Williams celebrates **Rendezvous Days** on Memorial Day and there's a **Cool Country Cruise-In and Route 66 Festival** in August.

CANYON GATEWAY RV PARK *(Open All Year)*

    Res and Info: (888) 635-0329, www.grandcanyonrvparks.com, canyonrvpk@aol.com
    Location: Williams, *N 35° 15' 46", W 112° 11' 34", 6,800 Ft*

103 Sites – The Canyon Gateway is one of the busiest RV parks in Williams, probably because it's easily visible on a hillside overlooking the freeway. There are 102 RV sites and one tent site. The sites are pull-thrus but there are 2 RVs in every 90-foot site. So in effect, there are really no pull-thrus if the park is busy. The parking is on red gravel. There are a few small trees between the sites but no other separation and there are no picnic tables or fires. Near the entrance is a picnic area with picnic tables. All of the RV sites have full hookups including cable TV. A data port is provided in the laundry room for internet access. A pay phone is inside the laundry room. There is no separate dump station, but the public is allowed to dump at a site for a $5 fee, use the showers for a $5 fee, or fill with water for a $5 fee. From I-40 take Exit 163 and drive up the hill to the campground.

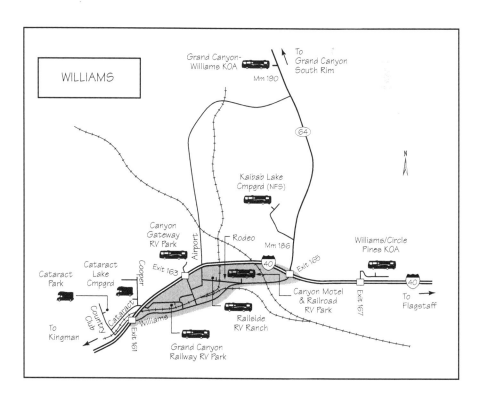

GRAND CANYON RAILWAY RV PARK *(Open All Year)*

Res and Info: (800) 843-8724, www.thetrain.com
Location: Williams, *N 35° 15' 00", W 112° 11' 48", 6,700 Ft*

124 Sites – This new campground, run by the Grand Canyon Railway itself, is probably the easiest place to stay in Willams and travel on the railroad up to the south rim of the Grand Canyon. The station is near the campground and packages are available which include staying at the RV park and traveling on the train. This is also the most modern campground in town with paved access roads, paved parking, and big sites. The sites are back-ins and pull-thrus to 65 feet. From I-40 take Exit 163 and travel south on Grand Canyon Blvd. for .3 mile. Turn right on Franklin Avenue (well signed) and watch for the convenience store where you stop and check in.

RAILSIDE RV RANCH *(Open All Year)*

Reservations: (888) 635-4077, www.thervranch.com
Information: (928) 635-4077, www.thegrandcanyon.com/railside
Location: Williams, *N 35° 15' 29", W 112° 10' 47", 6,700 Ft*

100 Sites – The Railside is a commercial RV park good for big RVs. It's a large gravel lot with a small amount of greenery between sites. Many people stay here while taking the train up to the Grand Canyon. The park will make your reservations to see the Grand Canyon by train, private tour, plane or helicopter. Most sites are full hookups with cable and some sites also have instant-on telephone connections. There are also a few tent sites. Good Wi-Fi internet is provided throughout the park at no extra charge. There is also a modem for other internet access. The office is in the general store which has a good selection of snacks and some grocery items. Other amenities include dry storage, a basketball court, horseshoes, dog run, and propane is sold. Leave I-40 at Exit 165 and drive south and then west on Business I-40 for 1.2 miles. Turn right on E Rodeo Rd, the campground is on the right in .5 mile.

CANYON MOTEL AND RAILROAD RV PARK *(Open All Year)*

Reservations: (800) 482-3955, RailroadRV@aol.com
Information: (928) 635-9371, www.RailroadRV.com, www.TheCanyonMotel.com
Location: Williams, *N 35° 15' 29", W 112° 10' 16", 6,700 Ft*

47 Sites – This is a well-run and friendly private RV park not associated with the railroad to the Grand Canyon, but it does have a railroad theme with several rail cars being used as rooms on the grounds. The park has newly built pull-thru RV sites to 70 feet with cable TV. There's an internet office with computers and Wi-Fi is provided. The swimming pool here is indoor. Also, there are 18 motel rooms, 3 rail car suites, and two suites in a 1929 classic caboose. The park specializes in arranging rail trips and tours to the Grand Canyon. The campground is conveniently located at the eastern entrance to town. Exit I-40 at Exit 165 and drive south and then west on Business I-40 for 1.2 miles. Turn right on E Rodeo Rd, the campground is directly ahead.

GRAND CANYON/WILLIAMS KOA *(Open March 1 to Nov 1)*

Reservations: (800) 562-5771, www.koa.com
Information: (928) 635-2307, gckoa@grandcanyonkoa.com, www.grandcanyonkoa.com
Location: 3 Miles NE of Williams, *N 35° 19' 38", W 112° 09' 24", 6,600 Ft*

88 Sites – The park has 62 RV sites, 26 tent sites, and 18 rental cabins. Many of the RV sites are pull-thrus to 65 feet. A data port is provided for internet access. Non guest are allowed to dump for a fee. Other amenities include horseshoes and a game room. During the summer the park offers steak dinners and pancake breakfasts. Reservations are made for train, air tours, van tours, horseback riding, and raft trips. Take Exit 165 from I-40 and drive north on SR-64. The campground is 1.7 miles north of the freeway.

WILLIAMS/CIRCLE PINES KOA *(Open All Year)*

Reservations: (928) 635-2626, www.koa.com
Information: (800) 562-9379, www.circlepineskoa.com, kamp@circlepineskoa.com
Location: 4 Miles E of Williams, *N 35° 15' 33", W 112° 07' 00", 6,900 Ft*

163 Sites – This is a very large KOA situated to provide a place to stay while visiting the Grand Canyon. They have a large number of tent sites, also cabins and big RV sites. All RV sites are pull-thrus, some are full-hookup and some are partial. The largest ones are about 70 feet long. Amenities include an indoor pool, a spa, mini golf, bicycle rentals, a sports activities area with a paved bicycle trail around it, an internet data port, free Wi-Fi to most sites in the park, groceries, and propane sales The campground is easily accessible off I-40 at Exit 167. It's on the north side of the freeway.

KAIBAB LAKE CAMPGROUND *(Open All Year)*

Reservations: (877) 444-6777, www.recreation.gov
Information: (928) 699-1239
Location: 2 Miles NE of Williams, *N 35° 16' 47", W 112° 09' 30", 6,800 Ft*

63 Sites – This is a large Kaibab National Forest campground with large sites set in pines next to Kaibab Lake. There are tent sites and a variety of RV sites including pull-thrus up to 75 feet long. The campground has flush toilets and a dump station ($5). During the winter there are no services but the campground remains open. There is fresh water fishing in the lake, a boat ramp and a dock. If you take Exit 165 from I-40 and drive north on SR-64 the campground entrance road is on the left in .7 mile.

CATARACT LAKE CAMPGROUND *(Open May 1 to Oct 1 - Varies)*

Reservations: (877) 444-6777, www.recreation.gov
Information: (928) 635-5600
Location: 1 Mile W of Williams, *N 35° 15' 02", W 112° 12' 46", 6,700 Ft*

18 Sites – This is a Kaibab National Forest campground. It is set on the shore of Cataract Lake under pine trees. None of the sites are right on the lake. The largest sites are pull-

ARIZONA

thrus and can accommodate RVs to 35 feet. None of the sites are very level and maneuvering room is limited. There is a boat ramp and freshwater fishing. Potable water in limited quantities is available. From I-40 take Exit 161. Drive toward town on Bill Williams Ave for 1.2 miles. Turn left on N 7th St and then after crossing the railroad tracks left again on Cataract Rd. Proceed ahead and under the freeway for another 1 mile. Turn right on Cooper Rd and you'll see the campground entrance on the left almost immediately.

CATARACT PARK *(Open May 1 to Sept 30 - Varies)*
   Information: (928) 774-5139, parks2@coconino.az.gov
   Location: 1.5 Miles W of Williams, *N 35° 14' 55", W 112° 13' 26", 6,700 Ft*

25 Sites – This is a Coconino County park on the west side of Cataract Lake. There are no hookups. The sites are all back-ins to a length of 70 feet, but maneuvering room limits RV size to about 35 feet. From I-40 take Exit 161. Drive toward town on Bill Williams Ave for 1.2 miles. Turn left on N 7th St and then after crossing the railroad tracks left again on Cataract Rd. Proceed ahead and under the freeway for another 1.9 mile. Turn right on Country Club Drive and in .6 mile you'll see the park entrance on the right.

WINSLOW AND THE HOPI MESAS

The small town of Winslow (population 10,000) has Route 66 attractions as well as being famous as the location of the corner in the Eagle's song "Take it Easy". The city is also an excellent base for a trip north to the Hopi Mesas. The most famous building in town is undoubtedly the **La Posada**, an old Fred Harvey Company hotel near the railroad tracks. It has been restored and you're welcome to tour the public rooms. The **Homolavi Ruins State Park**, just outside town, is a great place to camp and also has an interesting visitor center and some good hikes to and through the nearby ruins.

The three Hopi mesas are located 67 miles north of Winslow via SR-87. They're also accessible from the northwest near Tuba City on SR-264, the distance from Tuba City to the mesas is about 45 miles.

The Hopi Reservation is much smaller than that of the Navajos and completely surrounded by it. The Hopi live in some 13 villages on or near three mesas, named First, Second, and Third Mesas. The Hopi are well known for their art and their ceremonies and dances. It is possible to visit the towns but rules are changeable and many ceremonies are closed to outsiders. If you would like to visit the individual villages or attend a ceremony you can plan ahead by calling the Hopi Cultural Center (see campground description below) and asking when one might be scheduled and whether outsiders are allowed to attend.

A big help for visiting the mesas is the **Hopi Cultural Center** on SR-264 at the top of Second Mesa. It has a museum, a restaurant, a motel, and a campground. It's a convenient place to base yourself when visiting the area.

Winslow and the Hopi Mesas Campgrounds

HOMOLOVI RUINS STATE PARK *(Open All Year)*
   Information: (928) 289-4106, www.azstateparks.com, homolovi@pr.state.az.us
   Location: 3 Miles NE of Winslow, *N 35° 01' 53", W 110° 38' 52", 4,900 Ft*

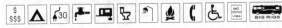

53 sites – This is a beautiful campground just off I-40 with nice big sites, many with electricity and water hookups. Access roads are paved and so are sites. Restrooms have flush toilets and there are showers. There's also a dump station. To reach the campground take Exit 257 from I-40 about 2 miles east of Winslow and head north. The State Park entrance is on the left in 1.4 miles.

WINSLOW PRIDE RV PARK *(Open All Year)*

Information: (928) 289-3201
Location: Winslow, *N 35° 01' 10", W 110° 40' 25", 4,900 Ft*

40 sites – This is a small older RV park right next to the interstate. At the time we went to press this campground was being gradually upgraded with a remodeled convenience store and improved restrooms. The campground is located at the eastern edge of Winslow, take Exit 255 and go north, you'll immediately see the campground on the left.

HOPI CULTURE CENTER *(Open All Year)*

Information: (928) 734-2401, www.hopiculturalcenter.com
Location: 67 Miles N of Winslow, *N 35° 50' 41", W 110° 31' 48", 6,300 Ft*

About 30 Sites – Next to the Cultural Center and Restaurant on the Second Mesa is a camping area. There are narrow lanes between juniper bushes, some picnic tables, and grills. Sites aren't clearly laid out, you park pretty much where you wish. Restroom are

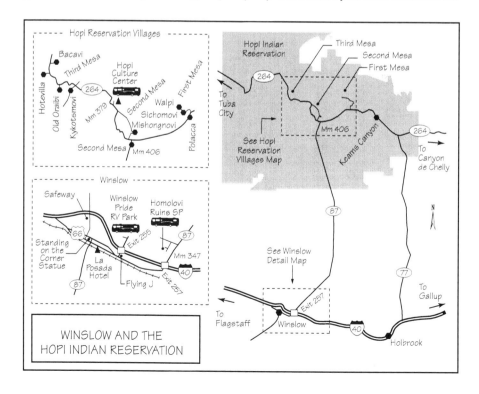

WINSLOW AND THE
HOPI INDIAN RESERVATION

in the Cultural Center next door. See the Hopi Mesas description above for the location of the Cultural Center.

YUMA

Yuma (population about 90,000) is one of the lowest areas in Arizona. That means that it has very comfortable winter weather, and extremely hot summer weather. This is Arizona's third largest metro area, behind Phoenix and Tucson. Note that in winter the population of Yuma more than doubles, and many of these visitors are RVers.

Historically Yuma was a convenient place to cross the Colorado River. It was originally called Yuma Crossing. **Yuma Crossing State Historical Park,** located at the site of the Army's old Yuma Quartermaster's Depot, celebrates the crossing and tells about its considerable history. There is a visitor center and museum and several other buildings on 9 acres along the Colorado River.

Nearby is the **Yuma Territorial Prison State Historical Park**. The famous prison here was only in existence from 1876 to 1909. After that, for a short time it was a high school. Make what you want out of that. With three-foot thick granite walls the prison remains well-preserved and great fun to explore. A big event here is the **Gathering of the Gunfighters** in January. There is a one-mile walking trail between the two historical parks along the Colorado.

If you are interested in a quick visit to Mexico Yuma is a good place to do it. Two nearby towns are good spots. **Los Algodones**, west of town with the crossing from California, is a nice little town, very popular with Yuma residents as a place to pick up medicine, get

CLARK'S GREBES ON THE COLORADO RIVER

dental work done or pick up some glasses, and perhaps have a good Mexican meal. From Yuma travel west on I-8 to Exit 166. Drive south and park in the big lot. You'll want to walk across, not drive, since you need special vehicle insurance to go into Mexico,

South of Yuma you can do pretty much the same thing to visit the town of **San Luis Río Colorado**. This is less of a gringo town, and for that reason perhaps more interesting but not as convenient for medical visits. Travel southwest from Yuma on US-95 for about 20 miles to San Luis on the US side, park, and walk across.

Just 18 miles east of Yuma are the **Imperial Sand Dunes**. The dune area runs for 40 north-south miles and 5 east-west. They were a barrier to travel for early wagon and motor travelers, a wooden plank road was used to cross them from 1915 to 1926. Today I-8 has replaced the plank road and the area is known as Imperial Dunes National Recreation Area and is used by thousands of off-road vehicle drivers each weekend. You can camp here too although it can be a dusty and noisy experience, see the camping description below.

For more about Yuma, and particularly snowbird winter RV parks, see the *Snowbird Destinations* chapter of this book. Many of the campgrounds listed in that chapter also have spaces for travelers, our charts in Chapter 8 give overnight rates for the ones that do.

Yuma Campgrounds

🚐 FORTUNA DE ORO RV RESORT *(Open All Year)*

    Reservations: (800) 839-0126
    Information: (928) 342-5051, www.fortunadeoro.com
    Location: Yuma, *N 32° 40' 08", W 114° 23' 53", 300 Ft*

900 Sites – This large RV resort is a good possibility for an overnight site even during the Snowbird season but call before heading that way. It's a 55 and over park. Sites are back-ins and pull-thrus to 50 feet. Amenities include a nine hole golf course, pool, and spa. Instant-on phones are available and there's a data port and Wi-Fi at a central location. Take Exit 14 from I-8 on the east side of Yuma and go north to the frontage roads. Turn right and you'll see the entrance on the left in .7 mile.

🚐 BLUE SKY RV PARK *(Open All Year)*

    Res and Info: (928) 342-1444, (877) 367-5220, www.blueskyyuma.com
    Location: Yuma, *N 32° 40' 11", W 114° 27' 21", 300 Ft*

210 Sites – A smaller park for Yuma, but with nice facilities including a good pool area. The park has back-ins and pull-thrus to 80 feet. Amenities include a pool and spa. Take Exit 12 from I-8 and go south to the frontage road. Head west and you'll see the campground entrance on the left in .7 mile.

🚐 RIVER'S EDGE RV RESORT *(Open All Year)*

    Res and Info: (760) 572-5105
    Location: 3 Miles W of Yuma, *N 32° 44' 08", W 114° 39' 02", 100 Ft*

494 Sites – The River's Edge is a large resort just west of Yuma along the Colorado River. It's actually in Winterhaven, California. They fill up like the Yuma parks but

often have a few sites available for overnighters. Sites here are all back-ins to 45 feet in long lines backing up to strips of trees. The trees provide quite a bit of shade. Amenities include a pool, spa, and boat ramp. Take Exit 170 from I-8 and turn south, you'll see the entrance immediately. Follow the entrance road about .4 mile to the campground.

▣ MITTRY LAKE AND WILDLIFE AREA *(Open All Year)*

Information: (928) 317-3200, www.az.blm.gov
Location: 15 Miles N of Yuma, *N 32° 49' 03", W 114° 28' 26", 100 Ft*

Scattered Boondocking – The Bureau of Reclamation runs this 700 acre wildlife area between the La Laguna and Imperial dams. The area is designated for free camping in established areas. Because this is a wildlife area, camping is limited to 10 days per calendar year. There are no facilities. Many of the camping areas are right along the lake. Some sites have rock fire rings. The road runs along the lake and there are places to pull in and park along the lake side as well as in larger areas on the bench above. From I-8 take Exit 2 in Yuma and head east on US-95. In 5.4 miles turn left on South Ave 7 E and drive north for 7.1 miles to a T. Here turn right and drive east for .5 mile to another T. Turn left on Ave 7½ and follow it north for about 2 miles to the Mittry Lake area.

▣ PILOT KNOB BLM LTVA *(Open All Year)*

Information: (928) 317-3200, www.az.blm.gov
Location: 9 Mile W of Yuma, *N 32° 44' 35", W 114° 45' 17", 300 Ft*

Scattered Boondocking – This is a convenient LTVA area just 9 miles west of Yuma. See the introductory material in this chapter for the BLM LTVA costs and rules. There is a dump station at the nearby gas station and there is also two associated 14-Day parking areas close by. Ask the onsite host at the LTVA for more specific instructions about how to locate them. The LTVA is located just southeast of Exit 164 (Sidewinder Road) from I-8, you can't miss it.

▣ IMPERIAL SAND DUNES RECREATION AREA *(Open All Year)*

Information: (760) 337-4400, www.blm.gov/ca/elcentro/ImperialSandDunes
Location: 17 Miles W of Yuma, *N 32° 44' 19", W 114° 53' 06", 100 Ft*

Scattered Boondocking – Between Exits 156 and 151 Grays Wells Road runs parallel to I-8 on the south side of the interstate This is one of the access roads to the Imperial Sand Dunes Recreation Area. Even more camping and riding areas are accessible off SR-78 to the north. The attraction here is obviously the sand dunes and everyone here has at least a few ATVs for exploring the dunes. A relatively complex fee scheme is in effect. Weekly ($25) and annual ($90) permits are available online (www.imperialsanddunes. net) and at off-site sales outlets or at higher rates ($40 weekly, $120 annual) from pay stations on-site.

▣ SLEEPY HOLLOW RV PARK AND ANDRADE EXIT BOONDOCKING *(Open All Year)*

Information: (760) 572-5101
Location: 6 Miles W of Yuma, *N 32° 43' 19", W 114° 43' 31", Near Sea Level*

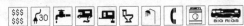

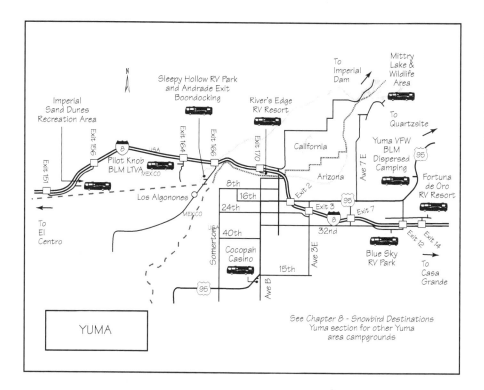

YUMA

See Chapter 8 - Snowbird Destinations
Yuma section for other Yuma
area campgrounds

150 Sites and Scattered Boondocking – The Sleepy Hollow is an Indian-run campground about .3 mile north of the crossing into Algodones, Mexico. This is a handy place to stay if you have dental or medical appointments in Algodones across the border. The campground is older and not in great shape, but it's adequate. There are a lot of long-term units here. This is a big park with all back-in sites. There are full and no-hookup sites. The restrooms and showers are located in the building which house the office. The laundry is near the middle of the park. There is a dump station with a $5 fee for dumping. Reservations are not accepted at this park. Dry camping includes use of dump station, water, restrooms w/showers and laundry room. To reach the campground take Exit 166 (marked Algodones) from I-8 just west of the Arizona/California line. Drive south for 1.9 mile, the campground is on the right. There are also many scattered boondocking sites north along the access highway all the way to the far side of I-10 that are on tribal land. There is a fee to park in this area of $95 for three months.

🚐 COCOPAH CASINO *(Open All Year)*
Information: (800) 23 SLOTS, www.cocopahresort.com
Location: 6 Miles S of Yuma, *N 32° 36' 17", W 114° 39' 12", 200 Ft*

50 Sites – The Cocopah Casino has a large paved parking area designated for RVs. They charge $5 for three days. There are no facilities but the casino is handy. From Yuma head south on US-95. You'll see the casino on the left about five miles south of Yuma.

ARIZONA

YUMA VFW BLM DISPERSED CAMPING AREA *(Open All Year)*
Information: (928) 317-3200, www.az.blm.gov
Location: 5 Miles N of Yuma, *N 32° 43' 43", W 114° 25' 21", 200 Ft*

Scattered Boondocking – See the introductory material in this chapter about the BLM 14-Day dispersed camping areas. This is one of the smaller BLM short term areas in the Southwest but also one of the most popular since it's so convenient to the Yuma area. It's located behind the VFW post and is not otherwise affiliated with it. From I-8 take Exit 12, just east of central Yuma. Drive north on Fortuna Road for 1.9 miles. Turn right on US-95 and drive 2.7 miles, the entrance is on the left.

Information Resources

See our Internet site at www.rollinghomes.com for Internet information links.

Ajo, Why, and Organ Pipe Cactus National Monument

Ajo District Chamber of Commerce, 400 Taladro, Ajo, AZ 85321; (520) 387-7742

Ajo Historical Museum, 160 Mission Street, Box 778, Ajo, AZ 85321; (520) 387-7105

Organ Pipe Cactus National Monument, Route 1, Box 100, Ajo, AZ 85321; (520) 387-6849, (520) 387-7661

Apache Trail

Goldfield Ghost Town, (480) 983-0333

Dolly Steamboat, Arizona Steamboat Cruises, PO Box 977, Apache Junction, AZ 85217; (480) 827-9144

Benson

Benson Visitor Center, 249 E 4th St, Benson, AZ 85602, (520) 586-4293

Kartchner Caverns State Park, PO Box 1849, Benson, AZ 85602; (520) 586-2283

San Pedro Valley Arts and Historical Museum, 180 South San Pedro Street, Benson, AZ 85602; (520) 586-3070

Bisbee and Naco

Bisbee Chamber of Commerce and Visitor Center, 1 Main St, PO Box BA, Bisbee, AZ 85603; (520) 432-5421, (866) 224-7233

Bisbee Mining and Historical Museum, 5 Copper Queen Plaza, Bisbee, AZ 85603; (520) 432-7071

Queen Mine Tour, (520) 432-2071, (866) 432-2071

Borrego Springs and Anza-Borrego State Park (California)

Borrego Springs Chamber of Commerce, 786 Palm Canyon Dr, PO Box 420, Borrego Springs, CA 92004; (800) 559-5524, (760) 767-5555

Anza-Borrego State Park, 200 Palm Canyon Drive, Borrego Springs, CA 92004; (760) 767-5311

Camp Verde

Camp Verde Chamber of Commerce, 385 S Main, Camp Verde, AZ 86322; (928) 567-9294

Fort Verde State Historic Park, (928) 567-3275

Montezuma Castle National Monument, (928) 567-3322

Casa Grande

Casa Grande Valley Historical Museum, 110 W Florence Blvd, Casa Grande, AZ 85222; (520) 836-2223

Casa Grande Ruins National Monument, 1110 Ruins Dr, Coolidge, AZ 85228; (520) 723-3172

Greater Casa Grande Chamber of Commerce, 575 N Marshall St, Casa Grande, AZ 85222 (520) 836-2125, (800) 916-1515

Chiricahua Mountains

Fort Bowie National Historic Site, (520) 847-2500

Coachella Valley (Palm Springs)

Fabulous Palm Springs Follies, (760) 327-0225

Indian Canyons, (760) 325-3400, (800) 790-3398

Indio Chamber of Commerce, 82-503 Highway 111, Indio, CA 92201; (760) 347-0676

Palm Springs Bureau of Tourism, 777 N Palm Canyon Dr, Palm Springs, CA 92262; (800) 347-7746

Palm Springs Aerial Tramway, One Tramway Rd, Palm Springs, CA 92262; (760) 325-1391, (760) 325-1149, (888) 515-TRAM

Palm Springs Air Museum, 745 N Gent Autry Trail, Palm Springs, CA 92262; (760) 778-6262

Palm Springs Desert Museum, 101 Museum Dr, Palm Springs, CA 92263; (760) 325-7186

Coronado Trail: Clifton to Springerville on SR-191

Casa Malpais Museum, 318 E Main St, Springerville, AZ 85938; (928) 333-5375

Phelps Dodge Morenci Copper Mine, (928) 865-4111

Douglas

Douglas Visitor Center, 1125 Pan American Ave, Douglas, AZ 85607; (520) 364-3468

El Centro (California)

Calexico Chamber of Commerce, 1100 Imperial Ave, Calexico, CA 92232; (760) 357-1166

El Centro Chamber of Commerce & Visitor's Bureau, 1095 South 4th St, El Centro, CA 92243; (760) 352-3681

Flagstaff

Flagstaff Visitor Center, 1 E Route 66, Flagstaff, AZ 86001; (928) 774-9541, (800) 842-7293

Museum of Northern Arizona , 3101 N Fort Valley Rd, Flagstaff, AZ 86001; (928) 774-5213

Lowell Observatory, (928) 774-2096

Walnut Canyon National Monument, (928) 526-3367

Sunset Crater Volcano National Monument, (928) 526-0502

Wupatki National Monument, (928) 679-2365

Globe

Besh Ba Gowah, (928) 425-0320

Globe-Miami Chamber of Commerce, 1360 N Broad St, Globe, AZ 85501; (928) 425-4495, (800) 804-5623

Gila Country Historical Museum, 1330 N Broad St, Globe, AZ; (928) 425-7385

Grand Canyon

Grand Canyon National Park, Information, (928) 638-7888

ARIZONA

Holbrook and Petrified Forest National Park
Holbrook Chamber of Commerce, 100 E Arizona St, Holbrook, AZ 86025; (928) 524-6558, (800) 524-2459

Petrified Forest National Park, (928) 524-6228

Imperial Dam Recreation Area
BLM Yuma, 2555 E Gila Ridge Rd, Yuma, AZ 85365; (928) 317-3200

Twentynine Palms and Joshua Tree National Park
Joshua Tree National Park, (760) 367-5500

29 Palms Chamber of Commerce, 6455 Mesquite Ave Ste A, Twentynine Palms, CA 92277; 760 367-3445

Kingman
Powerhouse Visitor Center, 120 W Andy Devine, PO Box 1150, Kingman, AZ 85402; (928) 753-6106, (866) 427-7866

Route 66 Museum, 120 W Andy Devine, Kingman, AZ 85402; (928) 753-9889

Mojave Museum of History and Arts, 400 W Beale St, Kingman, AZ 85402; (928) 753-3195

Lake Mead National Recreation Area
Alan Bible Visitor Center, 601 Nevada Hwy, Boulder City, NV 89005; (702) 293-8990

Hoover Dam Visitor Center, (702) 294-3523

Lake Havasu And The Parker Strip
Lake Havasu Area Chamber of Commerce, 213 London Bridge Road, Lake Havasu City, AZ 86403; (928)855-4115

Parker Chamber of Commerce, 1217 California Ave, Parker, CA 85344; (928) 669-2174

Las Vegas
Las Vegas Visitor Center, 3150 Paradise Rd, Las Vegas, NV 89109; (702) 892-7575

Lees Ferry
Glen Canyon National Recreation Area, Lees Ferry Ranger, 928-355-2234

Meteor Crater
Meteor Crater Enterprises, Inc, (800) 289-5898

Mohave Valley: Laughlin, Bullhead City, and Needles
Bullhead City Chamber of Commerce, 121 Hwy 95, Bullhead City, AZ 86442; (928) 754-4121

Lake Mead National Recreation Area, (702) 293-8990

Laughlin Visitors Center, 1555 S Casino Dr, Laughlin, NV 89029; (702) 298-3321, (800) 452-8445

Providence Mountains State Recreation Area (Mitchell Caves), (760) 928-2586

Navajo National Monument
Navajo National Monument, (928) 672-2700

Nogales
Nogales-Santa Cruz Chamber of Commerce, 123 Kino Park, Nogales, AZ 85621; (520) 287-3685

Tubac Presidio State Historic Park, (520) 398-2252

Tumacacori National Historic Park, (520) 398-2341

Page and Glen Canyon National Recreation Area
Glen Canyon Recreation Area, Carl Hayden Visitor Center, (928) 608-6404

Page-Lake Powell Chamber of Commerce, 644 N Navajo Dr, Page, AZ 86040; (928) 645-2741, (888) 261-7243

Powell Museum, 6 N Lake Powell Blvd, Page, AZ 86040; (928) 645-9496, (888) 597-6873

Rainbow Bridge National Monument, (928) 608-6404

Payson and the Mogollon Rim

Rim Country Museum, (928) 474-3483

Rim Country Regional Chamber of Commerce, Beeline Highway and Main St, PO Box 1380, Payson, AZ 85547; (928) 474-4515, (800) 672-9766

Tonto Natural Bridge State Park, (928) 476-4202

Phoenix

Arizona State Capitol, 1700 W Washington, Phoenix, AZ 85007; (602) 542-4675

Greater Phoenix Convention and Visitor's Bureau, 50 N 2nd St, Phoenix, AZ 85004; (602) 254-6500, (877) 225-5749

Heard Museum, 2301 N Central Avenue, Phoenix, AZ 85004-1323; (602) 252-8848

Phoenix Art Museum, Central Avenue & McDowell Road, 1625 N Central Avenue, Phoenix, AZ 85004-1685; (602) 257-1222

Pichaco State Recreation Area

Picacho State Park, (760) 996-2963

Pipe Spring National Monument

Pipe Spring National Monument, (928) 643-7105

Prescott

Sharlot Hall Museum, 415 W Gurley St, Prescott, AZ 86301; (928) 445-3122

Smoki Museum, 147 N Arizona, St, Prescott, AZ 86301; (928) 445-1230

Phippen Museum, 4701 N Hwy 89, Prescott, AZ 86301; (928) 778-1385

Prescott Chamber of Commerce, 117 W Goodwin St, PO Box 1147, Prescott, AZ 86302; (928) 445-2000, (800) 266-7534

Quartzsite

Quartzsite Business Chamber of Commerce, 101 W Main St, PO Box 2566, Quartzsite, AZ 85346; (928) 927-9321

Quartzsite Improvement Association, 235 E Ironwood St, Quartzsite, AZ 85346; (928) 927-6325

Safford

Graham County Chamber of Commerce, 1111 Thatcher Blvd, Safford, AZ 85546; (928) 428-2511, (888) 837-1841

Sedona, Cottonwood, and the Verde Valley

Cottonwood Chamber of Commerce, 1010 S Main, Cottonwood, AZ 86326; (928) 634-7593

Gold King Mine and Ghost Town, (928) 634-0053

Jerome Chamber of Commerce, 310 Hull Ave, Drawer K, Jerome, AZ 86331; (928) 634-2900

Jerome Historical Society Mining Museum, 200 Main Street Jerome, AZ 86331; (928) 634-5477

Jerome State Historic Park, (928) 634-5381

Sedona Uptown Gateway, N US-89A and Forest Rd, PO Box 478, Sedona, AZ 86339; (928) 282-7722, (800) 288-7336

Tuzigoot National Monument, (928) 634-5564

ARIZONA

Verde Canyon Railroad. 300 North Broadway , Clarkdale, AZ 86324; (800) 320-0718

Show Low and Pinetop-Lakeside Region

Fort Apache Historic Park and Apache Cultural Center and Museum, (928) 338-1392

Hon-Dah Ski and Outdoor Sport, (928) 369-7669, (877) 226-4868

Lakeside Ranger Station, 2022 W White Mtn Blvd, Lakeside, AZ 85929; (928) 368-5111

Pinetop-Lakeside Chamber of Commerce, 102-C W White Mtn Blvd, PO Box 4220, Pinetop, AZ 85935; (928) 367-4290, (800) 573-4031

Show Low Regional Chamber of Commerce, 81 E Deuce of Clubs, Show Low, AZ 85901; (928) 537-2326, (888) 746-9569

Sierra Vista

Sierra Vista Convention and Visitor's Bureau, 3020 E Tacoma St, Sierra Vista, AZ 85635; (520) 417-6960, (800) 288-3861

Fort Huachuca Museum, (520) 533-5736

Coronado National Memorial, (520) 366-5515

Ramsey Canyon Preserve, (520) 378-2785

Theodore Roosevelt Lake

Tonto National Monument, (928) 467-2241

Tombstone

Tombstone Courthouse State Historic Park, 3rd and Toughnut St, Tombstone, AZ 85638; (520) 457-3311

Tombstone Visitor Information Center, 4th and Allen St, PO Box 1314, Tombstone, AZ 85638; (520) 457-3929

Tucson

Arizona-Sonora Desert Museum, 2021 N Kinney Road Tucson, AZ 85743; (520) 883-2702

Arizona Historical Society Museum, 140 N Stone Avenue, Tucson AZ 85701; (520) 770-1473

Tucson Museum of Art and Historical Block, 140 N Main Avenue Tucson, AZ 85701; (520) 624-2333

Titan Missile Museum, 1580 W Duval Mine Rd, Sahuarita, AZ 85614; (520) 625-7736

Pima Air and Space Museum, 6000 E Valencia Rd, Tucson, AZ 85706; (520) 574-0462

Saguaro National Park West, (928) 733-5158

Old Tucson Studio, 201 S Kinney Rd, Tucson, AZ 85735; (520) 883-0100

Sabino Canyon Visitor Center, (520) 749-8700

Mission San Xavier del Bac, (520) 294-2624

Kitt Peak Observatory, (520) 318-8726

Tucson Visitor Center, 110 S Church Ave, Ste 7199, Tucson, AZ 85701; (520) 624-1817, (800) 638-8350

White Mountains

White Mountain Apache Indian Reservation, Wildlife and Outdoor Recreation Division, PO Box 220, Whiteriver, AZ; (928) 338-4385

Wickenburg

Wickenburg Chamber of Commerce, 216 N Frontier St, Wickenburg, AZ 85390; (928) 684-5479, (800) 942-5242

Desert Caballeros Western Museum, 219 N Frontier St, Wickenburg, AZ 85390; (928) 684-2272, (928) 684-7075

Vulture Mine, (602) 859-2743

Robson's Arizona Mining World, (928) 685-2609

Hassayampa River Preserve, Visitor Center, (928) 684-2772

Willcox and the Upper Sulphur Springs Valley

Amerind Foundation Museum, 2100 N Amerind Road, Dragoon, AZ 85609; (520) 586-3666

Chiricahua National Monument, Visitor Center, (520) 824-3560

Fort Bowie National Historic Site, (520) 847-2500

Rex Allen Arizona Cowboy Museum, 150 N Railroad Ave, Willcox, AZ 85643; (520) 384-4583, (877) 234-4111

Willcox Chamber of Commerce, Cochise Visitors Center, 1500 N Circle I Rd, Willcox, AZ 85643; (520) 384-2272, (800) 200-2272

Williams

Visitor Information Center, 200 W Railroad Ave, Williams, AZ 86046; (928) 635-4061, (800) 863-0546

Grand Canyon Railway; (800) 843-8724

Winslow and the Hopi Mesas

Winslow Chamber of Commerce, (928) 289-2434

Hopi Culture Center, PO Box 67, Second Mesa, AZ 86043; (928) 734-2401

Yuma

Yuma Crossing State Historical Park, 201 N 4th Ave, Yuma, AZ 85364; (928) 329-0471

Yuma Territorial Prison State Historical Park, 1 Prison Hill Rd, Yuma, AZ 85365; (928) 783-4771

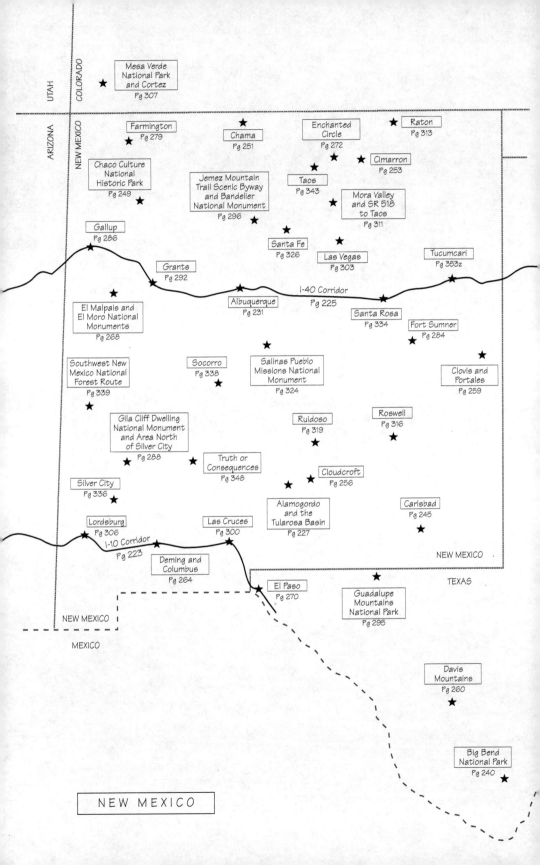

Mesa Verde
National Park
and Cortez
Pg 307

Farmington
Pg 279

Chama
Pg 251

Enchanted
Circle
Pg 272

Raton
Pg 313

Chaco Culture
National
Historic Park
Pg 249

Cimarron
Pg 253

Jemez Mountain
Trail Scenic Byway
and Bandelier
National Monument
Pg 296

Taos
Pg 343

Mora Valley
and SR 518
to Taos
Pg 311

Gallup
Pg 286

Grants
Pg 292

Santa Fe
Pg 326

Las Vegas
Pg 303

Tucumcari
Pg 353z

I-40 Corridor
Pg 225

Albuquerque
Pg 231

Santa Rosa
Pg 334

Fort Sumner
Pg 284

El Malpais and
El Moro National
Monuments
Pg 268

Southwest New
Mexico National
Forest Route
Pg 339

Socorro
Pg 338

Salinas Pueblo
Missions National
Monument
Pg 324

Clovis and
Portales
Pg 259

Gila Cliff Dwelling
National Monument
and Area North
of Silver City
Pg 288

Ruidoso
Pg 319

Roswell
Pg 316

Silver City
Pg 336

Truth or
Consequences
Pg 348

Cloudcroft
Pg 256

Carlsbad
Pg 245

Lordsburg
Pg 306

Las Cruces
Pg 300

I-10 Corridor
Pg 223

Alamogordo
and the
Tularosa Basin
Pg 227

NEW MEXICO

Deming and
Columbus
Pg 264

El Paso
Pg 270

TEXAS

Guadalupe
Mountains
National Park
Pg 295

NEW MEXICO

MEXICO

Davis
Mountains
Pg 260

Big Bend
National Park
Pg 240

NEW MEXICO

UTAH
COLORADO
ARIZONA
NEW MEXICO

Chapter 5

New Mexico

With a population of only about 1.8 million people in the fifth largest state in the United States (121,593 sq. miles) you would expect that there would be lots of opportunities to enjoy the outdoors in New Mexico. In fact, there's a lot more unoccupied land than you would expect since the majority of the citizens of the state occupy a narrow north-south strip along the Rio Grande.

The main reason that there are so few people in so much land is that New Mexico is not really an easy place to live. One important characteristic of the state is its altitude. The lowest place in the state is Red Bluff Reservoir near Carlsbad, it's at 2,850 feet. The Rio Grande Valley near Albuquerque is about 5,000 feet high while Santa Fe and Taos are near 7,000 feet. While summers are hot and dry the winters can be pretty cool.

The dry character of the climate in New Mexico means that most major population centers are along rivers. You'll also note that many of the campgrounds are located on the many reservoirs necessary for living and farming in this state.

Despite this New Mexico is a popular destination for visitors. The Santa Fe and Taos area get most of them but other parts of the state also have their attractions. We'll be talking about a lot of them in this chapter.

You'll probably be amazed to learn that New Mexico has only one national park, Carlsbad. There's a pretty good collection of monuments and historical parks though, and we'll talk about most of them below. We've also included the Guadalupe Mountains National Park although it's really in Texas and Mesa Verde National Park in Colorado.

An important aspect of New Mexico is its history. The state's name says a lot. The area was explored and settled well before most of the United States, and it was done by people who came north from Mexico. Today there is a huge Hispanic population in New Mexico, and the roots of many of these people in the state go back a lot farther than those of the Anglo residents.

Even older than the Hispanic roots, however, are those of the Indian population. Long before the Mexicans arrived there were large pueblo populations in the Rio Grande Valley and elsewhere. Today these people and their unique culture are one of the main attractions for visitors to the state.

REGIONS AND THEIR CAMPGROUND RESOURCES

The destinations in this book are listed alphabetically. To help you place them in a useful mental framework you might think of them as falling into the following regions of New Mexico.

Rio Grande Valley

The Rio Grande river runs right through the center of New Mexico from north to south. The river allowed the early inhabitants to farm and, with the addition of huge reservoirs, farming is still big in the valley. The major population centers are here too, including Albuquerque, Santa Fe, Las Cruces, and Taos. About two-thirds of the population of the state lives in this region.

For visitors the Rio Grande Valley is the mother lode. The state's largest city, Albuquerque, has lots to offer. Santa Fe and Taos are world famous. The Indian pueblos along the Rio Grande are big attractions. And the southern region with its big reservoirs and warmer winter weather attract large numbers of camping travelers in both the summer and winter.

In the far south there's a region that can be considered part of the Rio Grande Valley even though it's separated from the river by a low range of mountains. This it the very interesting Tularosa Basin with the White Sands National Monument and Missile Range. Most of the Tularosa is described in the *Alamogordo* section although some is also covered in the *Socorro* section.

Destinations in this book that are located in the Rio Grande basin include • *Albuquerque*, • *Alamogordo*, • *El Paso*, • *Las Cruces*, • *Santa Fe*, • *Socorro*, • *Taos,* and • *Truth or Consequences*.

Rocky Mountains

In North America we generally think of the Rocky Mountains as the continental divide. Water falling on the west side of the Rockies flows west into the Pacific. Water on the east side flows into the Atlantic.

It New Mexico things are different. Because the Rockies end in New Mexico it is possible for water from areas to the west of the mountains to sneak around the southern end (via the Rio Grande) and into the Gulf of Mexico. The Continental Divide in New Mexico is hardly noticeable if you're traveling either of the two east-west interstates. On both it is located about 50 miles east of the border with Arizona.

For our purposes we'll consider the Rockies to be the chain of mountain ranges that run from the Colorado border in the north and extend south to the Guadalupe Mountains.

This is probably pushing the traditional definition of the Rockies a little.

In the north the chain is split by the Rio Grande which runs between two arms of the range. Farther south the Rio Grande is to the west of the range until it reaches the Mexico border and curves around to follow the border all the way to the sea.

Many small mountain chains are part of the Rockies in New Mexico. In the north, west of the Rio Grande, are the San Pedro and Jemez Mountains. To the east of the river are the Sangre de Cristo Mountains, the Sandia Mountains, the Manzano Mountains, and the Sacramento Mountains.

Most of this high country is at least partly national forest land, either the Santa Fe National Forest or the Lincoln National Forest. For travelers the mountains offer comfortable summer destinations and snow in the winter.

Destinations in the Rocky Mountain Region in this book are: *Carlsbad,* • *Cloudcroft,* • *Enchanted Circle,* • *Jemez Mountain Trail Scenic Byway and Bandelier National Monument,* • *Mora Valley and SR-518 to Taos,* • *Ruidoso,* and • *Salinas Pueblo Missions National Monument.*

Great Plains

East of the Rockies are the Great Plains with the region east of the Pecos also known as the Llano Estacado or Staked Plains.

You'll hear lots of stories about how the Llano Estacado received its name. Some say that the flat area was so hard to navigate that early explorers had to drive stakes into the ground in order to find their way. Others say that the area was named after native plants which looked like large stakes scattered across the landscape or perhaps after stakes used to tie up horses or even after stakes used by the Indians to stake down their captives. More recently researchers have been saying that the name doesn't even translate into Staked Plains but into Palisade Plains or Stockade Plains. They say that Coronado, the Spanish explorer credited with naming the area, was impressed with the palisades of the Pecos and Canadian River forming the edge of the plain and named the whole area after them. There seems to be no definitive answer to this question so you're welcome to take your pick.

The plains are higher in the north than the south, much of eastern New Mexico is drained by the Pecos River in the south or the Canadian in the north. Most of the destinations listed for this region are along these rivers or one of their tributaries.

Two historical themes will be found in this region. In early days the Santa Fe trail crossed the northern part of the region. Raton, Cimarron, and Las Vegas all have Santa Fe trail history. Later this was cattle country and virtually every destination has that legacy.

The Great Plains destinations listed in this book are: • *Carlsbad,* • *Cimarron,* • *Clovis and Portales,* • *Fort Sumner,* • *Guadalupe Mountains National Park,* • *Las Vegas,* • *Raton,* • *Roswell,* • *Santa Rosa,* and • *Tucumcari.*

Colorado Plateau

Northwestern New Mexico is part of the Colorado Plateau. This elevated natural feature covers much of northwest New Mexico, northern Arizona, southwest Colorado, and southern Utah. The southern edge of the plateau is clearly defined by high cliffs in Arizona (the Mogollon Rim) but in New Mexico the transition is more gradual. The Colorado

Plateau is generally about 2,000 feet higher than areas to the south. In New Mexico the plateau stretches far south to the mountains near Silver City with the southern edge not as dramatic as the rim in Arizona. Some authorities also consider the mountains to the west of Santa Fe to be part of the plateau but for our purposes that region more closely resembles the Rockies.

Most of this region is either Indian or federal government land. Indian land includes the Navajo, Jicarillo Apache, Zuni , Acoma, and Laguna Reservations. Federal lands include extensive stretches of BLM land as well as all or part of the Carson, Santa Fe, Apache, Cibola and Gila National Forests. It is high country with both plateau and mountain terrain, and has hot summers and cool winters. There is very little water and a thin population.

The Colorado Plateau destinations listed in this book include the following: • *Chaco Culture National Historic Park*, • *Chama*, • *El Malpais and El Moro National Monuments*, • *Farmington*, • *Gallup*, • *Grants*, • *Gila Cliff Dwelling National Monument and Area North of Silver City*, • *Mesa Verde National Park and Cortez*, • *Silver City*, and • *Southwest New Mexico National Forest Route*.

I-40 Corridor

Many New Mexico travelers cross the state on I-40 and see little else. These travelers might consider New Mexico to be a pretty dry and not very scenic place since the route is mostly high, dry plateau and grasslands. I-40 crosses the Continental Divide about 48 miles east of the Arizona border, the altitude is about 7,300 feet, but you hardly notice it. It also crosses the Rio Grande in Albuquerque and climbs across a pass to the east where it rises to about 7,000 feet before descending again to the Great Plains. You should note that these altitudes are significantly higher than those along I-10 to the south, a good reason to consider that route for winter travel.

Route 66, the Mother Road, which was the primary route west from Chicago to Los Angeles for many years, followed the same route as I-40. You'll find that many of the towns along I-40 honor the memory with various attractions.

In fact, there are many things to see and do along the route, and we have included many destinations along it. Total distance across New Mexico along I-40 from the Arizona line to the Texas border is 373 miles. The following I-40 destinations, listed from west to east, are along this route (the mileage in parenthesis is the distance from the Arizona border): • *Gallup* (20 miles), • *Grants* (81 miles), • *El Malpais and El Moro National Monuments* (81 miles), • *Albuquerque* (155 miles), • *Santa Rosa* (275 miles), and • *Tucumcari* (332 miles). Because most of these destinations are in either the Colorado Plateau, Rio Grande, or Great Plains regions you'll find that we've listed them in those headings too. Mileage markers along I-40 and exit numbers run from west to east. For an overview see the *Interstate 40 Corridor – New Mexico* on page 225.

I-10 Corridor and the Southwest

The southern interstate across New Mexico crosses country that is, if anything, more barren than that along I-40. However, it is lower and is usually the preferred winter route. From the Arizona border to the Texas border the route is 165 miles. The almost unnoticeable high point is the Continental Divide at about 4,500 feet, some 54 miles east of the Arizona border. Destinations and distance from the Arizona border along this route are • *Lordsburg* (22 miles), • *Deming* (82 miles), • *Los Cruces* (140 miles), and • *El Paso*

(183 miles). Along this route too the mileposts and exit numbers climb from west to east. For an overview see *Interstate 10 Corridor – New Mexico* on page 223.

East Texas

Most of us think of the Southwest as ending at the eastern border of New Mexico, but there are some great destinations in Texas that are not far (at least by Texas standards) to the east. The city of El Paso is by far the largest population center in east Texas. The city marks the spot where the Rio Grande turns north into central New Mexico. Just to the northeast of El Paso is the seldom-visited Guadalupe Mountains National Park. Farther east another mountainous area, the Davis Mountains, serves as a popular playground for Texans and just to the south is the spectacular Big Bend National Park.

These Texas destinations are described in the following sections: ● *Big Bend National Park*, ● *Davis Mountains*, ● *El Paso*, and ● *Guadalupe Mountains National Park*.

GOVERNMENT LANDS AND THEIR CAMPGROUNDS

New Mexico State Campgrounds

If you like fishing and boating on reservoirs you'll love the New Mexico State Park system. We list 41 state park campgrounds in this book (more than one in some state parks) and 28 of them are associated with a reservoir.

The park system has 30 parks that offer camping. Twenty-nine of them are described in this book. Only Clayton Lake State Park, in far northeast New Mexico, is not included here.

CAMPING AT THE CITY OF ROCKS STATE PARK

New Mexico

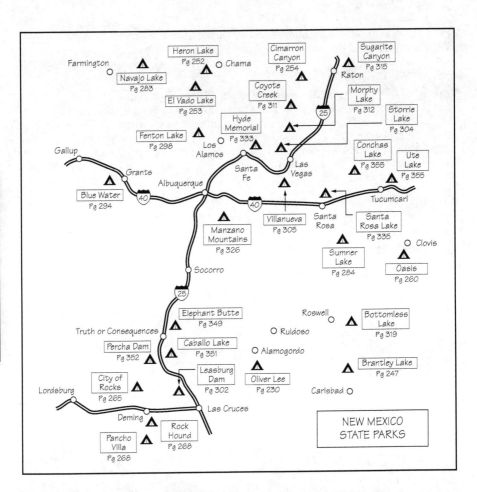

NEW MEXICO STATE PARKS

New Mexico state parks have their own unique system of classifying sites. Large areas with no facilities are often designated camping locations. These are called undeveloped sites or dispersed camping. They make great overflow areas so there is usually room for everyone at campgrounds that have these areas. A developed site is one with a parking pad and usually a picnic table and fire pit. Developed sites are sometimes serviced sites, ones with hookups, often electricity or electricity and water. In general we find that rates for state parks are usually lower than the rates for commercial parks in the same area. Many state park campgrounds have electrical and water hookups and dump stations. Most can handle larger RVs, see the individual listings in this book for more information.

Most state parks have a day fee that you are not required to pay if you are staying in the campground and paying for that. However, signs at entrance gates usually state that you must pay the fee to enter and that there is a fine if you do not. Payment vouchers ask for your site number, which you would not know if you did not have a reservation until you actually selected a site. When we pointed out that it is impossible to comply with the rules rangers usually just smile and indicate that they do not enforce the rule for campers. We suggest, however, that if there is a visitor center near the entrance you stop and check in before entering the park.

In most state parks you can pay for camping with cash or a check (made out to Arizona State Parks). State parks have no provision for receiving payment by credit card unless there is a visitor center. If so, during working hours, you can often use one. At other times check-in is self-service at an iron ranger (envelope deposit box) check-in station. New Mexico state parks have a 21-day stay limit.

Reservations can be made for almost all New Mexico State Parks either by telephone or using the internet. The telephone number is (877) 664-7787 (877 NM-4-RSVP). On the web go to www.nmparks.com for both information and reservations. In each listing we give an information number which is usually at the park itself. Reservations can be made up to 6 months in advance but no less than 1 day prior to your arrival. Telephone operators are familiar with site size and the website has sites sizes and even pictures so you should be able to reserve a site appropriate to your rig. There is a $10.60 per site fee for each reservation that you make.

Federal Campgrounds

In this chapter you'll find a variety of federal campground types. These include national forest campgrounds in 6 different national forests: Carson, Cibola, Gila, Lincoln, San Juan, and Santa Fe. There are also National Park Service campgrounds at Guadalupe Mountains National Park, Mesa Verde National Park, Bandelier National Monument, Chaco Culture National Historical Park, El Moro National Monument, and Gila Cliff Dwellings National Monument. The Bureau of Land Management (BLM) and Corps of Engineers also operate campgrounds in the state. In all you will find a total of 64 federal campgrounds located in New Mexico and listed in this book.

Most RVers think of federal lands campgrounds as best for tent campers and small RVs. Many are, but you'll also find some big-rig campgrounds including a few with utility hookups. Look in our *Alamogordo, Albuquerque, Chama, Gila Cliff Dwellings,* and *Southwest New Mexico National Forest Route* sections for federal campgrounds offering hookups. It is possible to use a big RV in some federal campgrounds and we've included a lot of information in this chapter that will help you decide which ones are right for you and your camping vehicle. Note that most federal campgrounds have a stay limit, often 14 days.

Seniors can get a discount on fees for most federal government campgrounds. If you're a US citizen or permanent resident and 62 years old you can buy a Golden Access Passport. The cost is $10 for life, it gets you half off on most federal campground fees as well as free access to national parks and other federal lands.

DESTINATIONS AND THEIR CAMPGROUNDS

INTERSTATE 10 CORRIDOR – NEW MEXICO

Interstate 10 (I-10) is one of two main corridors running across Arizona and New Mexico. In New Mexico both I-10 and I-40 are fairly high altitude routes but I-10 is flatter and does not have any passes. That means it's the preferred winter route although we don't think it's as scenic.

In New Mexico I-10 is 164 miles long. Mileage markers (and therefore highway exit numbers) start at the western border of the state. The campgrounds listed below are all in New Mexico. See the *Interstate 10 Corridor* section in the Arizona chapter for campgrounds in that state.

You will note that many of the campgrounds along the highway are described in other places in this book. Rather than including them twice we've given the page number where you can find the detailed descriptions.

Interstate 10 Corridor Campgrounds

➲ **Exit 22**

🚐 LORDSBURG KOA *(Listed under Lordsburg on page 306)*

➲ **Exit 81**

🚐 81 PALMS RV PARK *(Listed under Deming on page 267)*

➲ **Exit 82A**

🚐 HITCHIN POST RV PARK *(Listed under Deming on page 267)*

🚐 STARLIGHT VILLAGE RESORT *(Listed under Deming on page 268)*

➲ **Exit 85**

🚐 DREAMCATCHER RV PARK *(Listed under Deming on page 266)*

🚐 SUNRISE RV PARK *(Listed under Deming on page 267)*

🚐 WAGON WHEEL RV PARK *(Listed under Deming on page 266)*

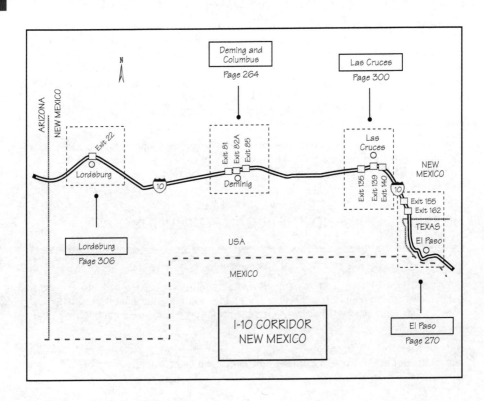

🚐 DEMING ROADRUNNER RV PARK *(Listed under Deming on page 266)*

🚐 LITTLE VINEYARD RV PARK *(Listed under Deming on page 266)*

➲ *Exit 135*

🚐 LAS CRUCES KOA *(Listed under Las Cruces on page 301)*

➲ *Exit 139*

🚐 COACHLIGHT INN AND RV PARK *(Listed under Las Cruces on page 301)*

🚐 SUNNY ACRES RV PARK *(Listed under Las Cruces on page 303)*

➲ *Exit 140*

🚐 HACIENDA RV AND RALLY RESORT *(Listed under Las Cruces on page 301)*

🚐 SIESTA RV PARK *(Listed under Las Cruces on page 302)*

➲ *Exit 155*

🚐 WESTERN SKY'S RV PARK *(Listed under El Paso on page 272)*

➲ *Exit 162*

🚐 EL PASO WEST RV PARK *(Listed under El Paso on page 272)*

INTERSTATE 40 CORRIDOR – NEW MEXICO

Interstate 40 (I-40) and Interstate 10 are the two main corridors running across Arizona and New Mexico. Of the two, I-40 is probably the most scenic. In New Mexico both I-40 and I-10 are fairly high altitude routes but I-10 is flatter and does not have any passes. In the winter I-10 is probably the best route.

In New Mexico I-40 is 372 miles long. Mileage markers (and therefore highway exit numbers) start at the western border of the state. The campgrounds listed below are all in New Mexico. See the *Interstate 40 Corridor* section in the Arizona chapter for campgrounds in that state.

You will note that many of the campgrounds along the highway are described in other places in this book. Rather than including them twice we've given the page number where you can find the detailed descriptions.

Interstate 40 Corridor Campgrounds

➲ *Exit 16*

🚐 USA RV PARK *(Listed under Gallup on page 288)*

➲ *Exit 26*

🚐 GALLUP KOA *(Listed under Gallup on page 287)*

➲ *Exit 33*

🚐 RED ROCK PARK *(Listed under Gallup on page 288)*

➲ *Exit 79*

🚐 BAR S RV PARK *(Listed under Grants on page 293)*

➲ *Exit 81*

🚐 BLUE SPRUCE RV PARK *(Listed under Grants on page 293)*

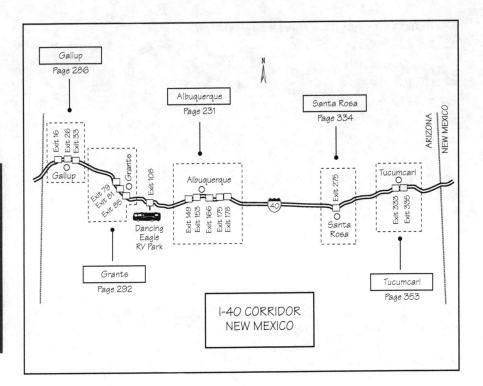

CIBOLA SANDS KOA *(Listed under Grants on page 293)*

➲ **Exit 85**

LAVALAND RV PARK *(Listed under Grants on page 294)*

➲ **Exit 108**

DANCING EAGLE RV PARK *(Open All Year)*
Res and Info: (877) 440-9969, (505) 552-1111, www.dancingeaglecasino.com/rv.html
Location: 42 Miles W of Albuquerque, *N 35° 01' 52", W 107° 28' 32", 5,900 Ft*

35 Sites – This new RV park is run by the Laguna Pueblo in conjunction with the new Dancing Eagle Casino across the parking lot. Sites here are long back-ins and pull-thrus in a fenced gravel lot. These are all electric and water sites with lengths to 70 feet. There is a dump station and laundry. The Travel Center across the road has showers and a store and the casino has a restaurant, all within easy walking distance of the campground. Take Exit 108 from I-40 about 42 miles west of Albuquerque. You'll see the campground next to the road on the south side of the highway.

➲ **Exit 149**

ENCHANTED TRAILS RV PARK AND TRADING POST *(Listed under Albuquerque on page 236)*

AMERICAN RV PARK *(Listed under Albuquerque on page 236)*

🚐 **HIGH DESERT RV PARK** *(Listed under Albuquerque on page 236)*

➲ *Exit 153*

🚐 **PALISADES RV PARK** *(Listed under Albuquerque on page 237)*

➲ *Exit 166*

🚐 **ALBUQUERQUE CENTRAL KOA** *(Listed under Albuquerque on page 237)*

➲ *Exit 175*

🚐 **TURQUOISE TRAIL RV CAMPGROUND AND RV PARK** *(Listed under Albuquerque on page 238)*

➲ *Exit 178*

🚐 **HIDDEN VALLEY RESORT** *(Listed under Albuquerque on page 238)*

➲ *Exit 275*

🚐 **SANTA ROSA CAMPGROUND** *(Listed under Santa Rosa on page 334)*

🚐 **SANTA ROSA LAKE STATE PARK – JUNIPER PARK CAMPGROUND** *(Listed under Santa Rosa, page 335)*

🚐 **SANTA ROSA LAKE STATE PARK – ROCKY POINT CAMPGROUND** *(Listed under Santa Rosa on page 336)*

➲ *Exit 333*

🚐 **MOUNTAIN ROAD RV PARK** *(Listed under Tucumcari on page 354)*

➲ *Exit 335*

🚐 **CACTUS RV PARK** *(Listed under Tucumcari on page 354)*

🚐 **EMPTY SADDLE RV PARK** *(Listed under Tucumcari on page 354)*

🚐 **KOA OF TUCUMCARI** *(Listed under Tucumcari on page 354)*

NEW MEXICO

ALAMOGORDO AND THE TULAROSA BASIN

Alamogordo (population about 35,000) sits up against the Sacramento Mountains and faces westward across the Tularosa Basin, a flat plain that has played an important part in the U.S. atomic and missile programs. There are a surprising number of interesting things to see and do in the region. The busiest RV season here is winter, snowbirds like the area. Summer, despite the heat, is also popular since there are so many attractions in the surrounding area. Still, you might consider basing yourself up high in Ruidoso with day trips to visit the Tularosa Basin.

In Alamogordo itself is the excellent **New Mexico Museum of Space History**. It is a large museum covering space flight. There is an IMAX theater and a planetarium.

White Sands National Monument is located about 22 miles west of Alamogordo. The park is a 275-square mile area of brilliantly white gypsum dunes. There's a visitor center, a sixteen-mile drive, and trails through the dunes. The whole thing is even more interesting since it sits in the middle of the White Sands Missile Testing area. Fortunately the park road is closed when rocket tests are being conducted. There is very limited walk-in tent camping in the monument, check at the visitor center if you are interested.

There's a museum that is open to the public at the White Sands Missile Range, the **White Sands Missile Range Museum and Missile Park**. The missile park has examples of

NEW MEXICO

THE WHITE SANDS NATIONAL MONUMENT

many missiles including a U.S. version of Germany's WWII era V-1, Nikes, the Red-stone, and others. The entrance road is 44 miles west of Alamogordo off US-70. Since it's on a military reservation you'll need to show your driver's license, vehicle registration, and proof of insurance.

The **Three Rivers Petroglyph National Recreation Area** is located about 32 miles north of Alamogordo. It's a little-visited site in rugged country that contains over 20,000 petroglyphs, most created by the Jornada Mogollon people about 1,000 years ago. There's a campground, see below for a description of the campground as well as instructions for getting there.

A bit north of the Three Rivers Petroglyph National Recreation Area is the **Valley of Fires BLM Recreation Area**. This is a lava flow area that is said to be the most recent in the U.S., about 1,500 years old. It too has a campground, see below.

Alamogordo and the Tularosa Basin Campgrounds

ALAMOGORDO ROADRUNNER CAMPGROUND *(Open All Year)*

Reservations: (575) 437-3003
Information: (877) 437-3003, www.roadrunnercampground.com,
          info@roadrunnercampground.com
Location: Alamogordo, *N 32° 55' 04", W 105° 57' 27", 4,300 Ft*

75 Sites – The campground was originally a KOA although it is no longer. It is well-

run and has been maintained in good condition. The main road in the park is paved and secondary roads are gravel. There are 63 RV sites, 10 tent sites, and 2 rental cabins. The sites have a combination of hookup offerings. There are many pull-thrus to about 50 feet. Trees and landscaping are used to separate the sites and some sites have brick lattice dividers. Each site has a cement picnic table on a paved patio and a raised barbecue grill. Internet access is available via a telephone data port, a DSL outlet, or Wi-Fi in the building. Those camped near the building pick up Wi-Fi at their sites. Soon a computer will be added for additional email access. There is a seasonal heated pool. A morning complementary breakfast is available. The office sells grocery items, RV supplies, gifts, and propane. In Alamogordo from northbound US -54 head east on 24th Street. The campground is on the right in a block and a half.

⬛ DESERT PARADISE RV PARK *(Open All Year)*

Res and Info: (575) 434-2266, www.geocities.com/desert_paradise_park,
desertparadisepark@yahoo.com
Location: Alamogordo, *N 32° 52' 03", W 105° 58' 58", 4,200 Ft*

32 Sites – The sites in this park are in 2 main areas. Entering the park there are 2 rows of mobile homes. One of the rows has 3 back-in spaces open for RVs. The outside row has 13 back-in spaces. These sites are as long as 70 feet. Behind the clubhouse is the second area of the park. It has is a row of 16 pull-thru sites also to about 70 feet in length. All of the sites have full hookups including cable TV. Parking is on gravel and there is a picnic

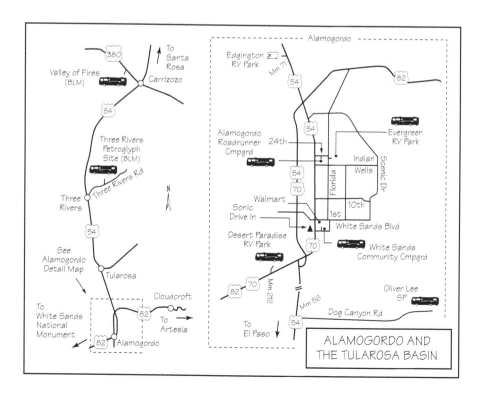

ALAMOGORDO AND
THE TULAROSA BASIN

table at each site. A data port is available for internet access and a courtesy phone in the office can be used for calling card calls. The clubhouse has a kitchen, sitting area, book library, and a TV. Winter is busy here with snowbird visitors. The campground is on the north side of US-82 some 1.1 miles west of the convergence of US-70 and US-54 at the south end of Alamogordo.

☎ EVERGREEN RV PARK *(Open All Year)*

Information: (575) 437-3721, evergreenpark@netmdc.com
Location: Alamogordo, *N 32° 55' 04", W 105° 57' 06", 4,200 Ft*

27 Sites – The RV park is part of a large mobile home park which is to the north with the RV park separate to the south. The RV park has 48 spaces, 21 of which are rented on an annual basis. Eighteen of the remaining spaces are usually rented by the season. The remaining 9 are kept for daily and weekly rentals. The sites are identical. They are all full hookup back-ins with cable TV, and are about 55 feet in length. There is a paved parking pad and a paved patio. A data port is available in the office for internet access. This park is for self contained rigs only. A bathroom in the activity center is not for general RV park use. There are no showers. A pool is located in the mobile home park section. A public laundry is about a block away. Reservations or credit cards are not accepted. In Alamogordo from northbound US-54 head east on 24th Street. Drive three blocks and turn right on North Florida Ave. The campground is on the left after the turn.

☎ WHITE SANDS COMMUNITY CAMPGROUND *(Open All Year)*

Information: (575) 437-8388
Location: Alamogordo, *N 32° 53' 07", W 105° 57' 24", 4,300 Ft*

86 Sites – A large part of this park is a mobile home park, but the RV park is in a separate area. The RV park has 2 sections. The older section has 50 sites, including 28 pull-thrus to 60 feet long. These sites have paved parking and a paved patio. The sites are separated by latticed brick dividers and have 30-amp power. The new section has 36 sites, all back-ins with 50-amp power. These sites are mostly 60 feet in length and very wide. Parking in the new section is on gravel and there are no patios. A gravel area in front of the site has a picnic table. All sites are full hookup including cable TV. A data port is available in the office for internet. Other amenities include a beauty shop, an exercise room, basketball, tennis, horseshoes, shuffle board, a clubhouse with a full service kitchen, pool table, and big screen television. The pool is new and very nice. The RV park is off the east side of US-54 in Alamogordo just south of East 1st Street.

☎ OLIVER LEE STATE PARK *(Open All Year)*

Reservations: (877) 664-7787, www.nmparks.com
Information: (575) 437-8284, (888) 667-2757,www.nmparks.com
Location: 14 Miles S of Alamogordo, *N 32° 44' 51", W 105° 54' 53", 4,300 Ft*

44 Sites – The sites in this campground are off two loops near the Sacramento Mountains overlooking the valley. Eighteen sites have electric and water hookups. Water is available to the other sites. Some sites have sheltered picnic tables and all have picnic tables and fire pits. The sites are wide parallel parking style sites, some long enough for RVs to 40 feet and all with plenty of width for slide-outs and tow cars too. There are wheel-

chair accessible bathrooms and showers. A pay telephone is at the visitor center near the entrance to the campground. Several trails leave from the park. Nearby is the Oliver Lee Ranch which is open to the public by guided tour on Saturday and Sundays at 3:00 pm. The ruin of Frenchy's Cabin is near the campground. Reservations are accepted for only 7 sites. The campground access road goes east from US-54 about 9 miles south of Alamogordo. It's 4.5 miles in to the campground on a good paved road.

▣ THREE RIVERS PETROGLYPH SITE *(Open All Year)*
Information: (575) 525-4300
Location: 32 Miles N of Alamogordo, *N 33° 20' 40", W 106° 00' 33", 5,000 Ft*

8 Sites – This is a BLM site with eight campsites. Two have electrical and water hookups for RVs to 45 feet. A few trees provide shade. There are six shelters with barbecue grills, campsites double as picnic sites. The fee for day use or no-hookup camping is only $2. A visitor center here is occasionally staffed by volunteers. Trails lead to thousands of petroglyphs created by the Jornada Mogollon people from 900 to 1400 A.D. The access highway is paved. From Alamogordo drive north on US-54 for some 27 miles to Three Rivers. There turn right on Three Rivers Road and drive 4.5 miles to the campground.

▣ VALLEY OF FIRES BLM RECREATION AREA *(Open All Year)*
Information: (575) 648-2241, (575) 627-0272
Location: 59 Miles N of Alamogordo, *N 33° 41' 05", W 105° 55' 12", 5,200 Ft*

23 Sites – This campground occupies a site surrounded by a lava flow. These are very large sites, both back-ins and pull-thrus. Some have electrical hookups. From Albuquerque drive north on US-54 to the intersection with US-380, a distance of 55 miles. Turn left on US-380, the entrance to the recreation area is on the left in another 3.9 miles.

ALBUQUERQUE

New Mexico's largest city (population about 800,000 in the metro area) isn't as popular with travelers as the two tourist Meccas to the north: Santa Fe and Taos. Still, the town definitely has its attractions including one of the most popular RV events in the nation, the Albuquerque Balloon Festival. You may find that you travel through Albuquerque frequently since it's right at the intersection of two of New Mexico's biggest highways: north/south I-25 and east/west I-40.

The **Albuquerque International Balloon Festival** has been held every October since 1972. One of the reasons the festival is held here is the so-called **Albuquerque Box**. The box occurs in October on about 30% of the mornings. It consists of a low-level wind that carries balloons south, with a higher level breeze that brings them back north, often allowing them to land at very near the same place they departed from. This makes Albuquerque a very good place for a huge balloon festival, and the city takes advantage of it. North of central Albuquerque you'll find **Balloon Fiesta Park** and the **Anderson-Abruzzo Albuquerque International Balloon Museum**. During the first week of October there will be nearly 750 balloons here, as well as the thousands of RVers who have come to watch the action. See the campground write-up below for information about how to attend the festival in your RV.

NEW MEXICO

STREET MARKET IN OLD TOWN ALBUQUERQUE

If you happen to be visiting Albuquerque outside Balloon Festival time there are other things to do. Probably the most interesting attraction is the **Old Town** which clusters around a Mexican-style square with the old **San Felipe de Neri Church** facing the north side of the square. This district has its share of tourist shops but it also has galleries with excellent artwork and some good places to eat. Along the edges of the district are a number of very good museums including the **Albuquerque Museum**, the **New Mexico Museum of Natural History and Science**, and the **Indian Pueblo Cultural Center**.

At the northwest edge of Albuquerque is **Petroglyph National Monument**. Trails lead through basaltic rocks with over 15,000 petroglyphs. Take Exit 154 from I-40 and follow signs five miles north to the monument.

The **Coronado State Monument** is located a few miles north of Albuquerque in the town of Bernalillo. There you'll find a museum with murals recovered from kiva walls during the excavation of the Kuaua Pueblo at the site. Outside the museum you can descend into a kiva and view replicas of the murals on its walls. At the entrance to the monument is Coronado Campground, described below. To reach the monument drive north from Albuquerque on I-25 to Exit 242. Drive westward for 1.6 miles to the monument entrance on your right.

A popular day trip from Albuquerque is a ride on the **Sandia Peak Tramway** up the west side of the Sandia Mountains to Sandia Peak. Up top are an observation point, a restaurant, and trails. This is also the top of the Sandia Peak Ski area so there are downhill as well as cross-country ski trails. It's also possible to drive up Sandia Peak from the east on the **Sandia Crest Byway**. Do this only in a smaller vehicle. To reach it drive east on I-40 from Albuquerque and take Exit 175. Drive north on SR-14 for 6.1 miles and turn left onto SR-536. This is the Sandia Crest Byway and it leads about 13 miles thought the piney Cibola National Forest to the Sandia Crest at 10,678 ft. Along the way you might stop at the **Museum of Archeology and Material Culture** in Cedar Crest and the **Tinkertown** Museum.

Actually, during the first part of this trip, while on SR-14, you were traveling another recommended local driving route. This is the **Turquoise Trail**. It's an alternative way of driving between Albuquerque and Santa Fe and leads 50 miles from the Tijeras intersection (Exit 175) on I-40 up to Santa Fe. Along the way it passes through the interesting former mining towns of **Golden, Madrid,** and **Cerrillos**.

During the year the Albuquerque area hosts a number of events. In addition to the Balloon Festival there's the **Gathering of Nations Powwow** in April, the **New Mexico Arts and Crafts Fair** in late June, and the **Bernalillo Wine Festival** in Bernalillo on Labor Day. The **New Mexico State Fair** is held in Albuquerque during September.

Albuquerque, like Taos and Santa Fe is surrounded by Indian reservations and pueblos. Two of these pueblos, Ácoma and Laguna, are off I-40 to the west. One, Isleta, is along the Rio Grande and I-25 to the south. Four; Sandia, San Felipe, Santo Domingo, and Cochiti; are along the Rio Grande to the north. An additional two, Santa Ana and Zia, are along the Jemez River which flows into the Rio Grande from the west. Additional pueblos in New Mexico are described in the Santa Fe, Taos, Jemez Mountain Trail, and Gallup sections of this chapter.

- **Ácoma Pueblo** is unique, one of only three original adobe pueblos still being occupied. The others are Taos and old Orabi on the Hopi Reservation in Arizona. The Ácoma Pueblo is also called "**Sky City**" because it occupies a site atop a 375 foot high butte. The Ácoma people produce a variety of pottery styles for sale as well as jewelry. To reach Sky City drive west from Albuquerque on I-40 a distance of 42 miles to Exit 108 and then drive south on Tribal Road 23 for 11 miles to the visitor center. This is where you depart for your tour of Sky City. The Ácoma Pueblo also maintains a casino, the **Sky City Casino**, along I-40. It's at Exit 102.

- **Laguna Pueblo** is located just east of Ácoma Pueblo, a little closer to Albuquerque. It occupies the I-40 travel corridor, the main Laguna village of **Old Laguna** is easily visible just north of I-40 near Mile 125. Look for the white San Jose de Laguna Mission which appears to dominate the village center. There are a number of shops in Old Laguna where crafts may be purchased. Easiest access is from I-40 at Exit 124, then drive old Route 66 eastward a mile to the town. The pueblo also owns a new casino, the **Dancing Eagle**, off I-40 at Exit 108. There is an RV park there which is described below as the Dancing Eagle RV Park.

- **Isleta Pueblo** is the only one located south of Albuquerque. The main attraction is the **Isleta Gaming Palace**, a casino, located off I-25 at Exit 215. Nearby is a golf course and campground, see **Isleta Lakes and Recreation Area** below for a description of the campground. The Isleta Pueblo itself is located just west of the Rio Grande about 3 miles south of the Casino and is accessible using SR-47, the highway that exits I-25 at Exit 215 and then runs past the Casino. Most tourists come to see the **San Augustine Catholic church** in the village. There are also some galleries and shops selling Indian art and crafts.

- **Sandia Pueblo** is located just north of Albuquerque. The pueblo operates a casino, the **Sandia Casino**. To reach it take Exit 235 from I-25 and drive east a short distance, it is on the left. On the right is the **Bien Mur Market Center**, the largest pueblo-operated market for arts and crafts in the area.

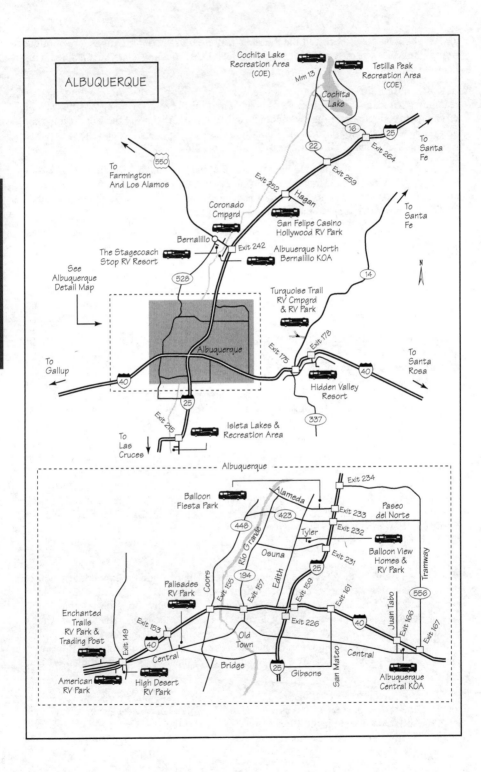

ALBUQUERQUE

- **Santa Ana Pueblo**, the farthest east of those along the Jemez River, operates the **Santa Ana Star Casino** and twenty-seven hole **Santa Ana Golf Course**. There's also a **Hyatt Regency** on the reservation which houses the tribe's **Tamaya Cultural Center**. To reach these facilities leave I-25 at Exit 242 and drive west for 2.5 miles on SR-44.

- **San Felipe Pueblo** is the next pueblo north from Santa Ana Pueblo along I-25. The tribe's **Casino Hollywood** is at Exit 252 of I-25 and has an RV park, see **San Felipe Casino Hollywood RV Park** below for more information. The village is on the opposite side of the freeway about 3 miles distant and is known for its **church** and also its **Corn Dance** which is held May 1.

- **Santo Domingo Pueblo**, midway between Albuquerque and Santa Fe off I-25 offers little in the way of tourist attractions. The village is located off I-25 at Exit 259, then northwest about 4 miles. This puts the village just north of San Felipe Pueblo's village. There are some shops in the village on the access road and also on the plaza at the church. The pueblo is known for its **Corn Dance** on August 4 and its **Labor Day weekend arts and crafts fair**.

- **Cochiti Pueblo** is the farthest north of the Keres-speaking Rio Grande pueblos. It's actually closer to Santa Fe than Albuquerque but is described here because it has much in common with the adjoining pueblos to the south. The village is located near the large Cochiti Dam and its reservoir, called Cochiti Lake. There are two campgrounds on the lake, see Cochiti Lake Recreation Area and Tetilla Peak Recreation Area write-ups below. The artists of this pueblo are known for their clay storyteller figures and for their drums. A new national monument, **Tent Rocks**, is located near the village and operated by the pueblo in conjunction with the BLM. The monument showcases an area of striking hoodoos. To reach the village take Exit 264 from I-25. Drive northwest on SR-16. After 8.2 miles you'll meet SR-22. Continue north on SR-22 for 2.5 miles. Turn left on BIA-84 and drive about 3 miles to the village. From here you can follow signs about 5 miles south to Tent Rocks National Monument.

- **Zia Pueblo** is a little off the beaten path. There are no major tourist developments related to the pueblo but there is a **Cultural Center** in the village where crafts are displayed and information about local artists is available. The Zias are known for their pottery and baskets, a Zia symbol is used on the New Mexico state flag. The village also has a very striking little church, **Nuestra Señora de la Asunción**. To reach the pueblo take Exit 242 from I-25 and drive west on SR-44. In 17 miles you'll see the village on the right.

Albuquerque Campgrounds

🚐 **BALLOON FIESTA PARK** *(Only Open During Balloon Festival)*
   Res and Info: (888) 422-7277, www.balloonfiesta.com
   Location: Albuquerque, *N 35° 11' 06", W 106° 35' 52", 5,100 Ft*

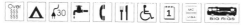

1,800 Sites – The Balloon Park is 320 acres. There is a large grass area for launching balloons with a row of 177 vendor sites along the side. The park has camping facilities for about 1,800 RVs. The only facilities other than hookups are portable toilets although kiosks do sell food. Each site is twice the width of an RV and 55 feet long. There are 4 four types and prices of sites, the following information was correct for 2008, it is likely that there will be some changes over time. The 900 Standard Sites have no hookups and cost $30. A $5/night discount is given if you reserve and pay for 9 or more nights. About

480 Premium Sites have 20-amp electricity (maybe 50-amp soon) and water. They cost $65 per night. The 300 VIP sites have no hookups but are adjacent to Fiesta Park and cost $85. The 120 most expensive sites are the Presidents Compound Sites, 60 for officials and 60 for the public. The charge for these is $150 per day. Premium and Presidents sites include entry to the festival which normally costs $6 on-line. Reservations are required for all sites and there is a 3-day minimum. Electric and water serviced sites normally are fully reserved sometime in May-June and the VIP sites a little later during June-July. The festival lasts for ten days beginning the Friday before the first Saturday of October. Easiest access is from Exit 233 of I-25, you should receive parking information when you make your reservations.

AMERICAN RV PARK *(Open All Year)*

Reservations: (800) 282-8885, info@americanrvpark.com
Information: (505) 831-3545, www.americanrvpark.com
Location: 3 Miles W of Albuquerque, *N 35° 03' 37", W 106° 47' 49", 5,700 Ft*

186 Sites – American RV Park is a nice modern park with good facilities. Many of the sites are pull-thrus, some as long as 65 feet. Fifteen of the back-in sites are available for tenting and several of these sites have a sand pad for pitching the tent. Wi-Fi is provided to the park by an independent vendor. A high-speed data port is provided for other internet access. There is a pool and a spa. The office building houses a store where grocery items are sold and there is a dining area with a fireplace, tables, and chairs. A free continental breakfast is served daily. Other amenities are basketball, horseshoes, a picnic/barbecue area, and recreation room. To drive to the campground take Exit 149 from I-40. This is just west of the city. Go south for just a short distance and turn right on Central Ave SW which parallels the freeway. Watch carefully and don't make the mistake of getting back on the freeway on-ramp there. The campground is on the left .6 miles west of the exit.

ENCHANTED TRAILS RV PARK AND TRADING POST *(Open All Year)*

Reservations: (800) 326-6317
Information: (505) 831-6317, www.enchantedtrails.com
Location: 3 Miles W of Albuquerque, *N 35° 03' 35", W 106° 48' 35", 5,700 Ft*

135 Sites – Almost all sites in this RV park are pull-thrus with full hookups. They are generally about 60 feet in length but there are also some even longer. There is a data port for internet access as well as Wi-Fi. Currently the building which houses the office has a large gift shop, a laundry, TV & billiards room and a clubhouse. Plans are to add a restaurant to this building. A seasonal swimming pool is located next to the office. Propane is for sale in the park. A new Camping World RV supply store is next door. To drive to the campground take Exit 149 from I-40. This is just west of the city. Go north to the access road that goes west along the north side of the highway, this is called Central Ave NW. Drive west for 1.3 miles to the RV park.

HIGH DESERT RV PARK *(Open All Year)*

Res and Info: (866) 839-9035, www.highdesertrvpark.com
Location: 3 Miles W of Albuquerque, *N 35° 03' 41", W 106° 47' 28", 5,700 Ft*

77 Sites – The sites in this park are back-ins and pull-thrus to 66 feet with parking in an open gravel lot. Wi-Fi is provided to the park by an independent contractor. There is a data port in the office and instant-on telephone is available at some sites. To drive to the campground take Exit 149 from I-40. This is just west of the city. Go south for just a short distance and turn right on Central Ave. SW which parallels the freeway. Watch carefully and don't make the mistake of getting back on the freeway on-ramp there. The campground is on the left .2 miles west of the exit.

ALBUQUERQUE CENTRAL KOA *(Open All Year)*

Reservations: (800) 562-7781, www.koa.com
Information: (505) 296-2729, www.albuquerquekoa.com, albuquerque@koa.net
Location: Albuquerque, N 35° 04' 21", W 106° 30' 30", 5,500 Ft

175 Sites – There are 167 RV sites, 8 tent sites (with electric), an open tenting area and 11 rental cabins. There are also 28 sites for RV storage. A good percentage of the sites are pull-thrus, some to 70 feet. Wi-Fi is provided to the park at no additional charge and a data port is provided for other internet access. The office building has a store which has a good stock of grocery items, RV supplies, and gifts. Propane is also available. This is also a rental location for Cruise American RV Rentals. There is a seasonal heated pool and an indoor spa open year-round. Take Exit 167 from I-40 on the east side of Albuquerque. Head west on Central Avenue for .8 miles. Turn right on Figueroa St. NE and the campground will be two blocks ahead.

BALLOON VIEW HOMES & RV PARK *(Open All Year)*

Res and Info: (800) 932-9523, (505) 345-3716
Location: Albuquerque, *N 35° 09' 20", W 106° 37' 01", 5,000 Ft*

87 Sites – This park is a combination mobile home park and RV park. Registration is in the clubhouse which is in the mobile home park area. There are 87 sites in the RV park. All of the sites except 14 are pull-thrus to about 45 feet in length. The sites are full hook-up including cable TV. Many of the sites are occupied by what appears to be monthly renters and the park looks a little shabby. The sites are all side-by-side with little separation between sites. Each site does, however, have a paved patio. There are no bathrooms in the RV park, but bathrooms and showers are available in the clubhouse (in the mobile home section). This is a little inconvenient, because it is quite a walk to get there. Also at the clubhouse there is an exercise room, spa, sauna, telephone and a data port for internet access. From I-25 in north Albuquerque take Exit 231 and drive west on Osuna Rd. NE. After 2.3 miles turn right on Edith Blvd NE and drive two blocks. Turn right on Tyler Rd NE and you'll see the campgrounds entrance on the right.

PALISADES RV PARK *(Open All Year)*

Res and Info: (505) 831-5000
Location: Albuquerque, *N 35° 04' 29", W 106° 44' 12", 5,100 Ft*

112 Sites – The Palisades seems to be primarily a park with permanent residents but there are 8 pull-thru sites out front for travelers. There are also two tent sites. The office sells

a few grocery items, but a big Albertson's is just down the street. Propane is available in the park. Easiest access to the park is by taking Exit 153 from I-40 in Albuquerque. Drive south on Nolasco Road NW for .9 miles. Turn left on Central Ave. NW, you'll see the campground entrance on the left in .4 mile.

HIDDEN VALLEY RESORT *(Open All Year)*

Reservations: (800) 326-2024
Information: (505) 281-3363
Location: 10 Miles E of Albuquerque, *N 35° 06' 14", W 106° 20' 21", 6,600 Ft*

119 Sites – This is a popular RV park to the east of Albuquerque. It is situated at a higher altitude than the city so summer temperatures are cooler than at the parks nearer to the city. Sites here are closely spaced but there are back-ins and pull-thrus to 65 feet. There are also tent sites. The pool area has a heated swimming pool, spa and recreation hall. A data port is provided for internet access. Other amenities include a basketball court, a pet exercise area, a dump station, a library and clubhouse exchange, RV storage, and a short hiking trail. The park is associated with Resorts of Distinction, Coast to Coast, and Caravan RPI. They also give AARP and Military Discounts. Take Exit 178 from I-40 east of Albuquerque. The campground entrance is on the south side of the highway, look for the sign just to the left, the campground isn't immediately visible since it is tucked into a small valley just out of sight.

TURQUOISE TRAIL RV CAMPGROUND AND RV PARK *(Open All Year)*

Res and Info: (505) 281-2005, debswe@earthlink.net
Location: 14 Miles E of Albuquerque, *N 35° 08' 34", W 106° 22' 01", 6,900 Ft*

87 Sites – The Turquoise Trail is another campground located east of Albuquerque at a higher altitude. In summer these are popular parks because temperatures are lower than in town. There are many tent sites. RV sites here are back-ins and pull-thrus to 70 feet. From Exit 175 of I-40 drive north on the Turquoise Trail, SR-14. In four miles turn left on Snowline Dr and proceed .3 mile to the campground.

ALBUQUERQUE NORTH/ BERNALILLO KOA *(Open All Year)*

Reservations: (800) 562-3616, www.koa.com
Information: (505) 867-5227
Location: 10 Miles N of Albuquerque, N 35° 18' 24", W 106° 32' 23", 5,100 Ft

87 Sites – This KOA, like most, has a variety of RV sites, tent sites, and camping cabins. RV sites include pull-thrus to 60 feet in length. There is a seasonal swimming pool. The office stocks grocery items, RV supplies, gifts, and sells propane. Every morning year-round a free pancake breakfast is served. Other menu items can be purchased. Other amenities include horseshoes, croquet, a meeting area, a game room, book trade, and movie rentals. A data port is provided for internet access. From I-25 north of Albuquerque take Exit 242. On the west side of the freeway turn south at the first road, S. Hill Rd., and follow it .6 mile to the KOA.

CORONADO CAMPGROUND *(Open All Year)*

Res and Info: (505) 980-8256, www.townofbernalillo.lib.nm.us
Location: 11 Miles N of Albuquerque, *N 35° 19' 30", W 106° 33' 37", 5,000 Ft*

35 Sites – Coronado is a City of Bernalillo campground. Sites are located in 2 areas. The main area has 27 sites which all have electricity and water hookups. A separate secondary area has 8 sites with water shared between sites and no electricity. Near the secondary area is an open tenting area. The main area sites are back-ins and pull-thrus up to 70 feet in length, some next to the river. Each has a pretty adobe picnic shelter decorated with southwest art. Wheelchair accessible bathrooms are located in both the main and secondary campground areas. The park does not have a laundry on-site, but there is one on Hwy 550 nearby. There is a $10 non-refundable fee for each campsite reserved. Prices go up to $30 a day for any site during the balloon festival. From I-25 north of Albuquerque take Exit 242. Travel west on US-550 for 1.5 miles. Immediately after crossing the Rio Grande the campground entrance is on the right.

THE STAGECOACH STOP RV RESORT *(Open All Year)*

Reservations: (888) 272-PARK
Information: (505) 867-1000
Location: 12 Miles N of Albuquerque, *N 35° 19' 23", W 106° 34' 14", 5,200 Ft*

83 Sites – All sites in this campground are pull-thrus, some to 60 feet. There are trees (cottonwoods and pines mostly) scattered throughout the park and some landscaping. All sites are full hookup including cable TV and all have a picnic table at the site. A high speed network hookup and also Wi-Fi are available in the office. The main building which houses the office also has a good size convenience store which sells grocery items and RV supplies. In this building are bathrooms and showers, an exercise room, and a very nice meeting/game room with a big fire place and nice living room style furniture. The swimming pool is seasonal and there is a spa. There are also 3 rental cabins and a picnic pavilion. From I-25 north of Albuquerque take Exit 242. Travel west on US-550 for 2.3 miles. Turn left on SR-528, the campground entrance is on the left in a half mile.

SAN FELIPE CASINO HOLLYWOOD RV PARK *(Open All Year)*

Information: (505) 771-5803
Location: 20 Miles N of Albuquerque, *N 35° 24' 53", W 106° 24' 06", 5,300 Ft*

100 Sites – This RV park is pretty basic. It is a big gravel lot sitting between the San Felipe Casino and the Hollywood Hills Speedway. This lot has 100 side-by-side parking lot style spaces which are all pull-thrus and have electrical hookups. There is a dump station and a water fill station. There are no other facilities specifically for the RVs. The casino has public bathrooms and restaurants. There is also a Phillips 66 gas station out front which has a small convenience store and a restaurant and also offers showers. Registration is at the guest services counter in the casino. Take Exit 252 from I-25 north of Albuquerque. The casino and RV parking area are on the east side of the freeway.

NEW MEXICO

◄ COCHITI LAKE RECREATION AREA *(Open All Year)*

Reservations: (877) 444-6777, www.recreation.gov
Information: (505) 465-0307, http://www.spa.usace.army.mil/recreation/cochiti/index.htm
Location: 45 Miles N of Albuquerque, *N 35° 38' 32", W 106° 19' 31", 5,400 Ft*

56 Sites – Cochiti Lake is a Corps of Engineers campground. The sites are off 2 loops - A (sites 1-34) and B (sites 35-56). All of the sites in loop A have electric (most have water) and a paved parking pad. These sites have picnic tables (some covered) and raised barbecue grills. B loop has no hookups but water is available. Parking in B loop is on gravel. The sites all have picnic shelter buildings and barbecue grills. Quite a few of the A and B loop sites are pull-thrus to as long as 80 feet. The back-in sites are mostly to 30 feet or less. There is also an overflow area which has about 25 sites for smaller rigs or tenting. It is mostly used for groups. Loop A has wheelchair-accessible flush toilets and showers and B loop has vault style toilets. There's a boat launch near the entrance to the campground. From I-25 take Exit 264 and drive northwest on SR-16. After 8.2 miles you'll meet SR-22. Continue north on SR-22 for 3.8 miles to the entrance of the camping area in the small town of Cochiti Lake.

◄ TETILLA PEAK RECREATION AREA *(Open April 1 to Oct 31 - Varies)*

Reservations: (877) 444-6777, www.recreation.gov
Information: (505) 465-0307, http://www.spa.usace.army.mil/recreation/cochiti/index.htm
Location: 45 Miles N of Albuquerque, *N 35° 38' 46", W 106° 18' 15", 5,500 Ft*

52 Sites – This campground is directly across the lake from the Cochiti Lake Recreation Site. It has back-in and pull-thru sites to about 45 feet. Some have electricity and water hookups, others are no-hookup sites. There are flush toilets and showers. This side too has a boat ramp and lake fishing is possible. Hiking trails leave from the park. From I-25 take exit 264 and drive northwest on SR-16. After 3.7 miles turn right and follow the access road for 11 miles to the campground.

◄ ISLETA LAKES AND RECREATION AREA *(Open All Year)*

Res and Info: (505) 244-8102
Location: 10 Miles S of Albuquerque, *N 34° 56' 44", W 106° 40' 21", 4,900 Ft*

140 – This is an Isleta Reservation campground. It has full-hookup back-ins and pull-thrus to 70 feet. There is a store which stocks grocery items, ice, fishing supplies, and sells propane. There is a recreation room and a pavilion. Fishing is possible in the lake which is stocked. Other amenities include basketball, badminton, volleyball, and a sports field. The dump station can be used by non guests for a fee. Nearby is the Isleta Casino and golf. This campground is just 15 minutes from Albuquerque. Take Exit 215 from I-25 south of Albuquerque and drive south on Broadway Blvd SE. In just .2 mile or so turn right for the entrance road to the campground.

BIG BEND NATIONAL PARK (TEXAS)

Big Bend National Park occupies the U.S. side of the big bend of the Rio Grande River in western Texas. The topography of the park, with the river valley at 1,800 feet and the Chisos Mountain peaks at over 7,000 feet, means that there's a lot of diversity in scenery and wildlife. There are really three different ecosystems: the river valley, the Chihuahuan Desert, and the mountains.

The main visitor center of the park is at Panther Junction. This is near the center of the park and the point where the access road from the north meets the access road from the west. It's also where the road down to the river at Rio Grande Village heads south. The visitor center is a great place to pick up information and see what's happening in the park.

Rio Grande Village is on the river 21 miles from **Panther Junction**. The access road is paved and fine for RVs. The village has the lowest elevation in the park at about 1,800 ft and can be very hot in the summer. There's a small store, a hookup RV park, and a no-hookup campground here. Attractions in the area include the **Boquillas Canyon Overlook** for views into Mexico and Boquillas Canyon, and the abandoned **Hot Springs Village** where you can soak in a rustic desert pool next to the Rio Grande with Mexico only a few hundred feet away across a stretch of the river that is often ankle deep.

The **Chisos Basin** is surrounded by peaks in the center of the Chisos Mountains. The altitude in the basin is about 5,500 feet, it's a mountainous setting with rugged cliffs and pine trees. A campground and a lodge occupy the basin. Some of the best hiking trails in the park lead up into the surrounding mountains. Access is by a road from near Panther Junction. It's a paved road but steep with curves and is not recommended for large RVs, see the Chisos Basin Campground write-up below for more about this.

The park's third big campground and destination is along the river at the west end of

COLORADO RIVER EMERGES FROM SANTA ELENA CANYON

the park. There's a campground here and also the **Castolon Visitor Center**, not much more than a small store and ranger's office. The big attraction in this area is **Santa Elena Canyon** where the Rio Grande emerges from an impressive gorge with rock walls rising over a thousand feet above the river. A trail leads a mile or so up the canyon and there's access to the river for canoes and kayaks.

In addition to the three formal campgrounds there are many remote campsites in the park. Some are accessed on hiking trails but most are off the jeep roads which thread through much of the park. If you're prepared for this type of travel the park has a lot to offer.

Bird watchers love Big Bend because they can easily see birds here that are scarce anywhere else in the U.S. The location close to the Mexican border means that there are species normally only seen in Mexico. Not only that, the park sits astride a bird migration route from South and Central America to locations far to the north. And the diverse ecosystems in the park attract a large variety of species, over 450 of them have been recorded here.

The park is in a very isolated location, no major cities are anywhere near. The small town of Marathon about 40 miles north of the Persimmon Gap (north) entrance has a small store, a gas station, and an RV park and campground. The town of Study Butte (and nearby Terlingua) is just outside the park's west entrance and it too has only small stores, gas stations, restaurants, and a few campgrounds. The most convenient nearby town for supplies is probably Alpine, and that's 80 miles north of the park's western entrance and is described in the Davis Mountains section elsewhere in this chapter.

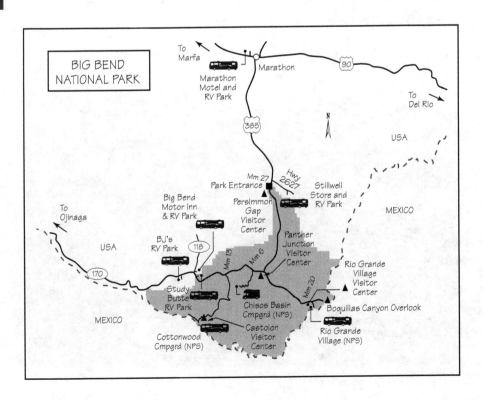

Big Bend National Park Campgrounds

RIO GRANDE VILLAGE CAMPGROUND – BIG BEND NATIONAL PARK *(Open All Year)*

Reservations: (877) 444-6777, www.recreation.gov
Information: (915) 477-2251, www.nps.gov/bibe/
Location: Big Bend National Park, *N 29° 10' 51", W 102° 57' 26", 1,800 Ft*

125 Sites – This is the largest of the three main campgrounds in the park. It is located near the Rio Grande so the altitude is the lowest in the park. It's a great birding location with large grassy areas and water near the campground. There are actually two campgrounds here, a 25 unit RV campground and a 100 unit tent and no-hookup RV campground. The RV hookup camping is back-in sites to 45 feet in a paved parking lot. Sites are full-hookup and there are picnic tables next to each site. Only self-contained rigs are allowed in this campground since there are no restrooms outside the hours when the store is open. The second campground is a large grassy area with back-in sites to 40 feet, each with picnic table and raised barbeque. This campground has restrooms with flush toilets. Between the two campgrounds and serving both of them is a store and restrooms with flush toilets and showers. The rates for the RV campground are shown with the icon above, the rates for the tent or no-hookup campground are the same as the rates for the other two campgrounds in the park. A paved road good for large RVs called Rio Grande Village Drive provides access to the campgrounds, it leads 21 miles south from the park visitor center at Panther Junction.

CHISOS BASIN CAMPGROUND – BIG BEND NATIONAL PARK *(Open All Year)*

Reservations: (877) 444-6777, www.recreation.gov
Information: (915) 477-2251, www.nps.gov/bibe/
Location: Big Bend National Park, *N 29° 16' 32", W 103° 18' 06", 5,400 Ft*

65 Sites – This could easily be the most scenic of the Big Bend campgrounds since it's located in a high-altitude basin and surrounded by rugged cliffs and pine-covered mountainsides. Access is via a paved road across Panther Pass which has 15 percent grades and sharp curves. The park service recommends use by campers with trailers no longer than 20 feet or coaches no longer than 24 feet. We've seen coaches to 28 feet in the campground but careful driving is required. There are 60 no-hookup sites here, each with a picnic table. Many are small and not level but there are a few level sites to 40 feet, some of these are pull-thrus. Each site has a picnic table and raised barbecue and there are restrooms with flush toilets and a dump station. From the visitor center at Panther Junction drive west on Maverick Drive for 3.4 miles. Turn left onto Basin Drive and follow it up and over Panther Pass to the campground, a distance of 6.5 miles.

COTTONWOOD CAMPGROUND – BIG BEND NATIONAL PARK *(Open All Year)*

Information: (915) 477-2251, www.nps.gov/bibe/
Location: Big Bend National Park, *N 29° 08' 19", W 103° 31' 24", 2,200 Ft*

35 Sites – Cottonwood is arguably the most remote of the main campgrounds in the park, it's in an interesting area near Castolon and the Santa Elena Canyon. This is a no hookup campground with flat back-in sites to 40 feet, each with picnic table and raised barbecue. Generator use is not allowed in this campground. Restrooms are vault toilets but water is

available, there's also the store at Castolon which is only .7 mile distant. From the visitor center at Panther Junction drive west on Maverick Drive for 12.7 miles. Turn south on Ross Maxwell Scenic Drive and follow it for 23 miles to the campground entrance on the left. Ross Maxwell is paved and fine for any RV.

STUDY BUTTE RV PARK *(Open All Year)*
Res and Info: (432) 371-2468
Location: Study Butte, *N 29° 18' 48", W 103° 31' 34", 2,500 Ft*

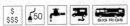

13 Sites – Study Butte is a small, very basic RV park convenient to the west entrance to the park. There are about 13 large pull-thru sites in a gravel yard. These are full hookup sites, only self contained rigs should use this park since there are not bathroom or shower facilities. Sites do have picnic tables and some have raised barbeque grills. The campground is in Study Butte, it's 2.5 miles west of the gate to Big Bend National Park.

BIG BEND MOTOR INN AND RV PARK *(Open All Year)*
Res and Info: (432) 371-2218
Location: Terlingua, *N 29° 19' 44", W 103° 32' 03", 2,500 Ft*

125 Sites – This is by far the largest of the RV parks in this region, it's a good big-rig park. It's located quite near to the west gate of the park. Sites are set in a very large gravel lot behind a motel, restaurant, gas station and convenience store. There are a variety of site types including full-hookup pull-thrus to 55 feet, partial hookup sites, and tent sites. Wi-Fi is provided but doesn't reach most of the park. The campground address is Terlingua but it really seems to be in Study Butte, it's 3.7 miles west of the gate to Big Bend National Park.

BJ'S RV PARK *(Open All Year)*
Res and Info: (432) 371-2259
Location: Terlingua, *N 29° 19' 19", W 103° 35' 33", 2,600 Ft*

25 Sites – This is a basic but clean big rig park with full hookup pull-thru sites and restrooms with hot showers. It's located on SR-170 near Terlingua Ghostown some 3.6 miles west of the intersection of SR 118 and SR-170. This is about 7 miles from the west gate of Big Bend National Park.

MARATHON MOTEL AND RV PARK *(Open All Year)*
Res and Info: (432) 386-4241, (866) 386-4241, www.marathonmotel.com,
                 frontdesk@marathonmotel.com
Location: 42 Miles North of Persimmon Gap Entrance of Big Bend National Park,
                 N 30° 12' 29", W 103° 15' 15", 4,000 Ft

40 Sites – Marathon is an attractive little town located to the north of the east entrance of Big Bend National Park. It's a good base for a visit if you have a large RV. This motel has pull-thru and back-in RV sites to 70 feet as well as a camping area for smaller RVs

not needing hookups or for tent campers. There's a nice little courtyard café at the motel or it's easy to walk the short distance to town for a restaurant visit or shopping. From the western intersection of US-90 and US-395 in central Marathon drive west on US-90 for 1 mile to the campground.

STILLWELL STORE AND RV PARK *(Open All Year)*

Res and Info: 432-376-2244, www.stillwellstore.com
Location: 9 Miles North of Persimmon Gap Entrance of Big Bend National Park.
N 29° 38' 41", W 103° 04' 45", 2,400 Ft

70 RV Sites, Many more boondocking and tent sites – This store and RV park occupy an isolated and historic ranch in the dry country just north of the park. It's a bit off the main highway but the access road is paved and access is easy. The campground has about 70 RV sites, most are big pull-thrus (some full-hookup, some water and electric). There are also large areas for no-hookup or tent camping, both near the store and in remote locations. In addition to the campground and restrooms there is a small store/gift shop and museum. From US-90 some 2.4 miles north of the Persimmon Gap entrance station drive east on FM-2627 for about 6.1 miles.

CARLSBAD

Carlsbad (population about 30,000) is a Pecos River town with a tourism, mining (potash), and farming economy. The tourism is of course related to the nearby Carlsbad Caverns, but also to the Guadalupe Mountains National Park a bit farther south.

CARLSBAD CAVERNS

NEW MEXICO

NEW MEXICO

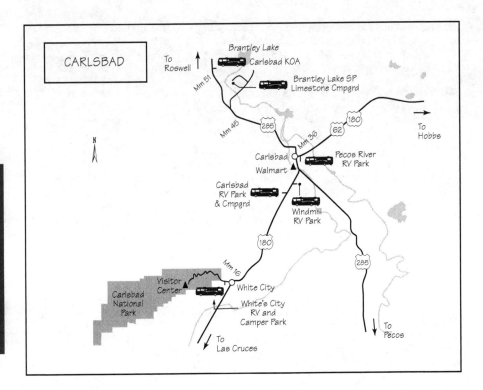

In the northeast section of town the Pecos River has been dammed to create a long lake called Lake Carlsbad. There is a bike path here as well as a swimming beach and boat rentals. During the Christmas season there are even Christmas light boat tours to see the lights along the river.

Northwest of Carlsbad is the **Living Desert Zoo and Gardens State Park**. It's dedicated to showing off the flora and fauna of the Chihuahuan Desert. You might think of it as being the counterpart of Tucson's Arizona-Sonora Desert Museum. There's a greenhouse for the cacti as well as lots of animals including gray wolves, black bears, javelina, mountain lions, bobcats, mule deer, antelope, elk, and bison. There's also an aviary.

Brantley Lake State Park is on the reservoir of a dam on the Pecos River about 10 miles to the north of Carlsbad. Like many other reservoirs in New Mexico it offers fishing and warm water sports. Due to recent findings of DDT in fish caught here the state recommends catch and release fishing.

And finally, there's the big draw. **Carlsbad Caverns National Park** is located about 23 miles southwest of Carlsbad. The caverns are definitely a wonder of the world and are also great fun to explore. If you're a walker you can enter the mouth of the cave and hike down into the cave on paved paths. No guide is required. If you'd rather ride there's an elevator that will whisk you 800 feet down to meet your friends who walked the two miles from the entrance. Another attraction here is a Mexican free-tail bat colony. From April to October they roost here and each evening visitors can watch them leave the cave in huge clouds. Early risers can watch them dive into the cave individually as they return at dawn. There's no campground in the park but there is an RV park just outside it where the entrance road leaves the highway. This is White's City and it's described below.

Please see the separate listing for the Guadalupe Mountains National Park.

Carlsbad Campgrounds

BRANTLEY LAKE STATE PARK – LIMESTONE CAMPGROUND *(Open All Year)*

Reservations: (877) NM-4-RSVP, www.nmparks.com
Information: (575) 457-2384, (888) 667-2757, www.nmparks.com
Location: 15 Miles N of Carlsbad, *N 32° 33' 50", W 104° 22' 49", 3,300 Ft*

51 Sites – This park has 51 sites off of a big loop. All site have electricity and water hookups. Two of the sites also have sewer, they cost $18 per night. Three of the sites are pull-thrus to 60 feet in length. A few of the back-in sites are as long as 45 feet. The sites all have blue metal covered picnic tables on paved patios and raised barbecue grills. Sites 3-28 can be reserved. The campground sits up above the lake and from about half of the sites there is a good lake view. The bathroom building has flush toilets and showers. The park offers over 2 miles of hiking trails, some leaving from the campground. There is a boat ramp at the day use area and a pay telephone at the entrance booth. The dump station is on the north side of the entrance road to the campground. From Carlsbad drive north on US-285 for 10 miles. The access road goes right, it's 5 miles in to the campground.

CARLSBAD KOA *(Open All Year)*

Reservations: (800) 562-9109, www.koa.com
Information: (575) 457-2000, www.carlsbadkoa.com
Location: 15 Miles N of Carlsbad, *N 32° 35' 12", W 104° 24' 59", 3,300 Ft*

118 Sites – This KOA is a big modern one with almost every facility you can imagine. There are 104 RV sites, 8 tent sites, a group tenting area, a tent village with 6 sheltered tent sites, 4 camping cabins, and 1 camping cottage. All of the RV sites are pull-thrus and are 40 feet wide by 70 feet long and very flat. The sites all have full hookups including satellite TV. The sites are separated by wide grassy lawns and each has a picnic table and most have fire pits. Wi-Fi is provided to the sites for no additional charge and there is a data port in the office. There is a seasonal pool and a spa which is open year round. The office building houses the bathrooms and showers, laundry, and a 6,000 sq ft clubhouse with a kitchen. During the summer barbecue is served and will be delivered to your RV. Other amenities include horseshoes, basketball, tether ball, volleyball, and a fenced "pooch park". The park is on the east side of US-285 about 15 miles north of Carlsbad.

CARLSBAD RV PARK AND CAMPGROUND *(Open All Year)*

Reservations: (888) 878-7275, camping@cavemen.net
Information: (575) 885-6333, www.carlsbadrvpark.com
Location: Carlsbad, *N 32° 22' 04", W 104° 14' 06", 3,200 Ft*

135 Sites – This campground has 41 tent sites, 95 RV sites, and 2 rental cabins. The tent

sites all have a shaded picnic table and many have a raised barbecue grill. The RV sites are full hookups, many are pull-thrus to 55 feet in length. They have picnic tables and a few also have grills. There are lots of trees in the park for shade and separation. Wi-Fi is provided to the sites for no additional charge and there is a data port . The indoor heated swimming pool is open year round. There is a large game room with video machines and a group meeting room. Breakfast is served daily for a nominal charge. The office stocks a good selection of groceries, RV supplies, and gifts. Other amenities include a group fire pit, horseshoes, and nightly entertainment (like movies). The campground is located toward the southern edge of town. It's on the west side of US-180 some 1.7 miles south of the intersection of US-180 and US-285.

PECOS RIVER RV PARK *(Open All Year)*

Information: (575) 887-9835, www.pecosriverrv.com
Location: Carlsbad, *N 32° 25' 05", W 104° 13' 22", 3,000 Ft*

19 Sites – This is a small park mostly full of long term rentals. Three of the sites are pull-thrus. The campground sits near the Pecos River and many of the sites are back-in sites along the river. Tenting is allowed. A mini mart is next to the park, so some groceries are available. The best feature of the park is the paved bicycle path which runs between the park and the river.

WINDMILL RV PARK *(Open All Year)*

Reservations: 888) 349-7275, windmillrvpark@yahoo.com
Information: (575) 887-1387, www.windmillrvpark.com
Location: Carlsbad, *N 32° 22' 41", W 104° 13' 34", 3,000 Ft*

62 Sites – All sites are full hookups and are all pull-thrus to about 55 feet in length. Tent camping is allowed in the regular h/u sites for the same price as an RV. Shade trees and grass separate the sites. Wi-Fi is provided to the sites for $3 daily by an outside vendor. The office building houses a meeting room and a laundry. A desk with a data port and courtesy phone is available in the meeting room for internet access and for local and calling card calls. The seasonal swimming pool is between the office and the sites. The RV park is just north of the Chevron gas station which has a convenience store. The campground is on the east side of US-180 some .8 miles south of the intersection of US-180 and US-285.

WHITE'S CITY RV AND CAMPERS PARK *(Open All Year)*

Reservations: (800) CAVERNS, whitescity@whitescity.com
Information: (575) 785-2291, www.whitescity.com
Location: 14 Miles S of Carlsbad, *N 32° 10' 32", W 104° 22' 36", 3,600 Ft*

132 Sites – White's is the closest campground to the park but it's an older campground and not very well maintained. There are 132 total tent and RV sites. Some of the RV sites are full hookup, some are partial, and they're in two areas. Forty seven sites are on

the highway side of Walnut Canyon near the road to the cavern. The remaining sites are on the far side of the little canyon and away from the highway. There are full hookup pull-thrus to 55 feet for larger RVs. Parking is mostly gravel but some sites have a small paved area. Each site has a picnic table and some have a shelter roof. Some sites have a fire pit and others have a raised barbecue grill. There are 2 old restroom buildings (high school-style showers) in the camping areas, it's best to avoid them. A computer in the lobby of the Best Western Hotel (where RVers register) is available for internet access and Wi-Fi is provided to sites for no extra charge although coverage is spotty. Groceries, a restaurant, a telephone, and a pool are also available at White's City. White's is located right at the intersection for the entrance road to Carlsbad Caverns National Park some 14 miles south of Carlsbad. It's another 7 miles to the cavern itself.

CHACO CULTURE NATIONAL HISTORIC PARK

Chaco Canyon is a shallow canyon over ten miles long and about a mile wide. It is surrounded by red cliffs along which are the ruins of many Puebloan buildings. This is an important site, most of the buildings are from the period beginning about 700 AD and ending about 1100 AD when Chaco Canyon was the heart of a powerful culture. Ruins like the ones at Aztec and the Salmon ruins near Farmington were part of it.

There are a number of ruins here. Some are quite large. They include Pueblo Bonito, Chetro Ketl and Casa Rinconada. Some have been partially reconstructed and others are little more than mounds. Self-guided trails lead through most ruins. Because this is such a remote site the ruins are seldom crowded.

Facilities at Chaco include a visitor center with exhibits and a bookstore as well as a

PUEBLO BONITO AT CHACO CANYON

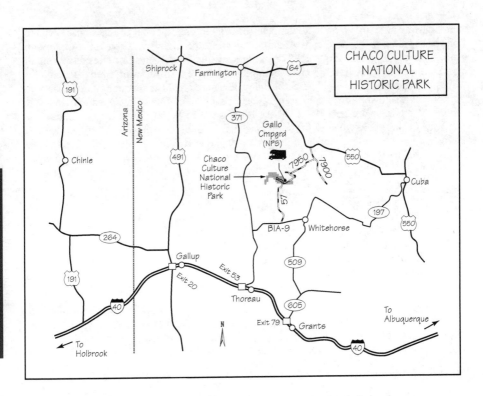

campground. The campground is described below. As you can see this campground is not suitable for larger RVs. Due to the rough roads you have to travel to get here you probably wouldn't want to bring a large RV in here anyway.

You can approach Chaco from either the north or south. It's located in empty country between Farmington and Grants. If you look at a map you'll see there aren't any major roads in that area. Chaco is right in the middle.

From the north drive south on US-550 for about 39 miles and then turn right onto gravel back roads following direction signs to the park. We're told there are about sixteen miles of rough gravel if you approach from this direction.

From the south take Exit 53 from I-40 and drive north on SR-371 for 28 miles. Turn right on BIA-9 and drive 13 miles. Turn left on SR-57, this is a gravel road. It's 20 miles on this road to the park entrance where the road once again is paved.

Chaco Culture National Historic Park Campground

🚐 **GALLO CAMPGROUND** *(Open All Year)*
Information: (505) 786-7014, www.nps.gov/chcu
Location: Chaco Canyon, *N 36° 02' 05", W 107° 53' 32", 6,200 Ft*

$$ ⛺ 🔥 ♿

49 Sites – There's only one campground in the park. Sites 1-34 are RV or vehicle sites off one loop road. A second smaller loop contains sites 35-49 which are tent only sites.

Each site has a tent pad, a picnic table, and a fire pit. The RV sites are mostly for RVs to about 25 feet, although a couple are large enough for 30 footers. There are also 2 group areas. Hiking trails leave from the campground and there's even a small ruin nearby. A dump station is on the left as you enter the camping area and there are spaces for 2 hosts. The visitor's center is nearby and there is a pay telephone and restrooms there. There is a 7 day stay limit.

CHAMA

Little Chama (population about 1,000) is best known as the southern terminal of the **Cumbres & Toltec Scenic Railroad**. This is a narrow gauge steam tourist railroad that runs from Chama some 65 miles north into Colorado to the town of Antonito. The railroad operates every day from mid May through mid October. The most popular time to ride the railroad is probably September and October when the changing colors of the leaves are very scenic.

Chama is a popular cross-country ski area in winter and hosts the **Chama Chile Classic Cross-Country Ski Race** in February. Other local celebrations are **Chama Days** during the first part of August and the **Chama Valley Music Festival** on Fridays and Saturdays each July.

Three large reservoirs along the Chama River south of Chama are big recreational draws. They offer water sport and fishing opportunities. These are **Heron Lake**, **El Vado Lake**, and the **Abiquiu Reservoir**. All have camping areas, see the descriptions below.

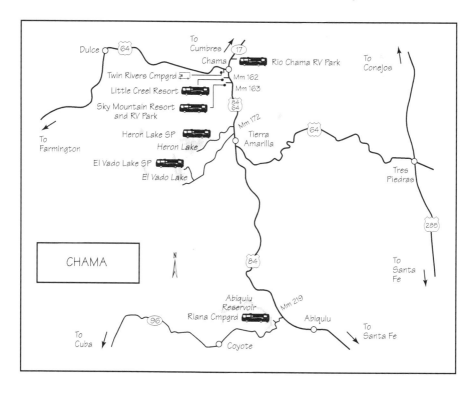

NEW MEXICO

Chama Campgrounds

LITTLE CREEL RESORT *(Open All Year)*

  Res and Info: (575) 756-2382, www.LittleCreelResort.com, lcresort@valornet.com
  Location: 1 Mile S of Chama, *N 36° 52' 18", W 106° 34' 57", 7,800 Ft*

62 Sites – The campground sits along the river. Most of the sites are pull-thrus to a length of 65 feet, there is also a tent-camping area. Guests are allowed to use the data port in the office for internet. Other amenities include tennis courts, a meeting hall which will seat 175 people, horse corral, and lots of hiking across the river. The campground is .8 mile south of the intersection of SR-17 and US-84 just south of Chama.

RIO CHAMA RV PARK *(Open May 1 to Oct 15)*

  Res and Info: (575) 756-2303, www.coloradodirectory.com/riochamarv,
                riochama.rv@verizon.net
  Location: Chama, *N 36° 54' 32", W 106° 34' 39", 7,900 Ft*

98 Sites – The campground sits along the Rio Chama not far from the C&TS Railroad Depot. There are 98 sites, which includes 20 tent sites and 78 RV sites. Many sites are pull-thrus to a length of 65 feet. The sites are set under good shade and have picnic tables, barbecue grills, and fire rings, firewood is sold. A central data port is provided for internet access. The dump station can be used by non guests for a fee. Other amenities at the park include horseshoes, volleyball, and a covered pavilion for group gatherings. Fishing and swimming are possible in the river and there are hiking trails from the park. From the intersection of SR-17 and US-84 just south of Chama drive north for 2 miles through town, the campground is on the right.

SKY MOUNTAIN RESORT AND RV PARK *(Open May 1 to Oct 31 - Varies)*

  Res and Info: (575) 756-1100, www.skymountainresort.com
  Location: 2 Miles S of Chama, *N 36° 51' 55", W 106° 34' 50", 7,700 Ft*

46 Sites – This is a big-rig campground with full hookup back-ins and pull-thrus to 45 feet. The campground is 1.2 miles south of the intersection of SR-17 and US-84 just south of Chama.

HERON LAKE STATE PARK *(Open All Year)*

  Reservations: (877) NM-4-RSVP, www.nmparks.com
  Information: (575) 588-7470, (575) 588-7247, (888) 667-2757, www.nmparks.com
  Location: 16 Miles S of Chama, *N 36° 41' 33", W 106° 39' 25", 7,300 Ft*

147 Sites – The state park has camping in 5 campgrounds and dispersed camping at other locations around the lake. The 5 campgrounds are called Willow Creek (sites 1-23) Blanco (sites 24-60), Brushy Point (sites 61-100), Island View (sites 101-129) , and Salmon Run (sites 130-147). Blanco has the largest sites, many are 60 feet in length, 10 are pull-thrus and all have electricity and water. Willow Creek has some sites which can accommodates RVs to 35 feet, some of which are pull-thrus and 18 of which have electric and water hookups. The other campgrounds have very little maneuvering room

and are limited to use by rigs under 22 feet. All of the sites have picnic tables, and fire pits. Some have raised barbecue grills and some have covered picnic tables. This is a large "no wake" lake good for canoeing, fishing, and swimming. Many of the sites are lakefront. To reach the campground turn west from US-64 on the entrance road about 10 miles south of the intersection of SR-17 and US-84 near Chama. It's 6 miles in to the visitor center.

EL VADO LAKE STATE CAMPGROUND *(Open All Year)*

Reservations: (877) NM-4-RSVP, www.nmparks.com
Information: (575) 588-7470, (575) 588-7247, (888) 667-2757, www.nmparks.com
Location: 24 Miles S of Chama, N 36° 36' 52", W 106° 44' 17", 6,900 Ft

80 Sites – This is a pretty park along the shore of El Vado Lake. The campground has two loops. The Elk Run Loop has sites 1-48, two of which are pull-thrus to about 100 feet in length and 19 having water and electric hookups. The back-in sites are up to 40 feet long. The sites and the roads on this loop are lined by hip-high posts spaced about 4 feet apart. There is a bathroom shower building which is wheelchair accessible. A pay telephone is located outside this building. The second loop is the Pinion Beach loop which houses sites 49-80. There are no hookups on this loop, but many are right above the lake shore. The dump station is located near the Elk Run Loop and a boat launch and a small dock are between the two loops. There is fishing and swimming in the lake. Most sites have covered picnic tables on a paved patio. To reach the campground leave US-64 some 12 miles south of Chama between Mile 172 and 173. Head west toward Heron Lake State Park. At 12 miles from the turn make a right into the entrance road to the park, you'll arrive in another .3 miles.

RIANA CAMPGROUND *(Open April 15 to Oct 15 - Varies)*

Reservations: (877) 444-6777, www.recreation.gov
Information: (505) 685-4561
Location: *54 Miles S of Chama, N 36° 14' 43", W 106° 25' 37", 6,500 Ft*

54 Sites – This Corps of Engineers campground sits up above and over looks Abiquiu Lake. The sites are on 4 loops: Puerco (sites 1-15), Chama (sites 16-30), Pedernal (sites 31-39), and a tent loop with walk-in tent sites (40-54). Small juniper trees are scattered around the park. The sites on the Puerco Loop have water and electricity hookups and are as long as 60 feet. These sites are mostly back-in, with a few parallel-parking style. Sites on the other loops do not have hookups. The Chama Loop sites are suitable for RVs to 30 feet and those on Pedernal Loop for RVs to 22 feet. All of the sites have covered picnic tables, fire pits, and some have raised barbecue grills (some of the grills even have lids). Flush toilets and showers are located in the Puerco loop, and all the loops (including Puerco) have vault style toilets. In the winter the there is no charge to come here, but there are no services either. Fishing and swimming in the lake are possible. On US-84 some 50 miles south of Chama turn right on SR-96. You'll reach the campground in 4 miles.

CIMARRON

Cimarron (population about 1,000) has a name that resonates in the history of the west. It was a stop on the Santa Fe Trail and was visited by various famous wild west personalities including Kit Carson, Charles Bent, Davy Crockett, Wyatt Earp, Jesse James, Annie Oakley, Black Jack Ketchum, Charles Kennedy, and Clay Allison. Buffalo Bill is said to have organized his Wild West Show in Cimarron. It was also one of the most violent towns in the west with frequent shootings and gunfights.

Today things are pretty quiet here. US-64 leaves the Rockies just to the west and heads out onto great plains. If you travel westwards for 24 miles you'll reach the heavily promoted Enchanted Circle at Eagle Nest. Along the way you'll pass through the **Cimarron Canyon**, now a state park. There are 4 campgrounds in the park, they are described below.

In Cimarron itself you can visit the historic area of town south of US-64 and the river. There's a museum in the old **Aztec Mill** and sites and buildings of interest include the **plaza**, the **Santa Fe Trail Inn**, the **St James Hotel** (site of twenty-six shootings), the **Dold Trading Post**, **Schwenk's Gambling Hall**, the **jail**, and the **Wells Fargo Station**.

Cimarron Campgrounds

CIMARRON INN AND RV PARK *(Open All Year)*

Reservations: (800) 546-2244, info@cimarroninn.com
Information: (575) 376-2268, www.cimarroninn.com
Location: Cimarron, *N 36° 30' 37", W 104° 55' 02", 6,400 Ft*

16 Sites – This park has 11 RV sites, 5 tent sites, 3 cabins and 12 rooms in the inn. The RV sites are all back-ins which will almost all accommodate a rig to 45 feet. All of the sites have full hookups including cable TV. The tent sites have a covered picnic table and fire pits. There is not a laundry or telephone at the campground, but both are located 1 block away. Guests are allowed to use the office phone for local and calling card calls. Internet is available at the town library and visitor center. Campground reservations are suggested in the summer. The campground is within walking distance of everything in town. The campground is located on the south side of the highway in Cimarron.

PONIL CAMPGROUND *(Open All Year)*

Res and Info: (575) 376-2343 or (575) 376-1010, ponilcamp@zianet.com
Location: Cimarron, *N 36° 31' 15", W 104° 53' 56", 6,400 Ft*

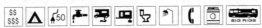

45 Sites – Ponil is a commercial campground just outside Cimarron to the east. The sites are in a grassy lot off the highway. There are 45 sites, twenty are full hookup sites, 10 have electricity and water only, and 15 are no hookup. Several of the sites are pull-thrus and can be as long as you want them to be. The back-ins are different sizes, some will accommodate long rigs. The sites are separated by trees and a lawn. The tenting sites are down by the creek. Other amenities include badminton, volleyball, and a sports field. The park is open all year with limited facilities in the winter. It is fully operational from March 1 - Nov 30. The campground is on the north side of US-64 just east of Cimarron.

CIMARRON CANYON STATE PARK – PONDEROSA CAMPGROUND *(Open All Year)*

Reservations: (877) NM-4-RSVP, www.nmparks.com
Information: (575) 377-6271, (888) 667-2757, www.nmparks.com
Location: 14 Miles W of Cimarron, *N 36° 32' 47", W 105° 07' 54", 7,500 Ft*

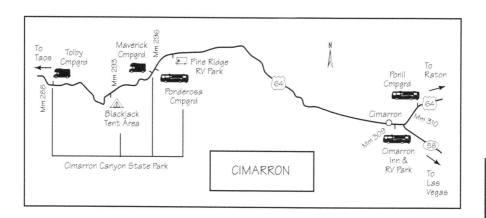

18 Sites – This campground is just south of the Cimarron River. It is a big paved circular lot. Around the exterior of the lot are parallel parking style sites (sites number 75-88) which are 45 feet in length. These sites have a picnic table and fire pit on a gravel pad next to the parking space. In the middle of this lot are 9 pull-thru parking spaces 55 feet long which are not numbered. To the back of the lot there are 4 walk-in tent site (site number 91-94). These sites also have picnic tables and fire pits. There are both wheelchair accessible vault toilets and flush toilets. Two water faucets are in the camping area. Seven sites in the campground can be reserved. The campground is located along US-64 14 miles west of Cimarron.

▣ CIMARRON CANYON STATE PARK – MAVERICK CAMPGROUND *(Open All Year)*

Reservations: (877) NM-4-RSVP, www.nmparks.com
Information: (575) 377-6271, (888) 667-2757, www.nmparks.com
Location: 14 Miles W of Cimarron, *N 36° 32' 42", W 105° 08' 02", 7,600 Ft*

43 Sites – This campground has 43 sites (sites number 30-72) off 2 loops set under a forest of pines. The sites all have a picnic table on a paved pad and a fire pit. The sites are all back-in and generally about 25 feet in length, but there are a few which will take 30 foot RVs. These sites are separated by vegetation and trees. Some of the sites sit along the side of a small fishing pond which is behind the park. The Cimarron River runs behind the fishing pond. There are water faucets scattered around the campground and there are wheelchair accessible flush toilets. The main trail to Touch Me Not and Green Mountain leave from here. Eight sites can be reserved. The Cimarron River is stocked with trout, usually rainbows. The campground is located along US-64 14 miles west of Cimarron.

▣ CIMARRON CANYON STATE PARK – BLACKJACK TENT AREA
(Open May 15 to Sept 15 - Varies)

Information: (575) 377-6271, (888) 667-2757, www.nmparks.com
Location: 16 Miles W of Cimarron, *N 36° 31' 51", W 105° 10' 17", 7,800 Ft*

5 Sites – This is a paved lot along the side of the highway. There are 2 wheelchair accessible vault toilets in the parking lot. These are the only restrooms for the camping area. A

trail leads from the parking lot (really a day use area) to the 5 walk-in sites (sites 25-29). The sites are all strung out along a trail along the creek. The sites each have a picnic table and a fire pit. There is no water at this campground other than the creek. The campground is located along US-64 16 miles west of Cimarron.

CIMARRON CANYON STATE PARK – TOLBY CAMPGROUND *(Open All Year)*

Reservations: (877) NM-4-RSVP, www.nmparks.com
Information: (575) 377-6271, (888) 667-2757, www.nmparks.com
Location: 20 Miles W of Cimarron, *N 36° 32' 17", W 105° 13' 23", 8,000 Ft*

22 Sites – The sites in this campground (site numbers 1-22) are all back-ins on one loop road. The Cimarron River runs between Highway 64 and the campground. The sites are very small – a couple of them will take an RV to 30 feet but several are only 15 feet long. Maneuvering room is tight. Each site has a picnic table on a paved pad and a fire pit. Some of the sites also have a raised barbecue grill. There are both wheelchair accessible flush toilets and vault toilets. The flush toilets close in the winter. Water is available in the park. There is also a day use area. Seven sites can be reserved. The campground is located along US-64 some 20 miles west of Cimarron.

CLOUDCROFT

Cloudcroft (population about 1,000) occupies the top of a pass through the Sacramento Mountains. At about 8,700 feet altitude this is a pleasant place to spend time during the summer as well as being a winter snow destination.

The town was founded in 1899 when the El Paso & Northeastern Railroad build a branch line to the pass to haul timber out. A lodge, originally build for railroad workers, eventually became a resort destination. The original lodge burned down long ago but it was replaced and is in operation. Today the town has a 9-hole golf course that is billed as the highest in the U.S. It also has the southernmost ski area in the United States, Ski Cloudcroft.

Cloudcroft is surrounded by the Lincoln National Forest. There are hiking trails (cross-country ski trails in winter), biking trails, and even ATV trails. Many national forest campgrounds are near the town.

The railroad no longer comes to Cloudcroft, it was closed down in 1947. Today the railroad right-of-way is used for hiking and is known as the **Cloud-Climbing Rail Trail**. The Sacramento National Forest Ranger Station in Cloudcroft has the details.

In **Sunspot**, about 20 miles south of Cloudcroft, are the National Solar Observatory and the Apache Point Observatory. During daytime hours you can take a self guided tour of the grounds and visit the interactive information center.

Cloudcroft Campgrounds

DEERHEAD CAMPGROUND *(Open May 15 to After Labor Day - Varies)*

Information: (575) 682-2551
Location: 1 Mile S of Cloudcroft, *N 32° 56' 38", W 105° 44' 45", 8,900 Ft*

29 Sites – This Lincoln National Forest campground is set under a forest of pines. There are 29 sites which are only big enough for car parking. The sites are tent only and are behind barriers made of heavy duty cables. All of the sites have picnic tables and fire rings. Bathrooms are vault style. Water is available with the first 5 gallons free and then 25 cents per gallon for more. Firewood is available for $5 a bundle. Showers are available at the nearby Silver Overflow lot for $3. There are lots of hiking trails in this area. At the western edge of the village of Cloudcroft SR-24 goes south from US-82. Follow it for 1 mile to the campground entrance. The route is signed.

PINES CAMPGROUND *(Open May 15 to After Labor Day - Varies)*
Information: (575) 682-2551
Location: 1 Mile NE of Cloudcroft, *N 32° 57' 59", W 105° 44' 06", 8,600 Ft*

43 Sites – This Lincoln National Forest campground has 21 single sites, 2 double sites, and 1 triple site. The interior roads and the sites are paved. Each site has a picnic table and fire pit. A sign at the entrance limits RV size to 35 feet. The bathrooms are wheelchair accessible vault style. Water is available and the first 5 gallon are free and thereafter the charge is 25 cents a gallon. A dump station ($5) and showers ($3) are available at the Silver Overflow area, described below. Firewood is available at this campground for $5 a bundle. There are lots of cross country ski trails in this area which are used for hiking in the summer. From the village of Cloudcroft drive east on US-82 for about a half mile. Turn left on US-244 and drive .4 miles to the campground.

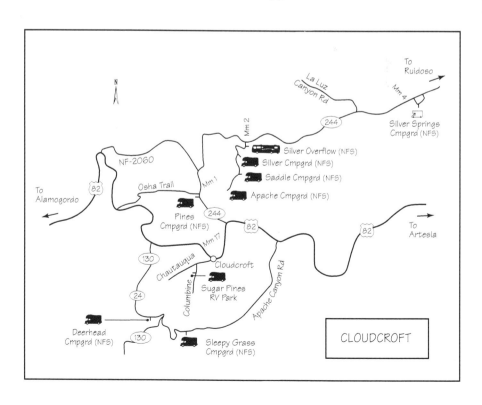

SILVER OVERFLOW, SADDLE, AND APACHE CAMPGROUNDS
(Open April 15 to Oct 15 - Varies)

Information: (575) 682-2551
Location: 2 Miles NE of Cloudcroft, *N 32° 58' 35", W 105° 43' 30", 9,000 Ft*

120 Sites – Off this one road (FR 24G) are 4 Forest Service Campgrounds. The Silver Overflow (GPS above) area is a big paved lot with room for 50 rigs. They could be as long as 45 feet. Here there is a dump station ($5) and bathrooms with flush toilets and shower ($3). Next down the road is Silver Campground with 30 sites, one of which is a pull-thru. Next is Saddle Campground with 16 all back-in sites. The last is Apache Campground with 24 sites, three of which are pull-thru. The maximum size rig appropriate for these three campgrounds is 35 feet although maneuvering rooms is scarce. The 3 campgrounds have paved roads and parking, picnic tables, fire pits, drinking water, and vault style wheelchair accessible toilets. Five gallons of water is free and more costs 25 cents per gallon. From Cloudcroft drive east on US-82 for about a half mile. Turn left on US-244 and drive 1.9 miles to the campground entrance on the right.

SLEEPY GRASS CAMPGROUND *(Open May 15 to after Labor Day - Varies)*

Information: (575) 682-2551
Location: 2 Miles S of Cloudcroft, *N 32° 56' 29", W 105° 44' 16", 9,000 Ft*

46 Sites – This Lincoln National Forest campground is set in a forest of pines. The sites are for tents, vehicle parking is nearby but there's not much room. All of the sites have picnic tables and fire rings. Bathrooms are wheelchair accessible vault style. Water is available with the first 5 gallon free and then 25 cents a gallon for more. Firewood is available for $5 a bundle. There are lots of hiking trails in the area and La Pasada Encantada trail leaves from the parking lot just before the campground entrance. At the western edge of the village of Cloudcroft SR-24 goes south from US-82. In a mile you'll come to Deerhead Campground. Continue past, take the left fork and then a quick right onto Apache Canyon Rd and you'll come to the campground in .6 mile.

SUGAR PINES RV PARK *(Open All Year)*

Res and Info: (505) 682-3375, http://sugarpinesrvpark.com
Location: Cloudcroft, *N 32° 57' 07", W 105° 44' 09", 8,700 Ft*

12 Sites – This small campground is in a residential area. It has 12 sites, 2 of them are pull-thrus. The sites are terraced off the side of a hill and are all full hookup including cable TV. Although some of the sites are pretty long, because of tight maneuvering room the campground is best for rigs to 35 feet. The office building has a small sitting room, a laundry, and a bathroom/shower room. Just east of Cloudcroft turn south off US-82 onto Spruce Street. In just a few hundred feet take the right fork onto Chautauqua Blvd. and in another 100 yards or so turn left into Columbine Blvd. The campground is just ahead on the right.

CLOVIS AND PORTALES

These two small towns are located near the eastern New Mexico border on US-60 to the east of Fort Sumner. Clovis (population about 40,000) is the county seat. Portales (population about 13,000) is located about 13 miles to the southwest and is the home of Eastern New Mexico University.

The name Clovis probably rings a bell because arrowheads found at the nearby **Blackwater Draw Archeological Site** were named after the town. The findings here were important because they proved that men had occupied North America about 11,000 years ago, quite a bit earlier than had been believed previously. The **Blackwater Draw Museum** (not located at the actual Blackwater Draw site) is located on US-70 about half way between Clovis and Portales.

Portales is a **peanut-growing center**, a good place to pick some up. There are several peanut processing plants in town. There's also a **peanut festival** in late October. There are several museums on the university campus including the **Roosevelt County Historical Museum**, the **Miles Minerals Museum**, and the **Natural History Museum**.

In Clovis you might want to visit the **Clovis Depot Model Train Museum** which is located in a restored train depot. Clovis celebrates Pioneer Days in early June which includes a rodeo. In June the town hosts the **Norman and Vincent Petty Music Festival** which focuses on early rock and roll, important to Clovis since this is the home of the **Norman Petty Studios**. They were used by Buddy Holly, Roy Orbison, and Roger Williams, among others. The studios can be toured during the festival.

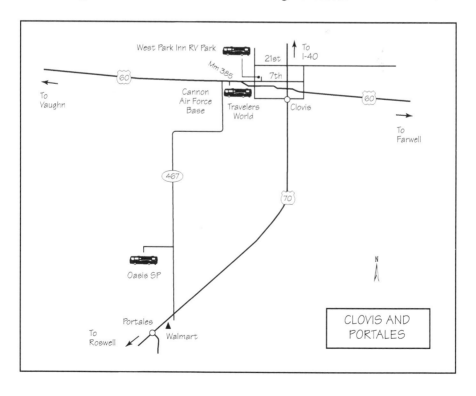

New Mexico

Clovis and Portales Campgrounds

🚐 **OASIS STATE PARK** *(Open All Year)*

Reservations: (877) NM-4-RSVP, www.nmparks.com
Information: (575) 356-5331, (888) 667-2757, www.nmparks.com
Location: 6 Miles N of Portales, *N 34° 15' 35", W 103° 20' 59", 4,000 Ft*

23 Sites – Oasis is a small but well-done state campground. Fourteen of the sites are pull-thrus with electrical and water hookups. The remainder are no-hookup sites. Most of the sites are pull-thrus suitable for RVs to 45 feet. A small man-made pond is the main amenity here, it's stocked with trout in the winter and channel catfish in the summer. The restroom building has flush toilets and hot showers and there is a dump station. From US-70 at the northern edge of Portales drive north on SR-467 for 3.8 miles. Turn left on Oasis Road and you'll reach the campground entrance in 1.8 miles.

🚐 **TRAVELER'S WORLD** *(Open All Year)*

Res and Info: (575) 763-8153, travelersworld@yahoo.com
Location: Clovis, *N 34° 24' 15", W 103° 15' 35", 4,300 Ft*

60 Sites – Sites in this RV park are both back-ins and pull-thrus to 70 feet. Most are full-hookup. From Clovis drive west on US-60. The campground is on the south side of the highway 3.8 miles west of the intersection of US-60 and US-70 in Clovis.

🚐 **WEST PARK INN RV PARK** *(Open All Year)*

Res and Info: (575) 763-7218
Location: Clovis, *N 34° 24' 17", W 103° 13' 25", 4,200 Ft*

12 Sites – This is a small park with some full-time resident RVs. Sites are back-ins with a few pull-thrus to about 65 feet. In Clovis drive west on 7th street. The campground is 1.5 mile west of SR-209 on the north side of the road.

DAVIS MOUNTAINS (TEXAS)

The Davis Mountains are a volcanic range in east Texas that runs in a northwest-southeast line from the vicinity of Alpine in the south to just south of US-10 in the north. They're not a particularly high range of mountains, the highest point is Mount Livermore with an altitude of 8,378 feet, but they rise above the surrounding plains and for this reason have a higher rainfall than most of west Texas. The trees here include pines and oaks, it can seem more like New Mexico than Texas.

The region is a tourist destination with a number of interesting sights. Most of these center around the cute little town of **Fort Davis** with its population of just over 1,000. It's the highest town in Texas and often in summer it's also the coolest. In town is the **Fort Davis National Historic Site** and about 20 miles to the north is the **McDonald Observatory** where on some nights visitors can use the telescopes to watch the night sky. Also nearby is the **Chihuahuan Desert Nature Center and Botanical Gardens**, they're located four miles south on Hwy 118.

Marfa (population 2,100), located 20 miles south of Fort Davis, and actually sitting on the plains south of the Davis Mountains, is another interesting destination. The town is known for its **Marfa Mystery Lights**, there's actually a viewing area along US-87 about nine miles east of town. Marfa has become an artist's town with several galleries and the **Chinati Foundation** contemporary art museum (tours by reservation only) located in the buildings of a former military base near town.

The largest town in the area is **Alpine** with a population of about 5,700. It's located 25 miles east of Marfa and 20 miles southeast of Fort Davis. At one time Alpine was the largest town in the largest county in the largest state of the union – of course when Alaska became a state that all ended. The town is home to the Sul Ross State University which has an excellent regional museum, **The Museum of the Big Bend**. Alpine is the place to pick up supplies or perhaps even base yourself, it has a number of good RV parks.

Davis Mountains Campgrounds

BALMORHEA STATE PARK *(Open All Year)*
Reservations: (512) 389-8900, www.tpwd.state.tx.us
Information: (512) 389-8900
Location: Balmorhea, *N 30° 56' 43", W 103° 47' 12", 3,400 Ft*

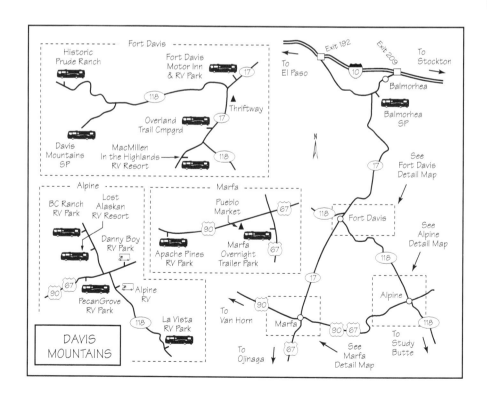

DAVIS MOUNTAINS

35 Sites – Balmorhea State Park is well known for it's huge spring-fed swimming pool. Travelers often stop for a dip or the night since the park is only a 6 miles off I-10. This water isn't hot, it stays between 72 and 76 degrees year-round. RV sites here are very nice. The access roads and sites are paved, most have a covered picnic table area and raised barbecue grills. There are pull-thrus to about 55 feet as well as shorter back-ins. Sites have electricity and water, there is a dump station. Tent camping is possible. The park has a $7.00 per person daily fee in addition to the camping rate indicated by the pictogram above. There is no additional fee for the pool. Take Exit 209 from I-19 and drive south west on SR-17. The park entrance is on the left in 6.8 mile.

DAVIS MOUNTAINS STATE PARK *(Open All Year)*

Reservations: (512) 389-8900, www.tpwd.state.tx.us
Information: (432)-426-3337
Location: 4 Mile North of Fort Davis, *N 30° 35' 58", W 103° 55' 45", 5,000 Ft*

100 Sites – This is a beautiful state park with the campground tucked into a valley north of the town of Fort Davis. Access roads and sites here are paved. They include full, partial and no-hookup sites, some are pull-thrus as long as 55 feet so it's a fine park for big rigs. Restrooms have flush toilets and hot showers. There are hiking trails and several bird-watching stations and feeders making this park a favorite with birdwatchers. Note that in addition to the camping fee indicated by the pictogram above there is an additional $2.50 per person entrance fee for this park. Watch for the entrance gate on the left as you head west on SR-118 from the intersection on SR-17 at the northern end of town. The campground is 2.8 miles from the intersection.

HISTORIC PRUDE RANCH *(Open All Year)*

Res and Info: (432) 426-3202, http://www.prude-ranch.com
Location: 6 Miles North of Fort Davis, *N 30° 36' 20", W 103° 56' 56", 4,900 Ft*

30 Sites – The Prude Ranch is a guest ranch offering trail rides, western riding lessons, tennis courts, hiking trails, and a restaurant and swimming pool. The sites are pull-thrus and back-ins to 45 feet with full hookups. Watch for the entrance gate on the right as you head west on SR-118 from the intersection on SR-17 at the northern end of town. The campground is 4.4 miles from the intersection, about 1.7 mile beyond the entrance to Davis Mountains State Park.

OVERLAND TRAIL CAMPGROUND *(Open All Year)*

Res and Info: (888) 478-5267
Location: Fort Davis, *N 30° 35' 28", W 103° 53' 33", 4,800 Ft*

32 Sites – The Overland Trail is conveniently located right in central Fort Davis. You can easily walk to restaurants and stores. Careful maneuvering is required by big rigs but the campground has pull-thru and back-in sites to 70 feet. Parking is on grass and dirt and tents are accommodated. The campground is located on the north side of SR-118 as it passes through town, between 5th and 6th Streets.

MacMillen in the Highlands RV Resort *(Open All Year)*
  Res and Info: (432) 426-2056, (877) 426-2055, www.macmilleninthehighlands.com
  Location: Fort Davis, *N 30° 34' 53", W 103° 54' 14", 4,800 Ft*

31 Sites – This small RV park is located just outside Fort Davis, a convenient location. There are back-in and pull-thru sites with patios to 65 feet. Amenities include a restaurant out front and a mini-mart. The campground is locate just southwest of town on SR-17 toward Marfa.

Fort Davis Motor Inn and RV Park *(Open All Year)*
  Res and Info: (432) 426-2112
  Location: Fort Davis, *N 30° 36' 27", W 103° 52' 57", 4,800 Ft*

14 Sites – This modern motel has back-in sites to 45 feet under trees with picnic tables, raised barbecues, and patios. These are full-hookup sites with cable TV, Wi-Fi is available in the lobby area. Several of the sites work well for tents. The motel is located east of Fort Davis. From the center of town drive northwest to the intersection of SR-17 and Canyon Drive (SR-118). Head east on SR-17, the motel is on the left in just .2 miles.

Marfa Overnight Trailer Park *(Open April 1 to Oct 31 - Varies)*
  Information: (432) 729-4405
  Location: Marfa, *N 30° 18' 21", W 104° 01' 11", 4,600 Ft*

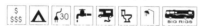

20 Sites – This little older campground has about 10 very long full-hookup pull-thru RV sites as well as tent camping on grass. The RV area has no shade but there are a few small trees in the tent area. Restrooms have toilets and hot showers. The campground is in Marfa off US-67 (South Highland Street) just .2 mile south of the intersection with US-90.

Apache Pines RV Park *(Open All Year)*
  Res and Info: (432) 729-4479
  Location: Marfa, *N 30° 18' 19", W 104° 02' 44", 4,900 Ft*

14 Sites – The Apache Pines is an RV park for self-contained RVs only, there are no restrooms. The 14 sites are pull-thrus to 50 feet and have full hookups. There are a few small trees but they won't provide much shade. The campground is located just west of Marfa on the south side of US-90, it's 1.5 miles west of the intersection of US-90 and US-67 in town and is outside the built-up area.

Pecan Grove RV Park *(Open All Year)*
  Reservations: (800) 644-7175
  Information: (432) 837-7175
  Location: Alpine, *N 30° 21' 17", W 103° 40' 49", 4,500 Ft*

40 Sites – The Pecan Grove is a nice shaded RV park on the west side of Alpine. It has tenting sites as well as pull-thru and back-in RV sites to 55 feet, both partial and full hookup. Sites have picnic tables. The campground is on the south side of US-90 some 1.6 miles west of the intersection of SR-118 and US-90 in the center of town.

LA VISTA RV PARK *(Open All Year)*
　　Res and Info: (432) 364-2293
　　Location:　　6 Miles South of Alpine, *N 30° 17' 22", W 103° 35' 40", 5,100 Ft*

14 Sites – The La Vista is a small campground in the hills south of Alpine, a wide-open unpopulated area with scattered small trees. Sites are full-hookup pull-thrus to 80 feet and there are restrooms with hot showers. The campground entrance is on the east side of SR-118 some 6.7 miles south of the intersection of US-90 and SR-118 in Alpine.

LOST ALASKAN RV RESORT *(Open All Year)*
　　Res and Info: (800) 837-3604, www.lostalaskan.com
　　Location:　　Alpine, *N 30° 22' 47", W 103° 40' 12", 4,400 Ft*

100 Sites – The Lost Alaskan is a good big-rig park with modern facilities. They have full-hookup pull-thru and back-in sites to 90 feet as well as a tent camping area. The grounds have many scattered pines, there's also a pool and gift shop. The park is on the west side of the Fort Davis Highway (SR-118) some 1.6 miles north of its intersection with US-90 in town.

BC RANCH RV PARK *(Open All Year)*
　　Res and Info: (432) 837-5883, www.bcranchrvpark.com
　　Location:　　2 Miles North of Alpine, *N 30° 23' 48", W 103° 40' 49", 4,800 Ft*

30 Sites – A bit farther out of town than the Lost Alaskan but on the same highway, the BC Ranch has pull-thru and back-in sites to 70 feet with trees for shade. The park is on the west side of the Fort Davis Highway (SR-118) some 2.9 miles north of its intersection with US-90 in town.

DEMING AND COLUMBUS

Deming (population 14,000) is one of the larger towns along I-10 as it crosses southern New Mexico. Once an important railroad town, the Deming area is now agricultural. This might seem surprising since there are no apparent rivers or reservoirs nearby. The nearby Mimbres River goes underground about 20 miles to the north and doesn't come back to the surface until it reaches Mexico.

Deming has an eclectic museum that's worth a look. The **Deming Luna Mimbres Museum** has Mimbres pots, some old cars, and many other even more varied items.

What Deming is really known for, though, is its duck races. The **Great American Duck Races** are held during the fourth week in August. Don't worry, if you don't have your own duck, or if yours is slow, you can rent one. Reservations are a good idea. As you can imagine this is a popular event.

NEW MEXICO

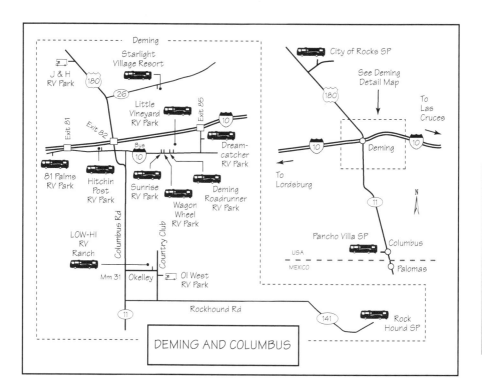

DEMING AND COLUMBUS

Deming is blessed with three excellent state parks, all with camping, and all within an hour or so. **Rock Hound State Park** is located on a hillside overlooking Deming from the southeast. You're allowed to haul out 15 pounds of rocks per person. The park is located about 12 miles southeast of Deming, for better instructions see the campground description below.

Northwest of town is **City of Rocks State Park**. The park nestles up to a series of tufa (a soft volcanic rock) towers. The no-hookup campsites here are particularly attractive, much like the ones in the granite rocks at Joshua Tree National Park. The park is about 28 miles northwest of Deming and the campground is described below.

Finally, down near the Mexican border in Columbus is **Pancho Villa State Park**. This park documents the raids by Pancho Villa against Fort Furlong in Columbus during the Mexican Revolution in 1916. There's a museum at the park. The state campground is an excellent one and the crossing into Mexico here is pretty good for RVs. It's the place to cross if you're headed for Nuevo Casas Grandes with its Paquime ruins or Mata Ortiz and its pottery.

Deming and Columbus Campgrounds

🚐 CITY OF ROCKS STATE PARK *(Open All Year)*

Reservations: (877) NM-4-RSVP, www.nmparks.com
Information: (575) 536-2800, (888) 667-2757, www.nmparks.com
Location: 28 Miles NW of Deming, *N 32° 35' 10", W 107° 58' 24", 5,200 Ft*

62 Sites – This state park has 10 pull-thru sites with water and electricity in a gravel lot. The rest of the sites are back-ins set in scenic locations near the big rocks that this park is named for. Some sites will take RVs to 45 feet. Each hookup site has a beige metal-covered picnic table on a paved patio. Roads leading from the main road to camp sites are typically gravel. The sites have fire pits with grills. There are flush toilets and showers. The no hookup sites have picnic tables which are not covered and fire rings. There is a large visitors center near the entrance to the park and an observatory for star-gazing. From Deming drive northwest on US-180 for 24 miles. Turn right on SR-61 and in another 3 miles you'll come to the park entrance road going left. It's another 1.5 miles into the park.

DREAMCATCHER RV PARK *(Open All Year)*

Res and Info: (575) 544-4004, www.escapees.com/dreamcatcher
Location: Deming, *N 32° 16' 20", W 107° 42' 42", 4,300 Ft*

117 Sites – The Dreamcatcher is conveniently located right off Exit 85 of I-10, the eastern Exit for Deming. The campground has very large pull-thru sites on gravel with full hookup. There are also large areas around the edge of the campground for dry camping in RVs. This is an Escapee Rainbow park so there are excellent deals for Escapee club members, particularly for the dry camping. Take Exit 85 and head south, the campground is on the left almost immediately.

LITTLE VINEYARD RV PARK *(Open All Year)*

Res and Info: (800) 413-0312, (575) 546-3560, www.littlevineyard.com
Location: Deming, *N 32° 16' 07", W 107° 43' 38", 4,300 Ft*

153 Sites – The Little Vineyard is a big rig campground with all pull-thru sites to 65 feet. There's an indoor heated swimming pool, a spa, and a recreation hall with planned activities in winter. The campground is located just east of the downtown district. Take Exit 85 from I-10 and follow the I-10 business loop south and then west for 1.1 miles as it make a 90 degree bend to the right, the campground entrance is on the right.

DEMING ROADRUNNER RV PARK *(Open All Year)*

Res and Info: (575) 546-6960, (800) 226-9937, www.zianet.com/roadrunnerrv
Location: Deming, *N 32° 16' 07", W 107° 43' 42", 4,300 Ft*

104 Sites – This commercial park in Deming has tent sites as well as RV sites. The RV sites include back-ins and pull-thrus to 65 feet. There's an indoor swimming pool and a spa. The office has a computer and a data port. The campground is located in a string of RV parks just east of central Deming. Take Exit 85 from I-10 and follow the I-10 business loop south and then west for 1.1 miles as it makes a 90 degree bend to the right, the campground is on the right.

WAGON WHEEL RV PARK *(Open All Year)*

Res and Info: (575) 546-8650
Location: Deming, *N 32° 16' 07", W 107° 43' 45", 4,300 Ft*

70 Sites – One of the less expensive parks in town, the Wagon Wheel is popular and has a lot of long-term residents all year long. The park has tent sites, back-ins, and pull-thrus to 50 feet. Take Exit 85 from I-10 and follow the I-10 business loop south and then west for 1.3 miles as it makes a 90 degree bend to the right, the campground is on the right.

Sunrise RV Trailer Park *(Open All Year)*
Res and Info: (505) 546-8565
Location: Deming, *N 32° 16' 07", W 107° 43' 50", 4,300 Ft*

81 Sites – The Sunrise is another good deal in Deming and it has all pull-thru sites to 55 feet. Take Exit 85 from I-10 and follow the I-10 business loop south and then west for 1.3 miles as it makes a 90 degree bend to the right.

Hitchin Post RV Park *(Open All Year)*
Res and Info: (575) 546-9146
Location: Deming, *N 32° 16' 05", W 107° 45' 54", 4,300 Ft*

40 Sites – This is a small park with the sites packed onto the property. Thee are both back-ins and pull-thrus, some to 55 feet. The park sits away from other RV parks in town and is just northwest of the central area. Take Exit 82A from I-10 and drive south on Gold Ave for a block. Turn right on Motel Drive (this is I-10 business loop) and go 5 blocks west, the campground is on the right.

81 Palms RV Park *(Open All Year)*
Res and Info: (575) 546-7434
Location: Deming, *N 32° 15' 57", W 107° 47' 29", 4,300 Ft*

106 Sites – This is a nice looking park, a cut above the others in town. It's also a 55+ senior park and a popular snowbird destination. It's a good big-rig park with back-ins and pull-thrus to 65 feet. There's a swimming pool and spa, also a recreation hall and planned activities. Easiest access to this park is from Exit 81 of I-10 at the west end of Deming. The campground is located off the access road on the south side of the highway, about .9 miles west of the exit.

LOW-Hi RV Ranch *(Open All Year)*
Information: (575) 546-4058
Location: 4 Miles SE of Deming, *N 32° 12' 38", W 107° 44' 06", 4,300 Ft*

50 Sites – This is the home park for an organization of single RVers known as Loners on Wheels. You don't have to be a member to stay in the park and they're a friendly group. The park has back-in and pull-thru sites to 55 feet in length. There are full-hookup and partial-hookup sites as well as a large dry camping area. There is a recreation hall, a communications room, and a bunk house. The communications room has a courtesy telephone and a data port for internet access. Take Exit 82A from I-10 and drive south on Gold Ave. South of town this becomes SR-11. Some 4.2 miles from I-10 turn left on Okelley Road SW. Drive east for .9 miles, the campground is on the left.

NEW MEXICO

ROCK HOUND STATE PARK *(Open All Year)*

Reservations: (877) NM-4-RSVP, www.nmparks.com
Information: (575) 536-2800, (575) 546-6182, (888) 667-2757, www.nmparks.com
Location: 12 Miles SE of Deming, *N 32° 11' 01", W 107° 37' 02", 4,600 Ft*

29 Sites – This park has an adobe building which houses the Visitor Center near the entrance. Rock hounds are encouraged to take home sample of up to 15 pounds of rocks. The mountains behind the park are called the Florida Mountains. The campground occupies a sloping site overlooking Deming and is landscaped with desert vegetation. Most sites here have electricity and water hookups but there are a few dry sites too. Some of the sites are pull-thrus and will take RVs to 45 feet. Sites have metal shaded picnic tables, some have both a raised barbecue grill and a metal fire pit, others just have just the fire pit. The bathroom building has flush toilets and free hot showers. A pay telephone is outside the bathroom. There is a dump station and water-fill station in the park. There is also a group area with covered picnic tables. The gate gets locked at dark. Easiest access is by heading south from I-10 at Exit 82A. Drive 5.3 miles which takes you through town and out on SR-11. Turn east on Rockhound Road and drive directly east for 6 miles. Bear right on SR-141 which will take you another 2.3 miles to the park entrance.

STARLIGHT VILLAGE RESORT *(Open All Year)*

Res and Info: (575) 546-9550, www.zianet.com/starlight
Location: 3 Miles N of Deming, *N 32° 17' 43", W 107° 44' 01", 4,300 Ft*

46 Sites – The Starlight is a big rig snowbird park north of town. Sites are back-ins and pull-thrus to 80 feet in a big gravel lot. The office has a data port for email. From Exit 82A drive north for 1.2 miles on US-180. Turn right on SR-26 and drive east for 1.7 mile, the resort entrance is on the right.

PANCHO VILLA STATE PARK *(Open All Year)*

Reservations: (877) NM-4-RSVP, www.nmparks.com
Information: (575) 531-2711, (888) 667-2757, www.nmparks.com
Location: Columbus, *N 31° 49' 36", W 107° 38' 32", 4,100 Ft*

This historical state park has 61 sites as well as a tent camping area. The RV sites are all pull-thrus, most have electricity and some are full-hookups. Only a few sites can be reserved. The campground has numerous historical exhibits and also a new museum and visitor center. The campground is easy to find in Columbus, 31 miles south of Deming.

EL MALPAIS AND EL MORO NATIONAL MONUMENTS

In the dry country south of Grants there are two interesting national monuments: El Malpais and El Moro.

El Malpais encompasses a lava flow. The name Malpais means bad country or "badlands" in Spanish and the name is appropriate. This is a fairly recent lava flow, only two to three thousand years old. It occupies an area between the Ácoma and Zuni pueblos and is crossed by a 7.5 mile long walking trail, the Zuni-Ácoma Trail.

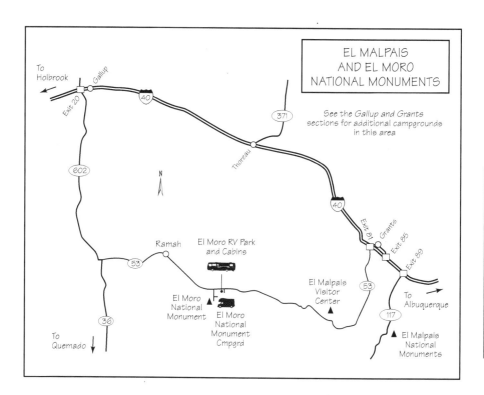

There are actually three visitor centers here. The first is near I-40 at Exit 85. It's just south of the freeway. This center covers public lands throughout the area and is run jointly by the BLM, the National Park Service, and the National Forest Service.

The second, on the east side of the monument, is a little isolated. It's run by the BLM and is located 5 miles south of Exit 89 from I-40. There are good views near here from overlooks across the flows. This really is the visitor center for the El Malpais National Conservation Area which surrounds the national monument. An attraction on this side of the flows is the La Ventana Natural Arch, the largest easily accessible sandstone arch in New Mexico.

The El Malpais National Monument visitor center is located 23 miles south of Exit 81 off I-40. This center is more accessible and conveniently located on SR-53 which connects it with El Morro National Monument. In this area you'll also find the privately owned **Bandera Crater Ice Caves**.

To the west of El Malpais, 18 miles from the monument visitor center is another interesting national monument, **El Moro**. In Spanish El Moro means "the headland", and that's what this monument is all about. El Morro, also often called Inscription Rock, was a well-known landmark for travelers in the west. Many of them scratched their names on the rock. Today you can see Indian petroglyphs, the names of Spanish explorers, and also those of later travelers who passed this way. The monument has an easy paved half-mile trail leading to the inscriptions, as well as a longer loop trail that climbs the headland and visits ruins of the Atsinna Pueblo there.

El Malpais and El Moro National Monuments Campgrounds

EL MORO NATIONAL MONUMENT CAMPGROUND *(Open All Year)*

Information: (505) 783-4226
Location: El Moro National Monument, *N 35° 02' 11", W 108° 20' 11", 7,200 Ft*

9 Sites – The monument has its own campground. It's very attractive, in an area of pines and junipers. Located about three quarters of a mile east of the visitor center there are 9 sites off a paved loop road. Most of these sites are suitable for vehicles up to about 25 feet but a few will take longer RVs. The park is best for RVs no longer than 30 feet due to limited maneuvering room. Tenters will find flat sand tent pads at each site. Water is available only in the summer. Parking is on gravel with picnic tables, fire pits, and raised barbecues.

EL MORO RV PARK AND CABINS *(Open All Year)*

Res and Info: (505) 783-4612
Location: 1 Mile E of El Moro National Monument,
                N 35° 02' 38", W 108° 19' 10", 7,200 Ft

30 Sites – For large RVs this is a good alternative to the campground at El Morro Monument. The sites in this campground are off a gravel loop road to the west of the Ancient Way Cafe. Each site has a picnic table and there are lots of juniper trees for shade. Twenty-three of the sites are full hookups, 1 has 20 amp power only, and 6 are without hookups. Two sites are very long pull-thrus, long enough for any size RV, and a few of the back-ins are also very large. About half of the sites can receive a Wi-Fi signal. There are also cabins available for rental. A pay telephone is located on the porch of the restaurant. The campground is located one mile east of the El Moro National Monument along SR-53.

EL PASO (TEXAS)

El Paso (metro area population about 715,000) is the second largest city along the U.S./Mexico border. While the town is in Texas it has close ties with New Mexico since it is at the southernmost end of the north-south Rio Grande corridor that forms the heart of New Mexico.

It's hard to even think of El Paso without being aware of Ciudad Juárez, Mexico's fifth largest city (population about 1,200,000), just across the border. The two cities really form one large metropolitan area, separated only by a political boundary. Ciudad Juárez, originally El Paso del Norte, has always been the largest of the two cities.

Interesting sights in El Paso include the University of Texas's **Centennial Museum** with exhibits explaining the history and natural history of the area. The **Museum of Archeology at Wilderness Park** covers some of the same information but also offers acres of poppies during the spring. It's located north of town and just east of the Franklin Mountains. Also popular is the **War Eagles Air Museum** which is actually located in the neighboring suburb of Santa Theresa, NM at the Doña County Airport. This museum houses aircraft and vehicles from World War II and later conflicts, some of the aircraft

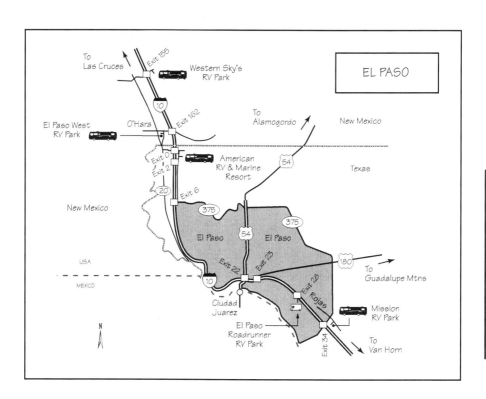

on display are: P-38, P-40, F-4U Corsair, Mustang, F-86, Mig-15, and Mig-21. El Paso's Zoo is considered a good one.

A popular driving route is the **Mission Trail** which visits three historical churches to the east of El Paso. From Exit 32 off I-10 drive south three miles to Mission Ysleta. From there follow Socorro Road three miles east to Mission Socorro. Finally, follow Socorro another 6 miles south to Presidio Chapel San Elceario.

El Paso Campgrounds

MISSION RV PARK *(Open All Year)*
    Res and Info: (915) 859-1133
    Location: El Paso, *N 31° 42' 03", W 106° 16' 50", 3,500 Ft*

188 Sites – Mission RV Park is conveniently locate just off I-10 to the east of central El Paso. Sites are back-ins and pull-thrus to 70 feet. There are also tent sites. There's an indoor swimming pool, a spa, a recreation room and a small store. From I-10 take Exit 34, it is marked Joe Battle and Americas Ave. After the exit go around the block to the north by turning north on Joe Battle to Rojas, turning right and then right again onto RV drive. You'll soon see the RV park on your left.

EL PASO WEST RV PARK *(Open All Year)*

Reservations: (800) 754-1543
Information: (575) 882-7172, www.1second.com/elpasowestrv.htm
Location: 22 Miles NW of El Paso, *N 32° 01' 11", W 106° 36' 14", 3,800 Ft*

102 Sites – The El Paso West is an older RV park with nice level gravel parking pads well separated by rows of trees. Sites are back-ins and pull-thrus to 75 feet. Many are full hookups. There is lots of shade and some sites have picnic tables. From I-10 take Exit 162. This is the first exit north of the New Mexico/Texas border. Drive west .8 miles to SR-460 and turn left. The campground is on the right in .3 miles.

AMERICAN RV AND MARINE RESORT *(Open All Year)*

Res and Info: (915) 298-5400
Location: 18 Miles NW of El Paso, *N 31° 58' 48", W 106° 34' 42", 3,900 Ft*

290 Sites – This is a big-rig campground. There are pull-thru and back-in sites to 80 feet set on a large gravel lot. There are no restrooms so all RVs must be self-contained. To reach the campground take Exit 2 from I-10 just south of the Texas/New Mexico border. Drive north along the access road on the eastern side of the freeway for 1.5 miles to the entrance road. There is a large RV sales operation with a Camping World in front of the RV park.

WESTERN SKY'S RV PARK *(Open All Year)*

Res and Info: (575) 233-2573
Location: 30 Miles NW of El Paso, *N 32° 07' 13", W 106° 38' 06", 3,900 Ft*

72 Sites – The Western Sky's RV Park is extremely convenient. It's really closer to Los Cruces than El Paso but it's good if you are approaching El Paso late in the day and are looking for a convenient place to stay. Sites here are almost all pull-thrus that will take a 45 foot RV. Take Exit 155 drive south on the access road on the east side of the freeway to the entrance, it's only about .4 miles

ENCHANTED CIRCLE

The Enchanted Circle is an 85-mile driving route circling Wheeler's Peak to the northeast of Taos. This is one of the most heavily promoted driving routes in the state, and it is truly scenic. Wheeler's Peak is New Mexico's highest mountain at 13,161 feet.

Traveling counter-clockwise the route climbs into the mountains east of Taos and crosses Palo Flechado Pass. At 21 miles it reaches the ski resort community of **Angel Fire**.

An interesting place to visit near Angel Fire is the **Vietnam Veterans National Memorial**. Dedicated to the GIs killed in Vietnam it occupies a hillside near the Angel Fire cutoff from US-64 and features a chapel which overlooks the valley and airstrip below.

Ten miles farther along the loop reaches **Eagle Nest**. At 8,000 feet this is a high and exposed location. You'd think it would be best visited during the summer but this is a popular winter cross-country skiing location. The lake here is a reservoir, it offers excellent trout fishing. The lake is also a popular wind surfing destination.

Traveling north and then northwest now on SR-38 you'll cross Bobcat Pass at 9,820 feet and descend steeply into the resort town of **Red River**, 17 miles from Eagle Nest. This is the most popular stop on the circle and offers lots of services for visitors. The town has a pleasant and protected valley location and serves as a ski destination in winter with the Red River Ski Area as well as the largest cross-country ski area in the state. In summer there are fishermen, hikers, mountain bikers, and 4-wheelers.

As the highway descends the Red River Valley it passes a number of excellent Carson National Forest campgrounds and after 12 miles reaches Questa. Here you might want to take a detour about 11 miles north and west to the **Wild River National Recreation Area**. Administered by the BLM the area has a series of very small campgrounds with spectacular views overlooking the junction of the Rio Grande and Red River which pass through the gorge far below. Some hiking trails lead down into the gorge to the rivers.

Back at Questa the route travels south on SR-522 to Taos, a distance of 25 miles.

Enchanted Circle Campgrounds

ENCHANTED MOON CAMPGROUND *(Open May 1 to Oct 15)*
Information: (575) 758-3338
Location: 11 Miles E of Taos, *N 36° 22' 18", W 105° 23' 08", 8,300 Ft*

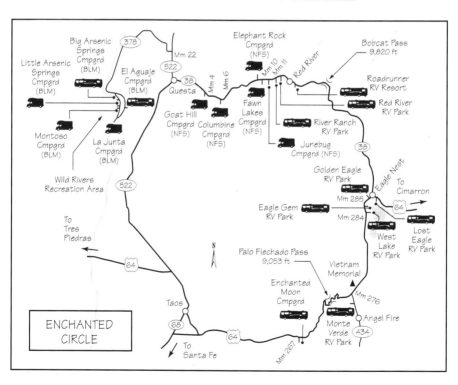

ENCHANTED CIRCLE

37 Sites – This park has 37 sites with a mix of partial and full hookups, back-in and pull-through sites. Tenting sites are available in a secluded area. The sites have picnic tables and fire pits and wood is available. Other amenities include a laundry, game/recreation room, recreation area, and play area. Fishing is possible in the stream and hiking trails leave from near the park. The campground is on the south side of US-64 about 11 miles east of Taos.

MONTE VERDE RV PARK *(Open May 15 to Oct 15 - Varies)*
Res and Info: (575) 377-3404
Location: Angel Fire, *N 36° 24' 42", W 105° 17' 37", 8,300 Ft*

28 Sites – This commercial park at Angel Fire has 28 sites in an oblong lot running back from SR-434. Twenty back-in sites with full hookups are located in the front of the lot and 8 pull-thru sites with water and electricity are located in the back of the lot behind the office. The longest of the back-in sites is 60 feet and the pull-thrus are 60 to 70 feet. Some of the sites have picnic tables, portable grills & fire pits are available. Firewood is available at the park. There is also one rental cabin. A data port is provided in the office for internet access and a courtesy phone for local and calling card calls. A village shuttle bus runs through the park to ski runs, golf course, restaurants and shopping. Propane is sold at the park. The tent rate is $7.25 per person plus tax. From US-64 drive 1.3 miles south toward Angel Fire on SR-434. The campground is on the right.

WESTLAKE RV PARK *(Open May 15 to Oct 1)*
Information: (575) 377-7275
Location: Eagle Nest, *N 36° 32' 11", W 105° 16' 31", 8,200 Ft*

28 Sites – The sites in this campground are all back-in sites around the perimeter of a lot. In the interior is an office building and a covered partially enclosed picnic pavilion. The sites sit up above and overlook the valley holding Eagle Nest Lake. Each site has a covered table with a bench on each side. There are 28 sites and they are all full hookups. A few of the sites along the bottom part of the lot could take rigs to any size. A bathroom building with showers and laundry is available. The state park boat ramp is at the end of the same road that services this park. The campground is right off the US-64 just 1.6 miles south of the intersection of US-64 and SR-38 in Eagle Nest.

EAGLE GEM RV PARK *(Open May 1 to Oct 15)*
Information: (575) 377-2214 or (575) 377-0533, strip2214@aol.com
Location: Eagle Nest, *N 36° 32' 25", W 105° 16' 30", 8,200 Ft*

68 Sites – This park has full-hookup back-in sites to 50 feet. There is also a dump station. There are 7 rental cabins. A central data port is provided for internet access and a courtesy phone is located in the park's large recreation hall for local or calling-card calls. The park is within easy walking distance of Eagle Nest Lake for fishing and a boat launch is available nearby at the state park. The campground is right off the US-64 just 1.3 mile south of the intersection of US-64 and SR-38 in Eagle Nest.

NEW MEXICO

GOLDEN EAGLE RV PARK *(Open All Year)*

Res and Info: (575) 377-6188, www.goldeneaglerv.com, golden@newmex.com
Location: Eagle Nest, *N 36° 33' 09", W 105° 16' 14", 8,200 Ft*

53 Sites – This campground has back-in and pull-thru sites to 70 feet in length. Most sits are full hookup. The sites have picnic tables but no fire pits. A data port and a desk are provided in the clubhouse for internet access and a courtesy telephone is available for local and calling card calls. The office building has a store which sells limited RV supplies and propane. A big club room is available in the same building. This park is close enough to walk to restaurants and shopping in Eagle Nest. Lake fishing is possible and the state park boat launch is nearby. A dump station is available and RVers not staying here are allowed to dump for a fee. Reservations are recommended for the summer season. The RV park is right off US-64 just .1 mile south of the intersection of US-64 and SR-38 in Eagle Nest.

LOST EAGLE RV PARK *(Open May 15 to Oct 31)*

Reservations: (800) 581-2374
Information: (575) 377-2374
Location: Eagle Nest, *N 36° 33' 14", W 105° 15' 45", 8,300 Ft*

41 Sites – Lost Eagle is an RV-only park, there are no restrooms. The campground has closely-space full-hookup back-in sites to 60 feet. Each site has a bright blue picnic table. You can walk to local stores and restaurants since the park is right in the middle of Eagle Nest. From the intersection of US-64 and SR-38 west of town it's just .2 miles east to the campground.

RED RIVER RV PARK *(Open All Year)*

Reservations: (800) 670-3711
Information: (575) 754-6187
Location: Red River, *N 36° 42' 35", W 105° 25' 17", 8,600 Ft*

31 Sites – This is a gravel lot between the highway and the Red River. All of the sites are back-ins to 40 feet along the exterior of the lot and are all full hookups. Some of the sites are right along the river and there are also rental cabins available along the river. A central data port is available for internet access. The building near the entrance houses the office, showers, laundry, and a recreation hall. The bathrooms are nice and have 4 individual shower rooms. Freshwater fishing is possible in the Red River which runs behind the park. The campground is located toward the western end of the town of Red River, right next to SR-38, the main thoroughfare. It's on the south side of the highway.

RIVER RANCH RV PARK *(Open All Year)*

Res and Info: (575) 754-2293, www.redrivernm.com/riverranch, riverranch@redrivernm.com
Location: Red River, *N 36° 42' 32", W 105° 25' 34", 8,600 Ft*

60 Sites – River Ranch has tent sites, rental cabins, and both back-in and pull-thru RV sites. Some RV sites are as long as 45 feet and both full and partial hookup sites are offered. Some sites are next to the river. A central data port is available for internet access. A convenience store sells limited grocery items, RV supplies, fishing tackle, and propane. Other amenities at the park include a game room and a recreation room. Riverside fishing is possible and the park has its own stocked fishing pond. This campground too is at the western edge of Red River on the south side of SR-38.

ROADRUNNER RV RESORT *(Open May 1 to Sept 30 - Varies)*
 Res and Info: (575) 754-2286, (800) 243-2286
 Location: Red River, *N 36° 41' 54", W 105° 23' 36", 8,700 Ft*

180 Sites – This is a big park with 180 full hookup sites. The main interior road are paved and secondary roads are gravel. There are back-ins and pull-thrus to 50 feet. The sites have tables and fire pits and wood is available for purchase. A central data port is provided for internet access. There is a convenience store which sells limited groceries, RV supplies, fishing tackle, ice, and propane. Other amenities at the park include a pavilion, an adult room, a recreation hall, a sports field, and tennis courts. River fishing is possible. This campground is on the far side of town from those listed above. On Main Street headed east continue straight when the highway veers left. The campground is about a half mile beyond this point.

JUNEBUG CAMPGROUND *(Open May 15 to Oct 1 - Varies)*
 Information: (575) 586-0520, (575) 758-6200
 Location: 1 Mile W of Red River, *N 36° 42' 30", W 105° 26' 13", 8,500 Ft*

23 Sites – The sites in this Carson National Forest campground are on one road with a turn-around. There are 23 sites which are mostly back-in with a few pull-thrus. Some sites are long enough for RVs to 35 feet. The sites have picnic tables and fire pits. The toilets are vault style. The campground is located .9 miles west of Red River on the south side of SR-38.

FAWN LAKES CAMPGROUND *(Open May 15 to Oct 1 - Varies)*
 Information: (575) 586-0520, (575) 758-6200
 Location: 2 Miles W of Red River, *N 36° 42' 26", W 105° 26' 57", 8500 Ft*

19 Sites – The camping sites in this park are set under pine trees next to the Red River on a loop with one spur. The spur is not appropriate for large RVs. The sites are almost all back-in sites (a couple are parallel parking style) with some on the main loop large enough for RVs to 35 feet. The sites have picnic tables and fire rigs. A few have raised barbecue grills. There are wheelchair designated sites, and the bathrooms are vault style with wheelchair access. Water is available at the park. Fishing is possible in the Red River and there are hiking trails nearby. The park also provides fishing access to two stocked ponds. The campground is located 1.7 miles west of Red River on the south side of the highway.

NEW MEXICO

ELEPHANT ROCK CAMPGROUND *(Open May 15 to Sept 15 - Varies)*
Information: (575) 586-0520, (575) 758-6200
Location: 2 Miles W of Red River, *N 36° 42' 21", W 105° 27' 20", 8,400 Ft*

21 Sites – A paved road loops under a forest of pine trees through this Carson National Forest campground which has recently been upgraded with paved road and sites. There are 22 mostly back-in sites (1 parallel parking style) each having a picnic table and fire pit. Three of the sites are equipped with ramps and are fully wheelchair accessible. The sites here are small and are only appropriate for RVs to about 30 feet. Water is available in the campground. Trout fishing is possible on the nearby Red River.

COLUMBINE CAMPGROUND *(Open May 15 to Oct 1 - Varies)*
Information: (575) 586-0520, (575) 758-6200
Location: 6 Miles W of Red River, *N 36° 40' 51", W 105° 30' 55", 7,900 Ft*

26 Sites – The sites in this Carson National Forest campground are off one big loop and a smaller star-shaped loop. There are 26 sites in total which include some that are walk-in tent sites. Six of the sites are long pull-thrus, but limited maneuvering room make the park really suitable for RVs to only 35 feet. The 8 sites which are on the star-shaped loop are all designed as wheelchair sites - everything in these sites is paved and the fires pits are raised. The vault style bathrooms are also wheelchair accessible. All of the sites have picnic tables and fire pits. Hiking trails leave from the campground. The campground is located 6.1 miles west of Red River on the south side of the highway.

GOAT HILL CAMPGROUND *(Open May 15 to Oct 15 - Varies)*
Information: (575) 586-, (575) 758-6200
Location: 8 Miles W of Red River, *N 36° 41' 21", W 105° 32' 27", 7,700 Ft*

5 Sites – This Carson National Forest campground is a small gravel lot right by the side of SR-38. It has parking under pines for 5 RVs to about 35 feet. The sites are loosely laid out under the trees either as pull-thrus or back-ins with some of the spaces right along the edge of the creek. There are 5 picnic tables and fire grills. The toilets are vault style. Because it's tough to gate this campground it tends to be used all year long, even when technically closed. The campground is located 7.7 miles west of Red River on the south side of the highway.

WILD RIVERS RECREATION AREA – EL AGUAJE CAMPGROUND *(Open All Year)*
Information: (575) 758-8851, (575) 770-1600
Location: 15 Miles NW of Questa, *N 36° 39' 58", W 105° 40' 22", 7,400 Ft*

7 Sites – El Aquaje is the largest of the campgrounds in the recreation area. There are 7 sites off a gravel road in a light forest of pines. Six of the sites are back-ins to a maximum length of 30 feet and 1 pull-thru site is about 100 feet in length. Each site has a covered picnic table, a paved patio, a fire pit, and a raised barbecue grill. There are wheelchair accessible vault toilets and water. Hiking trails leave from the campground. From Questa drive north on SR-522 for 2.5 miles. Turn left on SR-378 and drive for 8.9 miles to reach

the entrance to the fee area. Continue on to a Y in another 1.5 miles. Take the left fork and you'll reach the campground in 2 miles.

WILD RIVERS RECREATION AREA – BIG ARSENIC SPRINGS CAMPGROUND
(Open All Year)

Information: (575) 758-8851, (575) 770-1600
Location: 14 Miles NW of Questa, *N 36° 39' 27", W 105° 41' 05", 7,400 Ft*

6 Sites – The sites in this campground are set off 3 small loop roads. Sites 6-8 are on the first loop as you enter the park. These 3 sites are all very small back-in sites only suitable for pick-up campers, vans, or tenters. The middle loop has only one site, site 9. This is a pull-thru which is at least 70 feet in length. The last loop has sites 10 and 11 which although a little larger are still only suitable for pickup campers, vans and tents. Each site has a covered picnic table (with one wall and a roof), a paved patio, a fire pit, and a raised barbecue grill. In the first loop there is a wheelchair accessible vault toilet and there are additional vault toilets in the other loops. From Questa drive north on SR-522 for 2.5 miles. Turn left on SR-378 and drive for 8.9 miles to reach the entrance to the fee area. Continue on to a Y in another 1.5 miles. Take the right fork and you'll reach the campground in .7 miles.

WILD RIVERS RECREATION AREA – LITTLE ARSENIC SPRINGS CAMPGROUND
(Open All Year)

Information: (575) 758-8851, (575) 770-1600
Location: 14 Miles NW of Questa, *N 36° 40' 02", W 105° 40' 49", 7,500 Ft*

3 Sites – Little Arsenic has just 3 sites. The turn around is very tight and the interior roads are bordered closely by pines. Only pick-up campers vans, or tent campers should come into this campground. All 3 of the sites are spectacular as they sit right on the edge of the canyon and have great views. The 3 sites have a covered picnic table (with one wall and a roof), a paved patio, a fire pit, and a raised barbecue grill. There are handicap accessible vault toilets. Water is available. Trails run from the campground and connect with the Confluence Trail in the canyon. From Questa drive north on SR-522 for 2.5 miles. Turn left on SR-378 and drive for 8.9 miles to reach the entrance to the fee area. Continue on to a Y in another 1.5 miles. Take the right fork and you'll reach the campground in 1.4 miles.

WILD RIVERS RECREATION AREA – LA JUNTA CAMPGROUND *(Open All Year)*

Information: (575) 758-8851, (575) 770-1600
Location: 15 Miles NW of Questa, *N 36° 39' 27", W 105° 41' 05", 7,400 Ft*

3 Sites – This is a day use area and a trailhead parking area. The camping here is for walk-in tenting. There are 3 tent sites. Each site has a covered picnic table (with one wall and a roof), a paved patio, a fire pit, and a raised barbecue grill. There are wheelchair accessible vault toilets. Water is available. A group shelter is located in this area. This is also one of the overlook points. The Rio Bravo Nature Trail and the Confluence Trail leaves from the campground. From Questa drive north on SR-522 for 2.5 miles. Turn left on SR-378 and drive for 8.9 miles to reach the entrance to the fee area. Continue on to a Y in another 1.5 miles. Take the right fork and you'll reach the campground in 2.1 miles.

🚐 **WILD RIVERS RECREATION AREA – MONTOSO CAMPGROUND** *(Open All Year)*
Information: (575) 758-8851, (575) 770-1600
Location: 15 Miles NW of Questa, *N 36° 39' 56", W 105° 40' 51", 7,500 Ft*

2 Sites – There are only 2 sites in this camping area. One is a real beauty - it sits right along the edge and looks down into the canyon. Both sites have a covered picnic table (with one wall and a roof), a paved patio, a fire pit, and a raised barbecue grill. These sites are only appropriate for vans, pick-up campers, or tent campers. It is difficult to turn around on the interior road of the campground. There are vault toilets. Water is available. The Confluence Trail runs below and trails lead from near the campground down to the Confluence Trail. From Questa drive north on SR-522 for 2.5 miles. Turn left on SR-378 and drive for 8.9 miles to reach the entrance to the fee area. Continue on to a Y in another 1.5 miles. Take the right fork and you'll reach the campground in 1.6 miles.

FARMINGTON

Farmington (population about 40,000) is a major business and population center of the Four Corners region. It's located at the confluence of the Animas, San Juan, and La Plata Rivers. This region is a traditional home of the Navajo and Ute Indians. For campgrounds the busy season in this part of New Mexico is the summer, due to the high altitude the area is cool in winter.

From high spots in the area you can see **Shiprock Pinnacle** to the southwest, it's a sa-

HOUSEBOATS ON NAVAJO LAKE

cred spot for the Navajo Indians. For a closer look drive west on US-64 to the town of Shiprock.

Angel Peak, about 21 miles south of Bloomfield, is a rock formation traditionally believed to be a dwelling place of "sacred ones", by the Navajo. It's a desert badlands area and has trails, picnic areas, and a campground. See the campground write-up below for directions.

Aztec Ruins National Monument is located in Aztec, about 14 miles east of Farmington. The pueblo here was built and occupied between 1050 and 1300 AD. The outstanding attraction here is the Great Kiva which was reconstructed in 1934. It's said to be the only reconstructed kiva of its kind in North America. There's a commercial campground within walking distance, see the Ruins Road RV Park and Campground description below.

The **Salmon Ruins** were an outlying colony of Chaco Canyon. The **Salmon Ruins and Heritage Park** has a museum and the heritage park is a preserved homestead and group of replica Indian dwellings illustrating the history of the local area. The facility is located 10 miles east of Farmington on US-64.

Navajo Lake State Park on the shores of Navajo Lake is located about 45 miles east of Farmington. The lake was formed by damming the San Juan River. It's a huge recreational draw with campgrounds, houseboats, fishing, and lots of warm water water sports. There's also great trout fishing in the San Juan River below the lake. See the three state park campground descriptions below for more information.

An unusual destination near Farmington is the **B-Square Ranch**. It's a large wildlife preserve and an experimental farm. There are two museums on the property. One is the Bolack Museum of Fish and Wildlife with a large collection of mounted animals, 2,500 of them. The other is the Bolack Electromechanical Museum with exhibits illustrating use and development of electricity, telephones, farming and the oil field industry at the ranch. It's best to call ahead for an appointment but walk-ins are welcome if there's room. The ranch is located south of Farmington off US-64.

Farmington's San Juan County Fairgrounds hosts the **San Juan County Fair** in August. It's the largest county fair in the state of New Mexico.

The **Navajo Fair** is celebrated in nearby Shiprock in late September or early October. It features traditional dancing and a rodeo.

Farmington Campgrounds

MOM & POP RV PARK *(Open All Year)*

Reservations: (800) 748-2807
Information: (505) 327-3200
Location: Farmington, *N 36° 43' 13", W 108° 11' 13", 5,300 Ft*

34 Sites – Here's a campground with some personality, we think it's a great place to stay while checking out Farmington. The sites in this simple campground are set around the exterior of a lot with one row of pull-thrus down the center. There are 34 sites, 6 of them are pull-thrus to a length of 70 feet. The back-in sites are about 45 feet long. Every site has full hookups, a paved parking pad, and a picnic table. The bathrooms have a separate room which is wheelchair accessible. A data port is provided in the office for internet.

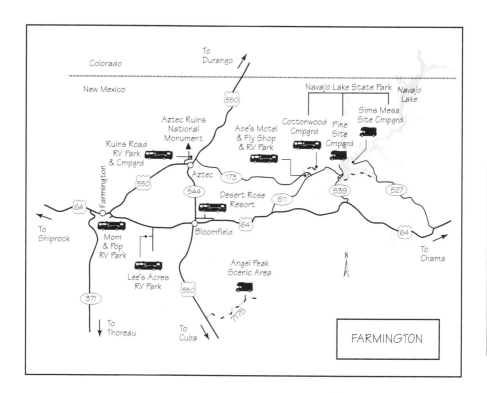

A public laundry is just about two blocks away. The campground owner has an outdoor and an indoor train village set up in the office and between the office and his residence. He'll tell you where everything in town is and what to do and see in the area, in fact he's put together an extensive written guide so you won't miss anything. The campground is toward the eastern edge of Farmington. It's in the interior of the Y formed where E Broadway and E Murray Drive join.

DESERT ROSE RESORT *(Open All Year)*

Res and Info: (866) 459-8339 or (505) 632-8339, www.desertrosepark.com
Location: 12 Miles E of Farmington, *N 36° 43' 07", W 107° 57' 22", 5,500 Ft*

79 Sites – This former KOA is actually located some distance east in Bloomfield. There are tent sites, camping cabins, and many pull-thru RV sites to 50 feet. A few sites sport raised barbecue grills, a few also have fire pits. Internet is available using a data port and Wi-Fi is available. There is an outdoor seasonal swimming pool and an indoor spa. The campground store offers Native American pottery and there is a restaurant. Other amenities include a game room with TV and a pool table, horseshoes, and volleyball. From Farmington head east on US-64, also known as Bloomfield Blvd. In 10 miles you'll reach Bloomfield. Turn north on US-550 in the center of town. In .5 mile turn right on E. Blanco Blvd. and head east, the campground is on the left in 1.2 miles.

LEE'S ACRES RV PARK *(Open All Year)*
Information: (505) 326-5207
Location: 6 Miles E of Farmington, *N 36° 41' 28", W 108° 05' 45", 5,300 Ft*

96 Sites – Lee's is a very basic campground with big sites. It's a big gravel lot with both back-in and pull-thru sites, all full hookup. There are no other facilities. Drive east from Farmington for about 5.5 miles. Just past Downs RV Park (see above) watch for the sign and turn right. The campground is south about a half mile next to the San Juan River.

RUINS ROAD RV PARK AND CAMPGROUND *(Open All Year)*
Res and Info: (505) 334-3160, www.ruinsroadrvpark.com
Location: Aztec, *N 36° 49' 48", W 108° 00' 00", 5,600 Ft*

53 Sites – For fans of Aztec Ruins National Monument this is the place to stay, it's within .3 mile of the monument, easy strolling distance. The campground has 53 sites, 45 of which are pull-thru sites to 60 feet in length. The sites are all full hookup. The facilities are basic with no restrooms. Trees border 3 sides of the park and there are a few shade trees between the sites. Grass strips separate the sites. There is one portable toilet in the park so tent campers can stay here. The park is near the Animas River and there is a hiking trail along the river. In Aztec you could just follow signs for Aztec Ruins National Monument to find the campground but here are better directions. Ruins Road goes north from US-550 about a half mile west of its intersection with SR-544. Follow Ruins Road north, the campground is on the right in .3 mile.

ANGEL PEAK SCENIC AREA *(Open All Year)*
Information: (505) 599-8900
Location: 21 Miles S of Bloomfield, *N 36° 32' 58", W 107° 51' 28", 6,600 Ft*

9 Sites – The campground has picnic tables on concrete patios and fire pits. Some sites have shelters over the tables. No water is provided. There are vault toilets and a nature trail as well as an overlook of Angel Peak. The access road limits RV size here to vans and pickup campers. From US-64 in Bloomfield drive south on US-550 for 15 miles. Turn east on gravel Road 7175 and follow it east for six miles to the campground.

ABE'S MOTEL AND FLY SHOP AND RV PARK *(Open All Year)*
Information: (505) 632-2194
Location: 6 Miles W of Navajo Dam, *N 36° 48' 18", W 107° 41' 43", 5,600 Ft*

14 Sites – This operation is a combination motel, fly shop, guided fly fishing (Born "N" Raised on the San Juan River Inc.), restaurant (El Pescador), and gas station. To the east of all of this is a gravel lot with 14 full hookup pull-thrus to about 60 feet in length. Each site has a picnic table and most have a raised barbecue grill. There are no bathrooms or showers for the campground although there are bathrooms in the fly shop/grocery store. There is a good selection of groceries in the store. A pay telephone is located in front of the fly shop. The campground is located very near the intersection of SR-173 from Aztec with SR-511, the road which follows the San Juan River westward from Navajo Dam.

That puts the place very near the San Juan River, just right for such a fishing-oriented operation.

NAVAJO LAKE STATE PARK – COTTONWOOD CAMPGROUND *(Open All Year)*

Reservations: (877) NM-4-RSVP, www.nmparks.com
Information: (505) 632-2278, (888) 667-2757, www.nmparks.com
Location: 9 Miles W of Navajo Dam, *N 36° 48' 37", W 107° 40' 41", 5,600 Ft*

48 Sites – This campground has a beautiful situation next to the San Juan River. It has 48 sites set on one loop road under cottonwood trees. Sites are back-ins and pull-thrus, some to 60 feet. All of the sites have a picnic table, fire pit, and a raised barbecue. Twenty-four of the sites have electric hookups. Water is not provided at the sites, but is readily available throughout the park. There is a trail to the river and parking for a day-use area nearby. The bathrooms have flush toilets which are wheelchair accessible, but no showers. There is a dump station near the entrance. Reservations are accepted May 15-Sept 15 for 12 of the sites. The only fly in the ointment is that there are 1.3 miles of dirt to be negotiated in reaching the campground. From SR-173 near Mile 17.5 turn north on the access road to the campground. The road is .8 miles west of the intersection of SR-173 and SR-511. The access road is dirt but easily negotiable by any vehicle. In 1.3 miles you enter Navajo State Park and the road turns to pavement. In another .7 mile you'll arrive at the campground.

NAVAJO LAKE STATE PARK – PINE SITE CAMPGROUND *(Open All Year)*

Reservations: (877) NM-4-RSVP, www.nmparks.com
Information: (505) 632-2278, (888) 667-2757, www.nmparks.com
Location: 1 Mile N of Navajo Dam, *N 36° 49' 13", W 107° 37' 10", 6,200 Ft*

160 Sites – Pine Site Campground has 4 areas - the Main Campground, Piñon Loop, Cedar Loop, and Juniper Loop. Campsites are mostly under junipers. The Main Campground has 5 loops: A-E. There are currently 9 full hookup sites and 54 electric sites, all in the Main Campground, with the full hookup sites on Loop A. Construction is underway in the Main Campground to add more electric hookups and to add water to the electric sites already there. The number of new electric sites is not know at this time. Showers are available on 2 of the Main Campground loops and in the Cedar Loop. Piñon Loop and Juniper Loop have only vault toilets. The sites have covered picnic tables, fire pits, and raised barbecue grills. This is a 40-year-old park with tight maneuvering room and only a few sites which could take 40 foot RVs, we recommend it only for RVs no longer than 30 feet. Large RV drivers will prefer Cottonwood Campground. The campground is located near the west shore of Navajo Lake about .8 miles north of the dam.

NAVAJO LAKE STATE PARK – SIMS MESA SITE CAMPGROUND *(Open All Year)*

Reservations: (877) NM-4-RSVP, www.nmparks.com
Information: (505) 632-2278, (888) 667-2757, www.nmparks.com
Location: Navajo Lake, *N 36° 49' 54", W 107° 35' 23", 6,100 Ft*

160 Sites – Sims Mesa Site campground is located on the east side of the lake. As the crow flies it's close to Pine Site Campground, but paved road access requires a drive of 41 miles from one to the other. Even if you're willing to follow gravel roads through the

NEW MEXICO

gas fields it's 9 miles. The campground has sites on two loops, Upper Loop (sites 1-19) and Main Loop (sites 20-39), and there is dispersed camping in two other areas, Lake Shore Camping and Ramp Area Camping. Twenty of the 2 loop sites have electric hook-ups. The sites are mostly back-in with a few pull-off style sites and they are near the lake in juniper trees. The sites are mostly shorter and appropriate for RVs to only about 30 feet in length. The sites have covered picnic tables on paved patios, a fire pit, and a raised barbecue grill. The restroom building is wheelchair accessible and has showers. The campground has a boat ramp, a marina, and a dump station. A visitor's center is located at the entrance to the campground. Reservations are accepted from May 15-Sept 15 for 11 sites in the park. There's also group camping and a group picnic pavilion. From the Navajo Dam drive south on SR-539 for 5.6 miles. Turn left on US-64 and drive another 14.4 miles. Finally, turn left and follow SR-527 for 20 miles to the campground.

FORT SUMNER

Fort Sumner, now a town of a little more than 1,000 people, began as a frontier fort. It is the site of the notorious Bosque Redondo, the area that served as a temporary reservation to the Navajo people after their defeat by troops under Kit Carson in 1862. The Navajos and also large numbers of Apaches were interned here until 1868. That year they were able to return to their traditional lands and the fort was abandoned.

The fort was then purchased by the largest cattle baron in the region, Lucien B. Maxwell. He turned it into a mansion. Eventually his son inherited it and that was when the second of the major events in the history of Fort Sumner occurred. One night Billy the Kid happened to be staying at the mansion, and that's where Pat Garrett found and killed him.

Both events, Bosque Redondo and the death of Billy the Kid, are well documented here. The old Fort Sumner is no longer standing, but there is **state monument** and visitor center at the site. To get there drive east out of town on US-60 and then south about four miles on SR-272 (Realwind Drive).

The **Old Fort Sumner Museum** is near the state monument. It has some information about the fort, and quite a bit about Billy the Kid. In fact, his grave is out back.

In town there's more Billy the Kid. The **Billy the Kid Museum** is privately owned and has lots of stuff related to Billy the Kid, local history, and the Indians of the area. The owners also operate the Valley View RV Park down the street.

Sumner Lake, about 15 miles north of town, is a reservoir behind a dam on the Pecos River. It is a state park and has several state park campgrounds. The lake is stocked for fishing and offers walleye, bass, crappie and channel catfish.

Fort Sumner Campgrounds

🚐 **SUMNER LAKE STATE PARK – EASTSIDE CAMPGROUND** *(Open April 1 to Sept 30)*
   Information: (575) 355-2541, (888) 667-2757, www.nmparks.com
   Location: 15 Miles N of Ft. Sumner, *N 34° 36' 44", W 104° 22' 31", 4,300 Ft*

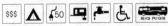

10 Sites – This campground sits on the east shore of Lake Sumner. There are 10 sites, 5 have electric hookups. The sites with electricity have an adobe style shelter covering a picnic table on a paved patio. The dry sites have a tin roofed shelter over the picnic table. The sites have raised barbecue grills. Two of the electric sites are pull-thrus. Sites are to

New Mexico

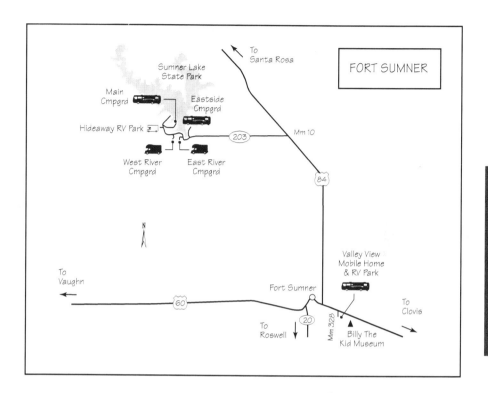

about 45 feet in length. There is a boat ramp in the camping area. Fishing and swimming are possible in the lake. Reservations are not taken at this camping area. A dump station is available, but it is across the dam near the Main Campground. From Ft. Sumner drive north about 9 miles on US-84 to SR-203, it's on the left. Drive west 5.3 miles to the entrance for the Eastside Campground.

⮕ SUMNER LAKE STATE PARK – MAIN CAMPGROUND *(Open All Year)*

Reservations: (877) NM-4-RSVP, www.nmparks.com
Information: (575) 355-2541, (888) 667-2757, www.nmparks.com
Location: 17 Miles N of Ft. Sumner, *N 34° 36' 56", W 104° 23' 23", 4,300 Ft*

24 Sites – The main campground has hookup sites called Pecos (sites 1-13) (to the right as you enter) and a no hookup sites to the left called Mesquite (sites 14-24). The Pecos sites have electricity at the sites and water is available. Three of the sites are pull-thrus suitable for any size RV. Six of these sites can be reserved. Some sites have fire pits and they all have a raised barbecue grill as well as an adobe-style picnic shelter on a paved patio. The Mesquite sites are all pull-thrus with no hookups, but water is available and they have a tin roofed shelter over the picnic tables. Four of these sites can be reserved. There is a bathroom building in the Pecos loop which has wheelchair accessible flush toilets and showers. There is a boat ramp in the camping area. Swimming and lake fishing for bass, crappie, channel catfish, and walleye are possible. From Ft. Sumner drive north about 9 miles on US-84 to SR-203, it's on the left. Drive west 7.3 miles and turn right at the sign for the Main Campground. You'll reach it in another .9 mile.

SUMNER LAKE STATE PARK – EAST RIVER CAMPGROUND *(Open All Year)*

Information: (575) 355-2541, (888) 667-2757, www.nmparks.com
Location: 15 Miles N of Ft. Sumner, *N 34° 36' 19", W 104° 23' 13", 4,100 Ft*

5 Sites – The East River Campground has 5 spaces. Each has a covered picnic table. Some of these sites have raised barbecue grills and others have fire pits. There is a wheelchair accessible vault toilet. Water is available only from the river. Showers, flush toilets, and a dump station are at the main campground. This campground is only suitable for tents, vans, or pickup campers. From Ft Sumner drive north about 9 miles on US-84 to SR-203, it's on the left. Drive west 6.4 miles and turn left at the camping area entrance.

SUMNER LAKE STATE PARK – WEST RIVER CAMPGROUND *(Open All Year)*

Information: (575) 355-2541, (888) 667-2757, www.nmparks.com
Location: 14 Mile N of Ft. Sumner, *N 34° 36' 12", W 104° 23' 18", 4,100 Ft*

4 Sites – The West River Campground has defined spaces for 4 very small vehicles to park. The 4 spaces each have a picnic table and a fire ring with a grill. There is a wheelchair accessible vault toilet but no potable water. From Ft Sumner drive north about 9 miles on US-84 to SR-203, it's on the left. Drive west 6.4 miles and turn left at the camping area entrance.

VALLEY VIEW MOBILE HOME & RV PARK *(Open All Year)*

Res and Info: (575) 355-2380
Location: Ft Sumner, *N 34° 28' 01", W 104° 13' 55", 5,500 Ft*

20 Sites – This campground has about 20 sites which are available for rental to travelers. There are 37 sites in total, several have permanent structures on them. Nine of the sites are pull-thrus to 100 feet in length. All sites are full hookup including cable TV. There are no bathroom or shower facilities. The campground has the same ownership as the Billy The Kid Museum which is 1 block farther east. There is a self registration booth at the campground or visitors can walk to the museum to register. Credit Cards are accepted only when registering at the museum. This is a very simple, clean, inexpensive place to stay while visiting Fort Sumner. It's right in the middle of the tiny town so you can walk to everything.

GALLUP

Gallup (population about 22,000) is often thought of as an Indian town. That's easy to explain, Gallup is strategically located between the Navajo and Zuni reservations and is also convenient to other Indian lands. The big event of the season in Gallup is the **Inter-Tribal Indian Ceremonial Gallup** at the end of July. It's held at Red Rock Park (see below for the campground there) and features an Indian rodeo and tribal dances. There's also the **Red Rock Balloon Rally** at the park in early December.

Gallup is also a **Route 66** town as you will see if you visit the historical center of town. You'll also find a large number of trading posts and galleries offering one of the best selections of Indian arts and crafts anywhere. For entertainment you might visit the **Gallup**

Cultural Center in the restored railroad station where each evening at 7 pm during the summer **Indian dances** are performed.

South of Gallup is the **Zuni Pueblo**. This is a unique pueblo, related to those of the Rio Grande valley but in an isolated location on the far side of the Continental Divide. Zuni is the largest of the New Mexico pueblos in land area and population, it also has the largest number of artisans by far. Specialties include silver jewelry, fetishes of animals carved from stone, pottery, some weaving, and even kachina dolls. The Zuni pueblo has a visitor center with a museum and heritage center. Tours are available at the center and it is also the location of the Zuni Arts and Crafts Enterprise, run by the pueblo. There are a number of other shops in the village. The other important attraction here is the mission church, **Nuestra Señora de Guadalupe**, with its impressive interior murals. To reach the pueblo drive south from Gallup on SR-602 for 30 miles. Turn right on SR-53 and you'll reach the visitor center in about 9 miles.

Gallup Campgrounds

 GALLUP KOA *(Open All Year)*
   Reservations: (800) 562-3915, www.koa.com
   Information: (505) 722-2333
   Location: Gallup, *N 35° 31' 51", W 108° 39' 52", 6,500 Ft*

53 Sites – This is a new KOA associated with the Quality Inn next door. It's an unusual KOA because it does not really have a variety of site types, in fact the camping area is a gravel lot. There are 43 RV spaces, 10 tent spaces, and 5 cabins. The sites are all full hookup including cable TV, they're pull-thrus to 80 feet. There is no separation between sites and no picnic tables or fire grills. Wi-Fi is being added to the park and should be in use by next season. There is a data port in the office. The hotel is associated with the La Quinta Inn next door. There is a swimming pool and spa at the inn which can be used by the RV guests. There is also a Denny's restaurant at the inn and a 10% discount is offered to guests of the RV park. Other amenities at the park include 3 picnic pavilions, an outside grill, and a camping kitchen. From I-40 in Gallup take Exit 26, the Quality Inn and campground are just to the east on SR-118.

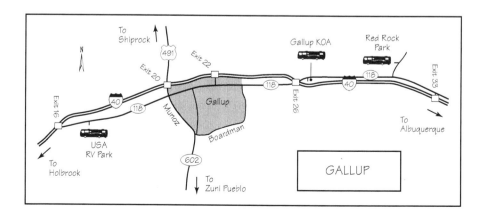

RED ROCK PARK *(Open All Year)*

Res and Info: (505) 722-3839
Location: 5 Miles E of Gallup, *N 35° 32' 29", W 108° 36' 30", 6,700 Ft*

140 Sites – The sites in this park all have water and electric hookups. Many of the sites are long pull-thrus or pull-offs, some as long as 70 feet. All sites have a picnic table and a fire pit. Trees are scattered throughout the park for shade. There are two dump stations. Check-in is at the Outlaw Trading post near the entrance. The Church Rock post office is located next door to the Trading Post and there is a telephone out front. There is usually not a manager on-site, payment is made by envelope with a slot near the on-site post office. From I-40 about 8 miles east of Gallup take Exit 33. Follow the road on the north side of the highway (Route 66) westward for 3.9 miles. Turn right at the sign and drive north .5 miles to the park.

USA RV PARK *(Open All Year)*

Res and Info: (505) 863-5021, www.usarvpark.com, reservations@usarvpark.com
Location: 3 Miles W of Gallup, *N 35° 30' 26", W 108° 48' 42", 6,500 Ft*

128 Sites – This older park has 128 sites. Some are full-hookup and some are partial. Many are pull-thrus as long as 80 feet. The sites are mostly side by side with no separation between but there are some trees for shade. The park is very clean. Wi-Fi is available and there is a data port. There is a heated pool in the summer. The office building houses a store which sells grocery items, gifts, and RV supplies. Propane is available. Other amenities at the park include a recreation hall, a game room, cowboy cookouts and pancake breakfasts in the summer, and planned activities. From I-40 west of Gallup take Exit 16. Drive east on SR-118 (I-40 business loop) for just .9 mile to the campground entrance, it's on the right.

GILA CLIFF DWELLING NATIONAL MONUMENT AND AREA NORTH OF SILVER CITY

The Gila Cliff Dwellings National Monument is located north of Silver City. Access is via two different roads, both are paved. The most direct route is to drive north through Pinos Altos on SR-15. The distance to the monument using this route is 42 miles. While the road is paved it is also narrow and winding. It is signed as only suitable for trailers to 20 feet so exercise caution. **Pinos Altos**, dating from 1859, is located on the Continental Divide at 7,080 feet just 7 miles north of Silver City. It's a small former mining town and has a campground.

A second route follows SR-152 eastward from Silver City and then SR-35 north through Mimbres. It meets the first route near Lake Roberts, about 18 miles south of the monument. This second route is better for larger rigs. The distance using this route is 65 miles from Silver City to the monument. Both routes take about the same time en route, over two hours.

Once you reach the Monument you'll find a main visitor center and, a mile or so away, a second contact station and the trail that accesses the ruins. From the contact station it's a very pleasant 1 mile walk up a small wooded canyon and then along the hillside past several modest cliff dwellings. The monument is also a popular jump-off point for hiking and horseback expeditions into the Gila Wilderness.

Along both routes to the monument is **Lake Roberts**. It's 22 miles south of the monument, has two campgrounds (see below), and is a popular fishing lake. The **Gila River** south of the monument is stocked and also offers decent fishing. A third nearby attraction along the route in to the monument is **Gila Hot Springs** with a couple of camping possibilities and some rustic hot pools.

Gila Cliff Dwelling National Monument and Area North of Silver City Campgrounds

🚍 CONTINENTAL DIVIDE RV PARK *(Open All Year)*
Information: (575) 388-3005
Location: 7 Miles N of Silver City in Pinos Altos, *N 32° 51'45", W 108° 13' 17", 7,000 Ft*

29 Sites – This small campground is in the little town of Pinos Altos, right atop the continental divide. Fourteen of the sites are hookup sites to about 35 feet. Some are pull-thrus. There is a shower house and a picnic pavilion. The campground is easy to find at the southern edge of the town, about 7 miles north of Silver City on SR-15.

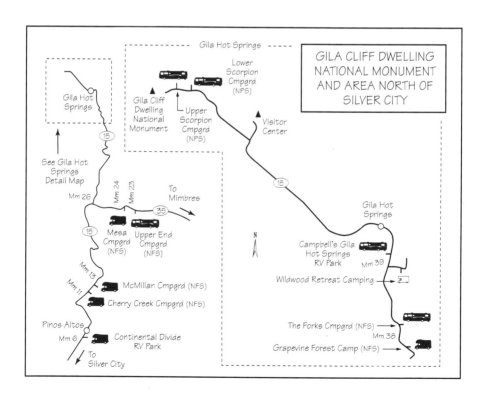

GILA CLIFF DWELLING NATIONAL MONUMENT AND AREA NORTH OF SILVER CITY

CHERRY CREEK CAMPGROUND *(Open All Year)*
Information: (575) 388-8201
Location: 12 Miles N of Silver City, *N 32° 54' 52", W 108° 13' 28", 6,800 Ft*

12 Sites – This little Gila National Forest campground has sites suitable for tent campers and RVs to about 22 feet. Most sites have picnic tables and fire pits and there are vault toilets. There is no potable water although the campground is along Cherry Creek. The campground is on the east side of SR-15 about 12 miles north of Silver City.

MCMILLAN CAMPGROUND *(Open All Year)*
Information: (575) 388-8201
Location: 14 Miles N of Silver City, *N 32° 55' 30", W 108° 12' 51", 7,100 Ft*

5 Sites – McMillan is another small Gila National Forest campground suitable only for very small RVs or tent campers. Most sites here have picnic tables and fire pits too, there is a vault toilet and no potable water although the creek is nearby. This campground is on the east side of SR-15 about 14 miles north of Silver City.

GRAPEVINE FOREST CAMP *(Open All Year)*
Information: (575) 388-8201
Location: 40 Miles N of Silver City, *N 33° 10' 45", W 108° 12' 16", 5,600 Ft*

Dispersed Camping – Camping is in the valley of the Gila River, just off the highway. Sites are scattered, some have fire rings and picnic tables, many do not. There are vault toilets but no potable drinking water. Due to uneven ground and lack of maneuvering room the camping area is not recommended for RVs over 25 feet. The campground is on the east side of SR-15 some 13 miles north of its intersection with SR-35 and about 6 miles south of the visitor center at Gila Cliff Dwelling National Monument.

THE FORKS CAMPGROUND *(Open All Year)*
Information: (575) 388-8201
Location: 40 Miles N of Silver City, *N 33° 11' 01", W 108° 12' 21", 5,500 Ft*

Dispersed Camping – Forks is a large dispersed camping area near the Gila River. There is an open clearing near the road that is flat and will allow you to park any size RV. From there roads continue on, they're narrow and sometimes steep and not recommended for RVs over 25 feet long. Facilities include vault toilets and some fire rings. No potable water is provided. The campground is on the east side of SR-15 about 13 miles north of its intersection with SR-35 and about 5 miles south of the visitor center at Gila Cliff Dwellings National Monument. RVs over 22 feet long should access this campground via Mimbres and SR-35.

MESA CAMPGROUND *(Open All Years)*
Information: (575) 388-8201
Location: 29 Miles N of Silver City, *N 33° 01' 56", W 108° 09' 20", 6,200 Ft*

24 Sites – Mesa is a Gila National Forest campground with some hookups. It's on a table (mesa) overlooking Lake Roberts. Vegetation here is pines and junipers. There are 10 sites with electricity and water arranged around the inside of the circular access road, the remaining sites on the outside do not have power. Some sites are long enough for RVs to 35 feet. Restrooms have flush toilets but not showers. The campground is on the south side of SR-35 about 4.6 miles east of the intersection of SR-35 and SR-15. This is about 22 miles southeast of Gila Cliff Dwellings National Monument. RVs over 22 feet should access this campground via Mimbres and SR-35.

UPPER END CAMPGROUND *(Open May 15 to Oct 15 - Varies)*
Information: (575) 388-8201
Location: 29 Miles N of Silver City, *N 33° 01' 40", W 108° 09' 02", 6,000 Ft*

12 Sites – Upper End is a Gila National Forest campground on the shore of Lake Roberts. The sites are big ones with a wide paved access road and paved parking pads. All sites have picnic tables, fire pits, and raised barbecue grills. Restrooms are wheelchair accessible vault toilets. There's a boat launch ramp at this campground. Upper End is located on the south side of SR-35 about 4.9 miles east of the intersection of SR-35 and SR-15. This is about 22 miles southeast of Gila Cliff Dwellings National Monument. Remember, RVs over 22 feet should access this campground via Mimbres and SR-35.

CAMPBELL'S GILA HOT SPRINGS RV PARK *(Open All Year)*
Information: (575) 536-9551
Location: Gila Hot Springs, *N 33° 11' 51", W 108° 12' 33", 5,700 Ft*

17 Sites – If you need hookups while visiting Gila Cliff Dwellings National Monument this is your only choice. Sites are pull-thrus along an access road. There's plenty of room for any size RV. Each site has full hookups and has a picnic table and a raised barbecue pit. The bathroom building is small but very good. There's even a spa behind it, an extra fee is charged its use. The campground is located on the west side of the road in Gila Hot Springs, about 3.3 miles south of the visitor center in the monument.

GILA CLIFF DWELLINGS NM – LOWER SCORPION CAMPGROUND *(Open All Year)*
Information: (575) 536-9461
Location: Gila Cliff Dwellings National Monument,
                  N 33° 13' 48", W 108° 15' 27", 5,700 Ft

5 Sites – The Lower Scorpion Campground has about five tent sites with picnic tables and fire pits. They can be used by tent campers or by RVs parked next to them in a small paved parking lot. RVs of any size can find a place to park in the lot. There are restrooms with flush toilets and there is a dump station nearby. As you enter the monument there is a Y in the road. To the right is the visitor center but if you take the left you'll see the dump station on your right in .1 mile, and then reach Lower Scorpion at 1.1 mile. Upper Scorpion is just beyond and then the ruins parking lot and trail.

▇ GILA CLIFF DWELLING NM – UPPER SCORPION CAMPGROUND *(Open All Year)*

Information: (575) 536-9461
Location: Gila Cliff Dwellings National Monument,
              N 33° 13' 50", W 108° 15' 40", 5,700 Ft

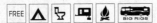

8 Sites – Upper Scorpion is set up just like lower Scorpion. Sites with picnic tables and fire pits are set in trees next to a paved parking lot. There is a restroom building with flush toilets. Here and at lower Scorpion the flush toilets are locked up when temperatures get cold. There are vault toilets just down the road at the parking area for the ruins parking area. As you enter the monument there is a Y in the road. To the right is the visitor center but if you take the left you'll see the dump station on your right in .1 mile, and then reach Lower Scorpion at 1.1 mile. Upper Scorpion is at 1.3 miles and the ruins parking lot at 1.5 mile.

GRANTS

Grants (population about 10,000) is located along I-40 about 65 miles west of Albuquerque and 55 miles east of Gallup. It's a good place to stay while visiting Chaco Culture National Historic Park some 85 miles to the north or El Malpais and El Moro National Monuments to the south. See the separate listings for these destinations in this chapter for more about them.

Grants was once an important uranium mining town. There's a museum in town covering

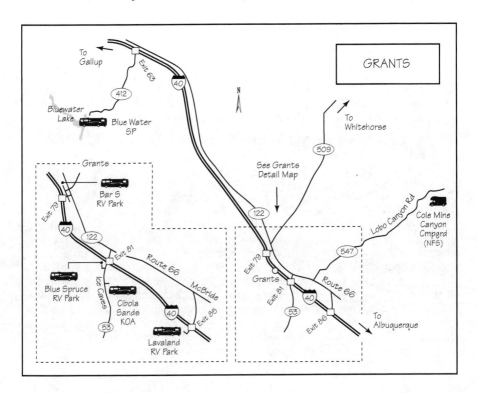

this, the **New Mexico Mining Museum**. The **Dinamations Discovery Museum**, just south of the freeway at Exit 85, has dinosaur displays.

Mt Taylor, sacred to the Navajo, is located just north of town. It is 11,301 feet high and in a smaller vehicle you can drive to the La Mosca Lookout at 11,000 feet. It's about 16 miles north of town on paved and then gravel roads.

Grants Campgrounds

BAR S RV PARK *(Open All Year)*

Res and Info: (505) 876-6002
Location: 3 Miles N of Grants, *N 35° 11' 12", W 107° 54' 03", 6,500 Ft*

64 Sites – The sites in this park are laid out in 4 rows. Three of the rows (46 sites) are very long pull-thru spaces, long enough for any possible type of rig. They advertise these as the longest pull-thru sites in New Mexico. Sites 47-62 are back-in spaces. The RV sites are full hookup including cable TV. The RV sites are in a very large gravel lot, but there is a pine tree at each of the sites. There are 2 tent sites near the front of the park. These are small spaces, but they each have a sheltered picnic table and a raised barbecue grill. There is a meeting area which has a laundry. Take Exit 79, the Milan Exit, just north of Grant. Drive east to SR-122 (this is also Route 66) and turn left. Drive a block and then turn left, drive another block and turn right, the campground is ahead on the right.

BLUE SPRUCE RV PARK *(Open All Year)*

Res and Info: (505) 287-2560
Location: 1 Mile W of Grants, *N 35° 09' 05", W 107° 52' 29", 6,500 Ft*

25 Sites – The sites here are back-ins and pull-thrus as long as 70 feet. Some are full hookup and some partial. There are also tent sites. None of the sites have picnic tables or fires. A data port is provided in the office building for internet access and a courtesy phone for local and calling card calls. The laundry and a sitting area with a kitchen are also in the main office building. This park has the same ownership as the Bar S RV Park. From I-40 take Exit 81 (coming from the SE) or 81A (coming from the NW), marked San Rafael, and head south on US-53 toward San Rafael. Almost immediately take the right on Zuni Canyon Rd. You'll see the campground immediately ahead on the right.

GRANTS/CIBOLA SANDS KOA *(Open All Year)*

Reservations: (888) 562-5608, www.koa.com
Information: (505) 287-4376, grantskoa@cia-g.com
Location: 1 Mile W of Grants, *N 35° 08' 42", W 107° 52' 25", 6,500 Ft*

43 Sites – The sites are in a big gravel lot with 3 rows of pull-thru spaces (37 sites), 6 back-in sites, 5 tent sites and 2 cabins. There is little separation between the sites. A few trees provide some shade. The campground has plenty of big-rig sites including back-ins and pull-thrus to 80 feet. The pull-thrus are all full hookup including cable TV. There is a nice tenting area back behind the store. The tent sites have tent pads, are partially separated by fences, and have tables. An outdoor kitchen and the restrooms are directly in

front of the tenting area. Wi-Fi is available and there is also a data port. Other amenities include a game room, meeting room, dog walk, and propane is sold. From I-40 take Exit 81 (coming from the SE) or 81A (coming from the NW), marked San Rafael, and head south on US-53 toward San Rafael. In .2 mile take the left on Cibola Sands Loop and you'll see the KOA on the left.

LAVALAND RV PARK *(Open All Year)*

Information: (505) 287-8665, www.lavalandrvpark.com
Location: 2 Miles SE of Grants, *N 35° 07' 20", W 107° 49' 58", 6,500 Ft*

50 Sites – Sites here are back-ins and pull-thrus to 60 feet. The sites are full hookup, including cable TV. There is also an area for tenting near the front of the park. A dump station is located at the back of one of the pull-thru rows and RVers from outside the park are allowed to dump for a fee. There is an older bathroom building with showers and a laundry. There is also a recreation room and a pavilion area. To reach the campground take Exit 85 from I-40 southwest of Grants. The campground is on the southwest side of the freeway

BLUE WATER STATE PARK *(Open All Year)*

Reservations: (877) NM-4-RSVP, www.nmparks.com
Information: (505) 876-2391, (888) 667-2757, www.nmparks.com
Location: 24 Miles W of Grants, *N 35° 18' 20", W 108° 06' 20", 7,400 Ft*

120 Sites – This park has 5 campgrounds (North Point, Meadows, Canyonside, Lakeside, and Pinon Cliff) on the eastern shore of Blue Water Lake accessible via Hwy 412. They are close together and you can't really tell where one ends and the next starts. There are about 120 developed sites, 14 of them have electric (in Canyonside). Electric sites are large enough for RVs to about 35 feet, but some sites in the other areas can take RVs to any size. The sites are mostly back-ins with some pull-thrus. Each site has a picnic table and fire pit with a grill. There are showers, flush toilets, a dump station, and water faucets scattered around the park. On the west side of the lake accessible via Hwy 612 at Exit 53 from I-40 is the Los Tusas area which has 7 developed sites and primitive sites. There are only vault toilets in that camping area. To reach the larger eastern shore campground take Exit 63 from I-40 and drive south on SR-412. The campground is 6 miles from the exit.

COAL MINE CANYON CAMPGROUND *(Open May 15 to Sept 30 - Varies)*

Reservations: 877-444-6777, www.recreation.gov
Information: (505) 287-8833
Location: 9 Miles NE of Grants, *N 35° 14' 02", W 107° 42' 12", 7,400 Ft*

14 Sites – This is a beautiful Cibola National Forest campground with the sites off a paved loop under pines and junipers. There are 14 sites, 6 of them are pull-thrus. The sites are as long as 60 feet but the narrow interior road with trees closely bordering the road make the campground suitable for RVs to about 35 feet. Each site has a paved parking pad, a picnic table, and a fire ring of metal or rock with a barbecue grill. There is no potable water. The campground lies below Mount Taylor (11,301 feet) which is one of 4 Navajo sacred mountains. There is a nature trail in the campground and longer hiking trails are available from the nearby forest service roads. From Grants head northeast on

Lobo Canyon Rd (SR-547) into the Cibola National Forest. The campground is 9 miles from Grants.

GUADALUPE MOUNTAINS NATIONAL PARK (TEXAS)

The Guadalupe Mountains National Park is located about 50 miles south of Carlsbad and 100 miles east of El Paso. It's just south of the Texas/New Mexico state line. The park is pretty much undeveloped with hiking the main way to see it. The park has 80 miles of trails and also Guadalupe Peak, at 8,749 feet the tallest mountain in Texas. There is a visitor center along US-180 on the southeast border of the park and a nearby camp-ground. Another remote campground is on the north side of the park. Both are described below. Probably the most popular area in the park is McKittrick Canyon which has been called the most beautiful spot in Texas. The most popular time to visit is late October and early November to see the fall colors. The canyon has its own contact station which is reached on an access road from US-180 about 40 miles south Carlsbad. The trail in to the canyon is 5 miles round trip, but you'll probably want to do more hiking once you reach the canyon.

Guadalupe Mountains National Park Campgrounds

PINE SPRINGS CAMPGROUND *(Open All Year)*

Information: (915) 828-3251, www.nps.gov/gumo, gumo_superintendent@nps.gov
Location: 55 Miles SW of Carlsbad, *N 31° 53' 47", W 104° 49' 41", 5,800 Ft*

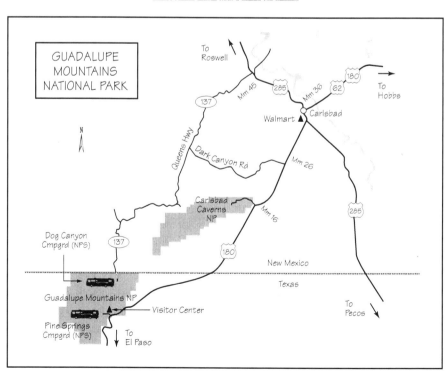

39 Sites – The Pine Springs Campground has a separate section for RVs and tents. The campground has strict rules dictating that no RVs are permitted in the tent area and no tents in the RV area. The RV camping area is a paved lot with 19 sites, 8 of which are pull-thrus. Some of the pull-thrus are to 45 feet and the back-ins are short, mostly to 25 feet. The back-ins have picnic tables, the pull-thrus do not, but there are tables in a grassy area in the middle of the parking lot. A bathroom with flush toilets, an outdoor utility sink, and a telephone are located here. The 20 sites in the tent area are mostly short walk-in sites. The tent sites are under junipers and the sites are separated with each one having a picnic table. Three water faucets are in the tent area. Parking is on a gravel road. Tenters use the bathroom in the RV area. No fires (even charcoal) are permitted in the park. A visitor center is nearby. To reach the campground drive south from Carlsbad. You'll cross into Texas and in 55 miles see the entrance road on your right.

Dog Canyon Campground *(Open All Year)*

Information: (915) 828-3251, (505) 981-2418, www.nps.gov/gumo,
                   gumo_superintendent@nps.gov
Location: 62 Miles E of Carlsbad, *N 31° 59' 41", W 104° 50' 02", 6,300 Ft*

13 Sites – This campground is located at the north entrance to the National Park, 62 miles (a 2 hour drive) from Carlsbad. Highway 137 is paved to the park and then becomes a good gravel road. The campground is 1/2 mile in on the gravel road. There is camping here for 4 RVs to any size and 9 walk-in tent sites. The RV spaces are in a gravel lot and are not delineated, RVs just park where they fit. The camping area has a bathroom with flush toilets and drinking water is available. A telephone is available at the nearby rangers station. No fires (including charcoal) are allowed in the park. Some hiking trails from the campground include the Indian Meadows Nature Loop (.5 miles), Lost Peak Trail, (6.4 miles) and the Marcus Overlook (4.5 miles round trip). From Carlsbad drive north about nine miles, then follow SR-137 southwest to the campground.

Jemez Mountain Trail Scenic Byway and Bandelier National Monument

To the west of the Santa Fe area are the Jemez Mountains. Running through them is an excellent alternate route for traveling between Albuquerque and Santa Fe. This is the Jemez Mountain Trail Scenic Byway. Much of the Byway runs through the piney reaches of the Santa Fe National Forest.

To follow the route from Albuquerque to Santa Fe drive north on I-25 for just a few miles to Exit 242. Then follow US-550 some 24 miles west to San Ysidro. At the intersection turn north on SR-4 and follow it 56 miles as it winds through national forest to Bandelier National Monument. From Bandelier it's only a 24 mile descent on SR-4 and SR-502 to the intersection with US-285 near San Ildefonso Pueblo about 16 miles north of Santa Fe.

Jemez Pueblo is located about 5 miles north of the intersection at San Ysidro. The **Walatowa Visitor Center** will introduce you to the pueblo and its customs and art. Jemez is known for its black on red pottery, but pueblo artists produce many styles of pottery and other work.

Some of the pueblo ruins you'll see in the western Rio Grande valley were excavated into a soft rock called tuff. This material is actually the ash from the eruption of Jemez

LADDER INTO A CAVE DWELLING AT BANDELIER NATIONAL MONUMENT

Volcano a million years ago. About 22 miles north of Jemez Springs (13 miles west of Bandelier National Monument) you'll pass a very large open treeless plain. This is the **Valle Grande**, it's the caldera of the volcano.

Bandelier National Monument is located on the Pajarito Plateau overlooking the Rio Grande Valley. In Frijoles Canyon you'll find a visitor center and easy walking trails to take you up canyon to the ruins. They're on the canyon floor and also above on the canyon walls. Bandelier has a campground which is described below.

Not on this route but just 11 miles north of Bandelier is **Los Alamos**. The town is known, of course, as the site of the development of the atomic bomb in World War II. It's certainly worth the drive over to visit **Bradbury Science Hall** and the **Los Alamos Historical Museum**.

There are a number of campgrounds along the byway. Most are governmental campgrounds with no hookups. The exception is the fairly remote Fenton Lake State Park which does have a few hookup sites. The campgrounds are listed below from south to north.

Jemez Mountain Trail Scenic Byway and
Bandelier National Monument Campgrounds

VISTA LINDA CAMPGROUND *(Open All Year)*
Information: (575) 829-3535 or (505) 438-7840
Location: 13 Miles N of San Ysidro, *N 35° 42' 56", W 106° 43' 17", 5,800 Ft*

14 Sites – This is a small Santa Fe National Forest campground. This is an in-and-out road with a pretty good turnaround circle at the end which a 45 foot rig should be able to turn in. The sites are mostly back-ins (one at the end is a pull-thru) to 45 feet in length and also wide. Each site has a picnic table, fire pit, and raised barbecue. Some of the sites have a shelter for the picnic table. The interior road and the parking are paved and pretty much obstacle free. The bathrooms are vault style. Water is available at faucets scattered through the park. From the south at the San Ysidro intersection follow SR-4 north for 13 miles.

SAN ANTONIO CAMPGROUND *(Open April 15 to Nov 15 - Varies)*
Reservations: (877) 444-6777, www.recreation.gov
Information: (575) 829-3535 or (505) 438-7840
Location: 28 Miles N of San Ysidro, *N 35° 53' 11", W 106° 38' 48", 7,800 Ft*

47 Sites – San Antonio is a Santa Fe National Forest campground. The sites in this campground are off of 3 loops under large pine trees. Sites are back-ins and pull-thrus to about 25 feet. Many of the sites are side-by-side parking for tent campers with walk-in sites. Each site has a picnic table and fire pit. Water faucets are scattered around the park. From the south at the San Ysidro intersection follow SR-4 some 26 miles north to the intersection with SR-126, turn left onto SR-126, and drive another 1.6 miles to the campground entrance.

FENTON LAKE STATE PARK *(Open All Year)*
Reservations: (888) NM-4-RSVP, www.nmparks.com
Information: (575) 829-3630, (888) 667-2757, www.nmparks.com
Location: 36 Miles N of San Ysidro, *N 35° 53' 09", W 106° 43' 27", 7,800 Ft*

37 Sites – This state park has sites off small loops on a long in-and-out road. The RV sites are on a loop by themselves. There are 5 sites on this loop. One site is a pull-thru and the other 4 are back-in. These sites are set under pine trees and are well separated. Maneuvering is tight and the recommended RV here is 30 feet even though the sites are larger. Thirty-two no-hookup sites are located further out the in-and-out road. Two of these sites are designated wheelchair and everything at the site is paved, including a trail to the wheelchair accessible vault toilet. All sites including the electric sites have picnic tables and fire pits. No sites are on Fenton Lake. The 35-acre lake is good for fishing and is stocked with trout, It has wheelchair accessible fishing piers. The lake is also popular for canoeing. Seven no-hookup sites and 2 electric sites can be reserved. From the San Ysidro intersection follow SR-4 some 26 miles north to the intersection with SR-126, turn left onto SR-126, and drive another 10 miles to the campground.

REDONDO CAMPGROUND *(Open April 15 to Nov 15 - Varies)*
Reservations: (877) 444-6777, www.recreation.gov
Information: (575) 829-3535 or (505) 438-7840
Location: 28 Miles N of San Ysidro, *N 35° 51' 41", W 106° 37' 39", 8,100 Ft*

60 Sites – Redondo is a Santa Fe National Forest campground. The sites in this campground are off of 3 loops under a forest of large pine trees. Sites are back-ins and pull-thrus to about 35 feet. Each site has a concrete picnic table and a rock fire ring. A sign in

the park says there is no water in this campground – the well has gone dry. From the San Ysidro intersection follow SR-4 some 28 miles north to the campground.

JEMEZ FALLS CAMPGROUND *(Open April 15 to Nov 15 - Varies)*
Information: (575) 829-3535
Location: 24 Miles W of Los Alamos, *N 35° 49' 26", W 106° 36' 23", 8,000 Ft*

52 Sites – This Santa Fe National forest campground has 52 sites off 2 loop roads under pine trees. Sites 2-32 are on one loop and 33-52 on the second loop. The sites are a combinations of back-ins and pull-thrus with some of both types long enough for RVs to 35 feet in length. Each sites has a picnic table, fire pits, and a raised barbecue grill. The bathrooms are wheelchair accessible vault style. Water faucets are scattered in the park. A short hiking trail leads to the Jemez Falls and a 1.5 mile trail leads across the mountains to the east ending at Battleship Rock. There is a 14 day stay limit at the park. It's a popular campground. Redondo Campground, listed above, often gets the overflow. From the intersection in San Ysidro follow SR-4 north 32 miles to the campground.

BANDELIER NATIONAL MONUMENT – JUNIPER CAMPGROUND *(Open All Year)*
Information: (505) 672-3861 x517, (505) 672-0343, www.nps.gov/band
Location: 54 Miles NE of San Ysidro, *N 35° 47' 43", W 106° 16' 44", 6,600 Ft*

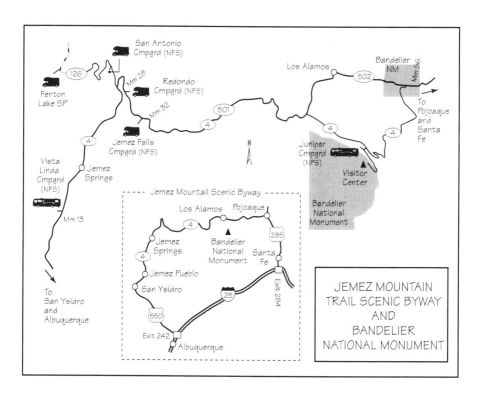

JEMEZ MOUNTAIN
TRAIL SCENIC BYWAY
AND
BANDELIER
NATIONAL MONUMENT

94 Sites – The sites in this campground are off of 3 loops, A-C. Only 6 of the sites are pull-thrus and these are in loop C. Most of the sites are suitable for RVs to 30 feet or less, but loop C has recently been remodeled and has some sites which will take RVs to 40 feet. There is a dump station near Loop A. Water is available in all three of the loops. A pay telephone is located between loops A and B. The park has a campground host and firewood is available from the host. There is an amphitheater and a big parking lot for the amphitheater. The Frey Trail leaves from the amphitheater parking lot and an overlook trail leaves from the amphitheater. The park has a self pay machine which accepts credit cards. There is a 14 day stay limit (total days) between Memorial and Labor days. The campground road is off SR-4 about .4 mile west of the intersection for the entrance road to the monument. From the intersection in San Ysidro follow SR-4 some 54 miles to the campground.

LAS CRUCES

Las Cruces (population about 80,000) is New Mexico's second largest city. The location has long been convenient to the Rio Grande trade route to the north. In fact, some people say Las Cruces is named for the crosses marking the graves of travelers along this route who were killed by Apaches. There are actually two towns here. Just south of Las Cruces is Mesilla which has a Hispanic heritage and was for a long time the largest of the two towns.

Downtown in Las Cruces is the Downtown Mall, where six blocks of Main Street are closed to vehicular traffic. Here you'll find **Branigan Cultural Center,** the **Museum of**

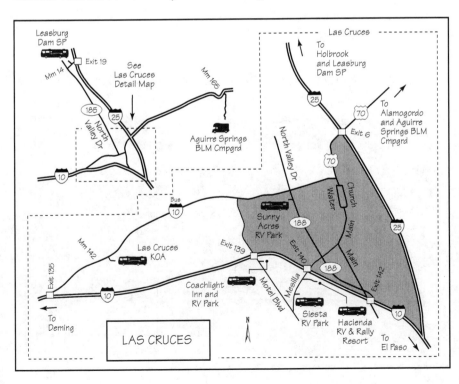

Fine Art and the City of Los Cruces Log Cabin Museum. Even better is the center of Mesilla, the Mesilla Plaza. It's surrounded by historical buildings from the 19th century and has lots of shops and restaurants.

Las Cruces has quite a few RV parks. Because of the low altitude here the region serves as something of a snowbird roost in the winter months with many RVers enjoying their time in the sun. See also the *El Paso* Listing where some parks listed are not far south of Las Cruces.

Las Cruces Campgrounds

COACHLIGHT INN AND RV PARK *(Open All Year)*

   Res and Info: (575) 526-3301, www.zianet.com/coachlight
   Location: Las Cruces, *N 32° 17' 31", W 106° 48' 27", 3,900 Ft*

46 Sites – The RV park sits in a fenced yard behind the Coachlight Inn. It has 46 sites, 36 of which are pull-thrus to about 40 feet in length and are full hookup. Although the sites are only 40 feet long the drive between rows is very wide so it is possible to get much larger rigs into the spaces. The remaining 10 sites have water and electric hookups only. Each site has a tree and a picnic table. Residents of the RV park are allowed to use the pool which is at the hotel. There is a data port in the office at the hotel for internet access and the park is working on putting in Wi-Fi. A restaurant with Mexican food, The Pit Stop Cafe, is located out front. Access is extremely easy. Take Exit 139 from I-10 as it passes through Las Cruces. Drive south about two hundred yards and turn into the Coachlight Inn driveway.

HACIENDA RV AND RALLY RESORT *(Open All Year)*

   Reservations: (888) 686-9090, info@haciendarv.com
   Information: (575) 528-5800, www.haciendarv.com
   Location: Las Cruces, *N 32° 17' 09", W 106° 47' 13", 3,900 Ft*

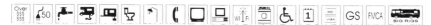

110 Sites – The Hacienda is a new first-class park. Rates are in the neighborhood of $35 per night. There are 110 sites, many are pull-thrus, and they're wide. The longest of the sites is 130 feet, and the normal site size is 55 to 60 feet. All of the sites are full hookup including cable TV and instant-on phone lines. Wi-Fi is provided to the sites by an outside vendor for a daily fee and there are also data ports. Bathrooms are individual rooms. The park has a big clubhouse with a living room with a fireplace, a meeting and activity room, group event area, hydro-therapy pool, exercise room, and a covered patio with a fireplace. The Hacienda specializes in club rallies. Rigs must be self contained to stay here even though there are restrooms with showers. Take Exit 140 from I-10 in Las Cruces. Go southwest on Avenida de Mesilla for just .1 mile and turn left into the entrance.

LAS CRUCES KOA *(Open All Year)*

   Reservations: (800) 562-1627, www.koa.com
   Information: (575) 526-6555, www.lascrucescampgrounds.com
   Location: Las Cruces, *N 32° 17' 34", W 106° 51' 32", 3,900 Ft*

95 Sites – This park sits on the top of a small hill with views across the valley. It has 81 RV sites, 14 tent sites, and 4 cabins. Most RV sites are full hookup including cable TV. Thirty three sites are pull-thrus to 55 feet in length. Some, but not all of the sites, have picnic tables. Wi-Fi is provided to the sites by an outside vendor. Other internet options include free data port, a high speed dedicated guest computer, and free wireless in the vicinity of the main building. The campground has a seasonal pool. There is a patio and a mountain view gazebo for guest use. The store stocks a good selection of grocery and gift items and propane is sold. Other amenities include a barbecue, pay telephone, and a fenced pet exercise area. The campground is most easily reached by exiting I-10 just west of town at Exit 135. Drive east on Business I-10 for 1.3 miles, the campground is on the right.

LEASBURG DAM STATE PARK *(Open All Year)*

Reservations: (877) NM-4-RSVP, www.nmparks.com
Information: (575) 524-4068, (888) 667-2757, www.nmparks.com
Location: 13 Miles N of Las Cruces, *N 32° 29' 26", W 106° 55' 06", 4,100 Ft*

24 Sites – The sites in this campground are in two areas. To the left as you enter the campground you'll see Greasewood Road. Off this road on two short loops are sites 1-14. Eight of the sites have water and electricity hookups and the other 6 sites have no hookups. The sites have covered picnic tables, fire pits, and paved parking pads. To the right as you enter the campground is the Cactus Patch Loop which has sites 15-24. These sites are on an in-and-out road with a good turn-around circle at the end. These are all pull-thrus 60 feet or longer. Each sites has electric and water hookups, a sheltered picnic table, fire pit, and paved parking pad. Six sites can be reserved. A wheelchair accessible bathroom with flush toilets and showers is located between the 2 camping areas. This park is north of Las Cruces. From I-25 take Exit 19 and head west on SR-157 for .8 mile and turn right. The camping area is .3 miles ahead.

SIESTA RV PARK *(Open All Year)*

Res and Info: (575) 523-6816, (800) 414-6816, siesta@zianet.com
Location: Las Cruces, *N 32° 17' 00", W 106° 47' 42", 3,900 Ft*

47 Sites – Seven of the sites in this older park are back-ins and the others are all pull-thrus to a length of 40 feet. There is room in the drives between rows for rigs to exceed the site size a bit so they are able to get larger rigs into the sites. Most sites have full hookups including cable TV. There is a tree and a short fence between most sites and each one has a picnic table. There is also a small tenting area. An email station with a computer and a data port is provided in the office for internet access. The office sells a good selection of groceries and gift items. Behind the office is a patio with a barbecue grill. Other amenities include horseshoes, a dump station, and spaces for RV storage. In Las Cruces take Exit 140 from I-10 and head south on Avenida de Mesilla. The campground is on the left in .5 mile.

SUNNY ACRES RV PARK *(Open All Year)*
Res and Info: (575) 524-1716, (877) 800-1716, www.zianet.com/sunnyacres
Location: Las Cruces, N 32° 18' 37", W 106° 47' 50", 3,900 Ft

70 Sites – This park was once totally a mobile home park. The section which is the RV park now still has about 15 mobile homes left among the RV sites. As the owners sell or move out, the mobile homes are being eliminated. Currently there are about 70 sites available for RVs. The sites are full hookup including cable TV. Forty-four of the sites are pull-thrus to at least 70 feet in length. Because the sites at one time were mobile home lots, they are very large. Some sites have paved patios. A row of trees between each site and a grass lawn separate the sites. Wi-Fi is provided to the sites for no additional charge and both dial-up and Ethernet data ports are available for other internet access. The bathrooms have 5 individual rooms, one of which is wheelchair accessible. The park has a clubhouse and activities in the winter. The easiest way to get to the park is to exit I-10 at Exit 139. Drive north on N Motel Blvd to US-70 which is also Business I-10, a distance of 1.2 miles. Turn right and drive 1.1 mile to North Valley Dr, turn right. Drive south about .1 mile, the park is on the right.

AGUIRRE SPRINGS BLM CAMPGROUND
Information: (575) 525-4300
Location: 18 Miles E of Las Cruces, *N 32° 22' 13", W 106° 33' 39", 5,700 Ft*

54 Sites – This BLM camping area is situated high on the east slope of the Organ Mountains and has fantastic views of the entire Tularosa Basin. It's a primitive campground with no hookups, sites are small making it a campground best for tent campers and RVs to about 25 feet. Sites have picnic tables on paved slabs, fire pits, and raised barbecue grills. Many tables have metal roofs for shelter from the sun, others rely on the scattered junipers. Restrooms are vault toilets. Trails lead from the campground up along the slope of the mountains. Access to the campground is a paved road leading from just east of the 165 mile marker on US-70, the highway running from Las Cruces to Alamogordo. This is about 14.5 miles east of the intersection of I-25 and US-70 and just beyond the crest of the San Augustin Pass as the highway crosses the Organ Mountains. From here it's 5.9 miles south to the campground entrance.

LAS VEGAS

New Mexico, like Nevada, has a town named Las Vegas. It's not surprising since the name in Spanish means "the meadows", a phrase that could apply to a number of places. While Las Vegas isn't really well known today, for a time during the late 1800s this was one of New Mexico's most important cities. The town is still New Mexico's largest east of the Rockies.

Las Vegas (population about 16,000) is located along I-25 between Santa Fe and Raton. It's 65 miles east of Santa Fe and 105 miles south of Raton. Due to its importance at the end of the 19th Century Las Vegas has a number of historical buildings, nearly 900 according to the National Register of Historic Places. Check at the Chamber of Commerce for maps with walking tours that will let you see some of them.

Las Vegas has a Hispanic history and feel. This is easy to see at the Fourth of July celebrations where you'll find plenty of Mexican music and dancing.

Probably the best places to stay near Las Vegas are the two state parks. Storrie Lake is conveniently near the town while Villanueva has a nice riverside location, a pleasant contrast to the many New Mexican state parks located on reservoirs.

Las Vegas Campgrounds

VEGAS RV PARK *(Open All Year)*
Res and Info: (505) 425-5640, vegasrv@zialink.com
Location: Las Vegas, *N 35° 37' 21", W 105° 13' 28", 6,500 Ft*

40 Sites – The Vegas is the only park actually in Las Vegas. It's on the north side of town near the Walmart. This is a wide open fenced lot next to a storage facility, very utilitarian. Sites are back-ins and pull-thrus to 65 feet. Take Exit 345 from I-25 and drive west on University Ave into town. In about 6 blocks turn right on 7th Ave. As you drive north this becomes SR-518 and 1.9 miles from the turn you'll see the Vegas RV Park on the right.

LAS VEGAS KOA *(Open March 1 to Nov 30)*
Reservations: (800) 562-3423, www.koa.com
Information: (505) 454-0180, koalvnm@desertgate.com
Location: 5 Miles S of Las Vegas, *N 35° 30' 40", W 105° 15' 09", 6,400 Ft*

56 Sites – This KOA is outside town in a pine forested area. There are 51 RV sites, 5 tent sites, 5 cabins, and 1 loft apartment. The RV sites are mostly pull-thrus, many to 60 feet in length. There are full, partial, and no hookup sites. Wi-Fi is provided to the sites for no additional charge and a data port is available. A courtesy phone is provided. At an outdoor cookout area breakfast and dinner are served from a menu daily. The store stocks a good selection of grocery items, RV supplies, and gifts. Propane is sold. Other amenities include a game room, horseshoes, volleyball, seasonal swimming pool, a group tent area, book exchange, free lending library of movies, ice cream socials, and bicycle rentals. RVers from outside the park can dump for a fee. The campground is located south of Las Vegas. Take Exit 339 from I-25. Drive about a hundred yards southeast on I-84. Turn right on the first road and follow it for .6 mile to the campground.

STORRIE LAKE STATE PARK *(Open All Year)*
Reservations: (877) NM-4-RSVP, www.nmparks.com
Information: (505) 425-7278, (888) 667-2757, www.nmparks.com
Location: 3 Miles N of Las Vegas, *N 35° 39' 26", W 105° 13' 56", 6,600 Ft*

50 Sites and Scattered Boondocking – This campground has 50 camping sites along the lake. Twenty sites have water and electricity hookups, 10 have water only, and the remaining 20 have no hookups, but water is near. The older section of the park is to the

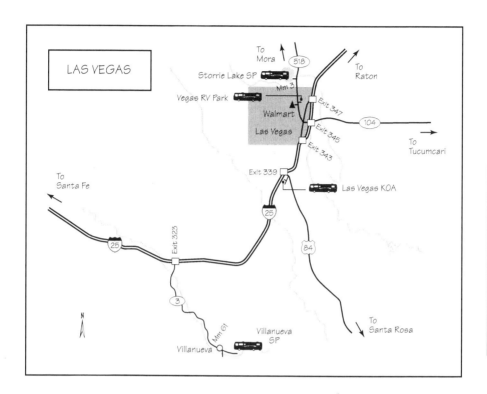

right as you enter and the newer section to the left. The non-electric sites (and the electric and water sites in the new section) have shelters. Ten of the sites in the old section have electricity. They are side-by-side back-ins with no picnic tables or fires. There are 2 large picnic shelters nearby. The new section has the other 10 electricity and water sites which are all large pull-thrus with a shelter. The old section bathrooms are vault style and in the new section there are flush toilets and showers. Dispersed camping is allowed on the grass near the lake. Reservations are accepted during the period from May 5 to Sept 5. Storrie Lake is located about 3 miles north of town on SR-518. See the Vegas RV Park for instructions on how to get onto SR-518 from I-25.

🚐 **VILLANUEVA STATE PARK** *(Open All Year)*
   Reservations: (877) NM-4-RSVP, www.nmparks.com
   Information: (575) 421-2957, (888) 667-2757, www.nmparks.com
   Location: 35 Miles S of Las Vegas, *N 35° 15' 50", W 105° 20' 17", 5,700 Ft*

31 Sites – The sites in this campground are off an in-and-out road with a turnaround at the end. Twelve sites have electrical hookups. Some have water and there are faucets scattered throughout the park. Ten sites are pull-thrus to a length of about 40 feet and some of the back-ins are also 40 feet. Many, but not all, of the sites have picnic shelters. There is a group picnic shelter on the river with a big rock fireplace. The bathroom building has flush toilets and showers and there is a dump station. The campground is set along the Pecos River and there is fishing and swimming in the river. Hiking trails leave from near

the campground. Drive south on I-25 from Las Vegas for about 22 miles and take Exit 323. Drive south on SR-3 for 13 miles, the park entrance road is on the left.

LORDSBURG

Lordsburg (population about 3,000) is the first town in New Mexico as you drive east along I-10. There's not much here, just one campground and a few stores, restaurants, and gas stations. It's a place to stop if you're traveling the freeway but it's also a place to stay while visiting nearby ghost towns.

Stein's Railroad Ghost Town is located north of I-10 at Exit 3. It's a privately owned town that is being gradually restored. You can visit and tour the place for a very reasonable price.

There are many other ghost towns in the region, mostly on private land. These include Shakespeare, Valedon, Roadforks, Richmond, Pyramid, Pratt, Sylvanite, Cloverdale, Bramlett, Playas and Walnut Wells.

Lordsburg Campground

LORDSBURG KOA *(Open All Year)*

Reservations: (800) 562-5772, www.koa.com
Information: (575) 542-8003, lordskoa@gilanet.com
Location: Lordsburg, *N 32° 20' 29", W 108° 43' 01", 4,200 Ft*

69 Sites – This KOA has 5 tent sites, 3 cabins, and 64 pull-thru RV sites to 70 feet. Both full and partial hookup sites are available. There's a swimming pool and recreation hall as well as phone, laundry, a small store, and a playground. The campground is located on the western edge of Lordsburg. From I-10 take the Lordsburg exit, Exit 22. Drive south for a block to Maple Street, then turn right and drive two blocks to Lead St. Turn left and the campground is straight ahead.

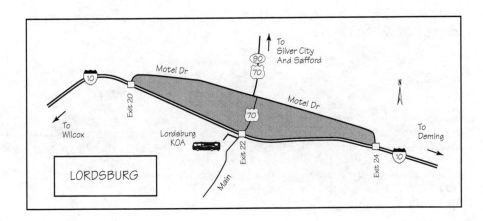

MESA VERDE NATIONAL PARK AND CORTEZ (COLORADO)

Mesa Verde National Park has some of the most impressive ancestral Puebloan ruins in the southwest. The large pueblos, tucked into caves in the sandstone cliffs, fit the mental picture many of us have of the way these ruins ought to look. The park occupies Mesa Verde, visitors climb up onto the mesa on a road from the north. It's a steep climb of 1,000 feet and a good reason not to bring that RV up into the park. Narrow park roads and lack of parking room are other reasons. There's a parking area just before the road starts up, it's a good place to leave your trailer or large RV before heading up to visit the park in a tow car.

Cortez (population about 9,000) is the main town servicing visitors to the park. It's about 8 miles west of the park entrance on US-160. The town has stores and a number of RV parks. In the town and nearby are other modern Indian and ancestral Puebloan attractions.

The **Colorado University Center Museum** has exhibits about the ancestral Puebloans. It also has the Cultural Park, an outdoor park offering crafts demonstrations and dancing by local Utes, Hopis and Navajos. There are evening programs almost every night Monday through Saturday in summer.

The **Anasazi Heritage Center** and the new **Canyon of the Ancients National Monument** are north of Cortez. The Heritage Center acts as the visitor and information center for the monument, you should visit before entering it. The center houses many of the finds from the monument area. It's located on SR-184 about 10 miles north of Cortez and

NEW MEXICO

THE IMPRESSIVE ANCESTRAL PUEBLOAN RUINS AT MESA VERDE

3 miles west of Delores. The area covered by the monument, 164,000 acres in southwest Colorado, has a very high density of ancestral Puebloan ruins. Some have or are being excavated but many others have not been disturbed. Access is by maintained gravel roads. There are no developed campgrounds in the monument but there is one near the Anasazi Heritage Center at McPhee Reservoir. You can get information about sites to visit at the Anasazi Heritage Center and the campground is described below.

Mesa Verde National Park and Cortez Campgrounds

MOREFIELD CAMPGROUND *(Open May 1 to Oct 15 - Varies)*
Reservations: (888) 896-3831, www.visitmesaverde.com
Information: (800) 449-2288
Location: Mesa Verde National Park, *N 37° 17' 50", W 108° 24' 53", 7,800 Ft*

435 Sites – This is the only campground in the park. It has 435 sites set on 10 loops and an eleventh loop for group camping. Fifteen of the sites on the Ute loop have full hookups, the rest of the campground has no hookups. A few of the sites on the Ute loop are as long as 35 feet, but for the most part the sites in the campground are only large enough for RVs to 25 feet. The sites are mostly back-ins with some parallel parking pull-off types. The Ute loop sites have picnic tables and raised barbecue pits and other loops have tables, fire rings and a designated spot for a tent. The camping spaces are mostly open with grass between sites. There are telephones and flush toilets in the camping areas. The campground is near Morefield Village where there is a gas station, grocery store, showers, telephone, laundry, LP gas for sale, firewood, and food services. No reservations are accepted and there is a 14 day stay limit. The park entrance goes south from US-160 some 8 miles east of Cortez. The campground is 7 miles inside the park.

SUNDANCE RV PARK *(Open All Year)*
Res and Info: (970) 565-0997
Location: Cortez, *N 37° 20' 53", W 108° 34' 28", 6,100 Ft*

68 Sites – The campground is in an oblong lot running back from Main Street. Sites 1-26 and 45-68 are back-in sites along the exterior of the park. One row of pull-thrus (17 sites) to about 50 feet in length runs down the middle of the lot. All of the sites are full hookup including cable TV. Parking at most sites is on gravel, but the four front pull-thrus have parking on grass. The back-ins along the west side of the lot have a grass area separating sites, but for all other sites, there is no separation. Trees are scattered around the park for shade. Wi-Fi internet is provided to the sites at no additional charge and there is a data port in the office building for other internet access. RVers not staying at the park are allowed to dump for a $5 fee. The park is within walking distance of central Cortez, very convenient. It's on the south side of the highway just east of the old town.

CORTEZ/MESA VERDE KOA *(Open April 1 to Nov 1)*
Reservations: (800) 562-3901, www.koa.com,
Information: (970) 565-0301, kortezkoa@fone.net
Location: Cortez, *N 37° 21' 09", W 108° 32' 43", 6,100 Ft*

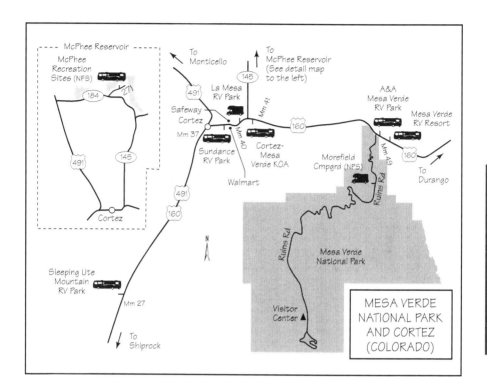

128 Sites – This campground has 56 tent sites, 71 RV sites, and 14 rental units including cabins and teepees. The 71 RV sites are all pull-thrus to a length of 60 feet. The sites are in a mostly clear gravel lot with a few trees for shade and not much separation between sites. Computer access is provided although there is a charge. The office has groceries, ice, wood, and gift items. The swimming pool is heated. There are two laundry rooms. Other amenities include basketball, volleyball, coin games, and horseshoes. Non guests are allowed to use the dump station for a fee. The campground is adjacent to Denny Lake where fishing is possible. The campground is on the eastern edge of Cortez on the south side of the highway.

🚐 **LA MESA RV PARK** *(Open All Year)*
    Information: (970) 759-1305, (970) 565-3610
    Location: Cortez, *N 37° 21' 08", W 108° 33' 18", 6,200 Ft*

43 Sites – This is a very basic camping facility with 5 tent and 38 RV sites. The sites are set along the exterior of a gravel lot with a paved circular road. All of the sites are back-ins, some to 55 feet, and each has a paved patio and a picnic table. A few have raised barbecue grills. There are shade trees along the exterior and down a grass strip which runs through the middle of the lot. A courtesy phone is provided for local and calling-card calls. The campground is on the north side of the highway on the eastern edge of Cortez.

NEW MEXICO

A&A MESA VERDE RV PARK *(Open April 1 to Nov 1)*

Reservations: (800) 972-6620, mesa@fone.net
Information: (970) 565-3517, www.mesaverdecamping.com
Location: 8 Miles E of Cortez, *N 37° 20' 25", W 108° 24' 24", 6,900 Ft*

71 Sites – This is one of two campgrounds east of Cortez near the entrance to Mesa Verde. The 71 sites here include 17 tent sites, 34 full hookup sites, 14 sites with electricity and water hookups, and 6 sites with no hookups. Thirty-two of the full hookup sites are pull-thrus to 70 feet in length. There are also 4 cabins. The sites have picnic tables and most have fire rings. Some tent sites have sheltered picnic tables. There is a covered gazebo and a group campfire area, as well as an outdoor pool, a spa, and an 18-hole mini-golf course. A store offers a good selection of grocery and gift items. Propane is sold. The recreation room has a pool table, TV, and kitchen facilities. There's a data port available for email access. Television is 22 channels using your antenna, not a cable hookup. The campground is located right at the exit from US-160 for Mesa Verde, that's 8 miles east of Cortez.

MESA VERDE RV RESORT *(Open All Year)*

Reservations: (800) 776-7421, mesaverdervresort@starband.net
Information: (970) 533-7421, mesa@fone.net
Location: 8.5 Miles E of Cortez, *N 37° 20' 13", W 108° 23' 48", 6,800 Ft*

54 Sites – This campground is near the entrance to Mesa Verde, a good alternative to the park campground. There are back-in and pull-thru sites to 60 feet. Most are full hookup sites. There is also a dump station. A repeater provides 22 TV stations including some cable (Fox, CNN). Wi-Fi is provided to the sites at no extra charge and there is a data port in the laundry room and the club house. There are 2 spas, one indoor and one outdoor. The clubhouse is very nice with a game table, sofas, satellite TV, and a fireplace. There are 3 ponds with walking trails around them. The campground is on the north side of US-160 about 8.5 miles east of Cortez and only a half-mile east of the entrance to Mesa Verde National Park.

SLEEPING UTE MOUNTAIN RV PARK *(Open March 1 to Nov 15)*

Reservations: (800) 889-5072
Information: (970) 565-6544
Location: 11 Miles S of Cortez, *N 37° 12' 23", W 108° 41' 18", 5,700 Ft*

76 Sites – Sleeping Ute is a modern big-rig campground located near a casino. The 76 sites including 30 full hookups, 31 sites with electricity and water, 10 dry sites, and 5 tent spaces. All hookup sites are pull-thrus and have cable TV. Sites are separated by a grass lawn and a gravel patio where the picnic table sits on a paved slab the size of the table. Tent sites have raised barbecue grills. There is a covered picnic pavilion with tables and

grills which anyone in the park may use. Internet access is available via a data port in the office building. The swimming pool and a kiddy pool are indoors and there is a sauna in the swimming building. RVers and tent campers not staying at the park can use the showers and the dump station for a fee. Camping at the casino is only allowed when the RV park is closed. The casino is a short walk or shuttle service is provided. There are restaurants at the casino. The nearby Mobil Travel Center has groceries. From Cortez drive west to US-160 and then south for 11 miles. You'll see the casino on the right, the RV park is at the rear.

МcPHEE RECREATION SITES *(Open May 1 to Oct 15 - Varies)*
> **Reservations:** (877) 444-6777, www.recreation.gov
> **Information:** (970) 882-7296, (970) 247-4874
> **Location:** 12 Miles N of Cortez, *N 37° 29' 55", W 108° 33' 35", 7,400 Ft.*

104 Sites – McPhee is a San Juan National Forest campground on a mesa overlooking McPhee Reservoir. Some sites here will take RVs to 50 feet. Access roads and parking are paved. Fourteen sites offer electrical hookups and another 12 are walk-in tent sites. There are flush toilets, showers, a laundry, and a dump station. Nearby is a boat ramp. From Cortez drive north on SR-145 for 7.8 miles. Take the left to continue north on SR-184 for another 3.7 miles. Turn right on Forest Road 271 and continue to the campground.

MORA VALLEY AND SR-518 TO TAOS

East of Taos and the Sangre de Cristo Mountains is a pleasant area of rolling pine-clad foothills called the Mora Valley. There are two small state campgrounds in his region that are very popular during the summer.

From the Mora Valley a two lane paved highway, SR-518, heads west through the mountains toward Taos, 47 miles away. The highway passes through the Carson National Forest, climbing the valley of the Mora River, passing Sipapu Ski Area, and then descending along the Rio Pueblo. Along the way it passes several National Forest Service campgrounds. They're also great places to spend time in the summer.

Mora Valley and SR-518 to Taos Campgrounds

COYOTE CREEK STATE PARK *(Open All Year)*
> **Reservations:** (877) NM-4-RSVP, www.nmparks.com
> **Information:** (575) 387-2328, (888) 667-2757, www.nmparks.com
> **Location:** 17 Miles N of Mora, *N 36° 10' 41", W 105° 14' 01", 7,700 Ft*

30 Sites – This is a small state campground with Coyote Creek running through the middle. There are a total of 30 sites, 17 of them offer water and electricity hookups. Some will take RVs to 35 feet. The hookup sites are basically side by side back-in parking spaces with no separation between sites. Behind each site is a picnic table and a metal fire pit with a grill. The tent sites are in another more secluded area with an individual parking area at each site and trees and vegetation for separation. Some will take RVs to about 25 feet. The restroom building has hot showers and flush toilets and a pay phone is located outside the building. There is a dump station in the park as well as a host on site. The Coyote River is known for it's stocked trout fishing. From Mora drive north on

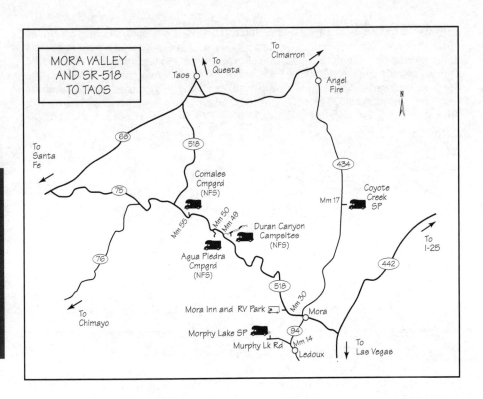

SR-434. This is a narrow country road so if you're in an RV caution is required. The state park is 17 miles north of Mora.

MORPHY LAKE STATE PARK *(Open All Year)*

Information: (575) 387-2328, (888) 667-2757, www.nmparks.com
Location: 7 Miles SE of Mora, *N 35° 56' 26", W 105° 23' 44", 7,900 Ft*

20 Sites – Morphy Lake State Park is probably the smallest campground in the state system. Developed sites with picnic tables and fire pits surround the lake which is stocked with trout, engines are not allowed on boats, just electric motors or paddles. Sites are small, RV size should be limited to about 25 feet. There is also a primitive tent-camping area. Toilets are vault-style and there is no potable water at the park. Hiking trails lead from the lake into the Pecos Wilderness. The three-mile access road has recently been paved so getting here is no longer much of a challenge. In winter the lake often freezes so ice fishing is a possibility. From Mora travel south on SR-94 to Ledoux, a distance of about 4 miles. Then turn right onto Murphy Lake Road and follow it 3 miles to the campground.

DURAN CANYON CAMPSITES *(Open May 15 to Oct 15 - Varies)*

Information: (575) 758-6200
Location: 19 Miles W of Mora, *N 36° 07' 37", W 105° 30' 19", 8,500 Ft*

12 Sites – The Carson National Forest Duran Canyon Campsites are located along FS-76, a gravel Forest Service road. Near the entrance from SR-518 there's an unattended pay station and sometimes a host. A stream runs alongside and there are lots of trees for shade. Some sites will take RVs to 30 or 35 feet, others are very small. There are fire rings but not picnic tables, toilets are vault style. There is no water at the sites but one pump is located about 3 miles into the canyon. From Mora head west on SR-518, the campground entrance road is on the right in 19 miles. This is just a mile east of Tres Ritos.

AGUA PIEDRA CAMPGROUND *(Open May 15 to Oct 15 - Varies)*
  Information: (575) 758-6200
  Location: 21 Miles W of Mora, *N 36° 08' 07", W 105° 31' 53", 8,400 Ft*

44 Sites – This Carson National Forest campground occupies a sloping hillside above the Rio Pueblo. Sites are off loops, most are back-ins although there are a few pull-thrus too. The Forest Service recommends RVs no longer than 36 feet in this campground, we might recommend even a little shorter. Several trails begin at the campground and there is a horse corral. The campground is located on the south side of SR-518 some 21 miles west of Mora near mile marker 50.

COMALES CAMPGROUND *(Open May 15 to Oct 15 - Varies)*
  Information: (575) 758-6200
  Location: 25 Miles W of Mora, *N 36° 09' 36", W 105° 35' 21", 7,900 Ft*

10 Sites – The ten sites of this Carson National Forest campground are located right next to the highway overlooking the Rio Pueblo. They have picnic tables and raised barbecue grills and are fine for RVs to 36 feet as the National Forest Service recommends. Watch for the campground entrance on the north side of SR-518 near mile marker 55. This is 25 miles west of Mora and only 20 miles from Taos.

RATON

Raton (population about 8,000) is located just a few miles south of where I-25 passes across 7,834-foot Raton Pass near the New Mexico/Colorado border. Raton has an interesting little museum but it's the nearby attractions that are of most interest.

Sugarite Canyon State Park is located 7 miles to the east. There are two lakes here, both stocked for fishing. The relatively high-altitude park also has hiking trails and two campgrounds, they are described below.

A few miles to the south of Raton is the National Rifle Association's **Whittington Center**. It's a fantastic operation covering over 50 square miles with many shooting ranges and other facilities including campgrounds.

The **Capulin Volcano National Monument** centers around the Capulin Volcano, a 2,200-foot cinder cone dating from volcanic activity about 50,000 years ago. There's a visitor center and a road that spirals up to the lip of the crater. From there you can hike down into the caldera. The monument is located 30 miles east of Raton along US-84.

NEW MEXICO

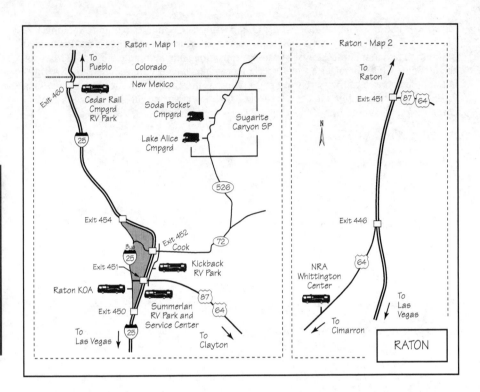

Raton Campgrounds

🚐 **CEDAR RAIL CAMPGROUND RV PARK** *(Open April 1 to Oct 31)*
  Res and Info: (575) 445-8500
  Location: 6 Miles N of Raton, *N 36° 59' 20", W 104° 28' 56", 7,800 Ft*

33 Sites – This park has both tent and RV sites. Five of the RV sites are pull-thrus as long as 55 feet and the back-in sites are about 35 feet in length. All of the RV sites are full hookup. A courtesy phone is provided for local and calling card calls. There is a convenience store which sells limited groceries and RV supplies. There is a dump station and campers from outside the campground can dump for a fee. Other amenities at the park include a recreation room, an exercise room, and horseshoes. The campground is at the top of Raton pass. From Raton drive north on I-25 for 6 miles to Exit 460. The campground is on the east side of the highway.

🚐 **SUMMERLAN RV PARK AND SERVICE CENTER** *(Open All Year)*
  Res and Info: (575) 445-9536
  Location: Raton, *N 36° 52' 55", W 104° 25' 52", 6,500 Ft*

44 Sites – This campground has 44 sites in 3 rows. Two of the rows (26 sites) are pull-thrus to as long as 75 feet. A tree and a small strip of grass separates the sites. The remain-

ing row of 18 sites are back-ins. All of the sites have full hookups including satellite TV. There is a tenting area over a small creek accessible by a foot bridge. Wi-Fi is provided to the sites for $2 a night. The phone line in the office can be used for other internet access. The office also carries a stock of RV supplies and propane is sold. RV service and repairs are done at the campground. A pay phone is located outside the office. From Exit 451 of I-25 in Raton go south on the first road east of the interchange, Cedar St. The campground is on the right in .2 miles.

KICKBACK RV PARK *(Open All Year)*
Res and Info: (575) 445-1200
Location: Raton, *N 36° 53' 24", W 104° 25' 39", 6,500 Ft*

35 Sites – The camping sites in this park are in are in 3 areas. In the front as you enter are 2 rows (17 sites) of pull-thru sites to as long as 65 feet. On the exterior of the park to the left is a row of 10 back-in sites. These are the main sites used by travelers, but in the back of the office building are 8 more sites and room for tenting on grass. All sites are full hookup including cable TV. The pull-thru sites have both 30 and 50 amp power, the 10 back-ins on the side have 30 amp power, and the 8 sites in the back have 30 and 50 amps. Sites are separated by newly planted small trees and a thin strip of grass and there is a picnic table at each site. A data port is available in the office for internet access and a courtesy phone for local and calling card calls. There is a game room. From Exit 451 of I-25 in Raton go north on the frontage road on the east side of the highway. The campground is on the right in .3 miles.

RATON KOA *(Open All Year)*
Reservations: (800) 562-9033, www.koa.com
Information: (575) 445-3488, ratonkoa@zianet.com
Location: Raton, *N 36° 52' 42", W 104° 26' 26", 6,500 Ft*

48 Sites – This campground has a tenting area, two rental cabins, and 48 RV sites. These are back-ins and pull-thrus to 75 feet. There are full, partial, and no-hookup sites. A central data port is provided for internet access. The office has a store which sells ice, fishing tackle, and propane. Other amenities include a basketball court, arcade, game room with a pool table, and horseshoes. In the summer there are ice cream socials and pancake breakfasts. The campground is near the center of town and just across the street are restaurants, a grocery store, and other shopping. RVers from outside the campground are allowed to use the dump station for a fee. Take Exit 451 from I-25 and drive west .4 mile to US-87 (also called Business I-25), and turn south. The campground entrance is on the right in .4 mile.

SUGARITE CANYON STATE PARK – LAKE ALICE CAMPGROUND *(Open All Year)*
Reservations: (877) NM-4-RSVP, www.nmparks.com
Information: (575) 445-5607, (888) 667-2757, sugarite@raton.com
Location: 7 Miles NE of Raton, *N 36° 57' 32", W 104° 23' 11", 7,100 Ft*

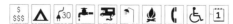

16 Sites – This campground has 16 sites off of 1 loop. Sites 1-12 are RV sites and 13-16

are tent sites. All of the sites (except 1) are back-in and some will take 35 foot RVs, but care is necessary because of trees close to the roads and limited maneuvering room. Site 12 (a long pull-thru site) is designated a wheelchair site. All of the RV sites have water and electricity and sites 6-9 also have sewer. The tent sites have a sand pad for setting up the tent. All sites have a picnic table and fire pit. There are 4 overflow sites available across the street from the entrance in a gravel lot. The bathrooms are wheelchair accessible vault style. Across from the nearby visitor center is a shower building. A pay telephone is also available at the visitor center. A fishing dock and boat ramp are available on Lake Maloya. Lots of trails run near the campground. From Exit 452 of I-25 in Raton head east and then north on SR-72. At the Y at 3.7 miles take the left fork onto SR-526. In another 3.2 miles you'll see the campground on the left.

🚐 SUGARITE CANYON STATE PARK – SODA POCKET CAMPGROUND
(Open May 15 to Oct 30 - Varies)

Information: (575) 445-5607, (888) NM-PARKS, sugarite@raton.com
Location: 8 Miles NE of Raton, *N 36° 58' 40", W 104° 23' 47", 7,900 Ft*

24 Sites – This campground has 24 back in sites. The sites are off an in-and-out road which has a turnaround at the end and a small loop off the side about half way in. Sites will take RVs to 35 feet although the steep entrance road makes getting larger RVs up here a first-gear operation at this altitude. The toilets are vault style. There is a campfire area, a group shelter, and a group camping area. Water is available in the park. The Deer Run Trail runs through the campground and a short nature loop trail is located off the turnaround loop at the end of the campground. It is 2 miles to the Visitors Center where there is a shower building. There is also a pay telephone at the Visitor Center. A fishing dock and boat ramp are available at Lake Maloya which is 1 mile away. From Exit 452 of I-25 in Raton head east and then north on SR-72. At the Y at 3.7 miles take the left fork onto SR-526. In another 4 miles the road to the campground goes left. It climbs steeply another mile to the campground.

🚐 NRA WHITTINGTON CENTER *(Open All Year)*

Res and Info: (575) 445-3615, www.nrawc.org, info@nrawc.org
Location: 10 Miles S of Raton, *N 36° 46' 24", W 104° 29' 08", 6,300 Ft*

215 Sites – The National Rifle Association's Whittington Center has a large RV campground as well as a tent campground. The 125-site RV campground has large pull-thru campsites with full hookups. There are an additional 50 sites at two of the ranges. The 35-site tent campground is limited to tents and small pop-up tent campers. There is a bathhouse with showers and laundry. Other amenities include 11 trap ranges, 4 skeet ranges, 2 five-stand ranges, and a 24 station sporting clays range. NRA membership is not required to use this facility, it's open to the public. From Raton drive south on I-25 for 3 miles to Exit 446. Follow US-64 south another 4 miles to the center.

ROSWELL

Roswell (population about 45,000) is probably best known as the site of a possible UFO crash in 1947. Despite US government assurance that the UFO was really a weather balloon, Roswell continues to cash in on the crash. You'll see alien figures everywhere,

ALIEN FIGURES ON A ROSWELL STOREFRONT

including a sign on the front of the local Walmart. You can visit the International **UFO Museum and Research Center** to find out all about it.

Roswell has another space connection too. The world's first liquid fuel rocket was launched here in 1926 by Robert Goddard. He conducted research in this area for about ten years. The **Roswell Museum and Art Center and Goddard Planetarium** will tell you all about it and a lot more. This center has galleries with the works of famous Southwest artists including Georgia O'Keefe. It also covers lots of local and regional history.

The **Bottomless Lakes State Park** was New Mexico's first state park, it dates from 1933. The park features red cliff towering over a series of small lakes. There is a campground here, it is described below. The park is about 13 miles east of Roswell.

Roswell Campgrounds

🚐 **RED BARN RV PARK** *(Open All Year)*

Res and Info: (575) 623-4897, (877) 800-4897, www.RedBarnRV.com
Location: 1.5 Mile E of Roswell, *N 33° 23' 38", W 104° 28' 55", 3,500 Ft*

15 Sites – The Red Barn is a small commercial RV park. There are 13 back-in sites (to 90 feet in length) around the exterior of a lot and 2 pull-thrus to 80 foot. The sites all have full hookups including cable TV. Behind the campground is a large grass field where tent camping is allowed. Most but not all of the sites have a picnic table. A data port and a desk are provided in the main office building just outside the restrooms and showers. A courtesy phone is also there for local or calling card calls. There is a dump station which

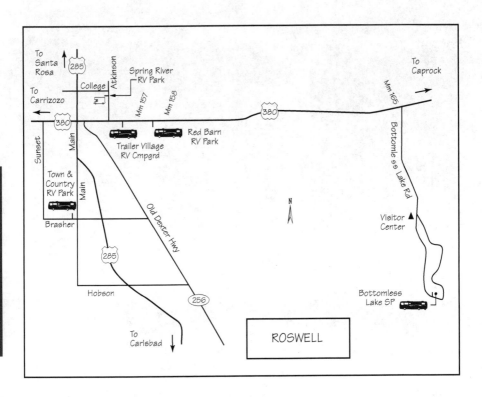

RVers from outside the campground are allowed to use for a fee. It's a popular campground, reservations are recommended. From Roswell head east on US-380. The campground is 2.4 miles from the intersection of US-380 and US-285 in the center of town.

🚐 **TOWN AND COUNTRY RV PARK** *(Open All Year)*

Reservations: (800) 499-4364
Information: (575) 624-1833, www.townandcountryrvpark.com,
             info@townandcountryrvpark.com
Location: Roswell, *N 33° 21' 08", W 104° 31' 31", 3,600 Ft*

75 Sites – This park has 70 sites for RVs and 5 for tents. The RV sites are back-ins and pull-thrus to 90 feet. All have full hookups including cable TV. Four of the sites have instant-on telephone which is available for $2.50 daily and there is a data port in the office. All sites have a picnic table and a raised barbecue grill. There is a line of trees down each row of RV spaces which provide some separation and shade. An outdoor sink is outside the bathrooms for tenters use. There is a seasonal swimming pool and a clubhouse. The campground is next to South Main Street, 3 miles south of the intersection of US-380 and US-284 in the center of town.

🚐 TRAILER VILLAGE RV CAMPGROUND *(Open All Year)*
Res and Info: (575) 623-6040
Location: .5 Mile E of Roswell, *N 33° 23' 37", W 104° 29' 54", 3,600 Ft*

53 Sites – This campground has a row of back-in sites (to 35 feet in length) around the back wall and the east side. Along the west side are 6 large parallel parking sites for big rigs. Down the interior of the park are 8 pull-thru sites to about 55 feet in length. All of the sites are full hookup including cable TV. There are trees between the sites which provide some separation and shade. Also between the pull-thru sites is a gravel area delineated by a concrete outline with a paved patio and a picnic table. The pull-thru and parallel parking sites have parking on gravel. The back-in sites along the east wall have parking on grass. These are the sites which are used for tenters. Wi-Fi is provided to the sites at no additional charge and a data port is available for other internet access. The office sells basic RV supplies. A public phone is available. From Roswell head east on US-380. The campground is 1.4 miles from the intersection of US-380 and US-285 in the center of town.

🚐 BOTTOMLESS LAKE STATE PARK *(Open All Year)*
Reservations: (877) NM-4-RSVP, www.nmparks.com
Information: (575) 624-6058, (888) 667-2757, www.nmparks.com
Location: 13 Miles E of Roswell, *N 33° 18' 58", W 104° 19' 51", 3,500 Ft*

45 Sites – Camping is in 2 different locations. Near the Visitor's Center a stub road with a turn-around provides access to 10 sites with shaded picnic tables on paved patios and raised barbecues. Water is available and there are wheelchair accessible vault toilets. The other area, the RV camping area at Lea Lake, has 35 sites. Six are full hookups, 26 have electricity and water, and 3 have no utilities. Nine sites are pull-thrus to as long as 100 feet. Some of the back-ins are to 40 feet. These sites have covered picnic tables on paved patios and raised grills. Camping is also allowed with no hookups at the day use area on Lea Lake. A recreation hall is used for performances in the summer. Lea Lake is good for swimming and there is a bath house. Three of the lakes near the Visitor Center are stocked with rainbow trout. Reservations are accepted for several of the Lea Lake sites. From the intersection of US-380 and US-285 in the center of Roswell drive east on US-380 for 10.3 miles. Turn south on Bottomless Lake Road and follow signs about 4 miles to the visitor center.

RUIDOSO

Ruidoso (population about 8,000) is a resort town on US-70 between Alamogordo and Roswell. The 7,000 foot altitude makes this a popular destination in both summer and winter. Near Ruidoso and part of the same area are the bedroom community of Alto to the north and Ruidoso Downs to the east along US-70.

The two biggest attractions in the area are probably Ruidoso Downs and Ski Apache. The **Ruidoso Downs Racetrack** is the summer attraction with horse races on Thursday through Sunday from late May to early September. The headline event is the **All**

American Futurity on Labor Day, a quarter horse race with a huge purse. Next to the race course is the **Hubbard Museum of the American West** with a huge display including art works by Frederic Remington and Charles M Russell as well as Indian pottery, saddles, stagecoaches, and pretty much anything else you can imagine having to do with the American west.

In winter the action switches to **Ski Apache**, probably the best skiing area in southeast New Mexico. It's hugely popular with folks from Texas, and also those from Albuquerque. The ski resort is located about 15 miles northwest of Ruidoso.

South and west of Ruidoso is the **Mescalero Apache Reservation** which has several attractions. These include the **Mescalero Apache Cultural Center Museum** and the **Inn of the Mountain Gods** casino and hotel

Ruidoso hosts lots of special events. The **Ruidoso Art Festival** is big time and held during the last weekend in July. The **Golden Aspen Motorcycle Rally** in late September sees many thousands of motorcycle visitors. There's **Aspenfest** on the first weekend of October with a chile contest and **Oktoberfest** on the third weekend of the same month. In between is the **Lincoln County Cowboy Symposium** at Ruidoso Downs, the whole month is a busy time in the Ruidoso area.

Ruidoso Campgrounds

TWIN SPRUCE RV PARK *(Open All Year)*

Res and Info: (575) 257-4310, www.ruidoso.net/twinsprue, twinspruce200@yahoo.com
Location: 2 Miles S of Ruidoso, *N 33° 18' 38", W 105° 38' 23", 6,600 Ft*

104 Sites – This is the most convenient and popular RV park in the area. There are back-in and pull-thru sites to 55 feet. Some sites are in the pines up and behind the roadside area. Tenting space is also available and there are 2 rental cabins. There are picnic tables and raised barbecue grills. Wi-Fi is provided to the sites for no additional charge and a data port is available in the lounge. The office has a store which sells groceries, gifts, and RV supplies. Propane is available. The campground is located next to US-70 about .1 mile southwest of the Mescalero Trail intersection.

PINE RIDGE RV CAMPGROUND *(Open All Year)*

Res and Info: (575) 378-4164
Location: 2 Miles SW of Ruidoso, *N 33° 18' 56", W 105° 37' 54", 7,200 Ft*

61 Sites – The sites in this park are terraced down the side of a good size slope. The interior roads are dirt/gravel and rutted from water runoff. Twenty-seven of the sites are pull-thrus as long as 50 feet and the back-ins are to 35 feet. Because of the rough, narrow interior roads, this park is best suited for RVs no longer than 35 feet, but carefully driven longer RVs do stay here. The park also has camping for tents. A central data port is provided for internet access. A bathroom building and laundry are located near the office. Follow Glade up the hill directly across from where the Mescalero Trail (the western most branch of SR-48) meets US-70. At the first intersection turn right and you'll see the campground.

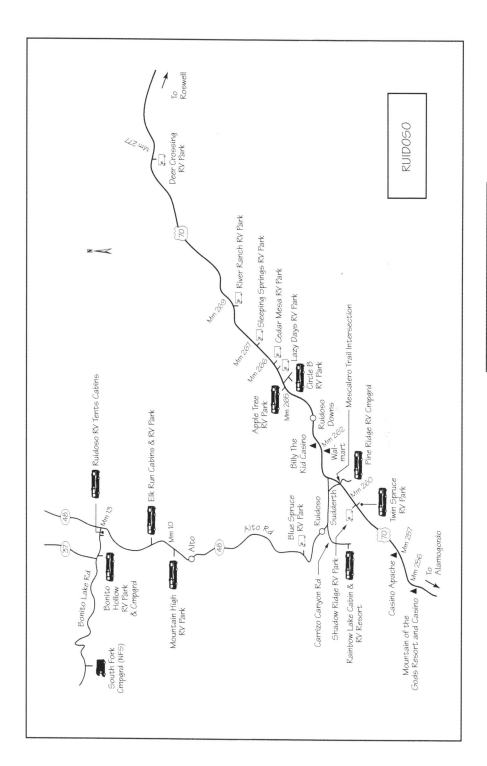

RUIDOSO

NEW MEXICO

☵ RAINBOW LAKE CABIN AND RV RESORT *(Open All Year)*

Reservations: (866) 808-3075, rlrvr@zianet.com
Information: (575) 630-2267, www.ruidoso.net/rainbow
Location: 2 Miles S of Ruidoso, *N 33° 18' 40", W 105° 40' 09", 6,700 Ft*

49 Sites – This campground has 49 RV sites and 18 rental cabins. The RV site rate is between $30 and $35. Three of the sites are pull-thrus. All sites are about 45 feet in length. The sites are all full hookups with cable TV. For the most part parking is in a big gravel lot. Some of the sites are separated by a small grass strip. The office sells some groceries and ice. A central data port is provided for internet access and a phone is available in the office for local and calling card calls. The park has a dump station and campers from outside the park are allowed to dump for a fee. The restaurant is open 6 am to 2:30 pm Thursday - Sunday. There is a recreation room. Wi-Fi is available. The campground has a picnic area with barbecue grills and fire rings. Two fishing lakes are within a mile of the campground. From SR-48 about 1.5 miles west of its intersection with US-70 follow Carrizo Canyon Rd. westward for about 1.5 mile to the campground.

☵ CIRCLE B RV PARK *(Open All Year)*

Res and Info: (575) 378-4990
Location: 4 Miles E of Ruidoso, *N 33° 20' 49", W 105° 34' 07", 6,300 Ft*

206 Sites – Most sites have full hookups. There are also 7 rental cabins. About half of the sites are pull-thrus to a length of 60 feet and the back-ins are to 50 feet. The sites are set under pine and juniper trees. A data port is provided for internet access. There is a store in the office building which sells basic groceries and RV supplies. There is a large group pavilion, a gazebo, and an indoor lounge and meeting room. The campground is on the south side of US-70 about 4 miles east of the easternmost intersection of SR-48 and US-70 just south of Ruidoso.

☵ APPLE TREE RV PARK *(Open All Year)*

Information: (575) 378-4995, www.appletreervpark.com
Location: 4 Miles E of Ruidoso, *N 33° 20' 53", W 105° 34' 10", 6,300 Ft*

80 Sites – The campground is terraced down the side of the hill from the highway. There are 80 sites, all with full hookups including cable TV. Most of the sites are back-ins and some are large enough for 40 foot motorhomes. The sites are separated by grass and there are some trees. Most sites do not have picnic tables. A data port is provided in the office which is the owners home and a courtesy phone is located there also for local and calling card calls. The park has a meeting room with a kitchen and 2 laundries. This park is mostly full starting in May for the summer. It is used by monthly tenants working at the downs. Getting in is hit or miss since the campground does not take reservations. The campground is on the south north of US-70 about 4 miles east of the easternmost intersection of SR-48 and US-70 just south of Ruidoso.

MOUNTAIN HIGH RV PARK *(Open April 1 to Oct 15 - Varies)*
Res and Info: (575) 336-4236
Location: 6 Miles N of Ruidoso, *N 33° 24' 36", W 105° 40' 17", 7,300 Ft*

65 Sites – This RV park has back-in and pull-thru sites suitable for RVs to 45 feet. There are no restrooms so only full-hookup self-contained RVs are accepted. The campground has picnic tables and fire pits, there's also a recreation hall. The campground is located north of Ruidoso. From Ruidoso drive north on SR-48 for 6.5 miles, the campground is on the left.

ELK RUN CABINS AND RV PARK *(Open All Year)*
Reservations: (800) 687-0620
Information: (575) 336-4240, www.ruidoso.net/elkrun
Location: 7 Miles N of Ruidoso, *N 33° 25' 07", W 105° 40' 10", 7,300 Ft*

19 Sites – The campground sits up on the hill behind the cabins under a forest of pines and alligator juniper. The park is upscale but not really a big RV park because maneuvering room is limited. There are 19 sites, 7 of them are pull-thrus. The longest sites are over 70 feet and the shortest is about 36 feet. The park prefers RVs no larger than 40 feet because maneuvering room is a little tight. Sixteen of the sites are full hookup, 2 have no sewer and 1 has no cable. Wi-Fi is provided to the sites by an outside vendor. No other internet access is available. The bathrooms and laundry are in the office building which is nearer to the cabins than the RV park. It is a short walk from the park. There is a group fireplace but the individual sites do not have fire pits. A courtesy phone is provided in the office for local and calling card calls. Also available are 5 two-story cabins and 2 one bedroom cabins. The campground is located north of Ruidoso. From Ruidoso drive north on SR-48 for 7 miles, the campground is on the right.

BONITO HOLLOW RV PARK AND CAMPGROUND *(Open May 1 to Oct 15)*
Information: (575) 336-4325, www.bonitohollow.com
Location: 10 Miles N of Ruidoso, *N 33° 26' 58", W 105° 40' 50", 7,000 Ft*

72 Sites – This campground is on the Bonito River and has 47 RV sites, 25 tent sites and 4 rental cabins. RV sites are either full or partial hookups. Sixteen of the RV sites are pull-thrus to a length of 65 feet and the back-in sites are 60 feet. A data port is provided for internet access. A general store sells grocery items, RV supplies, fishing tackle, ice, and firewood. Freshwater fishing is possible in the Bonita River. Other amenities include play equipment, badminton, volleyball, a pavilion, and hiking trails. The campground is located north of Ruidoso. From Ruidoso drive north on SR-48 for 9 miles. Turn west on SR-37 and in 1.3 miles you'll see the campground on the left.

RUIDOSO RV TENTS CABINS *(Open All Year)*
Res and Info: (575) 336-4444, http://sundancervcampground.com/
Location: 11 Miles N of Ruidoso, *N 33° 26' 53", W 105° 39' 55", 6,900 Ft*

25 Sites – This campground has pull-thru and back-in sites to 60 feet, many are right

along the Bonita River. All of the sites are full hookup. There is a footbridge across the river and tent camping is in a grass area by the river. There are also rental cabins. There is a bathroom and shower building. From Ruidoso drive north on SR-48 for some 9 miles. Turn left on SR-37 and drive for .2 mile, the campground is on the left.

SOUTH FORK CAMPGROUND *(Open May 15 to Sept 15)*
Information: (575) 257-4095
Location: 15 Miles N of Ruidoso, *N 33° 27' 12", W 105° 45' 05", 7,500 Ft*

60 Sites – This Lincoln National Forest campground is set under a forest of pine trees. There are about 60 sites, some of which are walk-in tent sites. Three sites are pull-thrus for RVs. The park is suitable only for RVs up to 35 foot because the roads are narrow and maneuvering room is limited. Water is available at the campground. Reservations are not accepted at this park and it is popular because of its location close to Bonita Lake so it fills in the summer. Bonita Lake is stocked and fishing is excellent. There are also hiking trails from near the campground. From Ruidoso drive north on SR-48 for some 9 miles. Turn left on SR-37 and drive for 1.2 mile. Turn left on Bonito Lake Rd and follow it for 5 miles to the entrance to the campground.

SALINAS PUEBLO MISSIONS NATIONAL MONUMENT

Running from north to south in the quadrant southeast of Albuquerque are the Manzano Mountains. Just east of them is the Salinas Valley. When the Spanish arrived in the area in the late 1600s they found that the Manzano Mountains were home to a pueblo popu-

THE SALINAS PUEBLO MISSION'S QUARAI CHURCH

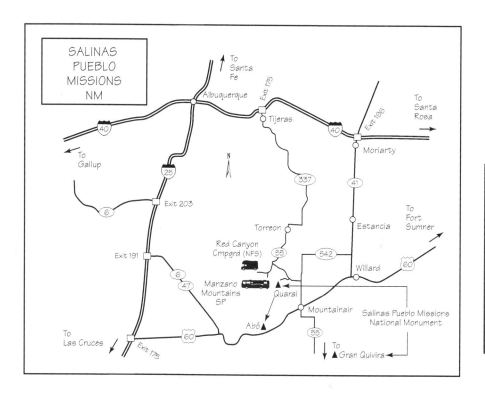

lation. The people here took advantage of their position between the Rio Grand pueblo Indians and the plains Indians and were engaged in trade with both of them. They farmed, hunted, and traded; they also collected valuable salt from the dried lake beds to the east.

The Franciscans were charged by the pope to convert the local Indians so in the early 1600s they came to live here. Missions were built at the large Indian pueblos in the region. Eventually, actually after only about fifty years, the Indians and Spanish abandoned the pueblos and moved east to the Rio Grande Valley. Historians blame the abandonment on problems with Apache raids from the east as well as dissatisfaction on the part of the Indians with the Spanish culture being pushed upon them.

The **Salinas Pueblo Missions National Monument** contains the ruins of three of the large churches built under the Franciscans. The monument headquarters (with the best introduction to the ruins) is in Mountainair while the churches are in three separate locations to the northwest, west, and south of Mountainair. The ruins of this national monument are impressive, perhaps the best examples of early Franciscan churches in North America.

Quarai is near Punta de Agua, about 8 miles north of Mountainair. Quarai has the ruins of a large church as well as the adjoining convents. A nearby mound marks the place of the unexcavated Indian pueblo.

Abó is located 9 miles west of Mountainair and also has the ruins of a church and convent as well as unexcavated Indian pueblo ruins.

Gran Quivira was the largest of the Salinas pueblos. It is located 25 miles southeast of Mountainair. Here you'll find the ruins of two churches, the adjoining convents, and some partially excavated pueblo ruins.

Salinas Pueblo Missions National Monument Campgrounds

🚐 **MANZANO MOUNTAINS STATE PARK** *(Open April 1 to Oct 31 - Varies)*
   Reservations: (877) NM-4-RSVP, www.nmparks.com
   Information: (505) 847-2820, (888) 667-2757, www.nmparks.com
   Location: 50 Miles SE of Albuquerque, *N 34° 36' 12", W 106° 21' 41", 7,200 Ft*

37 Sites – The campground has 37 sites. Seventeen are along the main ring road of the campground and the remaining 20 serve as a group and overflow area. Nine sites have electric hook ups. Most sites are back-ins but a few are parallel-style pull-offs. A few of the sites extend to 60 feet but most are in the 30-foot range. The sites are set under juniper and pines. All of the sites have picnic tables which sit on a paved pad and a fire ring with a grill. The bathrooms have flush toilets and hot and cold running water but no showers. Reservations are accepted and are necessary on weekends in summer unless you plan to arrive pretty early. There is a dump station at the entrance. An entrance gate is closed from sunset to 7:30 in the morning. From Exit 175 of I-40 east of Albuquerque drive south on SR-337 for 29 miles. Turn right on SR-55 and follow it for 12.3 miles. Turn right at the sign for the state park on county road BO63 and you'll reach the campground in another 3.4 miles.

🚐 **RED CANYON CAMPGROUND** *(Open April 15 to Oct 31 - Varies)*
   Information: (505) 847-2990
   Location: 50 Miles SE of Albuquerque, *N 34° 37' 01", W 106° 24' 10", 7,600 Ft*

50 Sites – This is a large Cibola National Forest campground. It offers access to several hiking trails that lead back into the Manzano Mountains and Manzano Mountains Wilderness. It's also a good base for exploring the Salinas Pueblo Missions National Monument. The campground has sites in two locations. The lower area has 38 sites while the upper area is designed for people camping with horses (there are small corrals) and has 12 sites. Most sites are back-ins suitable for RVs to about 25 feet but a few parallel-style pull-offs would take a 40 foot or even larger RV with very limited space for slide-outs and awnings. Each site has a picnic table, fire ring, and raised barbecue; the restrooms are vault toilets. From Exit 175 of I-40 east of Albuquerque drive south on SR-337 for 29 miles. Turn right on SR-55 and follow it for 12.3 miles. Turn right at the sign for the state park on county road B063. Just before the entrance to the state park at 2.3 miles turn right and follow the small road first on a narrow paved strip and then gravel some 2.5 miles to the campground.

SANTA FE

Santa Fe (population about 65,000) must be New Mexico's top tourist town. The attractions can keep you busy for days with lots of shopping, eating, and some great museums.

The place to start is probably the plaza. It's a traditional Hispanic square and is surrounded by shops and restaurants. To the east is the Romanesque cathedral, **St Francis**. Its builder, Archbishop Jean Baptiste Lamy, was immortalized in Willa Cather's novel *Death Comes for the Archbishop*. The plaza is also at the center of a group of outstanding museums and attractions. On the square itself is the **Palace of the Governors**. Indian vendors spread their items for sale outside its walls and inside it's an excellent historical museum. Three other great museums nearby, all really part of the Museum of New Mexico, are **the Museum of Fine Arts**, the **Museum of Indian Arts and Culture**, and the **Museum of International Folk Art**. Other great nearby museums are the **Georgia O'Keefe Museum** and the **Institute of American Indian Arts Museum**.

In addition to the St Francis Cathedral there are several other interesting nearby churches. **Loretto Chapel** is designed to be similar to St Chapelle in Paris, it's probably best known for its **Miraculous Staircase**. What may be the oldest church in the US is there too, it's the **San Miguel Mission** dating from 1625. Santa Fe also has the world's oldest shrine to Mexico's Our Lady of Guadalupe, the **Santuario de Guadalupe** which was built in 1776.

If shopping is your thing then don't just visit the plaza area. Two more great gallery and shopping areas are **Canyon Road**, about a mile and a half southeast of the plaza and the Guadalupe Sanbusco area about a half-mile southwest of it.

For an excellent day trip from Santa Fe consider a visit to **El Rancho de las Golondrinas**. This is an open-air historical museum. Old buildings and other exhibits have been collected from throughout the area to document the Hispanic ranching roots of the region. On some weekends the rancho is staffed with costumed actors demonstrating

THE ROMANESQUE ST FRANCES CATHEDRAL ON THE SANTA FE HISTORIC PLAZA

what life was like. Even during quiet times it's fun to wander the grounds and examine the exhibits.

Santa Fe also has a ski area, it's called **Ski Santa Fe**. The area is about a half-hour from the plaza about 15 miles up into the Sangre de Cristo Mountains. The base is at 10,350 feet and the top at 12,075. Three of the campgrounds listed below are on Hyde Park Road en route to the ski area.

Santa Fe holds **an Indian Market** in late August. Over a thousand Indian artists from around the country have booths on the plaza and compete for prizes. The **Santa Fe Fiesta** is another big event held the weekend after Labor Day.

The pueblos near Santa Fe are almost all easily accessible from US-285 running north of the city. For the pueblos south of Santa Fe see the Albuquerque section.

• **Tesuque Pueblo** is the closest to Santa Fe, it's a small pueblo with a population of only about 800. The plaza is surrounded by adobe buildings and is listed in the National Register of Historic places. The best-known artwork from Tesuque are small clay figures called Rain Gods. Tesuque has a casino, the **Camel Rock Casino** which is located along US-285 and has an arts and crafts store. The village entrance road leaves US-285 near Mile 173.5, directly across from the casino and south of the distinctive rock formation known as Camel Rock. The public is welcome to visit to watch dances during the San Diego feast day on Nov. 12, Christmas Day, the Three Kings Day celebration January 6 and for the Corn Dance on the first weekend in June.

• **Pojoaque Pueblo** is among the smallest of the pueblos in both population and size but has a very visible location right along US-285. You can't miss the tribe's **Cities of Gold Casino** and nearby **Poeh Cultural Center**. It houses art and exhibits as well as the largest arts and crafts store in northern New Mexico. There's also a new golf course.

• **San Ildefonso** is a popular and much-visited pueblo in a scenic location just west of US-285 near SR-502, the road to Los Alamos and Bandelier National Monument. The pueblo is known for it's black-on-black pottery, originally developed by María Povenka Martínez in the early 1900s. There is a visitor center as well as the **San Ildefonso Pueblo Museum** and also a **María Povenko Martínez Museum**. Pueblo dances open to the public are Corn Dances during June, August and September as well as the January 23 Comanche, and Buffalo Dances. From Santa Fe drive north on US-285 for about 17 miles and then turn left on SR-502 to the pueblo..

• **Nambé Pueblo** is located on the mountain side of US-285 near the beginning of what is described below as the high road to Taos. There is a reservoir on the reservation as well as a scenic waterfall. The campground near the waterfall is described below as Nambé Falls. Dances and celebrations normally open to the public include Three Kings Day on January 6, a July 4 arts and crafts fair at Nambé Falls, the feast day of San Francisco de Asis on October 4, and a Catholic mass and Buffalo Dance on December 24. Drive north from Santa Fe on US-285 about 17 miles and then turn right on SR-503 to reach the pueblo.

• **Santa Clara Pueblo** is located on the southern outskirts of Española. The town is known for its pottery and also the **Puye Cliff Dwellings**. It also operates a **Casino** in Española on Riverside Drive. You are generally welcome to visit artists shops in the pueblo. The village celebrates the San Antonio feast day on June 13 with Comanche Dances and the August 12 Santa Clara feast day with harvest and Corn Dances. In Española head out of town on SR-30, the Los Alamos Highway, the pueblo is on the left. For the Puye Cliff Dwellings continue on to Mile 5 and turn right onto Forest Service road #602. It's another seven miles an gravel road to the dwellings. Once there you can follow trails to the dwellings cut into tuff and also built on the cliff top.

• **San Juan Pueblo** is also located in Española but on the north side of town. Pueblo artists are best known for their incised redware pottery. The pueblo's casino is known as the **Ohkay Casino**. The **Oke Oweenge Crafts Cooperative** has a large shop located in the village center. There are a number of celebrations with dances normally open to out-siders including King's Day on January 6, a Corn Dance on June 13, the San Juan feast day on June 24, a Harvest Dance in September, a midnight mass on December 24, and Turtle Dances on December 26. To reach the pueblo drive north from central Española on SR-68 for about a mile and turn left just past the casino onto SR-74, it's about a mile to the village center.

There are two routes north from Santa Fe to Taos. The **low road** is the quickest, it's also the one to take if you're driving a larger or wider rig like an RV. From Santa Fe just follow multi-lane US-84 north through the pueblos. Near Espanola you'll turn north along the Rio Grande. The road soon becomes two-lane SR-68. Total distance is about 68 miles.

The **high road** is much more scenic and well worth the extra time and distance if you have a normal-sized vehicle. It's also worth the time to drive in a tow car if you have an RV. From Santa Fe drive north on US-84 for about 16 miles and turn right onto SR-503. This will take you east through Nambé Pueblo and then north. Some 7 miles from where you turned onto SR-503 turn left toward Chimayó. You'll soon pass though this little town, famous for both its sanctuary and its weaving. Near the center of town you'll meet SR-76. Follow this road to the right and it will lead you across the high slopes through Las Truchas, and Las Trampas to meet SR-75 near the Picuris Pueblo, a distance of 22 miles from Chimayó. Turn right again and drive eastward for just seven miles to meet SR-518. Turn left and descend the 17 miles into Taos.

There are several places you might want to stop along the way. **Nambé Pueblo** and its attractions are described above. The town of **Chimayó** is a not to be missed stop. The famous **Santuario de Chimayó**, dating from 1815, has a fascinating story and is a great photographic subject. Chimayó is also known as a weaving center, you'll find several galleries in town. Chimayó is also home to the well known **Rancho de Chimayó**, a great place to stop for lunch. There are two campgrounds near Chimayó, see the Santa Cruz Lakes write-ups below.

Las Truchas is also a weaving center, the town has many galleries. It was also the film-ing location for Robert Redford's *Milagro Beanfield War*. In **Las Trampas** it's worth the time to stop and take a look at the **Church of San José del Gracia**.

And finally, the attractions of **Picuris Pueblo** are described in the Taos section of this book.

Most of the campgrounds listed below for Santa Fe are outside the central area of town. If you want to visit the sights of central Santa Fe one stands out – Los Campos de Santa Fe. It's not right at the center of town but it has a handy location with good bus service, something none of the other campgrounds offer.

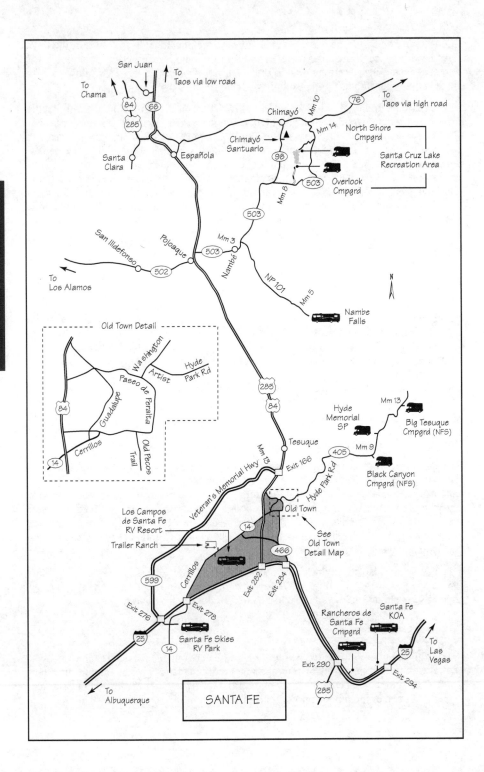

SANTA FE

Santa Fe Campgrounds

LOS CAMPOS DE SANTA FE RV RESORT *(Open All Year)*

Reservations: (800) 852-8160, loscampossf@aol.com
Information: (505) 473-1949, http://hometown.aol.com/loscampossf
Location: Santa Fe, *N 35° 38' 41", W 106° 00' 22", 6,600 Ft*

95 Sites – This is the most convenient campground for visits to central Santa Fe. Busses run right in front of the campground so there's no need to drive. The campground has back-in and pull-thru spaces to 70 feet long. They all have full hookups with cable TV as well as picnic tables on paved patios. Wi-Fi is provided to the sites at no extra charge and the office has DSL and dial-up data ports for other internet access. There is a seasonal swimming pool. Near the back of the park is a picnicking area with barbecue grills and a covered group pavilion, a pet walk area, and a playground. There are coin operated washers and dryers in both the men's and women's restrooms. Easiest access to the campground is from Exit 278 off I-25. Drive northeast on Cerrillos Rd for 3.4 miles to the campground, it's on the right.

SANTA FE SKIES RV PARK *(Open All Year)*

Reservations: (877) 565-0451, sfskysrv@swcp.com
Information: (505) 473-5946, www.santafeskiesrvpark.com
Location: 4 Miles SW of Santa Fe, *N 35° 35' 19", W 106° 02' 35", 6,400 Ft*

98 Sites – Santa Fe Skies is a big-rig campground. About half of the sites here are pull-thrus to 60 feet, some to 100 feet. Most sites have picnic tables, some have paved patio. Parking is on gravel. Wireless internet is provided to the sites by an outside vendor, wireless internet and a data port are available in the clubhouse for no charge. Many of the sites have instant-on telephone for a fee of $3.85 per day. The clubhouse has a full kitchen, a couple of rooms with tables and chairs, a theatre lounge with a large drop down screen, and a nice outdoor patio. A few non perishable grocery items are sold in the office. There is a larger convenience store on the entrance road to the park. To reach the park take Exit 276 from I-25 southwest of Santa Fe. Drive eastward on SR-599 for .5 mile to Cerrillos Rd. Continue straight ahead across Cerrillos onto Camino Alta, you'll see the park entrance on the left.

RANCHEROS DE SANTA FE CAMPGROUND *(Open March 15 to Nov 1)*

Reservations: (800) 426-9259, camp@rancheros.com
Information: (505) 466-3482, www.rancheros.com
Location: 7 Miles SE of Santa Fe, *N 35° 32' 44", W 105° 51' 52", 7,200 Ft*

127 Sites – This campground is located outside Santa Fe to the east along I-25. It has back-in and pull-thru sites to 50 feet and offers a variety of hook-up options. There are

also rental camping cabins. The office has a small store and other amenities include a central internet data port, free Wi-Fi in the park, nightly movies, a dog run, free cable TV, wood, recreation hall, coin games, a pavilion, and hiking trails. Take Exit 290 from I-25 about 6 miles southeast of Santa Fe. Follow the access road on the north side of the freeway (SR-300) toward the southeast for 1.1 mile to the campground entrance.

SANTA FE KOA *(Open March 1 to Nov 1)*
Reservations: (800) 562-1514, www.koa.com
Information: (505) 466-1419, www.santafekoa.com
Location: 10 Miles SE of Santa Fe, *N 35° 32' 45", W 105° 50' 11", 7,000 Ft*

66 Sites – This KOA has tent sites, cabins, and RV sites. Most RV sites are pull-thrus and they reach 60 feet in length. The sites have picnic tables, fire pits, raised barbecue grills and firewood is available for purchase. A central data port is provided for internet access. The store has grocery items, gifts, some RV supplies, and propane is sold. Other amenities at the park include a recreation room, a recreation field, a game room, free movie library, horseshoes, and basketball. Take Exit 294 from I-25 about 10 miles southeast of Santa Fe. Follow the access road on the north side of the freeway (SR-300) toward the southwest for .5 mile to the campground entrance.

BIG TESUQUE CAMPGROUND *(Open All Year)*
Information: (505) 753-7331 or (505) 438-7840
Location: 12 Miles NE of Santa Fe, *N 35° 46' 10", W 105° 48' 32", 9,600 Ft*

7 Sites – Big Tesuque is a small Santa Fe National Forest tent campground located right along SR-475 as it climbs toward the Ski Santa Fe area. There are about seven walk-in tent sites with picnic tables, fire pits, and barbecue grills. There is no potable water. A vault toilet is located right next to the parking slots along the highway. From Paseo de Peralta on the north side of central Santa Fe drive north on Washington Ave for just .2 mile. Turn right on Artist Road. Zero your odometer here and head up the hill. The road soon becomes Hyde Park Road and you'll reach the camping area in 11 miles.

BLACK CANYON CAMPGROUND *(Open May 15 to Oct 15 - Varies)*
Reservations: (877) 444-6777, www.recreation.gov
Information: (505) 753-7331
Location: 7 Miles NE of Santa Fe, *N 35° 43' 40", W 105° 50' 24", 8,300 Ft*

42 Sites – This is a Santa Fe National Forest campground located right next to Hyde Memorial State Park. It has been newly reconstructed with paved parking pads for RVs to about 35 feet. A state dump station associated with nearby Hyde Memorial State Park is just outside the campground. From Paseo de Peralta on the north side of central Santa Fe drive north on Washington Ave. for just .2 mile. Turn right on Artist Road. Zero your odometer here and head up the hill. The road soon becomes Hyde Park Road and you'll reach the camping area in 6.9 miles.

HYDE MEMORIAL STATE PARK *(RV Section Open All Year)*
Reservations: (877) NM-4-RSVP, www.nmparks.com
Information: (505) 983-7175, (888) 667-2757, www.nmparks.com
Location: 8 Miles NE of Santa Fe, *N 35° 44' 37", W 105° 50' 04", 8,900 Ft*

50 Sites – The Hyde Park Campground has several loops, all near each other off SR-475 as it climbs steeply toward Ski Santa Fe. We recommend no trailers and no RVs over 30 feet long for this campground because access through Santa Fe is difficult and maneuvering in the campground is tough. The Main Loop (sites 1-29) are no-hookup sites suitable for tents or RVs to 20 feet. Sites and roads are gravel. Sites 30-33 are similar but located off a separate road. Sites 34-36 are above the RV campground. The RV campground (sites 37-46) has 7 back-in sites with electricity suitable for RVs to 30 feet. The sites are paved, have picnic tables, fire pits, and water (not at the sites). The RV area also has an additional three sheltered tenting sites with covered picnic tables, fire pits, and raised barbecue grills. Three other sites (47-50) are near the visitor center. Toilets are vault style. A pay phone is at the visitor center and a dump station is nearby. Much of the campground is closed from May 15 to October 15 but the RV sites remain open when snow allows. From Paseo de Peralta on the north side of central Santa Fe drive north on Washington Ave for just .2 mile. Turn right on Artist Road. Zero your odometer here and head up the hill. The road soon becomes Hyde Park Road and you'll see the visitor center on the right in 7.2 miles. The entrance to the Main Loop is just beyond on the right and the RV camping area is a little bit farther and on the left.

NAMBÉ FALLS *(Open All Year)*
Reservations: (575) 455-2036, (575) 455-2304
Information: (575) 455-4444 (info), (575) 455-2304 (ranger)
Location: 22 Miles N of Santa Fe, *N 35° 51' 09", W 105° 54' 55", 6,500 Ft*

20 Sites – Below Nambé Falls the Nambé Pueblo maintains a campground for tents and small RVs, it has no hookups. There is also a dirt parking area for visitors to the falls that doubles as an RV camping area. It has shelter buildings with electrical and water hookups (50 amps) and room to park RVs to 45 feet long. The price is high, $25 for no hookup camping and $35 for hookups. Restrooms are portable toilets. There is a trail to an overlook above the falls. To reach the camping area drive north on US-285 from Santa Fe. Just north of Pojoaque turn east on SR-503 toward Nambé Pueblo. This is about 14 miles north of Santa Fe. In 3.1 miles turn right on NP-101, the parking lot entrance is 5.1 miles ahead. There is a pay station at the entrance.

SANTA CRUZ LAKE RECREATION AREA – NORTH SHORE CAMPGROUND
    (Open All Year)

Information: (575) 758-8851
Location: 31 Mile N of Santa Fe, *N 35° 58' 50", W 105° 54' 52", 6,300 Ft*

10 Sites – Santa Cruz Lake is an extremely scenic reservoir located behind Santa Cruz Dam. It's located directly southeast of Chimayó. The sites in this BLM campground are set off a gravel loop on the hillside behind the day-use area. The narrow access road and also the narrow campground road and sites with limited maneuvering and parking room

NEW MEXICO

making this campground only suitable for RVs to about 25 feet. Picnic tables with metal shelter roofs, fire pits, and some raised barbecues are provided. There are vault toilets and a boat ramp at the campground. From Chimayó head east on SR-76 for 1.6 miles. Turn right onto SR-503 and follow it as it switchbacks up the slope for 1.4 miles. Turn right into the campground entrance road, you'll reach the campground in another 1.3 miles.

SANTA CRUZ LAKE RECREATION AREA – OVERLOOK CAMPGROUND *(Open All Year)*
Information: (575) 758-8851
Location: 25 Miles N of Santa Fe, *N 35° 57' 53", W 105° 55' 10", 6,600 Ft*

12 Sites – Campsites in this campground have a spectacular view down over Santa Cruz Lake from the south. This BLM camping area isn't nearly as popular as the North Shore Campground, there is no water access. The views and uncrowded sites make up for that. There are 12 sites arranged off a loop road. Two are long pull-thrus and the other 10 are mostly long back-ins. Unfortunately, the access highways to this location limit the practical RV size to about 30 feet. Each site has a picnic table sheltered by a metal roof and a fire pit with a barbecue. Some sites also have raised barbecue grills. Juniper trees separate the sites. No water is available in the campground. From the intersection of SR-76 and SR-98 in Chimayó drive south on SR-98 for 3.6 miles. At the T where SR-98 meets SR-503 turn left, drive 1 mile to the campground entrance road on the left. The access road from here is gravel, it's about .9 mile.

SANTA ROSA

Santa Rosa (population about 25,000), is located on the Great Plains near the Pecos River. It's also located along I-40 and is a Route 66 town. In fact, it's a great Route 66 town since it's the location of the **Route 66 Auto Museum**. The museum has 22 autos from the Route 66 era as well as a vintage-style restaurant.

The Santa Rosa area is in desert country but is unusual because there are a number of small lakes in the vicinity. These are sinkholes in the local limestone terrain. One, the **Blue Hole**, is well known as a scuba diving location and is over 80 feet deep. There's even a dive shop at the hole. Many of these sinkholes are connected by water-filled caves.

Santa Rosa State Park, about 4 miles north of town, is on a reservoir behind a Pecos River dam. The lake offers fishing, boating, water-skiing and canoeing. Fish available include black bass, channel cats, walleye and crappie.

Santa Rosa Campgrounds

SANTA ROSA CAMPGROUND *(Open All Year)*
Res and Info: (575) 472-3126, (888) 898-1999, www.santarosacampground.com, santarosacampground@speakeasy.net
Location: Santa Rosa, *N 34° 56' 45", W 104° 39' 42", 4,700 Ft*

100 Sites – There are 100 RV sites, a tent camping area, and 1 rental cabin. Most of the sites are pull-thrus, some as long as 90 feet. Both water, electric only and full-hookup

(with cable) sites are available. There is a separate grassy area for tent camping. The tenting area has water, picnic tables and a grill area. There is a tree, a narrow line of grass, and some landscaping between the RV sites. Wi-Fi internet is provided to the sites for no additional charge and there is an Ethernet data port for other internet access in the office. A western barbecue restaurant is part of the park and it will deliver dinner to your RV. There is a seasonal swimming pool. The office sells groceries, gifts, RV supplies, and propane. Some sites have instant-on telephone. In Santa Rosa take Exit 275 from I-40 and head east on Business I-40 (also US-54). The campground is on the left in .6 mile.

▆ SANTA ROSA LAKE STATE PARK – JUNIPER PARK CAMPGROUND
(Open May 15 to Sept 15 - Varies)

Information: (575) 472-3110, (888) 667-2757, www.nmparks.com
Location: 7.5 Miles N of Santa Rosa, *N 35° 01' 43", W 104° 40' 54", 4,700 Ft*

26 Sites – Sites in this campground include 12 pull-thrus to as long as 50 feet and 14 back-ins to 45 feet. The sites are on two loops, an outer and an inner. All sites on the outer loop have no hookups, but water is available. The inner loop has 2 sites with electric hookups. One of these is used by a host and the other is a wheelchair accessible site. There are also 2 group shelters which both have electricity. The interior roads and sites are paved. Several sites are tenting sites with a parking spot for a vehicle and a short walk to the tent site. All sites have a covered picnic table on a paved patio and a raised barbecue grill. The sites in this campground are closer to the lake than those in Rocky Point

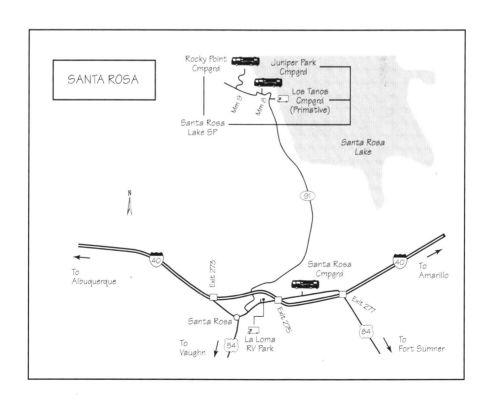

Campground. The bathroom has wheelchair accessible flush toilets. From Santa Rosa follow SR-91 north for 7.5 miles to the campground.

SANTA ROSA LAKE STATE PARK – ROCKY POINT CAMPGROUND *(Open All Year)*
Reservations: (877) NM-4-RSVP, www.nmparks.com
Information: (575) 472-3110, (888) 667-2757, www.nmparks.com
Location: 8.8 Miles N of Santa Rosa, *N 35° 02' 09", W 104° 41' 30", 4,800 Ft*

50 Sites – The sites in this campground are on 2 loops: A and B. A loop (sites A1-A23) is to the left as you enter the camping area and B loop (sites B1-B27) is straight ahead. A loop site all have electricity and some have also have water. Six of the sites on A loop are pull-thrus to 50 feet in length and the back-ins are to 45 feet. B loop sites have no hookups but water is available. Seven sites are pull-thrus and the sites are similar in length to those in A loop. All sites have a covered picnic table on a paved patio and a raised barbecue grill. Twelve sites in A loop and 4 in B loop can be reserved. A wheelchair accessible bathroom building with flush toilets and showers is between the two loops. Facilities at the park include a dump station, a boat ramp, visitor center, hiking trails, lake swimming, and fishing for bass, channel catfish, walleye, crappie, sunfish, yellow perch, & trout. From Santa Rosa drive north on SR-91 for 8.8 miles to the campground.

SILVER CITY

Silver City (population about 11,000) began in 1870 as a mining town after discovery of silver in the area. When the silver boom died Silver City became a copper town, there's still a huge mine, the Santa Rita Chino Open Pit Copper Mine, about 15 miles west of town. Silver City serves as a gateway to the Gila Cliff Dwellings National Monument. That monument and the routes to get there are discussed above in the *Gila Cliff Dwellings National Monument* section.

Silver City has two good museums. The **Silver City Museum** is the town's historical museum. The **Western New Mexico University Museum** has the largest collection of Mimbres pottery in the world but also covers local history.

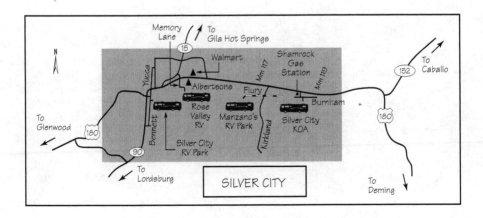

Silver City Campgrounds

SILVER CITY KOA *(Open All Year)*

Reservations: (800) 562-7623, www.koa.com
Information: (575) 388-3351, silvercitynm@mykoa.com
Location: Silver City, *N 32° 46' 42", W 108° 11' 28", 5,900 Ft*

74 Sites – This KOA has the normal tent and RV sites as well as camping cabins. There are back-ins and pull-thrus to 60 feet. Amenities include a pool and recreation hall. The campground is located east of town off US-180. From the intersection of SR-90 and US-180 in Silver City drive east on US-180 for 4.9 miles, the campground entrance is on the right.

MANZANO'S RV PARK *(Open All Year)*

Information: (575) 538-0918
Location: Silver City, *N 32° 46' 45", W 108° 13' 05", 6,000 Ft*

18 Sites – Manzano's is a smaller campground but is designed for larger RVs. There are back-in and pull-thru sites to 65 feet, all with full hookups. From the intersection of SR-90 and US-180 in Silver City drive east on US-180 for 3.9 miles. Turn right on Kirkland Road and follow it south for .3 mile. Turn right on Flury Lane and follow it .4 mile to the park.

SILVER CITY RV PARK *(Open All Year)*

Res and Info: (575) 538-2239
Location: Silver City, *N 32° 46' 42", W 108° 16' 20", 5,800 Ft*

21 Sites – This RV park near the center of Silver City has quite a few long-term residents but also spaces for travelers. The campground has tent sites as well as full-hookup back-ins and pull-thrus to 40 feet. From the intersection of SR-90 and US-180 in Silver City travel south on SR-90 for two blocks to 13th, turn left and drive a block to N Bennet St. Turn left and the campground is on the right.

ROSE VALLEY RV *(Open All Year)*

Res and Info: (575) 534-4277, (866) 787-2624, stay@rosevalleyrv.com
Location: Silver City, *N 32° 47' 02", W 108° 15' 23", 5,900 Ft*

57 Sites – This is a big-rig park with widely spaced sites. There are back-ins and pull-thrus to 70 feet, all with full hookups. From the intersection of SR-90 and US-180 in Silver City drive east on US-180 for 1.1 mile. Turn right on Memory Lane and follow it for .1 mile, the entrance to the campground is on the left.

SOCORRO

Socorro (population about 9,000) was once the largest town in Arizona. In the 1880s Socorro was a rich mining center serviced by railroad. The houses built during this era, as well as the Spanish era **San Miguel Mission**, are a Socorro tourist attraction, you can pick up a walking tour guide at the visitor center on the plaza.

Socorro is also home to the New Mexico Institute of Mining and Technology which has a **Mining Museum** with the largest collection of mineral specimens in the state.

The **Bosque del Apache National Wildlife Refuge** is located about 15 miles south of Socorro. The refuge was originally set up to protect the Whooping Crane, only 16 individuals were alive when the refuge was set up. The crane has come back and today visitors also come here to see them as well as snow geese, sandhill cranes, and other waterfowl. The best season for visits is late October to early April. There is a visitor center at the refuge and a 15-mile circular drive with trails and viewing platforms. The refuge hosts an annual **Festival of the Cranes** on the weekend before Thanksgiving.

East of Socorro 40 miles along US-60 is the **Very Large Array** radio telescope facility. Here 27 large antennas mounted on rails are scattered across the Plains of San Agustin. There is a visitor center. One of the campgrounds listed below, Datil Wells Recreation Site, is 24 miles west of the center access road.

Trinity Site is a 51,500-acre site that has been designated as a National Historic Landmark. It's located in the White Sands Missile Range. This is where the first atomic bomb was exploded on July 16, 1945. It is open to visitors only twice a year, on the first Saturdays of April and October. If you visit you'll be able to see Ground Zero where the bomb exploded, a crater filled with fused sand; the McDonald House where the bomb core was assembled; a "Fat Man" bomb casing; and one of the instrumentation observation bunkers. Information can be obtained by calling the White Sands Missile Range Public Affairs Office. To drive to Trinity Site head east from the Socorro area on US-380 from Exit 139 off I-25. After twelve miles a road leads south to Stallion's Gate and then another 22 miles to the site. Radiation levels now are now pretty low, officials say a visit to the site should expose you to about the same amount of radiation as a similar time spent in a jet airliner at cruising altitude.

In addition to the above, you might want to visit the **Valley of Fires National Recreation**

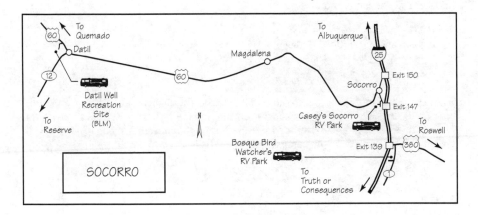

Area which is described in the Alamogordo section. It is also a campground. It's about 70 miles east of Socorro.

Socorro Campgrounds

🚐 CASEY'S SOCORRO RV PARK *(Open June 1 to Sept 30)*
    Reservations: (888) 674-2234
    Information: (575) 835-2234
    Location: Socorro, *N 34° 02' 34", W 106° 53' 36", 4,600 Ft*

84 Sites – This campground has back-in and pull-thru spaces with full-hookups including cable TV. The sites are large since access roads are very wide and long RVs can use them for extra space. The office also houses a gift shop and the laundry, propane is sold. A data port is provided in the office for internet access. There are pay phones out front. The bathrooms are old but have hot water showers. There is a seasonal swimming pool. The campground is located at the south end of Socorro where Business I-25 meets I-25 at Exit 147.

🚐 BOSQUE BIRD WATCHER'S RV PARK *(Open All Year)*
    Res and Info: (575) 835-1366
    Location: 13 Miles S of Socorro, *N 33° 52' 22", W 106° 52' 24", 4,500 Ft*

46 Sites – This campground is a popular spot for people who have come to visit the Bosque del Apache National Wildlife Refuge just to the south. There are tent sites as well as full hookup pull-thru RV sites to 60 feet. One easy access route is to take Exit 139 from I-25. Drive east for .7 mile into little San Antonio and turn right on SR-1 to head south. In another mile you'll see the campground on your right.

🚐 DATIL WELL RECREATION SITE *(Open All Year)*
    Information: (575) 835-0412
    Location: 62 Miles W of Socorro, *N 34° 09' 14", W 107° 51' 10", 7,400 Ft*

22 Sites – This BLM campground has sites suitable for both tenters and large RVs. Several sites are pull-thrus. There are no hookups but water is available. From Datil drive northwest on US-60 for one mile and enter the recreation site on the left.

SOUTHWEST NEW MEXICO NATIONAL FOREST ROUTE

In southeast New Mexico the Apache and Gila National Forests contain many square miles of remote forest. Much of this land is difficult to access in RVs or even automobiles but there are some decent highways. You can reach the area in any vehicle from the north from Gallup on I-40 by following SR-602, SR-36, SR-12 and US-180. From Silver City to the south US-180 is a good route, but you can also come in from Arizona via SR-78 from the Safford area.

Actually, the roads mentioned above provide a pretty decent route for any vehicle if you want to travel between I-40 and I-10 near the Arizona/New Mexico border. US-191, a north/south route in Arizona to the west is steep and winding, not good for larger vehicles.

The town of **Glenwood** is on US-180 about 60 miles north of Silver City and 195 miles south of Gallup. This is a small town with a relaxed atmosphere. The attraction here is the **Catwalk**, a trestle trail that hangs above Whitewater Canyon about five miles east of town. Glenwood has several small campgrounds suitable for tents and RVs, it make a good base for exploring the Mogollon area just to the north.

Mogollon is a virtual ghost town. To get there drive north from Glenwood on US-180 for about 4 miles to Alma and then eastward for 9 miles on SR-159. This road is paved but winding and steep, only attempt it in smaller vehicles. After Mogollon the road turns to a gravel forest service road, there are a number of forest service campgrounds as the road twists it's way back into the Mogollon Mountains toward the Gila Wilderness.

Farther north, a popular destination is the Gila National Forest's **Quemado Lake Recreation Area**. Quemado Lake, in the Gallo Mountains, is a reservoir with good fishing. There are also hiking and ATV trails in the area, not to mention excellent summer weather near 8,000 feet of altitude. The paved access road for the recreation area leaves SR-32 about 120 miles south of Gallup and 14 miles south of the small town of Quemado. Snuffy's, a privately operated store and restaurant near the entrance to the recreation area, provides the services and supplies necessary for a comfortable visit. There you'll find showers, a laundry, restaurant, bar, small general store, and rental boats There is a

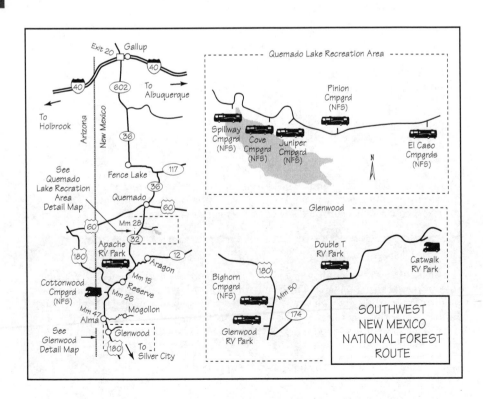

dump station at Piñon Campground, the only one in the recreation area. The first five campgrounds listed below are all inside this recreation area.

Southwest New Mexico National Forest Route Campgrounds

🚐 QUEMADO LAKE REC AREA – SPILLWAY CAMPGROUND *(Open All Year)*
Information: (575) 773-4678
Location: Quemado Lake Rec Area, *N 34° 08' 22", W 108° 29' 46", 7,600 Ft*

Scattered Boondocking – This parking area is the first of the campgrounds as you enter the National Forest Service managed Quemado Lake Recreation Area. The Spillway campground is nothing more than a large flat lot near the entrance and boat ramp. There's also a vault toilet nearby. There is no potable water.

🚐 QUEMADO LAKE REC AREA - COVE CAMPGROUND *(Open All Year)*
Information: (575) 773-4678
Location: Quemado Lake Rec Area, *N 34° 08' 15", W 108° 29' 26", 7,600 Ft*

Scattered Boondocking – A half mile beyond Spillway Campground, Cove Campground is just a parking area near the second launch ramp along the shore of the lake. RVs are allowed to park here overnight for free. The only facilities here other than the boat ramp are a vault toilet and water faucets.

🚐 QUEMADO LAKE REC AREA - JUNIPER CAMPGROUND *(Open May 1 to Sept 30)*
Information: (575) 773-4678
Location: Quemado Lake Rec Area, *N 34° 08' 14", W 108° 29' 19", 7,700 Ft*

38 Sites – Two tenths of a mile beyond Cove is Juniper Campground. Juniper is the only campground in the recreation area that has hookups. On one loop are eighteen sites with 30-amp electrical hookups. They're in groups of three with back-in side-by-side parking. They're pretty close together, not exactly what you go to a government campground looking for. The electrical sites are as long as 60 feet. The non-hookup sites on the campground's second loop are much nicer. They're individual sites, some overlooking the lake. Several are as long as 45 feet. All sites in this campground have a picnic table and fire pit, some have raised barbecue grills. Water is available and there are vault toilets.

🚐 QUEMADO LAKE REC AREA - PINION CAMPGROUND *(Open May 1 to Sept 30)*
Information: (575) 773-4678
Location: Quemado Lake Rec Area, *N 34° 08' 17", W 108° 28' 56", 7,700 Ft*

23 Sites – Four tenths of a mile beyond Juniper is Piñon Campground. Piñon is probably the nicest of the campgrounds in the recreation area even though it is away from the lake and has no hookups. A gravel loop road leads through a pine and juniper forest providing access to 23 sites. Those on the left side of the road are long back-ins and those on the right side are pull-off style sites which will accommodate RVs to about 40 feet. Each site has a nice gravel parking area, a picnic table, fire pit, and a raised barbecue grill. The campground also has 2 group areas. The bathrooms are vault style. There is a dump sta-

tion and water fill area and water faucets are scattered around the park.

QUEMADO LAKE REC AREA - EL CASO CAMPGROUNDS *(Open All Year)*

Information: (575) 773-4678
Location: Quemado Lake Rec Area, *N 34° 08' 14", W 108° 28' 17", 7,600 Ft*

40 Sites – Finally, six tenths of a mile beyond Piñon are the El Caso Campgrounds. The camping sites in these campgrounds are less formal than in Juniper and Piñon but not dispersed. There are designated camping sites which are very widely spaced under pine trees. The sites are arranged in 4 units. El Caso I, II, and III have separate entrances, there are about 25 unnumbered sites. Each has a picnic table and a fire pit with a grill. There are vault toilets in each of the units. No water is available at any of the units. Any size RV fits in these campgrounds but care must be exercised because of trees near the interior roads and overhanging branches. Farther out this road is El Caso IV with only vault toilets.

APACHE RV PARK *(Open All Year)*

Res and Info: (575) 533-6166, www.apachervpark.com
Location: 45 Miles N of Glenwood, *N 33° 48' 28", W 108° 39' 58", 6,300 Ft*

32 Sites – This is a simply designed commercial park with good big full-hookups sites. There are 32 sites in 4 rows. The interior 2 rows are pull-thrus and are long enough for any size rig. The sites are basic with gravel parking and full hookups but no picnic tables or patios. There is also a dump station. A metal building houses the office, laundry, and restrooms. Propane is sold and a dump station can be used by those not staying at the park for a fee. The campground is on the west side of US-180 about 45 miles north of Glenwood and 9 miles north of Reserve.

COTTONWOOD CAMPGROUND *(Open April 15 to Nov 15 - Varies)*

Information: (575) 539-2481
Location: 24 Miles N of Glenwood, *N 33° 37' 07", W 108° 53' 38", 5,800 Ft*

4 Sites – A gravel road under a forest of ponderosa pine and cottonwood trees provides access to 4 back-in camping sites in this small Gila National Forest campground. Sites are suitable for RVs to about 25 feet. Each site has a picnic table, a fire pit, and a raised barbecue grill. There is no water at the campground. The bathroom is a wheelchair accessible vault toilet. The campground is right off US-180 about 24 miles north of Glenwood and 13 miles south of Reserve.

GLENWOOD RV PARK *(Open All Year)*

Res and Info: (575) 539-2324
Location: Glenwood, *N 33° 19' 17", W 108° 52' 59", 4,700 Ft*

6 Sites – The Glenwood RV Park sits toward the northern entrance of Glenwood on the west side of the highway. It has six long back-in sites with full hookups. There are no restrooms so RVs must be self-contained and tenters cannot be accommodated. There are plans to expand this RV park over the next few years.

DOUBLE T RV PARK *(Open All Year)*

Res and Info: (575) 539-2812, www.doublethomestead.com
Location: 1 Mile E of Glenwood, *N 33° 19' 33", W 108° 52' 22", 4,700 Ft*

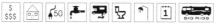

4 Sites – This is a pretty little campground on the road out to the Catwalk. There are only 4 sites and each site is a long pull-thru which can accommodate large RVs. The sites have a paved patio under a shelter, a picnic table, and a raised barbecue grill. Flowers are planted at the sites to provide some separation. The main building has 2 bathroom shower rooms and there are 1 and 2 bedroom guesthouses for rent as well as cabins. This is also a horse hotel with covered and uncovered stalls back behind the campground. The Little Whitewater Trail takes off from just across the road from the campground. From Glenwood drive east toward the Catwalk on SR-174. The campground is on the left in .7 miles.

CATWALK RV PARK *(Open All Year)*

Information: (575) 539-2329
Location: 2 Miles E of Glenwood, *N 33° 19' 49", W 108° 51' 47", 4,800 Ft*

10 Sites – This is a gravel lot with full hookup pull-thru camping spaces for 10 RVs. There are no picnic tables at the sites, but there is a small paved patio under a tree with a couple of dilapidated tables and a raised barbecue grill. There is no separation between the sites and no shade. Trees run along the edge of the gravel lot but there are none in the parking area. The sites are 35 feet long. This park is only suitable for self contained RVs because there are no restroom facilities. The park is not generally staffed and someone comes by in the evening to collect the fees.

BIGHORN CAMPGROUND *(Open All Year)*

Information: (575) 539-2481 or (505) 388-8201
Location: Glenwood, *N 33° 19' 22", W 108° 52' 57", 4,700 Ft*

5 Sites – Bighorn is a Gila National Forest campground. It's really more of a day use area along the highway just north of Glenwood but camping is allowed and there is room for five large RVs to parallel park next to picnic tables and fire pits. Tent camping is fine too. No potable water is available. There is a vault toilet and no other facilities.

TAOS

Taos (population about 7,000) has long been an important New Mexican town. The Taos Pueblo dates from the 1400s, the first Spanish mission here was established in 1598, the mountain men arrived in the 1700s, artists took up residence beginning in the early 1900s, and now there's even a ski resort. It's a blend of history, cultures, and people that makes Taos an interesting destination.

The **Taos Square** is the center of the action in town. There you'll find restaurants and galleries. On the surrounding streets are tourist destinations including the **Kit Carson Home and Museum**, the **Blumenschein Home and Museum**, the **Harwood Founda-**

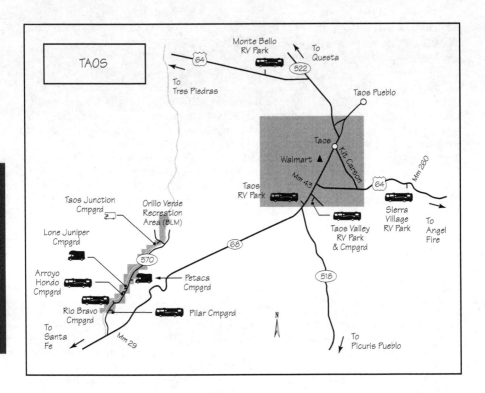

tion Museum, the **Governor Bent Museum**, and the **Van Vechten-Lineberry Taos Art Museum**.

The **Taos Ski Area** is considered a very challenging hill. It's located at 11,800 feet about 18 miles north of town. Many RVers use the RV parks in Taos as a base while skiing during the winter.

For a short drive you might go out to the bridge over the **Rio Grande Gorge**. It's on US-64 about 12 miles northwest of Taos. This is the second-highest suspension bridge in the US, the river is 650 feet below.

North of town about 10 miles, near the town of Arroyo Hondo on SR-522 is the **D H Lawrence Memorial**. Owned today by the University of New Mexico, the memorial is on the Kiowa Ranch where the writer lived for two years.

Just south of Taos in Ranchos de Taos you might want to visit the **San Francisco de Asis Church**. The striking design of this church was a popular subject for Georgia O'Keefe and other artists, it's just as popular today with many visiting photographers.

Probably the top destination in the area is the **Taos Pueblo** which is located just north of town. This adobe pueblo has been continuously occupied for about 1,000 years and is one of the very few original multistoried adobe complexes remaining. Only about 50 families live in the buildings today, there is no electricity or running water. However, the pueblo remains a center for ceremonies and most families live in more modern homes nearby. The Taos Pueblo also operates a casino, the **Taos Mountain Casino**, near the entrance to the pueblo. The San Geronimo Feast Days, September 29 and 30, are very popular with visitors. To visit the pueblo drive north from Taos for two miles. There is a parking area and entrance gate with restrooms, visitors can wander outside the two complexes without a guide after paying the entrance fee.

Picuris Pueblo is also near Taos. This pueblo is located in a high mountain valley along the high road between Santa Fe and Taos. The most popular attraction in the village is the **San Lorenzo Catholic Church** but Picuris also has a visitor center and museum as well as extensive adobe ruins. From Taos drive southeast into the mountains on SR-518 for 16 miles. Turn right onto SR-75 and drive another 7 miles to the pueblo.

If you are driving to Taos from Santa Fe there are two major routes, the high and low roads, and a number of attractions. See the Santa Fe section for more about these.

Along the low road, about 16 miles southwest of Taos, is the BLM's **Orilla Verde Recreation Area**. This recreation encompasses a pretty little section of the Rio Grande. It's a popular rafting area and there are a number of campgrounds here, they are described below. There's also a visitor center along SR-68 near the entrance to the area.

Taos Campgrounds

TAOS RV PARK *(Open All Year)*
> **Reservations:** (800) 323-6009, budhost@newmex.com
> **Information:** (575) 758-1667, www.taosbudgethost.com
> **Location:**   3 Miles S of Taos, *N 36° 21' 50", W 105° 36' 11", 6,900 Ft*

29 Sites – This campground is located in Ranchos de Taos which adjoins Taos to the south. The campground is a square gravel lot. There are 22 full hookup pull-thru sites, seven electricity and water sites which are all back-ins, and 1 teepee. The sites are about 40 feet in length. Each site has a blue or green picnic table, but there are no fire pits. The park has satellite TV which gives about 5 stations. Wi-Fi internet is provided for free in the office but won't reach most sites. There is also a data port available in the office for other internet access. There is a club house which has a television and a full kitchen. The park is affiliated with the Budget Host Inn which is next door. From Taos drive south on SR-68. The campground is right at the intersection with SR-518, about 3 miles south of Taos.

TAOS VALLEY RV PARK AND CAMPGROUND *(Open All Year)*
> **Reservations:** (800) 999-7571, camptaos@newmex.com
> **Information:** (575) 758-4469, www.taosnet.com/rv/
> **Location:**   3 Miles S of Taos, *N 36° 22' 11", W 105° 35' 33", 6,900 Ft*

92 Sites – The Taos Valley RV Park is the nicest of the parks in Taos. It's conveniently located south of town in Rancho de Taos. There are a combination of sites in the park including 35 sites with full hookups, 29 with electricity and water, and 28 with no utilities. Forty-six of the sites are pull-thrus, some to a length of 75 feet. About 20 of the sites have 50-amp power and the rest have 30 amps. The sites have picnic tables and a barbecue grill, no other fires are allowed. Some of the sites have A framed picnic shelters. There is no cable or internet access, but Wi-Fi is provided by an outside provider. A store with a few basic groceries and gift items and a lounge are in the main building which also houses the laundry and bathrooms. From Taos drive south on SR-68. Zero your odometer at

the intersection of SR-68 and US-64, turn left at .6 miles into Estes Rd. The campground is on the right in 350 yards.

⛟ MONTE BELLO RV PARK *(Open All Year)*

Res and Info: (575) 751-0774, www.taosmontebellorvpark.com, monte@taosnet.com
Location: 5 Miles NE of Taos, *N 36° 27' 38", W 105° 38' 11", 7,100 Ft*

23 Sites – The campground is set on an open plain northwest of Taos. There are 19 pull-thru sites to about 65 feet in length. Sixteen sites are full hookup and 3 have water and electricity only. There are also four tent sites which are on gravel pads near the back of the park. A picnic table is provided to each site, A covered picnic pavilion occupies the middle of the park. It has 2 barbecue grills and 2 picnic tables and is for all guests to use. A small swing set is available as a playground. The office also houses a convenience store which has a good selection of grocery items. The wheelchair accessible bathrooms are in the back of the office/store building. This is a simple campground, but has good facilities. From Taos head north on US-64 and stay on this highway as it forks to the west. You'll see the campground on the right about five miles northeast of town.

⛟ SIERRA VILLAGE RV PARK *(Open April 15 to Oct 15 - Varies)*

Res and Info: (575) 758-3660, kengreen@cybermesa.com
Location: 3 Miles E of Taos, *N 36° 22' 46", W 105° 30' 19", 7,500 Ft*

40 Sites – This park is set under trees beside the Rio Fernando de Taos River. The hillside to the south provides shade as do the trees. The park has 40 sites available to travelers in the summer. Seven of the spaces are pull-thrus and 10 spaces, including some back-ins, are as long as 54 feet. Twenty-one of the sites are full hookup and the others have electricity and water. There is a lodge building and 3 rental cabins. The park has satellite TV and Wi-Fi internet access is provided for no additional fee. There is also a phone line data port for other internet access. Reservations are taken by phone, but credit cards are not accepted. There is a nature trail which leaves from the camping area. From Taos head east on US-64. If you zero your odometer at the junction of US-64 with Kit Carson Rd you'll reach the campground at 2.9 miles.

⛟ ORILLA VERDE REC AREA – PILAR CAMPGROUND *(Open All Year)*

Information: (575) 751-4889
Location: 17 Miles SW of Taos, *N 36° 17' 08", W 105° 47' 10", 6,000 Ft*

9 Sites – This campground has 3 tent sites, 9 RV sites, and 2 day use sites on the far side of the road from the river. The sites are in an open lot with no trees for shade. The tent sites have covered picnic tables on a paved patio, a fire pit and a raised fire grill. The RV sites are pull-thru sites and some are to 60 feet in length. The RV sites have water and electric hookups, picnic tables, fire pits, and raised barbecue grills. There is a wheelchair accessible bathroom building which has flush toilets. Coin operated showers are located at the nearby Rio Bravo Campground. A boat launch is to the north at the Lone Juniper Recreation Site. Many hiking trails are accessible nearby including West Rim Trail, Petaca Point Trail, La Vista Verde Trail, and Las Minas Trail. There is a 14-day stay limit at the campground. A telephone is at the Visitor Center on Hwy 68. From a point 16 miles

southwest of Taos on SR-68 drive northwest on SR-570. The campground is on both sides of the road in 1.2 miles.

ORILLA VERDE REC AREA – RIO BRAVO CAMPGROUND *(Open All Year)*
Information: (575) 751-4889
Location: 18 Miles SW of Taos, *N 36° 17' 30", W 105° 46' 55", 6,000 Ft*

12 Sites – The sites in this camping area are back-in sites along the river under some shade trees. Eight of the sites are for tents with short parking spaces and there are 4 pull-thru RV sites to 70 feet in length. The tent sites have covered picnic tables on a paved patio, fire pits and raised barbecue grills The RV site have electricity and water at the sites, a picnic table, fire pit, and a raised barbecue grill. The restrooms have coin operated showers ($1 for 3 minutes). From a point 16 miles southwest of Taos on SR-68 drive northwest on SR-570. The campground is on the left in 1.7 miles.

ORILLA VERDE REC AREA – ARROYO HONDO CAMPGROUND *(Open All Year)*
Information: (575) 751-4889
Location: 18 Miles SW of Taos, *N 36° 17' 50", W 105° 46' 23", 6,000 Ft*

4 Sites – Because there is no water available, this campground is considered a primitive site and as such the price is only $5. There are 4 back-in sites along the river. One of these sites is about 50 feet long and can accommodate any size of RV. The other 3 sites are short and are suitable for RVs to about 25 feet. The sites have picnic tables and fire pits. There is a vault toilet. See the write-up above for Pilar Campground which describes other nearby facilities and hikes. From a point 16 miles southwest of Taos on SR-68 drive northwest on SR-570. The campground is on the left in 2.4 miles.

ORILLA VERDE REC AREA – LONE JUNIPER CAMPGROUND *(Open All Year)*
Information: (575) 751-4889
Location: 18 Miles SW of Taos, *N 36° 18' 01", W 105° 46' 19", 6,000 Ft*

1 Site – Here it is, the smallest campground listed in this guide. The 1 site in this small camping area sits in an open gravel lot between the road the river. The site is a back-in and suitable for a RV to 25 feet. There is a paved patio, picnic table, fire grill, and a raised barbecue pit at the site. There is also a vault toilet. There are a couple of day-use tables also available in the parking lot of this area. A boat launch and take-out is located just to the south of the site. See the write-up above for Pilar Campground which describes other nearby facilities and hikes. From a point 16 miles southwest of Taos on SR-68 drive northwest on SR-570. The campground is on the left in 2.6 miles.

ORILLA VERDE REC AREA – PETACA CAMPGROUND *(Open All Year)*
Information: (575) 751-4889
Location: 19 Miles SW of Taos, *N 36° 18' 27", W 105° 46' 00", 6,000 Ft*

5 Sites – This campground has 5 sheltered sites and a host site which has electricity. There is 1 site on the river side of the road and the other 4 and the host site are opposite

the river. The sites are about 25 feet long. All of the sites have a sheltered room, picnic table, fire pit ,and raised barbecue grill. The campground has vault toilets. See the write-up above for Pilar Campground which describes other nearby facilities and hikes. From a point 16 miles southwest of Taos on SR-68 drive northwest on SR-570. The campground is on both sides of the road in 3.2 miles.

TRUTH OR CONSEQUENCES

The town of Truth or Consequences (population about 7,000) was called Hot Springs until 1950. That year Ralph Edwards, creator of the radio program "Truth or Consequences" arranged with the town to change its name. It was a promotional opportunity for both Edwards and the town, and the town has outlasted the radio and television show.

The town was called Hot Springs because, of course, it has hot springs. Near the museum (see below) there's a spring said to have been used by Geronimo. Today there are **bath houses** in town, check with the Chamber of Commerce.

The town's museum is the **Geronimo Springs Museum**. You'll find out all about the name change but also a lot about the other history of the area including Indian pottery and minerals. **Callahan's Auto Museum** is also in T or C, it has cars from the 20s to the 60s.

The big attractions to this area are the two large reservoirs along the Rio Grande. **Elephant Lake** and **Caballo Lake** are huge draws with fishing and water sports. Each has

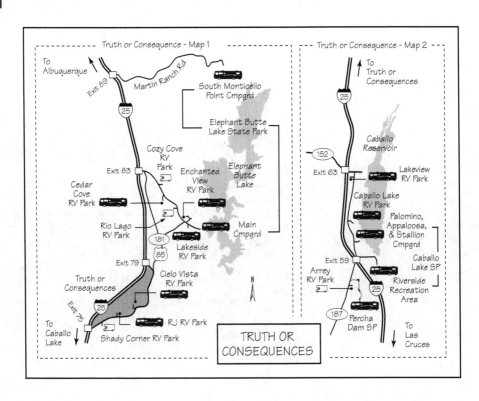

a state park with campgrounds, see the descriptions below for more information.

Campgrounds in the Truth or Consequences region are concentrated in three areas. There are a few parks, primarily snowbird parks, in town. North of town Elephant Butte State park has a number of camping areas, but also a cluster of snowbird campgrounds just west of the main entrance in the community of Elephant Butte. Finally, south of town near Caballo Lake there are both state and commercial campgrounds.

About 40 miles south of Truth or Consequences is the town of **Hatch**. The town is known as the chile-growing capital of the U.S. The big event here is a Chile Festival which is held on the Labor Day weekend.

Truth or Consequences Campgrounds

◆ CIELO VISTA RV PARK *(Open All Year)*
    Res and Info: (575) 894-3738, www.cielovistarvpark.com
    Location: Truth or Consequences, *N 33° 07' 39", W 107° 15' 43", 4,300 Ft*

72 Sites – The park is on the side of a hill and is terraced onto 3 levels. There are back-in and pull-thru sites to 58 feet. There is little separation between sites but there are some shade trees. Most sites have a small paved patio. The terraces are fenced with white picket fences. There is a phone and internet room with a computer data port and a courtesy phone which can be used for local and calling card calls. The sites have telephone available for extended stay guests which must be activated with the local phone company. There is a large recreation room with a banquet kitchen. Other amenities include a picnic and barbecue area, shuffleboard, horseshoes, and organized social activities. The campground is located right in T or C. From Exit 75 of I-25 drive east on Business I-25 (also called US-85 and Broadway) for 2.4 miles and turn left into the park entrance.

◆ RJ RV PARK *(Open All Year)*
    Res and Info: (575) 894-9777, www.newmexicorvparks.com, info@newmexicorvparks.com
    Location: Truth or Consequences, *N 33° 07' 21", W 107° 16' 36", 4,200 Ft*

47 Sites – This park has back-in and pull-through sites to 60 feet. All of the sites are full hookup (including cable TV) with 30 and 50 amp power. Most of the sites have cement patios and a picnic table. The park has a clubhouse with a kitchen, tables for group gatherings, and an outdoor patio. A data port for internet access is available in the clubhouse. The dump station may be used by RVers not staying at the park for $5. The campground is located right in T or C. From Exit 75 of I-25 drive east on Business I-25 (also called US-85 and Broadway) for 1.4 miles and turn left into the park entrance.

◆ ELEPHANT BUTTE LAKE STATE PARK – MAIN CAMPGROUND *(Open All Year)*
    Reservations: (877) NM-4-RSVP, www.nmparks.com
    Information: (575) 744-5421, (888) 667-2757, www.nmparks.com
    Location: 3.8 Miles NE of Truth or Consequences, *N 33° 10' 51", W 107° 12' 28", 4,400 Ft*

200 Sites and Scattered Boondocking – The main entrance to the park offers access to a number of campgrounds including some with full hookups, some with developed sites and no hookups, and also dispersed camping including beachfront camping area. There

are also swimming beaches, marinas and boat ramps. Easiest access is from Exit 83 of I-25. Follow SR-195 southeast for 4.3 miles to the entrance station.

ELEPHANT BUTTE LAKE STATE PARK – SOUTH MONTICELLO POINT CAMPGROUND *(Open All Year)*

Information: (575) 744-5421, (888) 667-2757, www.nmparks.com
Location: 18 Miles N of Truth or Consequences, *N 33° 17' 40", W 107° 11' 13", 4,500 Ft*

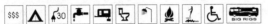

50 Sites – This campground is at the northern end of Elephant Butte Lake. The sites are off a big loop road (with 2 small loops off the main road near the lake). Some of the sites are very near the lake and have excellent views. The sites are about half pull-thrus and half back-ins. The pull-thrus are as long as 200 feet and the back-in can also accommodate the very largest RVs. All sites have electricity and water hookups, a level gravel parking pad, a sheltered picnic table on a paved patio, and a fire pit. In the middle of the park is restroom building with flush toilets and a shower and there are vault toilets on each end of the circle loop. A dump station is located to the left just as you enter the park. This is a perfect park for really large motorhomes. Access is from Exit 89 of I-25. Head east following signs to the campground, it's about 7 miles to the entrance.

CEDAR COVE RV PARK *(Open All Year)*

Res and Info: (575) 744-4472, www.cedarcovervpark.com, sheila@cedarcovervpark.com
Location: 5 Miles N of Truth or Consequences, *N 33° 11' 53", W 107° 14' 20", 4,500 Ft*

64 Sites – The sites here are in a very large gravel lot in an area away from any other development. Most sites are back-ins, with only 7 pull-thrus. There are plans to add 20 new sites which will all be pull-thrus. The sites are 50 feet long and there is plenty of room to exceed the site length so any size RV can be accommodated. All sites are full hookup. The pull-thru sites are divided by a line of rocks, other sites are slightly terraced or divided by a small rock wall. The park is only 5 years old so the trees are small. Wi-Fi is provided to the sites by an outside vendor for a fee. A data port and a courtesy phone are provided in the clubhouse which also has a kitchen and lounge area. There is a large covered patio with grill and picnic tables, restrooms are exceptionally nice. From Exit 83 of I-25 drive southeast on SR-195. In 1.8 miles turn right and you'll arrive at the park in another .4 mile.

ENCHANTED VIEW RV PARK *(Open All Year)*

Res and Info: (575) 744-5876, www.enchantedviewrv.com, enchantedviewrv@valornet.com
Location: 4 Miles N of Truth or Consequences, *N 33° 11' 16", W 107° 13' 12", 4,500 Ft*

37 Sites – This RV park is located in the Elephant Butte area near the main entrance to Elephant Butte State Park. The park is a dirt and gravel lot with mostly back-in (5 pull-thrus) parking in two rows. The sites are full hookups including cable TV. Most sites are to about 40 feet in length although a few reach 45 feet. There is no separation between the sites which are side by side parking. Wi-Fi is currently provided at no additional charge to about 1/2 of the park. There is also a data port in the clubhouse for other internet access and a courtesy phone is available for local and calling card calls. There is a deck on top of the clubhouse with a view of the lake and mountains. Other amenities include a covered

patio with barbecue grills and a new pool table and a card table in the clubhouse. Easiest access is from Exit 83 of I-25. Drive southeast on SR-195 for 3.3 miles, the RV park is to the left off Hawthorne Rd.

⊞ LAKESIDE RV PARK *(Open All Year)*

Reservations: (800) 808-5848, lakeside@riolink.com
Information: (575) 744-5996, (888) 667-2757, www.lakesiderv.com
Location: 4 Miles N of Truth or Consequences, *N 33° 10' 57", W 107° 13' 02", 4,500 Ft*

70 Sites – This RV park is also located in the Elephant Butte area near the entrance to the state park. Despite the name it is not along the side of the lake, or at least not very near it. There are 26 pull-thru sites to about 60 feet in length and the other sites are back-ins as long as 50 feet. The are two garden areas with sites which are very widely spaced and roomy. The Native Gardens section of the park has 9 big pull-thru sites set around a garden of cactus. The Desert Gardens has 19 very large widely spaced sites around a cactus garden. There is an extra $4 fee daily for sites in the garden areas. The other sides are terraced on the side of a slope behind the lounge. All sites are full hookup and cable is available at most sites for $2 daily. Wi-Fi is provided to the sites by an outside vendor for a fee. There is an activities lounge which has a data port, a courtesy phone, a television, an exchange library, and organized activities. There is also a covered patio with gas barbecue grills. Easiest access is from Exit 83 of I-25. Drive southeast on SR-195 for 3.6 miles, turn right on Country Club, and the park will be on your right.

⊞ CABALLO LAKE STATE PARK – PALOMINO, APPALOOSA,
AND STALLION CAMPGROUNDS *(Open All Year)*

Reservations: (877) NM-4-RSVP, www.nmparks.com
Information: (575) 743-3942, (888) 667-2757, www.emnrd.state.nm.us
Location: 19 Miles S of Truth or Consequences, *N 32° 54' 27", W 107° 18' 34", 4,200 Ft*

41 Sites plus Scattered Boondocking – There are three formal campgrounds here on the west side of the lake with a visitor center marking the entrance. Just to the north is the upper flats beach camping area which offers dispersed camping along the shore of the lake. Swimming is possible although there is no marked swimming beach. The formal camping areas offer large sites suitable for any RV; there are both full and partial-hookup sites. This area also has a dump station and a boat ramp. From Exit 59 off I-25 travel north on US-85 for .6 miles, the campground entrance is on the right.

⊞ CABALLO LAKE STATE PARK – RIVERSIDE RECREATION AREA *(Open All Year)*

Reservations: (877) NM-4-RSVP, www.nmparks.com
Information: (575) 743-3942, (888) 667-2757, www.nmparks.com
Location: 19 Miles S of Truth or Consequences, *N 32° 53' 39", W 107° 17' 36", 4,100 Ft*

19 Sites – Riverside Campground is located just below the dam. Sites here are also large, most are pull-thrus. These are water and electric sites, some with sewer. There is no dump station but there are flush toilets and a shower. There is another camping area with no utility hookups just above the dam as well as a rally campground just downstream from the Riverside Campground. From Exit 59 of I-25 drive directly east on the access road, in .6 mile the campground entrance is on the right.

PERCHA DAM STATE PARK *(Open All Year)*

Reservations: (877) NM-4-RSVP, www.nmparks.com
Information: (575) 743-3942, (888) 667-2757, www.nmparks.com
Location: 20 Miles S of Truth or Consequences, *N 32° 52' 08", W 107° 18' 21", 4,100 Ft*

50 Sites plus Scattered Boondocking – Little Percha Dam State Park is probably the nicest state park in the area although it does not offer much in the way of water sports since it's not on a lake. The dam here is a small one about two miles below the Caballo Lake Dam. This is a riparian area with trees, not an exposed area like the lakeshore campgrounds. The sites in this state park are off 2 loops. Straight as you enter the park is a loop with sites 1-30 which are all pull-thrus to a length of 50 feet. These sites all have electricity and water hookups and a covered picnic table on a paved patio. Some have a raised barbecue grill and others have a fire pit. At the entrance to this loop is a restroom building with flush toilets and hot showers. There is a visitors center with a telephone near the entrance. The second loop has 20 sites with no hookups. These sites have picnic tables, raised barbecue grills and rock fire rings. There are vault toilets in this section of the park. This park is popular for fishing in the Rio Grande and excellent bird watching. A dump station is available at nearby Caballo Lake State Park. From Exit 59 of I-25 travel south on SR-187. The campground entrance is on the left in 1.5 miles.

LAKEVIEW RV PARK *(Open All Year)*

Res and Info: (575) 743-2242, www.lakeview-rvpark.com, lakeview@zianet.com
Location: 14 Miles S of Truth or Consequences, *N 32° 57' 09", W 107° 18' 44", 4,300 Ft*

35 Sites – This park has 31 RV sites, 4 tent sites, and 2 rental cabins. The RV sites are set in 3 rows, 2 of them (18 sites) have pull-thrus while the back row has back-ins. The back-in sites are as long as 80 feet and the pull-thrus are about 70 feet. The back-in sites are used mostly by extended stay guests and the pull-thrus for short term. The back-ins have telephone lines which can be activated by the phone company. The sites are full hookup (no TV). There is no separation between sites but there are trees scattered around and between sites. A gas station and grocery store are run out of the front office. A data port is available in the office for internet access and a pay phone is outside. A good selection of groceries and propane is sold. RVers not staying at the campground are allowed to come in and dump for a fee of $10. There is some view of Lake Caballo from the park. The RV park is located just east of Exit 63 from I-25.

CABALLO LAKE RV PARK *(Open All Year)*

Res and Info: (575) 743-0502
Location: 17 Miles S of Truth or Consequences, *N 32° 55' 07", W 107° 19' 01", 4,300 Ft*

25 Sites – This small family-run campground has 18 pull-thru sites with full hookups. There are also 7 dry sites. The sites are 55 feet long by 35 feet wide. There are views from the campground sites of the mountains and the lake. Although there is no cable, good TV reception is available via a translator. There is a telephone data port in the owner's house for internet access and a courtesy phone for local or calling card calls. RVs must be totally self contained because there are no bathrooms or showers. The covered patio off the owners home is available for guests use. The park is 1/2 mile from a boat ramp on Ca-

ballo Lake. From I-25 at Exit 59 drive north on US-85 for 1.8 miles to the campground.

TUCUMCARI

Tucumcari (population 6,000) is a farming town located along I-40 in eastern New Mexico. It's a good place to spend the night if you're traveling the Interstate since towns along here are few and far between. Amarillo, Texas is about 100 miles to the east and Santa Rosa, New Mexico is about 55 miles to the west.

Tucumcari is a Route 66 town, the central east-west street is named Route 66 Blvd. When you drive through town you'll see that little seems to have changed since the 50s other than the addition of a somewhat faded looking K-Mart near the center of town. There are several Route 66 era motels and restaurants along the main drag, as well as souvenir shops.

The most interesting attraction in town is the **Mesalands Dinosaur Museum** with bronze castings of dinosaur bones. These castings are produced in the Mesalands Community College's own foundry. There's also a museum covering the local area, the **Tucumcari Historical Museum**. Located in an old schoolhouse, it's billed as a museum filled with old stuff, an accurate description.

The **Conchas Dam and Reservoir** on the Canadian River about 30 miles northwest of town is the source of irrigation water used in the area. Finished in 1940 it is a recreational

NEW MEXICO

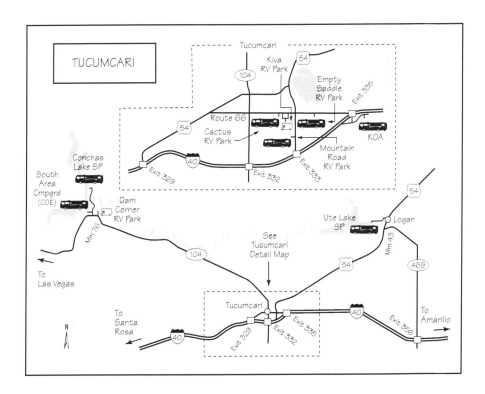

attraction too. The lake is 25 miles long and has 60 miles of shoreline. The Conchas Lake State Park provides boat launch and marina facilities a well as camping (see below). Recreational opportunities include swimming, water sports, and fishing for warm water species including walleye, black bass, channel catfish, bluegill, and crappie.

A second reservoir, **Ute Lake**, also provides recreational opportunities. It too hosts a state park, the Ute Lake State Park with camping facilities, see below. This is a long, narrow lake – 13 miles long and less than a mile wide. It's a popular fishing lake with walleye the main attraction, but there are also black bass, crappie, bluegill and channel catfish. Water sports are popular too, including windsurfing in the spring. Ute Lake is located about 20 miles northeast of Tucumcari.

Tucumcari Campgrounds

MOUNTAIN ROAD RV PARK *(Open All Year)*

Res and Info: (575) 461-9628
Location: Tucumcari, *N 35° 09' 44", W 103° 42' 09", 4,100 Ft*

60 Sites – The Mountain Road has full-hookup sites including pull-thrus to 60 feet. This campground has restrooms and showers as well as a data port for internet access. From I-40 take Exit 333 and drive north, the campground is on the left in .4 mile.

CACTUS RV PARK *(Open All Year)*

Information: (575) 461-2501
Location: Tucumcari, *N 35° 10' 17", W 103° 42' 37", 4,000 Ft*

44 Sites – The Cactus has pull-thru sites to 90 feet. This is an older park with trees that provide a bit of shade, a good choice if you want a convenient location with hookups. The RV park is on the south side of Route 66 Blvd as it passes through the center of Tucumcari. From Exit 335 of I-40 drive west on Route 66 Blvd, in 2 miles the campground is on the left.

EMPTY SADDLE RV PARK *(Open All Year)*

Res and Info: (575) 461-8623, www.emptysaddlerv.com, camp@emptysaddlerv.com
Location: Tucumcari, *N 35° 10' 18", W 103° 41' 37", 3,900 Ft*

35 Sites – The Empty Saddle is another Tucumcari campground with no restrooms. This one is a fairly new park with little in the way of shade. It's located just east of town off Route 66 Blvd. From Exit 335 of I-40 drive west on Route 66 Blvd, in one mile the campground is on the left.

KOA OF TUCUMCARI *(Open All Year)*

Reservations: (800) 562-1871, www.koa.com
Information: (575) 461-1841, tuckoa@direcway.com
Location: 2 Miles E of Tucumcari, *N 35° 10' 17", W 103° 40' 00", 4,000 Ft*

111 Sites – The KOA in Tucumcari offers the best camping facilities in town. There are tent sites as well as back-in and pull-thru RV sites to 70 feet. The campground also has a swimming pool. There is a data port in the office. The KOA is not as near town as the other campgrounds since it's on the far side of I-40 about two miles east of town. Take Exit 335 from I-40 and then follow the access road on the south side of the freeway toward the east for a half mile to the campground.

UTE LAKE STATE PARK *(Open All Year)*

Reservations: (877) NM-4-RSVP, www.nmparks.com
Information: (575) 487-2284, (888) 667-2757, www.nmparks.com
Location: 25 Miles NE of Tucumcari, *N 35° 21' 35", W 103° 27' 03", 3,800 Ft*

174 Sites – Ute Lake State Park has 5 camping areas. On the south shore of the lake are Mine Canyon Campground and South Area Campground, both have primitive camping with a few picnic shelters ($8). On the north shore of the park are 3 camping areas: North Area Campgrounds, Windy Point, and Logan Park Marina. The park headquarters and visitor center is at the North Campgrounds area. Sites here include nice tent sites as well as back-in and pull-thru RV sites to 200 feet with electric and water hookups. There is also a dump station and a boat ramp. Logan Park Marina has both water and electric sites and no-hookup sites (and a boat ramp) and Windy Point Campground has only primitive camping. In all there are 76 primitive and 98 developed sites at the park, something for everyone. From Tucumcari drive north on US-54 for 23 miles to the town of Logan. In the center of town head west on SR-540, you'll reach the entrance for the North Campgrounds in 2.3 miles.

CONCHAS LAKE STATE PARK *(Open All Year)*

Reservations: (877) NM-4-RSVP, www.nmparks.com
Information: (575) 868-2270, (888) 667-2757, www.nmparks.com
Location: 34 Miles NW of Tucumcari, *N 35° 25' 30", W 104° 11' 10", 4,200 Ft*

215 Sites – Camp sites are in two areas, the North Recreation Area and the Central Recreation Area. The North area has 3 campgrounds. Bell Campground has 33 sites with electric and water hookups, mostly back-ins with a few pull-thrus. North Campground has 29 sites with water, seven of them have electricity, sites are both pull-thrus and back-ins. Most sites will take RVs to 35 feet and a few to 45 feet (but note the weight restriction below). The nearby Cove Campgrounds has 10 developed sites and dispersed camping right on the water. Each of these campgrounds has a restroom with flush toilets and showers. The Central Recreation Area has 30 developed sites with no utilities and many primitive (dispersed) sites. Vault toilets are available. Total sites at the SP equal 112 primitive and 103 developed. The Tackle Box Lounge (and restaurant) is near the North Campground. Vehicle size in the North Recreation Area is limited by weight restriction on the dam which you must cross to get to the area, there is a 12 tons per axle or 15 ton maximum limit. To reach the campground start in Tucumcari and drive northwest on SR-104 for 30 miles. Turn right onto SR-433 at the sign for Conchas Lake State Park. The road will lead you north past the turnoff for the Central Recreation Area, across the dam, past the Corps of Engineers offices, to the North Recreation Area visitor center and campgrounds, a distance of about 4 miles.

CONCHAS LAKE – SOUTH AREA CAMPGROUND *(Open All Year)*
Information: (575) 868-2221, (505) 342-3601, http://corpslakes.usace.army.mil/visitors/
Location: 31 Miles NW of Tucumcari, *N 35° 22' 36", W 104° 11' 41", 4,100 Ft*

20 Sites – This campground is administered by the Corps of Engineers, it's not part of the state park. At one time this was a larger camping area and the back row of sites (away from the lake) even had electricity. Now there is one loop open with a total of 20 sites. The sites are all long but not necessarily flat. All of the sites have an adobe covered picnic table and a fire pit and each site has water at the site. There are no bathroom facilities except several portable toilets scattered around the camp area. There is a host at the campground. A boat ramp is near the campground and also a public golf course across the road. From Tucumcari drive northwest on SR-104 for 30 miles. Turn right onto SR-433 at the sign for the Conchas Lake State Park. Then, in just .2 mile, turn left into Lodge Road. The campground entrance is on the right in .7 mile.

NEW MEXICO

Information Resources

See our Internet site at www.rollinghomes.com for Internet information links.

State of Arizona

New Mexico Tourism Department, (800) 733-6396

Alamogordo

Alamogordo Visitor Center, 1301 N White Sands Blvd., Alamogordo, NM 88311; (575) 437-6120, (800) 826-0294

New Mexico Museum of Space History, Top of Hwy 2001, Alamogordo, NM 88310; (575) 437-2840, (877) 333-6589

Three Rivers Petroglyph National Recreation Area, (575) 525-4300

Valley of Fires BLM Recreation Area, (575) 648-2241

White Sands Museum and Missile Park, White Sands Missile Range, New Mexico 88002; (575) 678-8824

White Sands National Monument, PO Box 1086, Holloman Air Force Base, NM 88330; (575) 679-2599

Albuquerque

Ácoma Pueblo, Sky City Tours, (800) 747-0181, (505) 469-1052

Albuquerque Convention and Visitors Bureau, 20 First Plaza (PO Box 26866) , Albuquerque, NM 87125; (505) 842-9918, (800) 284-2282, (800) 733-9918

Albuquerque Museum, 2000 Mountain Rd NW, Albuquerque, NM 87104; (505) 243-7255

Anderson-Abruzzo Albuquerque International Balloon Museum, 9201 Balloon Museum Drive NE, Albuquerque, NM 87113; (505) 768-6020

Bien Mur Market Center, 100 Bien Mur Drive NE, Albuquerque, NM 87113; (505) 821-5400, (800) 365-5400

Coronado State Monument, 485 Kuaua Rd Bernalillo, NM 87004; (505) 867-5351

Indian Pueblo Cultural Center, 2401 12th Street NW, Albuquerque, NM 87104; (505) 843-7270

Museum of Archeology and Material Culture, 22 Calvary Road, Cedar Crest, NM 87008; (505) 281-4745

New Mexico Museum of Natural History and Science, 1801 Mountain Road NW, Albuquerque, NM 87104; (505) 841-2800

Petroglyph National Monument, (505) 899-0205

Sandia Peak Ski and Tramway, #10 Tramway Loop NE, Albuquerque, NM 87122: (505) 856-7325

Tent Rocks National Monument, (505) 761-8700

Tinkertown, 121 Sandia Crest Road, Sandia Park, NM 87047; (505) 281-5233

Big Bend

Big Bend Chamber of Commerce, PO Box 607, Terlingua, TX, 79852;

Big Bend National Park, PO Box 129, Big Bend National Park, Texas, 79834; (432) 477-2251

Marathon Chamber of Commerce, Front Street Books, 105 Hwy. 90 W, Marathon, TX 79842: (432) 386-4516

Carlsbad

Carlsbad Caverns National Park, 3225 National Parks Hwy., Carlsbad, NM 88220; (575) 785-2232 or (800) 967-2283

Carlsbad Chamber of Commerce, 302 S Canal St, Carlsbad, NM 88220; (575) 887-6516 or (800) 221-1224

Living Desert Zoo and Gardens State Park, (575) 887-5516

Chama

Chama Valley Chamber of Commerce, 2291 Main St, PO Box 306, Chama, NM 87520; (575) 756-2306, (800) 477-0149

Cumbres & Toltec Scenic Railroad, PO Box 789, Chama, NM 87520; (575) 756-2151, (888) 286-2737

New Mexico Welcome Center, At the Y coming into town; (575) 756-2235

Cimarron

Cimarron Chamber of Commerce, 104 North Lincoln Ave, PO Box 604, Cimarron, NM 87714; (575) 376-2417

Cloudcroft

Cloudcroft Chamber of Commerce, Box 1290, Cloudcroft, NM 88317; (866) 874-4447, (575) 682-2733

Sacramento National Forest Ranger Station, 61 Curlew Ave, Cloudcroft, NM; (575) 682-2551

Sunspot Visitor Center and Museum, (575) 434-7190

Clovis and Portales

Blackwater Draw Museum, 42987 Hwy 70, Portales, NM 88130; (575) 562-2202

Clovis Depot Model Train Museum, 221 W 1st Street, Clovis, NM 88101; (575) 762-0066

Eastern New Mexico University Natural History Museum, (575) 562-2723

Eastern New Mexico University Miles Mineral Museum, (575) 562-2651

Roosevelt County Historical Museum, (575) 562-2592

Davis Mountains

Alpine Visitor Bureau, 106 N 3rd St., Alpine, TX 79830; (800) 837 2326, (432) 837-2326

Chihuahuan Desert Nature Center and Botanical Gardens, Box 905, Fort Davis, TX 79734: (432) 364-2499

Chinati Foundation,(432) 729-4362

Fort Davis Chamber of Commerce, Town Square, Fort Davis, TX 79734: (800) 524 3015, (432) 426 3015

NEW MEXICO

Fort Davis National Historic Site, PO Box 1379, Fort Davis, TX 79734: (432) 426-3224
Marfa Chamber of Commerce, 207 N Highland, Marfa, TX 79834; (432) 729-4942
McDonald Observatory, Visitors Information Center, PO Box 1337, Fort Davis, TX 79734: (432) 426-3640
Museum of the Big Bend, Box C-101, Alpine, TX 79832: (432) 837-8143

Deming and Columbus
Deming Chamber of Commerce, 800 E Pine St, Deming, NM 88030; (575) 546-2674
Deming Luna Mimbres Museum, 301 South Silver, Deming, NM 88030; (575) 546-2382

El Malpais and El Moro National Monuments
Bandera Ice Caves, 1200 Ice Caves Rd, Grants, NM 87020; (888) ICE-CAVE
El Malpais National Monument, (505) 783-4774
El Morro National Monument, (505) 783-4226

El Paso
Centennial Museum, University of Texas at El Paso, El Paso, TX 79968; (915) 747-5565
El Paso Zoo, 4001 E Paisano, El Paso, TX 79905; (915) 521-1850
Mission Trail Association, 1 Civic Center Plaza, El Paso, TX 79901; (915) 534-0630
Museum of Archeology at Wilderness Park, 4301 Transmountain Road, El Paso, TX 79924; (915) 755-4332
War Eagles Air Museum, 8012 Airport Rd., Santa Teresa, NM 88008; (575) 589-2000

Enchanted Circle
Angel Fire Chamber of Commerce, Centro Plaza, Hwy 434, PO Box 547, Angel Fire, NM 87710; (575) 377-6661
Eagle Nest Chamber of Commerce, 54 West Therma Dr, PO Box 322, Eagle Nest, NM 87718; (575) 377-2420
Red River Chamber of Commerce, PO Box 870, Red River, NM 87558; (575) 754-2366, (800) 348-6444

Farmington
Aztec Chamber of Commerce, (505) 334-9551
Aztec Ruins National Monument, SR-516 #84, Aztec, NM 87410; (505) 334-6174.
B-Square Ranch and Bolack Museums, (505) 325-4275
Bloomfield Chamber of Commerce, (505) 632-0880
Farmington Convention and Visitor's Bureau, (800) 448-1240 or (575) 326-7602
Farmington Museum and Visitor Center, 3041 E Main St, Farmington, NM; (575) 326-7602
Salmon Ruins and Heritage Park, PO Box 125, Bloomfield, NM 87413; (505) 632-2013

Fort Sumner
Fort Sumner Chamber of Commerce, 707 N 4th St, Fort Sumner, NM 88119; (575) 355-7705
Fort Sumner State Monument, (575) 355-2573
Old Fort Sumner Museum, (575) 355-2942

Gallup
Gallup Cultural Center, 201 East Highway 66, Gallup, NM 87301; (505) 863-4131
Gallup Visitor's Bureau, 701 Montoya Blvd, Gallup, NM 87301; (505) 863-3841, (800) 242-4282

Gila Cliff Dwellings National Monument
Gila Cliff Dwellings National Monument, (575) 536-9461

Grants

Dinamations Discovery Museum, (505) 876-6999

Grants Chamber of Commerce, 100 Iron Street, Grants, NM; (505) 287-4802

New Mexico Mining Museum, (505) 287-4802

Guadalupe Mountains National Park

Guadalupe Mountains National Park, Main Visitor Center, (915) 828-3251

Jemez Mountain Trail Scenic Byway and Bandelier National Monument

Bandelier National Monument, (505) 672-3861, Extension 517

Bradbury Science Hall, 15th St & Central, Los Alamos, NM 87545; 505 667-4444

Los Alamos Historical Museum, 1921 Juniper Street, Los Alamos, NM 87544; (505) 662-4493

Walatowa Visitor Center, 7413 Hwy 4, Jemez Pueblo, New Mexico 87024; (575) 834-7235

Las Cruces

Branigan Cultural Center, 500 N Water Street, Las Cruces, NM 88004; (575) 541-2155

City of Las Cruces Log Cabin Museum, 671 Main Street, Las Cruces, NM 88004; (575) 541-2155

Las Cruces Chamber of Commerce, 760 W Picacho Ave, Las Cruces, NM 88005; (575) 524-1968

Las Cruces Convention and Visitor Bureau, 211 N Water, Las Cruces, NM 88004; (575) 541-2444, (800) 343-7827

Las Cruces Museum of Fine Arts, 490 N Water Street, Las Cruces, NM 88004; (575) 541-2137

Las Vegas

Las Vegas/San Miguel County Chamber of Commerce, 701 Grand Ave, PO Box 128, Las Vegas, NM 87701; (505) 425-8631

Lordsburg

Lordsburg Chamber of Commerce, 117 E 2nd St, Lordsburg, NM 88045; (575) 542-9864

New Mexico Welcome Center, Exit 20 from I-10; (575) 542-8149

Stein's Railroad Ghost Town, Box 2185, Roadforks, NM 88045; (575) 542-9791

Mesa Verde National Park and Cortez

Anasazi Heritage Center, 27501 Highway 184, Dolores, CO 81323; (970) 882-5600

Canyons of the Ancients National Monument, (970) 562-4282

Colorado University Center Museum, 25 N Market St, Cortez, CO 81323, (970) 565-1151

Colorado Welcome Center, 928 E Main St, Cortez, CO 81323; (970) 565-4048

Mesa Verde National Park, (970) 529-4461

Mora Valley and SR-518 to Taos

Mora Valley Chamber of Commerce, Route 518, PO Box 800, Mora, NM 87732; (505) 387-6072

Raton

Capulin Volcano National Monument, (575) 278-2201

Raton Tourist Information Center, 100 Clay Rd, PO Box 1211, Raton, NM 87740; (575) 445-8242

Raton Museum, 216 S 1st St, Raton, NM 87740; (575) 445-8979

NRA Whittington Center, PO Box 700, Raton, NM 87740; (575) 445-3615

Roswell

Hispano Chamber and Visitors Bureau, 426 N Main St, Roswell, NM 88203; (575) 624-0889

International UFO Museum and Research Center, 114 N Main St, Roswell, NM 88203; (575) 625-9495

Roswell Museum & Art Center & Goddard Planetarium, 100 W 11th St, Roswell, NM 88203; (575) 627-6744

Ruidoso

Ruidoso Chamber of Commerce, 720 Sudderth Dr, Box 698, Ruidoso, NM 88355; (575) 257-7395, (800) 253-2255

Hubbard Museum of the American West, 841 Hwy 70 West, Ruidoso Downs, NM 88346; (575) 378-4142

Mescalero Apache Cultural Center Museum, PO Box 176, Mescalero, NM 88340; (575) 671-4495

Ruidoso Downs Racetrack, 1461 Highway 70 East, Ruidoso Downs, NM 88346; (575) 378-4431

Salinas Pueblo Missions National Monument

Salinas Pueblo Missions National Monument, Visitor Center: Shaffer Hotel, Corner of Broadway & Ripley, Mountainair, NM 87036; (505) 847-2585

Santa Fe

El Rancho de las Golondrinas, 334 Los Pinos Road, Santa Fe, NM 87507; (505) 471-2261

Georgia O'Keefe Museum, 217 Johnson St, Santa Fe, NM 87501; (505) 946-1000

Institute of American Indian Arts Museum, 108 Cathedral Pl, Santa Fe, NM 87501; (505) 988-6281

Museum of Fine Arts, 107 W Palace Ave, Santa Fe, NM 87501; (505) 476-5072

Museum of Indian Arts and Culture 710 Camino Lejo, Santa Fe, NM 87505; (505) 982-5057

Museum of International Folk Art, Camino Lejo off Old Santa Fe Trail, Box 2087, Santa Fe, NM 87504; (505) 476-1200

Oke Oweenge Crafts Cooperative, (505) 852-2372

Palace of the Governors, 105 West Palace Ave, Box 2087, Santa Fe, NM 87504; (505) 476-5100

Poeh Cultural Center, (575) 455-3334

Puye Cliff Dwellings, 505-753-7326

Santa Fe Convention Center and Visitors Bureau, 201 W Marcy St, Santa Fe, NM 87501; (505) 955-6200, (800) 777-2489

Santa Rosa

Santa Rosa Chamber of Commerce, 486 Historic Route 66, Santa Rosa, NM 88435; (575) 472-3404

Route 66 Auto Museum, 2766 Old Route 66, Santa Rosa, NM 88435, (575) 472-1966

Silver City

Silver City Chamber of Commerce, 201 N Hudson St, Silver City, NM 88061; (575) 538-3785

Silver City Museum, 312 W Broadway, Silver City, NM 88061; (575) 538-5921

Western New Mexico University Museum, WNMU Campus; (575) 538-6386

Socorro

Bosque del Apache National Wildlife Refuge, PO Box 1246, Socorro, NM 87801; (575) 835-1828

Socorro Chamber of Commerce, (575) 835-0424

Mineral Museum at New Mexico Institute of Mining and Technology, (575) 835-5420

Very Large Array National Radio Astronomy Observatory (VLA), PO Box 0, Socorro, NM 87801; (575) 835-7243

White Sands Missile Range Public Affairs Office, (575) 678-1134 or (575) 678-1700

Southwest New Mexico National Forest Route

Whitewater Canyon Catwalk Trail, (575) 539-2481

Taos

Kit Carson Home and Museum, 113 Kit Carson Rd, Taos, NM; (575) 758-4741

Blumenschein Home and Museum, 222 Ledoux St, Taos, NM 87571; (575) 758-0505

Harwood Foundation Museum, 238 Ledoux St, Taos, NM 87571; (575) 758-9826

Governor Bent Museum, 117 Bent St, Taos, NM, 87571; (575) 758-2376

Van Vechten-Lineberry Taos Art Museum, 501 Paseo del Pueblo Norte, Taos, NM 87571; (575) 758-2690

Orilla Verde Recreation Area, (575) 758-4060

Truth or Consequences

Callahan's Auto Museum, 410 Cedar St, Truth or Consequences, NM 87901; (575) 894-6900

Geronimo Springs Museum, 325 Main St, Truth or Consequences, NM 87901; (575) 894-6600

Truth or Consequences Chamber of Commerce, 201 Foch St, Truth or Consequences, NM 87901; (575) 894-3536

Tucumcari

Tucumcari Chamber of Commerce, 404 W Tucumcari Blvd, PO Drawer E, Tucumcari, NM 88401; (575) 461-1694

Tucumcari Historical Museum, 416 S Adams Street, Tucumcari, NM 88401; (575) 461-4201

Mesalands Dinosaur Museum, 222 E Laughlin St, Tucumcari, NM 88401; (575) 461-3466

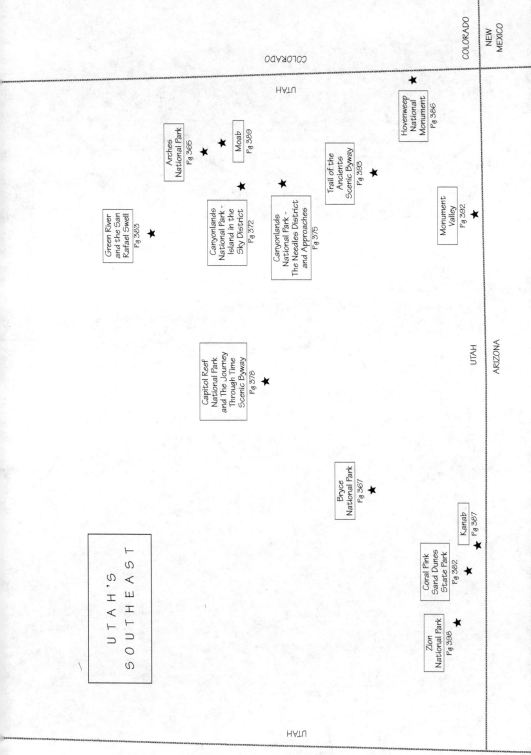

UTAH'S
SOUTHEAST

Zion
National Park
Pg 398

Coral Pink
Sand Dunes
State Park
Pg 382

Kanab
Pg 387

Bryce
National Park
Pg 367

Capitol Reef
National Park
and The Journey
Through Time
Scenic Byway
Pg 378

Green River
and the San
Rafael Swell
Pg 383

Arches
National Park
Pg 365

Moab
Pg 369

Canyonlands
National Park -
Island in the
Sky District
Pg 372

Canyonlands
National Park -
The Needles District
and Approaches
Pg 375

Trail of the
Ancients
Scenic Byway
Pg 393

Monument
Valley
Pg 392

Hovenweep
National
Monument
Pg 386

UTAH

COLORADO

COLORADO

NEW
MEXICO

UTAH

ARIZONA

NEVADA

UTAH

Chapter 6

Utah

The southeast quarter of Utah is one of the most scenic camping and RVing destinations in the entire country. It's an area where the geology reaches out and grabs you, not to be ignored. The State of Utah calls this area "Canyonlands", it's an appropriate name.

It helps to visualize this area as two north-south corridors. Travel east-west between the corridors can be tough, the canyons of the Colorado and Green rivers don't afford many crossing points and the sparse population means that there just don't have to be a lot of roads.

The easternmost corridor runs from Green River in the north on I-70 down to Monument Valley in the south on the Arizona – Utah border. In this chapter we've organized the stops along the way into the following destination descriptions: ● *Green River and the San Rafael Swell*, ● *Canyonlands National Park – Island In the Sky District*, ● *Arches National Park*, ● *Moab*, ● *Canyonlands National Park – The Needles District and Approaches*, ● *Trail of the Ancients Scenic Byway*, and ● *Hovenweep National Monument*.

The westernmost corridor runs from the area of Capitol Reef National Park in the north to the town of Kanab in the south. We've organized the route into the following sections: ● *Capitol Reef National Park and The Journey Through Time Scenic Byway*, ● *Bryce National Park*, ● *Zion National Park*, ● *Coral Pink Sand Dunes State Park*, and ● *Kanab*.

GOVERNMENT LANDS AND THEIR CAMPGROUNDS

Federal Campgrounds

In this part of Utah it's hard to ignore the national parks. There are 5 of them: Arches,

Bryce, Canyonlands, Capitol Reef, and Zion. All have campgrounds for vehicle campers, but not nearly enough for the summer crowds. Few of these in-park campgrounds offer hookups. Virtually all of the vehicle-accessible national park campgrounds in this area are described in this book, and so are alternative commercial and government campgrounds that are convenient to the parks. The National Park Service also runs campgrounds in national monuments, we've described the campgrounds in Natural Bridges and Hovenweep National Monuments too.

One national monument not run by the park service is the new Grand Staircase – Escalante National Monument. This large new monument is administered by the Bureau of Land Management. Formal campgrounds in the monument are scarce, but Calf Creek Recreation Area, which you'll find in our • *Capitol Reef National Park and The Journey Through Time Scenic Byway* section, is one of them. The BLM more commonly supervises land outside monuments. We've described additional BLM campgrounds in our • *Canyonlands National Park – Island in the Sky District,* • *Canyonlands National Park – The Needles District and Approaches,* • *Coral Pink Sand Dunes State Park,* • *Moab,* and • *Trail of the Ancients Scenic Byway* sections.

Finally, there are the national forests. You'll find national forest campgrounds listed in this book in these sections: • *Bryce National Park* (Dixie National Forest), • *Capitol Reef National Park and The Journey Through Time Scenic Byway* (Dixie National Forest), and • *Canyonlands National Park – The Needles District and Approaches* (Manti-La Sal National Forest).

Utah State Campgrounds

The state of Utah has only nine state parks with campgrounds in the area covered by this book. We've described all of them: Coral Pink Sand Dunes, Dead Horse Point, Escalante, Goblin Valley, Huntington, Goosenecks, Green River, Kodachrome, and Millsite. You can use the map below to find them.

Very few Utah state campgrounds have electrical hookups. In this area of the state only

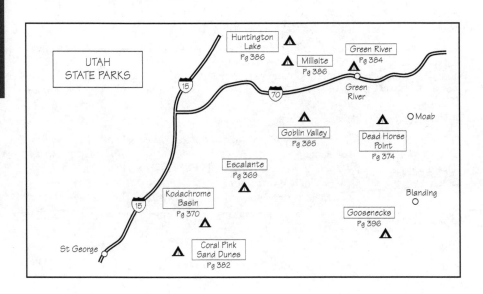

A FANTASTIC VIEW FROM GOOSNECKS STATE PARK

Dead Horse Point does, and these shelter-mounted electrical outlets seem more optimized for recharging a cell phone than hooking up an RV. All do have flush toilets however, as well as showers and dump stations.

Reservations are accepted at all Utah state parks listed in the book. You can make them by phone, call (801) 322-3770 if you're in Salt Lake City or (800) 322-3770 from anywhere else. You can also make them on the internet, go to www.stateparks.utah.gov and follow the Reservation link. Reservations can be made from 3 to 120 days in advance and a $8 fee is charged for each site reserved.

DESTINATIONS AND THEIR CAMPGROUNDS

ARCHES NATIONAL PARK

Arches National Park has the largest collection of natural arches in the world. It's a relatively small national park, the area is only 116 square miles, but there are close to 2,000 arches. Many are small, but there are also many spectacular ones.

The park has only 21 miles of roadway and one campground (see below). It tends to be crowded. If at all possible use a small vehicle to visit the park. The few people you'll see in RVs won't be enjoying themselves, parking is very tight and you'll want to park and take the short hikes out to the various arches near the road.

As you enter the park, just five miles north of Moab, you'll first come to the visitor center. Then the road climbs steeply. In 9 miles you'll reach a junction near Balanced Rock. To the right is the Windows Section, this road goes out 2.5 miles. Ahead the main road leads another 10 miles north to Devil's Garden and the campground.

Along all of the paved roads in the campground there are many pull-outs and short stub roads leading to parking spots and short hikes to see arches. Most you can see from the parking lot so you'll know whether you want to hike out or not. There are terrific photographic opportunities here.

Although there is only one campground in the park the camping possibilities outside it nearby are endless. Take a look at the following sections: *Canyonlands National Park – Island in the Sky District* and *Moab*.

Arches National Park Campground

DEVIL'S GARDEN CAMPGROUND *(Open All Year)*

Reservations: (877) 444-6777, www.recreation.gov
Information: (435) 719-2299, www.nps.gov/arch
Location: 18 Miles Inside Park Entrance, *N 38° 46' 48.8", W 109° 35' 26.5", 5,100 Ft*

52 Sites – Arches has only one campground, it is very popular. About half the sites can be reserved during the summer so if you don't have a reservation you'll want to arrive early at the visitor center, they start assigning campsites at 7:30 am. Sites are paved with fire grates and picnic tables and there are both back-ins and pull-thrus. There are flush toilets but no showers. Drinking water is available but filling RV tanks is not allowed

HIKING FROM THE CAMPGROUND IN ARCHES NATIONAL PARK

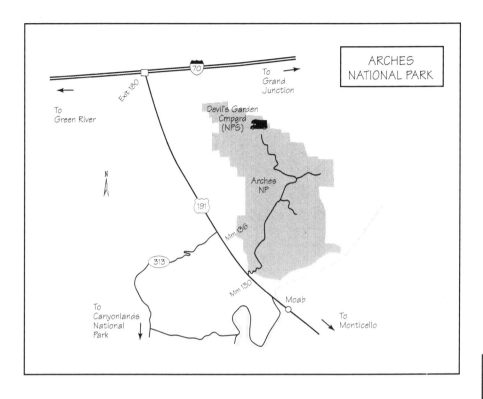

since water is scarce. Park regulations allow RVs to 30 feet although some sites would take longer ones. There is an addition al $9 charge for reservations. Follow the park road for 18 miles from the entrance station to the campground entrance.

BRYCE NATIONAL PARK

Bryce is one of the relatively small national parks. An 18-mile park road runs a bit inland from the lip of a cliff. Spur roads out the cliff let you overlook what is called the Pink Cliffs Formation. Really it's the uppermost of a series of cliff-like formations that run down to the north rim of the Grand Canyon. Most of the lower ones are inside the Grand Staircase-Escalante National Monument and form a staircase, hence the name of the monument.

Because there's just that one road this park can get very crowded in summer. There is a shuttle bus system in effect from early May until the end of September, busses run the entire length of the park road and are a great way to get around. The shuttle is voluntary and has been very effective in keeping the parking problems at the overlooks manageable. There are large lots outside the park and the busses run from these.

The altitude at Bryce is high and for that reason winter is cold. From November to April there is normally snow on the ground. Most park roads are plowed and one of the park campgrounds remains open all winter long. In summer the campgrounds inside the park fill early in the day. There are a number of campgrounds outside the park so it isn't necessary to camp inside. A selection of them is listed below.

Bryce National Park Campgrounds

🚐 **BRYCE CAMPGROUND NORTH** *(Open All Year)*
Reservations: (877) 444-6777, www.recreation.gov
Information: (435) 834-5322, www.nps.gov/brca, brca_reception_area@nps.gov
Location: Bryce National Park, *N 37° 38' 14", W 112° 10' 08", 7,900 Ft*

107 Sites – North Campground is the main campground for the park and the only one remaining open in winter. Reservations are only taken for the period from May 15 to September 30 and only about a third of the sites can be reserved. Sites are back-ins and pull-thrus off paved loops and have fire pits and picnic tables. There are no hookups. There are four loops. A and B have the largest sites, they're not huge but some will take RVs to 40 feet. Loops C and D are limited to vehicles under 20 feet so they are good for tent campers, particularly since generator use is not allowed on these loops. Near the camping area is a services area with general store, laundry, showers, telephone, campfire circle and dump station. The reservation fee is an additional $9 per site. The campground is just past the entrance to the park on the east side of the highway almost across from the entrance visitor center. The campground shuttle services the campground making getting around the park easy.

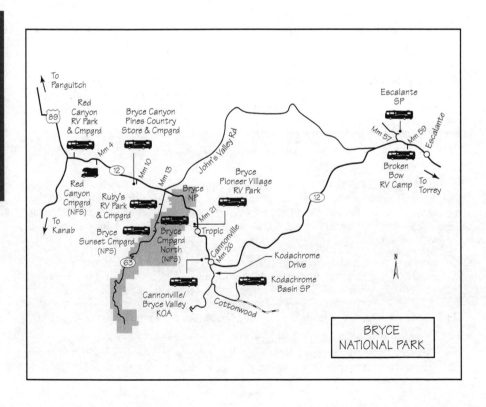

BRYCE SUNSET CAMPGROUND *(Open April 22 to Oct 10 - Varies)*

Information: (435) 834-5322, www.nps.gov/brca, brca_reception_area@nps.gov
Location: Bryce National Park, *N 37° 37' 20", W 112° 10' 19", 8,000 Ft*

101 Sites – The park's second campground closes in winter and does not accept reservations. Sites are off thee loops. Loop A has the largest sites, they're all back-ins with some to 40 feet. Generator use is allowed only on this loop. Loops B and C have smaller sites and are best for tent campers. Showers, a laundry, and a dump station are located at the nearby Sunrise Point General Store. The campground is on the west side of the park entrance road 1.3 miles from the entrance gate. There is a shuttle stop here.

RUBY'S RV PARK AND CAMPGROUND *(Open April 1 - Oct 31)*

Res and Info: (435) 834-5301 (April - Oct) or (435) 834-5341 (Nov - March),
                www.rubysinn.com, blainea@rubysinn.com
Location: 2 Miles N of Bryce National Park, *N 37° 40' 05", W 112° 09' 30", 7,700 Ft*

320 Sites – Ruby's is just outside the park, it's also on the shuttle run so access to the park and its sights is easy. The large facility has been here since 1923 and includes a lodge, restaurant, general store, post office, liquor store, western arts gallery, hair salon, and big campground and RV park. There are about 120 formal RV sites, many with full hookups. Some RV sites are as long as 100 feet and there are lots of pull-thrus. There is also lots more room for tent camping and no-hookup RV parking, probably an additional 200 sites or so. Parking is on packed dirt or gravel among pines, most sites have picnic tables. While full hookup sites are pricey at just over $30 for two people you can get a tent site for two for about $20. Additional people cost about $2 each. Ruby's is located along the park entrance road about 1.8 miles outside the park entrance.

BROKEN BOW RV CAMP *(Open All Year)*

Information: (888) 241-8785
Location: Escalante, *N 37° 46' 13", W 111° 36' 34", 5,800*

49 Sites – Broken Bow is a small commercial campground in the town of Escalante, about 48 miles east of Bryce National Park on SR-12. The campground has tent sites as well as pull-thru RV sites to 50 feet. Watch for the park as you pass through Escalante, it's right on the main road.

ESCALANTE STATE PARK *(Open All Year)*

Reservations: (800) 322-8770, www.stateparks.utah.gov
Information: (435) 826-4466, www.stateparks.utah.gov
Location: 1 Mile W of Escalante, *N 37° 47' 13", W 111° 37' 52", 5,600 Ft*

22 Sites – Escalante is a newer state park situated in Escalante Petrified Forest on the shore of Wide Hollow Reservoir. It's great for both tents and RVs. You can fish or swim in the reservoir and rental canoes are available. Two loop trails allow access to extensive

fields of petrified trees. The campground sites are off a paved loop road. Many of the sites are parallel parking pull-offs to 50 feet. All sites have picnic tables, fire pits, and raised barbecue grills on paved patios. From Escalante drive west on SR-12 for about a mile, then north on the access road for another half-mile to the campground.

BRYCE CANYON PINES COUNTRY STORE AND CAMPGROUND *(Open April 1 to Oct 31)*
Reservations: (800) 892-7923
Information: (435) 834-5441
Location: 6 Miles NW of Bryce National Park, *N 37° 42' 40", W 112° 13' 04, 7,700 Ft*

40 Sites – This campground is behind a Chevron station, store and restaurant. Since it's only 6 miles from the park it makes a good alternative place to stay. Horseback trail rides are offered in summer. The sites here are on gravel and set in pines. Many are pull-thrus suitable for RVs to 45 feet and longer. The campground is located on the south side of SR-12 about 4 miles west of the intersection for Bryce National Park.

BRYCE PIONEER VILLAGE RV PARK *(Open March 1 to Oct 31 - Varies)*
Information: (800) 222-0381
Location: Tropic, *N 37° 37' 21", W 112° 04' 55", 6,200 Ft*

20 Sites – This campground has 12 pull-thru sites for RVs to 45 feet and a grassy area for tent camping. The campground is located in the town of Tropic, 7.6 miles southeast on SR-12 from the intersection with the access road to Bryce National Park.

CANNONVILLE/BRYCE VALLEY KOA *(Open March 15 to Nov 15)*
Reservations: (888) 562-4710, www.koa.com
Information: (435) 679-8988, bvkoa@color-country.net
Location: Cannonville, *N 37° 34' 11", W 112° 03' 23", 5,900 Ft*

78 Sites – Cannonville/Brice is a full-service KOA. Like most KOAs it specializes in family camping groups with lots of things to keep the kids busy. Sites include full-hook-up pull-thrus to 90 feet as well as partial hookup and tent sites as well as rental cabins. The campground is located in Cannonville which is on SR-12 about 12 miles southeast of the junction with the Bryce National Park access road.

KODACHROME BASIN STATE PARK *(Open All Year)*
Reservations: (800) 322-8770, www.stateparks.utah.gov
Information: (435) 679-8562, www.stateparks.utah.gov
Location: 9 Miles S of Cannonville, *N 37° 31' 52", W 111° 59' 32", 5,800 Ft*

27 Sites – Kodachrome Basin is one of the most scenic campgrounds in the country. It is set in a basin surrounded by red sandstone cliffs and towers with the sites set between juniper trees. The campground will take large RVs with some parallel-parking pull-off sites to 60 feet. There are no hookups but there is a dump station, restrooms with flush toilets and hot showers, and a small store near the entrance with a few rental cabins. From

A SCENIC CAMPING SITE IN KODACHROME BASIN STATE PARK

Cannonville drive south on South Kodachrome Drive and then Cottonwood Road for 7.5 miles to the park entrance, then another 2.2 miles into the park to the campground. The route is all paved. The campground is 24 miles from the entrance to Bryce National Park.

RED CANYON CAMPGROUND *(Open May 1 to Oct 1 - Varies)*
Information: (435) 676-8815, (435) 676-9300
Location: 12 Miles W of Bryce National Park, *N 37° 44' 38", W 112° 18' 38", 7,200 Ft*

37 Sites – Red Canyon is a Dixie National Forest campground sitting on the south side of SR-12 to the west of Bryce National Park. Sites are back-ins and pull-thrus to about 35 feet set in pines and with views of the red rock cliffs bordering the canyon. Maneuvering room can be tight for larger RVs so care must be taken. Facilities are good for a national forest campground with flush toilets, showers, and a dump station. From the intersection of the Bryce Canyon access road and SR-12 drive west on SR-12 for 10 miles, the campground entrance is on the left.

RED CANYON RV PARK AND CAMPGROUND *(Open April 1 to Oct 15)*
Res and Info: (435) 676-2690
Location: 15 Miles W of Bryce National Park, *N 37° 44' 56", W 112° 21' 43", 6,800 Ft*

33 Sites – This is a simple commercial campground, not a bad place to base yourself for a visit to Bryce if you have an auto for transportation. The campground has back-in and

pull-thru sites to 60 feet as well as tent sites on grass. This area is grassland with few trees so there is no shade. The park is near the intersection of SR-12 with the north-south US-89. It is 13 miles west of the intersection of the park access road and SR-12.

CANYONLANDS NATIONAL PARK – ISLAND IN THE SKY DISTRICT

Canyonlands National Park actually has three districts: Island in the Sky, The Needles, and The Maze. The districts are separated by two rivers, the Colorado and the Green. These rivers flow from the north and merge before flowing south into Glenn Canyon Reservoir. The two districts covered in this book are this one, the Island in the Sky District, and The Needles, which follows. The third district, The Maze, is to the west of the Green River and has only difficult dirt road access so it is not covered in this book.

The Island in the Sky District is the area between the Green and Colorado Rivers before they merge. The most accessible section of this District is a high plateau which overlooks the Colorado and Green Canyons below. Paved roads lead to a number of overlooks, there is also one Canyonlands National Park campground in this section. The Islands in the Sky District is easily accessible from the Moab area which is only 30 miles from the entrance gate. Moab has lots of campgrounds and is great as a base for visiting both Arches National Park and the Island in the Sky District.

Once inside the gate there are only 19 miles of road. Although the Island in the Sky district is the busiest place in Canyonlands, it's still pretty quiet compared to Zion, Bryce, or Arches. From the entrance the main road leads two miles to the visitor center and then

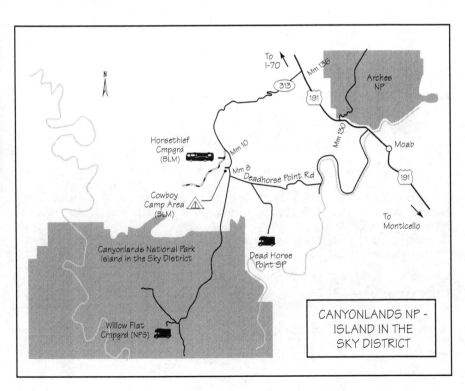

CANYONLANDS NP -
ISLAND IN THE
SKY DISTRICT

A VIEW OF CANYONLANDS ISLAND IN THE SKY DISTRICT

another 12 miles south to an overlook called Grand View Point. From a point 6 miles from the visitor center on Grand View Point Road another road goes northwest six miles to Upheaval Dome. And near the junction, from the Upheaval Dome Road, the campground road leads out to the cliff edge.

From the overlooks you are looking down into the Colorado and Green Rivers. It's about 1,000 feet down to a bench called the White Rim and then another 1,000 feet or so down to the rivers.

Just outside the gates of the Island in the Sky district is a much smaller state park – Dead Horse Point State Park. This state park has an overlook similar to those in the national park, and also a campground, see below.

The other campgrounds below are all BLM campgrounds located along the access highway that leads out to the Island in the Sky District and Dead Horse Point State Park.

Canyonlands National Park – Island in the Sky District Campgrounds

WILLOW FLAT CAMPGROUND *(Open All Year)*
Information: (435) 719-2313, www.nps.gov/cany
Location: 37 Miles W of Moab, *N 38° 22' 57", W 109° 53' 17", 5,900 Ft*

12 Sites – Willow Flats is a developed campground suitable for both tents and RVs located in Canyonlands National Park. It is located near the canyon rim overlooking the Island in the Sky area. The Park Service limits RV size to 28 feet. Restroom facilities are vault toilets. The access road and sites are paved and have picnic tables, fire pits, and

grills. Piñon pines and junipers dot the campground. There is no drinking water although it is available at the visitor center, about 7.5 miles distant. Since this is the only developed campground on top the rim in this area other than Dead Horse Point State Campground it is popular. Stays are limited to 7 days. SR-313 leaves US-191 about 10 miles north of Moab and heads west toward the park. After 18.6 miles you'll enter the park, then pass the entrance station, and in 1.8 miles see the visitor center on the right. From there continue another 6.1 miles to a Y, take the right fork. In another .3 miles take the left for the campground, then in 1.1 mile the campground entrance is on the left.

⛟ DEAD HORSE POINT STATE CAMPGROUND *(Open All Year)*

Reservations: (800) 322-8770, www.stateparks.utah.gov
Information: (435) 259-2614, stateparks@utah.gov
Location: 30 Miles W of Moab, *N 38° 29' 10", W 109° 44' 19", 6,000 Ft*

21 Sites – Dead Horse is even more popular than Willow Flats, perhaps because it offers reservations and electricity. Some sites here are pull-thrus but most are back-ins. Due to smaller sites and lack of maneuvering room RV size is limited to 28 feet. Sites have covered picnic tables and raised grills. Electricity is limited to an outlet at the picnic table, don't expect to pull many amps from it but you can keep the refrigerator and lights going. Restrooms are vault toilets and there is a telephone at the visitor center at the entrance to the park. In addition to the campground this park has viewpoints with spectacular views over the Island in the Sky district of Canyonlands National Park. SR-313 leaves US-191 about 10 miles north of Moab and heads west toward the park. After 14.2 miles turn left for Dead Horse State Park. In four miles you'll enter the park and in another 2.2 miles reach the fee station and visitor center. The campground is just beyond with a great overlook another 1.3 miles down the road. Your campground fee also covers the entrance fee for the park.

⛟ COWBOY CAMP AREA *(Open All Year)*

Information: (435) 259-2100
Location: 24 Miles W of Moab, *N 38° 33' 42", W 109° 47' 40", 6,200 Ft*

5 Sites – Cowboy is a small BLM tent camping area with eight walk-in sites, firepits, and a vault toilet. There is no drinking water. SR-313 leaves US-191 about 10 miles north of Moab and heads west. This campground is between Mile 8 and 9 on the right side of the highway. That's about 14.5 miles from the US-191 intersection.

⛟ HORSETHIEF CAMPGROUND *(Open All Year)*

Information: (435) 259-2100
Location: 24 Miles W of Moab, *N 38° 33' 42", W 109° 47' 40", 6,200 Ft*

60 Sites – Horsethief is a brand new campground built on a flat plateau. It has big sites suitable for RVs to 45 feet. There are vault toilets. It's a good overflow campground for Canyonlands and Deadhorse Point State Park. This campground is between Mile 10 and 11 on the right (west) side of the highway. That's about 12.5 miles from the US-191 intersection.

CANYONLANDS NATIONAL PARK – THE NEEDLES DISTRICT AND APPROACHES

Canyonlands National Park has three districts. They are described above in the *Island in the Sky* section. The Needles Section is accessed using SR-211, a highway that leaves US-191 from a point 37 miles south of Moab and 13 miles north of Monticello.

Monticello (population about 2,000) is the service center for the region and makes a good base for exploring the Needles District to the west. It has stores, restaurants, and several RV parks. It's the place to stay if you want hookups.

SR-211, the access highway for the Needles District, is a good paved highway. It runs westward through the Monti-La Sal National Forest, which has several campgrounds, until it reaches **Newspaper Rock** at about 12 miles. This rock is covered with petroglyphs and well worth a stop. There's a rest area and across the street a BLM dispersed camping area.

Nineteen miles farther along the road enters the **Needles District**. After the entrance station it's two miles to the visitor center. Then there's just seven miles of paved road out to Big Spring Canyon overlook. A number of hiking trails lead to interesting destinations and overlooks. The Needles District has one vehicle campground and also a commercial campground with no hookups accessible from a road just outside the entrance gate.

Another road goes westward from US-191 into an area known as the **Canyon Rims Recreation Area**. Needles Overlook Road leaves US-191 some 30 miles south of Moab

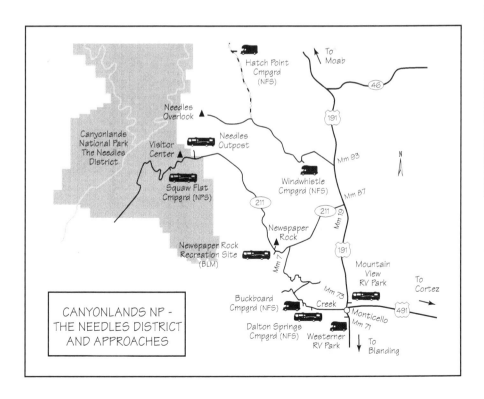

and 20 miles north of Monticello. You'll find two nice BLM campgrounds out there and, 22 miles from US-191 on paved road is another great overlook called, simply enough, **Needles Overlook**.

Canyonlands National Park – The Needles District and Approaches Campgrounds

🚐 **MOUNTAIN VIEW RV PARK** *(Open May 1 to Oct 31)*
   Res and Info: (435) 587-2974
   Location: Monticello, *N 37° 52' 54", W 109° 20' 33", 7,000 Ft*

30 Sites – Mountain View is a small privately owned campground in Monticello. It's older but in good repair. Sites are back-ins and pull-thrus to about 70 feet. The campground is toward the north side of town on the east side of US-91.

🚐 **WESTERNER RV PARK** *(Open April 15 to Oct 31 - Varies)*
   Information: (435) 587-2762, (801) 587-2762
   Location: Monticello, *N 37° 51' 54", W 109° 20' 35", 7,000 Ft*

25 Sites – The Westerner is on the south side of town, on the west side of US-91. Sites here are smaller, good for RVs to about 35 feet. There is an 18-hole golf course next door.

🚐 **BUCKBOARD CAMPGROUND** *(Open May 15 to Sept 30 - Varies)*
   Reservations: (877) 444-6777, www.recreation.gov
   Information: (435) 587-2041
   Location: 6 Miles W of Monticello, *N 37° 53' 02", W 109° 27' 06", 8,700 Ft*

11 Sites – This is a Manti-LaSal National Forest campground. It's in the high country west of Monticello and can be used to overnight when headed west into the Needles section of Canyonlands NP or as a cooler base for visiting the park. Amenities are limited to water faucets, vault toilets, picnic tables and fire rings. The sites are small although there are a few which will take RVs to 30 feet. From Monticello drive west on Creek Road for about 6 miles to the campground.

🚐 **DALTON SPRINGS CAMPGROUND** *(Open May 25 to Sept 30 - Varies)*
   Information: (435) 587-2041
   Location: 5 Miles W of Monticello, *N 37° 52' 28", W 109° 25' 53", 8,300 Ft*

16 Sites – Dalton Springs is a Manti-LaSal National Forest campground located near Buckboard Campground. It's similar to the Buckboard Campground but slightly lower in altitude and with some longer sites (including pull-thrus) that will take 40-foot RVs. Careful maneuvering is required since roads are narrow and swing room limited. From Monticello drive west on Creek Road for about 5 miles to the campground.

NEEDLES OUTPOST *(Open March 1 to Nov 30)*

Res and Info: (435) 979-4007, www.canyonlandsneedlesoutpost.com
Location: 46 Miles W of Monticello, *N 38° 10' 26", W 109° 44' 30", 5,000 Ft*

16 Sites – Needles Outpost is located a short distance outside the entrance to the Needles section of Canyonlands National Park. It offers a small grocery, restaurant, gas pump, and shower facilities. There are also 16 sites for camping in tents or RVs to about 30 feet. There are also two large group areas, if they aren't being used there is parking for RVs to about 40 feet. There are no hookups but there is a dump and water fill station. From Monticello drive north on US-191 for 13.5 miles to the intersection with SR-211, the Needles Section access road. Drive east on SR-211 for 33 miles to the campground access road which goes right. It's .5 mile up the access road to the campground.

NEWSPAPER ROCK RECREATION SITE *(Open All Year)*

Information: (435) 259-2100, www.ut.blm.gov
Location: 25 Miles W of Monticello, *N 37° 59' 16", W 109° 31' 09", 6,100 Ft*

10 Sites (Scattered Boondocking) – This is a undeveloped BLM camping area across the gravel highway from the Newspaper Rock Recreation Site. There are no facilities other than the vault toilets over at the parking area for visitors to the rock. A small stream runs alongside the camping area and does sometimes flood. For that reason exercise caution during the rain season. With careful maneuvering large RVs can find a place to park here although the flooding causes the situation to change from year to year. From Monticello drive north on US-191 for 13.5 miles to the intersection with SR-211, the Needles Section access road. Drive east on SR-211 for 12 miles to the campground. It's on the left opposite the parking area for Newspaper Rock.

SQUAW FLAT CAMPGROUND *(Open All Year)*

Information: (435) 719-2313, www.nps.gov/cany
Location: Canyonlands National Park, *N 38° 08' 56", W 109° 47' 46", 5,100 Ft*

26 Sites – This is the only developed campground inside the Needles section of Canyonlands National Park. It's a very scenic campground arranged around low sandstone bluffs. Although the Park Service recommends that only RVs to 28 feet use the park there are quite a few very long back-ins that would take RVs to 45 feet. The sites are off two loops, loop A has larger sites. Each campsite has a fire pit and picnic table and each loop has nice restrooms with flush toilets, outdoor utility sink, and water fountains. There are also additional vault toilets. While there are no phones in the campground itself there are public phones at the entrance station which is 2.9 miles from the campground. For showers people go to the Needles Outpost just outside the park entrance. From Monticello drive north on US-191 for 13.5 miles to the intersection with SR-211, the Needles Section access road. Drive east on SR-211 for 34 miles to the park entrance kiosk. After paying you'll see the visitor center on the right, stop here to pay if you want to use a credit card. The campground entrance is well-signed from here, it's 2.9 miles to the campground.

HATCH POINT CAMPGROUND *(Open All Year)*
Information: (435) 259-2100
Location: 43 Miles NW of Monticello, *N 38° 22' 55", W 109° 36' 58", 5,800 Ft*

10 Sites – Hatch Point is a BLM campground. Sites are back-ins and pull-thrus to 35 feet. Facilities include picnic tables and fire pits at each site as well as vault toilets. From mid April to mid October water is available at faucets throughout the campground. To reach Hatch Point campground drive north from Monticello for 20 miles. Then head west on the paved access road signed for Needles Overlook for 14.4 miles. Turn north at the Y on a gravel road for another 9 miles to the campground.

WINDWHISTLE CAMPGROUND *(Open All Year)*
Information: (435) 259-2100
Location: 26 Miles NW of Monticello, *N 38° 10' 39", W 109° 27' 44", 6,000 Ft*

15 Sites – Windwhistle is a BLM campground in an attractive setting below sandstone cliffs. Sites are back-ins to about 32 feet and there is also a group camping area. Amenities include picnic tables and fire rings at each site, vault toilets, and water from about mid April to mid October. There is often a host at this campground and there is a nice nature trail below the cliff face with a handout and numbered plant specimens. From Monticello drive north for 20 miles. Then head west on the paved access road for Needles Overlook for 5.5 miles, the campground entrance is on the left.

CAPITOL REEF NATIONAL PARK AND THE JOURNEY THROUGH TIME SCENIC BYWAY

Capitol Reef is the second largest park in Utah although you might be forgiven for thinking it is actually the smallest. Where the main access road crosses the park it's only 15 miles wide – but the park is almost 71 miles long. Capitol Reef encompasses a geologic feature known as the Waterpocket Fold. Here, long ago, the land folded upward. Since then it has been eroding and leaving an uneven landscaped filled with beautiful colors.

The visitor center is just off SR-24 where it cross the park. This area is known as Fruita and is also where the main campground is located. The main park road, known as Scenic Drive leads south from the visitor center for 12 miles. Most of the road is paved. A dirt road a little farther east, known as the Notom Road, also goes south, this time for almost 40 miles.

The Cathedral Valley section of the park, in the north, is accessed using dirt roads that lead north from points east of the park.

From Torrey, just west of the park, SR-12, designated as **The Journey Through Time Scenic Byway**, leads 112 miles to the southwest and Bryce National Park. SR-12 is paved the entire distance, and should be fine for any RV other than one section that concerns some drivers and not others. It's known as the "Hogback", see below. You may choose to use an alternate route to access Bryce if you have concerns about the climbing or braking abilities of your RV.

From Torrey SR-12 heads south. It soon climbs into the Dixie National Forest and cross-

UTAH'S SOUTHEAST

es **Boulder Mountain**. Views of the mountains to the east are great. The high point is about 9,000 feet and then the road descends into the town of Boulder where you can tour a partially excavated ancestral Puebloan ruin at **Anasazi State Park Museum**.

From Boulder the road ascends the "**Hogback**". Here the road runs along a ridge with great view in both directions. Signs warn of grades to 14 percent but the steep places are short and over 7 miles you lose about 1,500 feet. If you have any questions about your RV's brakes you may not want to travel this portion of the byway, but properly driven roadworthy RVs should find it easy.

Near the bottom of the grade is **Calf Creek Recreation Area**. There's a very scenic BLM campground here (tents or small RVs only, see below) as well a parking lot for those who wish to hike the three mile trail to Lower Calf Creek Falls.

Sixty-three miles after leaving Torrey you'll reach Escalante. Just west of town is **Escalante Petrified Forest State Park** with a great little campground and trails through an area of petrified trees.

Now you're approaching the Bryce area. But first turn south in Cannonville and visit **Kodachrome Basin State Park**. It's 24 miles from Bryce, close enough to use as your base while visiting the national park. Of course, that assumes you'd actually want to leave this beautiful location. Campgrounds in this area are listed in the Bryce National Park section since they're decent places to overnight while visiting the crowded national park.

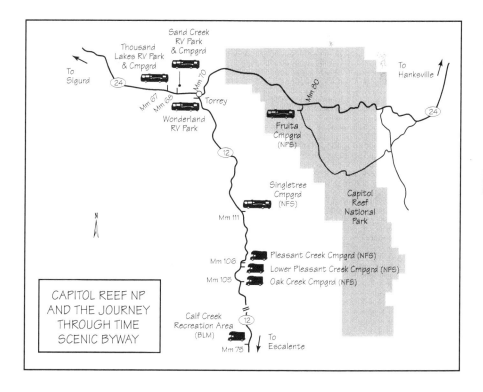

Capitol Reef National Park and The Journey Through Time Scenic Byway Campgrounds

FRUITA CAMPGROUND *(Open All Year)*

Information: (435) 425-3791, www.nps.gov/care
Location: Capitol Reef National Park, *N 38° 16' 56", W 111° 14' 49", 5,400 Ft*

71 Sites – Fruita is the main campground in Capitol Reef National Park. It's a very pleasant place for both tenters and RVs with sites spread under shady cottonwood trees. Sites are paved back-ins to 40 feet off paved interior roads with no hookups. There are picnic tables and raised fire grills, also restrooms with flush toilets but no showers. There's also a dump station. Trails lead back along the valley to the park visitor center. The visitor center for the park is located on SR-24 as it passes through the park. The campground is off Capitol Reef Road which goes south in front of the center. It's 1.4 miles to the campground.

WONDERLAND RV PARK *(Open March 1 to Nov 15 - Varies)*

Res and Info: (435) 425-3665
Location: Torrey, *N 38° 17' 54", W 111° 24' 09", 6,800 Ft*

58 Sites – This commercial campground is a good choice if you want hookups and large sites near Capitol Reef National Park. There are back-in and pull-thru sites to 70 feet with picnic tables and portable fireplaces for fires. Separate tent sites offer grass to pitch on and are separated by white fences. Restrooms offer flush toilets and showers, there are a few RV supplies in the office, there's a telephone and data port there too. Across the street is a Texaco which has some grocery items, a pay phone, and sells propane. The campground is right at the junction of SR-24 and SR-12 in Torrey. That's 10 miles west of the visitor center in Capitol Reef.

THOUSAND LAKES RV PARK AND CAMPGROUND *(Open March 1 to Nov 15 - Varies)*

Reservations: (800) 355-8995, 1000lakesrv@usmessage.net
Information: (800) 355-8995, www.thousandlakesrvpark.com
Location: 2 Miles W of Torrey, *N 38° 18' 02", W 111° 26' 41", 6,800 Ft*

67 Sites – Thousand Lakes is another good campground near the park. They have tent sites as well as back-in and pull-thru RV sites to 70 feet. There's a swimming pool as well as a cookout each evening offering excellent foot. There are bike and jeep rentals. The campground is located 2.4 miles west of the intersection of SR-24 and SR-12 in Torrey.

SAND CREEK RV PARK AND CAMPGROUND *(Open April 15 to Oct 7 - Varies)*

Res and Info: (435) 425-3577, www.sandcreekrv.com
Location: 2 Miles W of Torrey, *N 38° 17' 57", W 111° 25' 59", 6,800 Ft*

24 Sites – Sand Creek offers a bunkhouse for hikers and bikers as well as tent sites and 12 full hookup sites with pull-thrus to 60 feet. The campground is located 1.7 miles west of the intersection of SR-24 and SR-12 in Torrey.

SINGLETREE CAMPGROUND *(Open May 25 to Oct 15 - Varies)*
Information: (435) 425-3702
Location: 12 Miles S of Torrey, *N 38° 09' 41", W 111° 20' 04", 8,300 Ft*

31 Sites – This is a Dixie National Forest campground suitable for larger RVs. There are back-in sites to 60 feet, all are paved and are off a paved loop access road. There are both vault and flush toilets and each site has a picnic table, fire pit, and raised barbecue grill. The campground has a dump station. There are also group sites here as well as volleyball and horseshoe areas. The Singletree River runs through the campground. ATV use is not allowed. The campground is off SR-12 some 12 miles south of the Torrey junction which is just west of Capitol Reef National Park.

PLEASANT CREEK CAMPGROUND *(Open May 25 to Oct 30 - Varies)*
Information: (435) 425-3702
Location: 17 Miles S of Torrey, *N 38° 06' 07", W 111° 20' 13", 8,600 Ft*

11 Sites – This is a Dixie National Forest campground. About half the sites here are very short, the remainder reach as long as 36 feet. Each site has picnic table, fire pit, and raised barbecue. There is a vault toilet. ATV use is not allowed in the campground. The campground is off SR-12 some 17 miles south of the Torrey junction to the west of Capitol Reef National Park.

LOWER PLEASANT CREEK *(Open May 25 to Oct 30 - Varies)*
Information: (435) 425-3702
Location: 17 Miles S of Torrey, *N 38° 06' 02", W 111° 20' 13", 8,600 Ft*

5 Sites – Lower Pleasant Creek is a small Dixie National Forest campground. Sites here vary, signs indicate that trailers only to 20 feet are allowed. Maneuvering is tough but motorhomes to 30 feet would fit a couple of the sites. One at the entrance would actually take a 40 footer but we suspect it's usually occupied by a host. Sites have picnic tables, fire pits, and raised barbecue grills. There is a vault toilet. No ATV's (all-terrain vehicles) are allowed in this campground. The campground is off SR-12 some 17.1 miles south of the Torrey junction to the west of Capitol Reef National Park.

OAK CREEK CAMPGROUND *(Open May 20 to Sept 30 - Varies)*
Information: (435) 425-3702
Location: 18 Miles S of Torrey, *N 38° 05' 21", W 111° 20' 34", 8,900 Ft*

9 Sites – This is a small Dixie National Forest campground suitable only for tent campers and RVs to about 20 feet. Little Oak Creek runs next to the campground. Sites have picnic tables, fire rings and raised barbecues. There is a vault toilet. The campground is off SR-12 some 18 miles south of the Torrey junction which is west of Capitol Reef National Park.

🚐 CALF CREEK RECREATION AREA *(Open All Year)*

Information: (435) 826-5499
Location: 15 Miles W of Escalante, *N 37° 47' 29", W 111° 24' 51", 5,100 Ft*

13 Sites – Calf Creek, a BLM campground, is one of the most attractive campgrounds in the state, if not the country. It's small and RV size here is limited to 25 feet due to small sites, a narrow access road, and a ford across the small creek that runs through the campground. Sites are set among the rocks in a canyon, 3 are pull-thrus, the remainder back-ins. The highway runs along the edge of the campground but isn't particularly busy. Facilities in the campground are limited to picnic tables, fire pits, and vault toilets. The very popular Calf Creek Falls Trail (2.5 miles one way) departs from the campground so there is a large parking lot at the entrance as well as a restroom with flush toilets. The campground is located along SR-12 some 15 miles west of Escalante.

CORAL PINK SAND DUNES STATE PARK

This is a 3,700-acre state park about 20 miles west of Kanab. Most of the park is covered by beautiful pink sand. It's popular with off-road vehicle riders but also has good hiking routes in areas reserved for hikers. There's a nice state campground as well as a BLM campground nearby.

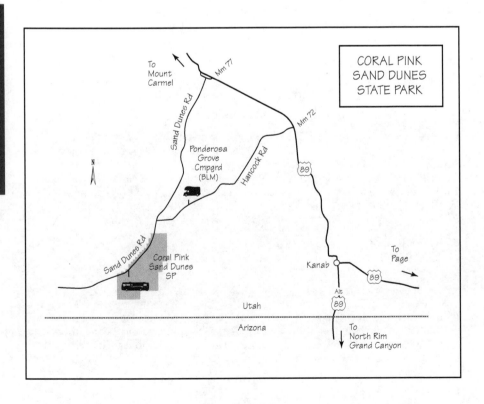

Coral Pink Sand Dunes State Park Campgrounds

CORAL PINK SAND DUNES STATE PARK CAMPGROUND *(Open All Year)*

Reservations: (800) 322-3770, www.stateparks.ut.gov
Information: (435) 648-2800, www.stateparks.ut.gov
Location: 21 Miles NW of Kanab, *N 37° 02' 12", W 112° 43' 51, 5,900 Ft*

22 Sites – This is another beautiful Utah state campground. The sites here are big, some are pull-thrus to over 100 feet. Each has a paved patio with picnic table, fire pit and raised barbecue grill. Restrooms have flush toilets and showers. A telephone and ice are available at the nearby entrance station. The dunes are adjacent for walking and ATV riding. To drive to the park and campground head north from Kanab on US-89 for 8 miles. Turn left and follow the paved entrance road for 13 miles to the park and campground.

PONDEROSA GROVE CAMPGROUND *(Open May 15 to Oct 31)*

Information: (435) 644-2672
Location: 15 Miles NW of Kanab, *N 37° 05' 17", W 112° 40' 18", 6,200 Ft*

8 Sites – This BLM campground offers back-in sites to 30 feet. Sites have picnic tables, fire pits, and raised barbecues and there is a pit toilet. Potable water is not available. There is no access from this campground for ATVs but there is hiking access to the dunes just across the road. From Kanab head north on US-89 for 8 miles. Turn left and follow the paved entrance road for 7 miles to the campground.

GREEN RIVER AND THE SAN RAFAEL SWELL

Green River (population about 1,000) is located where I-70 crosses the Green River. The town is popular as a place to start float trips down the Green River and also as a base for exploring the canyon country to the southwest and the San Rafael Swell to the west. The most visited attraction in town is probably the municipal **John Wesley Powell River History Museum**. Powell lead the first expedition to descend the Green River and Colorado through the Grand Canyon.

Green River says that it's the watermelon capital of the country, and they celebrate the fact with **Melon Days** in the second half of September.

West of Green River is the San Rafael Swell, a large uninhabited desert area with no major roads except the interstate. I-70 crosses the Swell west of Green River, it's one of the most spectacular stretches of interstate in the country.

The San Rafael Swell extends both north and south of I-70 for many miles. South of I-70 a great destination is **Goblin Valley State Park** and the nearby **Little Wild Horse Canyon**. The state park campground description and driving directions are given below. Goblin Valley is a wonderland of small wind and water-shaped sandstone mushrooms and goblins. The **nearby Wild Horse and Bell Canyon** loop trail is one of the best in Utah, it visits two slot canyons and is an easy but fairly long 8 mile loop. To reach the parking lot take the dirt road from just north of Goblin Valley State Park and drive west for five miles.

To see some of the north portion of the swell you'll want to turn north once you reach

SR-10, 71 miles west of Green River. This will take you up the west side of the swell. There are two state park campgrounds along the stretch of SR-10 between I-70 and the town of Price.

One popular destination is the **Cleveland-Lloyd Dinosaur Quarry**. Thousands of dinosaur bones have been taken from this quarry. In the visitor center you'll find a huge mounted skeleton as well as lots of other dinosaur exhibits, outside you can tour the diggings as well as walk to areas where dinosaur tracks can be seen in the stone. The route to the quarry goes east from SR-10 about 12 miles south of Price, there are 12 miles of unpaved roads en route to the quarry, the route is well signed.

Another good route into the swell leaves SR-10 a bit farther south. Leaving the highway about 2 miles north of Castle Dale it visits the **Wedge overlook of the San Rafael River**, the **Buckhorn Wash Pictographs**, and connects with I-70 east of Green River. This is a 45-mile gravel road. Check with the BLM in Price for more about travel in the San Rafael Swell, get some maps, and check road conditions locally before heading out. There are many more remote roads if you want to explore.

Green River and the San Rafael Swell Campgrounds

GREEN RIVER STATE PARK *(Open All Year)*

Reservations: (800) 322-3770, www.stateparks.utah.gov
Information: (435) 564-3633, (801) 538-7220, www.stateparks.utah.gov
Location: Green River, *N 38° 59' 23", W 110° 09' 14", 4,000 Ft*

40 Sites – This state park is a green strip running south from central Green River along the river. The northern part of the park is a 9-hole golf course, adjoining it to the south is the campground. As you might guess, many of the folks staying at this campgrounds take advantage of the opportunity to use the golf course. Sites here are all back-ins, several to 40 feet. There are no hookups but there is a dump station and the restrooms have flush toilets and showers. From central Green River .1 mile west of the Green River bridge on the west side of the golf course follow Green River Blvd .4 mile south to the park entrance.

A/OK RV PARK *(Open April 1 to Oct 1 - Varies)*

Res and Info: (435) 564-8209
Location: Green River, *N 38° 59' 16", W 110° 09' 14", 4,000 Ft*

77 Sites – This older park is a former KOA. There is tent camping on grass as well as back-in and pull-thru sites to 70 feet. From central Green River just west of the bridge and golf course follow Green River Blvd .6 mile south to the campground.

SHADY ACRES RV PARK *(Open All Year)*

Res and Info: (800) 537-8674, (435) 564-8290, www.shadyacresrv.com
Location: Green River, *N 38° 59' 43", W 110° 09' 13", 4,000 Ft*

88 Sites – The campground has tent sites as well as pull-thru sites to 90 feet. It is next to the golf course on the business loop of I-70 in central Green River.

UTAH'S SOUTHEAST

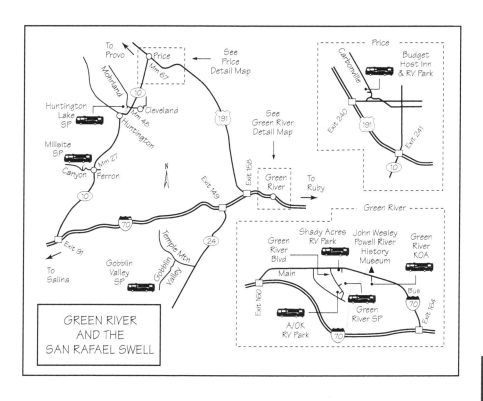

GREEN RIVER
AND THE
SAN RAFAEL SWELL

🚐 **GREEN RIVER KOA** *(Open All Year)*

Reservations: (800) 562-2734, www.koa.com
Information: (435) 564-8195, greenriverkoa@yahoo.com
Location: Green River, *N 38° 59' 32", W 110° 08' 28", 4,000 Ft*

80 Sites – The campground has tent sites as well as back-in and pull-thru sites to 75 feet. Amenities include a swimming pool and dump station. The campground is located right on the I-70 business loop in Green River, next to the bridge over the Green River and across from the museum.

🚐 **GOBLIN VALLEY STATE PARK** *(Open All Year)*

Reservations: (800) 322-8770, www.stateparks.utah.gov
Information: (435) 564-3633, www.stateparks.utah.gov
Location: 49 miles SW of Green River, *N 38° 34' 18", W 110° 42' 37", 5,000 Ft*

24 Sites – Sites in this little campground are back-ins and pull-thrus to 50 feet although many are much shorter. There are flush toilets and a shower. From Green River drive west 13 miles on I-70 to Exit 149. Drive south on SR-24 for 24 miles. Turn right onto Temple Mountain Road and follow it for five miles, then take the left onto Goblin Valley Road and you'll reach the park in another 7 miles.

🚐 MILLSITE STATE PARK *(Open April 15 to Nov 15 - Varies)*

Reservations: (801) 322-3770 (in Salt Lake City), (800) 322-8770, www.stateparks.utah.gov
Information: (435) 687-2491
Location: 41 Miles S of Price, *N 39° 05' 31", W 111° 11' 41", 6,200 Ft*

20 Sites – Millsite is an extremely popular park on the shore of Millsite Reservoir. The trout fishing is good here. Sites are back-ins and pull-thrus to 55 feet. There is also an overflow area with room for about 15 large RVs. The overflow sites are often full too, reservations are recommended. There are flush toilets and showers, also a boat ramp. From SR-10 about 44 miles south of Price in the town of Ferron head west on Canyon Road. The campground is 4.2 miles down the road on the south side of the reservoir.

🚐 HUNTINGTON LAKE STATE PARK *(Open All Year)*

Reservations: (801) 322-3770 (in Salt Lake City), (800) 322-8770, www.stateparks.utah.gov
Information: (435) 687-2491
Location: 19 Miles S of Price, *N 39° 20' 50", W 110° 56' 34", 5,900 Ft*

22 Sites – Huntington Reservoir is known for its warm-water species fishing, particularly large-mouth bass. This is also a popular warm water-sports lake. Reservations are highly recommended. Sites here are back-ins and pull-thrus to 60 feet. There are no hookups but restrooms have flush toilets and showers, there is also a boat launch. From SR-10 19 miles south of Price and 2 miles north of Huntington drive west on Mohrland Road for about 200 yards to the entrance.

🚐 BUDGET HOST INN AND RV PARK *(Open All Year)*

Res and Info: (435) 637-2424
Location: Price, *N 39° 36' 10", W 110° 49' 17", 5,500 Ft*

30 Sites – This is a simple campground behind a motel. The sites are back-ins and pull-thrus to 60 feet. Amenities include a heated pool. From US-191 as it bypasses Price on the southwest side of town take Exit 240 (1st North Street). Head east on North Street for .2 mile and turn left on Carbonville Road. Drive north 200 yards, the campground is on the left.

HOVENWEEP NATIONAL MONUMENT

Hovenweep National Monument is a very engaging ancestral Puebloan site located in a barren area near the Utah-Colorado border. There are many ruins here, mostly located in a small valley. A hiking trail runs around much of the rim of the valley offering great views and photo opportunities. These ruins are not large but they are unique. They are constructed of rocks and some are round towers.

Access is either from the west in Utah off US-191 about 10 miles north of Bluff or from the east off US-160 about 3 miles south of Cortez. Both routes are well marked. It's 30 miles from the cutoff north of Bluff, 39 miles from the cutoff south of Cortez. Both routes are paved and fine for any RV.

UTAH'S SOUTHEAST

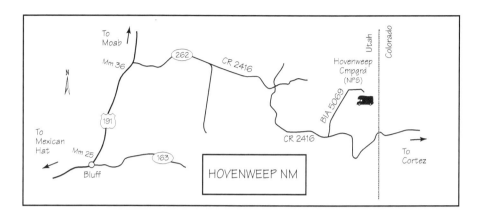

Hovenweep National Monument Campground

 HOVENWEEP CAMPGROUND *(Open All Year)*
Information: (970) 562-4282, www.nps.gov/hove
Location: Hovenweep National Monument, *N 37° 22' 59" W 109° 04' 17", 5,100 Ft*

31 Sites – There is only this one campground at Hovenweep. It's good for tents and smaller RVs but does not have room for large RVs. Some parallel parking type sites will take 35 footers but that's about it. Sites have picnic tables and raised barbecue grills but no fire pits. The visitor center is nearby and trails lead from the campground to the ruins. The campground is just .4 mile past the visitor center.

KANAB

Kanab, population about 4,000, has a position at the south and west side of the canyon country similar to that of Moab in the north and east. The town serves as a supply center and base of operations for many visitors to the area. Just some examples: Zion is 30 miles northwest, Bryce is 75 miles north, Page and Glen Canyon National Recreation Area are 73 miles west, the Grand Canyon North Rim is 80 miles south.

The town has several RV parks. Not far west is Coral Pink Sand Dunes State Park which has its own listing in this chapter.

Kanab Campgrounds

 **CRAZY HORSE RV CAMPARK** *(Open All Year)*
Reservations: (866) 830-7316, crazyhorse@kanab.net
Information: (435) 644-2782, www.crazyhorsecampark.com
Location: Kanab, *N 37° 02' 36" W 112° 30' 58", 4,900 Ft*

72 Sites – This is an older RV park toward the western edge of town. There are grassy tent sites as well as back-in and pull-thru sites to 45 feet. Sites have paved patios and picnic tables, some have fire pits and others have raised barbecues. There is a seasonal

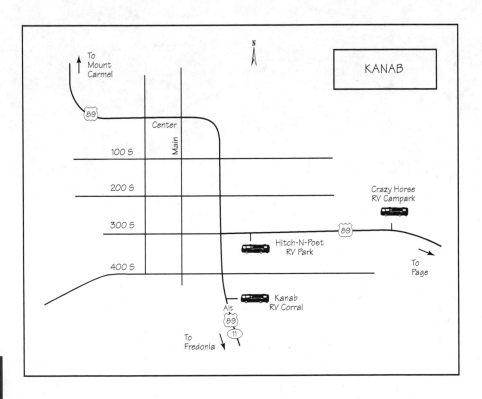

swimming pool, free Wi-Fi at sites nearer the office, and some grocery items in the office. A large supermarket and restaurants are within walking distance. The campground is on US-89 some .6 mile east of the intersection of US-89 and SR-11 in Kanab.

HITCH-N-POST RV PARK *(Open All Year)*

Reservations: (800) 458-3516
Information: (435) 644-2142, www.hitchnpostrvpark.com
Location: Kanab, *N 37° 02' 33", W 112° 31' 28", 4,900 Ft*

21 Sites – The Hitch-N-Post is a small but rather charming campground in the center of Kanab. There are a grassy tent-camping area, three rental cabins, and back-in and pull-thru RV sites to 45 feet. Maneuvering room for big RVs is tight. Picnic tables and moveable fire pits are available. Wi-Fi can be received if you're near the office. There is a dishwashing sink for tent campers. The laundromat next door has a pay phone and there's a drive-in and McDonalds across the street, not to mention many shops and other restaurants within walking distance. The campground is just east of the intersection of US-89 and SR-11, less than a block.

KANAB RV CORRAL *(Open All Year)*

Res and Info: (435) 644-5330, www.xpressweb.com/~rvcorral
Location: Kanab, *N 37° 02' 23", W 112° 31' 31", 4,900 Ft*

44 Sites – This is the nicest of the Kanab RV parks but it does not cater to tent camp-ers. It's neat and very clean. Sites are back-ins and pull-thrus to 50 feet. Restrooms are spotless although they are closed in winter when all customers must be self-contained. There's a seasonal swimming pool. Wi-Fi is available throughout the park and there is a data port in the office. The campground is located .25 mile south of the intersection or US-89 and SR-11 on the east side of US-89.

MOAB

Moab (population about 5,000) is the most populous town in this part of Utah. It serves as a supply center for outdoor activities in the area with grocery and gear stores as well as restaurants and entertainment. The town is becoming more upscale all the time.

Moab is best known as an off-road bicycle town. The most famous trails are just east and above town in the Sand Flats Road area. The Slickrock Trail (9.6 miles) is world famous, there's also a much shorter practice trail. Campgrounds in the area are listed below under *Sand Flats Recreation Area.*

The Moab Area has lots of rough outback roads throughout the area that make great **bike and jeep routes**. They were established as mineral exploration roads in years past. The **Colorado and Green Rivers** are very popular rafting rivers, several tour companies operate out of Moab.

Moab has a convenient location for visits to Arches National Park and Canyonlands Na-

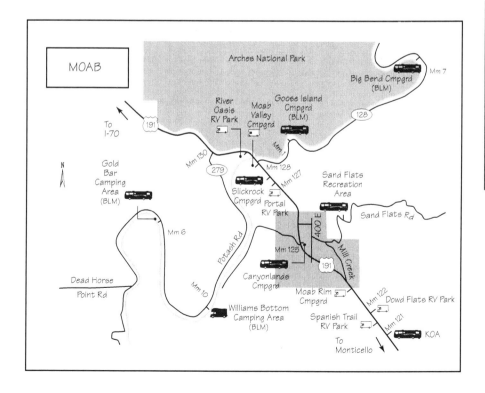

tional Park (Island in the Sky District). Neither has nearly enough camping so the Moab area takes up the slack. There are RV parks in town and also north and south of town, and BLM campgrounds in the surrounding area.

Moab Campgrounds

GOOSE ISLAND CAMPGROUND *(Open All Year)*
  Information: (435) 259-2100
  Location:　4 Miles NE of Moab, *N 38° 36' 35", W 109° 33' 28", 4,000 Ft*

18 Sites – Goose Island occupies a spectacular riverside location. Sites are back-ins, some to 75 feet. There is a vault toilet. The campground also offers group sites. There is no potable water, it is available a mile downstream at Matrimony Springs. To reach the campground travel north from Moab on US-191 for about 2 miles. Turn east on SR-128 to drive along the south shore of the Colorado River. You'll see the campground on the left in 1.5 miles

BIG BEND CAMPGROUND *(Open All Year)*
  Information: (435) 259-2100
  Location:　9 Miles NE of Moab, *N 38° 38' 55", W 109° 28' 47", 4,000 Ft*

23 Sites – Big Bend is located along the Colorado River. There are 23 sites, some exceeding 100 feet. There are also 5 overflow sites on the far side of the road. Sites have picnic tables and fire pits and there is a vault toilet. The campground has no potable water, it is available at Matrimony Springs, 1 mile downriver from Goose Island Campground, see above. To reach the campground travel north from Moab on US-191 for about two miles. Turn east on SR-128 to drive along the south shore of the Colorado River. You'll see the campground on the left in 7.5 miles.

WILLIAMS BOTTOM CAMPING AREA *(Open All Year)*
  Information: (435) 259-2100
  Location:　9 Miles NW of Moab, *N 38° 32' 19", W 109° 36' 13", 4,000 Ft*

18 Sites – This is a small campground with sites suitable for tent camping or RVs to 24 feet. There's an outhouse and sites have fire pits and raised barbecues, some have picnic tables. There is no potable water. Within a mile of the campground you'll see some rock art along the highway. From Moab drive north for 4 miles and turn left on SR-279, Potash Road. This road follows the north bank of the Colorado. The campground is located near mile marker 10, 5.3 miles from the highway.

GOLD BAR CAMPING AREA *(Open All Year)*
  Information: (435) 259-2100
  Location:　14 Miles NW of Moab, *N 38° 34' 26", W 109° 37' 59", 4,000 Ft*

8 Sites – Gold Bar is primarily a BLM group camping area but there are 8 sites for individual RVs. Since this is really a gravel lot there is room for large RVs. The campground is on the bank of the Colorado River. Restrooms are vault toilets, there is no potable

UTAH'S SOUTHEAST

water. From Moab drive north for 4 miles and turn left on SR-279, Potash Road. This road follows the north bank of the Colorado. The campground is located between Mile Markers 5 and 6, 9.7 miles from the highway.

SLICKROCK CAMPGROUND *(Open All Year)*
Reservations: (800) 448-8873
Information: (435) 259-7660, (435) 259-4152, www.slickrockcampground.com
Location: 1 Mile N of Moab, *N 38° 35' 39", W 109° 34' 03", 4,000 Ft*

182 Sites – This is an older campground with a variety of sites. They include tent sites and pull-thrus for RVs to 45 feet. Mature shade trees really help on hot days and there's a pool and spas. The campground is located about a mile north of Moab on the west side of US-191.

CANYONLANDS CAMPGROUND *(Open All Year)*
Reservations: (800) 522-6848, cancamp@frontiernet.net
Information: (435) 259-6848, www.canyonlandsrv.com
Location: Moab, *N 38° 33' 53", W 109° 32' 58", 4,100 Ft*

136 Sites – This is a large commercial campground located right in Moab, the only one we listed in this book. It is a large park with the entrance next to a gas station which has a small grocery store. There are tent sites as well as a variety of hookup sites including pull-thrus that will take RVs to 45 feet in a pinch. Lots of restaurants and stores are within walking distance. The campground is located on the east side of US-191 as it pass through Moab, there's a large sign.

MOAB KOA *(Open March 1 to Oct 31)*
Reservations: (800) 562-0372, www.koa.com
Information: (435) 259-6682, www. moabkoa.com, info@moabkoa.com
Location: 2 Miles S of Moab, *N 38° 31' 23", W 109° 29' 49", 4,600 Ft*

132 Sites – Like most KOAs this one offers a full range of amenities to appeal to family campers. There are tent sites and partial and full hookup RV sites to 55 feet. Also a heated pool and mini golf. The campground is located south of Moab on the east side of US-191, it's about two miles south of town.

SAND FLATS RECREATION AREA *(Open All Year)*
Information: (435) 259-2100
Location: 2 Miles E of Moab, *N 38° 34' 32", W 109° 31' 26", 4,600 Ft*

120 Sites – The slickrock bicycle trails in this BLM recreation area east of Moab are world famous. There are also a lot of basic camping sites here. There's a pay station at the

entrance for the area (for both camping and bicycle riding) and then parking for riding as well as 8 clusters of campsites and large overflow areas. Cluster A has the best sites for RVs, it would accommodate 40-footers. Other clusters would be best for tent campers. No potable water is provided. Most designated sites have picnic tables and fire pits as well as outhouses. From Moab head east on Sand Flats Road. You'll reach the entrance gate at 1.5 miles, the parking areas and campgrounds extend for several miles beyond.

MONUMENT VALLEY

Monument Valley is right on the border between Utah and Arizona. It must be one of the most beautiful places in the country. The valley is on Navajo land and is operated by them, this isn't a national park. The 17-mile Valley Drive loop runs through the valley with lots of places to stop and take pictures. It's a dirt road and very rough and uneven but certainly passable in any smaller vehicle as long as it's dry. If you don't want to do it in your own vehicle, however, you can take a tour in a truck from the visitor center.

There are two handy campgrounds here. One is a commercial campground to the west, but pretty close. The other is the Navajo campground right at the visitor center. Generally you'll find that 9 out of 10 visitors choose the facility at Goulding's.

Monument Valley Campgrounds

GOULDING'S MONUMENT VALLEY CAMPGROUND *(Open All Year)*
   Res and Info: (435) 727-3235, www.gouldings.com, campground@gouldings.com
   Location: Monument Valley, *N 37° 00' 23", W 110° 12' 56", 5,400 Ft*

66 Sites – Goulding's has a long history as the place to stay while visiting Monument Valley. In addition to the campground there's a lodge, a restaurant, a pretty good size grocery store, a gas station, and an airstrip. You'll see lots of tours flying in here. The campground is set in a red rock canyon which is sometimes hot, but sometimes nice because it's protected from the wind. There are tent sites as well as back-in and pull-thru RV sites to 60 feet. Access roads are paved but parking is on red dirt. The amenities building has

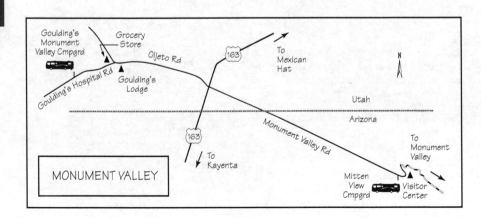

a small store and there is a shuttle bus to the restaurant. The hookup price here is about $36, tent sites go for $22. Tours of Monument Valley can be arranged at the campground. There is a computer for internet access as well as a data port. In winter, from November 1 until March 15, only the sites are open (with hookups). During that period sign in at Goulding's Market as you approach the park. From the Arizona-Utah border on US-163 it's only .4 mile north to the access road for Goulding's. Turn left and you'll pass the airstrip, lodge, and grocery store and arrive at the campground after 2.4 miles.

🚐 **MITTEN VIEW CAMPGROUND** *(Open All Year)*
   Information: (435) 727-5872, www.monumentvalleyonline.com
   Location: Monument Valley, *N 36° 58' 53", W 110° 06' 48", 5,600 Ft*

90 Sites – On the opposite side of US-163 from the access road to Goulding's is the access road to the Monument Valley visitor center and entrance. It's about 3.5 miles from the highway to the visitor center. As you drive toward the visitor center you pass back into Utah. The Navajo-run campground is on the right just before you reach the visitor center. The location is fairly exposed and can be windy. All camping is on gravel, there are tent sites as well as pull-thru sites for large RVs. Each site has a covered picnic table and raised barbecue. Restrooms have showers which require a token. Pay for camping at the adjacent visitor center (open 6 am to 8 pm in summer) which also has a restaurant and pay phones. A half-mile walking trail is adjacent to the campground, there's an $5 entrance fee to the park as well as the camping fee.

TRAIL OF THE ANCIENTS SCENIC BYWAY

The driving loop described here is in southeast Utah, north of Monument Valley and south of Moab and the Needles District of Canyonlands National Park. It's a 130-mile loop with a number of interesting attractions. This is really only a portion of the designated Scenic Byway which also includes *Monument Valley* and *Hovenweep*, described separately in this chapter. Note that larger RV drivers may want to avoid the Moki Dugway. That means they'll need to drive out to Natural Bridges from Blanding and then return, then continue south on US-191 and US-161 to Mexican Hat. We'll start in Blanding, just two miles north of the junction of US-191 and SR-95 and drive the loop.

Blanding (population about 3,000) is a good base for exploring the area for larger RVs because it has a hookup campground and a convenient location if you want to leave your RV while driving out to Natural Bridges. The main attraction in this small town is **Edge of the Cedars State Park**. It's at the western edge of town and features a partially excavated ancestral Puebloan ruin. There's also a modern museum with a great pottery collection.

Natural Bridges National Monument is located 37 miles west of Blanding along SR-95. There's a visitor center with a nearby campground (see below) and a nine mile loop road offering overlooks of and hiking trails to the three large natural bridges featured by this monument. Trailers are prohibited on the road, you can leave them at the visitor center. In addition to the campground in the monument, which only has sites to about 30 feet, there is a nearby BLM boondocking location, a former gravel pit, that can take big RVs.

From Natural Bridges National Monument you can drive south on SR-261 to the southernmost part of the loop near Mexican Hat. If you have a good map you'll notice that 29

VIEW OF MEXICAN HAT FROM VALLE'S TRADING POST AND RV PARK

miles south of Natural Bridges the road becomes very irregular. This is the **Moki Dug-way**. Here the highway turns to gravel and drops off the edge of the Cedar Mesa. It drops 1,100 feet in three miles. The State of Utah recommends that only vehicles less than 28 feet long and 10,000 pounds attempt to traverse it. The grade is about 10%, which isn't really bad. There are several switchbacks but semis negotiate them so any RV should be able to too. Once you reach the bottom the paving starts again and you can continue south toward Mexican Hat.

Six miles south of the Dugway take the access road west to **Goosenecks State Park**. The road out is paved and about 3.5 miles long. There's a great overlook of gooseneck bends of the San Juan River, the river itself is 1,000 feet below the lookout point. You can boondock in the parking area here, it's described as a campground below.

At the southernmost point of this loop is a BLM area known as the **Valley of the Gods**. A seventeen mile dirt road runs from SR-261 just south of the lower end of the Moki Dug-way east to meet US-163. This area is a miniature version of Monument Valley which is some distance to the south. Best of all, there's usually almost no one else here. When dry the road is usually suitable for RVs to 25 feet, some dips in the road would be difficult to negotiate in a larger RV. Boondocking is OK on already established parking areas.

From this southern end of the loop it's an easy drive south 3 miles to Mexican Hat. This small town on the San Juan River is known for the hat-like rock formation northeast of town, it also has an RV park. Farther south, 26 mile distant, is Monument Valley. The campgrounds here are described in another section of this chapter.

Driving north now you'll soon reach the small town of Bluff. A few miles south of town you'll see the sign for Sand Island BLM Campground. Even if you don't need to stop for the night you can drive in here and take a look at the **Sand Island Petroglyph Site**. This wall of petroglyphs is one of the best anywhere, and very easy to access.

From Sand Island it's an easy drive north through Bluff to return to Blanding. A good side trip is the drive out to Hovenweep, it is described separately in this chapter.

Trail of the Ancients Scenic Byway Campgrounds

GOFER-KAMPARK *(Open All Year)*
Res and Info: (435) 678-2991, (435) 678-2770, kampark@yahoo.com
Location: Blanding, *N 37° 36' 46", W 109° 28' 42", 5,900 Ft*

65 Sites – This is a commercial campground located behind a Shell station in Blanding. There's also a Taco Bell Express and a small store at the station, the town's small supermarket is across the street. Sites include tent sites and many large pull-thrus, large trees provide shade. This is a good big-rig campground. The campground is on the east side of US-191 as it passes through Blanding near the south edge of town.

BLUE MOUNTAIN RV PARK *(Open March 15 to Nov 1)*
Res and Info: (435) 678-2570
Location: Blanding, *N 37° 35' 50", W 109° 28' 49", 6,000 Ft*

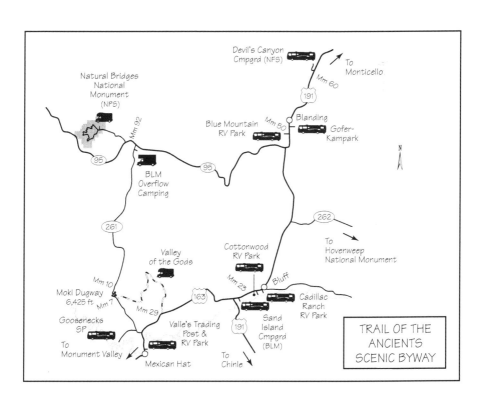

TRAIL OF THE
ANCIENTS
SCENIC BYWAY

37 Sites – The Blue Mountain is a nice big-rig park with great views, it's located just outside Blanding to the south. The sites here are back-ins and pull-thrus to 75 feet. There are also tent sites. The park is on the west side of US-191 about a mile south of Blanding.

DEVIL'S CANYON NATIONAL FOREST CAMPGROUND *(Open May 15 to Oct 15 - Varies)*
Information: (435) 587-2041
Reservations: (877) 444-6777, www.recreation.gov
Location: 9 Miles N of Blanding, *N 37° 44' 12.7", W 109° 24' 42.5", 7,100 Ft*

42 Sites – Devil's Canon is an easily accessible Manti-LaSal National Forest campground located right along US-191, the main north-south highway through this area. The campground is set in pines, there are two loops. Loop one is newer and has larger sites, including back-ins and pull-thrus that will take RVs to 45 feet. There are picnic tables and fire rings, those on loop A are on paved pads. The campground is on the west side of US-191 about nine miles north of Blanding.

NATURAL BRIDGES NATIONAL MONUMENT CAMPGROUND *(Open All Year)*
Information: (435) 692-1234, www.nps.gov/nabr
Location: Natural Bridges National Monument, *N 37° 36' 34", W 109° 59' 01", 6,400 Ft*

13 Sites – Natural Bridges National Monument has only one small campground. It is located about .3 miles from the visitor center at the entrance to the monument. Sites are all back-ins, a sign in the visitor center say the maximum RV size is 30 feet, at the campground another sign says 26 feet. A few sites will take 30-footers with careful driving. Most if not all sites have nice sandy tent-camping pads. The campground has no water but drinking water is available at the nearby visitor center as is a telephone. There are vault toilets at the campground, flush toilets at the visitor center, and no showers either place.

BLM OVERFLOW CAMPING FOR NATURAL BRIDGES NATIONAL MONUMENT
    (Open All Year)
Information: (435) 587-1500
Location: 7 Miles E of Natural Bridges Nat. Mon., *N 37° 34' 15", W 109° 52' 58", 6,700 Ft*

50 Sites – The BLM allows overnight camping at this gravel lot about 7 miles from Natural Bridges National Monument. It's handy since the monument has such a small campground and it will not take large RVs. There's lots of room for many RVs of any size. The lot is located just south of the intersection of SR 95 and SR-261 on the east side of SR-261.

GOOSENECKS STATE PARK *(Open All Year)*
Information: (435) 678-2238
Location: 4 Miles N of Mexican Hat, *N 37° 10' 28", W 109° 55' 38", 4,800 Ft*

UTAH'S SOUTHEAST

8 Sites – This state park is really a large parking area overlooking the spectacular Goose-necks of the San Juan River. Facilities for camping are limited to a large gravel lot and nearby vault toilet. There's lots of room to park and lots of room to maneuver. The park is located at the end of a 3.5-mile paved road that leaves SR-261 some 4 miles north of Mexican Hat.

VALLE'S TRADING POST AND RV PARK *(Open All Year)*
Res and Info: (435) 683-2226
Location: Mexican Hat, *N 37° 08' 59", W 109° 51' 27", 4,100 Ft*

15 Sites – The camping area is located behind an older café and small store in the tiny town of Mexican Hat. There are 13 sets of hookups, many have room for large RVs to pull alongside. There is also a fenced tent camping area for about 3 tents with a picnic table. It's nothing fancy but the owners are friendly and the views are excellent.

VALLEY OF THE GODS *(Open All Year)*
Information: (435) 587-1500
Location: 7 Miles NE of Medicine Hat, *N 37° 14' 07", W 109° 48' 53", 4,500 Ft*

Dispersed Camping – Camping in RVs is allowed in pull-off locations along the road through the valley. It must be an already established driving surface and it must be off the road. There are no facilities. The valley access road runs from US-163 in the east to SR-261 in the west. Most suitable parking sites are near the east entrance, about 7 miles northeast of Medicine Hat.

SAND ISLAND BLM CAMPGROUND *(Open All Year)*
Information: (435) 587-1500, UT-Monticello@blm.org
Location: 2 Miles SW of Bluff, *N 37° 15' 46", W 109° 36' 47", 4,300 Ft*

23 Sites – Sand Island is located on the shore of the San Juan River, it's popular with river rafters as well as fishermen. The area is also known for the extensive petroglyphs on a cliffside next to the campground. Camping sites are in two areas. Area A is reserved for smaller vehicles to 22 feet and tents, Area B has separated pull-thru and back-in sites to 75 feet. Both areas have some cottonwoods for shade and some sites are along the river. There are modern vault toilets and no showers. The campground has a boat launch area and a day-use area. It is located off US-191 about 2 miles southwest of Bluff.

COTTONWOOD RV PARK *(Open March 1 to Nov 30)*
Res and Info: (435) 672-2287
Location: Bluff, *N 37° 16' 47", W 109° 33' 58", 4,300 Ft*

27 Sites – A nice small campground with grassy tent sites as well as pull-thru and back-in RV sites to 65 feet. The campground is located in Bluff just a block off US-191, you'll see the sign pointing south on 4th Street near the western end of town.

▄ **Cadillac Ranch RV Park** *(Open All Year)*
Reservations: (800) 538-6195, cadranch@frontiernet.net or ranch@sanjuan.net
Information: (435) 672-2262, www.bluffutah.org
Location: Bluff, *N 37° 16' 57", W 109° 33' 04", 4,300 Ft*

30 Sites – This is a neat, well-run campground next to the owner's house. Red-rock cliffs across the road make this a pretty setting. Parking is on gravel, sites are back-ins and pull-thrus to 60 feet. There are also tent sites near a small pond. RV sites have picnic tables while tent sites have both fire pits and tables. There's also a dedicated dishwashing sink for tenters. Fishing is possible in the small lake, a license is not required. Paddle boats are also available. While the park has no laundry there is a laundromat about two blocks away. The campground is located on the south side of US-191 near the eastern edge of Bluff.

Zion National Park

Zion National Park is one of the most scenic parks anywhere. While the park is fairly large most of it gets little in the way of visitors. The popular part of the park is Zion Canyon which is relatively small. Here, unlike Bryce, the Grand Canyon, or Canyonlands, you're in the canyon looking up, not above looking down.

Most visitors enter the Zion Canyon area of the park from its west gate near Springdale. The visitor center here has large parking lots because Zion uses a shuttle system for visi-

ENTERING ZION NATIONAL PARK

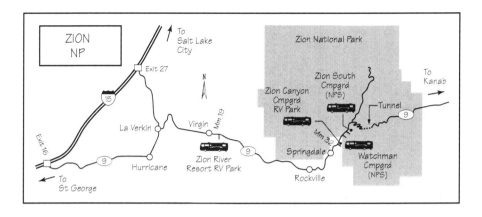

tors. There are also large parking lots outside the park in Springdale, and they're served by the shuttles too. The shuttles run from early April to late October, outside that period you can drive into the canyon. We used to hear people complaining about having to use the shuttles, now we're hearing people complain about not being able to use shuttles in the off season. The reduction in traffic due to the shuttles has really made the canyon a more pleasant place to visit.

If you approach the canyon from the east on SR-9 you have to pass through a tunnel. This is fine if you're small, but RVs are restricted. Vehicles over 7 ft 10 inches wide or over 11 ft 4 inches tall must travel in the center of the tunnel so opposing traffic must be stopped. In summer it's just a matter of driving up and paying a $10 fee, you'll be accommodated. In the off season, however, you have to call and make an appointment, the number is (435) 772-3256.

The park has two campgrounds in the canyon. If you can't get into one of these there are commercial campgrounds nearby including a large one just outside the entrance in Springdale which is very handy.

Zion National Park Campgrounds

WATCHMAN CAMPGROUND *(Open All Year)*

Reservations: (800) 365-2267 or (301) 722-1257 outside US or Canada, www.rescreation.gov
Information: (435) 772-3256, www.nps.gov/zion
Location: Zion National Park, *N 37° 11' 54", W 112° 59' 10", 3,900 Ft*

147 Sites – Watchman is a newly refurbished campground that is now set up for modern RVs. The setting is spectacular as it is overlooked by Zion's red cliffs. The campground is located behind the new visitor center just inside the west gate so it's very handy and the shuttle busses are easily accessible. Sites are off four loops, those on A and B have electrical hookups. Sites are as long as 55 feet, mostly back-ins but with a few pull-thrus. Most electrical sites are 30-amp, the few pull-thrus have 50-amp service. Reservations are available from April 7 to October 28 (varies), it's first-com, first-served outside that period. Restrooms have flush toilets but no showers. There's a dump and water fill station. The campground is located just inside the western park entrance.

ZION SOUTH CAMPGROUND *(Open March 15 to Oct 31 - Varies)*

Information: (435) 772-3256, www.nps.gov/zion
Location: Zion National Park, *N 37° 12' 16", W 112° 58' 59", 3,900 Ft*

127 Sites – Zion South has not been refurbished although we suspect it's coming. Interior roads are paved but camping is on dirt or gravel. The sites here are not well defined, some are long pull-thrus and others small tent sites. Restrooms have flush toilets and there's a dump station. No reservations are taken. If you enter the park at the west entrance continue only .5 mile, the campground entrance is on the right.

ZION CANYON CAMPGROUND RV PARK *(Open All Year)*

Res and Info: (435) 772-3237, www.zioncamp.com, zioncamp@infowest.com
Location: 1 Mile W of Zion West Gate, *N 37° 11' 37", W 112° 59' 33", 3,800 Ft*

220 Sites – This large campground is located behind a Quality Inn just outside the west entrance to Zion. It's a great location, very convenient to the park. The campground is on the bank of the Virgin river and some electric and water sites overlook the river. There are back-in and pull-thru sites to 50 feet. There is a swimming pool and both Wi-Fi and a data port are available. There's a small store at the campground but no restaurant. You have to walk next door for that. The motel and campground are on the south side of the highway .7 mile west of the entrance gate to the park.

ZION RIVER RESORT RV PARK *(Open All Year)*

Res and Info: (800) 838-8594, www.zionriverresort.com, info@zrr.com
Location: 13 Miles W of Zion West Gate, *N 37° 12' 10", W 113° 10' 40", 3,500 Ft*

131 Sites – Zion River Resort is an upscale RV park located a few miles west of Zion's west gate. It has tent sites as well as nice RV sites, some are pull-thrus to 65 feet. Amenities include Wi-Fi, instant-on telephones at the sites, swimming pool and spa, excellent gift shop, game rooms, a meeting/theater room, and a camper kitchen. A shuttle is available to Zion. Rates here run from about $35 to $45. The campground is located on the south side of SR-9 some 13 miles west of the west entrance of the park. It's just east of the town of Virgin.

Information Resources

See our Internet site at www.rollinghomes.com for Internet information links.

Arches National Park

Arches National Park, (435) 719-2299

Bryce National Park

Bryce National Park, (435) 834-5322

Canyonlands National Park

Canyonlands National Park, (435) 719-2313

Capitol Reef National Park and the Journey Through Time Scenic Byway

Anasazi State Park Museum, Post Office Box 1429, Boulder, Utah 84716; (435) 335-7308

Capitol Reef National Park, (435) 425-3791, extension 111

Escalante Petrified Forest State Park, 710 North Reservoir Road, Escalante, Utah 84726-0350; (435) 826-4466

Kodachrome Basin State Park, PO Box 180069, Cannonville, Utah 84718-0069; (435) 679-8562

Coral Pink Sand Dunes State Park

Coral Pink Sand Dunes State Park, PO Box 95, Kanab, Utah 84741-0095; (435) 648-2800

Green River and the San Rafael Swell

Bureau of Land Management, Price Field Office, 125 South 600 West, Price, Utah 84501; (435) 636-3600

Green River Visitor Center, 885 East Main Street, Green River, UT 84525; (435) 564-3526, (800) 635-6622

John Wesley Powell River History Museum, 885 East Main Street, Green River, UT 84525; (435) 564-3427

Goblin Valley State Park, PO Box 146001, Salt Lake City, UT 84114-6001; (801) 538-7220

Hovenweep National Monument

Hovenweep National Monument, (970)562-4282

Kanab

Kanab Travel Information Center, 78 S 100 East, Kanab, Utah 84741; (435) 644-5033, (800) 733-5263

Moab

Grand County Travel Council, PO Box 550, Moab, UT 84532; (435) 259-8825, (800) 635-6622

Moab Information Center, Corner of Main and Center, Moab, UT

Trail of the Ancients Scenic Byway

Edge of the Cedars State Park, 660 West 400 North, Blanding, UT 84511-0788; (435) 678-2238

Natural Bridges National Monument, (435) 692-1234

Goosenecks State Park, (435) 678-2238

Valley of the Gods, BLM Monticello Field Office, 435 N Main, Monticello, UT; (435) 587-1500

Monument Valley

Monument Valley Visitor Center, (435) 727-5874/5870, (435) 727-5875

Zion National Park

Zion National Park, (435) 772-3256

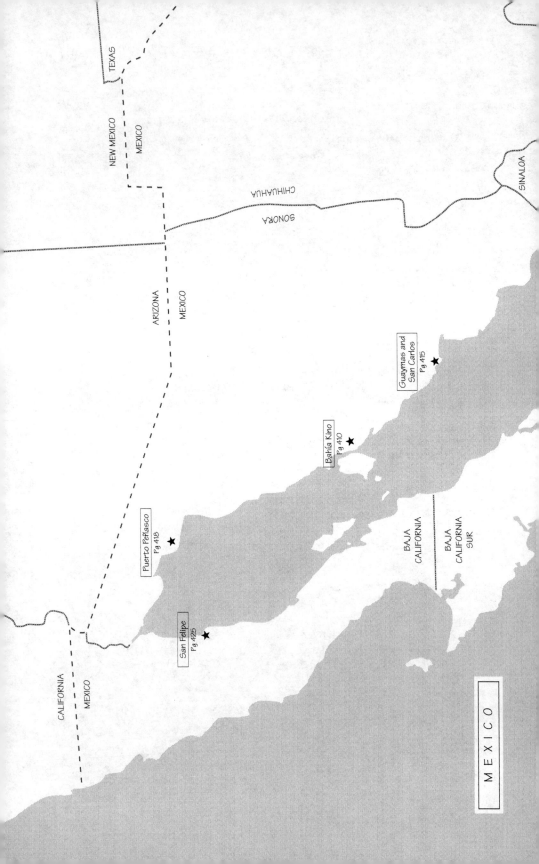

MEXICO

TEXAS

NEW MEXICO

MEXICO

CHIHUAHUA

SINALOA

SONORA

ARIZONA

MEXICO

Guaymas and
San Carlos
Pg 415 ★

Bahía Kino
Pg 410 ★

Puerto Peñasco
Pg 418 ★

BAJA
CALIFORNIA

BAJA
CALIFORNIA
SUR

San Felipe
Pg 425 ★

CALIFORNIA

MEXICO

M E X I C O

Chapter 7

Mexico Destinations

There are several popular Mexican camping destinations not far south of the border. Southwest RV travelers often visit these places. San Felipe and Puerto Peñasco, in particular, sometimes seem to have more American campers than locals.

One reason people take their RVs to these places is that it's so easy. Special regulations are in effect that apply to just a limited number of Mexican destinations. Visitors are not required to have the vehicle import permits required for visiting much of the rest of Mexico. Tourist cards are not required for some visits, although they are required in others. One thing you must take care of though, it's essential to have Mexican insurance before crossing the border with your RV. We'll talk more about that below.

Why do people even want to travel in Mexico? The reasons include beaches, food, culture, and prices. The southwest has no ocean beaches, but Mexican beaches are close by. The four destinations described here all have beaches, and RV sites right on the beach too. All are full of great restaurants, shops, and also great Mexican people. Folks from north of the border are more than welcome, and once you get that insurance out of the way, prices for almost everything, including fuel, are lower than in the States.

If you've never been to Mexico in a vehicle you'll probably find that Puerto Peñasco is the easiest first-time destination. Be aware though, that Puerto Peñasco is overwhelmed by people from north of the border.

San Felipe is probably the next easiest destination. The campgrounds aren't quite as good, but the town does have a slightly more Mexican atmosphere than Puerto Peñasco.

Kino Bay and Guaymas/San Carlos are a little more of a challenge to visit. Vehicle permits are no longer required to visit them but you must have tourist cards. Fortunately, there's a service center just south of Nogales so getting a tourist card is a snap. From there it's just a matter of driving south, not too difficult. Many visitors prefer Guaymas/San Carlos and Kino Bay to the easier to visit towns to the north. See below for much more about all of these towns.

If traveling to Mexico in a vehicle interests you but you would like more information than is contained in this book you can find it in two other books that we write and publish. *Traveler's Guide to Mexican Camping* (ISBN 0-97494-712-1) is a complete guide to camping throughout Mexico. *Traveler's Guide to Camping Mexico's Baja* (ISBN 978-0974947181) covers the Baja Peninsula as well as Puerto Peñasco.

Crossing the Border and The Drive South

If you're bound for **Puerto Peñasco** you'll want to cross at Lukeville/Sonoyta. There is an excellent 61 mile two-lane paved road running south to Puerto Peñasco from the border. The crossing itself is excellent. It is not crowded, has lots of room for RVs, and outside holidays and weekends generally takes only a few minutes to negotiate. In fact, you'll want to make sure that you avoid the crowds heading south on Friday afternoon and Saturday morning, and also those coming north on Sunday. On the US side of the border the roads are also pretty good, SR-85 south from Interstate 8 is 80 miles (129 km) long. If you would like to overnight before crossing the border there are conveniently located campgrounds in the area to the north of Lukeville, see our *Ajo, Why, and Organ Pipe Cactus National Monument* section. Mexican insurance is available in Lukeville. Vehicle-import permits are not required for a visit to Puerto Peñasco, nor are tourist cards if your visit is for less than 72 hours. For longer visits see the *Tourist Cards* section below.

The closest crossing point for **San Felipe** is Calexico/Mexicali. This is a large town, the population approaches a million people. The best crossing is east of town and is called Calexico East on the US side. From the crossing just follow the signs for San Felipe around Mexicali. The road south from Mexicali to San Felipe is 122 miles (200 km) long. Most if it is decent two-lane paved highway, some of the northern portion has four lanes. Many folks from southern California whip over to Mexicali on Interstate 8 for a quick weekend visit to San Felipe. Vehicle-import permits are not required for a visit to San Felipe, nor are tourist permits if your visit is for less than 72 hours. Otherwise see the *Tourist Permits* section below.

For both **Kino Bay** and **Guaymas/San Carlos** you'll want to cross at Nogales. Nogales is the preferred crossing for folks headed down Mexico's west coast since it is serviced by US Interstate Highway 17 from Tucson to the north and serves as the beginning of Mex 15, which is a four-lane highway all the way to Mazatlán. The Nogales crossing is unusual because you don't get your tourist card at the border crossing. Instead, there are modern facilities with quite a bit of parking room some 12 miles (19 km) south of the border on Mex 15. The place is known as the Km 21 Checkpoint.

The preferred crossing in Nogales is west of town. It is known as the Mariposa Gate on the US side and Garita #3 on the Mexican side. This crossing is designed for heavy truck traffic and is one of the best crossings into Mexico for RVs and other travelers because it connects with a toll bypass route that quickly takes you around busy Nogales, you'll hardly see any traffic at all once you cross the border.

New rules that came into effect in 2006 make it much easier to travel as far south as

Guaymas/San Carlos. Vehicle permits are no longer required as long as you only go as far as Guaymas/San Carlos. However if you want to go farther you need the vehicle permits, they can be obtained at a checkpoint south of Guaymas.

Tourist cards are still required for visits to Kino Bay and Guaymas/San Carlos, they can be obtained at the Km 21 Checkpoint. See the *Tourist Card* section below for more details.

While you are not required at this time to have a passport to travel to Mexico, you should know that the U.S. government is stiffening its requirements. Beginning June 1, 2009 all people crossing the border into the U.S. will be required to have either a passport or a passport card (available to US citizens in the second half of 2008).

Tourist Card

Any US or Canadian citizen entering Mexico must obtain a Tarjeta de Turista or tourist card from Mexican immigration. These are also sometimes called an FMT (Forma Migratoria Turista). The exception is short term visitors to Puerto Peñasco or San Felipe (for less than 72 hours). You must have proof of your citizenship to get your tourist card. Actually, you are required to have this identification for any visit to Mexico, even for short visits to border towns or Puerto Peñasco and San Felipe. The best proof of citizenship is a passport but a certified copy of your birth certificate is also acceptable. If you use your birth certificate instead of a passport you will also need a picture ID like a drivers license.

Tourist cards (FMTs) are issued for up to a 180-day stay and there is a charge, actually a tourist tax. You do not pay at the border immigration office, instead you take the card to any bank in Mexico and they collect about $23 and stamp the form. At some crossings they send you to a nearby bank to do this before issuing the tourist card, at others they issue the card and you are allowed to visit a bank and pay any time before returning to the US. You must have the stamped form to leave Mexico, and it is very important to return the form at the immigration office before leaving the country.

For visitors to Puerto Peñasco (if you are going to stay over 72 hours) there is an immigration office at the Sonoyta border crossing on the Mexican side. For visitors to San Felipe (if you are going to stay over 72 hours) there is one at the Mexicali crossings on the Mexican side and also one at the San Felipe airport. For visitors to Kino Bay or Guaymas/San Carlos there is an immigration office at the Km 21 checkpoint.

You will find many people in both Puerto Peñasco and San Felipe who don't worry about getting a tourist card for their visits, even if they are staying for long periods. The truth is that the tourist card rules are seldom if ever enforced in these two destinations. However, this may change at any time.

Insurance

Your automobile insurance from home will not cover you in Mexico. Mexico follows the Napoleonic code, you are guilty until proven innocent. If you have an accident and have no liability insurance to assure the authorities that you can pay for damages it is possible that you might be detained in jail for a considerable time.

People who go into Mexico for just a short time usually buy daily coverage. This is extremely expensive. Some people get this short-term coverage for the time it takes to get to their favorite campground. Once there they park the vehicle and don't use it until they buy more short-term coverage for the drive home.

Longer term coverage, for six months or a year, is much cheaper. It is comparable with the cost of insurance in the US. You can buy just liability insurance or you can buy a policy that also covers damage to your vehicle or vehicles. Check with your US insurance agency to see if damage to your vehicle while in Mexico might be covered by your US policy. No US policy will cover you for liability in Mexico, however. To keep costs down see if you can cancel your US insurance while you are in Mexico since it is not providing any coverage. Here are names and addresses for a few of the brokers that offer Mexican insurance. Call them well before you travel and compare coverage and costs. They will charge the policy to a credit card and mail it to you so that you do not have to worry about insurance at the last moment.

> ADA Vis Global Enterprises, Inc., 38790 Sky Canyon Dr, Murrieta, CA 92563; (800) 909-4457; Website: www.adavisglobal.com.

> Caravan Insurance Services, 127 Promise Lane, Livingston, TX 77351; (800) 489-0083 or (936) 328-5831; Website: www.caravaninsuranceservices.net.

> Discover Baja Travel Club, 3089 Clairemont Dr, San Diego, CA 92117; (800) 727-2252 or (619) 275-4225; Website: www.discoverbaja.com.

> Lewis and Lewis Insurance Agency, 8929 Wilshire Blvd, Suite 220, Beverley Hills, CA 90211; (800) 966-6830 or (310) 657-1112; Website: www.mexican-autoinsurance.com.

> Miller Insurance Agency, Inc., 5805 SW Willow Lane, Lake Oswego, OR 97035; (800) 622-6347; Website: www.MillerRVInsurance.com.

> Point South Insurance, 11313 Edmonson Ave, Moreno Valley, CA 92555; (888) 421-1394; Website: www.mexican-insurance.com.

> Sanborn's Mexico Auto Insurance, 2009 S 10th (SH-336), PO Box 310, McAllen, TX 78505-0310; (800) 222-0158; Website: www.sanbornsinsurance.com; Email: info@sanbornsinsurance.com.

> Vagabundos del Mar Boat and Travel Club, Adventure Tours, 190 Main St, Rio Vista, CA 94571; (800) 474-2252; Website: www.vagabundos.com.

What Can You Take Into Mexico?

Campers tend to bring more things along with them when they visit Mexico than most people. When you cross the border you may be stopped and your things quickly checked. You are actually allowed to bring only certain specified items into Mexico duty free and most RVers probably have more things along with them than they should. Fortunately Mexican border authorities seldom are hard-nosed, in fact they usually don't do much looking around at all. Lately we have heard that people bringing large quantities of food sometimes have problems getting it across the border. Now that Mexico has such good supermarkets there is really little need to bring in much food.

Do not even think about taking either **guns, ammunition,** or **illegal drugs** into Mexico. Any of these things will certainly get you in big trouble. Guns and ammunition are forbidden, so are prescription-type drugs unless you have a valid prescription in your possession. If you travel much on Mexican highways you'll eventually be stopped and searched. Possession of these things, at the border or in Mexico, can result in jail and confiscation of your vehicle.

Pets

You can take your dog or cat into Mexico. Birds and other pets are subject to additional restrictions, taking them to Mexico is not practical. We've not heard of anyone taking a pet into Mexico who has run into problems going south, whatever requirements are in effect do not seem to be observed, so the rules you want to watch for are the ones for bringing the animal back into the US. The US Customs web site says that dogs coming back into the US require a rabies vaccination certificate that is at least 30 days old with an expiration date that is not expired. Your vet will probably know the proper forms that are required, if not, check with customs. Coming north your dog or cat may be examined at the border to see if it seems to be sick, if there is a question you may be required to have it examined by a vet before it will be admitted to the US.

Money

Mexico, of course, has its own currency, called the peso. The exchange rate varies, it has recently fluctuated between ten and thirteen pesos to the dollar. Some visitors, particularly in San Felipe and Puerto Peñasco, never seem to have any pesos and use dollars for most purchases. They pay for the privilege, prices in dollars tend to be higher than if you pay in pesos. Outside of border areas and the Baja dollars are not readily accepted.

Cash machines are now widespread in Mexico and represent the best way to obtain cash. If you don't already have a debit card you should take the trouble to get one before heading south, make sure it has a four-digit international number. Both Cirrus (Visa) and Plus (MasterCard) networks are in place, not all machines accept both. Don't be surprised if a machine inexplicably refuses your card, bank operations and phone lines are both subject to unexpected interruptions. If you can't get the card to work try a machine belonging to another bank or just go directly to a teller inside the bank. You should consider bringing a backup card in case the electronic strip stops working on the one you normally use. Most cards have a maximum daily withdrawal limit, usually about $300 US. In Mexico this limit is sometimes lower than it is in the US. When you use your card be sure to grab it as soon as the machine spits it back out. Don't count your cash first. Mexican machines are sometimes programmed to suck the card back in within a short period of time (15 seconds) if it isn't snatched quickly. This is a safety measure but causes problems. It's almost impossible to get a card back once the machine takes it. Some people use only cash machines at bank branches, and only when they are open, for this very reason.

Visa and MasterCard credit cards are useful in Mexico, but cards are not as widely accepted as north of the border. Restaurants and shops, particularly in tourist areas, accept them. Outside metropolitan and tourist areas their acceptance is limited. A few Pemex gas stations are beginning to accept credit cards but they charge a significant fee for doing so. Some large supermarkets now accept Visa and MasterCard. It is also possible to get cash advances against these credit cards in Mexican banks but the fees tend to be high.

Water and Groceries

Don't take a chance when it comes to drinking Mexican water. Even water considered potable by the locals is likely to cause problems for you. It is no fun to be sick, especially when you are far from the border in an unfamiliar environment. The easiest solution is to drink bottled water. Everywhere in Mexico you can buy large 19 liter (approximately five-gallon) bottles of water. They are available at supermarkets, purified water shops, or from vendors who visit campgrounds. Water purchased this way is inexpensive. You can either keep one of the large bottles by paying a small deposit or actually empty them into your own water tank or other containers.

Another source of potential stomach problems is fruit and vegetables. It is essential that you peel all fruit and vegetables or soak them in a purification solution before eating them. Diluted bleach can be used for this, the directions are right on the label of most bleach sold in Mexico. You can also purchase special drops to add to water for this purpose, the drops are stocked in the fruit and vegetable department of most supermarkets in Mexico. The drops are better than bleach for this because they don't affect the taste of the vegetables.

There are large modern supermarkets in Puerto Peñasco and Guaymas. There are also large ones in Hermosillo, you'll pass them en route to Kino Bay which has only small grocery stores. San Felipe also does not have a large supermarket although there are rumors that one is coming soon.

Fuel

Choosing the brand of gas you're going to buy is easy in Mexico. All of the gas stations are Pemex stations. Pemex is the national oil company, it is responsible for everything from exploring for oil to pumping it into your car. Gas is usually sold for cash although a few stations now accept cards. There are usually two kinds of gas, Magna Sin in green pumps and higher octane Premium in red pumps. You'll probably start by using Magna Sin, with a nominal octane rating of 87. You may or may not find that it is acceptable. Diesel is carried at many stations. Note that at this time Mexican diesel is not ULSD. It does not meet manufacturers requirements for diesel vehicles built in 2007 and later. If you have one of these newer vehicles then using Mexican diesel would probably void your engine warranty. Do not fill a vehicle that requires ULSD in Mexico. If you can't reach the Mexican destinations described in this chapter and return using fuel purchased in the U.S. we suggest waiting until Mexico begins stocking ULSD for your visit to Mexico. Watch the updates on our website (www.rollinghomes.com) for more about this. At this time it looks like it may be several years before ULSD is available in Mexico.

Gas and diesel sell for the same price at all Pemex stations in an area. The region very near the border may have different prices than that a little farther south. In the winter of 2007/2008 prices in Mexico were: Magna Sin $2.46, Premium $3.09, diesel $2.09. These prices have, of course, been converted from pesos per liter to US dollars per gallon. Prices increase just a few cents per gallon each month on a very regular basis.

Telephones and Internet

In recent years it has become much easier to communicate in Mexico. The country has installed street-side pay phones in most cities, the cell phone network is as good as the one in the US (sometimes better), and internet cafés and even Wi-Fi in campgrounds are common.

In recent years phones in kiosks or booths, usually labeled Ladatel or Telmex, have appeared along the streets in more and more Mexican towns. To use them you buy a phone card, usually at a pharmacy. These are computerized smart cards charged with 10, 20, 30, 50, or 100 pesos. To buy one ask for a "tarjeta Ladatel". To use the phone you insert the card into the slot on the front of the phone and the amount of money left on the card appears on a readout. As you talk the time left counts down on the readout.

To dial an international call to the U.S. or Canada you dial 00 + 1 + area code + the local number. To place a collect call to the U.S. or Canada you dial 09 + 1 + area code + local number. To dial a Mexican long distance number you dial 01 + area code + local number. To dial a Mexican local number you dial the local number without the area code.

To call into Mexico from the U.S. or Canada you must first dial a 011 for international access, then the Mexico country code which is 52, then the Mexican area code and number. The telephone numbers given in this book assume you are calling from the US or Canada. From Mexico drop the 01152. Then follow the instructions above.

One good deal for calling the states is a Sam's Club or Costco pre-paid AT&T or MCI card. These cards can only be purchased in stores north of the border, not the Mexican stores. The rate is about $.34 per minute from most of Mexico. The cards are handy because you can add money to them over the phone by giving a credit card number, even from Mexico.

Cell phones are very popular in Mexico but using your US cell phone can cost quite a bit. The rate is usually about $1.50 per minute. Before you go to Mexico call your provider and have your phone set up for use in Mexico. Ask what the rate will be so you're not too shocked when you come home and see the bill.

The internet is a useful tool for communicating from Mexico. Internet cafes are common. Many Mexican homes do not have computers and good telephone connections so Mexicans (often students) commonly go to these cafes to use computers. You'll find them in any city.

We have found that quite a few RV parks have installed computers and even Wi-Fi systems to help their guests stay in touch with home. You'll find information about this in the campground write-ups.

Safety

Mexico would be full of camping visitors from the US and Canada if there was no uncertainty about safety. This uncertainty is the factor that crowds RVers into campgrounds just north of the border but leaves those a hundred miles south pleasantly uncrowded. People in those border campgrounds will warn you not to cross into Mexico because there are banditos, dishonest cops, terrible roads, and language and water problems. The one thing you can be pretty sure of when you get one of these warnings is that that person has not tried Mexican camping him/herself.

The best policy while traveling in Mexico is to exercise normal caution. Most RVers follow the following rules.

1. Don't drive at night. Mexican roads are not well marked so it's easy to have an accident if you do drive at night.

2. Stay in campgrounds. When you're unfamiliar with the language and the customs it's best to stay in a place that has been set aside for you.

Campgrounds

Mexican campgrounds vary a great deal. Near the border, and that includes all of the areas described in this book, many campgrounds are much like the ones you'll find in the rest of the Southwest. However, there are also many that are fairly primitive. You can choose.

MEXICO DESTINATIONS

Most of the larger campgrounds in Mexico, especially in the areas described here, have hookups for electricity, water and sewer. Almost all of the primary campgrounds covered in this book have them but the actual condition of the outlets, faucets, and sewer connections may not be very good. We find that in many campgrounds the hardware wasn't great when installed, and maintenance doesn't get done unless absolutely necessary. It is a good idea to take a look at the connections on a parking pad before pulling in, you may want to move to another one.

Mexican electrical service is usually at a higher voltage than in the US or Canada. We normally see from 125 to 130 volts if there aren't a lot of RVs in the campground. This can cause some problems if you have a sophisticated RV. Amperage in campgrounds can be 50 amps, but most are about 15 amps, the campground descriptions below give that information. Many campgrounds only have small two-slot household-type outlets so be sure that you have an adapter that lets you use these smaller sockets. Most sockets do not have a ground, either because the outlet is the two-slot variety without the ground slot, or because the ground slot is not wired. Test the electricity at your site before plugging in. You can buy a tester at your camping supply store before heading for Mexico that will quickly indicate the voltage and any faults of the outlet. This is cheap insurance. You might make yourself a two-prong adaptor that can be reversed to achieve correct polarity and that has a wire and alligator clip so you can provide your own ground.

Even if the voltage in a campground appears to be OK when you hook up it may not stay that way. Voltage usually fluctuates in Mexican campgrounds during the day. Many accessories and appliances in modern RVs are sensitive to this and can be damaged by very high or low voltages. Most experts say you are safe between 104 and 128 volts. You should monitor voltage to see if this is a problem. Many people with modern RVs have large battery banks and solar panels, consider using these instead of electrical hookups at times when voltages are outside acceptable limits.

Water connections are common in campgrounds, but you may not want to trust the quality of the water even if the campground manager assures you that it is good. See the *Water and Groceries* section of this chapter for details on how to cope with this.

Sewer connections in Mexican campgrounds are usually located at the rear of the site. You should make sure that you have enough hose to reach several feet past the rear bumper of your RV before you come south. You probably won't be able to buy any sewer hose or holding tank chemicals down south

DESTINATIONS AND THEIR CAMPGROUNDS

BAHÍA KINO, SONORA (BAH-HEE-AH KEY-NO)

Bahía Kino or Kino Bay (population about 5,000) is really two villages. Both towns, of course, are named for the famed Jesuit missionary Padre Eusebio Francisco Kino. Kino Viejo (Old Kino) is a fishing village with dusty streets arranged around a traditional square. Fishing is from skiffs or pangas, they are pulled up on the beach for unloading. Kino Nuevo (New Kino) is a resort with small hotels and RV parks strung along several miles of beach to the northwest. Only one RV park is in Viejo Kino but the old town is where many of the services are located, including restaurants and the handiest gas station. Small grocery stores in both towns provide limited supplies, for bigger shopping trips the huge supermarkets in Hermosillo are only 66 miles (107 km) distant on a decent two-

MEXICO IS A BIRD WATCHER'S DREAM

lane paved road. Closer, at 27 miles (44 km), along the road to Hermosillo is the farming town of Miguel Alemán with a population of 33,000. Miguel Alemán now has several medium-sized supermarkets. Kino Bay has street-side telephone booths but no banks.

Kino is Seri Indian country, some of them live in Bahía Kino but there are also villages located to the north along the coast and on Isla Tiburón. You can sometimes find **stands selling ironwood carvings** of dolphins and other animals in Kino Bay. Most of the ironwood carvings, however, are not authentic traditional Seri carvings, they are produced in small factories on the back streets of Kino Viejo. The town has a museum, **Museo de los Seris**, with displays of historical photographs and traditional articles of clothing and living utensils. There is also a shop where carvings can be purchased next to the museum.

The fishing is sometimes excellent off Kino Bay and there are miles of coast to explore along rough sandy roads to the north. Mexico's largest island, Isla Tiburón, is offshore and can only be visited with a Seri guide.

Bahía Kino Campgrounds

KINO BAY RV PARK *(Open All Year)*
Res and Info: (011-52) (662) 242-0216, kinobayrvpark@hotmail.com
Location: Kino Bay, *N 28° 51' 34", W 112° 01' 29", Near Sea Level*

200 Sites – Bahía Kino's largest trailer park is friendly, organized, and well run. There are 200 full hookup spaces at the Kino Bay. These are rather barren pull-thru spaces with 30-amp outlets (air conditioners are OK), sewer, water, and covered patios. They are large enough for big RVs. The restrooms are modern and clean, they have hot-water

MEXICO DESTINATIONS

showers. The campground has a huge fenced storage area for boats and RVs and a fish-cleaning house that is well separated from the living areas. The beach with a restaurant is right across the street. The folks at the reception office speak English and stand out because they are so helpful. They also offer two computers with internet hookups in the office. The campground is well-signed. If you zero your odometer as you pass Pemex #2660 at the entrance to Old Kino Bay and continue straight on the main highway you will find that the Kino Bay RV park is on your right at 5.7 miles (9.2 km).

KUNKAAK TRAILER PARK *(Open All Year)*
Res and Info: (011-52) (662) 242-0088, www.kunkaak.com
Location: Kino Bay, *N 28° 51' 40", W 112° 01' 23", Near Sea Level*

60 Sites – The Trailer Park Kunkaak is one of the few campgrounds in Bahía Kino that is not on Avenida Mar de Cortés along the water. It is not far away, however, it sits almost behind the Kino Bay RV Park. The location is nice and quiet, away from the cars traveling along the waterfront. The campsites of the Kunkaak are arranged around an attractive central building which houses the office, lounge, game room, restrooms and laundry room. There is no fence around this park, the spaces are attractively arranged and separated by rock walls and plants. The 60 spaces have 15-amp outlets with 30-amp breakers (air conditioners are OK), water, and sewer. They have tile-roofed patios with storage rooms. Some are fine for big RVs but there is restricted room for slide-outs. Restrooms are modern and clean and have hot water showers. To find the campground zero your

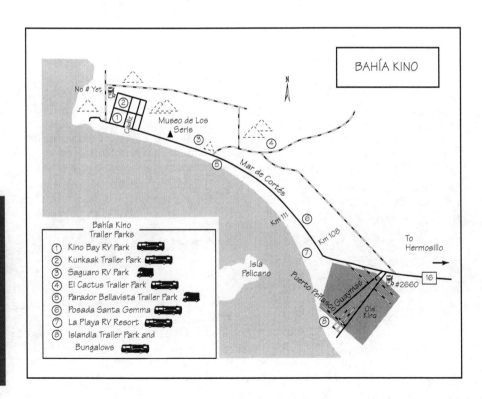

odometer as you pass Pemex #2660 at the entrance to Old Kino Bay and continue straight on the main highway. At 5.6 miles (9 km) turn right on Cadiz and drive a block inland alongside the small pitch-and-putt golf course, the trailer park will be on your left.

SAGUARO RV PARK *(Open All Year)*
Information: (011-52) (662) 242-0165
Location: Kino Bay, *N 28° 51' 18", W 112° 00' 12", Near Sea Level*

25 Sites – The Saguaro is one of the older trailer parks in Kino Bay. It sits across the road from the beach, many people prefer to keep their RVs away from the salt water. The campground has 25 spaces, they have 30-amp outlets, sewer, and water hookups. Eighteen of them have covered patios and many are pull-thrus. They're large enough for RVs to about 35 feet. Parking and drives are gravel. The restrooms are older and needed maintenance badly last time we visited, they sometimes have hot water showers. The Saguaro also has four rental rooms. To find the campground zero your odometer as you pass Pemex #2660 at the entrance to Old Kino Bay and continue straight on the main highway. At 4.4 miles (7.1 km) you'll see the Saguaro on the right near the foot of the small hill. English is spoken if the owner is living here but recently she has been away.

EL CACTUS TRAILER PARK *(Open All Year)*
Res and Info: (011-52) (662) 216-1643 (Hermosillo),
(011-52) (662) 258-1200 (Kino Bay Cell Phone)
Location: Kino Bay, *N 28° 51' 36", W 111° 59' 27", Near Sea Level*

29 Sites – The El Cactus is not located in Bahía Kino at all, it sits alone in the desert about a mile from the ocean. If you like your peace and quiet this is the place for you. All sites are back-ins with 15-amp outlets, sewer, water, satellite TV, and patios. Some have a little shade. The restrooms are clean and have hot water showers. There is a swimming pool. The campground is surrounded by a chain-link fence and lots of desert. Only limited English is spoken. To reach the El Cactus zero your odometer as you pass Pemex #2660 at the entrance to Old Kino Bay and continue straight on the main highway. Turn right at 4.3 miles (6.9 km) just before the small hill, there is a sign for the El Cactus Trailer Park. Follow the gravel road for .9 miles (1.5 km), the trailer park is on the left.

PARADOR BELLAVISTA TRAILER PARK *(Open All Year)*
Res and Info: (011-52) (662) 242-0139
Location: Kino Bay, *N 28° 51' 12", W 111° 59' 50", Near Sea Level*

16 Sites – The Parador Bellavista is a small beachside trailer park. The maneuvering room is limited but somehow RVs to about 35 feet manage to get in here each year. There are 16 spaces in the campground, nine along the front row overlooking the beach. All have electricity (15-amp or 30-amp outlets), sewer, and water hookups. Most of the spaces are back-in (or pull-in), two are parallel parking spaces. Most have patios, some with ramadas. The restrooms have hot showers and there is a laundry with a self-service machine. To find the Bellavista zero your odometer as you pass Pemex #2660 at the entrance to Old Kino Bay and continue straight on the main highway. The campground is on the left at 4.1 miles (6.6 km). Limited English is spoken.

POSADA SANTA GEMMA *(Open All Year)*

Res and Info: (011-52)(662) 214-5579 (Hermosillo), (011-52) (662) 242-0026 (Kino Bay)
Location: Kino Bay, *N 28° 51' 00", W 111° 59' 09", Near Sea Level*

14 Sites – This is another small campground next to the beach. The Posada Santa Gemma is also a motel. All sites are back-in or pull-in with 15-amp outlets, sewer, and water and covered patios. Some sites are suitable for RVs to 35 feet. An additional seven spaces with no hookups are located across the road. The seven spaces overlooking the beach are usually full, the others are usually empty. The restrooms are small but adequate and have hot-water showers. To find the Santa Gemma zero your odometer as you pass Pemex #2660 at the entrance to Old Kino Bay and continue straight on the main highway. The campground is on the left at 3.3 miles (5.3 km). Limited English is spoken.

LA PLAYA RV RESORT *(Open All Year)*

Res and Info: (011-52) (662) 242-0274, www.laplayarvhotel.com,
                 kinorvlaplaya@prodigy.net.mx
Location: Kino Bay, *N 28° 49' 48", W 111° 57' 18", Near Sea Level*

48 Sites – As you enter Nuevo Bahía Kino the first campground you'll see is the newest campground in town, the La Playa. It's definitely the most upscale of Kino's camp-grounds and plans are in the works to continue improving it. There are 48 full-hookup sites with 30 and 50-amp outlets on two terraces overlooking the beach. These are big sites. Many RVers have contracted to have structures erected on the patios and plan to return every winter. As a result most available sites for travelers are at the rear of the ter-races with little in the way of views. The restrooms are some of the nicest we've seen, of course they have hot showers. The owner of this campground is one of the town's top homebuilders, he is continuing work on the campground as time allows. A pool and spa have been planned for several years but were not yet installed when we last visited. To reach La Playa zero your odometer as you pass Pemex #2660 at the entrance to Old Kino Bay and continue straight on the main highway. The campground is on the left at 1.1 miles (1.8 km). Limited English is spoken here.

ISLANDIA TRAILER PARK AND BUNGALOWS *(Open All Year)*

Res and Info: (011-52) (662) 242-0081, islandia@hotmail.com
Location: Kino Bay, *N 28° 49' 23", W 111° 56' 45", Near Sea Level*

30 Spaces – The Islandia is the only one of the Kino Bay trailer parks located in Old Kino Bay. The location in the old town gives this campground an entirely different feel that any other campground in Kino Bay. We were very impressed with this campground when we last visited. Facilities were considerably upgraded from our prior visit and were in good condition. The water-front campground has 30 spaces with 30-amp type outlets (20-amp breakers), sewer, and water. Twelve spaces are back-ins, the remainder are pull-thrus. Some spaces are along the water but most sit back away from the beach. There's lots of room for big RVs. Restrooms are in good condition and have hot showers. There's a self-service laundry with two washers and also a boat ramp. There are also several rent-al bungalows scattered around the property. You can easily walk to the center of town in a few minutes. The town has dusty streets, a square, several small stores and restaurants,

and small fishing boats pulled up along the beach. To get to the campground watch for
Pemex #2660 as you enter Old Kino Bay on the main road from Hermosillo. Turn left
on the second road after the Pemex. This is a 45° turn onto Guaymas, which is a paved
street. Follow Guaymas for .4 mile (.6 km) and just before the road narrows turn right on
Puerto Peñasco along the fence of the campground and enter on your left. Some English
is usually spoken by the staff here.

GUAYMAS AND SAN CARLOS, SONORA (GWAY-MAS AND SAWN-KAHR-LOES)

You can think of Guaymas and San Carlos (combined population about 125,000) as twin
cities, fraternal twins, they are not at all alike. Guaymas itself is an old port, the first supply depot was set up here by the Jesuits in 1701 although they were driven out later by the
tough and resistant local Indians. Today the major industry is fishing. Guaymas has several modern supermarkets which are the best places to lay in supplies in the area. While
Guaymas itself isn't really a tourist town it does have its appeal. The town has a good
natural harbor, a central market, and because it's a port, Guaymas is one of Mexico's
towns that celebrates Carnival.

North of Guaymas is San Carlos, center of the tourist activity. The recent completion of
a four-lane boulevard through San Carlos has really changed the ambiance. The dust is
gone, now the town seems to be making real progress toward being an upscale resort.
There are marinas, hotels, a golf course, and restaurants. There are also several good RV
parks.

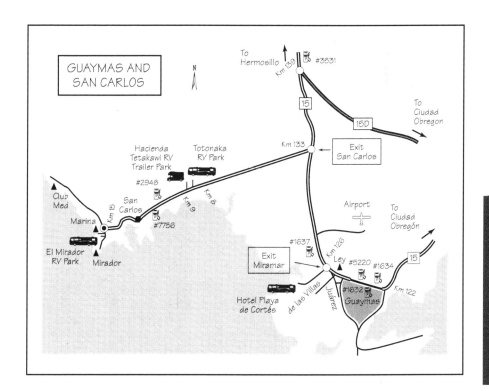

Between Guaymas and San Carlos is the small town of Miramar. The main reason you will want to know this is that Miramar is home to a popular RV park for visitors passing through the area, the venerable Hotel Playa de Cortés.

The toll highway bypasses Guaymas entirely, don't miss the Guaymas/San Carlos cutoff near Pemex #3531 and Km 139 when headed south from Hermosillo.

Guaymas and San Carlos Campgrounds

TOTONAKA RV PARK *(Open All Year)*

Res and Info: (011-52) (622) 226-0323, (011-52) (622) 226-0481,
www.mexonline.com/totonaka.htm, totonakarv@yahoo.com
Location: San Carlos, *N 27° 57' 48", W 111° 01' 28", Near Sea Level*

120 Sites - The Totonaka Trailer Park is located in central San Carlos. It's a nice park in a convenient location. This is our favorite place to stay in the Guaymas area. The campground has about 120 spaces, these are back-in sites with patios, electricity, water, sewer and TV. Electrical outlets are 15 amp style but most spaces have 30 or 40-amp breakers. Many sites will handle big RVs. The park has a cobblestone central avenue with packed gravel side streets and parking areas. Restrooms are in good condition, they have hot water showers. A laundry room has many coin-operated washers and dryers. There is a swimming pool at the front of the campground and restaurants within easy walking distance. The beach is across the street. There is a bus that runs along the waterfront and into Guaymas every quarter hour. The young English-speaking owner is something of an internet aficionado so there is free Wi-Fi internet access as well as a computer dedicated to internet access in the office. Zero your odometer as you take the cutoff from Mex 15 toward San Carlos. You will be driving on a nice four-lane highway that is virtually empty. At 5.6 miles (9.0 km) you will see the Totonaka Trailer Park on the right.

HACIENDA TETAKAWI RV TRAILER PARK *(Open All Year)*

Reservations: (011-52) (622) 226-0220
Location: San Carlos, *N 27° 57' 48", W 111° 01' 33", Near Sea Level*

The Hacienda Tetakawi is a nice Best Western Hotel with an older trailer park in the rear. You'll find people here who return every year and stay for the entire season. This campground is badly in need of maintenance, few travelers find the facilities to be adequate. There are about 40 spaces, they are back-ins with patios, 15-amp outlets with 15 or 30-amp breakers, sewer, and water hookups. They are suitable for RVs to about 32 feet. The hookups at many sites are not useable. There are many more sites in the rear but they have never been in use when we have visited. The bathrooms are clean, they have hot-water showers. There is a swimming pool with a bar/restaurant up front next to the motel. To find the campground just follow the instructions given above for reaching the Totonaka RV Park. The Hacienda Tetakawi is just beyond and located right next door.

EL MIRADOR RV PARK *(Open Sept 1 to April 30 - Varies)*

Res and Info: (011-52) (622) 227-0213, (011-52) (622) 227-0107,
www.elmiradorrv.com, mirador@tetakawi.net.mx
Location: San Carlos, *N 27° 56' 39", W 111° 05' 14", Near Sea Level*

THE EL MIRADOR RV PARK IN SAN CARLOS

90 Sites – This is the newest RV park in San Carlos. The park is actually built to US standards, many people think it is the best RV park in Mexico. If you judge strictly by the quality of the facilities it probably is. That's not to speak badly of the location either – the area is very scenic, the weather generally good, and it's an easy drive from the states. However, the campground itself is in an isolated location outside San Carlos. The campground has about 90 large back-in sites, almost all are suitable for the largest RVs. The parking pads are cobblestone and there are cement patios. Electrical outlets are 30 amps and each site also has water, sewer, and satellite TV connections. There is gravel between the sites and no shade. The amenities at this campground were excellent when built but have been neglected lately. There is a swimming pool and spa (often cold), an excellent restaurant, a laundry room with coin-operated machines, a game room with pool and ping-pong tables, and two tennis courts. If you want to spend time here it is a good idea to make reservations ahead, during the winter it seems that every caravan coming through San Carlos stays here, and this campground honors their reservations, unlike some in Mexico. That means that individual travelers without reservations are often turned away or can only stay a night or two. The campground is located west of central San Carlos. If you take the San Carlos exit from the highway north of Guaymas at the Km 133 marker and drive west you will reach San Carlos in about 4.4 miles (7.1 km), and reach a Y at 7.5 miles (12.1 km). Go right here following the sign to Algodones and climb up and over a low hill, then follow the road through a small area of holiday homes and then through a short valley between two hills. You will reach an intersection at 9.9 miles (16 km). Turn left here and the entrance to the campground is on the right at 10.4 miles (16.8 km). The route is well-signed for the entire distance.

MEXICO DESTINATIONS

HOTEL PLAYA DE CORTÉS *(Open All Year)*
Res and Info: (011-52) (622) 221-0135, (800) 782-7608
              http://hermosillovirtual.com/gandara/index.htm
Location: Guaymas, *N 27° 54' 44", W 110° 56' 42", Near Sea Level*

85 Sites – The Hotel Playa de Cortés was built in 1936 as a railway resort hotel and continues to have a nice but faded ambiance. It is located in Miramar between the San Carlos cutoff from Mex 15 and the town of Guaymas. Behind the hotel is a nice RV parking area with 52 very long full-hookup (30-amp outlets) back-in slots. Each has its own patio and drivers of long fifth-wheels will find that they do not need to unhook. Twenty-seven additional full-hookup (15-amp outlets) back-in sites with no patios have recently been added as well as 6 more sites with only electrical and water hookups. This is a full-service hotel, it has a restaurant, bar, swimming pool, beach area, tennis courts, and small boat charters are available for fishing or sightseeing. There are no permanently-located RVs here. Busses run in to Guaymas from near the hotel. The hotel is located at Playa Miramar, a beach community between Guaymas and Bahía San Carlos. Take the off-ramp from Mex 15 just west of Guaymas and follow the wide road 1.9 miles (3.1 km) to its end. You'll be at the hotel. Just through the gate turn to the left to enter the campground. Usually only very limited English is spoken at the front desk but this changes from one visit to the next.

PUERTO PEÑASCO, SONORA (PWEHR-TOE PEN-YAHS-KOE)

Puerto Peñasco (population about 45,000) is probably the easiest town in Mexico to visit in your RV. RVers from north of the border virtually own this town, noisy hordes of them fill RV parks and boondock in the vicinity. On weekends and holidays Puerto Peñasco is even more popular. After all, it is only a little over an hour's driving time south of the Arizona border, it is located in a free zone requiring little governmental paperwork, and there are beaches, desert, fishing, and Mexican crafts and food. Don't forget to pick up Mexican auto insurance, however.

Americans often call the town Rocky Point, you'll see why when you see the location of the old town. The road to Rocky Point was built by the American government during World War II when it was thought that it might be necessary to bring in supplies this way if the west coast was blockaded by Japanese submarines. That never happened, but the road, now paved and in good shape, makes the town easy to reach.

Campgrounds in Puerto Peñasco are in three areas. Three are northwest of the old town along Playa Bonita and Sandy Beach. Three older (quieter) ones are along the water east of the old town. Others are starting to appear north of town along the highway. The Sandy Beach area is a construction beehive, until recently condos were going up like mushrooms. Along with that construction come some benefits. There are now two operating golf courses in the Puerto Peñasco area. Another nice feather of Puerto Peñasco is a modern Ley supermarket. There's no need to bring a lot of groceries south. Almost all campgrounds in Puerto Peñasco have desk staff that can speak English.

THE NEW MAYAN PALACE GOLF COURSE IN PUERTO PEÑASCO

Puerto Peñasco Campgrounds

🚐 **BONITA RV PARK** *(Open All Year)*

Res and Info: (011-52) (638) 383-1400, www.playabonitaresort.com,
bonitarvpark@hotmail.com
Location: Puerto Peñasco, *N 31° 18' 44", W 113° 32' 48", Near Sea Level*

96 Sites – This is one of the newer parks in town. It's conveniently located near the beach and the tourist area of town. Unfortunately, the park itself is uninviting due to the surrounding wall. The campground has 96 full-hookup sites. These are back-ins with 30-amp power. There's lots of room here for big RVs, particularly as the campground is seldom even partly full. Restrooms are modern and offer hot showers, there's a lounge room with television.

As you enter town from the north watch for Pemex #2488 on the left. Four-tenths of a mile (.6 km) after the Pemex is a cross road marked with many large green signs on a pedestrian bridge over the road. Turn right here on Calle 13. Proceed across the railroad tracks and drive 0.4 mile (0.6 km). The campground entrance is on the right.

🚐 **CONCHA DEL MAR CAMPGROUND AND RV PARK**
(Open All Year)

Location: Puerto Peñasco, *N 31° 18' 59", W 113° 33' 04", Near Sea Level*

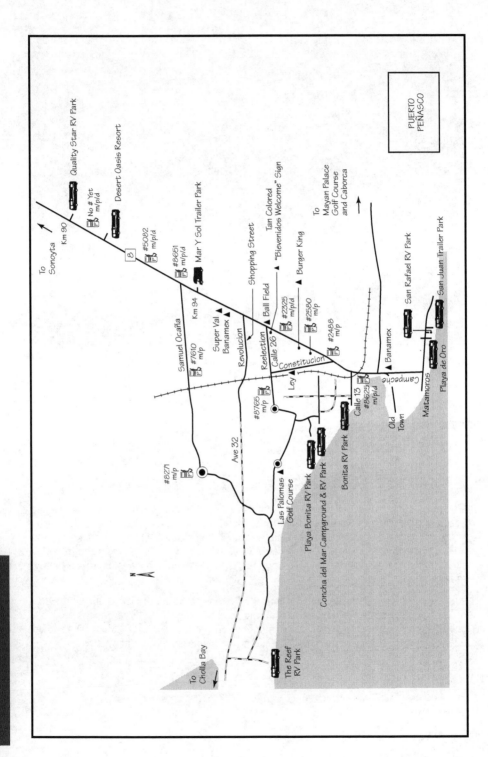

Concha del Mar is a large flat unimproved dirt and sand area near the eastern end of Playa Bonita between the Bonita RV Park and the Playa Bonita RV Park. It's a large area and can handle many rigs or tents. There's a restroom building with flush toilets and cold showers. There are no hookups. This park is surely a parcel of land in a holding pattern, we'll see if it ends up as a hookup RV park or condos.

As you enter town from the north watch for Pemex 2488 on the left. Four-tenths of a mile (.6 km) after the Pemex is a cross road marked with many large green signs on a pedestrian bridge over the road. Turn right here on Calle 13. Proceed across the railroad tracks and drive .3 mile (.5 km), turn right at the corner. Now drive north for .3 mile (.5 km) , a distance of five blocks (count the cross streets on your right). Turn left here and at the end of the road in .3 mile (.5 km) is an arch which serves as the entrance to the park. An attendant will collect your fee and you can enter.

⛟ PLAYA BONITA RV PARK *(Open All Year)*

Res and Info: (011-52) (638) 383-2596, www.playabonitaresort.com,
playabonitarvpark@hotmail.com
Location: 1 Mile W of Puerto Peñasco, *N 31° 19' 06", W 113° 33' 16", Near Sea Level*

300 Sites – This is a large campground located northwest of town on Playa Bonita. The Playa Bonita RV Park is affiliated with a nice hotel next door. This campground has good access to lots of four-wheeling so it's full of off-road folks and their equipment most weekends. All sites are back-in slots with 30-amp outlets, sewer, and water. Many big

BEACH FRONT CAMPING AT THE PLAYA BONITA RV PARK

MEXICO DESTINATIONS

RVs use this campground although the sites aren't really quite long enough and maneuvering room is restricted. Restrooms are clean and have hot water. The campground has a small recreation room with a TV, a self-service laundry, limited groceries, and the affiliated hotel next door has a restaurant. The campground has free Wi-Fi too. The beach out front is beautiful. One nice feature is the malecón (walkway) that fronts the entire park, a great place to walk and watch the action. There's also a spa tub. Evening fireworks displays by the guests are a tradition at this campground – great if you like them, bad if you don't like the noise.

As you enter Puerto Peñasco watch for Pemex #8651 on the left. Continue for another 1.3 miles (2.1 km) and turn right onto Calle 26. Follow Calle 26 westward for .4 mile (.6 km) past Pemex #8765 to a traffic circle. Drive 270 degrees around the circle and follow the road south. It will make a 90 degree bend to the right and just beyond the bend you want to turn left, the left turn is .3 mile (.5 km) from the traffic circle. In just .1 mile (.2 km) turn right, pass through a gate with a guardhouse (usually manned) and continue to the campground at the end of the road.

THE REEF RV PARK *(Open All Year)*

Res and Info: (011-52) (638) 383-5790, www.thereefrvpark.com,
thereefrvpark@prodigy.net.mx
Location: 3 Miles W of Puerto Peñasco, *N 31° 19' 38", W 113° 36' 12", Near Sea Level*

152 Sites – This used to be a popular boondocking spot. Now it's a large RV park offering full hookups above beautiful Sandy Beach.

This is a large RV park with 52 waterfront sites and over a hundred behind. These are all really big back-in sites with lots of room for big rigs. The parking surface is almost white crushed gravel, there isn't a bit of shade. About half the sites have full hookups with 50 and 30-amp outlets. Restrooms have hot showers. There's a popular upscale bar/ restaurant adjacent. There is also a boondocking area controlled by this campground that is along the beach on the town side of the park. There are no hookups, just a flat, well-packed area overlooking the beach. The price for boondocking is $5. The monthly beach rate for the RV park is $700, for spaces back from the water it is $500.

As you approach Puerto Peñasco watch for Pemex #8651 which is on the left. Just before you reach the Pemex turn right onto a paved road. Follow this road west for 2.3 miles (3.7 km) to a traffic circle. Drive around the circle about 270 degrees and drive south. Follow this road for 3 miles (4.8 km) behind several large condo high rises until you reach an intersection. Turn left and the campground is immediately ahead.

PLAYA DE ORO RV PARK *(Open All Year)*

Res and Info: (011-52) (638) 383-2668, www.playadeoro-rv.com, playadeororv@yahoo.com
Location: Puerto Peñasco, *N 31° 17' 52", W 113° 32' 07", Near Sea Level*

325 Spaces – This huge campground is one of the oldest ones in Puerto Peñasco. It bills itself as the only full service RV park in Rocky Point. Quiet a bit of the park has been recently redone, particularly the service buildings. It's looking pretty good. There are now 325 spaces at the Playa de Oro. They are located south of Matamoros Ave. along and back from the beach and also extending well inland to the north of Matamoros. The sites have 30-amp (some 50-amp) electricity, sewer, and water. They have gravel surfaces,

no shade, and no patios and will take RVs to 40 feet. The bathrooms are remodeled, the showers require a quarter for 4 to 5 minutes. The campground has a small, simple restaurant, a mini-mart, a self-service laundry, and a boat ramp. There is also a large long-term storage yard for those wishing to leave a trailer or boat when they go back north.

As you approach Puerto Peñasco from the north watch for Pemex #8651 on the left. Zero your odometer here and continue straight for 2.8 mile (4.5 km). You will see that the highway is going to bend to the right ahead, you want to go straight so get in the left lane and continue straight when it's clear. Now continue another .5 mile (.8 km) to a T. Turn left and you'll see the campground gate on the right in .4 mile (.6 km).

SAN RAFAEL RV PARK *(Open All Year)*
   Res and Info: (011-52) (638) 383-5044, (638) 383-2681
   Location: Puerto Peñasco, *N 31° 17' 49", W 113° 31' 58", Near Sea Level*

31 Sites – This is a smaller campground with no beachfront sites even though it is south of Calle Matamoros. All visitor sites have 30-amp outlets, sewer, and water. These are gravel-surfaced back-in spaces without patios or shade. Some are long sites suitable for big RVs. Permanent resident RVs occupy two sides of the park. The campground has clean modern restrooms with hot showers, a TV room, and a self-service laundry.

As you approach Puerto Peñasco from the north watch for Pemex #8651 on the left. Zero your odometer here and continue straight for 2.8 mile (4.5 km). You will see that the highway is going to bend to the right ahead, you want to go straight so get in the left lane and continue straight when it's clear. Now continue another .5 mile (.8 km) to a T. Turn left and you'll see the campground gate on the right in .5 mile (.8 km).

SAN JUAN TRAILER PARK *(Open All Year)*
   Res and Info: (602) 334-4175 (US), (011-52) (638) 388-0516
   Location: Puerto Peñasco, *N 31° 17' 47", W 113° 32' 02", Near Sea Level*

20 Sites – This is a campground on the beach side of the San Rafael RV Park. All sites are back-ins, half are waterfront. A few have 50-amp outlets, most have 30-amp. All spaces also have water and sewer outlets. Restrooms were under construction when we last visited, they will have hot water showers.

As you approach Puerto Peñasco from the north watch for Pemex #8651 on the left. Zero your odometer here and continue straight for 2.8 mile (4.5 km). You will see that the highway is going to bend to the right ahead, you want to go straight so get in the left lane and continue straight when it's clear. Now continue another .5 mile (.8 km) to a T. Turn left and drive .5 mile (.8 km) to the street beyond the San Rafael RV Park. Turn right at the corner and you'll find the campground at the end of the road on the right next to the beach.

HACIENDA DE MARCOS *(Open All Year)*
   Res and Info: (011-52) (638) 385-1030
   Location: 7 Miles N of Puerto Peñasco, *N 31° 25' 36", W 113° 28' 09", Near Sea Level*

20 Sites – This campground is located north of town on the road to Sonoyta. If you are

looking for a small friendly place you should stop in here. Each time we visit the place is even nicer. The sites are back-ins with full hookups (50 and 30-amp outlets). Big RVs will find lots of room to park and maneuver. There's a laundry and restrooms are modern and clean with flush toilets and hot water showers. The swimming pool is very nice, there's also a restaurant. The owner/managers are from north of the border. The Hacienda De Marcos is located on the east side of Mex 8 near Km 83, some 7.5 miles (12 km) north of Puerto Peñasco.

QUALITY STAR RV PARK *(Open All Year)*
Res and Info: (011-52) (638) 102-0062
Location: 3 Miles N of Puerto Peñasco, *N 31° 22' 08", W 113° 30' 21", Near Sea Level*

34 Sites – This is the most unusual campground in Puerto Peñasco, perhaps in Mexico. When you drive in the first thing you see is a furniture gallery, that's where the office is located. Then you notice that the sites look a little like a storage yard. Some RVs here really are in storage, but most are not. The unusual look derives from the high surrounding fence and the very high metal shade structures over every site in the park. Then, in the rear of the campground, you'll find a mini water park with pools and Jacuzzi.

All sites here are covered back-in sites suitable for any size RV and have full hookups including 30-amp outlets. The restrooms are modern and very nice with hot showers. There's a coin operated laundry and out back are swimming pools, they're open to the public and closed for part of the winter.

The campground is located east of the highway near Km 90. This is just outside Puerto Peñasco to the north.

DESERT OASIS RESORT *(Open All Year)*
Res and Info: (011-52) (638) 102-0222
Location: 3 Miles N of Puerto Peñasco, *N 31° 21' 52", W 113° 30' 28", Near Sea Level*

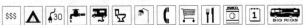

40 Sites – This is a modern motel and campground with a nice bar/restaurant and a mini market.

The campground has about 40 spaces with full hookups, a few are pull-thrus and many now have roofs over the sites. Good maneuvering room and large sites make it suitable for any rig. Power outlets are 30-amp and parking is on gravel. The restrooms have hot showers and flush toilets. There's also a coin-operated laundry. The monthly rate for an uncovered site is $320, for a covered on it's $485

The park is located at Km 91 which is 2.5 miles (4 km) north of Puerto Peñasco.

MAR Y SOL TRAILER PARK *(Open All Year)*
Res and Info: (011-52) (638) 383-3190
Location: Puerto Peñasco, *N 31° 20' 22", W 113° 31' 30", Near Sea Level*

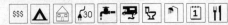

20 Sites – This trailer park adjoins the Mar y Sol Hotel on the south side. Thee back-in spaces are suitable for RVs to 35 feet. All spaces have full hookups with 30-amp outlets, there is no shade. Restrooms have hot showers. The hotel has a restaurant. The

campground is on the east side of the highway near Km 94 just as you arrive in Puerto Peñasco.

SAN FELIPE, BAJA CALIFORNIA (SAHN FAY-LEE-PAY)

Although San Felipe (population about 15,000) is a Baja town its location in the far northeast portion of the peninsula means that it is not normally part of a visit to the peninsula's destinations farther south. That doesn't mean that this isn't a popular place, like Puerto Peñasco this town is full of Americans looking for easily accessible sun and sand. The majority of them seem to be RVers.

Most of the action in San Felipe is found along its malecón (waterfront promenade) and the street one block inland – Mar de Cortez. Overlooking the malecón and the strip of sandy beach that fronts it is Cerro El Machorro, a tall rock with a shrine to the Virgin de Guadalupe at its top. This is a great place for photos. The bay in front of town goes dry at low tide, the panga fishermen who use the beach launch and retrieve their boats by driving out on the solid sand. Several of the campgrounds are located along the southern extension of Mar de Cortez so strolling in to central San Felipe is very easy. The town has a selection of decent restaurants and small shops as well as four Pemex stations.

Most of the important streets in town are paved and the rest present no driving problems. Watch for stop signs, however. They are in unexpected places. Sometimes the smallest dusty side street has priority over a main arterial.

It seems like San Felipe always has some kind of celebration in the works. Like many

WATCHING THE MOON RISE IN SAN FELIPE

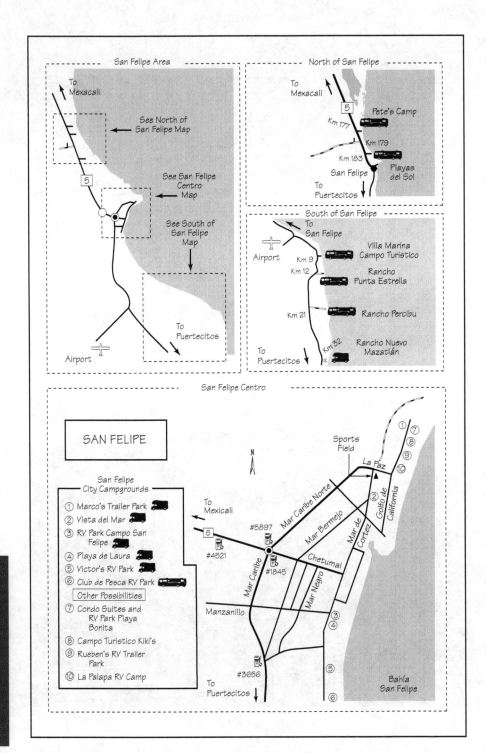

San Felipe Area

To Mexacali

See North of San Felipe Map

See San Felipe Centro Map

See South of San Felipe Map

To Puertecitos

Airport

North of San Felipe

To Mexacali

5

Pete's Camp

Km 177

Km 179

Km 183

San Felipe

Playas del Sol

To Puertecitos

South of San Felipe

To San Felipe

Airport

Km 9   Villa Marina Campo Turistico

Km 12   Rancho Punta Estrella

Km 21   Rancho Percibu

Km 32   Rancho Nuevo Mazatlán

To Puertecitos

San Felipe Centro

SAN FELIPE

San Felipe City Campgrounds

① Marco's Trailer Park
② Vista del Mar
③ RV Park Campo San Felipe
④ Playa de Laura
⑤ Victor's RV Park
⑥ Club de Pesca RV Park

Other Possibilities

⑦ Condo Suites and RV Park Playa Bonita
⑧ Campo Turistico Kiki's
⑨ Rueben's RV Trailer Park
⑩ La Palapa RV Camp

N

Sports Field

La Paz

① ⑦
⑧
⑨
⑩

②

Golfo de California

To Mexicali

Mar Caribe Norte

Mar Bermejo

Mar de Cortez

5

#5897

#4521

#1845

Mar Caribe

Chetumal

Mar Negro

③
④

Manzanillo

⑤

#3656

To Puertecitos

⑥

Bahía San Felipe

Mexican ports San Felipe celebrates Carnival (Mardi Gras) at the appropriate time in the spring. Spring Break is big here, just as on the rest of the peninsula, it happens during the third and fourth weeks of March. Semana Santa, the week up to and including Easter, is a big Mexican beach holiday and San Felipe is very popular as it hosts a number of sporting events. During the summer the town celebrates Día de la Marina on June 1. And in November there's the Shrimp Festival, one of the biggest celebrations of the year in San Felipe. Several times during the year there are major off-road races and in early March the Midwinter West Hobie Regatta.

In addition to all of the above San Felipe gets lots of visitors from Mexicali and California on weekends and any excuse for a holiday in either the States or Mexico. Many of the campgrounds are really set up for tent campers with ramadas for shade. Expect lots of noise and activity when these visitors are in town.

Campgrounds around San Felipe start many miles north of town. There are also many in town, then they continue south toward Puertecitos. Campgrounds below are listed from north to south.

San Felipe Campgrounds

🚐 **PETE'S CAMP** *(Open All Year)*
  Res and Info: (909) 676-4224 (US), www.petescamp.com, Rafael@petescamp.com
  Location: 7.5 Miles N of San Felipe, *N 31° 05' 26", W 114° 52' 10", Near Sea Level*

100 Sites – This is an older campground, actually more of a community, located along the beach north of San Felipe. There are many permanently located trailers here but also a large camping area below and next to the excellent beach. The camping area has dozens of thatched-roof ramadas (shade shelters) with room for small RVs to squeeze between them. Large RVs park behind the ramadas. There are no hookups but a dump station is available as is drinking water. There are restrooms with flush toilets and hot showers as well as a restaurant. The campground access road is at about Km 177.5. This is about 7.5 miles (12.1 km) north of the San Felipe entrance monument. There's a 1.1 mile (1.8 km) good oiled road east to the camp.

🚐 **PLAYAS DEL SOL** *(Open All Year)*
  Information: (011-52) (686) 576-0292, playasol@telnor.net
  Location: 4 Miles N of San Felipe, *N 31° 02' 21", W 114° 49' 32", Near Sea Level*

100 Sites – This is a large camping area on the beautiful beach north of San Felipe. Similar to Pete's but even simpler. There are many ramadas near the beach with parking for smaller RVs beside them or larger ones behind if things aren't too crowded. Flush toilets and hot showers are provided. The campground entrance is near Km 183, about 4 miles (6 km) north of the San Felipe entrance monument. Follow the somewhat grand divided entrance road east a mile to the beach.

🚐 **MARCO'S TRAILER PARK** *(Open All Year)*
  Information: (011-52) (686) 577-1875
  Location: San Felipe, *N 31° 02' 08", W 114° 49' 42", Near Sea Level*

20 Sites – Marco's isn't on the water and all San Felipe campers seem to want to be in a campground next to the beach, even if they're parked so far back that they never see the water. Nonetheless Marco's succeeds in staying relatively full, perhaps because it is almost next to the beach. The back-in sites are arranged around the perimeter of the campground. There is lots of maneuvering room but large RVs have some difficulty parking because the lot slopes and the leveled parking pads aren't very long. Each space has 15-amp outlets, sewer, water, and a nice little covered patio. There is even a little shrubbery to separate the sites, unusual in San Felipe. The restrooms are old but clean and in good repair, they have hot water showers. There is a small meeting room with a library and a sun deck on top.

From the glorieta (traffic circle) at the entrance to town take the road that leads northeast. This is Mar Caribe Norte and is the road to the left as you come from Mexicali. It will curve to the right at 0.8 miles (1.3 km) and come to a T at 1 mile (1.6 km). Turn left and you'll see the entrance to the campground on the left in one block.

⊞ VISTA DEL MAR *(Open All Year)*
Location: San Felipe, *N 31° 01' 50", W 114° 49' 51", Near Sea Level*

21 Sites – The Vista del Mar is another campground suffering from a location far from the water. The facility is really very good, but often virtually empty. There are 21 back-in spaces arranged on both sides of a sloping lot with a view of the ocean and hills to the north of town. Each space has 15 and 30-amp outlets, sewer, and water. Large RVs will have trouble parking because the level parking pad is not very long. The entire campground is paved, much of it with attractive reddish bricks. Each campsite has a tile-roofed patio with a table and barbecue. The restrooms are spic-and-span and have hot water showers. At the upper end of the campground is a group barbecue area.

From the glorieta (traffic circle) at the entrance to town take the road that leads northeast. This is Mar Caribe Norte and is the road to the left as you come from Mexicali. It will curve to the right at 0.8 miles (1.3 km). You must take the turn to the right at 0.9 miles (1.4 km) just before the fenced sports field, the campground is a short way up the hill on the left.

⊞ RV PARK CAMPO SAN FELIPE *(Open All Year)*
Res and Info: (011-52) (686) 577-1012, www.camposanfelipe.com
Location: San Felipe, *N 31° 01' 06", W 114° 50' 11", Near Sea Level*

34 Sites – You'll find the San Felipe to be very much like the Playa de Laura next door but in much better condition. It has the distinction of being the closest campground to central San Felipe.

The campsites are arranged in several rows parallel to the beach, the closer to the beach you are the more you pay. Sites have 30-amp outlets, sewer, water, and covered patios with tables. Most are pull-thrus. Another 5 are small and have sewer and water only. RVs to 35 feet can use some of the sites but maneuvering is difficult. The restrooms are clean and in good repair, they have hot water showers. There is a handy telephone next to the office.

As you enter town zero your odometer at the glorieta (traffic circle). Turn right toward the airport and drive 0.8 miles (1.3 km) to the Pemex. Turn left here and drive down the hill toward the beach. You'll come to a T at 1.2 miles (1.9 km). Turn left and almost immediately you'll see the Campo San Felipe on the right in 0.2 miles (0.4 km).

PLAYA DE LAURA *(Open All Year)*
Res and Info: (011-52) (686) 577-1128, (011-52) (686) 554-4712
Location: *San Felipe, N 31° 01' 05", W 114° 50' 09", Near Sea Level*

43 Sites – This older RV park doesn't seem to have been kept up to quite the same standards as the ones on either side. Still, it has a good location and is quite popular. Campsites are arranged in rows running parallel to the beach. The front row is really packed and limits beach access by campers in the rows farther from the beach. Pricing varies with beach slots more expensive than those farther back. Each camping space has 15-amp outlets, water and a covered patio with table and barbecue. Many have sewer hookups. Most of the spaces are pull-thrus but maneuvering space is limited, some sites are good for RVs to about 35 feet. Restrooms are older and need maintenance, they have hot water showers.

As you enter town zero your odometer at the glorieta (traffic circle). Turn right toward the airport and drive 0.8 miles (1.3 km) to the Pemex. Turn left here and drive down the hill toward the beach. You'll come to a T at 1.2 miles (1.9 km). Turn left and almost immediately you'll see the Playa de Laura on the right in 0.2 miles (0.3 km).

VICTOR'S RV PARK *(Open All Year)*
Res and Info: (011-52) (686) 577-1055, cortezho@telnor.net
Location: *San Felipe, N 31° 00' 49", W 114° 50' 12", Near Sea Level*

20 Sites – This 50-space campground is older with a lot of permanently located or long-term RVs. About 20 slots are available for daily rent. Victor's parking slots have 30-amp outlets, sewer, and water. Each space has a covered patio. Some are large enough for RVs to 35 feet. The restrooms are clean and showers have hot water. The campground has a meeting room near the front next to the beach and the motel next door has a swimming pool and restaurant for the use of campground residents. There is also a laundry. This campground is fully fenced, even along the beach, and usually has an attendant.

As you enter town zero your odometer at the glorieta (traffic circle). Turn right toward the airport and drive 0.8 miles (1.3 km) to the Pemex. Turn left here and drive down the hill toward the beach. You'll come to a T at 1.2 miles (1.9 km). Turn right and almost immediately you'll see Victor's on your left.

CLUB DE PESCA RV PARK *(Open All Year)*
Res and Info: (011-52) (686) 577-1180, clbdpaca@telnor.net
Location: *San Felipe, N 31° 00' 48", W 114° 50' 08", Near Sea Level*

60 Sites – This is an old San Felipe favorite. The campground has many permanents, but also some choice slots for tents and smaller RVs along the ocean and others toward the rear of the park. There are 32 slots along the beach with ramadas and with 30-amp outlets and water but no sewer hookups. These spaces are paved. We've seen RVs to 34 feet in

them but usually only shorter RVs park here. At the rear of the park are slots with 15-amp outlets, sewer, and water. Larger RVs fit here better, there's room for RVs to about 35 feet. Restrooms are neat and clean and have hot water showers. There is a small grocery store and a room with a ping-pong table next to the beach dividing the beachside sites.

As you enter town zero your odometer at the glorieta (traffic circle). Turn right toward the airport and drive 0.8 miles (1.3 km) to the Pemex. Turn left here and drive down the hill toward the beach. You'll come to a T at 1.2 miles (1.9 km). Turn right and you'll find the Club de Pesca at the end of the road.

VILLA MARINA CAMPO TURISTICO *(Open All Year)*
Res and Info: (011-52) (686) 577-1342, (011-52) (686) 590-7663
Location: 10 Miles S of San Felipe, *N 30° 54' 58", W 114° 42' 54", Near Sea Level*

26 Sites – This is definitely the nicest and most modern campground south of San Felipe. Campgrounds with a lot less to offer have much nicer signs, it's almost like this place is trying to hide. The campground has 26 full-hookup spaces. They have 15-amp electrical outlets. The camping area is located on a low bluff above a sandy beach. Sites on the front row have small covered patios, the second row sites are covered and have stairways leading to terraces on top with excellent views. Amazingly, sites are long enough, wide enough, and even high enough for most big RVs although you'll have to maneuver with care. Modern clean restrooms have flush toilets and hot showers. There's laundry service and this is a gated and attended campground.

The campground is located south of San Felipe. Zero your odometer as you reach the glorieta (traffic circle) at the entrance to town. Turn 90 degrees right toward the airport and head south. At 7.1 miles (11.5 km) the road makes a right angle turn to the left, the airport is straight. Turn left. In another 5.4 miles (8.7 km) you'll see the entrance on your left. The 0.3 mile (0.5 km) gravel road will take you to the park.

RANCHO PUNTA ESTRELLA *(Open All Year)*
Information: (011-52) (686) 565-2784 or (760) 357-6933 (USA), puntaestrella@mexico.com
Location: 12 Miles S of San Felipe, *N 30° 53' 00", W 114° 42' 28", Near Sea Level*

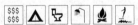

100 Sites – This is a large campground with simple facilities. There are miles of beach and desert behind. The camping sites are a long row of 100 wood-roofed ramadas stretched along the beach. They are intended for tent camping. The sand between the ramadas is soft, probably too soft for any RV parking. An electrical cord with light bulbs hanging from it has been strung along the front of the camping ramadas. Behind the row of ramadas the surface is harder so RVs can boondock there. Simple restrooms have flush toilets and hot showers. There's also a dump station.

The campground is located south of San Felipe. Zero your odometer as you reach the glorieta (traffic circle) at the entrance to town. Turn 90 degrees right toward the airport and head south. At 7.1 miles (11.5 km) the road makes a right angle turn to the left, the airport is straight. Turn left. In another 7.7 miles (12.4 km) you'll see the entrance on your left. It's 0.9 mile (1.4 km) to the campground.

MEXICO DESTINATIONS

RANCHO PERCIBU *(Open All Year)*

Location: 20 Miles S of San Felipe, *N 30° 48' 58", W 114° 42' 13", Near Sea Level*

25 Sites – The beach here at Percibu has long been a favorite for shell collectors from San Felipe. There's a restaurant and bar as well as about 25 sites, some with metal ramadas, for picnicking or camping. A restroom has flush toilets and hot showers.

The campground is located south of San Felipe. Zero your odometer as you reach the glorieta (traffic circle) at the entrance to town. Turn 90 degrees right toward the airport and head south. At 7.1 miles (11.5 km) the road makes a right angle turn to the left, the airport is straight. Turn left. In another 12.8 miles (20.6 km) you'll see the entrance on your left. It's 2.3 mile (3.7 km) to the campground.

RANCHO NUEVO MAZATLÁN *(Open All Year)*

Telephone: (686) 225-0724 or (686) 166-7124
Location: 27 Miles S of San Felipe, *N 30° 43' 18", W 114° 42' 24", Near Sea Level*

50 Sites – This campground is unique in the San Felipe area. Sites are situated under pines about 100 yards back from a pristine beach. Many sites have picnic tables and there are scattered water faucets. There's rooms for perhaps 50 camping rigs or tents, the campground is OK for RVs to about 30 feet. Restrooms have flush toilets and cold showers.

The campground is located south of San Felipe. Zero your odometer as you reach the traffic circle at the entrance to town. Turn 90 degrees right toward the airport and head south. At 7.1 miles (11.5 km) the road makes a right angle turn to the left, the airport is straight. Turn left. In another 19.7 miles (31.8 km) you'll see the entrance on your left. Follow signs toward the beach and campground.

Other Camping Possibilities

The campgrounds listed above only scratch the surface in San Felipe. Starting about 10 miles (16 km) north of town you will see many roads heading for the beach. Most of these roads end at small campgrounds with few services or facilities. The same situation prevails south of town. If you don't need hookups you can explore some of them and you may find a place that suits you.

In addition, there are several small campgrounds in a congested area at the north end of San Felipe near Marco's Trailer Park, described above. These include Condo Suites and RV Park Playa Bonita, Campo Turistico Kiki's, Ruben's RV Trailer Park, and La Palapa RV Camp. These campgrounds tend to have either very poor facilities or are very crowded and noisy with short term visitors. Take a look if that sounds good to you.

MEXICO DESTINATIONS

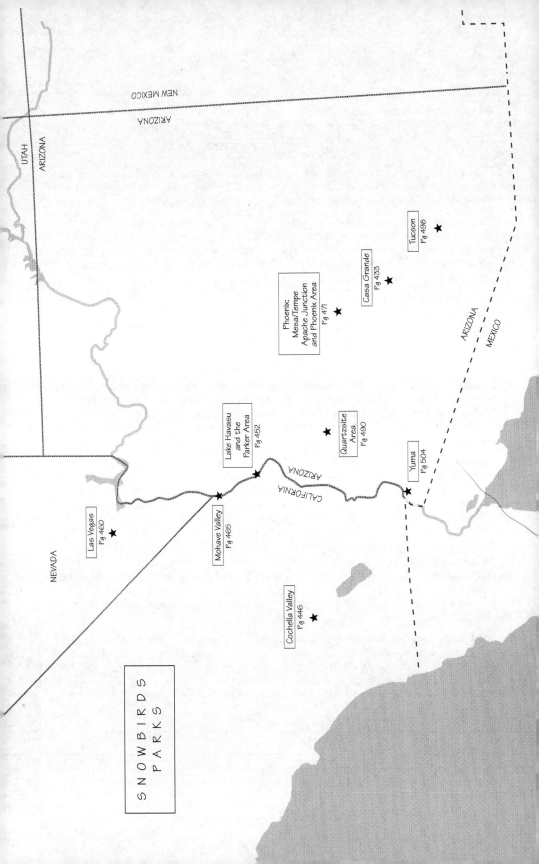

SNOWBIRDS
PARKS

Las Vegas
Pg 460 ★

NEVADA

Mohave Valley
Pg 465 ★

Cochella Valley
Pg 446 ★

CALIFORNIA

Lake Havasu
and the
Parker Area
Pg 452 ★

★

Quartzsite
Area
Pg 490

ARIZONA

Phoenix:
Mesa/Tempe
Apache Junction
and Phoenix Area
Pg 471 ★

Casa Grande
Pg 433 ★

Tucson
Pg 498 ★

Yuma
Pg 504 ★

ARIZONA
MEXICO

UTAH
ARIZONA

ARIZONA
NEW MEXICO

Chapter 8

Snowbird Destinations

INTRODUCTION

Arizona (and the southern desert area of California) has a huge number of Snowbird RV Parks. What's a Snowbird? Snowbirds are generally northern residents, from either the US or Canada, who come to the south to spend the winter. Not all Snowbirds are RVers, but many of them are. Arizona is just one of the Snowbird RV destinations in the US, others include the lower Río Grande Valley in Texas, the Gulf Coast, and of course, Florida. Mexico too has become a popular Snowbird destination.

Why is Arizona so popular? The most important reason is probably the weather. The desert is hot in the summer, but in the winter, at lower altitudes, it's ideal. Winter highs are in the 60s and 70s with evening lows in the 30s and 40s. Not only that, the sun shines almost every day.

Arizona is also popular because it's not too expensive. In many areas RV parks can be built much less expensively than in other places around the country. You'll see that some destinations are less expensive than others.

Snowbirds start arriving in October and November, but not in huge numbers. Many want to spend the holidays with their families up north. Then they make a break for the sunshine. The busiest months are January, February and March.

Some folks check in to one park for the season every year. They have found what they like and know the people and the area. Days are spent pursuing recreational activities, but not too hard. The lifestyle is very social for most Snowbirds; dinners, dances, and other get-togethers are common. Many parks have very extensive planned activities including clubs, hobby rooms, exercise and sports activities, and travel.

With today's large road-worthy RVs many Snowbirds don't stay in one park all season. It's easy to make a trip to Quartzsite or Mexico and then come back to your original park or move on to another. That way you can sample a variety of locations and lifestyles, and see some different friends.

Another trend attributable to modern RVs and technology is the huge desert Snowbird communities of boondockers. Many Snowbirds spend at least part of their winter on government lands in the desert. The cost is minimal and it's not hard to do, it just takes a little research and practice. It's also fun. Your nearest neighbor is as close or far away as you desire. You share your huge backyard with desert critters and plants of all kinds. Nights can be spent around the campfire under the stars. We don't talk about that kind of camping in this chapter, but there's a lot about it in *Chapter 4* in the *El Centro, Imperial Dam, Quartzsite Area*, and *Yuma* sections.

As spring arrives RVers start thinking about family, summer travels, or yard work and they start to hit the roads north. By May the RV parks are pretty much empty, the temperatures are rising, and only the few full-time residents are in the parks.

This chapter only lists some of the most popular Snowbird destinations. Other places that attract Snowbirds in the Southwest are *Deming, Las Cruces, Truth or Consequences, Willcox, Benson, Sierra Vista, Wickenburg, Ajo, Imperial Dam, El Centro*, and the eastern side of the *Salton Sea*. While we have not included those places in this Snowbird chapter you will find that we have described them and most of their campgrounds in the other chapters as traveling destinations. So if you have an interest in a smaller town for a winter destination you might want to take a look at those sections with Snowbird eyes.

What Should You Look For In Choosing a City

For most people the most important reason for choosing a city is probably a recommendation from a friend. After all, it's easy to trust the opinion of someone you know and it's also nice to know that your friends will be nearby so that you can spend time together. Hopefully we'll give you some additional worthwhile input in this chapter.

You could start by looking at the nearby tabulation of the results of our research which is titled *Snowbird Destination Comparison Table*. A quick look will show you that some places are a lot bigger and more popular than others. It will also show you that there is a difference in cost between the large Snowbird RVing destinations.

On the following pages we'll look at some of the things we think are important. For each city we'll look at: weather, living convenience and shopping, recreation, hospital facilities, and RV parks.

We'll make a note about the altitude of the city in the weather section. We do that because temperatures in the Southwest in the winter are very much dependent upon altitude. In fact, the accompanying altitude map illustrates that all of the major snowbird destinations in this chapter are under 3,000 feet. Higher areas just aren't as popular because they're cooler.

What Should You Look For in Choosing a Park

Once again, probably the main reason most people choose a park is because they have friends there. If you don't want to use that method, however, the tabulated sheets that follow should give you some information that will assist you in making your decision. Here are some other things to consider:

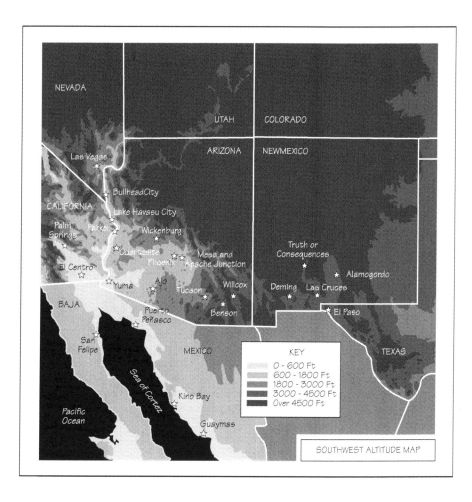

SOUTHWEST ALTITUDE MAP

- **Location** – Do you want to be close to shopping and restaurants or would you rather be in a quiet suburban or rural location. The accompanying maps show where each park is located.

- **Park Size** – This is more important than you may realize. Larger parks offer more in the way of facilities and more in the way of organized activities. On the other hand, some people don't care about that and prefer the simpler, more personal, and perhaps quieter existence offered by smaller parks.

- **Parking Sites** – The site is your home for months at a time. Are the connections what you need with adequate power, entertainment, and communications hookups? Will the site be big enough for your RV, your tow car, and your activities outside your RV? Is it pleasant, with shade, foliage or space to insulate you from your neighbors, and perhaps a patio and table.

- **Amenities** - Do you want a swimming pool and a recreation room? How about some of these other amenities we've seen in Snowbird parks: putting green, golf course, driving range, mini golf course, tennis courts, ballroom, recreation room, art room, crafts rooms, exercise room, library, spa, computer room, workshops, restaurant, stores, hairdresser, travel agent, shuffleboard courts, card rooms, pool tables, horseshoes, community fire pits, game rooms, boat ramps, walking trails, beaches, marinas, TV lounges, saunas, kitchen?

- **Activities** - Here is a listing of some of the activities offered by parks in the southwest:
  - » Professional stage entertainment
  - » Guest speakers – lots of different kinds of topics
  - » Special events and parties – Welcome Home, Octoberfest, Thanksgiving, Tree Trimming, Christmas Eve, Christmas Dinner, Mexican Fiesta, New Years Eve Dance, Valentine's Day Dinner and Dance, crafts shows, patio sales, St Patrick's Day parades and parties, dinner shows, variety shows, volunteer parties, Western Days, cabaret nights, fashion shows, talent shows, movie nights, jam sessions
  - » Socials – coffee klatches, pancake breakfasts, cookouts, barbecues, happy hours, ice cream socials, campfires, wiener roasts, coffee and doughnut gatherings, home-cooked holiday dinners
  - » Sports – aerobics, exercise classes, water aerobics, low impact aerobics, golf, billiards, shuffleboard, horseshoes, bowling, archery, tennis, water volleyball, softball, darts, cycling, pickle ball, ping pong bocce ball, croquet, washer tossing, fishing derbies, 4 wheeling expeditions, hiking
  - » Dancing – ballroom, line dancing, country and western, square dancing, clogging, tap dancing, belly dancing
  - » Games – card parties, chess, bridge, poker, pinochle, billiards, Scrabble, bingo, cribbage, Mexican Train, Texas Holdem, canasta
  - » Classes and Clubs – computers, ceramics, chorus, art, quilting, crochet and knitting, wood carving, rubber stamping, scrap booking, bible study, weight watching, photography, hiking, art lessons, cooking classes, Spanish classes, investment, singles clubs, digital photo clubs, Red Hat chapters, genealogy clubs
  - » Crafts – ceramics, wood carving, stained glass, oil painting, china painting, water color, quilting, porcelain dolls, lapidary, silversmithing, sewing, knitting, gourd art
  - » Travel – guided tours, sightseeing tours, casino trips
  - » Nature – nature walks, bird watching, hiking

Of course, not all parks have all these things. In general the larger parks offer more. Some of these events and activities are organized and run by the parks, others are organized by the park residents, and some are pretty unorganized. Some parks have an activity director on staff to help things along. Many people choose their park based upon the activities it offers.

- **Costs** – You'll find that the market is pretty efficient. The parks in each area are very competitive. They know what their neighbors offer and what they charge. RVers tend to be pretty good shoppers so in general, the market dictates that you'll get what you pay for. Just be sure you don't pay for something you don't need or want.

Our Park Listings and How to Use Them

The listings that follow contain the majority of the Snowbird parks in each locality that we cover. We've selected them based upon their size, their popularity, and the recommendations of others. We've also tried to select parks that are primarily Snowbird parks, not traveler parks or even year-round housing parks. If we've missed your favorite park we apologize, let us know and it might be in our next edition.

Here's a brief description of the information you'll find arranged by column:

1. Name and address. Note that the number of the park is the number shown on the area map so you can locate each one.

2. Contact Information and GPS – The information here is just a start. It is essential that you call any park you are considering and ask lots of questions. They're used to it, and if you don't like them on the phone you probably don't want to spend the winter with them. The GPS number is really location data. Try using this with Google Earth on a computer and you can look at a satellite picture of the park. It's also useful for finding the place on maps or with an electronic navigation system.

3. Sites Total/Sites Available – This data came directly from the park offices. The first number is easy, it's just the number of sites in the park and should be pretty reliable. The second number is the sites that are not filled with permanent RVs or mobile homes. Some parks had this number handy when we called and some just guessed. This is an important number because most Snowbirds with their own RVs are looking for parks that have a lot of other RV-driving visitors. Those parks tend to be more friendly and it is easier to get involved since there are fewer year-round residents who already know each other and have their own social circles.

4. Monthly Rate – This is the quoted monthly winter rate for a standard site. There are often premium sites that cost more. Note however, that parks often won't make reservations for just one month during the January to March period unless they know that they can't sell out to three month people. By late December they'll probably know and will accept monthly reservations. Electricity is usually not included in the rate. If it is we say so in the Comments column.

5. Overnight Rates – This is the same code we use Chapters 4, 5, 6, and 7. See the back cover of the book for a key. Parks with this data in the column accept overnight campers, often in a special section. However, in the middle of the Snowbird season you should call ahead to make sure there's room.

6. Longer Term Rates – In some localities it is customary to give an even further reduced rate if you agree to stay for a three or four month season. Other places don't offer this kind of deal, we'll talk about the custom in the text describing each destination in this chapter. If there's a check in the box, some kind of deal is normally available.

7. Age Restriction – Many of these parks have an age restriction. If there is one it is most likely to be a requirement that at least one person in the couple be 55 or older (and no children).

8. RV Restriction – This means that some RVs are not allowed. Usually it's a

small RV (no vans or pickup campers) or an age (perhaps no RVs over 10 years old), or an equipment (self contained only) restriction. If you see a check in this column take a look at the comments in the last column.

9. Site Surface – This one's easy: G is gravel, GR is grass, P is paved.

10. Patio – There is a check if there are patios and no check if there aren't. Some parks have a mix, the check indicates only that some have patios. Ask for one when you reserve if this is important to you.

11. Electric – The number is the maximum amperage available. If this is important make sure that you get the right hookups when you reserve, not all sites are necessarily the same.

12. TV – A symbol in the column indicates that a TV connection is available at the sites. A dollar sign indicates that there is an extra charge. This often means that you make arrangements with an outside provider for cable service which can be a very good thing if cable internet is available.

13. Phones at Sites – This indicates that phone hookups are at the individual sites. An I means that they are instant-on, and are turned on by the campground. A dollar sign means that there's an extra charge for this. An A indicates that you make arrangements with the phone company, there's always an extra charge for this. DSL internet service is available at some campgrounds with phone hookups, another thing to check into.

14. Internet – Indicates that there is a data port or a computer available at the park for your use.

15. Wi-Fi – An S indicates that the Wi-Fi signal can be received at the sites, a C means that you must take your computer to a central location to receive it. A $ means there's a charge and a F means it's free. Wi-Fi is very finicky and usually there are only some sites that get a good signal. Until the technology and installer ability improve you'll have to really manage this one. Make sure that the park understands that a Wi-Fi connection is extremely important to you so you get a site with good reception.

16. Swimming Pool – H means there's a heated pool, S means that it's solar heated, sometimes just not adequate in winter.

17. Spa – There's a hot tub or Jacuzzi.

18. Club House – A check indicates that there's a room set aside for social activities.

19. Planned Activities – There are planned activities. They may be managed by the park or the residents, ask lots of questions about this when you call.

20. Comments – There are notes here about unusual amenities or if clarification of some item is required.

Remember, don't even think of selecting a park without giving them a call and asking lots of questions.

Snowbird Destination Summary Table

The following Snowbird Destination Summary Table summarizes the data that follows in our tabulations of Snowbird campgrounds in the nine destinations that follow. Since this type of data is seldom available you may find it interesting.

SNOWBIRD DESTINATION SUMMARY TABLE

	Number of Parks	Total Park Sites	RV Sites	Average Monthly Rental Price	Percentage of Sites With Average Rentals			
					$0 - $250	$250 - $500	$500 - $750	$Over 750
Casa Grande	18	6,674	4,213	514	-	45%	55%	-
Coachilla Valley	19	6,806	4,153	936	-	13%	24%	63%
Lake Havasu And The Parker Strip	28	5,107	3,844	373	4%	85%	9%	2
Las Vegas	14	3,575	3,380	612	-	44%	47%	9%
Mohave Valley	21	2,469	1,963	295	18%	82%	-	-
Phoenix Area								
Mesa/Tempe	28	19,249	6,150	547	-	29%	63%	8%
Apache Jct	29	9,056	4,610	464	-	60%	40%	-
Phoenix	19	6.995	3,357	526	-	50%	47%	3%
Quartzsite	31	5,041	4,261	309	27%	73%	-	-
Tucson	20	7,099	3,288	558	-	26%	74%	-
Yuma	43	15,727	8,776	457	3%	65%	27%	5%
Total	270	87,798	47,995					

CASA GRANDE

Casa Grande (population about 30,000), located near the junction of I-8 and I-10, offers the RV Snowbird a relatively convenient location within an hour of both Phoenix and Tucson. The name of the town comes from the nearby Casa Grande ruins in Casa Grande Ruins National Monument. Casa Grande was originally a railroad construction town, then a mining town, and finally an agricultural town (dairy and cotton).

In recent years the town has become something of a bedroom community for people from Phoenix who commute to the city each day. That means that the day-to-day services that you need for a comfortable stay are available. RV parks here are scattered over a fairly large area and most are away from the concentration of business along the main drag, Florence Avenue, also known as SR-84/287.

For more information take a look the *Casa Grande* section in the *Chapter 4*.

Weather

The temperature chart shows that Casa Grande is just a little cooler than Yuma in the winter months. That's a little surprising considering the 1,400 foot altitude.

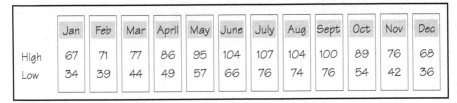

	Jan	Feb	Mar	April	May	June	July	Aug	Sept	Oct	Nov	Dec
High	67	71	77	86	95	104	107	104	100	89	76	68
Low	34	39	44	49	57	66	76	74	76	54	42	36

Living Convenience and Shopping

Casa Grande has an enviable location. You can drive to either Phoenix (40 miles) or Tucson (60 miles) in a little more than an hour but you're not stuck with the congestion of a major metropolis on a daily basis. Supermarkets and big box stores in Casa Grande include Albertson's, Fry's, Safeway, Food Cities, Home Depot, and a Walmart Supercenter. There is also an outlet mall out along I-10. If you're really a big store junkie there's a big collection of them north 35 miles along I-10 in Chandler.

Recreation

Recreational facilities and destinations in the Casa Grande area include:
- Seven Golf Courses
- Casa Grande Art Museum
- Casa Grande Valley Historical Society Museum
- Casa Grande Ruins National Monument
- Wild Horse Pass Casino
- Picacho Peak State Park
- O'Odham Tash Indian Days Celebration
- In addition, both Phoenix and Tucson with all that they offer are close enough for an easy visit.

Hospital Facilities

The Casa Grande region offers access to the following hospitals/medical centers:
- Casa Grande Regional Medical Center – In Case Grande
- Hu Hu Kam Memorial Hospital (in Sacatan) – 16 Miles N
- Chandler Regional Hospital (Chandler) – 33 Miles N
- Desert Samaritan Medical Center (Mesa) – 40 Miles N

Of course there are many more in both Phoenix and Tucson.

RV Parks

Considering the rural location it is surprising to find that Casa Grande has relatively high monthly rates. Of course Palm Springs and Las Vegas are higher but it's surprising to see both the Apache Junction area and Yuma lower. Rates here normally do not include electricity and the electricity rate is high, from $.11 to $.14 per kilowatt hour. There is also a city sales tax on monthly stays of 1.8%.

This is all somewhat softened by the fact that most parks here offer reduced three month rate since there is no large special event to attract Snowbird RVers and fill the parks for a month or so like Tucson and Quartzsite. Many parks are age-restricted to 55 and older. Parking is commonly on gravel with paved patios, cable TV is common, and TV reception with an aerial is pretty good so you can pick up both Phoenix and Tucson local channels. Most of the parks listed have heated swimming pools.

THE CITY OF CASA GRANDE IS NAMED FOR THE NEARBY CASA GRANDE RUINS

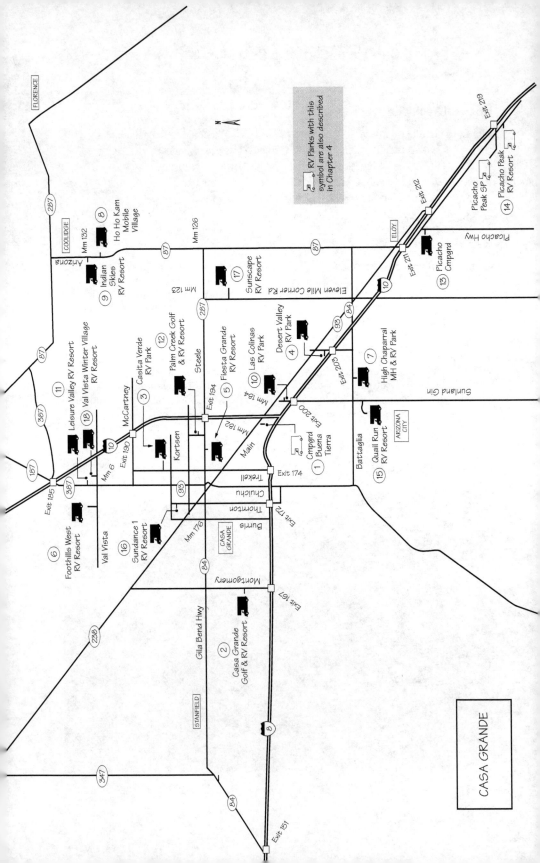

RV Parks with this symbol are also described in Chapter 4

N

FLORENCE

COOLIDGE

Arizona

Mm 132
Ho Ho Kam Mobile Village ⑧

Indian Skies RV Resort ⑨

87
Mm 126

Sunscape RV Resort ⑰

ELOY

87

Eleven Mile Corner Rd

Exit 212

Exit 219

Picacho Peak SP

Picacho Peak RV Resort ⑭

Picacho Hwy

Picacho Cmpgrd ⑬

Exit 211

287
Mm 123

Leisure Valley RV Resort ⑪
Val Vista Winter Village RV Resort ⑱

Casita Verde RV Park ③

Palm Creek Golf & RV Resort ⑫

Steele

Fiesta Grande RV Resort ⑤

Exit 194

Las Colinas RV Park ⑩

Mm 184

Desert Valley RV Park ④

Exit 203

93

84

10

High Chaparral MH & RV Park ⑦

Sunland Gin

387
387

187

10
Mm 6

Kortsen

Mm 182

Main

Exit 200

Cmpgrd Buena Tierra ①

Battaglia

ARIZONA CITY

Quail Run RV Resort ⑮

McCartney

Exit 190

Exit 185

387
93

Trekell

Chuichu

Thornton

Burris

Exit 174

Exit 172

CASA GRANDE

Foothills West RV Resort ⑥

Val Vista

Sundance 1 RV Resort ⑯

Mm 176

84

Montgomery

Exit 167

238

Gila Bend Hwy

Casa Grande Golf & RV Resort ②

8

STANFIELD

347

84

Exit 151

CASA GRANDE

#	Park	Sites Total/Available	Monthly Rate	Longer Term Rates	Overnight Rates	Age Restriction	RV Restriction	Site Surface	Patio	Electric	TV	Phone at Sites	Internet	Wi-Fi	Swimming Pool	Spa	Club House	Planned Activities	Comments
1	Campground Buena Tierra 1995 S Cox Rd Casa Grande, AZ 85222 (520) 836-3500 or (888) 520-8360 www.campgroundbuenatierra.com campgroundbuenatierra@yahoo.com N 32° 49' 53" W 111° 41' 18"	148 / 148	$400-450	✓	$$$$$$			G		50		A		C / F			✓	✓	6 premium sites have patios. Other amenities - desert golf, huge fire pits, hiking trails, horseshoes, bocce ball, horse pens, rec field
2	Casa Grande Golf & RV Resort 3290 South Montgomery Rd Casa Grande, AZ 85222 (520) 836-7210 www.casagrandegolfandrv.com information@casagrandegolfandrv.com N 32° 50' 59" W 111° 41' 18"	100 / 100	$450-500	✓	$$$$$$			G	✓	50			✓		✓	✓	✓	✓	An adult park but no specific age restriction. Popular golf course. Golf discounts for park residents. Large outdoor spa
3	Casita Verde RV Park 2200 N Trekell Rd Casa Grande, AZ 85222 (520) 836-9031 or (877) 362-6736 R www.rvonthego.com/casita-verde.html casitaverdervresort@mhchomes.com N 32° 54' 56" W 111° 43' 54"	192 / 120	$450-500	Over $$$$$$	$$$$$$	55		P	✓	50	✓ $	A	✓	S $	H	✓	✓	✓	Encore park. Cable activated by cable company. Other amenities - shuffleboard, horseshoes, game room, library. No tents
4	Desert Valley RV Resort 4555 W Tonto Road Eloy, AZ 85231 (520) 466-4500 or (866) 502-4700 www.desertvalleyrvpark.com info@desertvalleyrvpark.com N 32° 47' 14" W 111° 37' 41"	350 / 350	$450-500	Over $$$$$$	$$$$$$	55		G	✓	50	✓ $	- $	✓	S $	H	✓	✓	✓	Park opened in 2004. RVs, 5th-wheels, and trailers only. Satellite TV and telephones are activated by the office for a fee. 17,000 sq ft rec center
5	Fiesta Grande RV Resort 1511 Florence Blvd Casa Grande, AZ 85222 (520) 426-7000 or (888) 934-3782 www.rvonthego.com/fiesta-grande.html fiestagranderesort@mhchomes.com N 32° 52' 45" W 111° 43' 12"	767 / 417	$500-550	Over $$$$$$	$$$$$$	55		G	✓	50	✓ $	- $	✓	S $	H	✓	✓	✓	Encore park. Cable activated by cable company. Phones activated by office for fee. Other amenities - shuffleboard, computer room with 10 computers
6	Foothills West RV Resort 10167 North Encore Dr Casa Grande, AZ 85222 (520) 836-2531 or (877) 362-6736 R www.rvonthego.com/foothills-west.html foothills_west_rv_resort@mhchomes.com N 32° 58' 04" W 111° 46' 38"	192 / 114	$400-450	Over $$$$$$	$$$$$$	55		G	✓	50	✓ $	- $	✓	S $	H	✓	✓	✓	Encore park. Phone available by office for a fee. Activity director. Other amenities - shuffleboard, putting green, bocce ball
7	High Chaparral MH & RV Park 7575 Battaglia Rd Casa Grande, AZ 85222 (520) 466-5076 www.campingfriend.com sastms@alluretech.net N 32° 45' 54" W 111° 38' 53"	179 / 179	$300-350		$$$$$		✓	G	✓	50	✓ $	A	✓	S F	H	✓	✓	✓	Mobile home and RV park are next to each other but the sites are not intermixed
8	Ho Ho Kam Mobile Village 1925 S Arizona Blvd Coolidge, AZ 85228 (520) 723-3697 or (877) 723-3697 www.hohokamvillage.com info@hohokamvillage.com N 32° 57' 40" W 111° 31' 24"	202 / 90	$350-400	✓	$$$$$$	55		G	✓	50	✓ $	A	✓	S F	H	✓	✓	✓	Monthly rate includes electric. RVs to 40 feet only. Cable activated by cable company. Other amenities - shuffleboard, pool hall, library

Casa Grande Snowbird Parks
Page 2

#	Park / Address / Contact	Sites Total/Available	Monthly Rate	Overnight Rates	Longer Term Rates	Age Restriction	RV Restriction	Site Surface	Patio	Electric	TV	Phone at Sites	Internet	Wi-Fi	Swimming Pool	Spa	Club House	Planned Activities	Comments
9	Indian Skies RV Resort, 1050 S Arizona Blvd, Coolidge, AZ 85228; (520) 723-7831; www.indianskiesrvresort.com; info@indianskiesrvresort.com; N 32° 58' 00" W 111° 31' 29"	242 / 90	$350-400	✓	$$$$$$	55		G	✓	50	$	A	S	F	H	✓	✓	✓	6 month seasonal rates / Cable activated by cable company / Separate pet section / 38 ft maximum RV size / Shuffleboard, library
10	Las Colinas RV Park, 7136 S Sunland Gin Rd, Casa Grande, AZ 85222; (520) 836-5050; lascolinas55@yahoo.com; N 32° 48' 58" W 111° 40' 11"	150 / 80	$350-400	✓	$$$$$$	55		G	✓	50	$	A	S	$	H	✓	✓	✓	An overflow section can also be used by monthly guests / Other amenities - shuffleboard, horseshoes, game room, hiking trails
11	Leisure Valley RV Resort, 9985 N Pinal Ave, Casa Grande, AZ 85222; (520) 836-9449 or (800) 993-9449; www.leisurevalleyrvresort.com; info@leisurevalleyrvresort.com; N 32° 58' 15" W 111° 45' 20"	125 / 75	$450-500	✓	$$$$$$	55	✓	G	✓	50	$	A	C	F	H	✓	✓	✓	Cable activated by cable company / Other amenities - shuffleboard, horseshoes, bocce ball, big screen TV / No tents
12	Palm Creek Golf & RV Resort, 1110 N Henness Rd, Casa Grande, AZ 85222; (520) 421-7000 or (800) 421-7004; www.palmcreekgolf.com; info@palmcreekgolf.com; N 32° 53' 03" W 111° 42' 16"	1,850 / 1,200	$600-650	✓	Over $$$$$$	55	✓	G	✓	50	✓	I	S	F	H	✓	✓	✓	Park is about 9 years old / RVs, 5th-wheels, and trailers only / Phone activated by office - in park calls are free / Golf discounts for park residents
13	Picacho Campground, 18428 S Picacho Hwy, Picacho, AZ 85241; (520) 466-7401 or (888) 562-7453; kernelandsarge@aol.com; N 32° 42' 44" W 111° 29' 58"	65 / 65	$300-350	✓	$$$$$			G	✓	50		A					✓		Family park / Some sites have phone connections
14	Picacho Peak RV Resort, 17065 E Peak Lane, P.O. Box 300, Picacho, AZ 85241; (520) 466-7841; www.picachopeakrv.com; picachopeakrv@aol.com; N 32° 38' 36" W 111° 23' 17"	190 / 170	$350-400	✓	$$$$$$	55	✓	G	✓	50	✓	I - $	S	$	H	✓	✓	✓	2 pet limit / Phones activated by office for a fee / Other amenities - library, exercise room, shuffleboard / Older RVs require inspection
15	Quail Run RV Resort, 14010 S Amado Blvd, P.O. Box 1049, Arizona City, AZ 85223; (520) 466-6000 or (800) 301-8114; www.quailrunrvresort.com; quailrunrv@aol.com; N 32° 45' 11" W 111° 40' 56"	324 / 265	$400-450	✓	Over $$$$$$	55	✓	G	✓	50	$	I - $	S	$	H	✓	✓	✓	Phone activated by office for a fee / Older RVs require approval / Separate pet section / 9 hole mini golf, shuffleboard, exercise room, library
16	Sundance 1 RV Resort, 1920 N Thornton Rd, Casa Grande, AZ 85222; (520) 426-9662 or (888) 332-5335; www.sundance1rv.com; fun@sundance1rv.com; N 32° 53' 51" W 111° 46' 29"	711 / 565	$550-600	✓	Over $$$$$$	55	✓	G	✓	50	$	I - $	S	F	H	✓	✓	✓	Newer park - opened in 1999 / Cable and telephone activated by office for a fee / Separate pet section / Gated community

Casa Grande Snowbird Parks
Page 3

#	Park	Contact	Sites Total/Available	Monthly Rate	Longer Term Rates	Overnight Rates	Age Restriction	RV Restriction	Site Surface	Patio	Electric	TV	Phone at Sites	Internet	Wi-Fi	Swimming Pool	Spa	Club House	Planned Activities	Comments
17	Sunscape RV Resort 1083 E Sunscape Way Casa Grande, AZ 85294	(520) 723-9533 or (866) 678-6722 www.sunscapervresort.com sunscape@cgmailbox.com N 32° 51' 37" W 111° 33' 21"	525 / 20	$350-400	✓	$$$$$$	40	✓	G	✓	50		A	✓	S $	H	✓	✓	✓	This is an ownership park and all but about 20 sites are member owned Free Wi-Fi at hotspots in park Library, shuffleboard, mini golf
18	Val Vista Winter Village RV Resort 16680 W Val Vista Rd Casa Grande, AZ 85222	(520) 836-7800 www.jpkman.com vvwv@cybertrails.com N 32° 58' 05" W 111° 44' 47"	344 / 165	$550-600	✓	Over $$$$$$	55	✓	G	✓	50	$	A	✓	C F	H	✓	✓	✓	RVs, 5th-wheels, and trailers only Cable activated by cable company Arizona RV Park Of The Year - 2000 Activity director Library, shuffleboard, exercise room

COACHELLA VALLEY

The Coachella Valley includes a string of towns along SR-111: Palm Springs, Cathedral City, Rancho Mirage, Palm Desert, Indian Wells, La Quinta, and Indio. There's also Desert Hot Springs on the far side of the valley.

This area is so close to Los Angeles that it is heavily affected by the huge population over there. Many of the parks cater to folks planning to spend a short time in the area or people with big budgets and the willingness to pay for more amenities. On the other hand, there are less expensive parks, particularly in Palm Desert, that serve as an affordable place to spend the winter.

This can be a fun place to spend time with great restaurants, upscale shopping, and lots of golf. For more information take a look the *Coachella Valley* section in *Chapter 4*.

Weather

The near sea level altitude of Palm Springs means that winter temperatures are pretty pleasant, but not the summer. Expect a lot of wind in the north part of the valley, there's a reason they put those huge windmill farms up there.

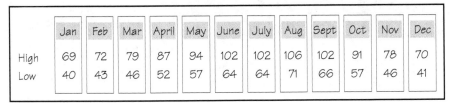

	Jan	Feb	Mar	April	May	June	July	Aug	Sept	Oct	Nov	Dec
High	69	72	79	87	94	102	102	106	102	91	78	70
Low	40	43	46	52	57	64	64	71	66	57	46	41

Living Convenience and Shopping

The Coachella Valley has a dense population along the mountains resulting in something of a traffic problem. It has been reported that SR-111 was first the place in history where a line was painted in the road to divide opposing lanes of traffic. This highway, which forms the backbone of a row of cities on the west side of the valley, is always packed with cars and you'll see some incredibly poor driving. It's a high-risk area. On the other hand, big boulevards to the north and east let you bypass much of this if you're willing to plan ahead. A good map is essential, this area is surprisingly hard to navigate once off SR-111.

The valley has always done a good job with luxury shopping. Today you can choose from the following destination shopping areas: downtown Palm Springs, The River at Rancho Mirage, El Paseo Drive, and old town La Quinta. Big malls include the Westfield Palm Desert, the Palm Springs Mall, the Indio Fashion Mall, and the Desert Crossing Shopping Center. For outlet shopping try one of the largest outlet malls in the country, Outlets at Cabezon, located about 20 miles west on I-10. Every grocery store chain seems to be represented in the Coachella Valley. Even the big box stores are here now, although it seems like they were slow in coming.

Recreation

Recreational facilities and destinations in the Coachella Valley area include:

- Over 80 Nearby Golf Courses

- Hot Springs
- Indian Canyons
- Indian Casinos
- Joshua Tree National Park
- Living Desert Reserve
- Moorten Botanical Gardens
- Palm Springs Aerial Tramway
- Palm Springs Air Museum
- Palm Springs Art Museum
- The Fabulous Palm Springs Follies

Hospital Facilities

- Desert Regional Medical Center – Palm Springs
- Eisenhower Medical Center – Rancho Mirage
- John F. Kennedy Memorial Hospital – Indio

RV Parks

RV parks are almost all in Cathedral City, Indio, or Desert Hot Springs. The prices in the Coachella Valley are higher than anywhere else in this chapter, but the higher priced parks pull the average up, and they do tend to be nice resort-style parks. Few of the parks here offer special rates for stays of over a month, probably because they find it easy to fill on weekends. For inexpensive parks take a look at locations on the northeast side of I-10.

PARKING UNDER THE PALM TREES IN DESERT HOT SPRINGS

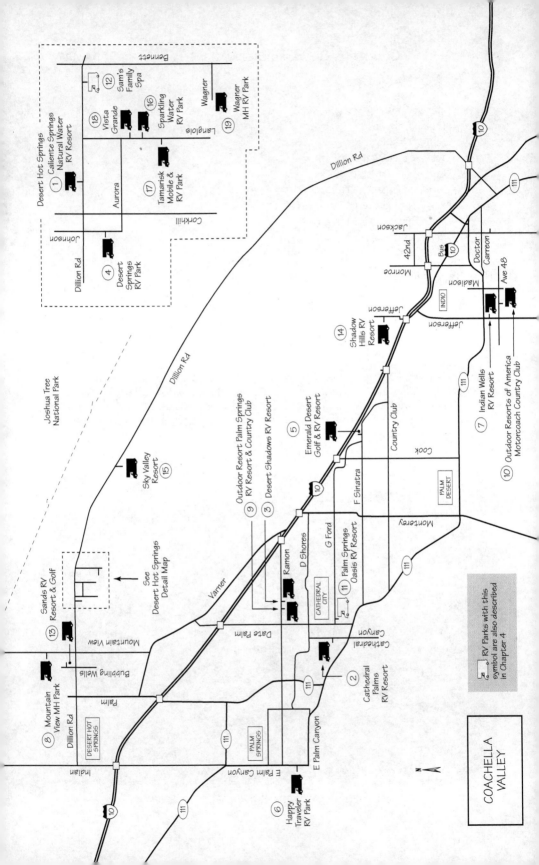

Desert Hot Springs

Bennett

⑫ Sam's Family Spa

⑯ Sparkling Water RV Park

Wagner

⑲ Wagner MH RV Park

Langlois

⑱ Vista Grande

① Caliente Springs Natural Water RV Resort

Aurora

Corkhill

⑰ Tamarisk Mobile & RV Park

Dillion Rd

Johnson

④ Desert Springs RV Park

Dillion Rd

Joshua Tree National Park

Dillion Rd

⑮ Sky Valley Resort

See Desert Hot Springs Detail Map

⑬ Sands RV Resort & Golf

Mountain View

Bubbling Wells

⑧ Mountain View MH Park

Palm

Dillion Rd

Indian

DESERT HOT SPRINGS

Varner

Date Palm

Ramon

D Shores

G Ford

CATHEDRAL CITY

⑪ Palm Springs Oasis RV Resort

Cathedral Canyon

② Cathedral Palms RV Resort

111

Outdoor Resort Palm Springs
⑨ RV Resort & Country Club

③ Desert Shadows RV Resort

⑤ Emerald Desert Golf & RV Resort

F Sinatra

Country Club

Cook

PALM DESERT

Monterey

111

Dillion Rd

⑭ Shadow Hills RV Resort

Jefferson

Jackson

42nd

Bus

Monroe

Madison

INDIO

Jefferson

111

Doctor

Carreon

Ave 48

⑦ Indian Wells RV Resort

⑩ Outdoor Resorts of America Motorcoach Country Club

10

111

PALM SPRINGS

E Palm Canyon

E Palm Canyon

111

⑥ Happy Traveler RV Park

111

10

RV Parks with this symbol are also described in Chapter 4

COACHELLA VALLEY

N

Coachella Valley Snowbird Parks
Page 1

#	Park / Address / Contact	Sites Total / Available	Monthly Rate Available	Longer Term Rates	Overnight Rates	Age Restriction	RV Restriction	Site Surface	Patio	Electric	TV	Phone at Sites	Internet	Wi-Fi	Swimming Pool	Spa	Club House	Planned Activities	Comments
1	Caliente Springs Natural Water RV Resort, 70-200 Dillon Road, Sky Valley, CA 92241 — (760) 329-8400 or (888) 894-7727, www.calientesprings.com, operations@calientesprings.com, N 33° 55' 34" W 116° 26' 12"	679 / 259	✓	$850-900	Over $$$$$$	55		G	✓	50	✓	A	C F	H	✓	✓	✓	✓	Cable internet at sites for a fee; Sites are pool or golf course - rate listed is the lower (pool); 9-hole golf course; Tennis, exercise room, shuffleboard
2	Cathedral Palms RV Resort, 35901 Cathedral Canyon Dr, Cathedral City, CA 92234 — (760) 324-8244, www.letsgocamping.com/resorts/Cathedral_Palms/index.htm, N 33° 47' 15" W 116° 28' 03"	155 / 125		$550-600	Over $$$$$$			G	✓	30	✓	A	C	H	✓	✓	✓	✓	Monthly rate includes electric; Tents are allowed; Some sites have 50-amp electric; Other amenities - shuffleboard, horseshoes, walking trails
3	Desert Shadows RV Resort, 69801 Ramon Road, Cathedral City, CA 92234 — (760) 321-7676 or (800) 235-2488, www.desertshadowsrv.org/, manager@DesertShadowsRV.org, N 33° 48' 56" W 116° 26'39"	460 / 460		$900-950	Over $$$$$$	55	✓	P	✓	50	✓	A	C F	H	✓	✓	✓	✓	Sites individually owned - available through homeowners association; RVs, 5th-wheels, and trailers only; Other amenities - tennis, exercise room, dance studio, shuffleboard
4	Desert Springs RV Park, 17325 Johnson Rd, Desert Hot Springs, CA 92241 — (760) 329-1384, www.desertspringsrvpark.com, hh1689@roadrunner.com, N 33° 55' 22" W 116° 26' 39"	96 / 93		$500-550	Over $$$$$$	55		G	✓	50	✓	A	S F	H	✓	✓	✓	✓	Cable activated by cable company; Unmanned entrance gate; About 45 sites are annual rentals - reserve early for a winter site; Minimum 7 night stay Jan-March
5	Emerald Desert Golf & RV Resort, 76-000 Frank Sinatra Dr, Palm Desert, CA 92211 — (760) 345-4770 or (800) 426-4678, www.emeralddesert.com, info@emeralddesert.com, N 33° 46' 22" W 116° 20' 19"	760 / 760		$1200-1250	55	55	✓	P	✓	50	$	A	C F	H	✓	✓	✓	✓	RVs, 5th-wheels, and trailers only (19 ft limit); Other amenities - 3 tennis courts, 9 hole golf course, exercise room, shuffleboard, convenience store
6	Happy Traveler RV Park, 211 W Mesquite Ave, Palm Springs, CA 92264 — (760) 325-8518, www.happytravelerrv.com, happytra@aol.com, N 33° 48' 29" W 116° 32' 50"	130 / 130	✓	$800-850	Over $$$$$$			P	✓	50	✓	A	S $	H	✓	✓	✓	✓	Closest park to Palm Springs; Monthly rate includes electric (no elec heat), cable TV, and taxes; Maximum length RV is 40 ft; No tent or tent trailers
7	Indian Wells RV Resort, 47-340 Jefferson St, Indio, CA 92201 — (760) 347-0895 or (800) 789-0895, www.carefreeresorts.com, N 33° 42' 15" W 116° 16' 06"	299 / 299		$850-900	Over $$$$$$			P	✓	50	✓	A	S $	H	✓	✓	✓	✓	180 of the sites are annual rentals; Other amenities - shuffleboard, exercise room, putting green and driving net
8	Mountain View MH Park, 15525 Mountain View Rd, Desert Hot Springs, CA 92240 — (760) 329-5870, http://rocvision.com/mtview.htm, montvumhp@aol.com, N 33° 56' 16" W 116° 28' 38"	110 / 55		$350-400	$$$$$$			G	✓	50	✓			H	✓	✓	✓	✓	Unmanned entrance gate; Sites were previously mobile home spaces so they are large enough for any size RV; Library

Coachella Valley Snowbird Parks
Page 2

#	Name / Address	Contact / GPS	Sites Total/Available	Monthly Rate	Longer Term Rates	Overnight Rates	Age Restriction	RV Restriction	Site Surface	Patio	Electric	TV	Phone at Sites	Internet	Wi-Fi	Swimming Pool	Spa	Club House	Planned Activities	Comments
9	Outdoor Resort Palm Springs RV Resort & Country Club, 69-411 Ramon Road, Cathedral City, CA 92234	(760) 324-4005 or (800) 843-3131, www.outdoorresort.com, email@outdoorresort.com, N 33° 48' 56" W 116° 26' 54"	1,213 / 10	$1300-1350	Over $$$$$$	$$$$$$	55	✓	P	✓	50	✓	A	$	S	H	✓	✓	✓	Sites are perimeter or on the golf course - listed lower rate; No tent trailers, truck campers, or Class B; 27 hole par 3 golf course, tennis
10	Outdoor Resorts of America Motorcoach Country Club, 80-501 Avenue 48, Indio, CA 92201	(760) 863-0721 or (888) 277-0789, www.motorcoachcountryclub.com, N 33° 41' 57" W 116° 15' 34"	419 / 419	$1950-2000	Over $$$$$$	$$$$$$	55	✓	P	✓	50	✓	A	$	S	H	✓	✓	✓	Sites are perimeter or premium - listed lower rate; 30-45 ft Class A RVs only; Some waterfront sites with docks; Golf, tennis
11	Palm Springs Oasis RV Resort, 36-100 Date Palm Drive, Cathedral City, CA 92234	(800) 680-0144 or (877) 362-6736 R, www.rvonthego.com, datepalmrvinfo@motorhomes.com, N 33° 47' 11" W 116° 27' 26"	140 / 130	$750-800	Over $$$$$$	$$$$$$	55	✓	P	✓	50	✓	A	$	S	H	✓	✓	✓	18 hole executive golf course; Other amenities - shuffleboard, library, sauna, tennis, billiards; Encore park
12	Sam's Family Spa, 70-875 Dillon Road, Desert Hot Springs, CA 92241	(760) 329-6457, www.samsfamilyspa.com, sams@samsfamilyspa.com, N 33° 55' 23" W 116° 25' 31"	334 / 175	$500-550	Over $$$$$$	$$$$$$	✓	✓	G	✓	50	✓	A	$	S	H	✓	✓	✓	Family park; Other amenities - exercise room, sauna, convenience store, 4 therapeutic pools
13	Sands RV Resort & Golf, 16400 Bubbling Wells Rd, Desert Hot Springs, CA 92240	(760) 251-1030 or (800) 772-7808, www.sandsrvresort.com, sandsrv@aol.com, N 33° 55' 41" W 116° 28' 58"	520 / 260	$450-500	Over $$$$$$	$$$$$$	✓	✓	G	✓	50	$	A	F	S	H	✓	✓	✓	Cable activated by cable company; Other amenities - 9-hole golf course, tennis courts, library, shuffleboard, convenience store
14	Shadow Hills RV Resort, 40-655 Jefferson, Indio, CA 92203	(760) 360-4040, www.shadowhillsrvresort.com, info@shadowhillsrvresort.com, N 33° 45' 14" W 116° 16' 09"	110 / 110	$900-950	Over $$$$$$	$$$$$$	✓	✓	P	✓	50	✓	A	F	S	H	✓	✓	✓	RVs must be less than 10 years old; Other amenities - horseshoes, shuffleboard, pool tables, excercise room, card room; $1 per day pet charge
15	Sky Valley Resort, 74-711 Dillon Road, Desert Hot Springs, CA 92241	(760) 329-8400 or (800) 800-9218, www.skyvalleyresort.com, N 33° 54' 08" W 116° 21' 32"	920 / 618	$650-700	Over $$$$$$	$$$$$$	55	✓	G	✓	50	✓	A	F	C	H	✓	✓	✓	Monthly rates depend on size and location - rate listed is lowest; Other amenities - tennis, pond, fishing, hiking trails
16	Sparkling Waters RV Park, 17800 Langlois Rd, Desert Hot Spgs, CA 92241	(760) 329-6551, N 33° 55' 10" W 116° 25' 51"	85 / 27	$650-700		$$$$$		✓	G	✓	50	✓	A			H	✓	✓	✓	Call for monthly rate; Other amenities - horseshoes, shuffleboard

	Sites Total/Available	Monthly Rate	Longer Term Rates	Overnight Rates	Age Restriction	RV Restriction	Site Surface	Patio	Electric	TV	Phone at Sites	Internet	Wi-Fi	Swimming Pool	Spa	Club House	Planned Activities	Comments
(17) **Tamarisk Mobile & RV Park** 18025 Langlois Rd Desert Hot Spgs, CA 92241 www.tamariskrvpark.com (760) 329-7943 N 33° 55' 02" W 116° 25' 55"	170 / 94	$350-400	✓	$$$$$$ Over	55		G	✓	30	$	A		C F	H	✓	✓	✓	Monthly rate includes 250 kwh of electricity Cable activated by cable company A few 50 amp sites RVs in separate area from mobiles
(18) **Vista Grande** 17625 Langlois Rd Desert Hot Spgs, CA 92241 (760) 329-5424 N 33° 55' 15" W 116° 25' 52"	112 / 40	$350-400	$$$$$$		55	✓	G	✓	30	✓	A			H	✓	✓		Self contained RVs only - bathrooms locked at night 2 or 3 sites have 50 amp power Some sites have patios
(19) **Wagner MH RV Park** 18-801 Roberts Road Desert Hot Spgs, CA 92241 (760) 329-6043 www.wagnermhandrvpark.com info@wagnermhandrvpark.com N 33° 354' 42" W 116° 25' 39"	94 / 89	$450-500	$$$$$$		55		G	✓	50		A			H	✓	✓	✓	2 hot mineral pools, 2 cool mineral pools

LAKE HAVASU AND THE PARKER STRIP

This area runs about 50 miles from north to south. In the north is Lake Havasu, a large reservoir behind Parker Dam. On the east side of the lake is the largest town in the area, Lake Havasu, with a population of about 55,000.

South of Parker Dam is a section of the Colorado river known as Moovalya Lake or the Parker Strip. This section of the river is narrow, but not free-flowing. It is behind the Headgate Rock Dam. Both sides of this lake are lined with recreational developments, many are RV parks.

At the south end of this area is the small town of Parker, actually on the Colorado River Indian Reservation. It serves as the supply town for the southern half of the region.

This region is unusual because it is a four-season destination. Even in the heat of the summer it attracts large numbers of lovers of water sports of all kinds from both Arizona and California. In winter, though, it's definitely a Snowbird haven.

For more information take a look at the *Lake Havasu And The Parker Strip* section in *Chapter 4.*

Weather

The altitude of this area ranges from 300 to 400 feet.

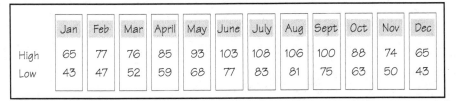

	Jan	Feb	Mar	April	May	June	July	Aug	Sept	Oct	Nov	Dec
High	65	77	76	85	93	103	108	106	100	88	74	65
Low	43	47	52	59	68	77	83	81	75	63	50	43

Living Convenience and Shopping

This is one of the more remote Snowbird destinations. The main shopping town is Lake Havasu City which has an Albertson's, two Basha's, a Food City, Safeway, Walmart, and Home Depot. Parker is much smaller and offers a Safeway. For more ambitious shopping expeditions you have to drive quite a distance; Yuma is 110 miles distant, Phoenix 150 miles, and Las Vegas about 150 miles also.

Parker is only 35 miles north of Quartzsite so you can easily visit in January during all of the activities there.

Recreation

Recreational facilities and destinations in Lake Havasu and the Parker Strip include:
- Four Golf Courses
- Blue Water Casino
- Colorado Indian Tribes Museum (Parker)
- Lake Havasu for boating and fishing
- Lake Havasu Museum of History (Lake Havasu)
- London Bridge and the Lake Havasu City tourist shops and attractions

- Parker Dam
- Parker Strip for boating and fishing

Hospital Facilities

- La Paz Regional Hospital – Parker
- Parker PHS Indian Hospital – Parker
- Havasu Regional Medical Center – Lake Havasu City

RV Parks

The parks in this area tend to have fewer amenities that some of the other Snowbird areas in this chapter. They rely on the river and the lake to attract guests. One thing they often do have, however, is a store. That can save you a long drive to get some milk.

Parks in Lake Havasu City, Parker, and nearby areas have a five to six percent tax on monthly space rentals. Make sure you inquire about this when you call to see if it's included in the rate.

Boondockers will note that in the *Lake Havasu City and the Parker Strip* section in our *Arizona* chapter we describe two free BLM Dispersed Camping areas near Lake Havasu City. Also, east of this area, near the Vidal Junction, there is BLM land with dispersed camping possibilities. Also note that Cattail Cove State Park sets aside sites for Snowbirds with a six month stay limit during the winter.

VIEW OF ARIZONA'S BLUE WATER CASINO FROM CALIFORNIA

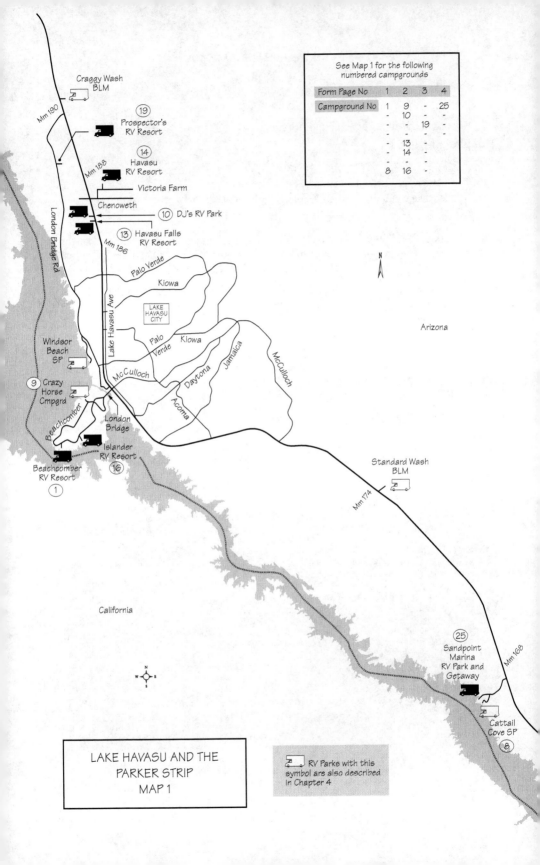

Craggy Wash
BLM

Mm 190

London Bridge Rd

⑲ Prospector's
RV Resort

⑭ Havasu
RV Resort

Mm 188

Victoria Farm

Chenoweth

⑩ DJ's RV Park

⑬ Havasu Falls
RV Resort

Mm 186

Palo Verde

Kiowa

LAKE
HAVASU
CITY

Lake Havasu Ave

Palo
Verde

Kiowa

Jamaica

McCulloch

Arizona

Windsor
Beach
SP

Daytona

McCulloch

⑨ Crazy
Horse
Cmpgrd

Acoma

Beachcomber

London
Bridge

Islander
RV Resort

⑯

Beachcomber
RV Resort

①

Standard Wash
BLM

Mm 174

California

N
W ◇ E
S

⑤ Sandpoint
Marina
RV Park and
Getaway

Mm 168

Cattail
Cove SP

⑧

N

See Map 1 for the following
numbered campgrounds

Form Page No	1	2	3	4
Campground No	1	9	-	25
	-	10	-	-
	-	-	19	-
	-	-	-	-
	-	13	-	
	-	14	-	
	-	-	-	
	8	16	-	

LAKE HAVASU AND THE
PARKER STRIP
MAP 1

🚐 RV Parks with this
symbol are also described
in Chapter 4

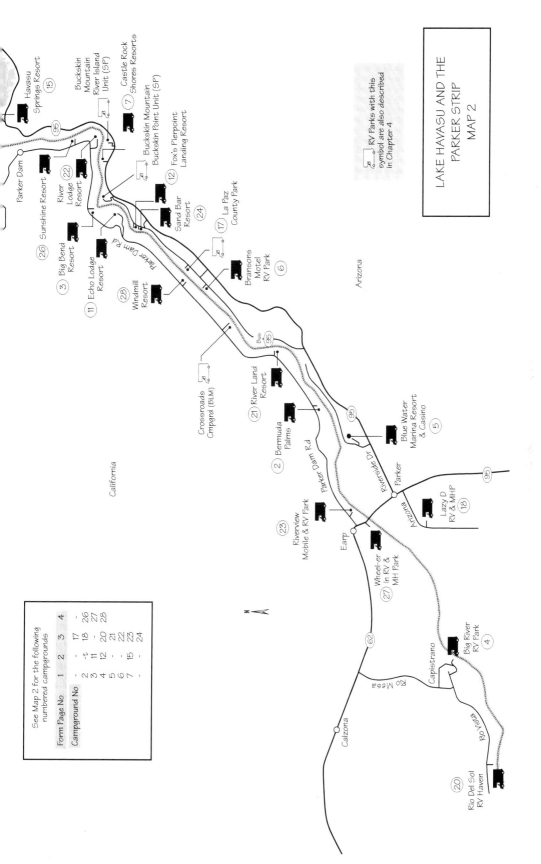

LAKE HAVASU AND THE
PARKER STRIP
MAP 2

RV Parks with this symbol are also described in Chapter 4

Havasu Springs Resort ⑮

Buckskin Mountain River Island Unit (SP)

Castle Rock Shores Resorts ⑦

Parker Dam

Buckskin Mountain Buckskin Point Unit (SP)

River Lodge Resort ㉒

Sunshine Resort ㉖

Fox's Pierpoint Landing Resort ⑫

Big Bend Resort ③

Sand Bar Resort ㉔

Echo Lodge Resort ⑪

La Paz County Park ⑰

Windmill Resort ㉘

Parker Dam Rd

Bransons Motel RV Park ⑥

Arizona

California

Crossroads Cmpgrd (BLM)

River Land Resort ㉑

Bermuda Palms ②

Blue Water Marina Resort & Casino ⑤

Bus 95

95

Parker Dam Rd

Riverview Mobile & RV Park ㉓

Riverside Dr

Parker

95

Earp

Arizona

Lazy D RV & MHP ⑱

Wheel-er In RV & MH Park ㉗

N

62

Capistrano

Rio Mesa

Big River RV Park ④

Calzona

Rio Vista

Rio Del Sol RV Haven ⑳

See Map 2 for the following numbered campgrounds

Form Page No	1	2	3	4
Campground No	-	-	17	-
	2	-t	18	26
	3	11	-	27
	4	12	20	28
	5	-	21	-
	6	-	22	-
	7	15	23	-
	-	-	24	-

Lake Havasu And The Parker Strip Snowbird Parks
Page 1

#	Park	Contact / Location	Sites Total/Available	Monthly Rate	Longer Term Rates	Overnight Rates	Age Restriction	RV Restriction	Site Surface	Patio	Electric	TV	Phone at Sites	Internet	Wi-Fi	Swimming Pool	Spa	Club House	Planned Activities	Comments
1	Beachcomber RV Resort 601 Beachcomber Blvd Lk Havasu City, AZ 86403	(928) 855-2322 N 34° 27' 09" W 114° 22' 10"	500 / 70	$500-550	Over $$$$$$				G		50	$	A		C F	H	✓	✓		Cable activated by cable company / Boat ramp / Wi-Fi can be received at some sites
2	Bermuda Palms HC Box 75 Earp, CA 92242	(760) 665-2784 N 34° 10' 50" W 114° 15' 01"	171 / 37	$150-200			55		G	✓	50	✓	A			H	✓	✓		No overnight sites / No dogs allowed / Reservations required early for a winter site
3	Big Bend Resort 501 Parker Dam Rd Parker Dam, CA 92267	(760) 663-3755 N 34° 15' 39" W 114° 10' 00"	150 / 150	$300-350	Over $$$$$$				G	✓	50	✓	A				✓	✓		Waterfront sites are priced slightly higher / Cable internet available for a fee
4	Big River RV Park 1 Marina Street Big River, CA 92242	(760) 665-9359 www.bigriverrvpark.com administration@bigriverrvpark.com N 34° 07' 41" W 114° 21' 36"	182 / 180	$300-350	Over $$$$$$				GR		50	✓	A	✓	S F		✓	✓		Swimming beach / Phone available at 70 sites / On the Colorado River / Boat launch
5	Blue Water Marina, Resort & Casino 1001 Bluewater Dr Parker, AZ 85344	(928) 669-2433 N 34° 09' 59" W 114° 15' 52"	191 / 189	$300-350	$$$$$				G	✓	50	✓	A		S		✓	✓		Limited 40 ft sites / 1st mth electric included in rate / Wi-Fi being installed at sites for 2008-09 season
6	Bransons Motel RV Park 7804 Riverside Dr Parker, AZ 85344	(928) 667-3346 N 34° 13' 13" W 114° 11' 56"	68 / 68	$300-350	Over $$$$$$				G	✓	50	✓	A		C F		✓	✓		No pets allowed / Reservations for 3 mths only / Wi-Fi received at sites near the clubhouse
7	Castle Rock Shores Resort 5220 Highway 95 Parker, AZ 85344	(928) 667-2344 or (800) 701-1277 www.castlerockshores.com info@castlerockshores.com N 34° 15' 25" W 114° 08' 43"	125 / 100	$300-350	Over $$$$$$				G		30	$	A		C F		✓	✓		Rate listed is for waterfront - terrace sites are less / Cable available from park for a fee / Some 50 amp sites available
8	Cattail Cove (SP) P.O. Box 1990 Lk Havasu City, AZ 86405	(928) 855-1223 www.azstateparks.com N 34° 21' 14" W 114° 10' 00"	61 / 61	$450-500	$$$$$				P		30									On the Colorado River / 6 mth stay allowed Oct-March in up to 50 of the sites / 5 sites have 50 amp power / Boat ramp

#	Name / Address	Contact	Sites Total/Available	Monthly Rate	Longer Term Rates	Overnight Rates	Age Restriction	RV Restriction	Site Surface	Patio	Electric	TV	Phone at Sites	Internet	Wi-Fi	Swimming Pool	Spa	Club House	Planned Activities	Comments
9	Crazy Horse Campgrounds, 1534 Beachcomber Blvd, Lk Havasu City, AZ 86403	(928) 855-4033, www.crazyhorsecampgrounds.com, crzyhrse@ctaz.com, N 34° 28' 08" W 114° 21' 25"	632 / 600	$300-350	✓	$$$$$$ Over			G	✓	50	✓	A	✓	S $	H	✓	✓	✓	The monthly rate varies depending on location and services (listed is cheapest) / On the Colorado River / 3 to 6 month stays are cheaper
10	DJ's RV Park, 3501 North Hwy 95, Lk Havasu City, AZ 86404	(928) 764-3964, www.djsrvresort.com, office@djsrvresort.com, N 34° 32' 18" W 114° 21' 09"	106 / 90	$350-400	✓	$$$$$$			G	✓	50	$	A	✓		H	✓	✓		5 mth seasonal discounts offered / Cable activated by cable company / No tents
11	Echo Lodge River Resort, P.O. Box 1088, Parker, AZ 85344	(760) 663-4931, www.echolodgeresort.com, N 34° 14' 58" W 114° 10' 23"	377 / 210	$300-350	✓	$$$$$			G	✓	30	✓	✓	✓		✓		✓		On the Colorado River / Boat launch / Beach with lake swimming / No pets allowed
12	Fox's Pierpoint Landing Resort, 6350 Riverside Dr, Parker, AZ 85344	www.foxsresort.com, (928) 667-3444 or (800) 335-3697, N 34° 14' 41" W 114° 10' 26"	70 / 70	$1000-1050	✓	$$$$$$ Over			G	✓	50	✓	A	✓	S F			✓		No monthly rate - charged weekly rate x 4 (includes electric) / 2 mth rate is $450/mth / Wi-Fi reaches some sites / Boating, fishing, mini-golf
13	Havasu Falls RV Resort, 3493 Hwy 95 North, Lk Havasu City, AZ 86404	(928) 764-0050 or (877) 843-3255, www.havasufallsrvresort.com, thefalls@npgcable.com, N 34° 32' 16" W 114° 21' 09"	129 / 129	$450-500	✓	$$$$$ Over	✓		P	✓	50	✓	– $	✓	C F	H	✓	✓		RVs must be self-contained / Phones activated by office for a fee / On the Colorado River / Reserve early for Jan-March
14	Havasu RV Resort, 1905 Victoria Farms Rd, Lk Havasu City, AZ 86404	(928) 764-2020 or (877) 407-2020, info@havasurvresort.com, www.havasurvresort.com, N 34° 15' 22" W 114° 08' 13"	269 / 250	$550-600	✓	$$$$$$	✓		P	✓	50	✓	A	✓	S F	H	✓	✓	✓	New park - open only 5 yrs / Monthly rate includes electric / 25 ft min RV and 10 yrs age / 9 hole putting green / Cable activated by cable company
15	Havasu Springs Resort, 2581 Highway 95, Parker, AZ 85344	(928) 667-3361, www.havasusprings.com, reservations@havasusprings.com, N 34° 17' 45" W 114° 07' 34"	136 / 136	$250-300	✓	$$$$$$ Over			G	✓	50	✓	A	✓	✓	✓	✓	✓	✓	Pool is not heated / On the Colorado River / Other amenities - marina, boat launch, beach, par 3 golf course / Free Wi-Fi at the restaurant
16	Islander RV Resort, 751 Beachcomber Blvd, Lk Havasu City, AZ 86403	(928) 680-2000, www.islanderrvresort.com, info@islanderrvresort.net, N 34° 27' 19" W 114° 08' 43"	519 / 250	$400-450	✓	$$$$$$ Over	✓		G	✓	50	✓	– $	✓	C F	H	✓	✓	✓	Sites include basic, premium (view), waterfront - rate listed is basic / Monthly rates only for 5 mth stays / RVs over 10 yrs age require approval / Phone activated by office for a fee

#	Park / Address	Contact	Sites Total/Available	Monthly Rate Available	Longer Term Rates	Overnight Rates	Age Restriction	RV Restriction	Site Surface	Patio	Electric	TV	Phone at Sites	Internet	Wi-Fi	Swimming Pool	Spa	Club House	Planned Activities	Comments
17	*La Paz County Park* 7350 Riverside Dr. Parker, AZ 85344	(928) 667-2069 www.co.la-paz.az.us parks@co.la-paz.az.us N 34° 13' 34" W 114° 11' 24"	114 / 114	$300-350	$$$$				GR	✓	50	✓	A	C F			✓			6 mth maximum stay No full hook-up sites On the Colorado River Boat ramp
18	*Lazy D RV & MHP* 1800 15th St Parker, AZ 85344	(928) 669-8797 oldfart@redrivernet.com N 34° 08' 19" W 114° 18' 06"	125 / 125	$200-250	$$$$				G	✓	50	$	A	C F			✓			Cable activated by phone company
19	*Prospector's RV Resort* 4750 N London Bridge Rd Lk Havasu City, AZ 86404	(928) 764-2000 www.prospectorsresort.com prospectorsrv@npgcable.com N 34° 33' 37" W 114° 22' 12"	212 / 125	$400-450	$$$$$$	Over	✓		G	✓	50	✓	A	C F	H	✓	✓	✓		New park - only 5 years old Older RVs subject to approval Other amenities - fitness room, TV lounge, game room
20	*Rio Del Sol RV Haven* 7905 Rio Vista Drive P.O. Box 2079 Big River, CA 92242	(760) 665-2981 www.riodelsolrvhaven.com riodelsol1@aol.com N 34° 06' 47" W 114° 24' 29"	101 / 97	$250-300	$$$$$			✓	G GR	✓	30	$	A				✓			On the Colorado River Other amenities - shuffleboard, river swimming, fishing, boat ramp Front row sites are seasonal only Daily rate includes cable
21	*Riverland Resort* 3401 Parker Dam Road Earp, CA 92242	(760) 663-3733 or (800) 811-6748 R www.reynoldsresorts.com reservations@reynoldsresorts.com N 34° 11' 39" W 114° 13' 34"	102 / 102	$250-400	$$$$$$				G	✓	30	✓	A	S $			✓			On the Colorado River Cable internet available for a fee Boat ramp
22	*River Lodge Resort* 675 Parker Dam Road Parker Dam, CA 92267	(760) 663-4934 or (800) 577-4837 www.riverlodgeresort.com reservations@riverlodgeresort.com N 34° 15' 39" W 114° 08' 22"	64 / 64	$350-400	$$$$$$	Over			G	✓	30	$					✓			On the Colorado River Monthly rate is for a waterfront site Some 50 amp sites Cable through park for a fee Private golf course, boat launch
23	*Riverview Mobile & RV Park* Box 47 Earp, CA 92242	(760) 665-9953 N 34° 09' 59" W 114° 17' 46"	350 / 330	$250-300	$$$$$				G	✓	50	✓	A	C F			✓	✓		On the Colorado River The park has mobile homes in a separate area Boat launch
24	*Sand Bar Resort* 6400 Riverside Dr Parker, AZ 85344	www.redrockresort.org (928) 667-3116 N 34° 14' 39" W 114° 10' 29"	73 / 73	$300-350	$$$$$$				G	✓	50			S $			✓			On the Colorado River Store Fox's Bar & Grill nearby Rate is for waterview (waterfront available only for 3 mth rentals)

Lake Havasu And The Parker Strip Snowbird Parks

	Sites Total/Available	Monthly Rate	Longer Term Rates	Overnight Rates	Age Restriction	RV Restriction	Site Surface	Patio	Electric	TV	Phone at Sites	Internet	Wi-Fi	Swimming Pool	Spa	Club House	Planned Activities	Comments
25 Sandpoint Marina RV Resort & Getaway P.O. Box 1469 Lk Havasu City, AZ 86405 (928) 855-0549 www.sandpointresort.com sandpoint@frontiernet.net N 34° 21' 12" W 114° 10' 18"	173 / 168	$350-400		$$$$$ Over		P	G	✓	50		A						✓	On the Colorado River 104 slip marina Boat ramp Other amenities - convenience store, restaurant
26 Sunshine Resort 1255 Parker Dam Road Parker Dam, CA 92267 (760) 663-3098 www.sunshineresort.info contactus@sunshineresort.info N 34° 16' 03" W 114° 08' 07"	61 / 29	$250-300		$$$$$$			G	✓	50	✓		✓	C F			✓		On the Colorado River 31 mobile spaces and 28 RV sites Considering extending Wi-Fi to sites Boat launch Convenience store
27 Wheel-er in RV & MH Park Box 46 Earp, CA 92242 (760) 665-8487 N 34° 09' 36" W 114° 18' 03"	56 / 56	$250-300		$$$$$$			G		50	✓	A				✓			On the Colorado River Internet available through cable co Other amenities - shuffleboard, river swimming, putting green convenience store
28 Windmill Resort 1451 Parker Dam Rd Earp, CA 92242 (760) 663-3717 N 34° 13' 34" W 114° 11' 52"	26 / 26	$300-350		$$$$$$			G	✓	30	$			S F			✓		Limited sites for 40 ft RVs Winter sites fill early in season All sites are on the water Cable through the park for a fee

LAS VEGAS

Las Vegas, with an area population approaching 600,000 people, doesn't play a huge part in the Southwest Snowbird scene but there are a significant number of spaces. The attractions of this town are obvious, Las Vegas makes a business of attracting travelers from all over the world.

For more information take a look at the *Las Vegas* section of *Chapter 4.*

Weather

With an altitude of 2,000 feet the winter weather in Las Vegas is cooler than any other Snowbird area in the chapter.

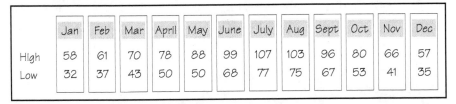

	Jan	Feb	Mar	April	May	June	July	Aug	Sept	Oct	Nov	Dec
High	58	61	70	78	88	99	107	103	96	80	66	57
Low	32	37	43	50	50	68	77	75	67	53	41	35

Living Convenience and Shopping

Las Vegas, like a few of the other cities in this chapter (Yuma, Phoenix) is one of the fastest growing cities in the country. That means that traffic congestion is more and more a consideration here. With a population of over a half-million people you can expect to be able to find any kind of shopping or other amenities you are likely to want.

Recreation

Las Vegas shines in the recreation area, both indoors and outdoors.
- Thirty-five Golf Courses
- Casinos
- Colorado River
- Hoover Dam
- Lake Mead National Recreation Area
- Red Rock Canyon State Park

Hospital Facilities
- Desert Springs Hospital
- Healthsouth Hospital at Tenaya
- Horizon Specialty Hospital
- Integrated Health Service of Las Vegas
- Kindred Hospital Las Vegas
- Mountain View Hospital
- Sunrise Hospital & Medical Center
- UMC of Southern Nevada
- Valley Hospital Medical Center

LAS VEGAS SNOWBIRD PARKS ARE NEAR THE CASINO ACTION

RV Parks

You'll see from the Snowbird Destination Comparison Table that Las Vegas has one of the highest average monthly rates in this chapter. Most parks do not include electricity in their rates and don't include tax either. There is a 9% tax on your first month's rental, none after that. One reason for the high rates here is that a number of parks have closed in recent years, and that means the others can afford to charge more. Also, three month seasonal rates are pretty much unknown here.

If you prefer the outdoors to the city you might consider the Lake Mead Recreation Area which is just east of Las Vegas. It has several RV parks with hookups in addition to the Park Service campgrounds. See the *Lake Mead Recreation Area* of the *Arizona* chapter for more information.

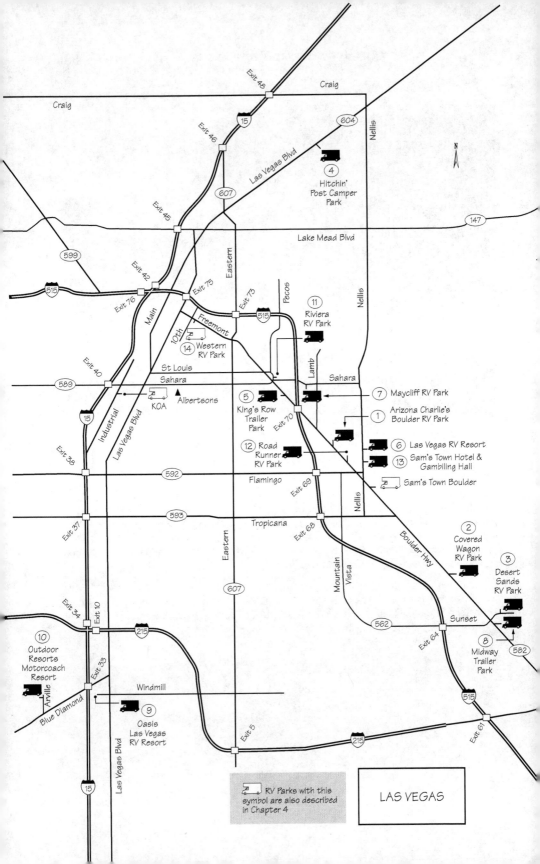

LAS VEGAS

Las Vegas Snowbird Parks
Page 1

#	Park / Address	Contact / Coordinates	Sites Total/Available	Monthly Rate	Longer Term Rates	Overnight Rates	Age Restriction	RV Restriction	Site Surface	Patio	Electric	TV	Phone at Sites	Internet	Wi-Fi	Swimming Pool	Spa	Club House	Comments
1	Arizona Charlie's Boulder RV Park, 4575 Boulder Hwy, Las Vegas, NV 89121	(702) 951-5911 or (800) 970-7280, www.arizonacharlies.com, N 36° 07' 29" W 115° 04' 36"	239 / 239	$650-700		$$$$$$ Over		✓	P		50		I F	✓	H	✓	✓		Minimum of 25 ft RVs. Monthly rate includes electricity. Telephone instant on for free. Other amenities - restaurant, shuffleboard, exercise room
2	Covered Wagon RV Park, 6635 Boulder Hwy, Las Vegas, NV 89122	(702) 454-7090, N 36° 04' 50" W 115° 01' 37"	207 / 207	$350-400		$$$$$		✓	G		50	✓	A		H	✓	✓	✓	RVs, 5th-wheels, and trailers only
3	Desert Sands RV Park, 1940 N Boulder Hwy, Henderson, NV 89015	(702) 565-1945, N 36° 03' 58" W 115° 00' 34"	245 / 245	$300-350		$$$$		✓	G		50	✓	A		H	✓	✓		RVs, 5th-wheels, and trailers only. Other amenities - sauna. DSL internet available through phone co
4	Hitchin' Post Camper Park, 3640 N Las Vegas Blvd, Las Vegas, NV 89115	(702) 644-1043 or (888) 433-8402, N 36° 13' 22" W 115° 05' 00"	196 / 196	$450-500		$$$$$$		✓	G		50	✓	A				✓		Gate park. 1 dog limit
5	King's Row Trailer Park, 3660 Boulder Hwy, Las Vegas, NV 89121	(702) 457-3606, N 36° 08' 22" W 115° 05' 04"	500 / 320	$300-350		$$$		✓	G	✓	50 $	✓	A		H	✓	✓		Cable activated by cable company. Swimming pool closed in winter
6	Las Vegas RV Resort, 3890 S Nellis Blvd, Las Vegas, NV 89121	(702) 451-8005, www.holidayrvpark.com, LasVegasInfo@HorizonRVResorts.com, N 36° 07' 08" W 115° 03' 51"	403 / 390	$550-600		$$$$$$ Over	21	✓	P		50	✓	A	✓	G F / H	✓	✓	✓	RVs, 5th-wheels, and trailers only for monthly sites
7	Maycliff RV Park, 4001 E Sahara, Las Vegas, NV 89104	(702) 457-3553, N 36° 08' 37" W 115° 05' 14"	128 / 128	$300-350				✓	P G		50		A						No daily sites - monthly or longer. Mostly annual rentals. RVs, 5th-wheels, and trailers only. Credit check and on time tax charged with first month rent
8	Midway Trailer Park, 125 E Mwelayne Dr #12, Henderson, NV 89011	(702) 564-0905, N 36° 03' 51" W 115° 00' 25"	52 / 50	$300-350				✓	G		50 $		A						No daily sites - monthly or longer only. RVs, 5th-wheels, and trailers only. Cable activated by park for a fee. Only 6 spaces for 40 ft RVs

Las Vegas Snowbird Parks
Page 2

#	Park	Sites Total/Available	Monthly Rate	Longer Term Rates	Overnight Rates	Age Restriction	RV Restriction	Site Surface	Patio	Electric	TV	Phone at Sites	Internet	Wi-Fi	Swimming Pool	Spa	Club House	Planned Activities	Comments
9	Oasis Las Vegas RV Resort 2711 Windmill Lane Las Vegas, NV 89123 (702) 260-2020 or (800) 566-4707 www.oasislasvegasrvresort.com reservations@oasislasvegasrvresort.com N 36° 02' 32" W 115° 10' 42"	700 / 700	$700-750	Over $$$$$$	$$$$$$		✓	P	✓	50	✓	I / F	S / $	H	✓	✓	✓	✓	Sites are standard, deluxe, and premium - rate is for standard RVs, 5th-wheels, and trailers only / Phone through office - free / 18-hole putting course
10	Outdoor Resorts of America LV Motorcoach Resort 8175 Arville St Las Vegas, NV 89139 (866) 897-9300 www.lasvegasmotorcoachresort.com orm.countryclub@verizon.net N 36° 02' 29" W 115° 12' 00"	300 / 300	$1800-1850	Over $$$$$$	$$$$$$	55	✓	P	✓	50	✓	A	S / F	H	✓	✓	✓	✓	30-45 ft Class A RVs only / Montly rate includes electric / Activities director / Other amenities - 9-hole putting course, exercise room, tennis
11	Riviera RV Park 2200 Palm St Las Vegas, NV 89104 www.rivierarvpark.com (702) 457-8700 rivierarvresort@embarqmail.com N 36° 08' 49" W 115° 06' 04"	136 / 136	$200-350	$$$$				P		50	✓		✓			✓			Early reservations necessary / No tents
12	Road Runner RV Park 4711 Boulder Hwy Las Vegas, NV 89121 (702) 456-4711 www.roadrunnerrvpark.com foursocks92@embarqmail.com N 36° 06' 57" W 115° 03' 48"	200 / 200	$400-450	$$$$				P	✓	50		A	✓			✓			Early reservations necessary / Daily rate first 3 days / Dogs up to 10 lbs
13	Sam's Town Hotel & Gambling Hall 4040 S. Nellis Blvd Las Vegas, NV 89122 (702) 454-8056 or (800) 634-6371 www.samstownlv.com/rvpark N 36° 06' 57" W 115° 03' 48"	200 / 200	$600-650	$$$$$$			G		✓	50	✓	I / F	S / $	H	✓	✓			Monthly rate includes electric (30 amp - higher for 50 amp) / 1st mth rate only includes tax / Instant phones at sites for free / Restaurant and casino next door
14	Western RV Park 1023 Freemont St Las Vegas, NV 89101 (702) 384-1033 N 36° 09' 58" W 115° 08' 04"	69 / 69	$500-550	$$$$			P			50									Nearest snowbird park to The Strip and Freemont

MOHAVE VALLEY

The Mohave Valley makes a very attractive Snowbird destination. It has good prices, good weather, and a lot to keep you busy.

The Mohave Valley area includes a little bit of three states: Nevada, Arizona, and California. It's the Colorado River Valley from the south end of Lake Mohave (behind Davis Dam) south to Needles and I-10.

The main cities are Laughlin, Bullhead City, and Needles. Laughlin has the casinos but little in the way of RV parks, just a traveler park for people needing convenient access to the casinos. Bullhead City is across the river from Laughlin and has a number of very good Snowbird RV parks. South across the Fort Mojave Indian Reservation is Needles, where you'll find the least expensive parks.

For more information take a look at the *Mohave Valley* section of the *Chapter 4.*

Weather

The altitude on the floor of the valley here is only in the neighborhood of 400 feet although the area is surrounded by higher terrain. Temperatures are very much like those in Quartzsite.

	Jan	Feb	Mar	April	May	June	July	Aug	Sept	Oct	Nov	Dec
High	65	71	78	87	97	107	112	110	103	90	75	65
Low	43	47	50	56	65	73	79	79	72	60	49	43

Living Convenience and Shopping

Laughlin has a population of about 8,000, Bullhead City has a population of about 35,000, Needles about 5,000. It's pretty easy to tell where the stores are going to be. Bullhead City has a Safeway, Albertson's, Food City, a Walmart Superstore, and a Home Depot. Needles has a Basha's and a Safeway, and Fort Mohave, about half-way between, also has a Safeway.

The closest place for much more in the way of shopping is Las Vegas, about 80 miles to the north.

Recreation

- Three Golf Courses in Bullhead City, One in Needles (Municipal), Two in Laughlin
- Colorado River – rafting, boating and fishing
- Lake Mohave National Recreation Area – boating, fishing, hiking
- Laughlin Casinos
- Mitchell Caverns
- Oatman (See Kingman section of Arizona chapter)

A COMFORTABLE BULLHEAD CITY SNOWBIRD RV PARK

Hospital Facilities

- Western Arizona Regional Medical Center – Bullhead City
- Colorado River Medical Center – Needles
- Kingman Regional Medical Center – Kingman
- Havasu Regional Medical Center – Lake Havasu City

RV Parks

As you might expect from the prices the parks here aren't really upscale with a lot of amenities, but they're not bad either. All in all, this area is a real value. You'll find that there are few three-month discounts available, people must already know that this is a good place to spend the winter.

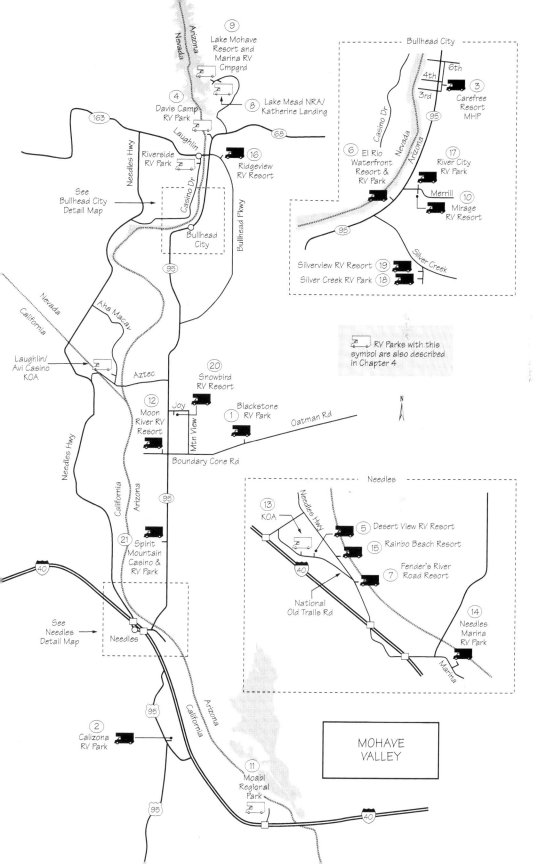

Nevada
Arizona

⑨ Lake Mohave Resort and Marina RV Cmpgrd

④ Davis Camp RV Park

⑧ Lake Mead NRA/ Katherine Landing

(163)

Needles Hwy

Laughlin

68

Casino Dr

Riverside RV Park

⑯ Ridgeview RV Resort

See Bullhead City Detail Map

Bullhead Pkwy

Bullhead City

(95)

Aha Macav

Nevada
California

Laughlin/ Avi Casino KOA

Aztec

⑳ Snowbird RV Resort

⑫ Moon River RV Resort

Joy

Mtn View

① Blackstone RV Park

Oatman Rd

Boundary Cone Rd

Needles Hwy

California
Arizona

(95)

㉑ Spirit Mountain Casino & RV Park

(40)

See Needles Detail Map

Needles

⑬ KOA

Needles Hwy

⑤ Desert View RV Resort

⑮ Rainbo Beach Resort

(40)

⑦ Fender's River Road Resort

National Old Trails Rd

⑭ Needles Marina RV Park

Marina

Needles

(95)

Arizona
California

② Calizona RV Park

(95)

⑪ Moabi Regional Park

(40)

Bullhead City Detail Map

Bullhead City

6th
4th
3rd

③ Carefree Resort MHP

Casino Dr

(95)

⑥ El Rio Waterfront Resort & RV Park

Nevada
Arizona

⑰ River City RV Park

Merrill

⑩ Mirage RV Resort

(95)

Silverview RV Resort ⑲

Silver Creek RV Park ⑱

Silver Creek

RV Parks with this symbol are also described in Chapter 4

N

MOHAVE VALLEY

Mohave Valley Snowbird Parks
Page 1

#	Name / Contact	Sites Total/Available	Monthly Rate	Longer Term Rates	Overnight Rates	Age Restriction	RV Restriction	Site Surface	Patio	Electric	TV	Phone at Sites	Internet	Wi-Fi	Swimming Pool	Spa	Club House	Planned Activities	Comments
1	Blackstone RV Park, 3299 Boundary Cone Rd, Bullhead Cty, AZ 86440, (928) 768-3303, blackstonervpark@yahoo.com, N 34° 58' 34" W 114° 32' 03"	136 / 136	$250-300	$$$$$				G	✓	50	✓	A	✓	S / F			✓	✓	Other amenities - grocery store, ATM machine, horseshoes
2	Calizona RV Park, P.O. Box 208, Needles, CA 92363, (760) 326-5679, www.calizonarvpark.com, calizona@citilink.net, N 34° 46' 15" W 114° 35' 43"	80 / 74	$150-200	$$$$				G	✓	50	✓	A		C / F			✓	✓	Other amenities - horseshoes, pool table
3	Carefree Resort/MHP, 350 Lee Ave, Bullhead Cty, AZ 86429, (928) 754-3438, www.durham-properties.com, N 35° 08' 47" W 114° 34' 02"	68 / 22	$350-400			55		G	✓	30	✓	A	✓	H			✓		Monthly rate includes first 500 kwh electric and cable. Primarily a montly park
4	Davis Camp RV Park, 2251 Hwy 68, Bullhead Cty, AZ 86429, (928) 754-7250 or (877) 757-0915, www.mcparks.com, N 35° 11' 06" W 114° 33' 57"	151 / 151	$350-400	$$$$				G	✓	50				S / F					Monthly rate includes electric. On the Colorado River. Additional fee for pets. Activities - river swimming, fishing, boating (boat launch)
5	Desert View RV Resort, 5300 Route 66, Needles, CA 92363, (760) 326-4000, www.desertviewrv.com, desertviewrv@citilink.net, N 34° 52' 06" W 114° 38' 25"	60 / 56	$250-300	$$$$$$		55		G	✓	50	✓	A	✓	S / F			✓		Other amenities - horseshoes. Full during winter months - call to reserve early. 2 pet limit
6	El Rio Waterfront Resort & RV Park, 1641 Hwy 95, Bullhead Cty, AZ 86442, (928) 763-4385, www.elriorv.com, elriorv@elriorv.com, N 35° 07' 33" W 114° 34' 43"	30 / 23		Over $$$$$$				G	✓	50				S / F			✓		Call for monthly rate. On the Colorado River. Boat launch, exercise room
7	Fender's River Road Resort, 3396 Needles Hwy, Needles, CA 92363, (760) 326-3423, www.fendersriverroadresort.com, fenfab5@aol.com, N 34° 51' 48" W 114° 37' 49"	24 / 24	$300-350	$$$$$				G		30	✓						✓		River and non-river sites - rate listed is for non-river. On the Colorado River. Boat launch. 2 sites have 50 amp power
8	Lake Mead NRA/Katherine Landing, 601 Nevada Way, Boulder Cty, NV 89005, (702) 293-8906 or (928) 754-3245, www.nps.gov/lame, lame_information@nps.gov, N 35° 13' 20" W 114° 33' 28"	170 / 170	$250-300	$$				P											Maximum stay limited to 90 days in any consecutive 12 monthos. Boat launch. Houseboat rentals and store at the resort

Mahave Valley Snowbird Parks
Page 2

#	Park / Address / Contact	Sites Total/Available	Monthly Rate	Longer Term Rates	Overnight Rates	RV Restriction	Site Surface	Patio	Electric	TV	Phone at Sites	Internet	Wi-Fi	Swimming Pool	Spa	Club House	Planned Activities	Comments
9	Lake Mohave Resort and Marina RV Campground, At Katherine Landing, Bullhead Cty, AZ 86430 — (928) 754-3245 or (800) 752-9669, www.sevencrown.com, N 35° 13' 13" W 114° 33' 51"	28 / 28	$400-450	$$$$$$	$$$$$$		G		50									Monthly rate includes electric. No reservations for RVs over 30 ft - limited room for larger RVs. Other amenities - grocery store, houseboat rentals, boat launch
10	Mirage RV Resort, 2196 Merrill Ave, Bullhead Cty, AZ 86442 — (928) 754-1177, N 35° 07' 39" W 114° 34' 22"	146 / 10	$400-450	$$$$$$	Over $$$$$$		G	✓	50	A			H	✓	✓	✓		The park is almost all park models. Monthly rate includes 500 kwh elec. 1st mth rate includes tax. Other amenities - gym, grocery store, restaurant
11	Moabi Regional Park, Park Moabi Rd, Needles, CA 92363 — (760) 326-3831, www.county-parks.com, moabi@ctaz.com, N 34° 43' 38" W 114° 30' 45"	155 / 155	$150-200	$$$$$			G	✓	50									Long term stay is limited to Nov - March. 96 sites are river front, 35 sites have full h/u. Monthly rate includes electric
12	Moon River RV Resort, 1325 Boundary Cone Rd, Mohave Valley, AZ 86440 — (928) 788-6666 or (866) 768-1649, www.moonriverresort.com, info@moonriverresort.com, N 34° 58' 09" W 114° 36' 09"	84 / 80	$300-350	$$$$$$			G	✓	50	A	✓	S / F	✓	✓	✓	✓		Monthly includes 500 kwh electric. 6 mth and annual rates. The swimming pool is not heated. Other amenities - dance floor, library, convenience store, kitchen
13	Needles KOA, 5400 National Old Trails Rd, Needles, CA 92363 — (760) 326-4207 or (800) 562-3407, www.koa.com, carla92992@frontiernet.net, N 34° 52' 07" W 114° 38' 35"	98 / 90	$250-300	$$$$$$			G	✓	30	A	✓	S / F	H	✓		✓		A few 50 amp sites available. Other amenities - convenience store, horseshoes, firewood, riverview picnic area
14	Needles Marina RV Park, 100 Marina Drive, Needles, CA 92363 — (760) 326-2197, www.needlesmarinapark.com, N 34° 50' 48" W 114° 36' 17"	157 / 157	$250-300	$$$$$$			G, GR	✓	50	A	✓	S / F	H	✓	✓	✓		Combined mobile home and RV park with RVs in a separate area. On the Colorado River. Marina and boat launch. $5 per pet per day
15	Rainbo Beach Resort, 3520 Needles Hwy, Needles, CA 92363 — (760) 326-3101, www.rainbobeachresort.com, beach@frontiernet.net, N 34° 52' 05" W 114° 38' 04"	122 / 122	$150-200	$$$$$			G	✓	50 $	A	✓		H	✓		✓		On the Colorado River. Sites on river slightly higher. 83 mobile homes and park models in a separate location. Boat launch
16	Ridgeview RV Resort - Sunrise Resorts, 775 Bullhead Pkwy, Bullhead Cty, AZ 86429 — (928) 754-2595 or (800) 392-8560, www.sunriseresorts.com, ridgerv@ctaz.com, N 35° 10' 17" W 114° 33' 19"	302 / 10	$400-450	$$$$$			G	✓	50	A	✓	C / F	H	✓	✓	✓		Membership park - 10 sites can be reserved monthly by non-members. Monthly rate includes electric. Cable TV activated by office for a fee

Mohave Valley Snowbird Parks
Page 3

#	Park / Address / Contact	Sites Total/Available	Monthly Rate	Longer Term Rates	Overnight Rates	Age Restriction	RV Restriction	Site Surface	Patio	Electric	TV	Phone at Sites	Internet	Wi-Fi	Swimming Pool	Spa	Club House	Planned Activities	Comments
17	River City RV Park, 2225 Merrill Avenue, Bullhead Cty, AZ 86442; (928) 754-2121; www.rivercityrvpark.com; info@rivercityrvpark.com; N 32° 42' 49" W 114° 39' 14"	132 / 132	$300-350	$$$$$				G	✓	50	✓	A	✓	H		✓	✓	✓	Mthly includes 1000 kwh electric. No reservations Nov - April. Many sites have phone which can be actiated by phone company
18	Silver Creek RV Park, 1515 Gold Rush Rd, Bullhead Cty, AZ 86442; (928) 763-2444; silvercreekrv@mohaveaz.com; N 35° 06' 45" W 114° 34' 19"	140 / 140	$300-350	✓	$$$$$			G	✓	50	✓	I / F	S / $	H					Reservations for 6 mths or longer. Instant telephone activated by office (included in rate). Other amenities - convenience store, horseshoes
19	Silverview RV Resort, 1501 Gold Rush Road, Bullhead Cty, AZ 86442; (928) 763-5500; www.silverviewrvresort.com; office@silverviewrvresort.com; N 35° 06' 47" W 114° 34' 19"	180 / 177	$350-400	✓	$$$$$			G	✓	50	✓	A	✓	H	✓	✓	✓	✓	Monthly rate includes electric. Sites are interior, edges, and bluff view - rate listed is the lowest view. Only 3 month reservations accepted in winter
20	Snowbird RV Resort, 1600 Joy Ln, Fort Mohave, AZ 86426; (928) 768-7141; www.sbrvresort.com; sbrv@mohaveaz.com; N 34° 59' 47" W 114° 35' 40"	124 / 124	$200-350	✓	$$$$$			G	✓	50	$	A	✓	S / $	✓	✓	✓	✓	Monthly rate includes 500 kwh of electricity. Cable activated by cable company. Manned entrance gate. 9 hole, par 3 golf course
21	Spirit Mountain Casino & RV Park, 8555 South Hwy 95, Mohave Valley, AZ 86440; (928) 346-1225; www.smrv.com; smrv@mojave.com; N 34° 54' 29" W 114° 35' 56"	82 / 82	$300-350		$$$$$			G		50	✓	I / F	✓				✓		Monthly rate includes electric, cable, and telephone. Telephone activated by park for no charge. Casino, driving range, miniature golf

SNOWBIRD DESTINATIONS

PHOENIX – MESA/TEMPE, APACHE JUNCTION, AND PHOENIX AREA

The Phoenix metropolitan area has by far the largest concentration of Snowbird parks in the Southwest. You'll see that we had to divide them between three maps and sets of tables: Mesa and Tempe, Apache Junction, and all the rest, just called the Phoenix Area.

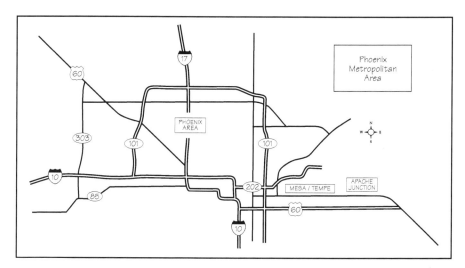

Phoenix is already one of the largest metropolitan areas in the country with a population approaching 4,000,000. It's also the fastest growing of the large metropolitan areas, and many of those people are coming for the same reason you probably are – great winter weather.

Are there any other attractions? More than you can count. This is a big city in an interesting area, almost anything you want to do you can do here or not far away. The only drawback is those furnace-like summers, a good time to be in the north. That's why you have an RV.

For more information take a look at the *Phoenix* section of *Chapter 4*.

Weather

The altitude here is only about 1,200 to 1,400 feet. Most people consider the winter temperatures here to be ideal.

	Jan	Feb	Mar	April	May	June	July	Aug	Sept	Oct	Nov	Dec
High	66	70	75	84	93	103	105	103	99	88	75	66
Low	41	44	49	55	64	72	80	79	72	61	48	42

Living Convenience and Shopping

The Phoenix metro area is extremely large with a network of freeways connecting it all together. Traffic can be bad, of course, but with no commute to worry about Snowbird visitors limit their travel to less busy traffic periods.

Shopping of all kinds is available. There are literally dozens of large malls and every other kind of store is located somewhere in the area. Just to give you an idea – there are nearly 50 Walmarts in the metro area.

Recreation

The Phoenix area is so large that there is anything you might be looking for. One standout attraction is the Cactus League Spring Training baseball games during March. There are games almost every day.

- Over 200 Golf Courses
- Adobe Dam Regional Park
- Arizona Diamondback (baseball), The Phoenix Suns (basketball), Arizona Cardinals (football), and The Phoenix Coyotes (hockey)
- Arizona Historical Society Museum
- Arizona Science Center
- Arizona Wing of the Commemorative Air Force at Falcon Field
- Cactus League Spring Training – Chicago Cubs, Seattle Mariners, San Diego Padres, San Francisco Giants, Milwaukee Brewers, Kansas City Royals, Oakland Athletics, Texas Rangers and the Anaheim Angels
- Cave Creek Regional Park
- Challenger Space Center
- Champlin Fighter Museum at Falcon Field
- Chandler Historical Museum
- Deer Valley Rock Art Center
- Desert Belle Paddleboat Cruises on Saguaro Lake
- Desert Botanical Gardens
- Estrella Mountain Regional Park
- Goldfield Ghost Town
- Hall of Flame Museum
- Harrah's Ak-Chin Casino
- Heard Museum
- Heritage Square
- Lake Pleasant Regional Park
- McDowell Mountain Regional Park
- Mesa Historical Museum
- Mesa Southwest Museum
- Mesa Symphony
- Papago Park
- Phoenix Art Museum
- Phoenix Greyhound Park
- Phoenix Symphony
- Phoenix Zoo and Harmony Farm
- Pueblo Grande
- Salt River Lakes
- Southwest Shakespeare Company

- Superstition Mountain Museum
- Taliesin West and the Frank Lloyd Wright Foundation
- Tovrea Castle
- Usery Mountain Recreation Area
- White Tank Mountain Regional Park

Hospital Facilities

Phoenix offers one of the largest selection of hospitals in the country.
- Arizona Heart Hospital
- Arizona State Hospital
- Desert Samaritan Medical Center
- Good Samaritan Regional Medical Center
- John C Lincoln Hospital North Mountain
- John C Lincoln Hospital – Deer Valley
- Kindred Hospital Arizona Phoenix
- Los Ninos Hospital
- Lutheran Heart Hospital
- Maricopa Medical Center
- Maryvale Hospital Medical Center
- Mayo Clinic Hospital
- Mayo Clinic Scottsdale/Phoenix
- Mesa General Hospital Medical Center
- Mesa Lutheran Hospital
- Paradise Valley Hospital
- Phoenix Baptist Hospital & Medical Center
- Phoenix Children's Hospital
- Phoenix Memorial Hospital
- PHS Indian Medical Center
- Select Specialty Hospital Arizona Inc
- St Joseph's Hospital Medical Center
- St Luke's Behavioral Health Center
- St Luke's Medical Center
- Valley Lutheran Hospital

RV Parks

The largest number of Snowbird parks in Phoenix are in the eastern suburbs of Mesa, Tempe, and Apache Junction. They stretch along a 15 mile east/west strip that is almost wall to wall RV parks. You'll find everything from very small parks offering just hookups to mega parks with over 1,000 sites and every amenity imaginable.

Away from the Mesa and Apache Junction area parks are much less dense. Still, there are plenty of them. One popular area is in the far northwest corner of the city where many RV Snowbirds enjoy being located near friends who own homes in one of the huge retirement subdivisions in that area.

The Phoenix-area Snowbird parks cover the range in terms of quality and amenities. You should be able to find exactly what you want. Parks here commonly offer discounts for stays of three months or longer.

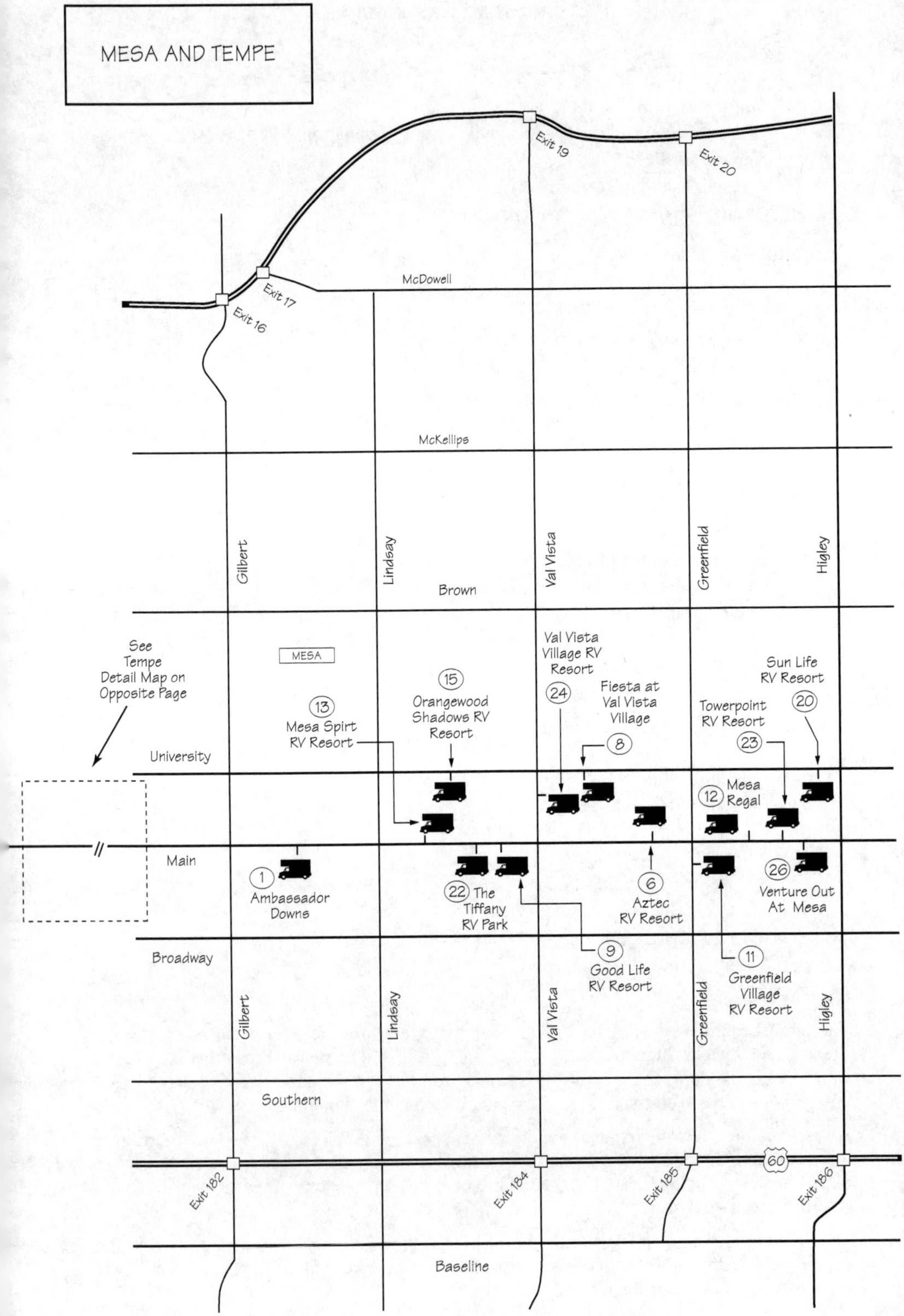

MESA AND TEMPE

Exit 19

Exit 20

Exit 17

Exit 16

McDowell

McKellips

Gilbert

Lindsay

Val Vista

Greenfield

Higley

Brown

MESA

See
Tempe
Detail Map on
Opposite Page

(13)
Mesa Spirt
RV Resort

(15)
Orangewood
Shadows RV
Resort

Val Vista
Village RV
Resort
(24)

(8)

Fiesta at
Val Vista
Village

Sun Life
RV Resort

Towerpoint
RV Resort
(23)

(20)

University

(12) Mesa
Regal

//

Main

(1)
Ambassador
Downs

(22) The
Tiffany
RV Park

(6)

Aztec
RV Resort

(26)
Venture Out
At Mesa

Broadway

(9)
Good Life
RV Resort

(11)
Greenfield
Village
RV Resort

Gilbert

Lindsay

Val Vista

Greenfield

Higley

Southern

Exit 182

Exit 184

Exit 185

60

Exit 186

Baseline

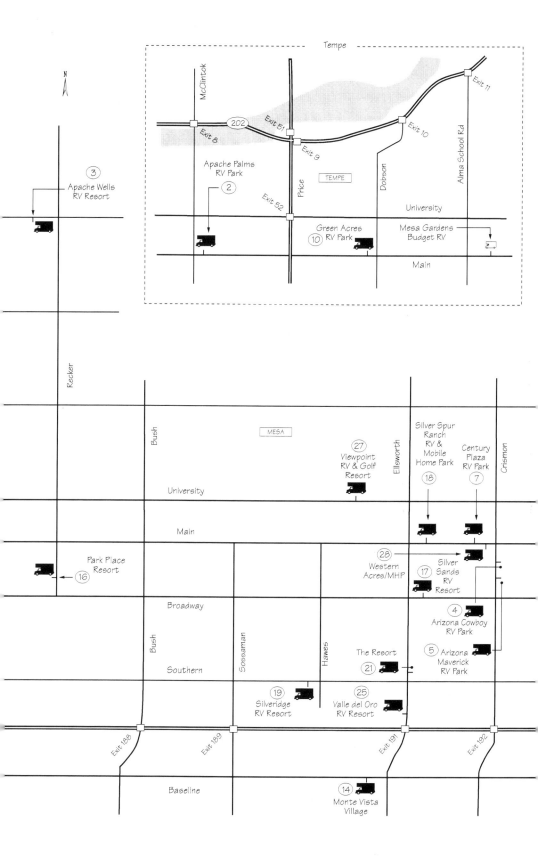

Mesa and Tempe Snowbird Parks
Page 1

Park / Contact	Sites Total/Available	Monthly Rate	Longer Term Rates	Overnight Rates	Age Restriction	RV Restriction	Site Surface	Patio	Electric	TV	Phone at Sites	Internet	Wi-Fi	Swimming Pool	Spa	Club House	Planned Activities	Comments
1. **Ambassador Downs** 2345 E Main St #150 Mesa, AZ 85213 (480) 964-8315 www.sunhome.biz N 33° 24' 55" W 111° 46' 48"	215 / 71	$250-300	$$$$$$	Over	55		G	✓	50	$	A		H			✓	✓	40 ft maximum RVs; Cable activated by cable company; Library, shuffleboard, horseshoes
2. **Apache Palms RV Park** 1836 E Apache Blvd Tempe, AZ 85281 (480) 966-7399 www.apachepalmsrvpark.com apachepalms@apachepalmsrvpark.com N 33° 24' 54" W 111° 54' 24"	80 / 80	$350-400	$$$$$$			✓	G	✓	50	✓	A	S	F	✓	✓			Monthly rate is for economy sites - higher rates apply for quality or super sites; RVs over 10 yr age require approval
3. **Apache Wells RV Resort** 2656 N 56th Street Mesa, AZ 85215 (480) 832-4324 or (888) 940-8989 www.cal-am.com reservations@cal-am.com N 33° 27' 56" W 111° 42' 35"	320 / 128	$450-500	$$$$$$	Over	55	✓	G	✓	50	$	A	C	F	✓	✓	✓	✓	RVs, 5th-wheels, and trailers only; Cable activated by cable company; Wi-Fi available at some sites; Other amenities - tennis, library, shuffleboard, exercise room
4. **Arizona Cowboy RV Park** 139 S Crismon Rd Mesa, AZ 85208 (480) 986-3333 or (800) 705-1181 www.arizonacowboyrvpark.com arizonacowboyrvpark@yahoo.com N 33° 24' 42" W 111° 36' 53"	75 / 75	$350-400	$$$$$$		55	✓	G	✓	50	✓	A	C	F	✓		✓		Gated community; RVs over 10 yr age require approval; Annual seasonal rates only; Other amenities - shuffleboard, horseshoes, putting green, library
5. **Arizona Maverik RV Park** 201 S Crismon Rd Mesa, AZ 85208 (480) 354-3700 or (888) 715-3700 www.campingfriend.com azmaverikrv@aol.com N 33° 24' 42" W 111° 36' 53"	38 / 38	$350-400	$$$$$$	Over		✓	G	✓	50	$	A	S	$	✓	✓	✓		Cable activated by cable company; Fills up early for the winter season; Gated security entrance; RVs must be less than 10 yr age
6. **Aztec RV Resort** 4220 E Main St Mesa, AZ 85205 (480) 832-2700 or (800) 848-6176 aztectrailerpark@quest.com N 33° 24' 57" W 111° 44' 24"	328 / 65	$500-550	$$$$$$		55	✓	G	✓	50	$	A	S	$	✓	✓	✓		RVs, 5th-wheels, and trailers only; Maximum RV site 39 feet; Cable activated by cable company; Other amenities - shuffleboard, horseshoes, game room
7. **Century Plaza RV Park** 9736 E Main St Mesa, AZ 85207 (480) 986-3076 N 33° 24' 57" W 111° 37' 12"	74 / 15	$250-300	$$$$$$	Over	55		G	✓	50	$	A			✓	✓			Jan-March minimum 3 mth reservation; Cable activated by cable company; Other amenities - shuffleboard, kitchen
8. **Fiesta at Val Vista Village** 3811 E University Dr Mesa, AZ 85205 (480) 832-6490 or (888) 940-8989 www.cal-am.com fiestaresort@aol.com N 33° 25' 20" W 111° 44' 53"	336 / 45	$550-600	$$$$$$	Over	55	✓	G	✓	50	$	A	S	F	✓	✓	✓		Deluxe site rates are higher; One of the 4 parks in Val Vista Village - see page 3 for Val Vista; RVs, 5th-wheels, and trailers only; Wi-Fi at sites near clubhouse

	Name / Address / Contact	Sites Total/Available	Monthly Rate	Longer Term Rates	Overnight Rates	Age Restriction	RV Restriction	Site Surface	Patio	Electric	TV	Phone at Sites	Internet	Wi-Fi	Swimming Pool	Spa	Club House	Planned Activities	Comments
⑨	Good Life RV Resort, 3403 E Main St, Mesa, AZ 85213, (480) 832-4990 or (800) 999-4990, www.goodliferv.com, info@goodliferv.com, N 33° 24' 55" W 111° 45' 27"	1,163 / 870	$400-450	✓	Over $$$$$$	55	✓	G	✓	50	$	A	✓	S $	H	✓	✓	✓	Self contained RVs only / Cable activated by cable company / Computer room with 16 computers / Other amenities - tennis, putting green, library, shuffleboard
⑩	Green Acres RV Park, 2052 W Main, Mesa, AZ 85201, (480) 964-5058, www.greenacresrvparkmesa.com, greenacresrvpark@aol.com, N 33° 24' 54" W 111° 52' 31"	64 / 64	$200-350		$$$$$	55	✓	G	✓	50	✓	A	✓	C F	H	✓	✓		Family owned / RVs over 15 yr age require approval / Sites in the back of park have 50 amp power and those in front have 30 amp
⑪	Greenfield Village RV Resort, 111 S Greenfield Rd, Mesa, AZ 85206, (480) 832-6400, www.greenfieldvillage.com, gvrresort@greenfieldvillage.com, N 33° 24' 49" W 111° 44' 09"	493				55	✓	P	✓	50	$	A	✓	S $	H	✓	✓	✓	RV sites are private owned / Number of available sites varies as does rental rate / No overnight sites during season / Only a few sites can take 40 ft RVs
⑫	Mesa Regal RV Resort, 4700 East Main St, Mesa, AZ 85205, (480) 830-2821 or (800) 845-4752, www.cal-am.com, reservations@cal-am.com, N 33° 24' 57" W 111° 43' 45"	2,005 / 950	$550-600	✓	Over $$$$$$	55	✓	G	✓	50	$	A	✓	S F	H	✓	✓	✓	Arizona's 2nd largest resort / Mthly rate does not include electric or sewer / Other amenities - shuffleboard, exercise room, tennis, 2 ballrooms
⑬	Mesa Spirit RV Resort, 3020 E Main St, Mesa, AZ 85213, (480) 832-1770 or (877) 924-6709, www.mesaspirit.com, mesaspirit@azrvpark.com, N 33° 24' 57" W 111° 45' 56"	1,800 / 800	$500-550	✓	Over $$$$$$	55	✓	G	✓	50	$	A	✓	S $	H	✓	✓	✓	RVs over 10 yr age require approval / Self contained RVs only / Cable activated by cable company / Other amenities - exercise room, tennis, computer lab, shuffleboard
⑭	Monte Vista Village, 8865 E Baseline Rd, Mesa, AZ 85209, (480) 833-2223 or (800) 435-7128, www.montevistaresort.com, info@montevistaresort.com, N 33° 22' 44" W 111° 38' 26"	832 / 40	$950-1000	✓	Over $$$$$$	55	✓	G	✓	50	$	A	✓	C F	H	✓	✓	✓	Mthly rates do not include utilities / No pets allowed / Other amenities - tennis, putting green, entertainment, exercise room, shuffleboard, game room,
⑮	Orangewood Shadows RV Resort, 3165 E University Dr, Mesa, AZ 85213, (480) 832-9080 or (800) 826-0909, www.orangewoodshadows.com, businessof orangewoodshadows.com, N 33° 25' 19" W 111° 45'46"	474 / 180	$500-550	✓	Over $$$$$$	55	✓	G	✓	50	$	A	✓	C F	H	✓	✓	✓	Cable activated by cable company / Over 800 citrus trees / Other amenities - shuffleboard, exercise room, ballroom / No pets
⑯	Park Place Resort, 306 S Recker Rd, Mesa, AZ 85206, (480) 830-1080, www.sunhome.biz, pptr@extremezone.com, N 33° 24' 37" W 111° 42' 08"	460 / 240	$350-400	✓	Over $$$$$$	55	✓	G	✓	50	$	A	✓	C F	H	✓	✓	✓	$75 mntly for electric / Cable activated by cable company / Other amenities - shuffleboard, library, mini golf, horseshoes, game room

Mesa and Tempe Snowbird Parks
Page 3

#	Park / Address / Contact	Sites Total / Available	Monthly Rate	Longer Term Rates	Overnight Rates	Age Restriction	RV Restriction	Site Surface	Patio	Electric	TV	Phone at Sites	Internet	Wi-Fi	Swimming Pool	Spa	Club House	Planned Activities	Comments
17	Silver Sands RV Resort 9252 E Broadway Rd Mesa, AZ 85207 (480) 984-6731 www.silversandsrvresort.com ssresort@aol.com N 33° 24' 30" W 111° 37' 52"	178 / 20	$400-450	✓	Over $$$$$		✓	G	✓	50	✓	A	✓	C / F	H	✓	✓	✓	Monthly rate includes electric and other utilities Adult park - no children Self contained RVs only Other amenities - library, mini golf
18	Silver Spur Ranch RV & Mobile Home Park 9310 E Main St #25 Mesa, AZ 85207 (480) 358-1618 www.rv-arizona.com enjoyarizona@rv-arizona.com N 33° 24' 56" W 111° 37' 46"	220 / 60	$300-350	✓	$$$$		✓	G / P	✓	50	$	A	✓	S / $			✓		Family Park Cable activated by cable company
19	Silveridge RV Resort 8265 E Southern Ave Mesa, AZ 85208 (480) 373-7000 or (800) 354-0054 www.silveridge.com officemg@silveridge.com N 33° 23' 35" W 111° 39' 11"	687 / 110	$550-600	✓	Over $$$$$$	55	✓	P	✓	50	✓	I	–		H	✓	✓	✓	Gated community RVs, 5th-wheels and trailers only Instant phones from office for a fee Activity director Wi-Fi free in clubhouse
20	Sun Life RV Resort 5055 E University Dr Mesa, AZ 85205 (480) 981-9500 or (877) 508-8886 www.cal-am.com reservations@cal-am.com N 33° 25' 21" W 111° 43' 18"	761 / 265	$550-600	✓	Over $$$$$$	55	✓	G	✓	50	✓	A	✓	S / F	H	✓	✓	✓	RVs, 5th-wheels, and trailers only Cable activated by cable company RVs over 10 yr age require approval Other amenities - tennis, computer center; shuffleboard, restaurant
21	The Resort 1101 S Ellsworth Rd Mesa, AZ 85208 (480) 986-8404 or (866) 386-1101 www.resortrvpark.com theresort@qwest.net N 33° 23' 42" W 111° 37' 54"	792 / 70	$500-550	✓	Over $$$$$$	55	✓	G	✓	50	✓	A	✓	C / F	H	✓	✓	✓	RVs, 5th-wheels, and trailers only Other amenities - shuffleboard, library, computer room, tennis, horseshoes
22	The Tiffany RV Park 3265 E Main St Mesa, AZ 85213 (480) 830-6337 http://park.dignet.us/ park@dignet.us N 33° 24' 57" W 111° 43' 32"	25 / 25	$300-350	✓	$$$$$		✓	G	✓	50	✓	A	✓	S / F	H				Family owned Adult park - no children Self contained RVs only
23	Towerpoint RV Resort 4860 E Main St Mesa, AZ 85205 (480) 832-4996 or (800) 444-4996 www.towerpointresort.com info@towerpointresort.com N 33° 24' 55" W 111° 45' 35"	1,112 / 240	$550-600	✓	Over $$$$$$	55	✓	G	✓	50	$	A	✓	S / $	H	✓	✓	✓	RVs, 5th-wheels, and trailers only No 1 mth reservations until near the winter season Cable activated by cable company Other amenities - tennis
24	Val Vista Village RV Resort 233 N Val Vista Drive Mesa, AZ 85213 (480) 832-2547 or (888) 940-8989 www.cal-am.com reservations@cal-am.com N 33° 25' 09" W 111° 45' 12"	1,016 / 400	$550-600	✓	Over $$$$$$	55	✓	G	✓	50	$	A	✓	S / F	H	✓	✓	✓	Deluxe site rates are higher One of the 4 parks in Val Vista Village - see page 1 for Fiesta RVs, 5th-wheels and trailers only Wi-Fi at sites near clubhouse

Mesa and Tempe Snowbird Parks
Page 4

#	Park / Contact	Sites Total/Available	Monthly Rate	Longer Term Rates	Overnight Rates	Age Restriction	RV Restriction	Site Surface	Patio	Electric	TV	Phone at Sites	Internet Wi-Fi	Swimming Pool	Spa	Club House	Planned Activities	Comments
25	Valle del Oro RV Resort, 1452 South Ellsworth Rd, Mesa, AZ 85209; (480) 984-1146 or (888) 940-8989; www.cal-am.com; reservations@cal-am.com; N 33° 23' 18" W 111° 37' 59"	1,762 / 562	$600-650	✓	Over $$$$$$	55	✓	G	✓	50	$	A	S / F	H	✓	✓	✓	RVs, 5th-wheels, and trailers only. Utilities not included in mthly rate. Other amenities - tennis, sewing room, driving range, shuffleboard, grocery store, horseshoes
26	Venture Out at Mesa, 5001 E Main St, Mesa, AZ 85205; (480) 832-0200 or (866) 410-0114; www.ventureoutrvresort.com; ventureoutgm@qwest.net; N 33° 24' 55" W 111° 43' 24"	1,749 / 33	$550-600		Over $$$$$$	55	✓	P	✓	30			C / F	H	✓	✓	✓	33 monthly side by side sites with 30 amp power and paved parking. Monthly rate includes electric and tax. No pets allowed
27	Viewpoint RV & Golf Resort, 8700 E University Dr, Mesa, AZ 85207; (480) 373-8700 or (800) 822-4404; www.viewpointrv.com; viewpointrvinfo@mhchomes.com; N 33° 25' 22" W 111° 38' 35"	2,035 / 435	$900-950	✓	Over $$$$$$	55	✓	G	✓	50	✓	I / F	S / $	H	✓	✓	✓	Cable and instant phone included in rate. 18 and 9-hole golf courses. Other amenities - shuffleboard, tennis, restaurant, horseshoes
28	Western Acres/MHP, 9913 Apache Trail, Mesa, AZ 85207; (480) 986-1158; westernacres@yahoo.com; N 33° 24' 54" W 111° 37' 01"	155 / 69	$350-400		$$$$$$			G	✓	50	$	A				✓	✓	Family Park. Limited sites for 40 ft RVs. Cable activated by cable company

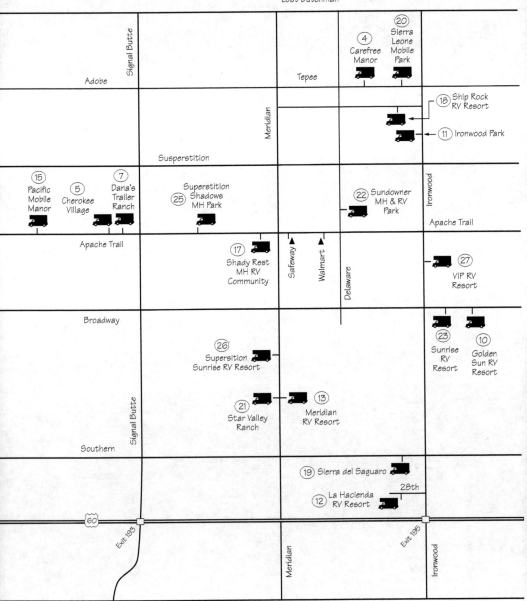

APACHE JUNCTION

RV Parks with this symbol are also described in Chapter 4

N

Lost Dutchman

Adobe | Signal Butte | Tepee

4 Carefree Manor

20 Sierra Leone Mobile Park

Meridian

18 Ship Rock RV Resort

11 Ironwood Park

Susperstition

15 Pacific Mobile Manor

5 Cherokee Village

7 Dana's Trailer Ranch

25 Superstition Shadows MH Park

22 Sundowner MH & RV Park

Ironwood

Apache Trail

Apache Trail

17 Shady Rest MH RV Community

Safeway

Walmart

Delaware

27 VIP RV Resort

Broadway

26 Supersition Sunrise RV Resort

23 Sunrise RV Resort

10 Golden Sun RV Resort

21 Star Valley Ranch

13 Meridian RV Resort

Signal Butte

Southern

19 Sierra del Saguaro

28th

12 La Hacienda RV Resort

60 Exit 195

Meridian

Exit 196

Ironwood

Baseline

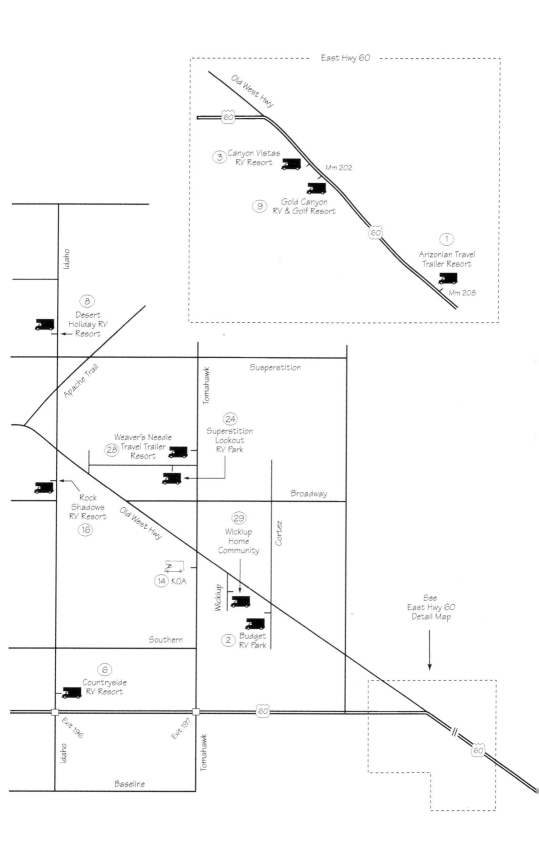

Apache Junction Snowbird Parks
Page 1

#	Park / Address	Contact / Coordinates	Sites Total/Available	Monthly Rate	Longer Term Rates	Overnight Rates	Age Restriction	RV Restriction	Site Surface	Patio	Electric	TV	Phone at Sites	Internet	Wi-Fi	Swimming Pool	Spa	Club House	Planned Activities	Comments
1	Arizonian Travel Trailer Resort, 15975 E Hwy 60, Apache Jct, AZ 85219	(480) 474-2974, www.apolloproperties.com/arizonan.htm, thearizonian@yahoo.com, N 33° 18' 10" W 111° 23' 34"	700 / 650	$400-450	✓	Over $$$$$$	55		G	✓	50	$	I	S $	H	✓	✓	✓	✓	Phone activated at office for a fee; Newer park - only 5 years old; 18-hole desert golf course; Other amenities - tennis, shuffleboard, wood shop, ceramics
2	Budget RV Park, 2024 S Cortez Rd, Apache Jct, AZ 85219	(480) 982-5856, N 33° 23' 49" W 111° 31' 13"	176 / 176	$250-300		Over $$$$$		✓	G	✓	50	$	A	C F		✓		✓		Electric included for extra $100 per month; No reservations accepted; Self contained RVs only
3	Canyon Vistas RV Resort, 6601 East Hwy 60, Gold Canyon, AZ 85218	(480) 288-8844 or (888) 940-8989, www.cal-am.com, reservations@cal-am.com, N 33° 21' 44" W 111° 28' 29"	637 / 480	$550-600	✓	Over $$$$$$	55		G	✓	50	$	I	C F	H	✓	✓	✓	✓	Self contained RVs only; Wi-Fi available at some RV sites; $25 mthly for trash and sewer; Park built in 1999; Amenities - tennis, library, ballroom
4	Carefree Manor, 1615 N Delaware, Apache Jct, AZ 85220	(480) 982-4008, www.carefreerv.net, infoatcarefreerv.net, N 33° 25' 48" W 111° 34' 12"	146 / 110	$350-400		Over $$$$$		✓	G	✓	50	$	A	S $	H	✓	✓			1 dog limit; Discounted yearly rates available; Adult park but not a 55+ park; Cable activated by cable company; Amenities - shuffleboard, pool tables
5	Cherokee Village, 10540 E. Apache Tr, Apache Jct, AZ 85220	(480) 986-4132, www.sunhome.biz, N 33° 24' 56" W 111° 36' 05"	408 / 178	$300-350	✓	Over $$$$$$	55		G	✓	50	$	A		H	✓	✓	✓	✓	Cable activated by cable company; $75 month for electric
6	Countryside RV Resort, 2701 S Idaho Rd, Apache Jct, AZ 85219	(480) 982-1537 or (866) 226-6090, www.mhcrv.com, countrysidervinfo@mhchomes.com, N 33° 23' 20" W 111° 32' 41"	560 / 520	$450-500		Over $$$$$	55		G	✓	50	$	A	S F		✓	✓			Encore park; 40 ft maximum RV size; RVs older than 10 years must be approved; Telephone instant on at the office
7	Dana's Trailer Ranch, 10712 E Apache Tr, Apache Jct, AZ 85220	(480) 986-1471, N 33° 24' 56" W 111° 35' 58"	177 / 57	$250-300		Over $$$$$		✓	G	✓	50	$	A			✓	✓	✓		Cable activated by cable company; Other amenities - shuffleboard, pool hall
8	Desert Holiday RV Resort, 840 N Idaho Rd, Apache Jct, AZ 85219	(480) 982-1876, www.desertholidayrv.com, office@desertholidayrv.com, N 33° 25' 24" W 111° 32' 48"	152 / 65	$400-450	✓	Over $$$$$$	55		G	✓	50	$	A	S F	H	✓	✓	✓	✓	Limited sites for 40 ft RVs; Cable activated by cable company; Other amenities - shuffleboard, horseshoes, exercise room

**Apache Junction Snowbird Parks
Page 2**

#	Park / Address / Contact / Coordinates	Sites Total/Available	Monthly Rate	Longer Term Rates	Age Restriction	RV Restriction	Site Surface	Patio	Electric	TV	Phone at Sites	Internet	Wi-Fi	Swimming Pool	Spa	Club House	Comments
9	Gold Canyon RV & Golf Resort, 7151 E Hwy 60, Gold Canyon, AZ 85218 — (480) 982-5800 or (877) 465-3226, www.robertsresorts.com, goldcanyonrv@aol.com, N 33° 21' 25" W 111° 28' 04"	754 / 219	$650-700	Over $$$$$$	55	✓	G	✓	50	$	A	S $	H	✓	✓	✓	Monthly rate includes electric; RVs, 5th-wheels, or trailers only; Cable activated by cable company; 9-hole golf course; Activity director
10	Golden Sun RV Resort, 999 W Broadway Ave, Apache Jct, AZ 85220 — (480) 983-3760 or (866) 226-6180, www.mhcrv.com, goldensunrvinfo@mhchomes.com, N 33° 24' 26" W 111° 33' 26"	329 / 128	$450-500	Over $$$$$$	55	✓	G	✓	50		A	S $	H	✓	✓	✓	Self contained RVs only; Activity director; Other amenities - shuffleboard, tennis, ballroom, library, exercise room, card room, billiards room
11	Ironwood Park, 1280 N Ironwood Dr, Apache Jct, AZ 95220 — (480) 982-3413, www.azrvresorts.net, osprops@aol.com, N 33° 25' 35" W 111° 33' 50"	106 / 61	$350-400	Over $$$$$$	55	✓	G	✓	50	✓	A	S F	H	✓	✓	✓	Recently remodeled facilities; Other amenities include bocci ball, shuffleboard, horseshoes
12	La Hacienda RV Resort, 1797 W 28th Ave, Apache Jct, AZ 85220 — (480) 982-2809, www.lahaciendarv.com, info@lahaciendarv.com, N 33° 23' 21" W 111° 33' 56"	280 / 60	$550-600	Over $$$$$$	55	✓	G	✓	50		A	S F	H	✓	✓	✓	Gated; RVs, 5th-wheels, or trailers only; 40 ft maximum RV size; Other amenities - computer lab, shuffleboard, putting green
13	Meridian RV Resort, 1901 S. Meridian Rd, Apache Jct, AZ 85220 — (480) 474-8900 or (866) 770-0080, www.meridianrvresort.com, info@meridianrvresort.com, N 32° 41' 58" W 114° 31' 40"	254 / 254	$550-600	Over $$$$$$	55	✓	G	✓	50	$	A	S $	H	✓	✓	✓	RVs, 5th-wheels, or trailers only; RVs over 10 yrs age require approval; Cable activated by cable company; Other amenities - library, exercise room, putting green, shuffleboard
14	Mesa Apache Jct KOA, 1540 South Tomahawk Rd, Apache Jct, AZ 85220 — (480) 982-4015 or (800) 562-3404, www.koakampgrounds.com, N 33° 24' 05" W 111° 31' 44"	150 / 150	$400-450	Over $$$$$$	55	✓	G	✓	50	$	A	S F	H	✓	✓	✓	3 mth minimum reservation; Must pay the 3 mth rental in advance; Other amenities - shuffleboard, store, horseshoes
15	Pacific Mobile Manor, 10220 E Apache Trail, Apache Jct, AZ 85220 — (480) 373-9790, www.azrvresorts.net, osprops@aol.z, N 32° 42' 49" W 114° 39' 14"	123 / 24	$250-300	Over $$$$$$	55	✓	G	✓	50	$	A	C F	H	✓	✓	✓	RV sites together at front of park; Cable activated by cable company; 40 ft maximum RV size; Other amenities - shuffleboard
16	Rock Shadows RV Resort, 600 S Idaho Rd, Apache Jct, AZ 85219 — (480) 982-0450 or (800) 521-7096, www.rockshadows.com, rockrv1@aol.com, N 33° 24' 34" W 111° 32' 48"	683 / 180	$500-550	Over $$$$$$	55	✓	G	✓	50	$	A	S $	H	✓	✓	✓	Cable activated by cable company; RVs, 5th-wheels, and trailers only; Considering Wi-Fi for this winter; Putting green, shuffleboard

No.	Park	Contact	Sites Total/Available	Monthly Rate ($)	Monthly Rate Available	Longer Term Rates	Overnight Rates	Age Restriction	RV Restriction	Site Surface	Patio	Electric	TV	Phone at Sites	Internet	Wi-Fi	Swimming Pool	Spa	Club House	Planned Activities	Comments
17	Shady Rest MH/RV Community, 11435 E Apache Trail, Apache Jct, AZ 85220	(480) 986-6997 N 33° 24' 52" W 111° 34' 59"	120 / 20	$300-350			Over $$$$$	55	✓	G	✓	50	$	A	C/F	H		✓	✓	✓	Seasonal rates are annual only. Limited space for 40 ft RVs. $5 pet fee. Other amenities - shuffleboard, horseshoes, library
18	Ship Rock RV Resort, 1700 W. Shiprock St., Apache Jct, AZ 85220	(480) 505-1300 www.azrvresorts.net osprops@aol.com N 33° 25' 38" W 111° 33' 53"	120 / 120	$500-550	✓		$$$$$	55	✓	G	✓	50	$	I $	S/F	H	✓		✓	✓	4 mth reservation required for Jan-March. RVs, 5th-wheels, and trailers only. RVs over 10 yrs age require approval. Cable activated by cable company
19	Sierra del Saguaro, 1855 West Southern Ave, Apache Jct, AZ 85220	(480) 982-2444 www.sierradelsaguaro.com sierradelsaguaro@aol.com N 33° 23' 35" W 111° 33' 57"	225 / 65	$400-450			$$$$$	55	✓	G	✓	50	$	A		H	✓		✓	✓	Family owned. No pets. Self contained RVs only. Other amenities - shuffleboard, horseshoes, game room
20	Sierra Leone Mobile Park, 1804 W Tepee St, Apache Jct, AZ 85220	(480) 982-5962 www.azrvresorts.net osprops@aol.com N 33° 25' 48" W 111° 33' 56"	94 / 23	$300-350			Over $$$$$	55	✓	G	✓	50	$	A			✓		✓		Limited space for 40 ft RVs. Seasonal rates are annual only. Other amenities - shuffleboard
21	Star Valley Ranch, 950 S Meridian Rd, Apache Jct, AZ 85220	(480) 986-0699 www.starvalleyranchaz.com manager@starvalleyranchaz.com N 33° 23' 52" W 111° 34' 51"	110 / 55	$500-550	✓		Over $$$$$	55	✓	G	✓	50	$	A	C/F	H	✓		✓		Monthly rate includes electric. Cable activated by cable company. Other amenities - tennis, putting green, shuffleboard, horseshoes, exercise room, billiard room, library
22	Sundowner MH & RV Park, 105 N Delaware Dr, Apache Jct, AZ 85220	(480) 982-2521 www.sunhome.biz sundownerpark@aol.com N 33° 24' 59" W 111° 34' 16"	246 / 80	$250-300	✓		Over $$$$$	55	✓	G	✓	50	$	A		H	✓		✓		Flat rate of $60 charged for electric. The Sundowner is comprised of three parks with a total of 246 sites. Other amenities - shuffleboard, horseshoes
23	Sunrise RV Resort, 1403 W Broadway Ave, Apache Jct, AZ 85220	(480) 983-2500 or (866) 787-2754 www.robertsresorts.com sunrisev@aol.com N 33° 24' 26" W 111° 33' 37"	501 / 250	$500-550	✓		Over $$$$$	55	✓	G	✓	50	$	A		H	✓		✓	✓	Monthly rate includes electric. RVs over 10 yrs age require approval. 24 ft minimum RV size. Cable activated by cable company. Gated community
24	Superstition Lookout RV Park, 1371 E Fourth Ave, Apache Jct, AZ 85219	(480) 982-2008 www.azrvresorts.net osprops@aol.com N 33° 24' 39" W 111° 31' 54"	188 / 120	$450-500	✓		Over $$$$$	55	✓	G	✓	50	$	A	S/F	H	✓		✓	✓	RV age restricted without approval. Cable activated by cable company. Limited sites for 40 ft RVs. Other amenities - shuffleboard, horseshoes, game room

	Sites Total/Available	Monthly Rate	Longer Term Rates	Overnight Rates	Age Restriction	RV Restriction	Site Surface	Patio	Electric	TV	Phone at Sites	Internet	Wi-Fi	Swimming Pool	Spa	Club House	Planned Activities	Comments
25 Superstition Shadows MHI Park 11100 E Apache Trail Apache Jct, AZ 85220 (480) 984-9633 N 33° 24' 57" W 111° 35' 26"	104 / 35	$350-400	Over $$$$$$		55		G	✓	30	$	A	✓	S $	H	✓	✓		40 ft spaces restricted to mobile home section Phone at some sites No pets
26 Superstition Sunrise RV Resort 702 S Meridian Apache Jct, AZ 85220 (480) 986-4524 or (800) 624-7027 www.superstitionsunrise.com info@superstitionsunrise.com N 33° 24' 07" W 111° 34' 52"	1,119 / 211	$500-550	Over $$$$$$		55		G	✓	50	$	A	✓	S $	H	✓	✓		Cable offered by park for a fee Other amenities - shuffleboard, exercise room, driving range, putting green, ballroom, computer lab
27 VIP RV Resort 401 S Ironwood Dr Apache Jct, AZ 85220 (480) 983-0847 N 33° 24' 43" W 111° 33' 44"	128 / 40	$250-300	$$$$$		55	✓	G	✓	50	$	A	✓	S F		✓	✓		Cable activated by cable company Clubhouse offers free Wi-Fi - reaches some sites Self contained RVs only Other amenities - shuffleboard
28 Weaver's Needle Travel Trailer Resort 250 S Tomahawk Rd Apache Jct, AZ 85219 (480) 982-3683 www.weaversneedle.com weaversneedle@yahoo.com N 33° 24' 46" W 111° 31' 45"	400 / 210	$450-500	Over $$$$$$			✓	G	✓	50	$	A	✓	S F	H	✓	✓		Cable activated by cable company Other amenities - shuffleboard, exercise room, wood shop, art room, library, computer room
29 Wickiup Home Community 2015 Old West Hwy Apache Jct, AZ 85219 (480) 982-6604 www.sunhome.biz wickiup@sunhome.biz N 33° 23' 55" W 111° 31' 25"	111 / 69	$250-300	$$$$$$		55	✓	G	✓	50		A					✓		Other amenities - shuffleboard, pool tables

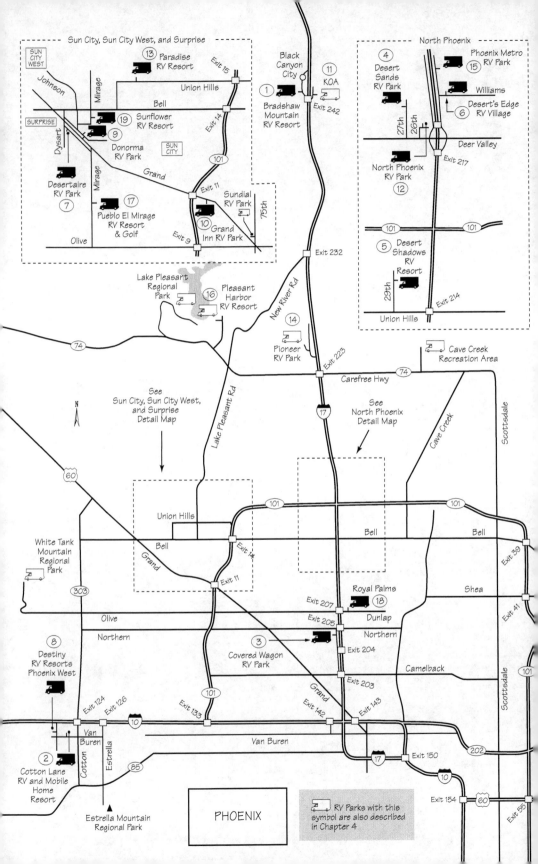

Sun City, Sun City West, and Surprise

- SUN CITY WEST
- SURPRISE
- SUN CITY
- Johnson
- Mirage
- Dysart
- Mirage
- Bell
- Grand
- Olive
- Union Hills
- 75th
- Exit 15
- Exit 14
- Exit 11
- Exit 9
- 101

- (13) Paradise RV Resort
- (19) Sunflower RV Resort
- (9) Donorma RV Park
- (7) Desertaire RV Park
- (17) Pueblo El Mirage RV Resort & Golf
- Sundial RV Park
- (10) Grand Inn RV Park

North Phoenix

- (4) Desert Sands RV Park
- (15) Phoenix Metro RV Park
- Williams
- (6) Desert's Edge RV Village
- 27th
- 26th
- Deer Valley
- Exit 217
- (12) North Phoenix RV Park
- 101
- 101
- (5) Desert Shadows RV Resort
- 29th
- Union Hills
- Exit 214

- Black Canyon City
- (1) Bradshaw Mountain RV Resort
- (11) KOA
- Exit 242
- Exit 232

- Lake Pleasant Regional Park
- (16) Pleasant Harbor RV Resort
- New River Rd
- (14) Pioneer RV Park
- Exit 223
- 74
- Carefree Hwy
- 74
- Cave Creek Recreation Area

- See Sun City, Sun City West, and Surprise Detail Map
- N
- See North Phoenix Detail Map

- 60
- White Tank Mountain Regional Park
- 303
- Union Hills
- Bell
- Grand
- Olive
- Northern
- Exit 14
- Exit 11
- 101
- Bell
- Bell
- Exit 39
- Shea
- Exit 41
- Cave Creek
- Scottsdale

- Royal Palms
- (18)
- Exit 207
- Exit 205
- Dunlap
- (8) Destiny RV Resorts Phoenix West
- (3) Covered Wagon RV Park
- Exit 204
- Northern
- Camelback
- Exit 203
- Scottsdale
- 101
- Exit 124
- Exit 126
- Exit 133
- 101
- Exit 142
- Grand
- Exit 143
- 10
- Van Buren
- Cotton
- Estrella
- Van Buren
- 10
- Exit 150
- 202
- 17
- (2) Cotton Lane RV and Mobile Home Resort
- 85
- Estrella Mountain Regional Park
- Exit 154
- 60
- Exit 55

PHOENIX

RV Parks with this symbol are also described in Chapter 4

Phoenix Snowbird Parks
Page 1

#	Park	Contact	Sites Total/Available	Monthly Rate	Longer Term Rates	Overnight Rates	Age Restriction	RV Restriction	Site Surface	Patio	Electric	TV	Phone at Sites	Internet	Wi-Fi	Swimming Pool	Spa	Club House	Planned Activities	Comments
1	Bradshaw Mountain RV Resort, 33900 S Old Blk Canyon Hwy, Blk Canyon Cty, AZ 85324	(623) 374-9800 or (877) 580-9800, www.bradshawmtnrvresort.com, reservations@bradshawmtnrvresort.com, N 34° 04' 18" W 112° 09' 09"	115 / 90	$550-600	Over $$$$$		55		G	✓	50	✓	A	S F	H	✓	✓	✓		$95 mthly utility fee not included / 25 miles north of Bell Road in Phoenix / Other amenities - pavilion, horseshoes, hiking trails, wooded
2	Cotton Lane RV & Mobile Home Resort, 17506 W Van Buren, Goodyear, AZ 85338	(623) 853-4000 or (888) 907-7223, www.arizonarvresorts.com, cottonlane@arizonarvresorts.com, N 33° 27' 03" W 112° 26' 07"	400 / 300	$400-450		$$$$$	55		G	✓	50	✓	– $	S $	H	✓	✓	✓	✓	Fairly new facilities - 9 years old / Discounts only for annual stay / Instant telephone access for a fee / Practice executive golf course with some sites on the course
3	Covered Wagon RV Park, 6540 N Black Canyon Hwy #53, Phoenix, AZ 85017	(602) 242-2500, wagonmasteraz@aol.com, N 33° 31' 58" W 112° 06' 46"	47 / 44	$600-650	Over $$$$$				G	✓	50		✓				✓			Family Park / Lower monthly rate for early reservations / Cable activated by cable company
4	Desert Sands RV Park, 22036 N 27th Ave, Phoenix, AZ 85027	(623) 869-8186, www.campingfriend.com, desertsandrvpark@yahoo.com, N 33° 41' 13" W 112° 07' 03"	70 / 70	$400-450	Over $$$$$			✓	G	✓	50	$	A	S $	H	✓	✓	✓		Deluxe and Premium sites offered / Cable activated by cable company / Swimming pool is not heated / Winter reservations only accepted about 1 week in advance
5	Desert Shadows RV Resort, 19203 N 29th Ave, Phoenix, AZ 85207	(623) 869-8178 or (800) 595-7290, www.arizonarvresorts.com, desertshadows@arizonarvresorts.com, N 33° 39' 36" W 112° 07' 17"	638 / 150	$550-600	Over $$$$$		42		G	✓	50	$	A	S $	✓	✓	✓	✓	✓	Discounts only for annual stay / Self contained RVs only - bathrooms locked after 10 pm / Cable activated by cable company / Activities director
6	Desert's Edge RV Village, 22623 N Black Canyon Hwy, Phoenix, AZ 85027	(623) 587-0940 or (888) 633-7677, www.desertsedgerv.com, info@desertsedgerv.com, N 33° 41' 28" W 112° 06' 38"	211 / 208	$550-600	Over $$$$$				G	✓	50	✓	A	S $	H	✓	✓	✓		Monthly rate includes elec and tax / Sites are standard, premium, desert, & double economy, basic, clasic, premium, premium delux - rate listed is the lowest
7	Desertaire RV Park, 12959 W Grand Ave., Surprise, AZ 85374	(623) 972-4518, N 33° 37' 46" W 112° 20' 22"	29 / 29	$400-450	Over $$$$$				G	✓	50		A		H	✓	✓	✓		400 kwh of electricity is included in the monthly rate / Adult park / Installation of satelite Wi-Fi in process in 2008
8	Destiny RV Resorts - Phoenix West, 416 N Citrus Rd, Goodyear, AZ 85338	(623) 853-0537 or (888) 667-2454, www.destinyrv.com, phoenixquestions@destinyrv.com, N 33° 27' 05" W 112° 26' 41"	284 / 264	$350-400	Over $$$$$				G	✓	50	✓	A	S F	H	✓	✓	✓	✓	Sites are standard, deluxe, and premium - rate listed is lowest / Some sites have phone connections available / Store, shuffleboard, exercise room

Phoenix Snowbird Parks
Page 2

#	Park / Address / Contact	Sites Total / Available	Monthly Rate Available	Longer Term Rates	Overnight Rates	Age Restriction	RV Restriction	Site Surface	Patio	Electric	TV	Phone at Sites	Internet	Wi-Fi	Swimming Pool	Spa	Club House	Planned Activities	Comments
9	Donorma RV Park, 15637 Norma Ln, Surprise, AZ 85374 — (623) 583-8195, tassingbm@aol.com, N 33° 37' 33" W 112° 19' 55"	66 / 48	$400-450	$$$$$ Over	55			G	✓	50		✓	C	F					Other amenities - horseshoes
10	Grand Inn RV Park, 8955 NW Grand Ave, Peoria, AZ 85345 — (623) 979-7200, N 33° 35' 24" W 112° 15' 03"	75 / 75	$650-700	$$$$$$				P	✓	50			S	F					Monthly rate includes electric and telephone service; No reservations accepted; 40 ft RV maximum
11	KOA Black Canyon City, Exit 242 off I-17, Blk Canyon Cty, AZ 85324 — (623) 374-5318 or (800) 562-5314 R, www.koakampgrounds.com, koabccaz@yahoo.com, N 34° 03' 38" W 112° 08' 31"	46 / 46	$400-450	$$$$$ Over				G	✓	50	✓	I		F	H	✓	✓	✓	Other amenities - game room, horseshoes, hiking trails, store
12	North Phoenix RV Park, 2550 W Louise Dr, Phoenix, AZ 85027 — (623) 581-3969, www.campingfriend.com, npcrvpark@yahoo.com, N 33° 41' 08" W 112° 06' 52"	195 / 195	$250-300	$$$$$	55			G	✓	50	✓	A	S	F	H	✓	✓	✓	Adult and family sections; Other amenities - store, pool tables, night security; $1 per day for pets - $10 max per mth
13	Paradise RV Resort, 10950 W Union Hill Dr, Sun City, AZ 85373 — (800) 847-2280 or (877) 362-6736 R, www.mhcrv.com, paradise_rv_reservations@mhcrv.com, N 33° 39' 13" W 112° 17' 43"	950 / 100	$750-800 ✓	$$$$$$ Over			✓	G	✓	50	$	A			H	✓	✓	✓	RVs, 5th-wheels, and trailers only; Other amenities - shuffleboard, exercise room, tennis, computer center, ballroom, putting green
14	Pioneer RV Park, 36408 N Blk Canyon Hwy, Phoenix, AZ 85086 — (623) 465-7465 or (800) 658-5895, www.arizonarvresorts.com, pioneer@arizonarvresorts.com, N 33° 49' 21" W 112° 08'53"	585 / 285	$450-500	$$$$$ Over	42	✓	✓	G	✓	50	✓	A	S	$	H	✓	✓	✓	42 yr age restriction for monthly tenants; Self contained RVs only; Cable activated by phone company; Activities director
15	Phoenix Metro RV Park, 22701 N Blk Canyon Hwy, Phoenix, AZ 85027 — (623) 582-0390 or (877) 582-0390, www.phoenixmetrorvpark.com, info@phoenix.metrorvpark.com, N 33° 41' 35" W 112° 06' 46"	310 / 310	$400-450	$$$$$	55		✓	G	✓	50	$	A			H	✓	✓	✓	1 small pet limit; Mostly extended stay sites in the winter; RVs, 5th-wheels, and trailers only
16	Pleasant Harbor RV Resort, 8708 W Harbor Blvd, Peoria, AZ 85383 — (800) 475-3272, www.pleasantharbor.com, mwd@pleasantharbor.com, N 33° 50' 58" W 112° 15' 04"	294 / 294	$550-600 ✓	$$$$$ Over			✓	G	✓	50	✓	A	C	F	H	✓	✓	✓	Sites priced by size and location - rate listed is lowest; Self contained RVs only; $1 per day fee per pet; Marina, store

Phoenix Snowbird Parks
Page 3

#	Park / Address / Contact	Sites Total/Available	Monthly Rate	Longer Term Rates	Overnight Rates	Age Restriction	RV Restriction	Site Surface	Patio	Electric	TV	Phone at Sites	Internet	Wi-Fi	Swimming Pool	Spa	Club House	Planned Activities	Comments
17	Pueblo El Mirage RV Resort & Golf 11201 N El Mirage Rd El Mirage, AZ 85335 (866) 787-2754 or (800) 445-4115 www.robertsresorts.com info@robertsresorts.com N 33° 35' 18" W 112° 19' 26"	1,075 / 475	$700-750	✓	Over $$$$$$	55	✓	G	✓	50	$	I $	✓	S $	H	✓	✓	✓	Monthly rate includes electric and tax. RVs, 5th-wheels, and trailers only. Phone and cable activated by park for a fee
18	Royal Palm 2050 West Dunlap Phoenix, AZ 85021 (602) 943-5833 www.continentalcommunities.com royalpalm@continentalcommunities.com N 33° 34' 03" W 112° 06' 13"	448 / 124	$400-450	✓	Over $$$$$$	55	✓	G		50	$	A	✓	S $	H	✓	✓	✓	Gated Community. Cable activated by cable company. Other amenities - shuffleboard, library, putting green
19	Sunflower RV Resort 16501 N El Mirage Rd Surprise, AZ 85374 (623) 583-0100 or (888) 940-8989 www.cal-am.com reservations@cal-am.com N 33° 38' 03" W 112° 19' 25"	1,155 / 250	$600-650	✓	Over $$$$$$	55	✓	G	✓	50	$	A	✓	C F	H	✓	✓	✓	21 ft minimum RV size. Cable activated by cable company. Wi-Fi available at some sites. Other amenities - shuffleboard, exercise room, ballroom

QUARTZSITE AREA

Quartzsite and its January rockhound and RV shows are well known, but there's more to the area than just the shows. Many folks spend the winters near Quartzsite and the January show season is just icing on the cake.

In addition to Quartzsite and its many RV parks there are other areas nearby that we like to think of as part of the Quartzsite scene. Of course there are the BLM boondocking areas outside town, they're described in *Chapter 4* under *Quartzsite Area*. Some nearby communities with lots of Snowbird RV parks include Blythe (20 miles west), Bouse (25 miles northeast), Brenda (15 miles east) and Salome (35 miles east).

For more information take a look at the *Quartzsite Area* section of *Chapter 4*.

Weather

The altitude of the Quartzsite area is about 900 feet. The little bit of altitude makes Quartzsite slightly cooler than Yuma.

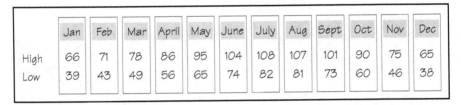

	Jan	Feb	Mar	April	May	June	July	Aug	Sept	Oct	Nov	Dec
High	66	71	78	86	95	104	108	107	101	90	75	65
Low	39	43	49	56	65	74	82	81	73	60	46	38

Living Convenience and Shopping

Most of the year there is very little traffic on the roads in Quartzsite, but during January and early February the main thoroughfares are virtually gridlocked for several hours each day. Experienced Quartzsite visitors plan ahead and find a place to camp that is near the places they'll want to visit. Many boondockers bring along quads, scooters, or other off-road vehicles so they can easily travel pretty much anywhere they want without worrying about the traffic.

There's lots of shopping in Quartzsite, but most of it is in the booths and tents of the shows and swap-meets. For groceries there are several small grocery stores on Main St. If you're willing to travel a bit, Blythe (20 miles west) has an Albertson's and Parker (35 miles north) has a Safeway. Farther afield, Yuma is 80 miles to the south and offers pretty much any store you're looking for.

Recreation

Recreation in Quartzsite means the RV and Rock shows. See the *Quartzsite Area* section in Chapter 4 for details.
- One 9-Hole and One 18-hole Golf Course
- Celia's Rainbow Botanical Gardens
- Gem and mineral and RV shows in January and February
- Hi Jolly Monument
- Jeep Trails
- Kofa National Wildlife Refuge
- Sonoran Desert
- Tyson Wells Museum

THE JANUARY ROCKHOUND AND RV SHOWS DRAW THOUSANDS OF RVERS

- World's largest Saguaro cactus with 47 arms

Hospital Facilities

Quartzsite has 3 nearby medical centers and year round ambulance and medivac heliport

- Palo Verde Hospital – Blythe, 20 miles west
- La Paz Regional Hospital – Parker, 35 miles north
- Parker PHS Indian Hospital – Parker, 35 miles north

RV Parks

The RV park market in Quartzsite is dominated by the big events during January and early February. While lots of people boondock on BLM lands others prefer hookups, and most spaces in town are taken during the show season. For that reason you won't find three-month discounts in Quartzsite. However, because Quartzsite is so quiet in the summer you will find many parks in town that charge about the same thing for a year that you would expect to pay for three or four months somewhere else.

Amenities in most of the Quartzsite parks are pretty basic. Parking on gravel with just hookups and a restroom is pretty standard. That's one of the reasons that rates here are so low.

Farther out, in Blythe, Brenda, and Salome there are nice larger parks with good facilities and more amenities. Don't forget about these if you're thinking about Quartzsite. Many people boondock for several months in this area, see the *Quartzsite Area* section of *Chapter 4* for information about the BLM lands near Quartzsite. Finally, Parker and its parks are just 35 miles to the north, see *Lake Havasu and the Parker Strip* in Chapter 4.

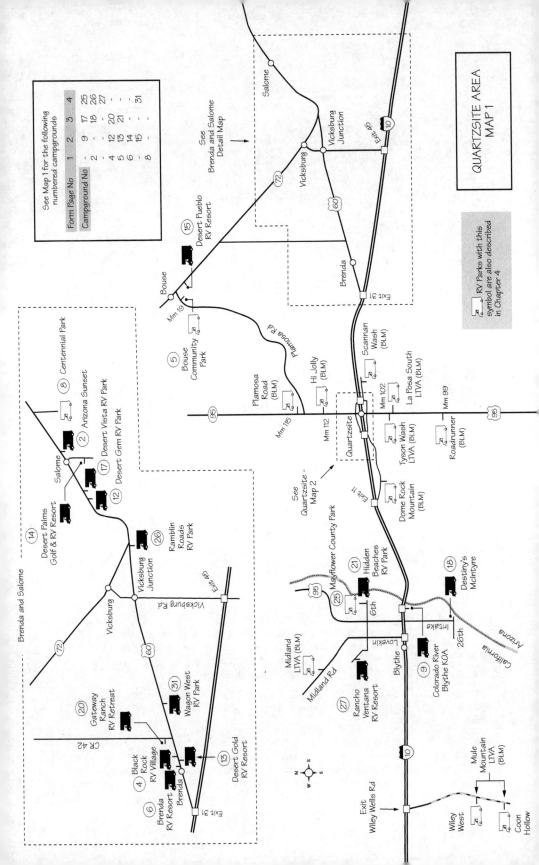

QUARTZSITE AREA
MAP 1

RV Parks with this symbol are also described in Chapter 4

See Map 1 for the following numbered campgrounds

Form Page No	1	2	3	4
Campground No	-	9	17	25
	2	-	18	26
	-	-	20	27
	4	12	21	-
	5	13	-	-
	6	14	15	31
	-	8	-	-

See Brenda and Salome Detail Map →

Salome

Vicksburg Junction

Vicksburg

Exit 45

72

60

Brenda

Exit 31

Bouse

⑮ Desert Pueblo RV Resort

Mm 19

⑤ Bouse Community Park

Palmosa Rd

Plamosa Road (BLM)
Mm 115

Hi Jolly (BLM)
Mm 112

Scannan Wash (BLM)

La Posa South LTVA (BLM)
Mm 102

Mm 99

95

95

Quartzsite

See Quartzsite - Map 2 →

Tyson Wash LTVA (BLM)

Roadrunner (BLM)

Dome Rock Mountain (BLM)

Exit 11

Mayflower County Park

⑳ Gateway Ranch RV Retreat

CR 42

④ Black Rock RV Village

⑥ Brenda RV Resort

Exit 31

⑬ Desert Gold RV Resort

㉛ Wagon West RV Park

60

Vicksburg

Vicksburg Junction

Vicksburg Rd

Exit 45

㉖ Ramblin Roads RV Park

⑫

⑰ Desert Gem RV Park

② Desert Vista RV Park

⑧ Centennial Park

Arizona Sunset

Salome

⑭ Desert Palms Golf & RV Resort

72

Brenda and Salome

㉕

⑦ Hidden Beaches RV Park

6th

95

⑱ Destiny's McIntyre

26th

California
Arizona

Intake

Blythe

⑨ Colorado River Blythe KOA

Lovekin

Midland LTVA (BLM)

Midland Rd

㉗ Rancho Ventana RV Resort

Exit Wiley Wells Rd

10

Wiley West

Mule Mountain LTVA (BLM)

Coon Hollow

N
W E
S

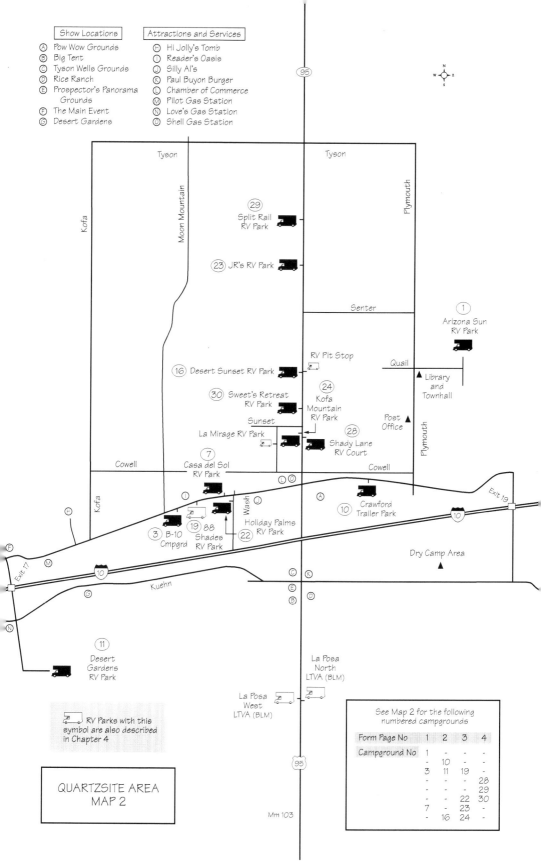

Show Locations
- (A) Pow Wow Grounds
- (B) Big Tent
- (C) Tyson Wells Grounds
- (D) Rice Ranch
- (E) Prospector's Panorama Grounds
- (F) The Main Event
- (G) Desert Gardens

Attractions and Services
- (H) Hi Jolly's Tomb
- (I) Reader's Oasis
- (J) Silly Al's
- (K) Paul Buyon Burger
- (L) Chamber of Commerce
- (M) Pilot Gas Station
- (N) Love's Gas Station
- (O) Shell Gas Station

Tyson   Tyson

Kofa   Moon Mountain   Plymouth

(29) Split Rail RV Park

(23) JR's RV Park

Senter

(1) Arizona Sun RV Park

RV Pit Stop   Quail

(16) Desert Sunset RV Park   ▲ Library and Townhall

(30) Sweet's Retreat RV Park

(24) Kofa Mountain RV Park

Sunset   Post Office ▲

La Mirage RV Park   (28) Shady Lane RV Court   Plymouth

Cowell   (7) Casa del Sol RV Park   Cowell

Kofa   (O)(L)(O)

(I)   (A)

(J)   (10) Crawford Trailer Park   Exit 19

(H)   Wash   I-10

(3) B-10 Cmpgrd   (19) 88 Shades RV Park   Holiday Palms RV Park   (10)

(F) Exit 17   (22)

(M)   Dry Camp Area

I-10   (C)   (K)   ▲

(G)   Kuehn   (E)

(N)   (B)   (D)

(11) Desert Gardens RV Park

La Posa North LTVA (BLM)

La Posa West LTVA (BLM)

[🚐] RV Parks with this symbol are also described in Chapter 4

95

QUARTZSITE AREA MAP 2

Mm 103

See Map 2 for the following numbered campgrounds

Form Page No	1	2	3	4
Campground No	1	-	-	-
	-	10	-	-
	3	11	19	-
	-	-	-	28
	-	-	-	29
	-	-	22	30
	7	-	23	-
	-	16	24	-

Park	Sites Total/Available	Monthly Rate	Monthly Rate Available	Longer Term Rates	Overnight Rates	Age Restriction	RV Restriction	Site Surface	Patio	Electric	TV	Phone at Sites	Internet	Wi-Fi	Swimming Pool	Spa	Club House	Planned Activities	Comments
① Arizona Sun RV Park 715 E Quail Trail P.O. Box 2783 Quartzsite, AZ 85346 (928) 927-5057 azsunrv@localnet.com N 33° 40' 34" W 114° 12' 14"	133 / 133	$200-250	✓	$$$$$		55		G		50		A						✓	Monthly fee is for January - Feb monthly - remainder of the year is lower
② Arizona Sunset 67330 E Hwy 60 Salome, AZ 85348 (928) 859-3995 N 33° 47' 10" W 113° 36' 09"	31 / 31	$150-200		$$$$				G	✓	50		A	S/F				✓	✓	
③ B10 Campground Overnighters P.O. Box 789 Quartzsite, AZ 85346 (928) 927-4393 b10campground@yahoo.com N 33° 39' 53" W 114° 13' 38"	157 / 157			$$$$$				G		50	✓	A	✓						Open Oct 1 - March 31 Call for monthly rate
④ Black Rock RV Village 46751 E Hwy 60 Salome, AZ 85348 (928) 927-4206 www.blackrockrvvillage.com manager@blackrockrv.com N 33° 40' 48" W 113° 56' 44"	408 / 169	$350-400		Over $$$$$$			✓	G		50	✓	A	S/$				✓		No monthly rates - weekly rates $195 - 215 RVs over 10 yr age require approval Other amenities - shuffleboard, pitch & putt golf, restaurant
⑤ Bouse Community Park La Paz County Parks 73510 Riverside Drive Parker, AZ 85344 (928) 667-2069 www.co.la.paz.az park@co.la.paz.az.us N 33° 55' 41" W 114° 01' 13"	25 / 25	$50-100		$$		55	✓	G		50	✓	A							No reservations 11 sites have electricity and water and the others are dry Other amenities - putting green, ramada
⑥ Brenda RV Resort 46251 E Hwy 60 Salome, AZ 85348 (928) 927-5249 or (877) 927-5249 www.grapevine7.com/brenda.htm g7resorts@hotmail.com N 33° 40' 42" W 113° 57' 12"	204 / 100	$250-300		$$$$$			✓	G		50	✓	A	S/F			✓	✓		Self contained RVs only Wi-Fi free to daily, available to mthly No pet area Other amenities - exercise room, shuffleboard, kitchen
⑦ Casa del Sol RV Park P.O. Box 110 Quartzsite, AZ 85346 (928) 927-6319 N 33° 39' 58" W 114° 13' 15"	100 / 75					55		G		50		A				✓	✓		Open Oct 1 - May 1 Call for monthly and daily rates Separate pet area
⑧ Centennial Park La Paz County Parks 73550 Riverside Drive Parker, AZ 85344 (928) 667-2069 www.co.la.paz.az park@co.la.paz.az.us N 33° 47' 20" W 113° 33' 36"	26 / 26	$50-100		$$				G				A							No electric No reservations Par 3, 18-hole golf course Other amenities - shaded cabana, tennis court, hiking trail

#	Park	Sites Total/Available	Monthly Rate	Longer Term Rates	Overnight Rates	Age Restriction	RV Restriction	Site Surface	Patio	Electric	TV	Phone at Sites	Internet	Wi-Fi	Swimming Pool	Spa	Club House	Planned Activities	Comments
9	Colorado River Blythe KOA, 14100 Riviera Drive, Blythe, CA 92225 / (760) 922-5350 or (800) 562-3948 / www.koa.com / blythekoa@yahoo.com / N 33° 36' 13" W 114° 32' 08"	300 / 293	$400-450	Over $$$$$$	$$$$$$			GR	✓	50	✓	A	✓	S $	H	✓	✓		On the Colorado River / Some sites have patios / Boat launch
10	Crawford Trailer Park, 315 E Main St, P.O. Box 2420, Quartzsite, AZ 85346 / (928) 927-6594 / real@tds.net / N 33° 40' 00" W 114° 12' 42"	63 / 63	$250-300		$$$$$			G		50								Open Sept 1 - March 31 / Jan rate is $450-500 range / Other amenities - shuffleboard, horseshoes
11	Desert Gardens RV Park, P.O. Box 619, Quartzsite, AZ 85346 / (928) 927-6361 or (866) 472-8793 / www.desertgardensrvpark.com / desertgardensrv.net / N 33° 39' 16" W 114° 14' 16"	270 / 180	$150-200	$$$$$		55		G		50	$	A	✓	S $		✓	✓	✓	No reservations / Same rate all year / Cable activated by cable company / Considering adding Wi-Fi / Shuffleboard, horseshoes
12	Desert Gem RV Park, 6450B E Hwy 60, Salome, AZ 85348 / (928) 859-3373 or (888) 285-0270 / www.desertgemrvpark.com / desertgem@tds.net / N 33° 45' 35" W 114° 39' 13"	56 / 56	$150-200	$$$$$		55		G		30		A				✓	✓	✓	Annual rates are offered / Other amenities - cook house, patio dining
13	Desert Gold RV Resort, 46628 Hwy 60, Salome, AZ 85348 / (928) 927-7800 or (800) 927-2101 / www.grapevine7.com / g7resorts@hotmail.com / N 33° 40' 42" W 113° 56' 49"	549 / 493	$450-500	$$$$$$		55		G	✓	50	✓	A	✓	S $	H	✓	✓	✓	Annual rates are offered / Wi-Fi free for daily guests / Other amenities - exercise room, miniature golf, library, game room, dance floor
14	Desert Palms Golf & RV Resort, 39258 Harquahala Rd, Salome, AZ 85384 / (928) 859-2000 or (866) 725-6778 / www.desertpalmsrv.com / info@desertpalmsrv.com / N 33° 45' 52" W 113° 36' 39"	320 / 200	$350-400	✓	$$$$$$	55		G	✓	50	✓	A	✓	S $	H	✓	✓	✓	Nice modern park / 9-hole golf - executive par 3 course / Sites on the golf course / Other amenities - horseshoes, bocce ball
15	Desert Pueblo RV Resort, 28726 Hwy 72, Bouse, AZ 85325 / (928) 851-2206 / www.desertpueblorv.com / dprv@cox.net / N 33° 55' 03" W 113° 59' 41"	89 / 89	$150-200	✓	$$$$			G		50		A				✓	✓		5 mth and yearly seasonal rates
16	Desert Sunset RV Park, 480 N Central Blvd, Quartzsite, AZ 85346 / (928) 927-6443 / www.desertsunresorts.com / N 33° 45' 42" W 113° 39'00"	100 / 70	$250-300	$$$$$				G		50		A	✓	C $		✓	✓	✓	Jan only rate is $350-400 category / Lower rate for smaller RVs / Wi-fi available to some sites / Wi-Fi free to for daily guests / Other amenities, library, dance floor

#	Park / Address / Contact	Sites Total/Available	Monthly Rate	Monthly Available	Longer Term Rates	Overnight Rates	Age Restriction	RV Restriction	Site Surface	Patio	Electric	TV	Phone at Sites	Internet	Wi-Fi	Swimming Pool	Spa	Club House	Planned Activities	Comments
17	Desert Vista RV Park, 64812 Harcuvan Dr, Salome, AZ 85348 — (928) 859-4639 — N 33° 40' 27" W 114° 13' 02"	125 / 125	$200-250		$$$$$$	Over			G	✓	50	✓	A	S	H		✓	✓	✓	Annual rates offered; Other amenities – miniature golf, horseshoes, pool tables
18	Destiny's McIntyre, 8750 E 26th Ave, Blythe, CA 92225 — (760) 922-8205 — www.destinyrv.com — mcintyrequestions@destinyrv.com — N 33° 40' 27" W 114° 33' 56"	222 / 222	$200-250	✓	$$$$$$				GR		50							✓		On the Colorado River; Boat ramp; 5 month rate offered; Convenience store
19	Eighty Eight Shades RV Park, 575 W Main St, Quartzsite, AZ 85346 — (928) 927-6336 or (800) 457-4392 — www.grapevine7.com — g7resorts@hotmail.com — N 33° 39' 54" W 114° 13' 32"	230 / 104	$350-400		$$$$$	Over			G	✓	50	✓	A	S	$		✓	✓	✓	Annual rates offered; Wi-Fi free to daily guest
20	Gateway Ranch RV Retreat, 44660 Ave 42E, Salome, AZ 85348 — (928) 927-7770 — N 33° 41' 15" W 113° 55' 27"	100 / 66	$150-200	✓	$$$$		55		G	✓	50		A							Annual rates offered; All sites are wired for telephone and can be activated by telephone company; Wi-Fi may be available in 2009
21	Hidden Beaches RV Park, 6951 6th Ave, Blythe, CA 92225 — (760) 922-7276 — N 33° 39' 45" W 114° 31' 32"	90 / 90	$250-300		$$$$$$	Over			G	✓	50	✓		S	F		✓	✓	✓	On the Colorado River; Self contained RVs only; Boat launch
22	Holiday Palms RV Park, 355 W Main St, Quartzsite, AZ 85359 — (928) 927-5666 or (800) 635-5372 — www.grapevine7.com — g7resorts@hotmail.com — N 33° 39' 56" W 113° 13' 22"	244 / 244	$350-400		$$$$$				G	✓	30	✓	A	S	$		✓	✓	✓	Wi-Fi free to daily guest; 150 spaces are taken by annual residents; Annual rate offered; Same rate during January
23	Jr's RV Park, Box 669, Quartzsite, AZ 85346 — (928) 927-5774 — N 33° 40' 51" W 114° 13' 02"	187 / 187	$200-250		$$$$$		55	✓	G	✓	50	✓	A					✓		Open Sept 1 – April 30; Season rates offered; Self contained RVs only; Shuffleboard, horseshoes
24	Kofa Mountain RV Park, 170 N Central Blvd, Quartzsite, AZ 85346 — (928) 927-6778 — kofa170@rulogon.com — N 33° 40' 12" W 114° 13' 03"	54 / 54	$200-250	✓	$$$$$$		55		G	✓	50		A	S	$			✓	✓	Jan/Feb in $300-350 category; 1st and 2nd day Wi-Fi free to daily guests; 3 mth and annual rates offered; No pets

Quartzsite Area Snowbird Parks
Page 4

#	Park / Address / Contact	Sites Total/Available	Monthly/Available	Monthly Rate	Longer Term Rates	Overnight Rates	Age Restriction	RV Restriction	Site Surface	Patio	Electric	TV	Phone at Sites	Internet	Wi-Fi	Swimming Pool	Spa	Club House	Planned Activities	Comments
25	Mayflower County Park 4980 Colorado River Rd Blythe, CA 92225 (760) 922-4665 www.co.riversidecountyparks.org N 33° 40' 12" W 114° 32' 02"	152 / 152		$250-300	$$$$$				GR		30									On the Colorado River Monthly rates in winter only Boat launch
26	Ramblin Roads RV Park 60655 E US Hwy 60 Hope, AZ 85348 (928) 859-3187 or (800) 569-6027 www.ramblinroads.com ramblinroads@tds.net N 33° 43' 22" W 113° 42' 14"	177 / 166	√	$350-400	$$$$$$				G		50	√	A	S $			√	√	√	Open Labor - Memorial day Other amenities - 18-hole desert golf course, putting green Mini market
27	Rancho Ventana RV Resort 4410 Arrowhead #216 Blythe, CA 92225 (760) 921-3600 www.ranchoventanarv.com ranchoventanahoa@npgcable.com N 33° 40' 23" W 114° 38' 29"	212		$350-400			55		G	√	50	√	A	√	H		√	√		Private owned lots - call for monthly rates Sites are golf course and non golf course - rate listed is the lower 18-hole golf course
28	Shady Lane RV Court 185 N Hwy 95 P.O. Box 88 Quartzsite, AZ 85346 (928) 927-6844 N 33° 40' 11" W 114° 12' 59"	118 / 118		$200-250	$$$$$				G		50		A	S F			√	√		No monthly rate in Jan - weekly rate is $185 (2009) Wi-Fi available centrally and at some sites Open Sept 15 - April 15
29	Split Rail RV Park 1258 N Central Blvd P.O. Box 2811 Quartzsite, AZ 85346 (928) 927-5296 N 33° 41' 05" W 114° 13' 03"	80 / 80		$50-100	$$$$				G	√	50		A	S $			√	√		Jan monthly rate $360 Annual rate offered Wi-Fi offered in clubhouse and sites nearby Other amenities - library, dance floor
30	Sweet's Retreat RV Park 310 N Central Blvd Box 2464 Quartzsite, AZ 85346 (928) 927-5733 N 33° 40' 18" W 114° 13' 02"	67 / 67		$200-250	$$$$$				G		50		A	S $			√			Jan rate in $350-400 category Seasonal rates No pets
31	Wagon West RV Park 50126 E Hwy 60 Salome, AZ 85348 (928) 927-7077 wagonwest@tds.net N 33° 41' 33" W 113° 53' 06"	215 / 215	√	$300-350	$$$$$		55		G		50	√	A	S $			√	√		Jan monthly rate is in $400-450 category Desert golf course

TUCSON

With a population of close to a million the city of Tucson can be a great place to spend the winter. There are fewer Snowbird parks here than you might expect, not even half as many as Yuma.

One of the important features of the RVing scene in Tucson is the Tucson Gem and Mineral Showcase during the last few days of January and about ten days of February. This attracts many RVers to the city during that period.

Weather

At 2,400 feet Tucson is the highest of the Snowbird destinations in this chapter. It also has some of the cooler temperatures.

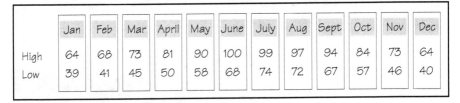

	Jan	Feb	Mar	April	May	June	July	Aug	Sept	Oct	Nov	Dec
High	64	68	73	81	90	100	99	97	94	84	73	64
Low	39	41	45	50	58	68	74	72	67	57	46	40

Living Convenience and Shopping

Tucson is a big city with all that that brings. There is traffic but also excellent shopping and lots to see and do.

Recreation

Tucson has some really outstanding outdoor destinations including Mt. Lemmon, Madera Canyon, Sabino Canyon, and Saguaro National Park. There's also a lot of Hispanic history in this town, and great Mexican food.

- 28 Golf Courses In Tucson
- Arizona State Museum
- Arizona-Sonora Desert Museum
- Cactus League Spring Training – Arizona Diamondbacks, Chicago White Sox, Colorado Rockies
- Catalina State Park
- Colossal Cave Mountain Park
- Davis-Monthan Air Force Base Tours
- DeGrazia Gallery
- Desert Diamond Casino and Casino of the Sun
- Flandrau Science Center and Planetarium
- International Wildlife Museum
- Kitt Peak National Observatory
- Madera Canyon
- Mt. Lemmon
- Old Tucson Studios
- Pima Air and Space Museum

- Reid Park Zoo
- Sabino Canyon
- Saguaro National Park
- San Xavier Mission
- Titan Missile Museum
- Tohono Chul Park
- Tubac
- Tucson Museum of Art
- Tumacacori National Historic Park
- Tucson Botanical Gardens

Hospital Facilities

- Carondelet Saint Joseph's Hospital
- Carondelet St Mary's Hospital
- El Dorado Hospital
- Kindred Hospital
- Kino Community Hospital
- Northwest Medical Center
- Summit Hospital of Southeast Arizona
- Tucson Heart Hospital
- Tucson Medical Center
- University Medical Center

RV Parks

Unlike Phoenix you'll find the Tucson RV parks scattered all around the edges of the city, mostly just off the freeways. Many parks here are fairly new and upscale, which is reflected in the high average monthly rental figure shown in our comparison chart.

Pima County's $.50 per night tax on RV sites is quite controversial and applies to both short and long-term stays. Many folks won't come here in protest, others just don't like the hit to their budgets. The tax is usually included in the quoted rate but you might check on this. The money is dedicated to paying for a baseball stadium.

You'll note that few parks in Tucson offer discounts for three-month stays. This may reflect the fact that they get a great deal of business in late January and early February from the Gem and Mineral Showcase.

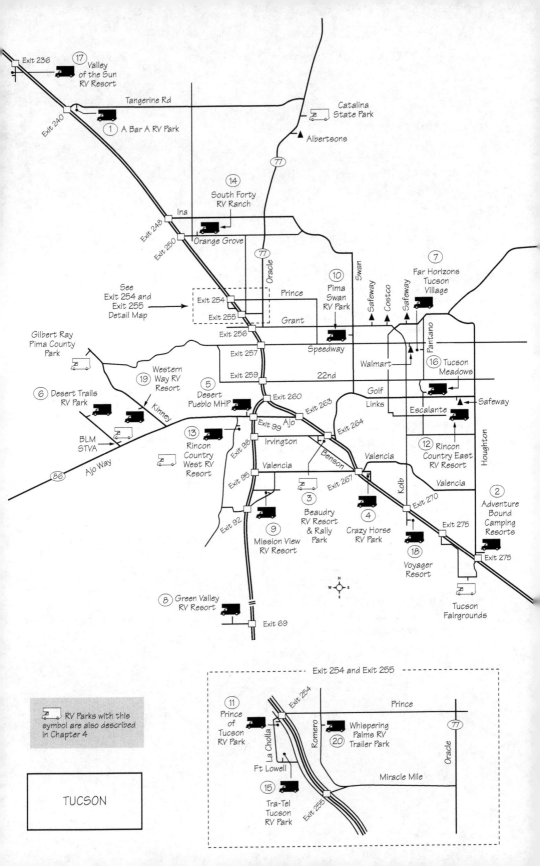

Exit 236
(17) Valley of the Sun RV Resort

Tangerine Rd

Exit 240
(1) A Bar A RV Park

Catalina State Park

▲ Albertsons

77

(14) South Forty RV Ranch

Exit 248
Ina

Exit 250
Orange Grove

Oracle

77

Prince

(10) Pima Swan RV Park

Swan

Safeway

Costco

Safeway

(7) Far Horizons Tucson Village

See Exit 254 and Exit 255 Detail Map →

Exit 254

Exit 255

Grant

Exit 256

Speedway

Gilbert Ray Pima County Park

Western Way RV Resort
(19)

Exit 257

Exit 259

22nd

Walmart

Pantano

(16) Tucson Meadows

(6) Desert Trails RV Park

Kinney

(5) Desert Pueblo MHP

Exit 260

Ajo
Exit 99

Exit 263

Golf

Links

▲ Safeway

Escalante

BLM STVA

(13) Rincon Country West RV Resort

Exit 98

Irvington

Benson

Exit 264

Valencia

(12) Rincon Country East RV Resort

Houghton

86

Ajo Way

Exit 95

Valencia

Valencia

(2) Adventure Bound Camping Resorts

Exit 267

Exit 270

Exit 92

(3) Beaudry RV Resort & Rally Park

Kolb

Exit 275

(9) Mission View RV Resort

(4) Crazy Horse RV Park

(18) Voyager Resort

Exit 275

W ⊕ E
N
S

(8) Green Valley RV Resort

Exit 69

Tucson Fairgrounds

🚐 RV Parks with this symbol are also described in Chapter 4

TUCSON

Exit 254 and Exit 255

Exit 254

Prince

77

(11) Prince of Tucson RV Park

Romero

Oracle

La Cholla

Whispering Palms RV Trailer Park
(20)

Ft Lowell

Miracle Mile

(15) Tra-Tel Tucson RV Park

Exit 255

Tucson Snowbird Parks
Page 1

#	Park / Address / Contact	Sites Total/Avail	Monthly Rate	Longer Term Rate	Overnight Rates	Age Restriction	RV Restriction	Site Surface	Patio	Electric	TV	Phone at Sites	Internet	Wi-Fi	Swimming Pool	Spa	Club House	Planned Activities	Comments
1	**A Bar A RV Park** — 9015 W Tangerine Farms Rd, Tucson, AZ 85653 — (520) 682-4332 — abaraaz@netscape.net — N 32° 25' 29" W 111° 09' 27"	85 / 85	$250-300	$$$$$				G		50		A			H		✓		RVs over 10 yr age require approval. Most sites have Wi-Fi at the site. Other amenities - shuffleboard, horseshoes, game room, hiking trails
2	**Adventure Bound Camping Resorts** — 10195 S Houghton Rd, Tucson, AZ 85747 — (520) 574-3000 or (800) 777-8799 — www.cactuscountryrv.com — cactuscountryrv@aol.com — N 32° 04' 03" W 110° 45' 52"	263 / 234	$500-550	$$$$$$ Over		✓		G	✓	50	✓	A	F	S	H	✓	✓	✓	
3	**Beaudry RV Resort & Rally Park** — 5151 S Country Club, Tucson, AZ 85706 — (888) 500-0789 — www.beaudryrvresort.com — info@beaudryrvresort.com — N 32° 09' 33" W 110° 55' 34"	346 / 346	$500-850	$$$$$$ Over			✓	G	✓	50	✓	F	F	C	H	✓	✓	✓	Rates range from $500 in the summer to $850 in Feb. Older RVs require approval
4	**Crazy Horse RV Park** — 6660 S Craycroft Rd, Tucson, AZ 85706 — (520) 574-0157 or (800) 279-6279 — czyhorse@mindspring.com — N 32° 07' 51" W 110° 52' 31"	154 / 135	$350-400	$$$$$		✓		G	✓	50	✓	$	F	S	H	✓	✓	✓	Seasonal rate for 5 months. Most sites have Wi-Fi at the site. Monthly rate includes tax - not electric
5	**Desert Pueblo MHP** — 1302 West Ajo Way, Tucson, AZ 85713 — (520) 889-9557 — www.desertpueblo.com — desertpueblooffi@qwest.net — N 32° 10' 42" W 110° 59' 32"	422 / 75	$400-450	$$$$$$ Over		55	✓	G	✓	50		A			H	✓	✓	✓	RVs, 5th-wheels, and trailers only. Cable activated by cable company. Only 1 pet (20 lb or less) allowed. Other amenities - shuffleboard, library, sauna, putting green
6	**Desert Trails RV Park (Formerly Justins)** — 3551 S San Joaquin Rd, Tucson, AZ 85735 — (520) 883-8340 or (888) 883-8340 — www.deserttrailsrvpark.com — info@deserttrailsrvpark.com — N 32° 10' 50" W 110° 08' 55"	240 / 240	$400-450	$$$$$		55	✓	G	✓	50	$	A	F	S	H	✓	✓	✓	Adult only park Nov - Mar. RVs over 10 yrs age require approval. Other amenities - game room, hiking trails, shuffleboard, horseshoes
7	**Far Horizons Tucson Village** — 555 N Pantano Rd, Tucson, AZ 85710 — (520) 296-1234 or (800) 480-3488 — www.tucsonvillage.com — vacation@tucsonvillage.com — N 32° 13' 44" W 110° 49' 27"	514 / 114	$600-650	$$$$$$ Over		55		G	✓	50	✓	A	$	S	H	✓	✓	✓	Sites include standard, premium, and patio - rate listed is standard. Patios only at some sites. Cable free at patio sites - at other site available for a fee
8	**Green Valley RV Resort** — 19001 S Richfield Ave, Green Valley, AZ 85614 — (520) 625-3900 — www.greenvalleyrvresort.com — info@greenvalleyrvresort.com — N 31° 54' 15" W 110° 59' 28"	304 / 85	$600-650	$$$$$$		55		G	✓	50	✓	A	$	S	H	✓	✓	✓	Monthly rate includes electric and tax. Separate pet section. Other amenities - shuffleboard, exercise room, horseshoes

Tucson Snowbird Parks
Page 2

#	Park / Address / Contact	Sites Total/Available	Monthly Rate Available	Longer Term Rates	Overnight Rates	Age Restriction	RV Restriction	Site Surface	Patio	Electric	TV	Phone at Sites	Internet	Wi-Fi	Swimming Pool	Spa	Club House	Planned Activities	Comments
9	Mission View RV Resort, 31 W Los Reales Rd, Tucson, AZ 85706 — (520) 741-1945 or (800) 444-8439, www.missionviewrv.com, missnview2@aol.com, N 32° 07' 04" W 110° 58' 18"	342 / 150	$500-550	✓	Over $$$$$	55		G	✓	50		A	S	$	H	✓	✓	✓	This park has a family section and a separate adult section. The swimming pool is indoors. Other amenities - shuffleboard, horseshoes, exercise room, library
10	Pima/Swan RV Park, 4615 E Pima St, Tucson, AZ 85712 — (520) 881-4022, N 32° 14' 38" W 110° 53' 40"	35 / 31	$250-300		$$$$			G	✓	30	$	A	S	F		✓		✓	Cable activated by cable company. Limited sites for larger than 34 ft RVs
11	Prince of Tucson RV Park, 3501 N Freeway Rd, Tucson, AZ 85705 — (520) 887-3501 or (800) 955-3501, www.princeoftucsonrvpark.com, princeoftucson@comcast.net, N 32° 16' 06" W 111° 00' 40"	177 / 130	$450-500		$$$$$	55	✓	G	✓	50		A	S	$	H	✓	✓	✓	1990 and newer RVs accepted. Other amenities - shuffleboard, convenience store, and pool tables. Good Sam park
12	Rincon Country East RV Resort, 8989 E Escalante Rd, Tucson, AZ 85730 — (520) 886-8431 or (888) 401-8989, www.rinconcountry.com, east@rinconcountry.com, N 32° 10' 40" W 110° 48' 06"	460 / 100	$600-650		$$$$$$			G	✓	50	$	A	S	$	H	✓	✓	✓	5 month seasonal rates. Cable activated by cable company. Other amenities - shuffleboard, exercise room, library, putting green, horseshoes, rec field
13	Rincon Country West RV Resort, 4555 S Mission Rd, Tucson, AZ 85746 — (520) 294-5608 or (800) 782-7275, www.rinconcountry.com, west@rinconcountry.com, N 32° 10' 09" W 111° 00' 13"	1,100 / 350	$600-650		Over $$$$$$	55		G / P	✓	50		A	S	F	H	✓	✓	✓	Sites are value and premium - the monthly rate listed is for value. 5 month seasonal rates. Premium sites have a patio. Cable offered by office for a fee
14	South Forty RV Ranch, 3600 W Orange Grove Rd, Tucson, AZ 85741 — (520) 297-2503, www.southfortyrvranch.com, southfortyrvranch@yahoo.com, N 32° 19' 26" W 111° 02' 32"	229 / 170	$500-550		$$$$$$			G	✓	50		A	S	F	H	✓	✓	✓	Adult park. Other amenities - billiards room, card room, exercise room, shuffleboard
15	Tra-Tel Tucson RV Park, 2070 W Ft Lowell, Tucson, AZ 85705 — (520) 888-5401 or (800) 444-7822, www.tra-tel.com, info@tra-tel.com, N 32° 15' 55" W 111° 00' 34"	70 / 63	$250-300		Over $$$$$			G	✓	50	$	A	C	F	S	✓	✓	✓	Most sites have phones which can be activated by phone company
16	Tucson Meadows Winter Haven RV Park, 2121 S Pantano Rd, Tucson, AZ 85710 — (520) 298-8024, www.tucsonmeadows.com, office@tucsonmeadows.com, N 32° 11' 49" W 110° 49' 24"	579 / 144	$550-600	✓			55	✓	G	✓	50	$	A	C	F	H	✓	✓	✓	Minimum stay is weekly. Older RVs require approval. No pet walking in RV park. Cable activated by cable company. Shuffleboard, exercise room, library

Tucson Snowbird Parks
Page 3

Park	Sites Total/Available	Monthly Rate	Longer Term Rates	Overnight Rates	Age Restriction	RV Restriction	Site Surface	Patio	Electric	TV	Phone at Sites	Internet	Wi-Fi	Swimming Pool	Spa	Club House	Planned Activities	Comments
(17) Valley of the Sun RV Resort 13377 North Sandario Rd Marana, AZ 85653 (520) 682-3434 www.valley-of-the-sun-rv-park.com alspall@cox.net N 32° 27' 10" W 110° 49' 24"	130 / 80	$350-400	$$$$$$				G	✓	50	$	A	✓	S F	H	✓	✓	✓	RV sites in a separate area from park models and mobile homes Cable activated by cable company Other amenities - shuffleboard, horseshoes, library
(18) Voyager Resort 8701 S Kolb Rd Tucson, AZ 85706 (520) 574-5000 or (800) 424-9191 www.voyagerrv.com info@voyagerresort.com N 32° 05' 37" W 110° 50' 26"	1,576 / 600	$700-750	$$$$$$	Over	55	✓	P G	✓	50	✓	I F	✓	S $	H	✓	✓	✓	Annual seasonal rate only Self contained RVs only Phones activated at office for no charge 9-hole golf, sauna, tennis, library
(19) Western Way RV Resort 3100 S Kinney Rd Tucson, AZ 85713 (520) 578-1715 or (800) 292-8616 www.wwrvresort.com info@wwrvresort.com N 32° 11' 05" W 111° 05' 34"	304 / 80	$600-650	$$$$$$	Over	55		G	✓	50	$	A	✓	S F	H	✓	✓	✓	Monthly rate includes electric Cable activated by cable company Only a few 40 ft RV spaces Other amenities - ballroom, library, shuffleboard, exercise room
(20) Whispering Palms RV Trailer Park 3445 N Romero Rd Tucson, AZ 85705 (520) 888-2500 or (800) 266-8577 www.whisperingpalmsrv.net mperrycwl@msn.com N 32° 16' 15" W 111° 00' 11"	18 / 16	$250-300	$$$$$				G		50	$	A	✓	S F	H		✓	✓	Cable activated by cable company Pool closed in the winter Other amenities - shuffleboard

YUMA

Yuma, with a population of about 90,000, is one of the fastest growing cities in the US. Not only that, with the influx of Snowbirds in the winter, some with RVs and some without, the population actually doubles. The city has a military presence too, there's a US Marine Corps Air Station here. It is said to be the busiest Marine airfield in the country.

Most people don't realize how isolated Yuma is from the rest of the population centers in Arizona. San Diego is a bit closer to Yuma than Casa Grande, not to mention Phoenix or Tucson.

Weather

With an elevation of just 200 feet Yuma is among the warmest of the Snowbird destinations in the chapter. Records show that Yuma is the hottest city of its size in the US and gets the most sunny days too.

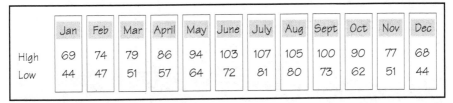

	Jan	Feb	Mar	April	May	June	July	Aug	Sept	Oct	Nov	Dec
High	69	74	79	86	94	103	107	105	100	90	77	68
Low	44	47	51	57	64	72	81	80	73	62	51	44

Living Convenience and Shopping

Many people like Yuma because it's big enough to have all the conveniences yet small enough to avoid many of the hassles involved in living in a large city. Most of the big box store chains are in Yuma and there are a variety of grocery stores. Even though the population doubles in the winter it seems that there are enough services being provided to cover the increase, crowding is seldom a problem.

An added benefit to Yuma's location is that it is so close to the Mexican border. The small Mexican town of Los Algodones is just across the border a few miles west of town. Many folks visit it for its restaurants, dentists, and pharmacies.

Recreation

- Nine Golf Courses
- Algodones Dunes
- Center of the World
- Cocopah Casino
- Cocopah Museum
- Dome Valley Museum
- Fort Yuma & Quechan Indian Museum
- Historic Downtown Yuma
- Imperial Dam Recreation Area
- Imperial Date Gardens
- Kofa National Wildlife Refuge
- Los Algodones, Mexico

MITTRY LAKE WILDLIFE REFUGE NEAR YUMA

- Marine Corps Air Station (tours)
- Mittry Lake Wildlife Refuge – birding and fishing
- Quechan Paradise Casino
- San Luis Río Colorado, Mexico
- St Thomas Indian Mission
- Yuma Crossing State Historic Park
- Yuma Territorial Prison State Historic Park
- Yuma Valley Railway

Hospital Facilities

- Yuma Regional Medical Center – Yuma
- PHS Indian Health Service Hospital – Winterhaven
- Pioneers Memorial Hospital District – Brawley, CA

RV Parks

Yuma offers a wide range of RV parks. There are older very basic parks as well as modern big parks with full amenities. Most parks offer a discount for three months.

Yuma is also very close to some of the most popular government boondocking areas. In Chapter 4 take a look at *Yuma* and also the *Imperial Dam Recreation Area*.

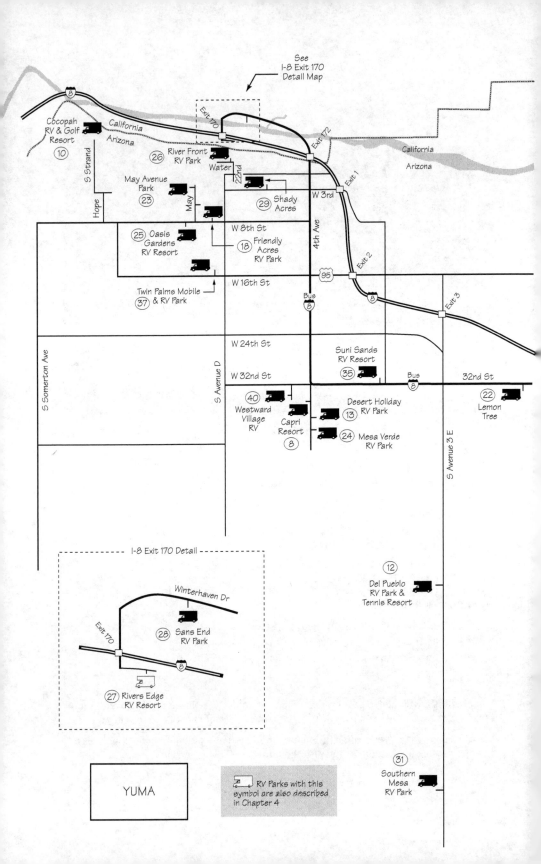

See
I-8 Exit 170
Detail Map

Cocopah
RV & Golf
Resort
(10)

California

Arizona

S Strand

Hope

(26) River Front
RV Park
Water

22nd

Exit 172

California

Arizona

May Avenue
Park
(23)

May

(29) Shady
Acres

W 3rd

Exit 1

(25) Oasis
Gardens
RV Resort

W 8th St

(18) Friendly
Acres
RV Park

4th Ave

Exit 2

W 16th St

95

Twin Palms Mobile
& RV Park
(37)

Bus
8

8

Exit 3

W 24th St

Suni Sands
RV Resort

W 32nd St

(35)

Bus
8

32nd St

S Avenue D

(40)
Westward
Village
RV

Capri
Resort
(8)

Desert Holiday
RV Park
(13)

(24) Mesa Verde
RV Park

(22)
Lemon
Tree

S Avenue 3 E

S Somerton Ave

I-8 Exit 170 Detail

Winterhaven Dr

(28) Sans End
RV Park

Exit 170

8

(27) Rivers Edge
RV Resort

(12)

Del Pueblo
RV Park &
Tennis Resort

YUMA

RV Parks with this
symbol are also described
in Chapter 4

(31)

Southern
Mesa
RV Park

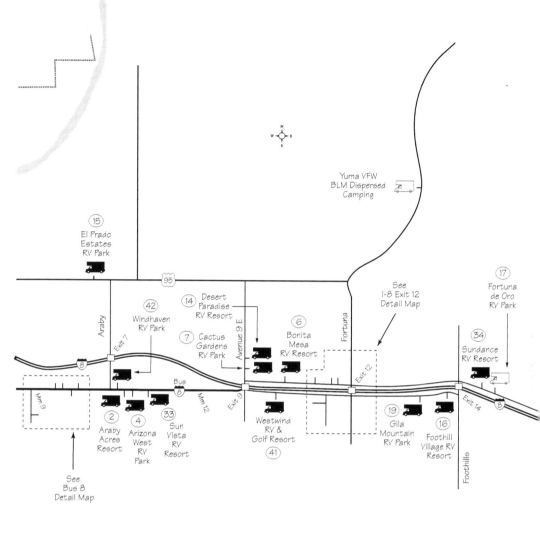

(15) El Prado Estates RV Park

Yuma VFW BLM Dispersed Camping

(95)

(17) Fortuna de Oro RV Park

Araby

Exit 7

(42) Windhaven RV Park

(14) Desert Paradise RV Resort

Avenue 9 E

(7) Cactus Gardens RV Park

(6) Bonita Mesa RV Resort

Fortuna

See I-8 Exit 12 Detail Map

(34) Sundance RV Resort

(8)

Bus (8)

Mm 12

Exit 9

(2) Araby Acres Resort

(4) Arizona West RV Park

(33) Sun Vista RV Resort

Westwind RV & Golf Resort

(41)

Exit 12

(19) Gila Mountain RV Park

(16) Foothill Village RV Resort

Exit 14

Foothills

(8)

Mm 9

See Bus 8 Detail Map

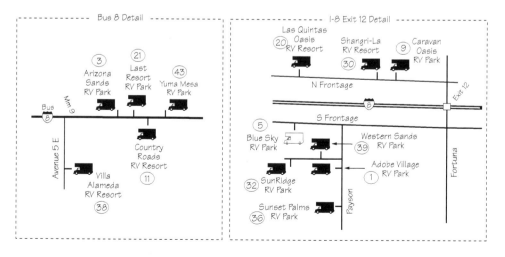

Bus 8 Detail

(3) Arizona Sands RV Park

(21) Last Resort RV Park

(43) Yuma Mesa RV Park

Bus (8)

Mm 9

Avenue 5 E

Country Roads RV Resort

(11)

(38) Villa Alameda RV Resort

I-8 Exit 12 Detail

(20) Las Quintas Oasis RV Resort

Shangri-La RV Resort (30)

(9) Caravan Oasis RV Park

N Frontage

Exit 12

(8)

S Frontage

(5) Blue Sky RV Park

Western Sands RV Resort

(39)

(32) SunRidge RV Park

Adobe Village RV Park (1)

(36) Sunset Palms RV Park

Payson

Fortuna

Yuma Snowbird Parks
Page 1

#	Park / Contact	Sites Total/Available	Monthly Rate (Available)	Longer Term Rates	Overnight Rates	Age Restriction	RV Restriction	Site Surface	Patio	Electric	TV	Phone at Sites	Internet	Wi-Fi	Swimming Pool	Spa	Club House	Planned Activities	Comments
1	Adobe Village RV Park 11350 South Payson Drive Yuma, AZ 85365 (928) 345-1154 yumaparks.com yumaparks@aol.com N 32° 39' 58" W 114° 27' 11"	118 / 85	$250-300	$$$$$		55		G	✓	50	✓	A	✓	$ S			✓	✓	Self contained RVs - bathroom facilities are locked at night. Cable DSL for internet available
2	Araby Acres Resort 6649 East 32nd Yuma, AZ 85365 (800) 833-6046 www.mhcrv.com araby_acresinfo@mhchomes.com N 32° 40' 11" W 114° 31' 04"	330 / 25	$550-1,150	$$$$$	Over $$$$$	55	✓	GR	✓	50	$	A	✓	$ S	H	✓	✓	✓	Mthly rates from $560 (Dec) to 1,150 (Jan/March) and 1,150 (Feb). Cable activated with cable company. Other amenities - fitness room, shuffleboard, putting green, library
3	Arizona Sands RV Park 5510 E 32nd St Yuma, AZ 85365 (928) 726-0160 www.arizonasandsrvpark.com azsandsrvpark@aol.com N 32° 40' 13" W 114° 32' 19"	204 / 197	$350-400	$$$$$		55	✓	G	✓	50	$	A	✓	$ S		✓	✓		Cable activated with cable company. Approval required for RVs 15 years & older
4	Arizona West RV Park 6825 E 32nd St Yuma, AZ 85365 (928) 726-1481 or (866) 726-1481 www.azwestrv.com info@azwestrv.com N 32° 40' 10" W 114° 30' 52"	227 / 207	$400-450	$$$$$		55	✓	G	✓	50	✓	A	✓	$ S	H		✓	✓	Monthly rate includes electric. 1 pet allowed. Seasonal reservations only. Cable DSL available for internet access
5	Blue Sky RV Park 10247 S Frontage Rd Yuma, AZ 85365 (928) 342-1444 or (877) 367-5220 R www.blueskyyuma.com manager@blueskyyuma.com N 32° 40' 11" W 114° 27' 21"	276 / 210	$350-400	$$$$$	Over $$$$$	55	✓	G	✓	50	✓	A	✓	$ S	H	✓	✓	✓	RVs must be self contained. Tents are allowed. Other amenities include billiard tables, horseshoes, shuffleboard, lending library, and a mailroom
6	Bonita Mesa RV Resort 9400 N. Frontage Rd Yuma, AZ 85365 (928) 342-2999 www.bonitamesa.com info@bonitamesa.com N 32° 40' 18" W 114° 28' 13"	470 / 200	$500-550	$$$$$	Over $$$$$	55	✓	G	✓	50	$	I $	✓	$ S	H	✓	✓	✓	Cable activated with cable company. Telephone instant from the office for a fee. Other amenities - library, exercise room, TV room, shuffleboard
7	Cactus Gardens RV Park 10657 S Avenue 9E Yuma, AZ 85365 (928) 342-9188 or (866) 315-9534 www.mhcrv.com cactus@digitaldune.net N 32° 40' 28" W 114° 28' 39"	428 / 158	$450-500	$$$$$	Over $$$$$	55		G	✓	50	✓	A	✓	$ S	H	✓	✓	✓	Encore park. Mthly rates from $450-525. Other amenities include an exercise room, shuffleboard, pitch n putt. Golfers league
8	Capri RV Resort 3380 S 4th Ave Yuma, AZ 85365 (928) 726-0959 or (800) 576-7596 R www.mhcrv.com caprirv@digitaldune.net N 32° 40' 01" W 114° 37' 29"	306 / 203	$400-450	$$$$$		55	✓	G	✓	30	$	A	✓	$ S	H	✓	✓	✓	Encore park. 35 feet maximum RV size. Jan-March min res 3 month. Activity director. Mthly rate $425-474

Yuma Snowbird Parks
Page 2

#	Park / Contact	Sites Total / Available	Monthly Rate	Longer Term Rates	Overnight Rates	Age Restriction	RV Restriction	Site Surface	Patio	Electric	TV	Phone at Sites	Internet	Wi-Fi	Swimming Pool	Spa	Club House	Planned Activities	Comments
9	Caravan Oasis RV Park, 10500 N 1-8 Frontage Rd, Yuma, AZ 85365 — (928) 342-1480 or (800) 348-1480 R — www.caravanoasisresort.com — infor@caravanoasisresort.com — N 32° 40' 17" W 114° 26' 54"	742 / 692	$400-450	✓	Over $$$$$$		✓	G	✓	50	✓	A	S $	H	✓	✓	✓	✓	Self contained RVs only. Sites are regular, delux, and premium (rate listed is regular). Other amenities - 5,000 sq ft recreation hall, shuffleboard
10	Cocopah RV & Golf Resort, 6800 Strand Ave S, Yuma, AZ 85364 — (928) 343-9300 or (800) 537-7901 — www.cocopahrv.com — info@cocopahrv.com — N 32° 44' 07" W 114° 41' 27"	805 / 480	$450-500	✓	Over $$$$$$		✓	G	✓	50	✓	A		H	✓	✓	✓		RVs, 5th-wheels, trailers only - no more than 10 years of age. Sites separated into pet and non pet areas. 18-hole PGA par 3-4 golf course
11	Country Roads RV Resort, 5707 East Hwy 80 #170, Yuma, AZ 85365 — (928) 344-8910 — www.countryroadsyuma.com — crrentals@countryroadyuma.com — N 32° 40' 10" W 114° 32' 03"	1,294	$550-600	✓		55	✓	G	✓	50	✓	A	S $	H	✓	✓	✓	✓	RV sites are private owned - call for availability and rates. Number of available sites varies. Monthly rate includes electric. 1 mth rentals are hard to get
12	Del Pueblo RV Park and Tennis Resort, 14794 Ave 3E, Yuma, AZ 85366 — (928) 341-2100 — www.delpueblorv.com — info@delpueblorv.com — N 32° 36' 51" W 114° 34' 55"	475 / 475	$500-550	✓	Over $$$$$$	55	✓	G	✓	50	✓	I $	S F	H	✓	✓	✓	✓	RVs, 5th-wheels, trailers only - over 10 yrs of age requires approval. Newer park - opened in 2002. Other amenities - tennis, putting green, shuffleboard, gym
13	Desert Holiday RV Park, 3601 S 4th Ave, Yuma, AZ 85365 — (928) 344-4680 — www.rvdesertholiday.com — rvdesertholiday@yahoo.com — N 32° 39' 43" W 114° 37' 26"	221 / 150	$450-500	✓	Over $$$$$$		✓	G	✓	50	✓	A	S $	H	✓	✓	✓	✓	Cable activated with cable company. Other amenities - shuffleboard, horseshoes, 2 recreation halls
14	Desert Paradise RV Resort, 105337 S Avenue 9E, Yuma, AZ 85365 — (928) 342-9313 or (866) 315-9331 — www.mhcrv.com — desertparadiservinfo@mhchomes.com — N 32° 40' 36" W 114° 28'39"	260 / 150	$450-500	✓	Over $$$$$$	55	✓	G	✓	30	✓	A	S $	H	✓	✓	✓	✓	Encore park. Jan-March RV size restricted to 32 feet and no slides. Other amenities - shuffleboard, full kitchen, fitness area, card room
15	El Prado Estates RV Park, 6200 E Hwy 95, Yuma, AZ 85365 — (928) 726-4006 or (800) 618-4219 R — N 32° 41' 58" W 114° 31' 40"	125 / 125	$200-250	✓	$$$$$$	55	✓	GR	✓	30	✓		C F		✓	✓	✓	✓	Dec rate is lower. Family park with no age restrictions. Data port for internet
16	Foothill Village RV Resort, 12705 S Frontage Road, Yuma, AZ 85365 — (928) 342-1030 or (866) 315-9332 — www.mhcrv.com — foothillvillagervinfo@mhchomes.com — N 32° 40' 08" W 114° 24' 49"	342 / 160	$400-450	✓	Over $$$$$$	55	✓	G	✓	30	✓	A	S $	H	✓	✓	✓	✓	Some 50 amp power - mostly 30. Other amenities - shuffleboard, library, billiards, pool tables, computer center. Jan-March 36 ft limit

Yuma Snowbird Parks
Page 3

#	Park / Address	Contact	Sites Total/Available	Monthly Rate	Longer Term Rates	Overnight Rates	Age Restriction	RV Restriction	Site Surface	Patio	Electric	TV	Phone at Sites	Internet	Wi-Fi	Swimming Pool	Spa	Club House	Planned Activities	Comments
17	Fortuna De Oro RV Park, 13650 N Frontage Rd, Yuma, AZ 85367	(928) 342-5051 or (800) 839-0126 R, www.fortunadeoro.com, fortunadeoro@roadrunner.com, N 32° 40' 08" W 114° 23' 53"	1,296 / 900	$500-550	✓	$$$$$$	55		G	✓	50	✓	- $	✓	C	H	✓	✓	✓	Self contained RVs only. Phones activated in the office. Other amenities - 9-hole golf course, exercise room, library, shuffleboard, darts, crafts room, pool tables
18	Friendly Acres RV Park, 2779 W Eighth St, Yuma, AZ 85364	(928) 783-8414, www.friendly-acres.com, info@friendly-acres.com, N 32° 42' 49" W 114° 39' 14"	380 / 70	$300-350	✓	$$$$	55		G	✓	50	$	A	✓	C F	H	✓	✓	✓	Limited sites for 40 ft RVs. 1 pet limit. After Oct 1 no reservations taken. Other amenities - kitchen, craft hall, library, shuffleboard
19	Gila Mountain RV Park, 12325 S Frontage Rd, Yuma, AZ 85367	(928) 342-1310, N 32° 40' 11" W 114° 25' 22"	253 / 12	$300-350	✓	$$$$$$	55		G	✓	50	✓	- $	✓		✓	✓	✓		Phones activated in the office for a charge. Recreation director. Other amenities - shuffleboard, horseshoes
20	Las Quintas Oasis RV Resort, 10442 E 1-8 Frontage Rd, Yuma, AZ 85365	(928) 305-9005 or (877) 975-9005 R, www.lasquintasrvresort.com, lasquintasresort@rvwifi.com, N 32° 40' 17" W 114° 27' 11"	460 / 350	$300-350	Over $$$$$$	$$$$$$	55		G	✓	50	✓	- $	✓	S F	✓	✓	✓	✓	Popular park - reservations needed early to get a site. Phones activated in the office. Other amenities - activity director, shuffleboard, and exercise room
21	Last Resort RV Park, 5590 E US Hwy 80, Yuma, AZ 85365	(928) 580-7383, N 32° 40' 13" W 114° 32'13"	40 / 40	$250-300	✓	$$$$	55		G	✓	50	$				✓		✓		Cable activated with cable company. Some sites have patios
22	Lemon Tree, 4695 E Hwy 80, Yuma, AZ 85367	(928) 726-0973, N 32° 40' 10" W 114° 33' 17"	135 / 25	$150-200	✓	$$$$	55		G	✓	50	✓	A							Park fills early in season. Cable activated with cable company
23	May Avenue Park, 304 May Avenue, Yuma, AZ 85364	(928) 783-0883, N 32° 43' 19" W 114° 39' 33"	146 / 26	$350-400	✓	$$$$$$	55		GR	✓	50	✓	A	✓		✓	✓	✓	✓	Only a couple of sites can take a 40 ft RV. Limited overnight sites - call for rate and availability
24	Mesa Verde RV Park, 3649 S 4th Ave, Yuma, AZ 85365	(928) 726-5814, www.mesaverderesort.com, mesaverde@digitaldune.net, N 32° 39' 39" W 114° 37' 26"	259/20	$500-550	Over $$$$$$	$$$$$$	55		G	✓	50	$	A	✓	S $	H	✓	✓	✓	Can accept RVs to 38 feet. Feb rate in $650-700 category. No pets allowed in the park. Other amenities - shuffleboard, horseshoes, game room

#	Park	Sites Total/Available	Monthly Rate	Longer Term Rates	Overnight Rates	Age Restriction	RV Restriction	Site Surface	Patio	Electric	TV	Phone at Sites	Internet	Wi-Fi	Swimming Pool	Spa	Club House	Planned Activities	Comments
25	Oasis Gardens RV Resort, 3225 W 8th St, Yuma, AZ 85365 — (928) 782-2222 — N 32° 42' 55" W 114° 39' 35"	146 / 20	$300-350	✓		$$$$$$	55	✓	G	✓	50	✓	A		H	✓	✓	✓	Jan-April rate - $400-500 category / No pets allowed / Accepts only RVs, 5th-wheels, or trailers / Limited overnight sites
26	River Front RV Park, 2300 W Water St, Yuma, AZ 85364 — (928) 783-5868 — N 32° 43' 47" W 114° 38' 54"	170 / 170	$200-250			$$$$$			G	✓	50	✓	A			✓		✓	On the Colorado River in Arizona / Activities - fishing / Other amenities - shuffleboard / horseshoes
27	River's Edge RV Resort, 2299 W Winterhaven Dr, Winterhaven, CA 92283 — (760) 572-5105 — www.riversedgervresort-2.com — yumapark@aol.com — N 32° 44' 08" W 114° 39' 02"	494 / 494	$350-400			$$$$$$			G	✓	50	✓	A	C / F	H	✓	✓	✓	On the Colorado River / Boat ramp / Activities - fishing, boating, canoeing / Shuffleboard courts
28	Sans End RV Park, 2209 W Winterhaven Dr, Winterhaven, CA 92283 — (760) 572-0797 — www.members.aol.com/sansendrv/ — sandsend@aol.com — N 32° 44' 23" W 114° 38' 31"	186 / 186	$350-400	✓		$$$$$$	55		G	✓	50	✓	A	C / $	H	✓	✓	✓	No reservations accepted / Other amenities - game room, horseshoes, shuffleboard
29	Shady Acres, 1340 W 3rd Street, Yuma, AZ 85364 — (928) 783-9431 — shadyacresrv@juno.com — N 32° 43' 19" W 114° 38' 11"	160 / 75	$250-300			$$$$$	55		G	✓	50	✓	A			✓	✓	✓	Maximum RV size 35 ft / Other amenities - shuffleboard and horseshoes / Wi-Fi being installed for 08/09 winter season
30	Shangri-La RV Resort, 10498 N Frontage Rd, Yuma, AZ 85365 — (928) 342-9123 or (877) 742-6474 R — www.shangrilarv.com — info@shangrilarv.com — N 32° 40' 17" W 114° 26' 58"	302 / 140	$500-550	Over		$$$$$$			G	✓	50 $	✓	A	S / $	H	✓	✓	✓	Good Sam park / Other amenities include game room, shuffleboard, horseshoes, pet section, volleyball, bingo, dancing, arts and crafts
31	Southern Mesa RV Park, 18540 South Avenue 3E, Yuma, AZ 85365 — (928) 726-5167 — N 32° 33' 35" W 114° 34' 51"	176 / 160	$300-350	Over		$$$$$$		✓	G	✓	50 $	✓	A	S / F	H	✓	✓	✓	3 day minimum stay / No extremely old RVs / Mile marked walking path in park / Other amenities - pond and waterfall, shuffleboard
32	SunRidge RV Park, 10347 East 34th Street, Yuma, AZ 85365 — (928) 345-4280 — www.yumarvparks.com — yumaparks@aol.com — N 32° 39' 59" W 114° 27' 18"	281 / 210	$300-350	✓		$$$$$$	55	✓	G	✓	50	✓	A		H	✓	✓	✓	5 mth reservation only / Self contained RVs - bathroom facilities are locked at night / Cable DSL for internet available / Small pets only

Yuma Snowbird Parks
Page 5

#	Park Name / Address / Contact	Sites Total/Available	Monthly Rate	Monthly Rate Available	Longer Term Rates	Overnight Rates	Age Restriction	RV Restriction	Site Surface	Patio	Electric	TV	Phone at Sites	Internet	Wi-Fi	Swimming Pool	Spa	Club House	Planned Activities	Comments
33	San Vista RV Resort, 7201 East 32nd St, Yuma, AZ 85365 — (928) 726-8920 or (800) 423-8382 R — www.sunvistarvresort.com — funtimes@sunvistarvresort.com — N 32° 40' 10" W 114° 30' 36"	1,230 / 450	$800-850	✓	$$$$$$ Over		55		G	✓	50	✓	A	✓	S $	H		✓	✓	2 month reservation required. Recreation director. Other amenities - exercise room, shuffleboard, computer room, horseshoes, game room
34	Sundance RV Resort, 13502 N Frontage Rd, Yuma, AZ 85367 — (928) 342-9933 — www.sundanceyuma.com — info@sundanceyuma.com — N 32° 40' 12" W 114° 24' 11"	499 / 200	$450-500	✓	$$$$$$ Over		55		G	✓	50	✓	I $	✓	S $	H		✓	✓	Jan-Mar rate in $500-550 category. Limited spaces for 40 ft RVs. Telephone activated by office for fee. Other amenities - shuffleboard, horseshoes, library, game room
35	Suni-Sands RV Resort, 1960 E 32nd Street, Yuma, AZ 85365 — (928) 726-5941 or (866) 315-9326 R — www.mhcrv.com — sunisandsrvinfo@mhchomes.com — N 32° 40' 12" W 114° 36' 04"	336 / 312	$400-450	✓	$$$$$$		55		G GR	✓	30	✓	A	✓	S $	H	✓	✓	✓	34 pull-thrus have 50 amp power - some of the pull-thrus can take RVs to 40 feet. Activity director. Walmart next door
36	Sunset Palms RV Park, 11450 South Payson Drive, Yuma, AZ 85365 — (928) 345-1159 — www.yumarvparks.com — yumaparks@aol.com — N 32° 39' 52" W 114° 27' 11"	117 / 100	$250-300	✓	$$$$$		55	✓	G	✓	50	✓	A	✓				✓		5 mth reservation only. Self contained RVs - bathroom facilities are locked at night. Cable DSL for internet available. Limited daily sites
37	Twin Palms Mobile & RV Park, 2660 West 16th Street, Yuma, AZ 85364 — (928) 782-2063 — N 32° 41' 56" W 114° 39' 16"	65 / 41	$300-350	✓	$$$$				GR	✓	50	$	A	✓						Monthly rate includes electric
38	Villa Alameda RV Resort, 3547 S Ave 5E, Yuma, AZ 85365 — (928) 344-8081 — villaalmeda@aol.com — N 32° 39' 47" W 114° 32' 46"	302 / 175	$400-450	✓	$$$$$$ Over		55		G	✓	50	$	A	✓	S F	H	✓	✓	✓	6 mth seasonal rate offered. Cable activated with cable company. Other amenities - shuffleboard, horseshoes, game room, exercise room
39	Western Sands RV Park, 10459 South Frontage Rd, Yuma, AZ 85365 — (928) 342-6133 — www.yumarvparks.com — yumaparks@aol.com — N 32° 40' 02" W 114° 27' 13"	156 / 133	$250-300	✓	$$$$$		55	✓	G	✓	50	$	A	✓				✓		5 mth reservation only. Self contained RVs - bathroom facilities are locked at night. Cable DSL for internet available. Limited daily sites
40	Westward Village RV, 3300 South 8th Avenue, Yuma, AZ 85365 — (928) 726-1417 — N 32° 40' 01" W 114° 37' 46"	106 / 43	$400-450	✓			55		G	✓	50	$	A	✓			✓	✓		Mthly rate includes electricity. Limited daily - call for rate. Cable activated with cable company. 10 shops in a village setting are part of the park complex

#	Park / Contact	Sites Total/Available	Monthly Rate	Longer Term Rates	Overnight Rates	Age Restriction	RV Restriction	Site Surface	Patio	Electric	TV	Phone at Sites	Internet	Wi-Fi	Swimming Pool	Spa	Club House	Planned Activities	Comments
41	**Westwind RV & Golf Resort** 9797 E 32nd St, Yuma, AZ 85365 (928) 342-2992 or (866) 440-2992 R www.westwindrvgolfresort.com info@westwindrvgolfresort.com N 32° 40' 11" W 114° 27' 48"	1,075 / 600	$600-650	✓	$$$$$$	Over 55	✓	G	✓	50	✓	I $	✓	S $	H	✓	✓	✓	Self contained RVs only The telephone is instant on at the office for a fee Other amenities - 9-hole golf, store, library, ballroom, shuffleboard
42	**Windhaven RV Park** 6580 East Highway 80, Yuma, AZ 85365 (928) 726-0284 www.windhavenrvpark.com windhavenyuma@yahoo.cm N 32° 40' 14" W 114° 31' 10"	144 / 119	$350-400	✓	$$$$$$	Over		G	✓	50	$	A	✓	S F	H	✓	✓	✓	Cable activated by cable company Considering expanding Wi-Fi to sites Other amenities - shuffleboard, game room, horseshoes RV side of park is only 10 yrs old
43	**Yuma Mesa RV Park** 5990 E Hwy 80, Yuma, AZ 85365 (928) 344-3369 yumamesa@aol.com N 32° 40' 14" W 114° 31' 53"	188 / 188	$300-350	✓	$$$$$$			G	✓	30	$	A	✓	S F	H	✓	✓	✓	Family park Cable activated by cable company Limited sites can accommodate 40 ft RVs Other amenities - shuffleboard

Information Resources

See our Internet site at www.rollinghomes.com for Internet information links.

Casa Grande

City of Casa Grande, 510 E Florence Blvd, Casa Grande, AZ 85222; (520) 421-8600

Greater Casa Grande Chamber of Commerce, 575 N Marshall St, Casa Grande, AZ 85222; (520) 836-2125, (800) 916-1515

Coachella Valley

Desert Hot Springs Chamber of Commerce, 11-711 West Drive, Desert Hot Springs, CA 92240; (760) 329-6403

Indio Chamber of Commerce, 82921 Indio Blvd, Indio, CA 92201; (760) 347-0676

Palm Springs Chamber of Commerce, 190 West Amado Road, Palm Springs, CA 92262; (760) 325-1577

Palm Springs City Hall, 3200 E Tahquitz Canyon Way, Palm Springs, CA 92262; (760) 323-8299

Palm Springs Desert Resorts Convention and Visitors Authority, 70-100 Highway 111, Rancho Mirage, CA 92270; (760) 770-9000

Lake Havasu and The Parker Strip

Lake Havasu Convention and Visitor's Bureau, 314 London Bridge Road, Lake Havasu City, AZ 86403; (928) 453-3444

Parker Area Chamber of Commerce, 1217 California Avenue, Parker AZ 85344; (928) 669-2174

Las Vegas

Las Vegas Chamber of Commerce, 3720 Howard Hughes Parkway, Las Vegas, NV 89169; (702) 735-1616

Mohave Valley

Bullhead Area Chamber of Commerce, 1251 Highway 95, Bullhead City, AZ 86429; (928) 754-4121, (800) 987-7457

City of Bullhead City, 1255 Marina Blvd, Bullhead City, AZ 86442; (928) 763-9400

Laughlin Chamber of Commerce, 1725 Casino Dr, PO Box 7777, Laughlin, NV 89028; (702) 298-2214

Needles Chamber of Commerce, PO Box 705, Needles, CA 92363; (760) 326-2050

Phoenix – Mesa/Tempe, Apache Junction, and Phoenix Area

Apache Junction Chamber of Commerce, 567 W Apache Trail, Apache Junction, AZ 85220; (480) 982-3141

Greater Phoenix Chamber of Commerce, 201 N Central Ave #2700, Phoenix, AZ 85004; (602) 254-5521

Mesa Chamber of Commerce, 120 N Center St, Mesa, AZ 85201; (480) 969-1307

Quartzsite

Quartzsite Business Chamber of Commerce, 101 W Main St, PO Box 2566, Quartzsite, AZ 85346; (928) 927-9321

Quartzsite Improvement Association, 235 E Ironwood St, Quartzsite, AZ 85346; (928) 927-6325

Tucson

Tucson Metropolitan Chamber of Commerce, PO Box 991, 465 W St Mary's Rd, Tucson, AZ 85701; (520) 792-1212

Yuma

Yuma Convention and Visitor's Bureau, 377 S Main St, Yuma, AZ 85364; (928) 783-0071, (800) 293-0071

Text Index

516

Map Index

Campground Index

Shadow Hills RV Resort	Coachella Valley SB Parks	Commercial	450
Shadow Ridge RV Resort	Ajo, Why, and Organ Pipe Cactus NM	Commercial	60
Shady Acres RV Park	Green River and the San Rafael Swell	Commercial	384
Shady Acres RV Park	Yuma Snowbird Parks	Commercial	511
Shady Lane RV Court	Quartzsite Snowbird Parks	Commercial	497
Shady Rest MH/RV Community	Apache JCT Snowbird Parks	Commercial	484
Shangri-La RV Resort	Yuma Snowbird Parks	Commercial	511
Sharp Creek Campground	Payson and the Mogollon Rim	NFS	144
Ship Rock RV Resort	Apache Jct Snowbird Parks	Commercial	484
Show Low Lake County Park CG	Show Low and Pinetop-Lakeside Region	Local	177
Sierra del Saguaro	Apache Jct Snowbird Parks	Commercial	484
Sierra Leone Mobile Park	Apache Jct Snowbird Parks	Commercial	484
Sierra Village RV Park	Taos	Commercial	346
Siesta RV Park	Las Cruces	Commercial	302
Silver City KOA	Silver City	Commercial	337
Silver City RV Park	Silver City	Commercial	337
Silver Creek RV Park	Mohave Valley SB Parks	Commercial	470
Silver Overflow, Saddle, and Apache CG	Cloudcroft	NFS	258
Silver Sands RV Resort	Mesa/Tempe Snowbird Parks	Commercial	478
Silver Spur Ranch RV & Mobile Home PK	Mesa/Tempe Snowbird Parks	Commercial	478
Silveridge RV Resort	Mesa/Tempe Snowbird Parks	Commercial	478
Silverview RV Resort	Mohave Valley SB Parks	Commercial	470
Sims Mesa Site Campground	Farmington	State	283
Singletree Campground	Capitol Reef National Park	NFS	381
Sink Hole Campground	Payson and the Mogollon Rim	NFS	144
Sky Mountain Resort and RV Park	Chama	Commercial	252
Sky Valley Resort	Coachella Valley SB Parks	Commercial	450
Slab City	Salton Sea East Side	State	169
Sleeping Ute Mountain RV Park	Mesa Verde NP	Commercial	310
Sleepy Grass Campground	Cloudcroft	NFS	258
Sleepy Hollow RV PK and Andrade CA	Yuma	Tribal	208
Slickrock Campground	Moab	Commercial	391
Snowbird RV Resort	Mohave Valley SB Parks	Commercial	470
Soda Pocket Campground	Raton	State	316
South Fork Campground	Ruidoso	NFS	324
South Forty RV Ranch	Tucson Snowbird Parks	Commercial	502
Southern Mesa RV Park	Yuma Snowbird Parks	Commercial	511
Sparkling Waters RV Park	Coachella Valley SB Parks	Commercial	450
Spencer Canyon Campground	Tucson	NFS	191
Spider Rock RV Park and Camping Too	Canyon de Chelly NM	Commercial	77
Spillway Campground	Payson and the Mogollon Rim	NFS	146
Spirit Mountain Casino	Mohave Valley SB Parks	Commercial	470
Split Rail RV Park	Quartzsite Snowbird Parks	Commercial	497
Spring Creek Inn and RV Resort	Theodore Roosevelt Lake	NFS	183
Squaw Flat Campground	Canyonlands NM - The Needles	NPS	377
Squaw Lake Campground	Imperial Dam Recreation Area	BLM	108
Stampede RV Park	Tombstone	Commercial	185
Standard Wash BLM Dispersed Camping	Lake Havasu/Parker Strip	BLM	117
Star Valley Ranch	Apache Jct Snowbird Parks	Commercial	484
Starlight Village Resort	Deming and Columbus	Commercial	268
Stewart Campground	Chiricahua Mountains	NFS	81
Stillwell Store and RV Park	Big Bend National Park	Commercial	245
Storrie Lake State Park	Las Vegas	State	304
Strayhorse Campground	Coronado Trail	NFS	86
Study Butte RV Park	Big Bend National Park	Commercial	244
Sugar Pines RV Park	Cloudcroft	Commercial	258
Summerlan RV Park and Service Ctr	Raton	Commercial	314

Sun Country Adult RV Park	I-10 Corridor	Commercial	54
Sun Life RV Resort	Mesa/Tempe Snowbird Parks	Commercial	478
Sun Ridge RV Park	Yuma Snowbird Parks	Commercial	511
Sun Vista RV Resort	Yuma Snowbird Parks	Commercial	512
Sunbeam Lake RV Resort	El Centro	Commercial	92
Sundance 1 RV Resort	Casa Grande Snowbird Parks	Commercial	444
Sundance RV Park	Mesa Verde NP	Commercial	308
Sundance RV Resort	Yuma Snowbird Parks	Commercial	512
Sundowner MH and RV Park	Apache Jct Snowbird Parks	Commercial	484
Sunflower RV Resort	Phoenix Snowbird Parks	Commercial	489
Suni-Sands RV Resort	Yuma Snowbird Parks	Commercial	512
Sunny Acres RV Park	Las Cruces	Commercial	303
Sunny Flat Campground	Chiricahua Mountains	NFS	81
Sunrise Campground	White Mountains	Tribal	194
Sunrise Park RV Campground	White Mountains	Tribal	194
Sunrise RV Resort	Apache Jct Snowbird Parks	Commercial	484
Sunrise RV Trailer Park	Deming and Columbus	Commercial	267
Sunscape RV Resort	Casa Grande Snowbird Parks	Commercial	445
Sunset Palms RV Park	Yuma Snowbird Parks	Commercial	512
Sunset View Campground	Navajo National Monument	NPS	135
Sunshine Resort	Lake Havasu/Parker SB Pks	Commercial	459
Superstition Lookout RV Park	Apache Jct Snowbird Parks	Commercial	484
Superstition Shadows MH Park	Apache Jct Snowbird Parks	Commercial	485
Superstition Sunrise RV Resort	Apache Jct Snowbird Parks	Commercial	485
Sweet's Retreat RV Apark	Quartzsite Snowbird Parks	Commercial	497
Tamarisk BLM LTVA	El Centro	BLM	92
Tamarisk Mobile & RV Park	Coachella Valley SB Parks	Commercial	451
Taos RV Park	Taos	Commercial	345
Taos Valley RV Park and Campground	Taos	Commercial	345
Taylor Lake Camp	Picacho State Recreatin Area	State	152
Temple Bar Resort	Lake Mead NRA	NPS	123
Ten X Campground	Grand Canyon South Rim	NFS	102
Tetilla Peak Recreation Area	Albuquerque	Corps of Eng	240
The Flintstones Campground	Grand Canyon South Rim	Commercial	103
The Forks Campground	Gila Cliff Dwellings NM	NFS	290
The Reef RV Park	Puerto Peñasco, Sonora	Commercial	422
The Resort	Mesa/Tempe Snowbird Parks	Commercial	478
The Springs at Borrego RV Resort	Borrego Springs and Anza-Borrego SP	Commercial	72
The Stagecoach Stop RV Resort	Albuquerque	Commercial	239
The Tiffany RV Park	Mesa/Tempe Snowbird Parks	Commercial	478
Thousand Lakes RV Park and CG	Capitol Reef National Park	Commercial	380
Three Rivers Petroglyph Site	Alamogordo/Tularosa Basin	BLM	231
Thunderbird Motorhome and RV Park	Sierra Vista	Commercial	180
Tier Drop RV Park	I-10 Corridor	Commercial	54
Tolby Campground	Cimarron	State	256
Tombstone RV Park and Resort	Tombstone	Commercial	185
Tombstone Territories RV Park	Tombstone	Commercial	185
Tortilla Campground	Apache Trail	NFS	65
Totonaka RV Park	Guaymas/San Carlos, Sonora	Commercial	416
Towerpoint RV Resort	Mesa/Tempe Snowbird Parks	Commercial	478
Town and Country RV Park	Roswell	Commercial	318
Trailer Village RV Campground	Roswell	Commercial	319
Trails End RV Park	Camp Verde	Commercial	75
Tra-Tel Tucson RV Park	Tucson Snowbird Parks	Commercial	502
Traveler's World	Clovis and Portales	Commercial	260
Tucson Meadows Winter Haven RV PK	Tucson Snowbird Parks	Commercial	502
Turquoise Trail RV CG and RV Park	Albuquerque	Commercial	238
Turquoise Triangle RV - Trailer Park	Sedona, Cottonwood, Verde Valley	Commercial	172

Turquoise Valley Golf and RV Park	Bisbee and Naco	Commercial	70
Tuthill County Park	Flagstaff	Local	94
Twentynine Palms Resort	Joshua Tree NP and 29 Palms	Commercial	109
Twin Buttes RV Park	Douglas	Commercial	89
Twin Palms Mobile & RV Park	Yuma Snowbird Parks	Commercial	512
Twin Spruce RV Park	Ruidoso	Commercial	320
Upper End Campgrund	Gila Cliff Dwellings NM	NFS	291
Upper Scorpion Campground	Gila Cliff Dwellings NM	NPS	292
USA RV Park	Gallup	Commercial	288
Usery Mountain Regional Park	Phoenix	Local	150
Ute Lake State Park	Tucumcari	State	355
Vacation Inn and Suites	El Centro	Commercial	91
Val Vista Village RV Resort	Mesa/Tempe Snowbird Parks	Commercial	478
Val Vista Winter Village	Casa Grande Snowbird Parks	Commercial	445
Valle del Oro RV Resort	Mesa/Tempe Snowbird Parks	Commercial	479
Valle's Trading Post and RV Park	Trail of the Ancients Scenic Byway	Commercial	397
Valley of Fire SP - Arch Rock CG	Lake Mead NRA	State	120
Valley of Fire SP - Atlatl Rock CG	Lake Mead NRA	State	120
Valley of Fires BLM Recreation Area	Alamogordo/Tularosa Basin	BLM	231
Valley of the Gods	Trail of the Ancients Scenic Byway	BLM	397
Valley of the Sun RV Resort	Tucson Snowbird Parks	Commercial	503
Valley View Mobile Home and RV Park	Fort Sumner	Commercial	286
Vegas RV Park	Las Vegas	Commercial	304
Venture In RV Resort	Show Low and Pinetop-Lakeside Region	Commercial	177
Venture Out of Mesa	Mesa/Tempe Snowbird Parks	Commercial	479
Victor's RV Park	San Felipe, Baja California	Commercial	429
Viewpoint RV & Golf Resort	Mesa/Tempe Snowbird Parks	Commercial	479
Villa Alameda RV Resort	Yuma Snowbird Parks	Commercial	512
Villa Marina Campo Turistico	San Felipe, Baja California	Commercial	430
Villanueva State Park	Las Vegas	State	305
VIP RV Resort	Apache Jct Snowbird Parks	Commercial	485
Vista del Mar	San Felipe, Baja California	Commercial	428
Vista Grande	Coachella Valley SB Parks	Commercial	451
Vista Linda Campground	Jemez Mountain Trail	NFS	297
Voyager at Juniper Ridge RV Resort	Show Low and Pinetop-Lakeside Region	Commercial	178
Voyager Resort	Tucson Snowbird Parks	Commercial	503
Wagner MH RV Park	Coachella Valley SB Parks	Commercial	451
Wagon West RV Park	Quartzsite Snowbird Parks	Commercial	497
Wagon Wheel RV Park	Deming and Columbus	Commercial	266
Wahweap RV Park	Page and Glen Canyon NRA	Commercial	140
Waltner's RV Park	Show Low and Pinetop-Lakeside Region	Commercial	177
Watchman Campground	Zion National Park	NPS	399
Watson Lake Park	Prescott	Local	154
Weaver's Needle Travel Trailer Resort	Apache Jct Snowbird Parks	Commercial	485
Wells Fargo RV Park	Tombstone	Commercial	184
West Park Inn RV Park	Clovis and Portales	Commercial	260
West River Campground	Fort Sumner	State	286
Western Acres/MHP	Mesa/Tempe Snowbird Parks	Commercial	479
Western RV Park	Las Vegas	Commercial	125
Western RV Park	Las Vegas Snowbird Parks	Commercial	464
Western Sands RV Park	Yuma Snowbird Parks	Commercial	512
Western Sky's RV Park	El Paso	Commercial	272

Western Way RV Resort	Tucson Snowbird Parks	Commercial	503
Westerner RV Park	Canyonlands NM - Needles	Commercial	376
Westlake RV Park	Enchanted Circle	Commercial	274
Westward Village RV	Yuma Snowbird Parks	Commercial	512
Westwind RV & Golf Resort	Yuma Snowbird Parks	Commercial	513
Wheel-er in RV and MH Park	Lake Havasu/Parker SB Pks	Commercial	459
Whispering Palms RV Trailer Park	Tucson Snowbird Parks	Commercial	503
White Sands Community Campground	Alamogordo/Tularosa Basin	Commercial	230
White Spar Campground	Prescott	NFS	156
White's City RV and Campers Park	Carlsbad	Commercial	248
Wickiup Home Community	Apache Jct Snowbird Parks	Commercial	485
Williams Bottom Camping Area	Moab	BLM	390
Williams/Circle Pines KOA	Williams	Commercial	203
Willow Flat Campground	Canyonlands NP - Island in the Sky	NPS	373
Willow Lake RV and Camping Park	Prescott	Commercial	155
Windhaven RV Park	Yuma Snowbird Parks	Commercial	513
Windmill Resort	Lake Havasu/Parker SB Pks	Commercial	459
Windmill RV Park	Carlsbad	Commercial	248
Windwhistle Campground	Canyonlands NM - Needles	BLM	378
Windy Hill Recreation Site	Theodore Roosevelt Lake	NFS	183
Winslow Pride RV Park	Winslow and the Hopi Mesas	Commercial	205
Wonderland RV Park	Capitol Reef National Park	Commercial	380
Woody Mountain Campground	Flagstaff	Commercial	94
Yavapai Campground	Prescott	NFS	155
Yuma Mesa RV Park	Yuma Snowbird Parks	Commercial	513
Yuma VFW BLM Dispersed CA	Yuma	Commercial	210
Zane Grey RV Park	Camp Verde	Commercial	75
Zion Canyon Campground RV Park	Zion National Park	Commercial	400
Zion River Resort RV Park	Zion National Park	Commercial	400
Zion South Campground	Zion National Park	NPS	400

ABOUT THE AUTHORS

For the last nineteen years Terri and Mike Church have traveled in Alaska, Mexico, Europe, Canada, and the western U.S. Most of this travel has been in RVs, a form of travel they love. It's affordable and comfortable; the perfect way to see interesting places.

Over the years they discovered that few guidebooks were available with the essential day-to-day information that camping travelers need when they are in unfamiliar surroundings. *Southwest Camping Destination, Pacific Northwest Camping Destinations, Traveler's Guide to Alaskan Camping, Traveler's Guide to Camping Mexico's Baja, Traveler's Guide to Mexican Camping, Traveler's Guide to European Camping, and RV and Car Camping Vacations in Europe* are designed to be the guidebooks that the authors tried to find when they first traveled to these places.

Terri and Mike live full-time in an RV: traveling, writing new books, and working to keep these guidebooks as up-to-date as possible. The books are written and prepared for printing using laptop computers while on the road.

For information on buying books by Mike and Terri Church and Rolling Homes Press go to **www.rollinghomes.com** and click on the "How To Buy" tab. Retailers and individuals can also buy books from our distributor:

Independent Publisher's Group   (800) 888-4741 or (312) 337-0474
814 North Franklin Street   www.ipgbook.com
Chicago, Illinois 60610

542

Pacific Northwest Camping Destinations
6" x 9" Paperback, 720 Pages, Over 180 Maps
ISBN 978-0982310120

Third Edition - Copyright 2012

S eashores, snow-capped mountains and visitor friendly cities have made the Pacific Northwest one of the most popular RV and tent camping destinations in North America, and this guide takes you to more than 100 destinations and 700 campgrounds throughout Oregon, Washington, and British Columbia.

Combining the functions of a campground directory and a sightseeing guide, each entry describes a vacation spot and its attractions and recommends good camping locations in the area, including privately owned, federal, state, and county campgrounds. Each campground is described in detail including a recommendation for the maximum size RV suitable for the campground. Written driving instructions as well as a map are provided showing the exact location. Tourist destinations are described and several itineraries are provided for driving on scenic routes throughout the region.

Traveler's Guide To Mexican Camping
6" x 9" Paperback, 576 Pages, Over 250 Maps
ISBN 978-0982310106

Fourth Edition - Copyright 2009

M exico, one of the world's most interesting travel destinations, is just across the southern U.S. border. It offers warm sunny weather all winter long, beautiful beaches, colonial cities, and excellent food. Best of all, you can easily and economically visit Mexico in your own car or RV.

The third edition of *Traveler's Guide To Mexican Camping* is now even better! It has become the bible for Mexican campers. With this book you will cross the border and travel Mexico like a veteran. It is designed to make your trip as simple and trouble-free as possible. Maps show the exact location of campgrounds and the text gives written driving instructions as well as information regarding the size of RV suitable for each campground. In addition to camping and campground information the guide also includes information about cities, roads and driving, trip preparation, border crossing, vehicle care, shopping, and entertainment.

RV and Car Camping Vacations in Europe
6" x 9" Paperback, 320 Pages, Over 140 Maps
ISBN 978-0965296892

First Edition - Copyright 2004

P eople from North America love to visit Europe on their vacations. One great way to travel in Europe is by RV or car, spending the night in convenient and inexpensive campgrounds. It's a way to travel economically and get off the beaten tourist trail. It's also a great way to meet Europeans. Many of them travel the same way!

Most of us lead busy lives with little time to spend on planning an unusual vacation trip. With this book a camping vacation in Europe is easy. It tells how to arrange a rental RV or car from home, when to go and what to take with you. It explains the process of picking up the rental vehicle and turning it back in when you're ready to head for home. There's also information about shopping, driving, roads, and other things that you should know before you arrive. Then it describes a series of tours, each taking from a week to two weeks. The ten tours cover much of Western Europe and even the capitals of the Central European countries. The book has details about the routes and roads, the campgrounds to use, and what to do and see while you are there.

Traveler's Guide To Alaskan Camping
6" x 9" Paperback, 486 Pages, Over 100 Maps
ISBN 978-0982310113

Fifth Edition - Copyright 2011

A laska, the dream trip of a lifetime! Be prepared for something spectacular. Alaska is one fifth the size of the entire United States, it has 17 of the 20 highest peaks in the U.S., 33,904 miles of shoreline, and has more active glaciers and ice fields than the rest of the inhabited world. In addition to some of the most magnificent scenery the world has to offer, Alaska is chock full of an amazing variety of wildlife. Fishing, hiking, kayaking, rafting, photography, hunting, and wildlife viewing are only a few of the many activities which will keep you outside during the long summer days.

Traveler's Guide To Alaskan Camping makes this dream trip to Alaska as easy as camping in the "Lower 48". It includes almost 500 campgrounds throughout Alaska and on the roads north in Canada with full campground descriptions, appropriate RV size for each campground, and maps showing exact locations. It also is filled with suggested things to do and see including fishing holes, hiking trails, canoe trips, wildlife viewing opportunities, and much more.

Traveler's Guide To Camping Mexico's Baja
6" x 9" Paperback, 256 Pages, Over 65 Maps
ISBN 978-0982310137

Fifth Edition - Copyright 2012

S un, sand, and clear blue water are just three of the many reasons more and more RVers are choosing Mexico's Baja as a winter destination. The Baja is fun, easy, and the perfect RVing getaway. Only a few miles south of the border you'll find many great campsites, some on beaches where you'll camp just feet from the water.

Traveler's Guide To Camping Mexico's Baja starts by giving you the Baja-related information from our popular book *Traveler's Guide To Mexican Camping*. It then goes further. We've added more campgrounds, expanded the border crossing section, and given even more information about towns, roads, and recreational opportunities. Unlike the Mexico book, the Baja book is arranged geographically following Transpensinsular Highway 1 south. The book also covers nearby Puerto Peñasco. Like all our books, this one features easy-to-follow maps showing exactly how to find every campground listed.

Traveler's Guide To European Camping
6" x 9" Paperback, 640 Pages, Over 400 Maps
ISBN 978-0965296885

Third Edition - Copyright 2004

O ver 350 campgrounds including the best choice in every important European city are described in detail and directions are given for finding them. In many cases information about convenient shopping, entertainment and sports opportunities is included.

This guide will tell you how to rent, lease, or buy a rig in Europe or ship your own from home. It contains the answers to questions about the myriad details of living, driving, and camping in Europe. In addition to camping and campground information *Traveler's Guide To European Camping* gives you invaluable details about the history and sights you will encounter. This information will help you plan your itinerary and enjoy yourself more when you are on the road. Use the information in this book to travel Europe like a native. Enjoy the food, sights, and people of Europe. Go for a week, a month, a year. Europe can fill your RV or camping vacation seasons for many years to come!

UNITS OF MEASURE

1 km = .62 mile	1 mile = 1.61 km
1 meter = 3.28 feet	1 foot = .30 meters
1 liter = .26 U.S. gallon	1 U.S. gallon = 3.79 liters
1 kilogram = 2.21 pounds	1 pound = .45 kilograms

convert from °F to °C by subtracting 32 and multiplying by 5/9
convert from °C to °F by multiplying by 1.8 and adding 32

KEY TO SYMBOLS

	Tents	Flush Toilets	Wi-Fi	No Pets
Rentals	Showers	Free Wi-Fi	Reservations
20 Amp Electric	Fires	Groceries	Credit Cards
30 Amp Electric	Swimming	Restaurant	Good Sam
50 Amp Electric	Playground	Laundry	Escapee
Water	Telephone	Propane	FMCA
Sewer	TV	Ice	Passport America
Dump	Internet	Handicap	Coast to Coast

 40 Foot Rigs

KEY TO CAMPGROUND PRICES

FREE	Free	$ / $$$	Over $15 and up to $20 U.S.
$	Up to $5 U.S.	$$ / $$$	Over $20 and up to $25 U.S.
$$	Over $5 and up to $10 U.S.	$$$ / $$$	Over $25 and up to $30 U.S.
$$$	Over $10 and up to $15 U.S.	Over $$$ / $$$	Over $30 U.S.

MAP LEGEND

84	Major Freeway	97	Secondary Road No.	State Border
	Other Paved Roads	20	Other Road No.	Country Border
	Unpaved Roads	Railroad	) (Mountain Pass
	Freeway Off-ramp		Ferry Route	▲ Area of Interest
Exit 2	Off-ramp - Name Indicated	O	City, Town, or Village	Campground (40 ft) (See Page 38)
5	Freeway Number	•	Roundabout	Campground (RVs Under 40 ft)
	City Center		Major Airport	Campground - Location Only, No Description
			Other Airport	⚠ Tent Only Campground